Introduction

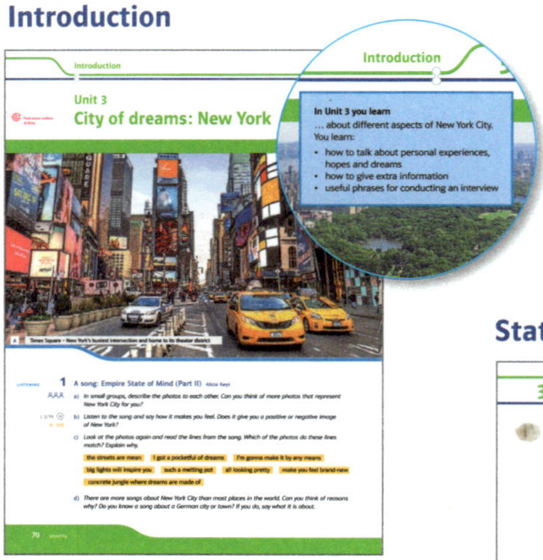

Die ersten beiden Seiten stimmen dich auf das Thema der Unit ein. In der blauen Kompetenzbox siehst du, was du in dieser Unit lernen wirst.

Die roten Dreiecke zeigen dir, dass du hinten im Diff pool z. B. Hilfen und leichtere oder weiterführende Aufgaben findest.

Stations

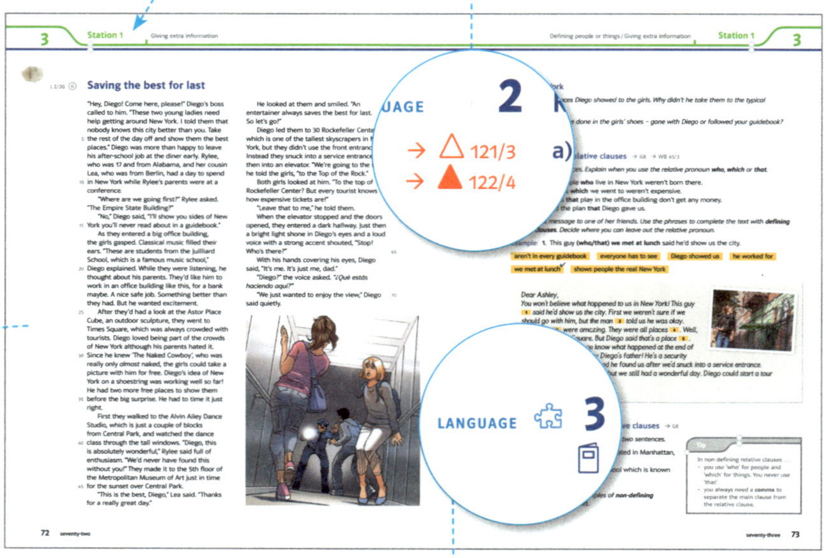

In den beiden Stations jeder Unit findest du deinen neuen Lernstoff, tolle Texte und passende Aufgaben.

Die Aufgaben mit dem Puzzle-Symbol unterstützen dich besonders dabei, deine Lernziele zu erreichen und helfen dir bei der Vorbereitung der Unit task.

Unit task

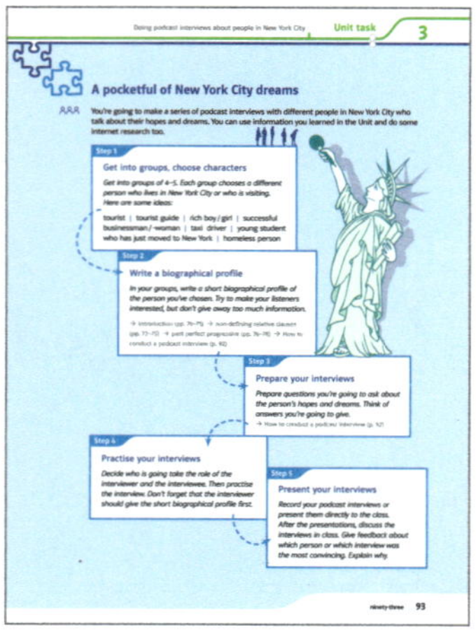

Und so kommt zum Schluss alles zusammen. Anhand dieser großen Unit-Aufgabe kannst du deine neu erworbenen Fähigkeiten schrittweise überprüfen und festigen und dabei auf kreative Weise zeigen, was du nun kannst.

Story

Hier findest du spannende Geschichten mit interessanten Aufgaben.

Action UK/USA!

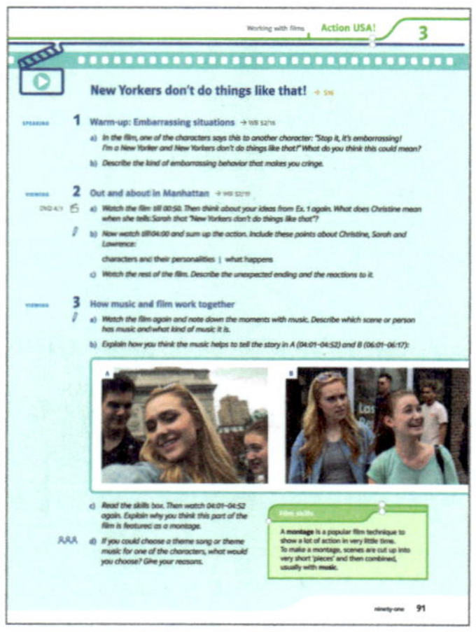

Und auf diesen Seiten gibt es tolle Filme aus UK und den USA!

Text smart

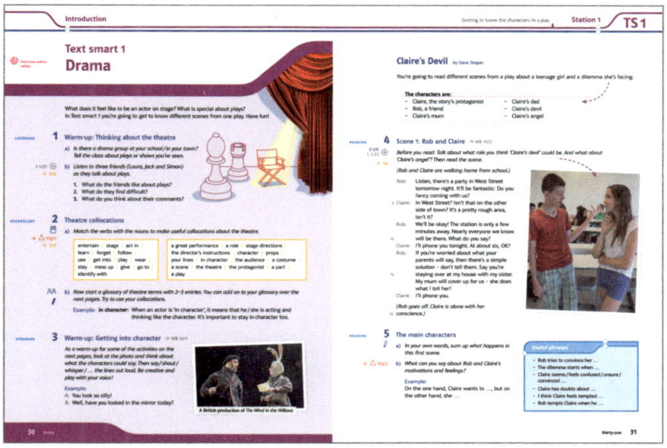

Auf den *Text smart*-Seiten lernst du, wie du mit authentischen Texten (z. B. Sachtexten, Werbetexten) umgehst und sie im Anschluss für deine eigenen Arbeiten nutzen kannst.

Across cultures

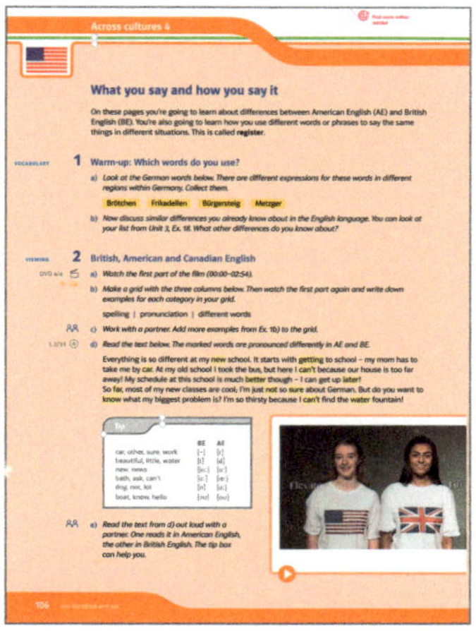

Vergleiche auf diesen Seiten deinen Alltag mit der Alltagskultur Großbritanniens und der USA und lerne, mit verschiedenen Begegnungssituationen umzugehen.

Diff pool

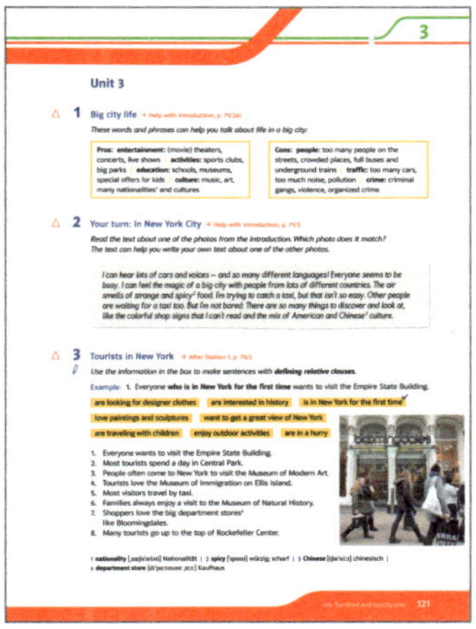

Skills

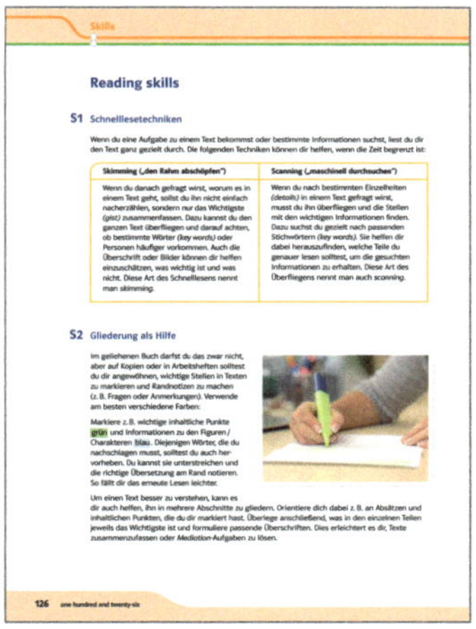

Grammar, Vocabulary

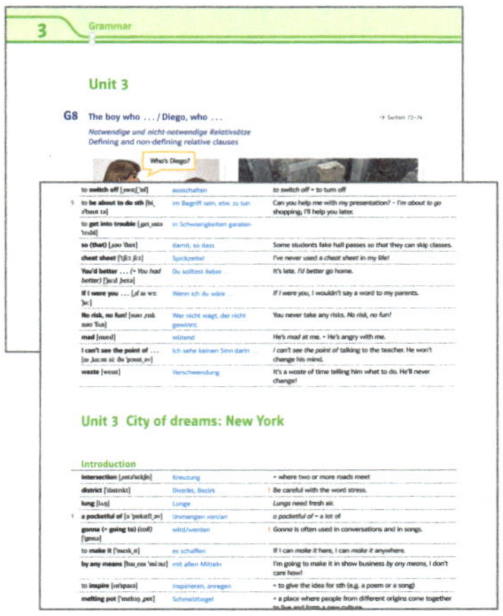

Im hinteren Buchteil stehen dir hilfreiche Anhänge zur Verfügung. Achte auf die Verweise in den Units, die dir sagen, in welchem Anhang du nachschlagen kannst.

Symbole

→ △ 121/3	Verweis auf leichtere Aufgaben / Hilfen im Diff pool
→ ▲ 122/4	Verweis auf anspruchsvollere Aufgaben im Diff pool
→ WB 7/4	Verweis auf eine Übung im Workbook
→ G2	Verweis auf die Grammatik im Anhang
→ S2	Verweis auf die Skills im Anhang
(Partnersymbol)	Partnerarbeit
(Gruppensymbol)	Gruppenarbeit
(Portfoliosymbol)	Hier entsteht ein Produkt für dein Portfolio.
(Stift)	Schreiben (geschlossen / einfach)
(Stift)	Schreiben (offen / kreativ)
S 1/14 ◎	Verweis auf die Schüler-CDs im Workbook (Audio)
L 1/19 ◎	Verweis auf die Lehrer-CDs (Audio)
DVD 3/7	Verweis auf die Lehrer-DVD (Film)
(Globus)	Code auf www.klett.de eingeben und Zusatzmaterial nutzen
(Puzzle)	Übungen, die die Unit task besonders vorbereiten
(Flaggen)	Across cultures

Green Line 4 G9 für Klasse 8 an Gymnasien

Herausgeber: Prof. Harald Weisshaar, Bisingen

Autorinnen und Autoren: Jennifer Baer-Engel, Göppingen; Carolyn Jones, Beckenham; Jon Marks, Ventnor; Harald Weisshaar, Bisingen; Alison Wooder, Ventnor sowie Cornelia Kaminski, Fulda; Elise Köhler-Davidson, Exeter; Katja Krey, Reutlingen; Bernd Wick, Neckartenzlingen

Beratung: Paul Dennis, Lahnstein; Cornelia Kaminski, Fulda; Nilgül Karabulut, Aachen; Hartmut Klose, Seevetal; Antje Körber, Merseburg; Jörg Nieswand, Berlin; Jörg Schulze, Dresden

Zusatzmaterial für Schülerinnen und Schüler zu diesem Band:

Workbook + Audio-CD + Übungssoftware	978-3-12-854248-5
Workbook + Audio-CD	978-3-12-854245-4
Fit für Tests und Klassenarbeiten mit Lösungsheft und CD-ROM	978-3-12-854247-8
Trainingsbuch mit Audio-CD	978-3-12-854304-8
Vokabellernheft	978-3-12-854284-3
Vokabeltraining aktiv	978-3-12-854334-5

sowie eine Reihe von abgestimmten *English Readers*

ISBN 978-3-12-854240-9 (fester Einband)
1. Auflage 1 8 7 6 5 4 | 2023 22 21 20 19

ISBN 978-3-12-854241-6 (flexibler Einband)
1. Auflage 1 6 5 4 3 2 | 2023 22 21 20 19

Redaktion: Michael Mattison; Anette Mohamud; Martina Reckart; Lektorat editoria: Cornelia Schaller, Fellbach
Herstellung: Anita Bauch; Anne Leibbrand; Cristina Dunu

Gestaltung: Petra Michel, Essen
Umschlaggestaltung: know idea, Freiburg; Koma Amok, Stuttgart
Illustrationen: Peer Kramer, Düsseldorf; jani lunablau, Barcelona
sowie Christian Dekelver, Weinstadt *(Karten)*; Denise Drews, Zürich *(Time line)*
Satz: Satzkiste GmbH, Stuttgart, Fotosatz Kaufmann Stuttgart
Reproduktion: Schwaben-Repro, Stuttgart
Druck: Himmer GmbH Druckerei, Augsburg

Printed in Germany

Green Line 4 G9

von
Jennifer Baer-Engel
Carolyn Jones
Jon Marks
Harald Weisshaar
Alison Wooder
Cornelia Kaminski
Elise Köhler-Davidson
Katja Krey
Bernd Wick

herausgegeben von
Harald Weisshaar

Ernst Klett Verlag
Stuttgart · Leipzig

Inhalt

Unit 2 Kids in America

Text smart 2 Advertisements

Across cultures 3 School life – dos and don'ts

Unit 3 City of dreams: New York

Legende

- Kompetenzaufgabe
- *Across cultures* (UK)
- *Across cultures* (US)
- < > fakultativ

Die in diesem Band aufbereiteten Inhalte stellen ein Angebot dar; sie sind nicht obligatorisch durchzunehmen. Maßgeblich für die Auswahl der Texte und Übungen ist der Lehrplan Ihres Bundeslandes bzw. Ihr schulinternes Curriculum.

Find more online: 8ak7n4

Unit 1
On the move

SPEAKING

1 Reasons for travelling → WB 2/1

a) *Look at the photos above. What are the people doing? What might they be thinking?*

b) *Why do you think these people are travelling? Share your ideas in class. The words and phrases in the box can help you.*

c) *Collect more reasons for travelling.*

Word bank

class trip | family holiday | have fun | escape from hard life | get to know other cultures | hope for a better future | visit family | learn a foreign language | have a break | meet exchange partners

LISTENING

2 Travel situations

a) *What can happen when you're travelling to another country? Share your ideas in class.*

L 1/1–5

b) *Listen to different travel situations. Match the speakers with the problems they're talking about. You don't need all the ideas.*

→ S15

feel seasick | get lost | have too much luggage | have communication problems | be afraid of flying | lose money | forget tickets | miss train / plane

B

C

In Unit 1 you learn

… how to talk about travel experiences and reasons for travelling. You learn:

- how to report what people have said
- how to report questions, commands and requests
- words and phrases for talking about travel

D

VOCABULARY

3 Travel words → WB 2/2–3

→ S17

a) *Make a grid and sort the words into the following categories:*

transport | places | people | things you need

departure lounge | by bike / car / bus | passport | boarding card | check-in desk | on foot | visa | passenger | flight attendant | train station | by train / plane | customs | suitcase | public transport | tickets | guide | airport | by boat / ferry / ship | tourist | passport control | arrivals hall | luggage | foreign currency | duty-free shop

b) *Can you think of more travel words? Add them to the grid.*

c) *Your turn: Choose five of the words from your grid and use them to write a short text about your last holiday or trip.*

Example: Sometimes we go by car to another town to visit my grandparents. During our last holiday we went by plane to … We left for the airport very early in the morning …

SPEAKING

4 Your turn: Your travel plan

→ △ 108/1

What type of travelling would you like to do when you're older? Where would you like to go? Get into groups of three and share your ideas. Then tell the class how your plans are similar or different.

L1/6

You told us there was free wifi!

My first trip away from home was really exciting, and I tried to enjoy every minute of it. But my best friend Steve is completely different. I'll tell you why.

On the way to France with our athletics team, Steve and I were out on the top deck of the ferry. It was a nice, quiet moment. Then Steve's phone rang.

"YEAH?" he said, in his big loud special telephone voice. "No, sorry, I didn't have time. Uh huh … Uh huh … WHAAAT?! Ha ha ha! OK, see you!"

"Who was that?" I asked.

"It was my friend Eddie," Steve answered. "He said he was at the leisure centre with Amarjit. He told me they were having crisps and drinks from the vending machine."

"Wow," I said. "That's so much more interesting than a ferry trip to another country. Why did you go 'WHAAAT'?"

"Er … oh yeah. Eddie said Amarjit had just spilt his drink over his crisps."

"Amarjit's crisps or Eddie's crisps?"

"Oh, I've forgotten. Hang on, I'll send them a message to ask."

It's only an hour from Dover to the French coast, and we could already see the houses of Calais. French houses often have shutters at the windows. British houses never have shutters. I love things that remind me I'm in a different country.

Ms Woodruff, the coach, came out of a door and onto the deck.

"It's time to get back on the coach," she said. Then she saw that Steve was still busy with his phone.

"I promised your parents I wouldn't let you use your phone in France!" she said. "You know it's really expensive to use it abroad!"

"But we aren't in France yet," said Steve. "We're still on the ferry."

"Where do you think the signal is coming from?" she said.

With a big groan Steve gave her his phone.

"Can I have it back when we arrive? You told us there was free wifi at the hostel. My parents said I could use my phone over wifi. They did. Honest!"

"Really? They told *me* you were an addict, and they thought you needed a break from your smartphone. You can have your phone for half an hour in the evenings, OK?"

"This is going to be an awful trip," muttered Steve.

"This is going to be a great trip," I thought.

READING

1 Understanding the text → WB 3/4

→ S1–3

a) *What do the narrator and Steve like / not like about the trip? Make a grid and write down what the text tells you about the two characters.*

b) *What does the coach decide about Steve's smartphone? Do you agree with her decision? Explain why or why not.*

c) *Your turn: Can you identify more with Steve or with the narrator? Say what's important for you when you travel.*

LANGUAGE

2 From direct to indirect speech → WB 3/5 → G1

→ △ 108/2
→ ▲ 109/3

a) *The following sentences are in the text, but in indirect speech. Copy the grid. Write down the sentences in direct speech. Then add the sentences in indirect speech from the text. Underline the words that change from direct to indirect speech.*

Direct speech	Indirect speech
1. Eddie: **I'm** at the leisure centre with Amarjit.	Eddie said **he was** at the leisure centre with Amarjit.

2. "We're having crisps and drinks from the vending machine." 3. "Amarjit has just spilled his drink over my crisps." 4. "I won't let Steve use his phone in France." 5. "There's free wifi at the hostel." 6. "You can use your phone over wifi." 7. "Steve is an addict. He needs a break from his smartphone."

b) *How do tenses change when you report what someone has said? Look at the sentences from a) and write down the verb forms.*

Example: I'm → he was **simple present → simple past**

c) *Read these sentences from the text. Report what the people say. Use **indirect speech**.*

1. Steve: I didn't have time. 2. Steve: I've forgotten. I'll send them a message to ask. 3. Ms Woodruff: It's time to get back on the coach. 4. Steve: We aren't in France yet. We're still on the ferry. 5. Coach: You can have your phone for half an hour in the evenings.

d) *Which verbs are used to introduce indirect speech in the text? Can you think of more verbs? Make a list.*

Example: He **told** me they were …

LANGUAGE

3 Steve's latest post → WB 3/6, 4/7–8 → G2

You're a friend of Steve's. While he was in France with his athletics team, he wrote this post. A few days later, you tell a friend about it. Look at the sentences with the words in green. Report them to your friend. Change the words in green to the words below. Then explain why you need to do this.

Start like this: Steve wrote a post a few days ago. He said that **he was having** a really good time **there**. …

that | there (2x) | that day | the next day | the day before

Just a quick post. (I'm only allowed half an hour on my phone!) 😉 You won't believe it. I'm having a really good time here. Today we went into a cute little town. I thought it was a holiday because all the shops were closed. Then I found out that French shops close for lunch! I think lunch is a big deal in France. Anyway, it's all been *fantastique* here. Well, apart from the food! Yesterday we had a kind of soup with lots of herbs and garlic in it. Ugh! But I guess that's typical of French cooking.
This evening we had 'burger au cheval'. I thought that meant 'burger in the style of a town called Cheval' but then I realised that it was MADE OF HORSE! Some people just ate the chips and salad, but I thought, "Well, why not finish it?" To be fair, it tasted OK. Got to go and get some sleep now. The event starts tomorrow. *A bientôt!*

SPEAKING → △ 109/4 → S11

4 Role play: Around the world

a) A: *You're a film star. For your latest film, you act in some amazing places around the world. First make notes about where you are now, what you did last week, and what you're going to do next.*

B: *You're a magazine reporter who wants to interview the film star. You're going to call him/her and ask about his/her journey. First make notes about the questions you're going to ask. After the role play, report to the class what A told you. Just report the most important information!*

Start like this: I interviewed … He / she said he / she was …

b) *Now change roles: B is the film star and A is the reporter.*

WRITING → △ 109/5

5 What happened? → WB 5/9–10, 6/11

a) *The Jones family had some problems during their holiday. Now their friends want to know about everything that went wrong. Look at the pictures and write down what they tell their friends.*

→ △ 109/6

b) *Your turn: Think of a funny, scary or embarrassing situation which you experienced during your last holiday or on a trip. Tell your partner about it. Try to make it as interesting as possible.*

LISTENING L1/8 → S15

6 ‹ A song: Island in the sun › Weezer

When you're on a holiday
You can't find the words to say
All the things that come to you
And I wanna feel it too

On an island in the sun
We'll be playing and having fun
And it makes me feel so fine
I can't control my brain

When you're on a golden sea
You don't need no memory
Just a place to call your own
As we drift into the zone

On an island in the sun
…

We'll run away together
We'll spend some time forever
We'll never feel bad any more

a) *Listen to the song. Which words/phrases tell you how the main character feels?*

b) *Write an extra verse for the song. Think of words that rhyme first.*

Start like this: When you're on a lonely beach … / When you're feeling really cool …

L1/9 Idiot nephew?

Rafiq: Did I tell you about my trip to Bangladesh last month?

Anya: No, you didn't. How was it?

Rafiq: Not bad, thanks, although it didn't start very well.

Anya: What happened?

Rafiq: At passport control, the man asked me what the purpose of my visit was. I was really surprised, and I just couldn't think of an answer. So I said I didn't know.

Anya: Ha! That wasn't very clever.

Rafiq: I know. I think he thought I was some kind of idiot. But it was my parents' idea for me to visit my family in Bangladesh. Next the man asked me if I was travelling with my parents.

Anya: What did you say?

Rafiq: I told him I was travelling alone. So then he asked me how old I was.

Anya: And you said you were fourteen, right?

Rafiq: I was really tired. I forgot about my last birthday, and I said I was thirteen. Then he looked at the date of birth on my passport, and it didn't match. I think that's when he started to get suspicious. He told me not to lie to him.

Anya: Oh dear. What happened then?

Rafiq: He told me to go into a side room to answer some more questions. I was lucky I had the address and phone number of my uncle and aunt with me. The airport security people called them, and asked if they knew who I was.

Anya: And they said, "No, we don't have an idiot nephew who can't even remember how old he is."

Rafiq: Very funny. Anyway, my uncle said my aunt was waiting for me at the airport, and gave them her mobile number. They called her, and asked her to come to the immigration office in the arrivals hall. Then a security guard took me there to meet her. When we got there, he asked her if I really was her nephew.

Anya: Did the security guy believe her?

Rafiq: Yeah. I think he knew she was telling the truth because she didn't seem worried.

READING

7 At passport control → WB 6/12

→ S1 **a)** *Explain Rafiq's problem when he arrives in Bangladesh.*

b) *How do you think Rafiq felt during his conversation with the man at passport control? And how do you think he felt when he left the airport?*

Start like this: Rafiq feels **embarrassed** because the man at passport control thinks that he's lying to him. He's **worried** …

→ S11 **c)** *Role play: Act out the scene between Rafiq and the man at passport control.*

LANGUAGE

8 Find the rule: Indirect questions → G3

a) *Look at the following sentences. What do you need to make indirect questions? Write down the rules for questions with and without question words.*

"What's the purpose of your visit?" → The man **asked me what** the purpose of my visit **was**.
"Are you travelling with your parents?" → He **asked me if** I **was travelling** with my parents.

b) *Find more examples of indirect questions in the text on p. 13. Write them down in your grid from Station 1, Ex. 2, and add the direct questions that go with them.*

LANGUAGE

9 Rafiq's questions → WB 6/13

→ △ 110/7
→ ▲ 110/8

Before the trip to Bangladesh, Rafiq had a lot of questions for his parents. Turn them into ***indirect questions****.*

Start like this: Rafiq asked his parents if they …

1. "Did you give Aunt Sadia my flight details?"
2. "Do I need a large suitcase for the trip?"
3. "Does the flight take long?"
4. "Don't you want to come too?"
5. "What can I bring them as a present?"
6. "Where will I meet them at the airport?"
7. "Where have you put my passport?"
8. "Why do I have to go at all?"

LANGUAGE

10 Getting around in Dhaka and London → WB 7/14 → G4

→ △ 110/9
→ ▲ 111/10

a) *Find the sentences that report these commands and requests in the text on p. 13. Write them down in your grid. What do you need to make indirect commands and requests?*

1. Man at passport control: Don't lie to me!
2. Man at passport control: Go into this side room to answer some more questions.
3. Airport security people: Please come to the immigration office in the arrivals hall.

b) *Rafiq is talking to Masud, his cousin from Dhaka, the capital of Bangladesh. What do they tell each other to do? Use* ***indirect commands and requests****.*

Start like this: Masud tells Rafiq to visit …

Masud: You must visit the old centre of Dhaka. It's quite small, but it's very interesting.
Rafiq: OK, I will. What's the best way to get there?
Masud: Walk. The traffic here is *very* slow. It's usually quicker to walk.
Rafiq: But it's so hot! I don't want to walk.
Masud: Then take a taxi. They're very cheap, but only if you agree on the price first.
Rafiq: OK, I'll remember that. When you go to London next month, use buses or the Tube. They're *much* cheaper than taxis.
Masud: Thanks for telling me. Send me a transport map when you are back in London. I want to study it before I travel.
Rafiq: You can download one from the internet. Just search for 'Transport for London'. Their website has all the information you need.
Masud: Yes, OK. I'll do that.

LANGUAGE **11**

A travel joke → WB 7/15

a) *Read what happened to Jenny, a young business traveller, while she was waiting for her flight to Seattle.*

In the departure lounge, Jenny sat down next to an old man who was looking very nervous.

"Sorry to bother you," he said. "Could I ask your advice about something?"

Jenny took off her headphones. "I'm sorry," she said. "Could you repeat that?"

"I'm going to meet my daughter in Seattle," the old man told her. "I'm worried about the flight because air travel always makes my ears hurt. Can you suggest anything to help?"

"Don't worry. Use chewing gum during take-off and landing. It always helps me."

Seven hours later, the plane landed in Seattle. When Jenny was waiting for her luggage, she saw the old man.

"How was your flight? Did my advice help?"

"Sorry, I didn't catch that," he said.

Jenny repeated her question.

"The chewing gum worked very well, thank you," replied the old man, "but … can you tell me how to get it out of my ears?"

b) *At the airport in Seattle, Jenny tells a friend what happened between her and the old man. Write down what she says.*

c) *Make a grid with the following headings:* ***asking for information, asking for advice, asking for clarification / repetition*** *and* ***apologising****. Find examples for these categories in the text. Can you think of more examples? Write them down in the grid.*

MEDIATION **12**

Airport announcements → WB 8/16

L1/11

→ S13, 15

a) *After a holiday in Great Britain, you're waiting with your family at London Heathrow for your flight back to Berlin. You're taking British Airways flight BA 0982 at 9:15. While you're waiting, you hear several announcements. First read the skills box. Then listen to the announcements. Which of them are important for you? Take notes. The key words in the box can help you.*

b) *Your parents were busy when the announcements were made. Report the most important points to them in German.*

Mediation skills

Announcements at airports or train stations often contain new words, and background sounds make them difficult to understand. It can help you to focus on important words, e.g. names of people or places, numbers or times, nouns and verbs as key words.

flight number | boarding time | gate | delay / why? | luggage

SPEAKING **13**

Your turn: Travel plans → WB 8/17–18

→ △ 111/11

Choose a foreign capital you'd like to visit. Use websites in English to find out how to get there by plane. Which airport will you use? How long will the flight take? What would you like to do there? Take turns to tell each other about your plans. Then report to the class what your partner told you.

S 1/4–7 L 1/13–16

Where I belong

SPEAKING

1 Before you read

With your partner, talk about reasons why people might want to leave their country.

A My father grabbed my arms and looked down at me. "Listen," he said. "You can't do anything here. It's getting harder and harder for people like us who travel around with our animals. Soon we'll have nothing left. If you go to England, you'll be able to help the whole family. And maybe, one day, you can come back and help Somalia too."

A week ago, I'd been nothing but a girl who would lead the same kind of life as her mother. I thought I would have a husband one day, and children to look after and teach. But now, suddenly, I was responsible for my whole family – and the future of my country too.

For a moment I was too scared to answer my father. But I knew he wouldn't change his mind. He had chosen me for this task and I had to accept it. "Yes," I said. "Yes, I will."

There was no time for anything else. My father jumped back into his car, turned round quickly and drove off, his face like a mask. I walked down the road to join the man who was taking me away.

Stop and think:
What do you think the narrator's journey will be like?

B The smuggler first took me to Kenya in a boat. Those journeys are very dangerous because the boats are always overloaded and the sea is full of sharks. Many people have died while they were trying to do what I was doing. But I didn't know that until much later. While we were at sea, I had other things to worry about.

It was a little boat, and I was crushed between men I had never seen before. It was the first time I had ever been in a boat, and Uncle didn't tell me that it would rock so badly as the waves smashed against it. I was scared, and I thought every moment that I was going to be sick.

I closed my eyes and repeated the things that Uncle had told me to learn.

My name is Khadija Ahmed Mussa. I'm thirteen years old. I'm going to England to join my mother and my brother and sisters. My sisters' names are Fowsia, Maryan and Sabra. Fowsia is eleven, Maryan is seven and Sabra is four. And my brother Abdi is fourteen.

I didn't try to imagine their faces or what they were like. They weren't people at all, just words that I had to learn. *My name is Khadija …*

Those hours in the boat were the worst hours of my life. I survived by closing myself away from what was happening, and when we landed in Kenya, I felt like a different person.

C What happened to me is called piggyback. Uncle was giving me a 'piggyback' to England. That was his business, and he did exactly what my father had paid for. Nothing else.

After we had left the boat, we travelled by road and then by plane, and every time we went through a checkpoint Uncle smiled at me. That was part of his routine. When we were through, the smile was put away together with my passport and he ignored me again, even when we were sitting next to each other.

I could have run away when we changed planes in Dubai. He showed me a seat in the airport and told me to sit there until he came back. But where would I have run to? I didn't know anything about that place and I had no passport except the one in Uncle's pocket. My father had paid for me to go to England and that was where I had to go.

I felt cold in the air-conditioning, and I concentrated on repeating the same words inside my head. *My name is Khadija …*

Stop and think:

How do you think Britain will be different for the narrator?

D When we landed in England, the sky was grey, and it was raining. Not clean, heavy rain, like the *gu*, but a steady, depressing drizzle. I didn't see how it was going to make anything grow because everywhere I looked the ground was covered with concrete. I felt hard and cold, like that concrete ground. If I hadn't, maybe everything would have happened differently and the officials would have sent me home. But they didn't. They looked at my face and then at my passport and let me into the country.

On the train, there were people from all over the world – they were all taking care not to look at each other. Was the whole city like that? Thousands of people who were all pretending that nobody else was there?

We travelled through streets of tall, yellow-grey buildings, and all the time the useless rain went on falling. When I looked up at the sky, I couldn't see any sign of the sun. Was it always invisible here?

I thought Uncle would take me to my new family's house. But when we got off the train, he took some coins out of his pocket and gave them to me. "Can you use a telephone?" he said.

I looked at him. "Of course I can!"

"You see the phone there?" He pointed down the road. "Call the number I give you. Then stay in the phone box. The person who answers the phone will come and fetch you."

I was too surprised to do anything except stare at him. "Don't waste time," he said. "People will notice you. Go!" The piggyback was over and suddenly I was on my own, walking down this strange road.

The phone was different from the phones I had used before, but it was easy to see how to use it. I pressed the buttons very carefully: I had no more money to put in if I made a mistake the first time.

"Hello," said a boy's voice. He spoke Somali, but his accent was very strange. "Are you in the phone box?"

"Yes," I said. "But I don't know where –"

"Just wait," he said. "I'm coming."

I knew it was him as soon as he came round the corner. A tall Somali boy who came straight towards me. He opened the door and stared at me.

"I'm Abdi," he said. When I hesitated, he said his full name this time. "I'm Abdirahman Ahmed Mussa."

He was much older than my brother Mahmoud, and tall too, but he was – more of a boy. That was when I really understood how far I had travelled. I was far away from Somalia, and far from myself, in a place where the people were going to be different. And I had to learn how to live there.

I stared straight back at Abdi. "And I'm Khadija Ahmed Mussa," I said.

From: *Where I belong* by Gillian Cross

SPEAKING

2 Your reaction

a) *Do you like the story? Explain why or why not.*

b) *Have you heard or read about people who try to come to Europe as refugees? How are these stories similar to the narrator's experience? The ideas from the introduction pages can help you.*

READING

3 Understanding the story → WB 9/19–20

→ S1–4

a) *Explain why the narrator must leave her country.*

b) *Look at the map on p. 16 and the text again. How does the narrator get from Somalia to England? Copy the grid and fill in the first line.*

	Part A	Part B	Part C	Part D
How?	by boat, overloaded			
Feelings?	I was scared … (l. 35)			

c) *How does the narrator feel during her journey? Find lines in the text that tell you about her feelings. Add them to your grid from b).*

d) *Imagine you'd have to go on a journey like the narrator in the story. What would be the scariest part for you? Share your ideas with a partner.*

READING

4 Reading between the lines

→ △ 111/12

First read the skills box. Then find information in the text that answers these questions.

1. What's the situation of the narrator's family?
2. What do you think the relationship is between the narrator and her father?
3. What kind of person is Uncle, the smuggler who takes the narrator to England?

Reading skills

Sometimes important information is not mentioned directly in a text. You need to **read between the lines** to get ideas about the characters and their relationships.

Example: When the narrator's father drives away, his face is like a mask. (l. 21) That might tell us that he tries to hide his feelings.

WRITING

5 More thoughts about the story → WB 9/21

a) *After she was picked up by Abdi at the phone box, the narrator meets her 'new' family. What do you think will happen? What might be new for the narrator compared with her old life? Make notes. The ideas in the box can help you.*

Word bank

different culture | new gadgets | modern house | different climate | no friends | be homesick | go to school | new rules

b) *Get into groups of 3–4. Together write a plan of how you think the story might continue. Present your ideas to the class.*

The guitar lesson → S16

SPEAKING

1 Warm-up

What do you think of when you hear the words "I go wherever the wind takes me"?

VIEWING

2 Ciara and Hayley → WB 10/22

DVD 3/7

a) *Watch the film and collect information about Ciara and Hayley. Think of the topics below. Then compare the two women.*

future plans / dreams

origin | work

travel destinations (past and future)

b) *What do you think of Ciara and Hayley? Would you like to meet them? Say why / why not.*

Word bank

friendly | outgoing | interesting | nice | boring | cool | sad | easy-going | strange | silly | rude | funny | happy | quiet | clever | crazy | odd

VIEWING

3 Film genres

a) *Read the skills box. What elements match the film 'The guitar lesson'?*

b) *Make a list with the genres from the box and add two films you've already seen (or heard of) for each genre.*

Film skills

There are many different **kinds of films**, or 'film genres'. Films from one genre usually have similar **main elements**. Here are some examples:

Science fiction: inventions in science / technology; often set in the future; time travel; aliens; unreal atmosphere

Romance: relationship between two characters; love; adventure; happy ending

Historical: set in specific historical era; often about real historical person / event; often lavish costumes / props

Fantasy: story about magic or supernatural forces; set in mythical time; often tells the story of a hero / heroine

WRITING

4 A film poster

Design a film poster for your favourite film from Ex. 3b).

How to tell a travel story

1 Listening: One travel story – two versions

L 1/17–18 → S15

a) *Listen to a young man's travel story and say if you find it interesting or not. Give reasons for your opinion.*

b) *Listen to another version of the same travel story. Compare the two versions.*

c) *Note down which phrases from the box you can hear in the story.*

Useful phrases

Did I tell you about …? | As I've already told you, … | … and then I realised / remembered that … | The next thing I knew … | A few seconds later … | The weirdest / funniest / scariest thing happened to me the other day. | After a while … | Anyway, it turned out that … | In the end, I decided to …

2 What makes a good travel story? → WB 11/24

→ S4

a) *Talk about what makes a travel story a* ***good*** *travel story. List your points.*

b) *Read this travel story. Find examples of the points you listed in a).*

The weirdest thing happened to me last year. I was on holiday in Italy. We visited a really nice little hill town, and then we decided to have a picnic. We walked out of the town into a small forest. It seemed like the perfect place to stop for a picnic. The next thing I knew, I started to have a really strange feeling. There was something about the place I just didn't like, and I *really* wanted to leave. I told my parents. At first they thought I was joking, but after a while they realised I was serious. I think they were disappointed I didn't want to stay, but they're cool (well, when it isn't about the music I like!) and they agreed. We left the forest area and found another place to have a picnic. Anyway, a few days later, I looked up the town on the internet. I found that a lot of people had died there in a war in the 16th century. Some soldiers had killed almost all the people in the town – women, children, old men. And guess where it had happened? In that forest! I don't believe in ghosts, but something weird definitely happened to me while I was there!

3 Write a travel story

→ S7–9

a) *This travel story is very short and it wouldn't be very interesting to listen to. Rewrite it as you'd tell it to a friend. Use the phrases from Ex. 1 and your ideas from Ex. 2 for help.*

I was on holiday in Egypt. I made a mistake when I ate with my left hand. My brother and I met some Egyptian guys about our age in a café. They invited us to play dominoes with them. Then they ordered some food to share with us. My brother and I started eating with our left hands. Then we realised that was a mistake. In Egypt and other Arab countries you should only eat with your right hand because people think the left hand isn't clean.

b) *Take turns to tell your travel story and give each other feedback.*

True or not true?

You're going to have a storytelling competition in two teams! Your task is to think of travel stories which you must present to the other team. The other team then has to guess if your team's stories are true or not.

Step 1

Plan your travel story → WB 12/26

Divide your class up into two teams. In each team there are five groups of 2–3 students. Each group thinks of two travel stories – one true and one not. In your groups, first collect ideas for your travel stories. These questions can help you:

- Where did you go?
- Why did you go there?
- What happened?
- What was funny / scary / embarrassing about it?

If your story isn't true, try to make it sound as convincing as possible. If it's true, it's important to make the other team believe that you've invented it. So be creative!

Step 2

Write a prompt card → WB 12/27

Write a prompt card for each travel story. Remember not to write whole sentences, but just key words with the most important points. Don't forget to include useful phrases that will make your story more interesting or exciting. → indirect speech (pp. 10–12, pp. 13–15) → How to tell a travel story (p. 20)

Step 3

Practise telling your stories → WB13/28

Decide who will present your group's travel stories to the other team. Then practise your presentation. The other group member(s) should make suggestions about how you could improve each story. → How to tell a travel story (p. 20)

Step 4

Start your competition

Get into the two teams and take turns to tell the different groups' stories. When the other team guesses correctly, they get a point. The team with the most points wins.

Step 5

Give your feedback → WB 13/29

After the competition, think of the travel stories you've heard. What did you find good / not so good about them? Explain why.

Find more online: 9s82pk

Dos and don'ts

SPEAKING

1 Good or bad behaviour? → WB 15/1

→ S11

a) *Work with a partner. Look at the situations in the pictures. Then look at the dos and don'ts below which are typical for English-speaking countries (and for others too). Which ones can you use to describe each situation? Explain why.*

A

B

C

D

Say thank you. | Don't stare. | Don't point. | Be polite. | Don't stand in the way. | Hold the door open for others. | Don't jump the queue. | Don't talk with your mouth full. | Smile. | Say hello back. | Don't litter. | Don't stand too close to others.

b) *What counts as good or bad behaviour in your family / your school / among your friends? You can look at the dos and don'ts in a) for help.*

SPEAKING

2 Your turn: Your experiences → WB 15/2

Can you remember a situation in which someone behaved differently to what you'd normally expect (in Germany or in another country)? Tell your partner about what happened. How did you feel about it? How did you react?

Useful phrases

Just imagine what happened to me when … | I saw something really funny / strange / odd when … | I was really surprised. | I couldn't believe my eyes / ears. | I didn't understand what was going on. | Well, I guess every country has its own customs. | For me, it looked like good / bad behaviour, but then I realised …

VIEWING

3 Aliens in London!

DVD 3/6

Just imagine: Aliens have landed in central London. It's a strange experience for everyone. Find out more!

a) *Watch the film. What did the aliens do wrong from a British point of view? Take notes.*

→ S16

b) *Look at the stills. What's the situation and what goes wrong? Work with your notes from a).*

A

B

WRITING

4 Role play: Breaking the ice

→ S11

a) *You're at a train station and your train is late. Another person is waiting for the train too. The person looks friendly and smiles at you. Write down a conversation you could have with him/her. Look at the icebreakers in the box for ideas.*

b) *Act out your conversation in class.*

Useful phrases

Icebreakers

I hope the train will arrive soon. | How long do you think we'll have to wait for ...?! | How long have you been ...? | I'm glad it isn't so crowded / busy / hot / cold here today. Yesterday it was so ... | Cool T-shirt! You must be a ... fan. | I've heard the film / show / band / ... is really good. | Have you seen the latest film with ...?

WRITING

5 Tips for aliens → WB 15/3

→ S7–9

Work in groups of 3–4. Write a leaflet for aliens who have come to visit earth. Give them tips about how to behave.

Tips for aliens

It's good / bad manners to ...
You should always ...
You shouldn't ever ...
People here (don't) usually ... when ...
It's a good / bad idea to ... because ...
People (don't) like it when you ...

LISTENING

1 Do as I say, not as I do

L1/20

a) *Listen to the first part of a conversation between Ricky and his parents. Where are they going? Why is Ricky not happy? Then listen to the second part. What happens at the train station?*

b) *Listen to both parts again. What do Ricky's parents tell him not to do? Which of those things do his parents do? Make notes.*

c) *Why is the title 'Do as I say, not as I do?'*

d) *Role play: Partner A: You are queueing at a station ticket office. Your train leaves in ten minutes. It's your turn next, but somebody jumps the queue and goes to the ticket office window in front of you. What are you going to say? Partner B: You are at a station ticket office. Your train leaves in two minutes, and you don't have time to queue for a ticket. Jump the queue.*

VOCABULARY

2 Airport talk

a) *Match the sentence halves.*

1. Collect your luggage	a. at passport control.
2. Get a visa and some foreign currency	b. at the check-in desk.
3. You can take public transport	c. before you travel.
4. Show your boarding card	d. in the arrivals hall.
5. Show your passport and visa	e. in the departure lounge.
6. Show your ticket	f. to the flight attendant.
7. Wait for your flight	g. to your hotel.

b) *Number the sentences in the most logical order. Compare with your partner.*

c) *Think about a journey you took recently by plane or any other type of public transport. Write at least six numbered sentences to describe your journey.*

Example: 1. I went to the train station by bus. 2. I bought a ticket from the ticket office … etc.

WRITING

3 An awful journey

a) *Write a travel story based on the pictures. Use these words:*

ferry | traffic | queue | seasick | passports | official

b) *Think of three other things that could go wrong on a journey. Write a short travel story which tells what happened.*

LANGUAGE

4 Messages from a ferry

*Use the words given to complete the text messages with the **present perfect simple** (I have done …) or the **present perfect progressive** (I have been doing …). Add **for / since** where necessary.*

I'm bored already! I … (sit on this ferry | an hour).

… (you | ever | go on a ferry | before?)

This is my first time, but there's nothing to do. I … (already | see all the ferry).

… (you | see the outside deck | yet ?)

No. It … (rain | we got on the ferry). I hope the weather will be better when we get to France.

I … (just check | the weather forecast online). It said it was going to be nice for the rest of the week.

Great! I … (look forward | to this holiday | a long time). I don't want bad weather to ruin it!

LANGUAGE

5 A post from Austria

a) *Read the blog post from a British teenager, who is staying at an activity centre in Austria. Your friend is going to spend the next two weeks at the same activity centre. Tell him / her about the rules and activities he / she will find there. Use **will / won't + be allowed to / have to**.*

I've finally arrived at the activity centre in Austria. There are kids from lots of other countries here, which is great. The first thing I learned is that we mustn't only hang out with kids from our own country. I think that's a good rule, but I'm not sure about some of the others. For example, getting up time is 7 am. Ouch! If you're 14 or older, you may leave the centre in a group, but if you're under 14 you must stay in the centre. I'm 13 and 11 months! There are lots of great activities to choose from. It's not necessary to do any particular activity, but we must choose something each morning and afternoon. We can't just do nothing, but that's not going to be a problem. I want to do almost all of the activities, starting with climbing!

b) *Read the next entry from the blogger in exercise above. Write the dialogue as it must have happened.*

It was about 8.30, and I was relaxing after dinner, chatting with my new friends. I told them I'd had a really nice first day, and one girl said they'd all enjoyed meeting me. Then she stood up and said it was nearly time for bed. I laughed and said she was joking, but then she told me that everybody had to be in bed by 9 o'clock. I couldn't believe it! One of the 'instructors' (that's what they call the adults who work here) was there too. I told him that I couldn't go to bed when it was still light outside. He told me that everybody else would be in bed – even the instructors – so I'd be alone. I said that was fine, but then he told me that it was the rule, and I had to follow it. I said it was like being in prison, but he just told me that I'd get used to it. So now I'm in my bed typing this on my phone. It's dark outside now, so perhaps I'll be able to go to sleep soon.

6 About the weather → WB 17/2

LANGUAGE

a) *Tell the story of what happened on a school trip to the mountains. Use* ***indirect speech*** *to report the things the teacher, the students and the driver said.*

Teacher: The weather forecast is good. We'll have a really nice trip.
Later, on the coach in the mountains:
Student A: The sky is getting darker. I think it's going to rain.
Student B: That isn't clouds. It's fog[1].
Student A: Fog is a cloud down on the ground.
The fog gets worse.
Driver: I've never seen such bad fog.
The fog gets even worse.
Driver: I can't drive any further because it's too dangerous. We'll have to stop and wait until the fog clears.
Teacher: Everything's going to be OK. We'll just be a little late getting home.
They don't get home until midnight.

VOCABULARY

b) *Use the words to complete the text.*

sun | climate | cloudy | windy | drizzle | raining | hot | clear

Britain is famous for having a cool, wet **1**. Every year, millions of Britons escape the **2** skies and **3** of a typical British summer, and fly south for some Mediterranean[2] **4**. But before you book a flight, remember the south of Europe does not always have **5**, blue skies. The Mediterranean coast can be **6** at all times of the year, which may be good for windsurfing but it's not so good for swimming. The sun can also be too **7** for people who are not used to it. Perhaps a traditional cold, wet holiday in Cornwall isn't so bad after all. It may be **8**, but at least you won't get sunburnt[3].

7 Airport worries

LANGUAGE

What did Dawn think when she was at the airport? What really happened? Write the complete sentences.

Example: I thought I was in the wrong part of the airport, but it was the right part.

I'm in the wrong part of the airport. ✔ | I've lost my plane ticket. | They won't give me anything to eat or drink on the plane. | My flight is going to arrive late. | There's going to a big queue at passport control. | It will be difficult to get from the airport to the city centre.

1. … but it was the right part. ✔ 2. … but then I found it in my jacket pocket. 3. … but a flight attendant gave me a delicious meal and a nice drink. 4. … but it really arrived a few minutes early. 5. … but I only had to wait for a few minutes. 6. … but in the end it was really easy. There were buses every ten minutes.

1 **fog** [fɒg] Nebel | 2 **Mediterranean** [ˌmedɪtrˈeɪniən] Mittelmeer- | 3 **to get sunburnt** [ˌget ˈsʌnbɜːnt] einen Sonnenbrand bekommen

MEDIATION

8 A cancelled[1] flight

You are waiting for an evening flight at a British airport when you hear a conversation at a help desk. The passenger is German and doesn't speak English, and the help desk assistant doesn't speak German. Help them and mediate the German into English and the English into German.

Passenger:	*Als ich am Check-in war, sagte man mir, dass mein Flug gerade gestrichen wurde.*
You:	He says that the people at the check-in desk told him …
Assistant:	Are you on the flight to Frankfurt?
You:	…
Passenger:	*Ja. Warum können wir nicht fliegen? Am Check-in wusste es niemand.*
Assistant:	I don't know for sure, but somebody told me there was a problem with the plane.
Passenger:	*Man sagte mir, ich könnte ein Ticket für einen Flug morgen bekommen. Bin ich hier an der richtigen Stelle dafür?*
Assistant:	Yes it is. I can give you a ticket now.
Passenger:	*Man sagte mir auch, dass die Fluglinie mir für heute Nacht ein Hotelzimmer bezahlt.*
Assistant:	That's right. They told me a few minutes ago that they would organise a bus to take you and the other passengers to the hotel. They said it would be here soon.

VOCABULARY

9 Bad news, good news

Match the bad news on the left with the good news on the right. Then write the sentences.

Example: 1. There was a lot of traffic on the road to the airport,
but my flight was delayed so I didn't miss it.

1. a lot of traffic / road to airport	a. got / last seat / not have to stand
2. flight / took off / late	b. lots of / phone boxes / could call home
3. hungry / at the station	c. landed on time / not late for meeting[2]
4. train / very crowded	d. ticket and passport / in pocket / took the flight anyway
5. left suitcase / bus to airport	e. flight / delayed / not miss it
6. mobile phone / not work / abroad	f. vending machine / snacks

SPEAKING

10 How was your journey? (Student A)

Look at the pictures and plan a travel story. Then talk to your partner about the experiences you each had.

Start like this: How was your journey?

1 **cancelled** ['kænsld] gestrichen | 2 **meeting** ['mi:tɪŋ] Besprechung

SPEAKING

11 How was your journey? (Student B)

Look at the pictures and plan a travel story. Then talk to your partner about the experiences you each had.

Start like this: How was your journey?

LANGUAGE

12 Lost in New Delhi

Write the dialogue with the taxi driver and with the people at the shopping centre.

Start like this: Tourists: Can you take us the India Gate, please?

I was in New Delhi with my dad. It's a really big city, and it's not easy to get around it. We got into a taxi, and asked the driver to take us to the India Gate. It's a big historic monument in the middle of the city. The driver asked us if we wanted to do some shopping. We wanted to buy some souvenirs, so I said we did. After a while, the driver said that we were there and stopped. We got out of the taxi and looked for the India Gate but all we could see was a big shopping centre.

Then we saw the sign: India Gate Shopping Centre. A man and a woman came up to us and asked us if we were lost. We asked them where we were. They said we were several miles away from the city centre. The woman told us not to worry. She told us they lived in the centre, and asked us if we'd like to go there with them in their car. I said we'd like that very much.

LANGUAGE

13 We're just about to close → WB 18/4

The narrator from the exercise above is now at a museum near the India Gate. Rewrite the dialogue as a travel story. Use only ***indirect speech*** *to report what was said. You will need to use* ***asked him / us if*** *… and* ***asked / told us to*** *… .*

Attendant:	I'm sorry, we're just about to close.
Father:	Oh dear. Can we come in anyway, just for a few minutes? This is our last day in New Delhi.
Attendant:	I'm sorry. I really can't let you in.
Father:	Never mind. Thank you anyway.
Attendant:	Where are you from?
Narrator:	We're from Birmingham.
Attendant:	Really? My brother lives in Birmingham. He has restaurant there. It's called the Delhi Kitchen. Do you know it?
Narrator:	Yes, we do. We've been there several times. We like it very much.
Attendant:	OK, come in, but don't tell anybody I let you. You can stay for about half an hour.

VOCABULARY

14 Fiesta!

Complete the travel story with the words in the box.

afraid of | air-conditioning | although | coast | crowded | energy | garlic | leaflet | outgoing | steady

I was on holiday with my family on the east [1] of Spain. Some other tourists told us to go to a city called Alicante, and gave us a tourist [2] about it. It looked interesting, so we decided to visit. When we arrived, we found that they were having a big festival with bonfires and fireworks. We all thought it was amazing, [3] my sister is a bit [4] fireworks. There was lots of fantastic street food too. I had some mushrooms with more [5] than I'd ever tasted before. It was all great! It was lucky we had booked a hotel, as the city was really [6]. When we were tired, we went back to the hotel, and tried to sleep, but it was impossible. There was some loud music playing in the street just outside the hotel – a [7] *Thud! Thud! Thud! Thud!* It was also really hot in the room, and the [8] wasn't working. So we put on our clothes, and went back to join the party. It went on until about 5 a.m.! The local people we spoke to were all so cool – really friendly, [9] and full of [10]. It was a wonderful experience.

VOCABULARY

15 Personality adjectives

a) *Put these personality adjectives into two lists (positive – negative). Then think of more words to add to the lists.*

annoying | calm | easy-going | gentle | grumpy | kind | odd | outgoing | rude | silly

b) *Have you ever been grumpy, silly or annoying? (Be honest!) Have you ever met anybody who was especially outgoing, calm, gentle or easy-going? Tell your partner about it.*

WRITING

16 Holiday photos

Use the words in brackets with the ***past progressive*** *to complete the dialogue.*

Artie: Here, these are some of my holiday photos. Those people are some friends I made at the activity centre.
Pete: ___ (why | they | wear) Christmas hats?
Artie: I was in Australia, remember. Christmas is in the middle of summer there.
Pete: ___ (That guy | take) a selfie while ___ (you | take) the photo!
Artie: He took about 200 selfies every day.
Pete: ___ (What | that boy | carry)?
Artie: It was an old suitcase. He found it in the sea, and ___ (he | bring) it onto the beach.
Pete: ___ (why | you | have) a bonfire? ___ (you | have) a barbecue?
Artie: No, it was just for fun. That's me, with the guitar. A friend took the photo.
Pete: I didn't know you could play the guitar.
Artie: ___ (I | not play) it. ___ (I | just hold it) it for the photo.

Text smart 1
Drama

Find more online: xa56yr

What does it feel like to be an actor on stage? What is special about plays?
In Text smart 1 you're going to get to know different scenes from one play. Have fun!

LISTENING

1 Warm-up: Thinking about the theatre

a) *Is there a drama group at your school / in your town? Tell the class about plays or shows you've seen.*

L1/21 → S15

b) *Listen to three friends (Laura, Jack and Simon) as they talk about plays.*

1. What do the friends like about plays?
2. What do they find difficult?
3. What do you think about their comments?

VOCABULARY

2 Theatre collocations

→ △ 112/1
→ S17

a) *Match the verbs with the nouns to make useful collocations about the theatre.*

entertain | stage | act in | learn | forget | follow | use | get into | play | wear | stay | mess up | give | go to | identify with

a great performance | a role | stage directions | the director's instructions | character | props | your lines | in character | the audience | a costume | a scene | the theatre | the protagonist | a part | a play

b) *Now start a glossary of theatre terms with 2–3 entries. You can add on to your glossary over the next pages. Try to use your collocations.*

Example: **in character:** When an actor is 'in character', it means that he / she is acting and thinking like the character. It's important to stay in character too.

SPEAKING

3 Warm-up: Getting into character → WB 19/1

As a warm-up for some of the activities on the next pages, look at the photo and think about what the characters could say. Then say / shout / whisper / … the lines out loud. Be creative and play with your voice!

Example:
A: You look so silly!
B: Well, have *you* looked in the mirror today?

A British production of *The Wind in the Willows*

Claire's Devil by Dave Draper

You're going to read different scenes from a play about a teenage girl and a dilemma she's facing.

The characters are:

- Claire, the story's protagonist
- Rob, a friend
- Claire's mum
- Claire's dad
- Claire's devil
- Claire's angel

READING

4 Scene 1: Rob and Claire → WB 19/2

S 1/9 L 1/22 → S4

Before you read: Talk about what role you think 'Claire's devil' could be. And what about 'Claire's angel'? Then read the scene.

(Rob and Claire are walking home from school.)

Rob: Listen, there's a party in West Street tomorrow night. It'll be fantastic: Do you fancy coming with us?

Claire: In West Street? Isn't that on the other side of town? It's a pretty rough area, isn't it?

Rob: We'll be okay! The station is only a few minutes away. Nearly everyone we know will be there. What do you say?

Claire: I'll phone you tonight. At about six, OK?

Rob: If you're worried about what your parents will say, then there's a simple solution – don't tell them. Say you're staying over at my house with my sister. My mum will cover up for us – she does what I tell her!

Claire: I'll phone you.

(Rob goes off. Claire is alone with her conscience.)

READING

5 The main characters

a) *In your own words, sum up what happens in this first scene.*

→ △ 112/2

b) *What can you say about Rob and Claire's motivations and feelings?*

Example:
On the one hand, Claire wants to …, but on the other hand, she …

Useful phrases

- Rob tries to convince her …
- The dilemma starts when …
- Claire seems / feels confused / unsure / convinced …
- Claire has doubts about …
- I think Claire feels tempted …
- Rob tempts Claire when he …

READING

S1/10–11
L1/23–24

6 Scene 2: The angel and the devil → WB 19/3

a) *In Scene 2, Claire's 'angel' and 'devil' speak for the first time. Before you read the scene, read the skills box.*

b) *Now read how the angel and the devil try to tell Claire what to do.*

Drama skills

Most stories feature characters in **typical roles.** There might be a hero / heroine on the one side and a villain on the other ('good guy' / 'bad guy'). These characters have good or bad motives. What characters from plays / films / books do you know in typical 'good' or 'bad' roles?

The trouble with you is that you never take risks. You always worry about what your parents tell you. What's the matter with you? Just have a little fun!

How boring can you get?! Do you want to lose *all* your friends? They'll all be there, and you'll be at home in front of the TV, like a good little girl.

Let's face it – you're scared! You always back down from things.

All kids lie to their parents. And it would only be a small lie, a white lie. Say you're going to stay with Rob's sister; that's partly true: You can sleep at their house after the party.

What if something bad happened? What if there's a fight? And you're not old enough to go. They'll see that you're not old enough; you'll end up embarrassed and miserable in front of Rob. Tell him you're sorry but you can't go.

Rob is exaggerating as usual. Most of your school friends won't be allowed to go because their parents are as sensible as yours.

It wouldn't be right to lie to your parents. You know they love you, and only want what's best for you. If they found out you had lied they'd never trust you again.

READING

7 Understanding Scene 2

→ S1–3

a) *What makes the devil and angel 'typical roles'? Read what these three students say about it. Say why you agree or disagree. (You can also look back at the skills box on p. 32.)*

Example:
A: That's easy! The devil is mean. He's a bad guy.
B: I agree that he's a typical bad guy, but I don't agree that a bad guy is always mean. This devil is pushy, but not mean. But what about the angel?
C: The angel sounds so scared. Is that typical for an angel? Maybe it is …

b) *Sum up the arguments of the devil and angel. Say which arguments you find the most convincing, and why.*

Example:
The devil says, "Just have a little fun!" Well, I think he's right.
How can you beat *that* argument?

c) *How would you decide if you were Claire?*

SPEAKING

8 White lies

→ △ 113/3

a) *Go back to Scene 2 and read the devil's suggestion for a 'white lie' in lines 11–14. Explain what a white lie is, and if there's a difference between a white lie and a normal one.*

b) *Your turn: Have you ever told a white lie? What was it, and why did you tell it? Tell a partner.*

SPEAKING

9 Getting into character: Reading a scene out loud → WB 20/4

→ S11

a) *Think – pair – share: Read the skills box. Then look at the words below the box. Which ones describe how a 'devil' voice or an 'angel' voice should sound? Which words match **both** voices? Write down your ideas and exchange them with your partner. Then tell the class what you've both agreed on.*

Drama skills

When you read the lines of a play, think about how they'll sound on stage. **Play with your voice** so you can get into character.
A voice on stage can be many things: angry, happy, loud, quiet, …

helpful | sweet | nice | quiet | fearful | loud | tempting | angry | scary | fast | pushy | friendly

b) *Warm-up: Take turns with your partner to read lines 1–14 in a devil voice and lines 15–26 in an angel voice.*

c) *Reading in chorus: Half your class reads the devil's lines out loud together, the other half reads the angel's lines together. Think about which key lines need more 'angel' or 'devil' feeling than the others.*

→ △ 113/4

d) *In groups of four, practise **the whole scene**. The angel and devil use their voices, but Claire never speaks: She only uses her face and gestures to show her dilemma. And one of you is the director; you give the others feedback. Then swap roles and find out which part each of you can read best. When you're ready, read your version of the scene to the class.*

READING

S 1/13–15
L 1/26–28

10 Scene 3: Claire and her parents

→ WB 20/4

Before you read: In the next scene, Claire makes her decision. How do you think she'll decide: Has she listened to her angel or her devil? Explain why you think so.

(Later at Claire's house. Claire is talking to her mum and dad.)

Claire: Mum, is it okay if I stay over at Jenny's house on Saturday night?

Mum: I didn't know you two were friendly.

Claire: Well, I like her a lot.

Mum: I hope you're not getting involved with that brother of hers. Rob isn't the sort of boy you should be mixing with.

Claire: Rob isn't as bad as people think.

Mum: From what I've heard, he's heading for trouble. So be warned!

Claire: Rob has his own circle of friends – we hardly ever speak to each other. Is it okay then, Mum?

Mum: All right. But check with your dad first.

(Claire's mother goes out. Claire is alone with her conscience.)

Angel: See! So many lies already. She'll be terribly hurt if she finds out you've been so dishonest. She trusts you, Claire!

Devil: She'll sleep easy and you can have a great time. Now, you need a good story to convince your dad.

(Later, Claire is with her dad.)

Claire: Dad, Mum says it's okay for me to stay at Jenny Costello's on Saturday, as long as you agree too.

Dad: As long as her parents don't mind, then, that's fine! Have I met her?

Claire: No, she's new in my class. We're working on a design project and I need money for materials.

Dad: What sort of design work is it?

Claire: Er … it's a dress design project. Could I have £25?

Dad: That's a lot! What's this dress going to be made out of? Silk?

Claire: Of course not. But we'd like to do really well on the project so we're buying a couple of books to help us.

Dad: Well, I don't mind paying out if it's to help with schoolwork. Here you are.

(He gives Claire £25 and leaves.)

READING

11 Understanding Scene 3

a) *Compare your answer from Ex. 10 with Claire's decision. Explain why Claire makes this decision.*

b) *Now answer these questions:*

1. Are Claire's parents worried about her? If yes, what do they say to express it?

   Example: Well, when the mother says, "I didn't know you two were friendly," that shows that she is surprised and unsure about who her daughter's friends are.

2. What lies does Claire tell in Scene 3?

c) *Discuss with your partner why you think Claire's decision was right or wrong.*

SPEAKING

12 Acting out Scene 3 → WB 20/5–6

In Ex. 9, you had the chance to practise 'getting into character' with different roles, and how it feels to read them out loud. Here, you'll take a step further: It's your turn to act out a whole scene.

→ △ 113/5
→ S11

a) *First, read the skills box. Then read out and* ***act*** *out Scene 3. Focus on your voice, your face and your gestures. (Decide if the five roles are enough, or if you need a director again too.)*

b) *Do you think it helps to understand the characters more when you act out a scene like this?*

Example:
A: When I was playing the angel, I almost felt like I needed to help Claire. I think I was 'in character' as an angel, as someone who helps.
B: Yeah, when I played Claire, I really had to fake an 'extra friendly' face when I was lying to my parents. I felt a bit fake myself!

Drama skills

Think about these ideas before you act out a scene:
- Decide **who is going to play which role**.
- First **read out your role**, but look up from the page again and again to learn your part, bit by bit.
- Try out **different voices**.
- **Get into character**: Sometimes it helps to think of a person you know who is similar to the person you're playing.
- On stage, your **face** and **gestures** are almost as important as your lines. Make sure your face matches your lines, and make sure that you sit, stand or move in the right way too.

READING **13**

Scene 4: Farewell

S 1/16
L 1/29

Before you read: Look at these lines from the next scene. Which characters from the play do you think will say each line? Explain why.

You've got to make the most of your youth while you still have it!

You'll have to live with that on your conscience.

You've been dishonest.

One lie nearly always leads to another.

Stop preaching!

Devil: Easy, wasn't it? Now everyone's happy: Your parents think you're a really keen student and that they're supporting you. What could be better?

Angel: But you've been dishonest and you'll have to live with that on your conscience. Once you start being dishonest it is hard to stop. One lie nearly always leads to another.

Devil: It's their own fault. If they were a bit more tolerant and easy-going then there'd be no need to lie to them.

Angel: Wouldn't you feel safer if your parents knew where you were and what time to expect you?

Devil: Safer? Where's the danger? A lively night out with a group of friends: Sounds safe enough to me. You've got to make the most of your youth while you still have it! Enjoy yourself while you've got the chance.

Claire: Yes! It's time I started living.

(On Saturday evening at Claire's house, with her dad and mum.)

Claire: Bye, then. I'll see you tomorrow lunchtime.

Mum: Have a good time. Why not bring Jenny round here next weekend? It would be nice to meet your new friend. Perhaps I should ring Jenny's mother later this evening. Just to check it's still okay for you to stop the night. It'll give me the chance to thank her.

Claire: There's no need. Anyway, you can't. Their phone is out of order.

Mum: But I thought Jenny rang you a little while ago. You did say it was Jenny, didn't you?

Claire: Er ... Yes, it was. She had to ring from somewhere else. Bye, now.

Angel: See? What did I tell you? Lies lead to more lies. It never stops.

Devil: Stop preaching! It was an excellent piece of quick thinking. Well done, Claire! Now for a night out on the town! Let's go!

READING

14 Understanding Scene 4

a) *Were you right about who said the different key lines in Ex. 13? Were there any surprises at all? Tell the class.*

b) *Explain Claire's sentence "It's time I started living". Why is it a key line in the play?*

→ △ 113/6

c) *Imagine you're acting the play for your school's Drama Club and you're practising the scene when Claire leaves the house for her night out ("Bye, now", line 40). In groups of six, show the* ***freeze frame*** *of* ***Claire, her parents*** *– and her* ***angel*** *and* ***devil*** *too! One of you is the* ***director****: He / She takes a photo and makes sure you're all in character. Before you do your freeze frame, make a grid with important words to help you to get into character for this scene. The word bank can help you. (Some words fit more than one role.)*

Word bank

shocked | happy | confused | fearful | guilty | angry | fantastic | worried

Claire	Mum	Dad	Devil	Angel
…	confused …	…	…	fearful …

LISTENING

15 A happy ending? → WB 21/7

a) *Now think about the whole story. For each of the four scenes, write a short summary of 2–3 lines.*

b) *With a partner, think about an ending for the play: a happy / sad / surprising / strange ending? Then present your ideas to the class.*

L 1/30 **c)** *Listen to the original ending of the play* Claire's Devil. *What happens?*

d) *Now that you know the whole story, do you feel the story has a message? If yes, a message for whom? Write about it in 5–6 lines.*

16 Options: Bring the story to life → WB 21/8

→ △ 114/7

Choose one of these options and bring Claire's Devil *to life!*

Option A: Stage the play

You've practised reading and acting different roles and one scene. Now you can stage the whole play. Look back at the tips on these pages for help, and you'll find helpful tips in your Workbook too. Think about:

- casting
- costumes and props
- where to stage your play
- learning your lines by heart
- playing with your voice

Option B: Write a photo story

In different groups, take photos of the key parts of each scene with yourselves as the actors. Your 'freeze frame' skills can help you. When you have the photos you need, do the following:

- Write speech bubbles for the characters.
- Write short texts to explain more background information from the plot / action that isn't in the bubbles.

Find more online: bf599t

The USA: Country of contrasts

How many contrasts can a country have? If you're talking about the United States of America (or 'the US'), the answer is: Lots! Find out for yourself on these pages and in the rest of this book.

urban and rural (opposites) area

A In New York City, the 'city that never sleeps', there are more than 13,600 taxis. But outside the big urban centers, in the endless, sparsely populated rural areas of the US, you can drive for hours and hours and not see a single car. (Well, maybe a tractor.)

american landscapes and weather

B In Arizona the summers are hot – and the winters too. In the desert Southwest, temperatures often climb to 110°F or more. No problem for a cactus! But if you fly about two hours to the northwest, you'll be in a much cooler climate zone: The Pacific Northwest has green forests and huge mountains, like Mt. Rainier in Washington State.

USA
historic america

C The country which started as a British colony and later became the United States was built on immigration. In the 19th and 20th centuries, immigrants were usually Europeans and arrived by ship at Ellis Island in New York. Today, most immigrants come from Asia and Latin America. Together, all the immigrants have created a country rich in cultural contrasts.

big trees/big towers

D The biggest, the best, the fastest: You can find lots of superlatives in the US!

For example, the world's tallest trees are found in California, like this huge redwood here. They can be 250 ft., 300 ft. tall or even taller!

In the early 20th century, Chicago and New York gave the world the first really tall skyscrapers. In 1931, the Empire State Building in New York became the world's tallest building at 1,454 ft. It isn't the tallest anymore, but it's probably still the world's most *famous* skyscraper.

USA (american) flags everywhere

E You can see American flags all over the country – at sports events, at schools, in front of homes, in big cities and in small towns. Each state also has its own flag.

People fly flags to show who or what they identify with. For some first-time visitors to the US, all the flags are a contrast to their own countries, where you don't see as many.

different Lifestyles

F Lifestyles can be hugely different in the US. More than 45 million Americans are poor: This means a family of four has only about $24,000 a year. At the same time, there are about 10 million millionaires in America – that's more than the population of Austria or Sweden. And billionaires? There are more of them in the US than in all of China, India and Russia together.

SPEAKING

1 Getting to know the US → WB 24/1

a) *Describe the scenery or the situation in each photo on pages 38–39. What can you see? These words and phrases can help:*

Word bank

crowded | sparsely / densely populated | urban | rural | out in the country | landscape | region | scenery | distances | open spaces | dry | wet | hot | cool | rain | water | climate | desert | mountainous | flat | tall | high | low | gigantic | tiny | rich | wealthy | poor | wasteful | luxury | lifestyle | love your country | leave your old life behind | start a new / better life | refugee | immigrant

Tip

Americans usually call their country 'the United States', 'the US' or simply 'America'. They don't often say 'the USA'.

Useful phrases

- The picture on the left shows … while the picture on the right is an example of …
- The picture of … shows / represents / symbolizes …
- The picture is a way to say that people in America …

b) *Now describe how the four photo pairs (A, B, D, F) show contrast in the US.*

c) *Write a heading for the four photo pairs and for the two single photos.*

d) *If **you** had chosen the photos to show the US as a 'country of contrasts', would you have chosen other ones? Which? Based on what information? Explain your reasons.*

VOCABULARY

2 Word-building: Adjective + noun collocations → WB 24/2

→ S17

a) *Lots of the words that you see on these pages are used in typical **adjective** + **noun** collocations: **rural area**, **hot climate** etc. These collocations are useful for describing people and places. With your partner, make as many collocations as you can with the words below.*

Adjectives:
high | low | dry | wet | hot | cool | harsh | mountainous | flat | extreme | open | crowded | sparsely / densely populated | rural | urban | cultural | wealthy | healthy | beautiful | interesting

Nouns:
region | landscape | climate | climate zone | area | scenery | lifestyle | standard of living | temperature | space

b) *Once you have your collocations, arrange them in **categories** that interest you (climates, landscapes, regions). As you learn more information and vocabulary about the US in this book, add on to your list / lists to make a mini-dictionary.*

Example: **Rural areas:** sparsely populated; open spaces; beautiful scenery; …

WRITING

3 Your turn: Contrasts in your country

What photos would you choose to show contrasts in Germany? Choose one topic (nature, food, buildings etc.) and find two photos for that topic which represent it well. Write a short text (5–6 sentences) for your topic and photos. Share your results with the class.

READING

4 Do you know how big everything is here?!

L2/1

Tristan and Callum's families became friends on vacation in Cornwall some years ago. Tristan lives in San Diego; Callum in London. Right now they're chatting online.

Dude, our summer vacation starts on June 10. When will you get to San Diego?

We're going to leave London on 12 June and stay in America for 5 (!) weeks.

5 weeks of surfing. AWESOME!

Sorry, first NYC and a Broadway play for Mum. Then surfing.

So 2–3 days in NYC and then a 6-hour flight to SD. CU on the 15th?

Wait, how many US states are there?

50. Why?

My mum and dad want to see half. Do you think we can see that many?

Hey, your mom and dad have no clue! Do you know how big everything is here?!

It isn't like it would take YEARS to see it all. And hey, we've got 5 whole weeks.

Not enough. My route planner says NYC to SD is 2,800 miles! 41 hours by car!!! And that's just time in the car. NO STOPS.

Wow, that IS far. So besides SD, what should we see? Boston?

Brits in Boston? Ever heard of the Boston Tea Party? American colonists who threw all the British tea into the harbour?

Oh, sounds like history. Don't tell my dad, he'll want to go. What about the South?

Callum, wrong direction! California is out WEST. Hello!

There are lots of states in the middle there. What could we see in the Midwest?

Endless corn and wheat fields. Some mountains too. The Rockies.

Sounds like lots of open space. Cool! Not like England. Good for riding horses?

Maybe, but not for riding WAVES. Get to Cali, man. Surfing! Fun in the sun!

Mum says we'll be in SD on the 4th of July. Isn't that the day with all the fireworks?

Epic, that's Independence Day! HUGE beach party on the 4th of July every year.

Massive! But wait: I'm going to celebrate how you guys became independent from us Brits?! I don't know about that …

Chill out. That was a long time ago. JUST GET HERE!

a) *Look at the map of the US at the back of your book and find all the places that are mentioned in the chat. Which place would you be most interested in? Explain why.*

b) *Understanding the text:*

1. Point out the moments in which Tristan could have given Callum more or better information about his country, for a more complete picture of the US.
2. Explain why you think Tristan *doesn't* offer more information. Isn't he interested?

c) *Your turn: Which places could you visit about 2,800 miles from where you live? Do some internet research on one place. In a short text with photos, describe how you could travel there and what you could do and see when you get there.*

Find more online: 8n27xv

Unit 2
Kids in America

A

B

VOCABULARY

1 Teen life in the US: First impressions

a) *Describe what you see in each picture. You can look at the word bank on the next page for ideas.*

b) *If you wanted to find out more about the topic 'Kids in America' on the internet, which words from the word bank (or other words) would you use as key words for search engines? Which of the photos give you ideas for your research? Explain why.*

SPEAKING

2 Preparing to live in America

On p. 43, you'll hear about a group of European teenagers who have just arrived in America for a year. Their families have moved to the US for work reasons.

Think – pair – share: What aspects of the three topics on the right would you want to know about if you moved to the US? On your own, think of 1–2 questions you might have. Exchange ideas with your partner before you both share your ideas with the class.

family life

school life

free time activities

In Unit 2 you learn

… how to talk and write about everyday life in the United States. You learn:

- about school life, family life and free time
- how to describe and analyze pictures
- what goes into a school yearbook
- how to use gerund and infinitive constructions to express your ideas

C

LISTENING 3 Orientation weekend: Welcome to America! → WB 25/1–2

L 2/2-3

→ △ 115/1

→ S15

a) *Josh, an American teenager, is giving a talk for European teenagers at an orientation weekend in New York. What information does he start with? Listen to the first part and then sum it up. The word bank can help here too.*

b) *Listen to the rest of Josh's talk. Take notes and sum up what he says about* ***neighborhood / family life, school life*** *and* ***free time activities****.*

c) *Which of your questions from Ex. 2 does Josh answer? What else would you have asked him about?*

Word bank

urban / city life | rural / country life | suburb | suburban | lots of / not enough space | long / short distances | apartment | front yard | backyard | swimming pool | lifestyle | shopping mall | rich | poor | quiet | noisy | safe | dangerous | middle school | high school | hallway | hall pass | dress code | restroom | locker | have fun | make friends | be the new boy / girl

d) *Your turn: Talk about what you find surprising / interesting / strange / different about life in America. Think of what you know from Across cultures 2 and from these pages.*

L 2/4

Living here isn't bad

Matt (from Cambridge) and Lena (a German-American from Hamburg) are two of the teenagers from the New York orientation weekend.

Hi Matt! I can't believe it's only been a week since we met in New York. So much has happened! Living here in rural Pennsylvania isn't bad – but it sure isn't like in the movies. Our house is huge – I love having a big bedroom. You should see my huge walk-in closet! There are a few young people around and I like hanging out with Madison, the girl down the road. They have a swimming pool in their backyard! But there isn't much to do here where the suburbs end and the country begins. Madison has talked about organizing a party for Thanksgiving, but that's not until NOVEMBER! There's a huge shopping mall with 400 stores on the other side of Pittsburgh, but getting there is difficult; it's a long drive. Madison's 16-year-old brother has a car (!), but he doesn't always want his little sister and her friends along for the ride. ☹☹☹ And all the families around here have strict curfews for their kids – Madison has to be home very early each night. ☹☹☹ Same in your neighborhood? – Anyway, I'm homesick for Germany! I miss seeing my old friends and I'm scared of changing too much so they won't like me anymore when I go back. I enjoyed meeting you in New York; how about meeting up in Pittsburgh soon? Lena

Hey Lena. Sounds like our experiences here are quite different. I don't miss my life in England at all! Being in a city is cool – Pittsburgh is big and we live in an apartment close to downtown. I'm still getting used to living on the 22nd floor – the elevator is a BIG part of my life! Can you imagine walking up 22 floors if it stopped working? I miss having a garden (= yard!) so I go out a lot. I take the bus everywhere; the buses are cheap. And luckily we've got shops, cafés, parks and cinemas (or 'movie theaters', as the Americans say) super close to where we live. I'm looking forward to starting school and making new friends next week. I'm good at swimming and football (= soccer!); maybe that will help at Birchview Middle School. But stop worrying about losing your old friends or your identity – just jump in and enjoy the experience. – Hey, I'm afraid I'm very busy right now; meeting up isn't easy. Do you remember Sophie from orientation? She's going to move to Pittsburgh soon – it'll be cool to see her again! Well, keep in touch. CU! ☺ Matt (PS: I keep forgetting your dad is American; no wonder your English is so good!)

READING

1 Two different experiences in America → WB 26/3

→ S1

a) *Sum up Lena's and Matt's situation in America. Whose situation sounds better to you? Say why.*

b) *Compare how Lena and Matt have been experiencing the US. What's the same, what's different?*

c) *Write another message from Matt to Lena to cheer her up with advice.*

READING 2 **Thanksgiving: A very American holiday** → WB 26/4

a) *Lena mentioned an important American holiday: Thanksgiving. Read the box and talk to your partner about festivals and holidays that are celebrated in Germany.*

Across cultures

Thanksgiving is one of the most important national holidays in the United States – and a very important day for families too. On the fourth Thursday in November each year, families all over the country get together for a big, wonderful meal. The meal is a symbol of everything one should be thankful for. This tradition started nearly 400 years ago …

In late 1620, the Pilgrims left England for America so they could practice their religion freely. The first American winter was very hard; the Pilgrims had to build houses and they had to find food. By spring more than half of them had died. The survivors then asked the Native Americans for help with planting food. With that help, the harvest in 1621 was a success. The colonists gave thanks with a big meal which they enjoyed together with the Indians. **What was on the menu?** Roast turkey, cranberry sauce, sweet potatoes and pumpkin pie – the same dishes you'll still find on lots of Thanksgiving tables today.

The first Thanksgiving, 1621

A typical Thanksgiving meal

b) *Your turn: What do you have to be very thankful for? Write about it in 5–6 sentences.*

c) *Why do you think Lena can't wait for Thanksgiving?*

LANGUAGE 3 **Different categories of gerunds** → G5

Each of the left-hand sentences below features a ***noun****. To the right of each sentence you see a sentence which is almost the same, but with a* ***gerund*** *instead of a 'normal' noun. This shows you how gerunds are really verbs which work as nouns:*

1. **Homework** isn't bad.	→ **Living** here isn't bad.
2. I like **burgers**.	→ I like **hanging out** with Madison.
3. I'm good at **football**.	→ I'm good at **swimming**.
4. I'm looking forward to **our trip** to New York.	→ I'm looking forward to **starting** school.

a) *The sentences above are examples of the four gerund categories you see on the right. Match each category to one of the four gerund sentences above.*

a) gerund after adjective + preposition
b) gerund after verb + preposition
c) gerund as sentence subject
d) gerund as sentence object

→ △ 115/2

b) *Go back to Lena's and Matt's messages. Find four different gerund examples which work in the same way as the four examples above. Make a grid.*

LANGUAGE

4 [Gerunds as subject or object] → WB 27/5

→ △ 116/3

Sophie was another girl at orientation in New York. She has posted her first thoughts about the US on a social media page for the others who were there. Use the words on the right to complete her post with gerunds as ***subject*** *or* ***object****.*

travel · move · live · hang out · be · share · cycle (2x) · have

Help! I didn't mind **moving** from Germany to America, but I never imagined 1 in the middle of nowhere! Luckily, we're only staying here with my aunt and uncle until our apartment in Pittsburgh is ready. 2 a bedroom with my messy cousin really gets on my nerves! I just can't get used to 3 such a messy room. Anyway, Dad always says how beautiful it is out here in the country, but where's the *action*?! 4 bored is no fun! I miss 5 with my friends. And, can you believe this? 6 to the next mall takes TWO HOURS by car! My cousin has just suggested 7 somewhere this afternoon – but I don't feel like 8 anywhere. I mean, where to anyway? We're in the middle of nowhere!

LANGUAGE

5 Gerunds in phrases

Now read Matt's reply to Sophie's post. Put in the missing ***verb + preposition*** *or* ***adjective + preposition*** *to make complete gerund phrases.*

Don't 1 feeling bored. When you get to Pittsburgh, you'll soon have to 2 being busy all the time! It's a great place, with lots to do. I'll never be 3 living here! I'm already very 4 finding my way around the city and I'm not at all 5 getting lost. I'm 6 going to my first baseball match soon. Do you 7 meeting up and going together? I'm 8 seeing you when you get here. Can't wait!

looking forward to · worry about · feel like · thinking of · tired of · good at · scared of · get used to

SPEAKING

6 Gerunds to talk about likes and dislikes → WB 27/6

→ △ 116/4

Gerunds are often helpful when you want to talk about likes and dislikes. Here, Lena is talking to her new friend, Madison. Rewrite their sentences with the phrases on the right and with ***gerunds****. Don't change the meaning!*

keep · look forward to · start · don't mind · stop · think of · be interested in · love

Lena

1. I'm a bit shy when I meet new people, but it's OK.
   → I **don't mind meeting** new people.
2. Maybe I'll go to the mall; I'm not sure yet.
3. Mom tells me to unpack every day!
4. There's a dress code so I don't wear crazy T-shirts to school anymore.

Madison

5. My brother learned to drive when he was 16.
6. Would you like to meet some more people in the area?
7. I can't wait to plan our Thanksgiving party!
8. I listen to music all the time!

SPEAKING 7

Your turn: Likes and dislikes

→ △ 116/5

a) *With the words on the right, tell your partner about things you like and dislike. (Tip: It might help to write out some of your ideas first. Also, the vocabulary box on p. 175 can help.)*

love | hate | enjoy | dislike | dream of | be tired of | be interested in | be scared of | be worried about | be good at | be crazy about

Example:

A: I'm never crazy about being the 'new person'. It always makes me feel so insecure. What about you?

B: For me, trying new things is great! You'll never know you're good at something until you try.

b) *Go back to p. 43 and 'climb into' photo C. Imagine **you** are there in the hallway on your first day at school. In 5–6 sentences, describe what's going through your mind.*

SPEAKING 8

How to: Describe pictures → WB 28/7–9

→ S5

What does America look / feel like for teens in rural areas? And in the city? After you read the skills box, work with a partner and answer the questions below. He / She chooses one of the pictures; you choose the other. The useful phrases box can help you too.

1. Describe your picture. Who's in it? What's happening?
2. Do you think your picture is a good example for showing what America might look like for Americans the same age as you? Why do you think so? Explain your ideas.

Speaking skills

When you talk about pictures (photos, cartoons), do it in steps:

1. First, **describe** what is happening. For this, you use the **present progressive**. It's also important to talk about what you can see in the foreground, middle and background.
2. After that, you can **analyze** a picture: You can give your opinion about it or explain what you think it means. For this you use the **simple present**.

Look at the phrases box below for examples.

A

Useful phrases

Describing pictures:

- In picture X, a person is talking / running / having fun with … / asking … | Somebody else is laughing / shouting / …
- In the foreground, there's a/an … / there's some …
- In the background, you see a/an … / lots of …

Analyzing pictures:

- In my opinion, the picture is a typical example of … because it shows …
- The picture represents … / shows …
- The picture tries to show … but I think a picture with … instead of … would work better because …

B

L 2/6

That's the worst thing to do!

Matt is on Birchview's yearbook committee. They decide what goes into the yearbook – and what doesn't. Matt is sitting with two of the most popular 8th-graders, Scott and Eva.

Scott, Eva and Matt were looking at different layouts in second period when Scott stopped to say something in Matt's direction. "Hey, let's go for lunch together."

"Yeah, with us this time, Matt. You don't want to sit with Henry and Tyler again, do you?" Eva added with a funny look on her face. "Stop talking to them. They're geeks."

"If you want to be popular, that's the worst thing to do!" Scott agreed.

Matt went on looking at the different layouts in front of him; he needed time to think – what a dilemma! "So, they want me to be friends with them," he thought to himself. "But why are they so mean about the boys I had lunch with yesterday, the 'geeks'?"

"The geeks are no fun to hang out with because they never *have* fun."

"Yeah, I mean, who wants to be around people whose idea of fun is to go to the mall and shout at the shoppers?"

Matt was confused. "I don't understand."

"They keep on talking about changing the world. So whenever there's a protest against child labor and sweatshops, the geeks are always the first to shout at the people who buy cheap sweatshop clothes."

"I mean, I agree: Child labor is awful," Eva went on. "But now the geeks want us to write about it in the yearbook. That isn't what it's for. A yearbook should be for fun things, for the highlights of our year!"

Another girl in the room had a different opinion: "Sorry Eva, but demonstrating for children's rights *is* a highlight of the year!"

Matt agreed. But all he could say was, "Well, I guess it isn't so easy to decide what goes into the yearbook!" He was smiling, but inside he didn't know what to think. "Do Scott and Eva expect me to drop my new friends just because they're different? I was looking forward to hanging out with them again," he thought. "Should I go to lunch with the in-crowd?" He didn't know. Yesterday had been his first day at this school, with two surprises: The day started with the Pledge of Allegiance – very different to the UK! And then in the cafeteria came another surprise: He was looking for a place to sit when two boys invited him to their table. They seemed a bit different and at first they talked a lot about their protests, but then they went on to talk about other things too. Matt liked them. Did he really need to choose between them and the others?

READING

9 Matt's dilemma → WB 29/10

a) *Eva and Scott are part of the popular in-crowd, and they talk about Henry and Tyler as 'the geeks'. What do you think of cliques like this at school?*

b) *What is Matt's dilemma? Describe it in your own words.*

c) *How would you react in Matt's situation? Write him an e-mail with your advice.*

→ ▲ 117/6

READING 10 L2/7

Everyday life in American schools → WB 29/11

Across cultures

Most American students take the **Pledge of Allegiance** every morning. They stand, face the American flag, put their right hand over their heart and say:

"I pledge allegiance to the Flag of the United States of America, and to the Republic for which it stands, one Nation under God, indivisible, with liberty and justice for all."

a) *What do you think of the Pledge of Allegiance?*

b) *With your partner, talk about other ways people show that they belong to a country / group / school / club / …*

LANGUAGE 11

→ △ 117/7–8
→ ▲ 118/9

Find the rule: Infinitives with question words → G6

a) *When you talk about what people ask themselves, you often use* ***infinitive constructions****. Look at these examples. Make a rule for questions with and without question words.*

Matt asked himself, "What should I think?" → Matt didn't know **what to think**.
He thought, "Should I go for lunch with the in-crowd?" → He wasn't sure **whether to go** for lunch with the in-crowd.

b) *Matt had a lot of questions during his first days at school. Make sentences about him.*

Start: He wanted to know **where to go** for a drink of water.

- Where can I go for a drink of water? ✔
- Should I use my own laptop?
- Should I buy lunch or bring my own?
- How much money must I bring for lunch?
- When can I use my locker?
- What do I have to wear for PE?

LANGUAGE 12

Infinitives after superlatives

Superlative phrases *with* ***infinitives*** *are easy to use. Look at the example below. Then use the words on the right to complete what some students in the school café are saying to each other.*

1. You eat so quickly. You're always **the first to finish**!
2. You take so long to choose your food! You're always …
3. You're having salads?! I want a burger! Am I …?
4. We shouldn't eat too much before swimming. That's …
5. The pizza here is fantastic. I always think it's …
6. If you don't have much money, soup is …
7. I like having lunch with you guys. You're …

the only one / eat meat
the cheapest thing / have
the first / finish
the funniest people / sit with
the worst thing / do
the last / sit down and eat
the best thing / order

LANGUAGE 13

Object + infinitive: Expressing wishes and expectations

a) *Change the sentences below into German. Then compare the German and English constructions:*

1. Scott: Come on, Matt. Sit at our table today!
↓
2. Scott wants Matt to sit at their table today.

→ △ 131/10
→ ▲ 131/11

b) *What do these people want or expect others to do? Look at the example and rewrite the other sentences in the same way. The yellow grid below can help too:*

Example: Scott: Don't sit with Henry and Tyler, Matt.
→ Scott doesn't **want Matt** to sit with Henry and Tyler.

1. Eva: No, sit with us instead. → Eva **would prefer** …
2. Matt to himself: They don't think that I should be friends with Henry and Tyler. → They **don't want** …
3. Tyler: We're happy when people think we're different. → We'**d like** …
4. Henry: We hope they'll start thinking about where their clothes are made.
5. Tyler to Matt: The teachers say we can't work on our protest events during class.
6. Matt to himself: Scott and Eva always think that everybody should agree with them.

want / would like would prefer would expect		**object (noun or pronoun)**		**infinitive with *to***
I (don't) want I expect I'd like I'd prefer	+	me you him / her / it us them	+	to …

erwarten ←

Tip

Be careful! It's a typical mistake not to use an **infinitive with *to*** in sentences with *want you to …* or *expect you to …* because the sentence structure is different in German.

LANGUAGE 14

Infinitives with and without *to* → WB 30/12

Read this e-mail from Sophie to Matt. Complete it with the verbs below. Use the infinitive form, with or without ***to***.

get | meet up | take | come | have | keep | do (2x) | control | calm down

Tip

The Grammar will help you to decide where to use ***to***. (→ G6)

Hi Matt – You know we wanted **1** in Pittsburgh next week? Well, sorry but I can't. My parents have been worried about me all the time since we moved to the big city and they don't let me **2** anything. They're crazy! They've decided **3** everything I do! Today, I had planned **4** a coffee with friends after school but they made me **5** straight home. I think it's probably better just **6** as they say – but soon I'll make my escape! They should **7** and relax – but it might **8** a while! I promise **9** in touch – let's **10** together soon. xo 🙂 Sophie

LANGUAGE

15 Gerund or infinitive: It depends on the meaning → G7 → WB 30/13

a) *Some verbs (begin, like, prefer etc.) can be followed by an infinitive or a gerund with no difference in meaning. But with a few verbs, the meaning changes. It's important to learn by heart when you need a gerund and when you need an infinitive. First, write these two sentences in German to find out how the meaning of* ***remember*** *changes:*

1. He **remembered** saying goodbye to his friends back home; it made him feel sad.
2. She **remembered** to tell her parents what time she was coming home.

→ △ 119/12

b) *In the text on page 18, the verbs* ***go on*** *and* ***stop*** *are each used with an infinitive and with a gerund. Talk about how the meaning changes for each verb. Then write the sentences in German; this will help you to see the difference more clearly.*

c) *Read these sentences from an argument Sophie had with her mother and complete them with a* ***gerund*** *or an* ***infinitive****.*

Sophie: I'll never forget **1** (hear) that you were taking me away from all my friends in Germany!
Mom: Don't forget **2** (call) me when you arrive at your friend's house!
Sophie: Please stop **3** (give) me rules and curfews all the time!
Mom: Can't you stop **4** (have) some lunch? I'm tired of arguing with you!
Sophie: Try **5** (listen) to me sometimes. I just want to make friends and fit in! Why don't you try **6** (understand) how I feel?
Mom: Playing sport is a good way to meet friends.
Sophie: Sure, but it means **7** (stay) after school – and you won't let me!
Mom: I don't mean **8** (upset) you. But America is new for all of us and I worry.

MEDIATION

16 Clean out your attics for the clothing drive! → WB 31/14–15

→ △ 119/13
→ S13

Birchview Middle School is having a clothing drive for a homeless shelter. The committee for the project has written a flyer for it. On video chat, Lena wants to tell some students at her old school in Hamburg about it. One of you plays Lena and describes the main ideas in the flyer; 2–3 others play students who ask Lena questions about it.

HELP THE HOMELESS!
Birchview Middle School Clothing Drive

Are you tired of looking at all the old clothes in your closet? Worried about what your next new outfit will be? Well, some people wish they had problems like that. The Lakeview Homeless Shelter needs our help, and Birchview has ALWAYS been good at helping.
So … **Donate as many old clothes as you can!**
(We'll accept clothing for kids and adults, and also shoes, belts, toys and bikes.) **The benefits:** Our school will get 15 cents a pound for all of the items we donate. And YOU'LL get a great feeling of knowing you helped homeless people, your school *and* your parents! (Remember, cleaning out the attic and garage is something they really expect you to do!) 🙂 THANK YOU!

(Clothing drop-offs: Mo–Fr this week in the cafeteria, before or after school)

S1/19–26
L2/9–16

Nightmare at the mall!

SPEAKING

1 Before you read

What teen films have you seen that felt believable at first, but then went in a direction that didn't seem believable at all? What was that moment? Use the words and phrases below to help you explain your ideas.

exaggerated actions / feelings / …

unrealistic situation / language / coincidence

actions which didn't match the character / the role

A Lena was excited. Madison's mom was finally driving them to the big mall on the other side of Pittsburgh. It was a long drive through lots of suburbs. After three weeks of waiting far outside the city, where the suburbs end, she was going to see the *real* America and have an afternoon away from her boring life. She could still hear her own mom's voice in her ears: "If you lose your friends, call me – and don't do anything silly!"

In the car, Madison's older brother Josh explained to Lena what was happening at the mall that day. "We're going to see a really famous baseball player, Wayne Larson," he explained. "He's going to open a new sports store, so expect big crowds. He might even sign a T-shirt for you!"

B When they finally arrived, Lena was amazed. So many stores, so many people, so much noise! For a moment she felt scared – but only for a moment. "This will be fun!" she thought. "Mom will come back later," said Madison. "If we lose each other, we need to meet here at these benches at 5 o'clock."

"Don't worry. I'm going to stay right next to you!" said Lena. But exactly at that moment, there was a huge cheer and she was suddenly pushed into a big crowd of hundreds of people; everyone was trying to get a look at Wayne Larson. Lena tried to grab Madison's arm, but the crowd was moving too fast and she soon realized that she had lost her friends – after only five minutes at the mall!

C Lena tried to turn around as the crowd pressed against her but she couldn't move at all. She started to feel sick and dizzy. The voices all around her were getting louder, then some voices became even louder than the rest …

"Down with child labor!" …
"What if they were YOUR children?!"

What was going on? Wayne Larson was looking very worried as his bodyguards helped him to escape from the crowd. Who were the protesters? Lena was just able to see a group of young people who were all carrying signs and shouting. Then the crowd started pushing again. This time, her feet didn't touch the ground and she flew through the air. She landed very close to the protesters. Then she felt a very strong pair of hands which then took her away.

D "I've got one of the troublemakers right here!" a man shouted. "So what do you have to say for yourself, young lady?"

Lena couldn't believe it! Now the police were arresting her! She tried to speak but nothing came out. "I …, I …,"

"Well, you'd better think of some good answers to our questions quickly or you'll find yourself in big trouble!" said the police officer. Lena could easily imagine spending a night in prison and she was starting to panic when a voice shouted from behind her.
"LEAVE HER ALONE!" Who was that?

E "She isn't doing anything wrong! She isn't from here. Let her go!" the voice continued. She tried again to speak "I …, I …"

"Sshh," whispered the voice. Pretend you don't speak English!"

She turned around and came face to face with … Matt?! From the New York weekend?! "What are YOU doing here?!" she asked.

"Er, rescuing you!" he answered. "Now, don't say anything else. I'll get you out of here." Lena waited while Matt spoke to the police officer and soon she was free to go.

F "What are you really doing here?" she asked Matt as they pushed through the crowds.
"Oh, I've come to support the protesters – they're my friends, from my new school in Pittsburgh."

Lena wanted to ask more questions, but then she remembered. What was she thinking? Matt had clearly told her that he didn't want to meet up with her – while he had made it very obvious that he wanted to meet *Sophie!* Lena found a small gap in the crowd and hurried away from Matt.

G What a nightmare! Lena wasn't enjoying her afternoon at the mall at all. Where were Madison and the others in this sea of people? Lena was going up and down escalator after escalator; she looked everywhere and just couldn't find them. She needed to call her mom and felt silly about it – surely she was old enough to look after herself better than this? But Lena accepted that it was time to give up and call her mom, so she opened her bag to get her phone and – it wasn't there.

H As Lena moved down *another* escalator, still looking all around her for Madison, she was trying so hard not to cry that she almost didn't notice the boy in front of her – Josh!

"Lena!" he shouted when he saw her. "We couldn't find you! Madison has already gone home with Mom – but don't worry. My friend, Nick, has a car. Come on!"

Lena didn't think twice: "Yeah, sure!"

"Cool, I'll drive you!" smiled Nick. But then Lena knew she really shouldn't go. She didn't know Nick and she didn't like his smile. And, her mom would go crazy … But really, she was too tired to care. She was just walking along slowly with the boys when from behind her she suddenly heard a voice she knew. "Lena! Here you are. I lost you! Look, here's your phone. You dropped it!" Matt was all smiles.

"He's just saved my life – for the *second* time today!" Lena thought. "I can't forgive him yet for liking Sophie more than me …" But then she said: "Let's have a coffee before I call my mom." They both smiled.

READING

2 Understanding the story → WB 32/16

a) *Match one of these headings to each of the eight parts of the story.*

1. Next stop: Prison?!
2. I can't be his friend
3. Alone already?!
4. Too old to be in this mess
5. Rescued again!
6. Escaping from home – finally!
7. Protests and shopping don't mix!
8. A friend to the rescue

b) *The title of the story is 'Nightmare at the mall'. Can you think of a title which would work better? Write it down and tell the class why you chose it.*

READING

3 Believe it or not?

Which of these events in the story did you find believable – or not? Explain your reasons.

1. Lena lost her friends at the mall.
2. Matt was at the same mall as Lena.
3. Lena was stopped by the police.
4. Matt found Lena's phone.
5. Lena agreed to get into Nick's car.
6. Matt found Lena twice.
7. Lena invited Matt for a coffee.
8. The mall was so crowded.

WRITING

4 An exaggerated storyline: Make it more realistic → WB 32/17

→ S7–9

Writing skills

Storylines are often exaggerated for more action and excitement. Examples:

- **coincidence:** *She turned around and came face to face with Matt.* (lines 70–71)
- **exaggerated language:** *He's just saved my life!* (line 118); *What a nightmare!* (line 89)
- **unrealistic situation:** *She felt a very strong pair of hands which then took her away.* (lines 49–51)
- **extreme action:** *Her feet didn't touch the ground; she flew through the air.* (lines 47–48)
- **extreme reaction:** *Pretend you don't speak English!* (lines 68–69)
- **out-of-character actions:** *Lena didn't think twice.* (line 108)

a) *Collect all the coincidences and unrealistic situations in the story.*

b) *Decide which situations in a) you would have left out of the story. Explain why.*

→ △ 119/14

c) *Creative writing: Choose one part of the story to rewrite so that it's more believable.*

SPEAKING

5 ‹ Your turn: Are you telling the truth? ›

a) *What* **true stories** *can you think of which are exaggerated and almost impossible to believe? Which stories can you think of which would be fun to tell but* **didn't really happen**? *Make notes about a story you can tell in b).*

b) *Play a game: Now tell your stories to the class. Everyone can show if they believe your story or not: A* **green** *card means "I believe it" and a* **red** *card means "No way, I don't believe it!" Each person needs to explain his / her green or red card.*

Go on, text her!

→ S16

SPEAKING

1 Warm-up: What do you look for in others?

→ WB 33/18

Share your ideas in your group about what you find attractive in others. The words / phrases in the boxes can help you.

Useful phrases

- I look for … in a friend / boyfriend / girlfriend.
- The person should have / be …
- The most important thing to me is …
- It's attractive if the person is / has …

nouns:
positive attitude | nice smile | good looks | sense of humor | sense of style | good listener | lots of the same interests

adjectives:
honest | fair | funny | attractive | smart | popular | outgoing | laid-back

VIEWING

2 The characters

DVD 4/1

a) *Watch the two scenes with Wesley and Jessica (till 04:09). Then describe each character in the story so far: Wesley, Jessica and also Leanne. What are their roles in the storyline?*

b) *Now watch again and answer these questions:*

1. Describe what Jessica means at these moments with her advice for Wesley:

Don't you think that's overdoing it? It's not really you. | Just relax and be yourself. | Remember not to eat anything with garlic. | Clothes aren't everything.

2. Explain why it's good advice – or not.
3. What advice would you give Wesley?

VIEWING

3 The date

a) *How does Wesley change between the scene on the left (03:34) and the scene on the right (05:25)? Describe what happens (in 5–6 sentences) and how these two stills show the difference. Think of how Wesley acts, talks and looks.*

b) *Do you think Wesley and Leanne have a chance together? Go back to Ex. 1. Think of what Wesley and Leanne might find attractive and interesting in each other.*

How to write in the appropriate style

This page can help you to find the right style and tone when you write different kinds of texts.

1 Listening: Students on the yearbook committee

L2/17

a) *Listen to two students who are discussing yearbook pages. Take notes about these points:*

the three main sections in yearbooks | typical content for each section | the appropriate language for each section

→ S15

b) *Listen again. Which of these photos and texts are good and which ones need to be changed? What changes do the students suggest?*

OMG, how cute is Austin Ford's smile?! No surprise that he won 'Boy with the Best Smile'! (What toothpaste does he use?)

((Dear yearbook team – we still need a text here!))

Why does Janie ALWAYS have to be in the middle of EVERY photo? Here she is again! She'll never learn, will she?

2 Find the right writing style → WB 34/20

In pairs, make a grid with three columns for ***Student Superlatives, Highlights of the Year*** *and* ***Clubs and Sports****. What language tone do you need for each category? What style of photos? What phrases are typical? Fill in your grid with ideas and phrases from the boxes below.*

3 Write a short yearbook text

Now go back to Ex. 1b). Write the text for photo 2 and improve the text for photo 3. Peer-edit each other's texts. Are the tone and the language appropriate?

→ S9

Word bank

Language tone:
funny | serious | ironic | simple | informative

Style of photos:
silly | natural | serious | individual / group | a silly / serious / … pose

Useful phrases

The swim / soccer / … team had their best season ever. | Being in / Participating in the Drama Club / the Yearbook Committee was … special / different / interesting this year because … | The Art Club started the year with … | Wasn't the Spring Dance / the championship basketball game the best ever? | We'll always remember the day when … | Here he / she is again with … | He / She will never learn! | We wanted you to see THIS! | How could we ever forget …?

An American-style yearbook

Here you get the chance to create some typical double pages in English for an American-style yearbook about your own school.

Step 1

Form groups

*Divide up into six groups. There should be **two groups** for each of the **three categories** of typical yearbook content you see on the right.*

- Student Superlatives
- Highlights of the Year
- Clubs and Sports

Step 2

Think about typical content for your pages → WB 35/21

*Each group is going to plan **a model double page** for its category. First you need to think about what kind of content is typical for your category. Think about these points as you brainstorm your ideas:*

- What kind of **texts** will you need: short / long; factual / funny?
- What kind of **photos**: individual / group; serious / funny; several / few / just one?
- What kind of a **design** would look best for your pages?
- What **examples** of school and free time activities from this unit can give you ideas for your own pages? What funny / strange / interesting things are there to report?
- What **vocabulary** and **language** from the unit could help you?

Tip

For the category 'Highlights of the Year', many yearbook commitees feature **free time** activities and events too (e.g. something that happened at the mall / a concert / at a party / …)

→ Vocabulary about teenage life (Introduction) → Likes / dislikes (Station 1) → Describing pictures (p. 47) → Questions and superlative phrases (Station 2) → Using the appropriate style and tone / Yearbook phrases (p. 56)

Step 3

Make a poster for your plan → WB 35/22

On a poster, make a plan that shows what your double page could look like. Then trade posters with the other group that has your category. Make sure you aren't doing the same things!

Step 4

Create your pages

Now divide up the work in your group: Collect photos, write texts, peer-edit each other's work. Also, somebody will need to present your pages to the class.

Step 5

Present your pages

Present your pages to the class. Explain why the topics, photos and texts are good examples. Other groups will say which parts of your pages they liked best, and give their reasons.

LISTENING

1 Moving

L 2/18

a) *Listen to the conversation between Kim and her best friend Tina. What is Kim's problem? What does Tina tell her?*

b) *Listen again and find examples of exaggerated language and extreme reaction. How does this match the turning point in the girls' conversation?*

c) *Partner A: You're going to move to another town / country with your family and you're really sad to leave your friends. Partner B: One of your best friends is going to move to another town / country. What do you tell him / her to make him / her feel better? Collect ideas and act out your conversations first together and then for the class.*

VOCABULARY

2 Urban vs. rural → WB 38/2

a) *Replace[1] the words and phrases in **bold** with the adjectives below to make the text more interesting. Sometimes you have to add the verb **be**.*

awesome | wealthy | dizzy | endless | flat | amazed | insecure | natural | gigantic | homeless

When I first saw New York City, I was **very surprised** by all the lights in the city. They seemed to be everywhere and to be on 24 hours a day! Sometimes when I looked up, I felt **like everything was spinning**[2] because all the buildings were **very, very big**. New York is a city of contrasts too. I saw people who were **very rich** and people who **didn't have a home**.

After three days in New York, I was ready to leave the city, but out in the country I felt small too because the landscape **had no mountains** and the sky **never stopped**. Everywhere I went people were **really, really great**. At first I **didn't feel very sure of myself**, but the Americans I met were all so friendly that soon it was **completely normal** for me to speak English with everybody!

b) *Use five of the adjectives from a) to write your own sentences.*

LANGUAGE

3 I'm looking forward to ...

*Use the words and phrases to rewrite the conversation with **gerunds**.*

Start like this: A: I'**m looking forward to seeing** you on Friday!

be good at | keep | look forward to ✔ | stop | be used to | be worried about

A: I can't wait to see you on Friday! ✔
B: Me too! I'm counting the days.
A: I'm not so sure if I should take the train.
B: Don't worry! It's easy to use the train.
A: Yeah, for you it's easy. You take the train all the time.
B: Yes, I do. But when I'm late, I have a problem. I can't run like you can!

1 **to replace (by/with)** [rɪˈpleɪs] ersetzen (durch) | 2 **to spin** [spɪn] sich drehen

LANGUAGE

4 Sophie's bedroom → WB 38/3

a) *What do the things in Sophie's bedroom and her telephone conversation say about her? Use the words and phrases to make sentences with* ***gerunds****.*

Example: Sophie **loves buying** new shoes.

decide against | dream of | be crazy about | be excited about | be good at | love ✔

dance | watch | go | listen | travel | buy ✔

I want to buy new shoes …

b) *Think about things in your room. What do they say about you? Write three sentences with* ***gerunds****.*

WRITING

5 America is different

a) *Imagine you've spent some time in America. Think of three things that are different there. Write down tips for someone who is visiting America for the first time.*

Start like this:
If you have to use the toilet in America, don't ask where the 'toilet' is. Instead …

b) *Your turn: What is different in Germany? Work with a partner and write down three tips for people who are visiting Germany for the first time.*

LANGUAGE

6 Too many rules

Put the words in the right order to make sentences with ***gerunds as subject or object****.*

1. the rules | isn't | following | cool
2. what everyone else | I | don't like | does | doing
3. with my parents | arguing | is awful | about my curfew
4. isn't | with a troublemaker | a good idea | being friends
5. don't mind | with the popular kids | I | hanging out
6. but | having | I | my own ideas | love

LANGUAGE

7 Celebrating Thanksgiving

a) *Use the verbs to complete the text with **gerunds as subject or object**.*

be | bother | celebrate | eat (2x) | play | talk | wait | watch

1 Thanksgiving is good and bad. I don't mind 2 turkey every year because my mom makes the best turkey ever. 3 polite and 4 my grandma's potatoes although I don't like them is hard. One of the worst parts is 5 with my annoying little cousins. They never know when to stop 6 me. 7 for dessert is probably the worst part. The adults spend so much time 8 before we get our pie. There's another big Thanksgiving tradition. I love 9 football on TV with all my uncles.

b) *What do you like / don't you like about holidays with your family? Make sentences with **gerunds** and share them with your partner. These ideas can help you:*

Celebrating holidays with my family is … | On holidays I really like / don't like … | … is the best part of holidays. | I always look forward to …

MEDIATION

8 Fair for everyone → WB 37/1

Lena is showing Matt a website about a fair trade group in Germany. Answer Matt's questions.

1. Why are they showing the picture of a clothes store? 2. What do they say about being fair?
3. The children in the picture are wearing school uniforms. What is said about this in the text?

FAIR FÜR ALLE – Wir setzen uns ein, damit alle fair handeln können.

Immer mehr Leute wollen Produkte kaufen, die „fair" hergestellt wurden, egal ob es sich um Lebensmittel oder Kleidung handelt. Oft wissen sie aber nicht, welche Produkte sie kaufen sollen und was „fair" genau bedeutet. Unser Ziel ist es, dass mehr Menschen sich für das Thema „fairer Handel" interessieren.

Und „fair" hat viele verschiedene Aspekte. Einer davon ist die Kinderarbeit, denn in manchen Ländern müssen die Kinder arbeiten, um zum Familienunterhalt beizutragen. Wir sind der Meinung, dass etwas dagegen getan werden muss. Alle Kinder sollten die Chance haben, eine Schule zu besuchen.

LANGUAGE

9 In the yearbook office

*Use **infinitive constructions** to rewrite the sentences.*

Example: 1. Tom loves the yearbook. He is always **the first to arrive** at the office.

1. Tom loves the yearbook. He is always the first person who arrives at the office. ✔
2. Julie has a good camera. So she is the only one who takes pictures.
3. Sue is very careful. She is always the first person who finds mistakes in the captions.
4. David is responsible. He is the last person who looks at the yearbook.
5. The last yearbook was amazing. It was the only one that won a prize.

SPEAKING

10 Student superlatives

In some yearbooks students are asked to vote in different categories, e.g. 'Most likely[1] to succeed', 'Most likely to become president[2]'.

a) *Describe the cartoon. If you need help, go back to the skills box on p. 47.*

b) *Explain the message of the cartoon. The useful phrases in the box can help you.*

Useful phrases

In my opinion, the cartoon's message is … | I think the cartoon wants to show / tell us that … | The cartoonist wants us to think about … / wants to make fun of[3] …

Talk about Snooty. She was listed as 'most likely to be googled' in the class yearbook.

LANGUAGE

11 Pocket money

a) *Use the prompts to make sentences with **object + infinitive**.*

Example: 1. Jill doesn't have any money. She **wants her father to lend** her some.

1. Jill doesn't have any money. her father | lend her some | she | want ✔
2. Her father thinks Jill is lazy. get an after-school job | he | her | would like
3. Jill says she doesn't have enough time. give her more pocket money | her parents | expect | she
4. Jill's father believes there is an easy solution. tell | he | her | to get a calendar
5. Jill gets angry. her father | her | to be polite | warn
6. Suddenly Jill is very sweet again. her father | remind | she | to give her her pocket money. Today is the first of the month!

b) *What do your parents like or expect you to do? And what do you like or expect your parents to do? Make a list and share your ideas in class.*

1 likely ['laɪkli] wahrscheinlich | **2 president** ['prezɪdnt] Präsident/-in | **3 to make fun of** [ˌmeɪk 'fʌn‿əv] sich lustig machen über

VOCABULARY

12 English in Britain and America

a) *Look at these words in American English. Find British English words which have the same meaning.*

vacation | yard | restroom | movie | downtown | elevator | movie theater | soccer | apartment | period | store

b) *Answer the following questions about American English.*

1. What do the Americans mean when they talk about a 'holiday'? 2. Where's the first floor in America? 3. Why do the Americans use the word 'soccer'? 4. Why is the temperature in America always so high?

LANGUAGE

13 At the shopping mall

Change the infinitive constructions back into ***questions****.*

Example: There were so many entrances to the mall. Lena didn't know which to use.
→ Lena: Which entrance should I use?

1. She wanted to know where to buy a new winter jacket.
2. She didn't know which store to go to first.
3. She wasn't sure whether to buy a jacket now or wait.
4. She asked herself what to do.
5. She didn't know who to ask about a restroom.
6. She wasn't sure when to take the bus home.

LANGUAGE

14 How to get around → WB 39/4–5

a) *Change the verbs into* ***gerunds*** *or* ***infinitives****.*

I'd always dreamed of **1** (travel) across America, but I wasn't sure how **2** (do) it. By bus? By train? By plane? I decided **3** (use) all different kinds of transportation[1]. I don't really like **4** (fly) so I did that first and flew to New York City. The next morning I went to the train station and was the first one **5** (buy) a ticket. My mother wants me **6** (take) lots of pictures on my trip so my first photos were of the train that arrived at the station. **7** (ride) on the train to Florida was nice, but I was tired of just **8** (sit) so next I rented a car and drove myself all the way to Chicago. **9** (drive) in America is easy because the roads are flat and wide and I'm good at **10** (concentrate). In Chicago I was really excited about **11** (get) a motorcycle, but I took the bus to the Grand Canyon instead. That's where I got a horse. At first I was worried about **12** (fall) off, but **13** (ride) it was so great that I rode it all the way to California!

b) *Think of places you'd like to visit in the US. Share your ideas with a partner. Tell him / her why you'd like to go there. Then present your partner's ideas in class.*

1 **transportation** ***(AE)*** [ˌtrænspɔːˈteɪʃn] Verkehrsmittel; Transport

SPEAKING

15 Who do you want to help?

a) *Look at the pictures. Say what the people are doing. Can you think of more ways to help other people? Collect ideas and share them in class.*

b) *Which of the three people or groups would you like to help? Explain why. Discuss your ideas with a partner.*

VOCABULARY

16 Across the USA

Complete the text with the words in the box.

attitude | colonists | European | harvest | populated | population | rights | rural | symbolizes | temperatures | tractors | vacation | wealthiest | attractive | demonstrated | skyscrapers | religion | urban | shopping malls

If you want to spend your **1** in the United States, there are many different destinations to choose from. Let's start on the East Coast. Many people say that this is the most **2** region in America; maybe because that's where most of the **3** in the 1600s were from. The East Coast is also densely **4** and has many big cities such as Boston, Washington, D.C., New York and Philadelphia. If you want to see **5**, you should start in New York City. In contrast, the rest of New York State is quite **6**.

States in the South are known for their warm **7**. That's one of the reasons these states have an older **8**. In the South many people practice a **9** so there are a lot of churches, and this is also where, in the past, many people **10** so that black and white people could have the same **11**.

In the middle of the US there are a lot of farms. People here enjoy living in the country and far away from cities. It's normal here for teenagers to drive **12** and to help with the **13**. But they also enjoy spending time at **14** just like **15** teens.

For some people the West Coast **16** an easy-going lifestyle and a relaxed[1] **17**. But the West Coast is more than Hollywood and beaches. It is also a very **18** location for the computer industry and some of the **19** Americans have started their companies here.

1 **relaxed** [rɪˈlækst] entspannt; locker

Find more online: n6sx2g

Text smart 2
Advertisements

You can see advertisements for products just about anywhere you look. How and why do advertisers try to win customers over? What are key features of most print ads? Find out here!

VOCABULARY

1 Warm-up: Are you a dream customer?

→ S17

a) *Describe what you think of when you hear the word 'advertisement'. Explain why you think that way.*

b) *Are you an advertiser's dream customer? Take the test and find out!* Yes ↓ No ↓

Start here

On the radio, they mention a big sale at a clothes store in the mall. They're offering two T-shirts for the price of one. And it's your favorite brand!

If you can avoid it, you don't pay attention to ads on the radio, on TV or anywhere.

You decide to go to the mall immediately to look for the T-shirts from the radio ad.

You're going to go to the mall anyway, so you'll have a look at them while you're there.

At the mall, they don't have any T-shirts in your favorite color. But you love a bargain, so you decide to buy two anyway.

You don't need one new T-shirt, so why would you need *two*? Forget it!

You don't like the T-shirts in the sale. But you see another T-shirt that looks really great. Maybe you'll buy it.

They're giving away free samples of a new chocolate bar, but you walk away; you'd feel guilty about not buying one.

They're giving away free samples of a new chocolate bar. You take one. Mmm, good! Then you decide to buy one.

They're giving away free samples of a new chocolate bar. You take one but won't buy one later. You never fall for *that* trick!

You see your favorite movie star on a new shampoo. You buy it because he / she has *perfect* hair.

You see your favorite movie star on a new shampoo. You aren't really happy with the product you're using now. Maybe you'll try this one; maybe not.

You never buy products that are advertised by celebrities. They earn enough money already.

You seem to be an advertiser's dream customer! You're receptive to ads and interested in buying new products.

You're interested in new things but you don't react immediately to every new temptation the advertisers try to sell you.

You seem to be sceptical about advertising and having new things. Ad people won't have an easy time with you!

c) 1. Say why you agree or disagree with your test results.
2. Give a short definition of what you think an advertiser's dream customer is.
3. Explain which *one* situation above comes closest to describing how *you* typically react.

d) *Your turn: Give an example of how an ad has succeeded in making you buy something.*

Did you see that new ad?

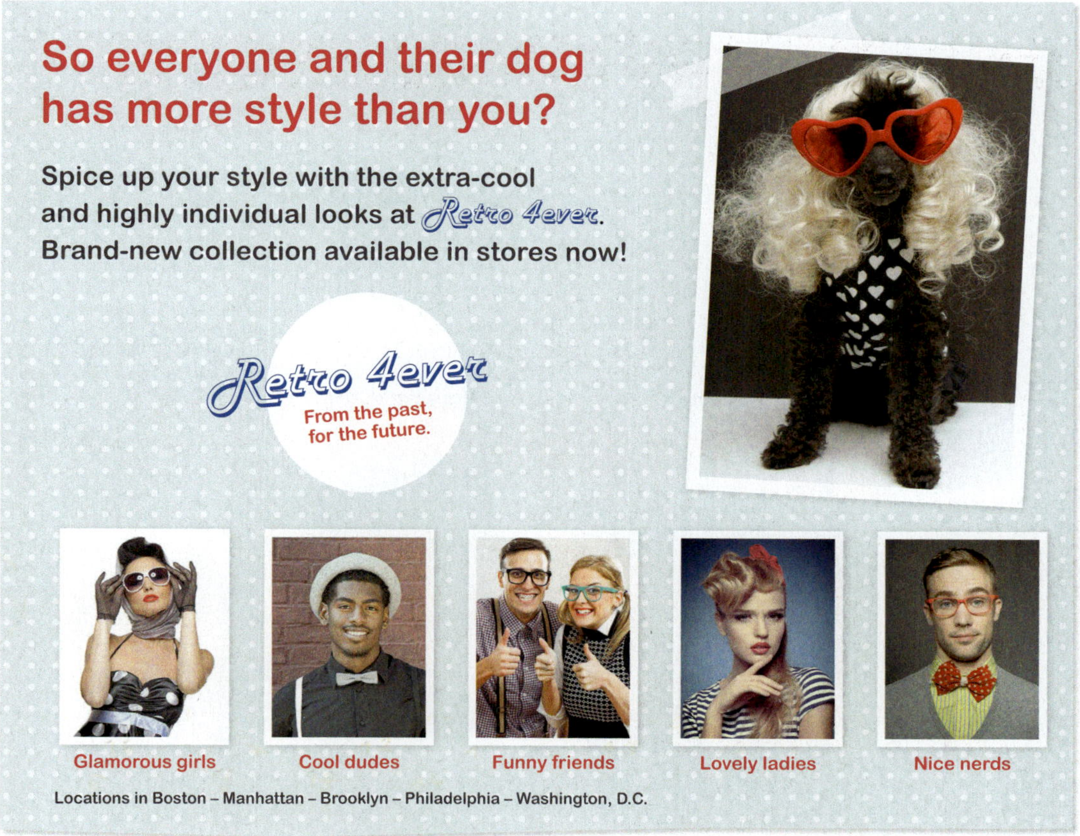

READING

2 The features of print ads → WB 40/1–2

→ S7 **a)** *Study the ad above.*

1. Describe what product the advertisers are trying to sell to their customers.
2. Say who you think the target group of customers is.

→ △ 120/1 **b)** *How is the ad above put together to sell the product? Point out the different features. (The skills box can help you.)*

c) *Now think about the language of the ad. Give examples of how these features work in the ad copy:*

humor   adjectives

Reading skills

With print advertisements, be aware of the **typical building blocks** that work together to sell the product:

- an **eye-catcher** (a visual and / or a text)
- a **slogan**
- the **ad copy** (the text parts of an ad)
- one or more **images** of the product
- **contact** and **location** information

d) *Your turn: If you were the customer and saw the ad above in a magazine, on a poster or on a billboard, would you be interested? Explain your opinion.*

SPEAKING

3 Slogans: A closer look

a) *'From the past, for the future' is the slogan for the* **Retro 4ever** *ad. In your group of 4–6, discuss reasons why you think it fits – or doesn't fit – the product.*

b) *Go back to the Retro 4ever ad. Together, think up a better slogan for the product. Why is it better? Compare your slogan with another group's.*

READING

4 Print ads: Similar product, different approach → WB 41/3

→ △ 120/2

a) *Study the ad below and answer these questions:*

1. Describe what product the advertisers are trying to sell.
2. Say who you think the target group is.

b) *Point out which features of print ads you can find in this ad and describe them.*

c) *Give your opinion on the quality of the ad:*

1. Explain how effective it is for the target group the advertisers are trying to attract.
2. Explain what 'fabulous' means here.

WRITING

5 Comparing the two ads

a) *Think – pair – share: Use the headings below to make a grid for each ad. On your own, write down key words for your opinion of the different features. Then talk about your ideas with a partner from your group in Ex. 3. In a classroom discussion, point out the differences and similarities between the two ads.*

visuals | slogan / ad copy | humor | product | target group | effectiveness

→ △ 120/3

b) *With your partner, use your ideas from a) to improve the two ads. You choose ad 1, your partner chooses ad 2. Make changes that you feel would be improvements. Then swap ads. Afterwards, explain to each other why you made your changes.*

WRITING

6 Options: Create your own ads → WB 41/4

→ S7–9

Option A: Trash to treasure

a) *Each of you finds an object at home you think is useless / ugly / awful / too old. It should be something you think nobody would buy!*

b) *Now slip into the role of the advertiser: What kind of an ad could make one of your objects sound like a great product? Together, write and design an ad for it.*

c) *Present your product to the class. How many classmates think your ad is convincing?*

→ S7–9

Option B: Create an ad around the visual

a) *Choose one of the photos below. What kind of a product could a print ad be about with a photo like that? Think of how you could combine the typical features of print ads to make your product sound wonderful for your target group! Together, write and design your ad.*

b) *Present your product to the class. How many classmates would buy your product?*

Find more online: 2px5br

School life – dos and don'ts

SPEAKING

1 Your turn

Talk about rules at your school. Look at the different situations below and the phrases on the right.

corridor | cafeteria | gym | laboratory | classroom | computer room | library | outside

Useful phrases

We can / can't | are / aren't allowed to | have to / don't have to
be late | eat / drink water | use our cell phones | shout | wear a uniform | be there without a teacher | skip classes | cheat | leave bags on the floor | …

If we break the rules / get caught …
- we have to stay after school | do extra work | stand outside | see the principal | …
- we are suspended | sent home
- we get detention
- our parents get a letter / phone call

VIEWING

2 A look at a US school

a) *Look at the film still. What do you think the problem is?*

DVD 4/2
→ S16

b) *Watch the film. Describe the situation. What's the problem with Ruby?*

Tip

If you break a rule in a US school, your teacher might give you **detention**.
This means that you have to stay in the classroom with a teacher in your free time – at lunchtime or after school. The teacher will give you some work to do and you have to do it in silence. You must complete all the work before you can leave the room.

Useful phrases

- If she …, she'll …
- If she doesn't …, her teacher might …
- She shouldn't … because …
- It's a bad idea for her to … because …
- If I were Ruby, I'd …
- Otherwise, she'll …

c) *Watch the film again. What are the consequences for Ruby? The phrases in the box can help you.*

d) *Give your opinion: What do you think about the way Ruby is acting? Does she deserve the consequences? Why / Why not?*

OCABULARY

3 A further look at rules → WB 43/1

a) *Match the verbs with the phrases. Then write down the correct rule (positive or negative!).*

Example: Don't bring stuff into the classroom!

get ✓ | use ✓ | bring ✓ | skip ✓ | stand in line (*AE*) | be (2x) ✓ | stand

1. stuff into the classroom ✓
2. late
3. in the hallway
4. for lunch
5. in the corridor without a hall pass
6. classes
7. detention
8. your cell phones

b) *Look at what the teacher is saying to her students. What do you think the student has or hasn't done in each situation?*

1. The class started 10 minutes ago!
2. Please put your bag into the locker!
3. Where were you this morning?
4. Switch it off right now, please!
5. You call this 'homework'?!

WRITING

4 Reasons behind the rules

Look at the rules from Ex. 3 again. Take turns to write a rule and to explain the reasons behind that rule.

Example:
A: 'No texting friends during class' means that they want students to listen to the teacher and focus on their work.

SPEAKING

5 Role play

→ S11

a) *Your friend doesn't agree with a school rule and is about to break it. You don't want your friend to get into trouble so you try to persuade him / her not to break the rule. Choose from one of the situations below and write the conversation. The phrases in the box can help you.*

fake hall pass so that he / she can skip classes

cheat in a test / use a cheat sheet

b) *Act out your conversation in class.*

Useful phrases

Persuading someone to change their behavior
- You're going to get into so much trouble!
- You're so going to get detention!
- You'll be suspended if you …
- They have that rule because …
- I see your point but …
- You might be right but …
- You'd better … / You should… / Why don't you …?
- If I were you, I'd …

Expressing an attitude
- No risk, no fun!
- They want me to …
- They make me so mad!
- Why can't I …?
- They can't stop me …!
- I can't see the point of …
- It's a waste of time telling him / her …
- I don't understand why …

Unit 3
City of dreams: New York

Find more online:
dr3h3e

A Times Square – New York's busiest intersection and home to its theater district

LISTENING

1 A song: Empire State of Mind (Part II) Alicia Keys

a) *In small groups, describe the photos to each other. Can you think of more photos that represent New York City for you?*

L 2/19 → S15

b) *Listen to the song and say how it makes you feel. Does it give you a positive or negative image of New York?*

c) *Look at the photos again and read the lines from the song. Which of the photos do these lines match? Explain why.*

the streets are mean | I got a pocketful of dreams | I'm gonna make it by any means | big lights will inspire you | such a melting pot | all looking pretty | make you feel brand-new | concrete jungle where dreams are made of

d) *There are more songs about New York City than most places in the world. Can you think of reasons why? Do you know a song about a German city or town? If you do, say what it is about.*

In Unit 3 you learn

… about different aspects of New York City.
You learn:

- how to talk about personal experiences, hopes and dreams
- how to give extra information
- useful phrases for conducting an interview

B The Chrysler Building in Midtown Manhattan

C Central Park – New York's big green lung

D In Chinatown

E Homeless people in the streets

LISTENING **2** **Big city life**

→ 121/1

a) *Think – pair – share: Imagine you lived in a big city like New York with your family. What do you think you'd enjoy most? What wouldn't be so great about it? Exchange ideas with a partner before you both share your ideas in class. Here are some topics to start with:*

people | entertainment | activities | education | culture | traffic | crime

L 2/20

b) *Listen to the interview with David, a teenager from New York. What does he or doesn't he like about life in the city? Take notes.*

→ S15

c) *Compare your ideas from a) with David's answers. What's the same, what's different?*

WRITING **3** **Your turn: In New York City** → WB 44/1–2

→ 121/2

Look at the photos again. Which photo could you imagine yourself in? Write a short text about what you're doing in the photo and what you can feel (see, hear, smell, taste).

L 2/21 Saving the best for last

"Hey, Diego! Come here, please!" Diego's boss called to him. "These two young ladies need help getting around New York. I told them that nobody knows this city better than you. Take the rest of the day off and show them the best places." Diego was more than happy to leave his after-school job at the diner early. Rylee, who was 17 and from Alabama, and her cousin Lea, who was from Berlin, had a day to spend in New York while Rylee's parents were at a conference.

"Where are we going first?" Rylee asked. "The Empire State Building?"

"No," Diego said, "I'll show you sides of New York you'll never read about in a guidebook."

As they entered a big office building, the girls gasped. Classical music filled their ears. "These are students from the Juilliard School, which is a famous music school," Diego explained. While they were listening, he thought about his parents. They'd like him to work in an office building like this, for a bank maybe. A nice safe job. Something better than they had. But he wanted excitement.

After they'd had a look at the Astor Place Cube, an outdoor sculpture, they went to Times Square, which was always crowded with tourists. Diego loved being part of the crowds of New York although his parents hated it. Since he knew 'The Naked Cowboy', who was really only *almost* naked, the girls could take a picture with him for free. Diego's idea of New York on a shoestring was working well so far! He had two more free places to show them before the big surprise. He had to time it just right.

First they walked to the Alvin Ailey Dance Studio, which is just a couple of blocks from Central Park, and watched the dance class through the tall windows. "Diego, this is absolutely wonderful," Rylee said full of enthusiasm. "We'd never have found this without you!" They made it to the 5th floor of the Metropolitan Museum of Art just in time for the sunset over Central Park.

"This is the best, Diego," Lea said. "Thanks for a really great day."

He looked at them and smiled. "An entertainer always saves the best for last. So let's go!"

Diego led them to 30 Rockefeller Center, which is one of the tallest skyscrapers in New York, but they didn't use the front entrance. Instead they snuck into a service entrance and then into an elevator. "We're going to the top," he told the girls, "to the Top of the Rock."

Both girls looked at him. "To the top of Rockefeller Center? But every tourist knows how expensive tickets are!"

"Leave that to me," he told them.

When the elevator stopped and the doors opened, they entered a dark hallway. Just then a bright light shone in Diego's eyes and a loud voice with a strong accent shouted, "Stop! Who's there?"

With his hands covering his eyes, Diego said, "It's me. It's just me, dad."

"Diego?" the voice asked. *"¿Qué estás haciendo aquí?"*

"We just wanted to enjoy the view," Diego said quietly.

READING

1 Diego's New York

→ S1

a) *Sum up which places Diego showed to the girls. Why didn't he take them to the typical New York sights?*

b) *What would you have done in the girls' shoes – gone with Diego or followed your guidebook? Explain why.*

LANGUAGE

2 Revision: Defining relative clauses → G8 → WB 45/3

→ △ 121/3
→ ▲ 122/4

a) *Look at these sentences. Explain when you use the relative pronoun* ***who, which*** *or* ***that****.*

1. Most of the people **who** live in New York weren't born there.
2. The restaurants **which** we went to weren't expensive.
3. The musicians **that** play in the office building don't get any money.
4. We followed the plan **that** Diego gave us.

b) *Read Rylee's message to one of her friends. Use the phrases to complete the text with* ***defining relative clauses****. Decide where you can leave out the relative pronoun.*

Example: 1. This guy **(who/that) we met at lunch** said he'd show us the city.

aren't in every guidebook | everyone has to see | Diego showed us | he worked for | we met at lunch | shows people the real New York

Dear Ashley,
You won't believe what happened to us in New York! This guy 1 *said he'd show us the city. First we weren't sure if we should go with him, but the man* 2 *told us he was okay. The things* 3 *were amazing. They were all places* 4*. Well, except for Times Square. But Diego said that's a place* 5*. It was amazing! And you know what happened at the end of our tour: We got caught by Diego's father! He's a security man at Rockefeller Center and he found us after we'd snuck into a service entrance. That was a bit embarrassing, but we still had a wonderful day. Diego could start a tour company* 6*.*
Miss you! xoxo – Rylee

LANGUAGE

3 Find the rule: Non-defining relative clauses → G8

a) *Explain the difference between these two sentences.*

1. The Juilliard School, which is located in Manhattan, is known around the world.
2. My cousin goes to a music school which is known around the world.

b) *Find at least five more examples of* ***non-defining relative clauses*** *in the text.*

Tip

In non-defining relative clauses …
- you use 'who' for people and 'which' for things. You never use 'that'.
- you always need a **comma** to separate the main clause from the relative clause.

LANGUAGE

4 What happened before

*Read what happened before Rylee and Lea met Diego. Decide if the sentences have **defining** or **non-defining relative clauses**. Put in commas where you need them.*

After the girls had said goodbye to Rylee's parents, Rylee who had never been to New York before decided to give her cousin a tour of the city. Rylee lived in a city that was home to only 10,000 people, but she wasn't worried at all. She told herself that she was a person who never got lost. The two girls took the subway to Lower Manhattan. Rylee planned to follow their guidebook which suggested a walking tour through Chinatown. 20 minutes later, the two girls were back at Wall Street Subway Station which is where they'd started. "So that's what you call an amazing tour," Lea groaned.

LANGUAGE

5 Flying to New York

*Combine the two sentences into one. Use **non-defining relative clauses**.*

Example: 1. Our plane is going to leave from Stuttgart Airport, which is close to our house.

1. Our plane is going to leave from Stuttgart Airport. This is close to our house.
2. We're going to fly to JFK International. This is one of the busiest airports in the US.
3. We're going to visit my Aunt Nancy. She works in the Empire State Building.
4. Aunt Nancy speaks six languages. She gives tours of the building.
5. The Empire State Building was built in 1931. It has 102 floors.
6. The elevator is really fast. It only takes one minute to get to the 80th floor.

LANGUAGE

6 Make the text more interesting → WB 45/4

→ △ 122/5

*Use **non-defining relative clauses** to add the extra information below.*

The Statue of Liberty is one of New York's most famous sights. But did you know that this symbol of freedom was a present from France? It was designed by the French artist Auguste Bartholdi. The statue was completed in France in 1884 and then brought to America. There it was rebuilt on Bedloe Island. In her right hand, 'Lady Liberty' is holding a torch, and in her left, a tablet with the date July 4th, 1776. The seven spikes on her crown stand for the seven seas and the seven continents of the world. Today the Statue of Liberty is a popular tourist attraction. You can even go up to the Statue's crown!

1. The Statue of Liberty stands in New York harbor.
2. This symbol of freedom has become so important for American culture.
3. Bartholdi based his figure on the Roman Goddess of Liberty.
4. The statue took nine years to build.
5. Bedloe Island is now known as 'Liberty Island'.
6. The torch stands for 'enlightenment'.
7. July 4th, 1776 is the date of America's independence from Britain.
8. The Statue of Liberty is visited by millions of people each year.

SPEAKING

7 Your turn: Give extra information

*Get into two teams. One team gives the main clause and the other team has to add a **non-defining relative clause**. Take turns.*

Example: My friend Ben has a dog. → My friend Ben, who is sitting next to me, has a dog.

READING

8 Food in New York City

Read the box about different food in New York. Then talk to your partner about food and places to eat where you live.

Across cultures

Life in New York City has been strongly influenced by its millions of immigrants from all over the world. You can best experience this when you start looking for New York **ethnic food**. From the outside, some restaurants look like just a hole in the wall, but inside you can find delicious Indian food like samosa, which is a fried pastry with a vegetarian filling. Another famous New York dish is bagel and lox – typical Jewish food.

Walking down the street is a great way to find delicious food too. New York has hundreds of **food trucks and carts** around the city which sell everything from hot dogs – New York's most famous snack – to schnitzel or tacos. New Yorkers are still combining flavors and specialities to create new dishes, e.g. the cronut – a combination of croissant and doughnut.

MEDIATION

9 What do you eat? → WB 46/5

→ △ 122/6
→ S13

On their tour of New York City, Lea told Diego about some typical German food. A few days later, Diego sends her an e-mail and asks about more typical food from her region. Lea finds this article on the internet. In their next video chat she tells Diego about it.

Say what Lea tells Diego. Use ***non-defining relative clauses*** *to give extra information.*

> Ein weiteres beliebtes Gericht aus der Mitte Deutschlands ist „Himmel und Erde". Hinter dem Wort „Himmel" versteckt sich der Apfel, der am Baum in den Himmel ragt. „Erde" bezieht sich auf die Kartoffel, die bekanntlich in der Erde wächst. Das sind die Hauptzutaten für dieses vegetarische Gericht. In manchen Regionen werden die gekochten, zerkleinerten Äpfel und Kartoffeln vermischt und mit Brot serviert. Häufig isst man dazu auch Blutwurst, Speck oder Leberwurst. Und bitte die Röstzwiebeln nicht vergessen …

WRITING

10 Your turn: Your city on a shoestring → WB 46/6, 47/7–9

a) *You're helping to write a guidebook about your hometown or region. In small groups, choose 3–4 interesting facts you want to include. These ideas can help you:*

the best view | the best thing for free | the best lunch under €10 | the highest spot | …

b) *Write short texts for each of the points you chose in a). Remember to give extra information.*

Example: The highest spot in our town, which is in a castle, is easy to get to. It's …

L 2/23

Life is a trip

Diego's father, Emilio, had been waiting in his taxi for just 20 minutes before his first passenger came. He lifted the young man's big suitcase into the trunk and then asked him where he wanted to go. "To the airport," the man groaned, "I'm done with this city." He'd come to New York when he was 19 and had been hoping for his big break for five years. All this time he'd gone to hundreds of auditions and had sung thousands of songs, but nobody had wanted him. He'd been thinking about his decision for quite some time and that morning, when he got another rejection e-mail, he'd decided the time had come. Now he was going home to Wisconsin, where he had an offer to teach music at a high school. "My dream just didn't come true here," he explained. "At least as a teacher I can make music every day."

Emilio wished the young man good luck and thought of his own dreams. They hadn't been as big when he'd come to America, but he still understood what it meant to get disappointed.

When Emilio got back in his car, another passenger was waiting on the sidewalk. Emilio knew the type – successful businessman but not necessarily happy. The man gave Emilio an address on Wall Street. And then something surprising happened. The man started talking to him, asking him questions. Emilio told him about his son, Diego, and how he and his wife had such big hopes for him. They'd been saving for his education since he was born, working two jobs each and now Diego said he wanted to be an entertainer. Emilio was sure this rich businessman would understand how disappointed Emilio felt. However, when they arrived in Manhattan, the man said something completely different. "Let your son follow his dreams. It's better to have a son with dreams you aren't happy about than not to have your son at all." He pressed a large bill into Emilio's hand and quickly got out of the taxi without his change.

Emilio's taxi wasn't empty for long. Two teenage girls and about 20 shopping bags got in. The girls didn't say hello; they just gave him an address on Park Avenue. Emilio listened to them as they talked about a life so different from his and yet so typical of New York. They'd been walking around Manhattan since 10 o'clock and now they were tired after all the shopping. They complained that today it was hard to find any good clothes in New York. Obviously they'd been shopping at the same stores for hours when they realized that London might be the better place to shop. Needless to say, they didn't give Emilio a tip. And needless to say, they didn't give the homeless woman on the sidewalk a single look as they got out of the taxi.

READING

11 A day in the life of Emilio → WB 48/10

→ S1

a) *Collect information about Emilio's passengers. Think of what is said about them in the text, but also about what they say or how they act. Make a mind map.*

b) *Use your mind map from a) to compare the different passengers.*

c) *Role play: Choose one of Emilio's passengers – the musician, the businessman or one of the rich girls. With your partner, write down five questions you'd like to ask this person and the answers this person might give. Then act out the dialogue.*

LANGUAGE

12 Revision: Present perfect progressive

→ △ 122/7

Remember: You can use the present perfect progressive for activities which began in the past and have been going on until now. Use the prompts to make sentences with the ***present perfect progressive*** *and* ***since*** *or* ***for****.*

Example: 1. It's already 10 o'clock. We**'ve been waiting** for our taxi since 9:30.

1. It's already 10 o'clock. We | wait for our taxi | 9:30. ✔
2. Can we leave? We | listen to the piano player | one hour.
3. We'll never get to the show on time. We | walk | hours.
4. Look how tall the skyscraper is already. They | not build | long.
5. I got a part in a play! I | dream about this | I arrived in New York.
6. It's so sad. He | live on the streets | he was 16.

LANGUAGE

13 Find the rule: Past perfect progressive → G9 → WB 48/11

a) *Look at these two sentences. Say which verb forms you need to form the* ***past perfect progressive****.*

1. Emilio **had been waiting** for 20 minutes.
2. They **had been walking** around Manhattan since 10 o'clock.

b) *Find more examples of the* ***past perfect progressive*** *in the text.*

c) *Look at the tip box and the sentences from a) and b). Write down the rule of how the* ***past perfect progressive*** *is used. Compare it to the use of* ***present perfect progressive****.*

Tip

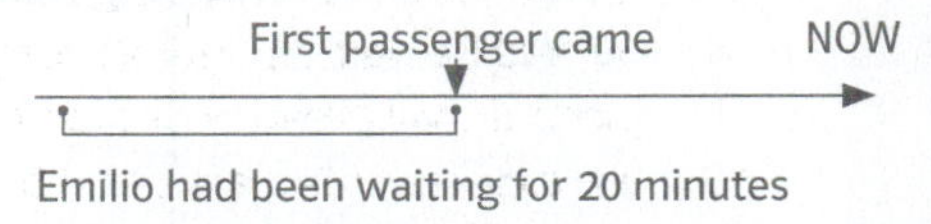

LANGUAGE

14 What had Meredith been doing?

Complete the sentences with the ***past perfect progressive****.*

1. Meredith (talk) about becoming an actor even before she saw her first Broadway play.
2. She (plan) to move to New York for eight years before she finally arrived there.
3. When she went to her first audition, she (not live) in New York for very long.
4. She was very tired that day because she (practice) all night long.
5. She (wait) for two hours when they told her that they didn't need any more people.
6. Her friends didn't know how long she (walk) around the city before she came home at midnight.
7. They knew she (hope) for a part in the play, but they told her that tomorrow was another day!

LANGUAGE **15**

Why were they tired when Emilio's taxi arrived? → WB 49/12

→ △ 123/8
→ ▲ 123/9

When Emilio arrived in Central Park at 11 o'clock yesterday, he saw different people who needed a taxi. Why were they tired? Make sentences with the ***past perfect progressive*** *and* ***since*** *or* ***for****.*

Example: 1. The young girl **had been running** for one hour / **since** 10 o'clock.

LANGUAGE **16**

What had been happening before?

→ △ 123/10

Complete these sentences with your own ideas. Use the ***past perfect progressive*** *and an* ***expression of time*** *(since / for …, all morning / day / week / night / year etc.).*

Example: When I looked out of the window this morning, the ground was all wet.
It **had been raining all night**.

1. I was very tired when I got home after school because I'd been …
2. Dave got the best grade on the test because he …
3. We … when there was a heavy storm and we had to go back.
4. When Kelly arrived at the café, her friends …
5. Our dog was very dirty. He …
6. Lisa thought her friend would never call. She …
7. Mary's eyes were very red. She …

SPEAKING **17**

Your turn: Your experiences in a new place

Do you remember the last time you were in a foreign city / a new place? What kind of people did you meet? What did you experience, see, hear, feel, smell? Tell your partner about it and ask each other about your experiences.

LISTENING

18 Differences between British and American English → WB 49/13

L 2/24 → S15

a) *Listen to a conversation between a British and an American student. What are they talking about? What differences do you notice in the way they speak?*

b) *Listen to the conversation again. Then look at these sentences. Change the British words to American and the American words to British.*

1. Buskers perform on the street to make a living.
2. It is easiest to take the subway when you want to explore the city.
3. Traffic is so slow here, let's use the freeway instead.
4. If you want to transport something that is big and heavy, you'll need a lorry.

c) *Can you think of more words that are different between British and American English? Start a list.*

READING

19 Living in New York City → WB 50/14–15

a) *In her song about New York Alicia Keys sings: "If I can make it here, I can make it anywhere." What does this tell us about how people see New York?*

b) *Read the box about life in New York. Have you seen huge contrasts like this where you live?*

Across cultures

As a city of superlatives, New York attracts people from all different social backgrounds – rich and poor, young and old, from the US and from abroad. They all come to New York with their **hopes and dreams**. A lot of them live their own 'rags to riches' success story, but others fail to make their living.

Today New York is one of the cities with the widest **gap between rich and poor** in the US. There are one-bedroom apartments for $5 million, and in New York's most expensive apartment building a penthouse was sold for $100 million. On the other hand, there are almost 60,000 homeless people who live on the streets or in poor conditions.

c) *Imagine you're either very rich or homeless. What would be different compared to your real life? Share your ideas with a partner.*

SPEAKING

20 Before you read

a) *You're going to read a graphic novel which is set in New York City. Read the quotation below from OG, one of the main characters in the story. Think about what he could mean.*

"Here is where you are. There is where you want to be. But you can't get there from here." (Harrison Blanchard aka OG)

b) *What might the graphic novel be about? Keep in mind what you've read in the Across cultures box.*

Asphalt Tribe

by Stefani Kampmann

Our city was as hectic and busy as usual.
MADAME TUSSAUDS
AMSTERDAM
ONE WAY
7 AV
MARY POPPINS
CHASE
QUICKSILVER
QUICKSILVER

This is where we lived.
Hilton
FREE
This was our home.
FREE
Hey!
Thieves! Stop!

Faster, Maybe!
They can't catch us.
Idiots.
They're just too stupid.
Come on, show me what's in there!

Just a bunch of junk. No cash.
Shit!
What do those chicks need all this stuff for?
Maybe! Rainbow!
Hey, Tears!
Where have you been?
ROCK

Behind the deli.
Cool!
Fast food from the dumpster.
There's enough for everyone.
Come on, let's look for the others. This will be a feast.

Aw, Maggot!
Your spray is ruining my manicure.
DON'T WORRY DIE HAPPY!
SMASH
Come off it, Jewel.
You could learn a lesson or two from 2Moro. Look how she's using her delicate fingers.
Hey guys! Supper is ready!

APITALISM!
Mmmm, delicious. Cold with mayo.
Aren't you going to bitch about the capitalistic throw-away society?
Never! Viva el capital!
Shit! The police!
POLICE

When the cops came with their van, we had to run.
POLICE
Otherwise they'd stick us in a juvenile home.

SPEAKING

1 Your reaction

What do you think of the graphic novel? With a partner, agree on three aspects you like or don't like about it. Explain why.

READING

2 Understanding the story → WB 51/16

a) *Divide the excerpt from the graphic novel into scenes. Sum up each scene in 2–3 sentences.*

b) *Compare your summaries with a partner's. Explain how you found out about what is happening in each scene.*

READING

3 How a graphic novel works

a) *Look at the first panel of the graphic novel (p. 50). Describe the picture and the atmosphere. Why do you think the artist used this picture as a lead-in to her story?*

b) *Now have a closer look at pages 54 and 58. What are the differences between them? Make a grid and fill in the information for both pages. Use these headings:*

content | sizes and shapes of panels | sequence of panels | shots

Reading skills

Graphic novels are divided into **panels** (the individual pictures) which can be different sizes and shapes. Some of the panels have **speech** or **thought bubbles** and / or **captions**. The short caption texts tell part of the story from the perspective of a first- or third-person narrator.

The **sequence** (or order) of the panels can play an important role. Sometimes panels are not arranged consecutively, but they overlap. This means that some smaller panels are laid over a larger one.

Just like in films, graphic novels make use of different kinds of **shots**. There can be **long** or **medium shots** (the camera is at a great or medium distance from the object that is being filmed) and **close-ups** (the camera is very close to the object).

→ △ 124/11

c) *Look at your grid from b) and the two pages from the graphic novel again. Describe the effects the stylistic elements have. How does that match the content? The useful phrases in the box can help you.*

d) *Explain how the choice of black and white matches the story. Do you know any other graphic novels? If you do, does the artist's choice / style of visuals match the story?*

Useful phrases

create suspense / a quiet atmosphere | make the reader live through / experience the story | show reactions / feelings of characters | introduce fast action / speed | create a distance

WRITING

4 What happens next?

What do you think happens when the kids run away from the police? Make a plan for the next two pages of the graphic novel. Think of content, sizes and shapes of panels, sequence of panels and shots. If you like being creative, you can even draw the panels.

READING

5 < Comparing the genres > → WB 51/17

a) *The graphic novel* Asphalt Tribe *is based on the novel* Can't Get There from Here *by* Todd Strasser. *Read this short excerpt. Think about how the artist might convert the scene into panels.*

Chapter One: New Year's Eve

It was one of those nights when there wasn't much traffic on the streets of New York. Most people were done with their stupid New Year's celebrations and back in the four-walled cells they called apartments. Prisoners of the system, Maggot said. Out here in the cold where we weren't walled in, we were free to go where we wanted to.

"Guess the cops have the night off," Maggot said, his brown dreadlocks stringy from the mist.

"The rest of the world too," muttered 2Moro. She was wearing a red-and-orange patchwork jacket, a tight black skirt, and high black boots. The piercings in her ears and eyebrow and nose glinted in the streetlight. Tattooed around her neck was a circle of black barbed wire.

I drank cold coffee from a paper cup. At night we drank coffee to stay awake. It was safer to sleep during the day.

A man and a woman came around the corner wearing raincoats and sharing a red umbrella. They slowed down when they saw us. The woman slid her arm through the man's and said something in his ear. Probably wanted him to turn around and go another way. But the man shook his head.

When they got near, the woman wrinkled her nose like something smelled bad.

"Have fun tonight?" Maggot asked, kind of menacing.

The couple stopped. "Yes, we did," the man answered.

"No work tomorrow, huh?" Maggot said.

"That's right."

"Day after that it's back to the old nine-to-five routine," Maggot said.

"You could say that," answered the man.

"Happy New Year," said 2Moro, not in a friendly way.

"Same to you," said the man. He and the woman hurried past. She kept glancing over her shoulder at us until they reached the next corner.

"Robots," Maggot said. "Just following the rules. Work till they die. Then new robots replace them."

b) *Give a summary of the excerpt in 2–3 sentences.*

c) *With your partner, make a list of the differences between a graphic novel and a novel. How are they effective in different ways?*

d) *What would you prefer to read – the graphic novel or the novel? Give reasons for your choice.*

WRITING

6 < Writing the novel version of a scene >

→ △ 124/12

a) *Look back at the scenes you were working with in Ex. 2a). Divide up the scenes among the class. Then write a short novel text for your scene. Keep in mind the differences between a graphic novel and a novel which you collected in Ex. 5c).*

b) *With a partner, peer-edit each other's texts.*

New Yorkers don't do things like that! → S16

SPEAKING

1 Warm-up: Embarrassing situations → WB 52/18

a) *In the film, one of the characters says this to another character: "Stop it, it's embarrassing! I'm a New Yorker and New Yorkers don't do things like that!" What do you think this could mean?*

b) *Describe the kind of embarrassing behavior that makes you cringe.*

VIEWING

2 Out and about in Manhattan → WB 52/19

DVD 4/3

a) *Watch the film till 00:50. Then think about your ideas from Ex. 1 again. What does Christine mean when she tells Sarah that "New Yorkers don't do things like that"?*

b) *Now watch till 04:00 and sum up the action. Include these points about Christine, Sarah and Lawrence:*

characters and their personalities | what happens

c) *Watch the rest of the film. Describe the unexpected ending and the reactions to it.*

VIEWING

3 How music and film work together

a) *Watch the film again and note down the moments with music. Describe which scene or person has music and what kind of music it is.*

b) *Explain how you think the music helps to tell the story in A (04:01–04:52) and B (06:01–06:17):*

A

B

c) *Read the skills box. Then watch 04:01–04:52 again. Explain why you think this part of the film is featured as a montage.*

d) *If you could choose a theme song or theme music for one of the characters, what would you choose? Give your reasons.*

Film skills

A **montage** is a popular film technique to show a lot of action in very little time. To make a montage, scenes are cut up into very short 'pieces' and then combined, usually with **music**.

How to conduct a podcast interview

For the unit task you're going to do podcast interviews about different people in New York City. This page will give you some useful phrases and a model for your interview.

1 Before the interview: A short biographical profile → WB 53/21

a) *In a podcast interview, the interviewer often gives his / her listeners a short profile of the person he / she is going to interview. With a partner, think of general kinds of biographical information that listeners might like to know before the actual interview. Make a list.*

b) *Read the biographical profile about Rita Moreno, an immigrant from Cuba who lives in New York. Compare the information with your list from a).*

Rita Moreno came to New York from Cuba when she was 16 years old. Her aunt and uncle, who had already been living there for three years, gave Rita a bedroom, but she had to work hard for everything else. Her dream was to become a dancer. In Cuba she'd already been going to a dance school for ten years, but she and her family saw no future for her there; the country was just too poor. Rita's path to success was very long and hard. She cleaned offices, sold tickets in a theater and always went to auditions. It took her almost three years before she got her first dancing job. Today she makes her living by dancing on stages around New York and the world, but she also helps young dancers who have their own hopes and dreams.

c) *You want to find out more about what Rita likes or doesn't like about her life in New York. Write down five questions you'd ask her in an interview.*

2 Conducting an interview: Daniel's Do-it-yourself Diner

L 2/29 → S15

a) *Listen to the interview. Then sum up what you've found out about Daniel and his New York City dreams. Why is his diner called 'Do-it-yourself'?*

b) *Listen to the interview again. Note down which phrases from the box you hear in the interview.*

c) *What's important for a good interview? Make a list of criteria with your partner.*

Useful phrases

Small talk: This is a beautiful office / area / room. | How long have you been living / working here? | Where did you grow up?

Follow-up: Can you tell me more about …? | That's interesting. Tell me a little more about that. | But don't you think that …? | Can you explain that to me? | Sorry, I didn't catch that.

Getting specific: How long have you …? | How many …? | When did you …? | How often …? | How long had you been … (+-ing) before you became … / went … / found …

Open questions: What are your feelings about …? | What do you think about …? | What are your goals?

At the end: Thanks, I enjoyed talking to you. | Thank you very much for this interesting talk.

d) *Write a short biographical profile about Daniel. Keep in mind the points you collected in Ex. 1.*

A pocketful of New York City dreams

You're going to make a series of podcast interviews with different people in New York City who talk about their hopes and dreams. You can use information you learned in Unit 3 and do some internet research too.

Step 1

Get into groups, choose characters → WB 53/22

Get into groups of 4–5. Each group chooses a different person who lives in New York City or who is visiting. Here are some ideas:

tourist | tourist guide | rich boy / girl | successful businessman / -woman | taxi driver | young student who has just moved to New York | homeless person

Step 2

Write a biographical profile → WB 54/23

In your groups, write a short biographical profile of the person you've chosen. Try to make your listeners interested, but don't give away too much information.

→ Introduction (pp. 70–71) → Giving extra information (pp. 72–75) → Talking about personal experiences (pp. 76–78) → Writing a biographical profile (p. 92)

Step 3

Prepare your interviews → WB 54/24

Prepare questions you're going to ask about the person's hopes and dreams. Think of answers you're going to give.

→ Conducting an interview (p. 92)

Step 4

Practise your interviews

Decide who is going to take the role of the interviewer and the interviewee. Then practise the interview. Don't forget that the interviewer should give the short biographical profile first.

Step 5

Present your interviews

Record your podcast interviews or present them directly to the class. After the presentations, discuss the interviews in class. Give feedback about which person or which interview was the most convincing. Explain why.

LISTENING

1 I ♥ NYC

L 2/30

a) *Listen to Makenna as she talks about her hometown New York. What does she say about these topics? Take notes.*

Stuyvesant High School | crime | people in New York | activities

b) *Make notes about your school and your hometown. Use your ideas to write a short text like Makenna's.*

MEDIATION

2 Getting around in New York → WB 56/1

You're spending a year as an exchange student in New York and your parents are visiting you for five days. They want to do some sightseeing on their own and ask you which subway ticket you think is best for them. You find this information about the MetroCard on a website. Tell them about the different options. Then say which ticket you think is best and why. Use a dictionary to look up new words.

To find out about the different ticket options, press 'Start', then 'MetroCard' and next 'Get new card'. Now you have to decide between an 'unlimited' and a 'regular' card. An unlimited MetroCard for seven days costs $31. This card is good if you want to use the subway a lot – even if you're going to be in New York for less than seven days. It's the best deal if you're going to use the subway at least 12 times, or do six round trips. Then each ride costs $2.38. The more you ride, the cheaper each ride is! If you ride 25 times, it's only $1.24 per ride. But remember – only one person can use the card! If you don't want to use the subway that often, you can buy a pay-per-ride or regular MetroCard. Up to four people can share the same card. You choose the amount that you want to put onto your card. The more you put on it, the more you save because you get an 11% bonus for every $5.50 you purchase. You can pay at the machines with cash, an ATM card or a credit card. If you pay in cash, your change will be all in coins.

LANGUAGE

3 Who is who?

You're new in New York and you don't know the people who live next door – Mr. Singh, Mr. Masengi and Mr. Nelson – very well, but you need a ride to the airport. Find out who the taxi driver is. Read the clues and make a grid in your exercise book.

The neighbor who lives in the yellow house doesn't drive a taxi.

Mr. Masengi, who is a security man, doesn't like the color red.

The actor, who doesn't live in a yellow house, is Mr. Nelson.

The house that Mr. Singh has been living in for five years isn't red.

LANGUAGE

4 More facts about New York → WB 57/2

*Write 2–3 sentences about each topic below. Use **non-defining relative clauses** where possible.*

Example: New York, **which is the largest city in the US**, is located on the East Coast.

New York	New York taxis
– largest city in the US – located on the East Coast – about 8 million live here; 1.6 million on island of Manhattan – Manhattan: most famous of NY's five boroughs[1]	– bright yellow in color – can be seen all around the city – many of the taxi drivers born outside the US – transport about 241 million passengers each year
The Brooklyn Bridge	**The Staten Island Ferry**

– connects[2] Manhattan and Brooklyn – designed by John A. Roebling in 1869 – completed after Roebling's death by his son – one of NY's top tourist attractions – cost $15 million to build	– in service[3] since 1817 – operates[4] 24 hours a day, 7 days a week – transports about 21 million passengers each year – free of charge[5]

LANGUAGE

5 Moving to NYC

a) *Put in a **gerund** or an **infinitive with to**.*

1. ___ (move) to New York City was the best decision I've ever made!
2. I was the first one in my family ___ (leave) our town.
3. At first my parents were afraid of ___ (let) me go on my own.
4. But I've always been crazy about ___ (try) new things.
5. I decided ___ (leave) as soon as I was done with high school.
6. My family didn't expect me ___ (stay) in New York for more than a year.
7. But I keep ___ (surprise) them with new dreams and ideas.
8. Now my brother is thinking of ___ (follow) me to NYC!

b) *What's the best decision that you've ever made? What happened because of this decision? Tell your partner about it.*

1 **borough** ['bʌrə] Stadtteil | 2 **to connect** [kə'nekt] verbinden | 3 **to be in service** [ɪn 'sɜːvɪs] in Betrieb sein | 4 **to operate** ['ɒpreɪt] in Betrieb sein | 5 **free of charge** [ˌfriː əv 'tʃɑːdʒ] kostenlos

READING

6 New York in a poem

Untitled by Jasbel
In this city
full of buildings
big, small, brown, orange
tiny windows
1 out of 1000
small and black
but still you and I
look outside
see the bridge
or the trees
mostly cars
and yellow taxis
cheese buses
and MTA buses
But where am I
If I go downtown alone
no one knows me
If I go to Brooklyn
no one knows me
alone in the middle of the big apple
places unexplored unknown to me
clueless[1], lost
In the middle of this jungle

a) *Read the poem. Find lines that show how Jasbel feels about New York City.*

b) *Discuss if this poem gives a good description of New York in your opinion. Explain why, why not.*

LANGUAGE

7 Defining or non-defining? → WB 57/3

Decide if these sentences have ***defining*** *or* ***non-defining relative clauses****. Put in commas where you need them.*

1. Diego who we met at a diner showed us some fantastic sights.
2. Some of the sights that Diego showed us were fantastic.
3. Rockefeller Center which is located in the heart of Manhattan is a huge shopping and entertainment center.
4. Rockefeller Center is a huge shopping and entertainment center that is located in the heart of Manhattan.
5. The Chinese dumplings[2] which we bought for lunch from a food truck on 14th Street tasted delicious.
6. The best restaurant for falafels is in Greenwich Village which is on the west side of Lower Manhattan.
7. In Times Square we saw the Naked Cowboy who is a famous street artist.
8. In Times Square we saw a street artist who was almost completely naked.

LANGUAGE

8 New in New York → WB 58/4–5

Put the verbs into the ***past perfect progressive****. Use* ***since*** *or* ***for*** *where it is needed.*

In August, Tyler and Missy finally left for New York City. They [1] (save) their money for the trip ever [2] they finished high school. They took the bus from Idaho to New York, and when they finally arrived in Manhattan, they [3] (already travel) [4] 24 hours. They [5] (hope) to stay with Missy's sister, but when they called, nobody answered the phone. Missy's sister [6] (not expect) them until the week after, and now they didn't know where to go! They [7] (look) at their map [8] a long time when a man asked if they needed help. He told them it was their lucky day. He [9] (help) people to find rooms in New York [10] 2005. That's when he had first arrived in New York without a room and someone had helped him!

1 clueless ['klu:ləs] ahnungslos | **2 dumpling** ['dʌmplɪŋ] Kloß

SPEAKING

9 New York's nicknames[1]

a) *There are many different names for New York. Which one do you think describes the city best? Exchange ideas with your partner.*

The melting pot | The center of the universe[2] | The city that never sleeps | The Big Apple | The city so nice they named it twice

b) *Think of nicknames for your hometown. They can be realistic or funny.*

LANGUAGE

10 What had people been doing?

a) *Use the prompts to write sentences with the* ***past perfect progressive****.*

Example: 1. Meredith came home late for dinner. She **had been shopping** since 10 o'clock.

1. Meredith came home late for dinner. She | shop | 10 o'clock.
2. Sam was feeling very tired. He | wait to get into the Empire State Building | two hours.
3. When Maisie came back to the hotel, she looked very red from the sun. She | walk | in the sun | all day.
4. Alex didn't know which subway station was next. He | sleep | 15 minutes.
5. Joe left the diner at 8 o'clock. He was very upset with his friends. He | wait | for them | 7 o'clock.
6. When Julie's mom arrived home at 10 p.m., the TV was still on. Julie | watch videos | all evening.

b) *Your turn: Partner A asks a question, Partner B answers. Use the* ***past perfect progressive****.*

Example: A: Why were you so tired last night?
B: I'**d been playing** football with my friends for three hours.

OCABULARY

11 Avoiding mistakes

a) *Look at these three words. Explain their different meanings.*

my cousins | my cousin's | my cousins'

b) *Complete the sentences with the correct form of the nouns.*

1. When I first came to New York, I lived in my ___ (sister) apartment.
2. She had crazy ___ (ideas) and we had lots of fun together.
3. One day we went to a party at her ___ (friends) place.
4. They lived in one of ___ (New York) tallest skyscrapers.
5. It was amazing to see the ___ (city) lights from up there.
6. And guess what? My best ___ (friend) brother came to the party.
7. He and his sister lived near my ___ (grandparents) house when we were kids.
8. He is one of the most attractive ___ (guys) I've ever met!

1 nickname [ˈnɪkneɪm] Spitzname | **2 universe** [ˈjuːnɪvɜːs] Universum

LANGUAGE

12 An interview with Colin

a) *A reporter from TeenMusicMag interviewed Colin, a young musician who plays his piano in Washington Square Park. Complete the interview. Decide if you need the* ***present perfect progressive*** *or* ***past perfect progressive****.*

TMM: Were you born in New York, Colin?
Colin: No, I'm originally from Tennessee, but I **1** (live) here for five years.
TMM: And why did you come here?
Colin: I **2** (dream) about it forever! And then one day I was finally brave enough to do it.
TMM: Colin, why did you decide to play your piano outside?
Colin: Well, I **3** (work) in a bar as a musician for two years, but I didn't like working every night.
TMM: Did you look for a new job then?
Colin: Yes, but I **4** (not look) for long when I decided to play in the park.
TMM: And do you make enough money with that?
Colin: I **5** (not expect) that before I started, but I do make enough.
TMM: How long **6** (perform) in Washington Square Park?
Colin: I **7** (do) it for two years now.
TMM: What do you do if the weather is bad?
Colin: I stay home! But one day I **8** (play) for only half an hour when it suddenly started to rain.
TMM: What did you do? Your poor piano!
Colin: The people who **9** (listen) helped me to cover it and then I quickly pushed it home.
TMM: And how long **10** (play) the piano altogether[1]?
Colin: I **11** (take) lessons since I was five.
TMM: Are you still taking lessons?
Colin: Well, not at the moment. My audience is my teacher!

b) *Write down questions you'd like to ask your partner. Then take turns to interview each other. Use the* ***present perfect progressive*** *and* ***past perfect progressive****.*

Example: A: How long **had you been playing** basketball before you joined our team?
B: **I'd been playing** basketball for one year.
A: And how long **have you been playing** basketball altogether?
B: **I've been playing** basketball since I was 12.

VOCABULARY

13 New York collocations

a) *Combine the words from the two boxes to make collocations you've learned in Unit 3.*

classical | melting | brand | follow | social | make | ethnic | food | city | office | concrete

a living | background | building | jungle | life | music | new | pot | a dream | cart | food

b) *Write a sentence for each of the phrases from a), but leave a gap where the phrase should go. Then exchange sentences. Your partner needs to find out which phrase goes in which sentence. Take turns.*

1 **altogether** [ˌɔːltəˈɡeðə] insgesamt

WRITING

14 I want to go to New York!

If you want to go on a student exchange, you usually have to fill out an online application[1] form. Answer the following questions about yourself in full sentences.

1. Which foreign languages have you studied, and for how many years?
2. What are your favorite school subjects?
3. Are you active in sports? If yes, which sports?
4. Which (if any) foreign countries have you visited?
5. What are your favorite hobbies, interests etc.?
6. Use one adjective to describe yourself. Explain why you have chosen it.

LANGUAGE

15 9/11 – New York had to rebuild

a) *As you've already learned, you can only use the modal verbs in the simple present. With other tenses, you use their substitute forms:* ***be allowed to, be able to*** *and* ***have to****. Rewrite these sentences in the simple past. Use the right substitute form.*

1. I can't call us a taxi because my phone is broken. We must take the subway.
2. We needn't buy tickets for the museum. Our class can go in for free.

b) *Complete the text with the verbs and the right substitute form:* ***be allowed to, be able to*** *or* ***have to****.*

On September 11, 2001, several terrorists **1** (hijack[2]) two planes and fly them into the twin towers of the World Trade Center in New York. At first nobody knew what had happened. One survivor said, "All I knew was that I **2** (get) out of the building." Of course the people in the World Trade Center **3** (not use) the elevators because of the fires. Firefighters[3] from all over New York came to help, but they **4** (not rescue) a lot of the people and at some point they **5** (leave) the scene because the buildings collapsed[4]. More than 3,000 people died. Until several months later, people who had lived near the World Trade Center **6** (not move) back into their apartments. Soon after 9/11, however, New Yorkers decided that they **7** (find) hope again. In 2014, One World Trade Center was opened as a new office building. At the place where the twin towers once stood there is now a memorial[5] and a museum, which tells the story of 9/11.

1 application [ˌæplɪˈkeɪʃn] Bewerbung | **2 to hijack** [ˈhaɪdʒæk] entführen | **3 firefighter** [ˈfaɪəˌfaɪtə] Feuerwehrmann/-frau | **4 to collapse** [kəˈlæps] einstürzen | **5 memorial** [məˈmɔːriəl] Denkmal

Find more online: a5rt5p

Text smart 3
Internet texts

In Text smart 3 you're going to take a look at typical kinds of online texts. Who writes them, what are their typical features, how reliable is the information you get online?

VOCABULARY

1 Warm-up: The internet in everyday life

a) *How would you finish this sentence: "If I had to spend a whole Saturday without my smartphone / my tablet, it would be so inconvenient because …"*

L 2/31–32 → S15

b) *Part 1: Tim and Marlon meet each other on the bus.*

1. Describe what Tim's problem is and how Marlon can help.
2. Then sum up what both boys say about the internet. The words below can help you.

Word bank

get quick information with apps | stay up-to-date on social media | watch tutorials | do research for school projects | follow / read blogs | follow social media profiles | post an opinion / comment on blogs / social media websites / …

c) *Now listen to part 2.*

1. Describe the problems Tim and Marlon mention.
2. Discuss how you feel about those problems.

SPEAKING

2 Your turn: Your reasons for using the internet

What were your main reasons for using the internet during the last 2–3 days? Compare your experiences with your partner's.

SPEAKING

3 America and the moon landing

On the following pages, you're going to work with internet texts about the first moon landing.

Read the box. Then say what other great moments or inventions in science and technology you can think of. Describe one for your partner.

Across cultures

On July 20, 1969, NASA astronaut Neil Armstrong became the first human on the moon. The **moon landing** is considered one of the greatest moments in the history of science and technology.

An online wiki text

The moon landing

The first moon landing took place on July 20, 1969, as the climax of NASA's Apollo 11 mission. Hundreds of millions of TV viewers watched on live TV as the landing module Eagle touched down on the moon's surface. Astronaut and Apollo 11 commander Neil Armstrong announced to mission control in Houston: "The Eagle has landed," words which soon became famous. More famous words followed six hours later when Armstrong stepped out of the Eagle and onto the moon: "That's one small step for (a) man, one giant leap for mankind." Armstrong was then joined by astronaut Buzz Aldrin. Together they took pictures to document the historic event and collected 46 pounds of moon rocks. After 21 hours, Armstrong and Aldrin returned to the command module Columbia, where astronaut Michael Collins had been waiting in orbit.

Years before, in 1961, the moon landing had become one of President John F. Kennedy's top priorities. He challenged the engineers and scientists at NASA to put a man on the moon by the end of 1969. It was clear to all that this would be the biggest challenge ever. It was also clear that it would be very political: During the Cold War, a triumph like the first moon landing was a prize that both the US and the Soviet Union wanted very much.

READING

4 Understanding the text → WB 59/1

→ S1–3 **a)** *Read the wiki text above. Sum up what happened in your own words.*

b) *Find phrases in the text that make the style factual and convincing. This box can help you:*

Reading skills

- A **factual text** should concentrate on **facts**. Opinions don't belong here.
- Factual texts about history focus on **times**, **dates**, **places** and **people**. Information like this can be easily checked at other text sources.

Tip

- **Wiki texts** are written to give information in the style of an encyclopedia. But wiki texts can be written or changed by any reader.
- Wikis try to be as **factual** as possible. But with so many authors, the regulators of wiki websites can't always keep their content completely free of opinions. So it is important to always look for **other reliable sources of information**. Don't rely only on wiki texts.

A blog post

READING

5 Hoaxes and conspiracy theories

→ △ 125/1

Across cultures

In the English-speaking world, there have been some famous hoaxes and conspiracy theories. The internet is full of such stories.

- When somebody stages a **hoax**, the person is playing a trick on the public. A typical hoax often features realistic photos that show something unbelievable like a UFO, or a monster.
- A **conspiracy theory** often involves an event or situation that a group of people would like to keep secret in a cover-up. The conspiracy theorists often see governments at the center of cover-ups. A famous example: Is the US government trying to keep real aliens a secret at the Area 51 air-force base?

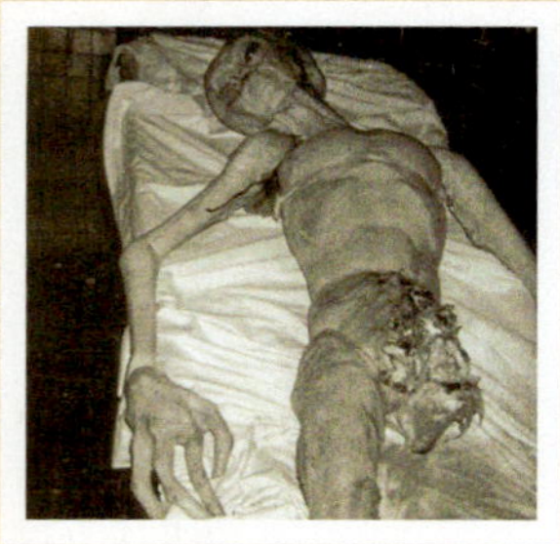

Read the box. Then talk about these questions in class:

1. Think of reasons why people would want to stage a hoax.
2. Explain why people often believe in conspiracy theories.

READING

6 A blog post on the moon landing: Was it all just a hoax?!

a) *Pre-reading: Some conspiracy theorists say the moon landing was just a hoax! But who could stage something so big? Share your ideas. The phrases below can help you.*

b) *Now read the blog post. Point out the main argument the blogger uses to claim that the moon landing never happened.*

c) *Give your opinion about the blogger's argument.*

Was it all just a hoax?! YES!

If this was possible then (with all that ANCIENT technology) why is nobody flying to the moon TODAY?!
The way I see it, this argument is still one of the strongest. It makes sense. I mean, my smartphone has more computing power than the Eagle had, and that was the height of engineering at the time. So a small computer would be enough to run all the software you'd need to control the landing module.

If that is correct (and it IS correct), why haven't we been there since 1972? NASA doesn't want to go? Of course they want to go! Did our tech improve? Of course it improved! Do we know more about the moon today than we did 40 years ago? Of course we do! So WHY, WHY, WHY?! It must have been a conspiracy. There's NO WAY we could have been there in 1969.

POSTED BY MR_WISEGUY ON NOV. 7 AT 8:43 PM

Useful phrases

You can't believe everything you read / see / … | With enough money / power, you can stage / fake / … | I bet a powerful company / the government / Hollywood could … | Something that big / complicated would be easy / impossible / … to fake.

Tip

A **blog** is a website which the blogger uses as a platform for his / her **blog posts** on a personal-interest subject. There are blogs for just about any topic. The word 'blog' is made up from the words *web* + *logbook*.

WRITING

7 Characteristics of a blog post

a) *Read the skills box. What key points would you add; what would you leave out?*

b) *Go back to the blog post in Ex. 6. Which key points from the list can you find there? Write down as many examples as you can find.*

Writing skills

Blog posts are written for others, not just for the blogger. These are **key points** many bloggers follow:

1. **Opinions** can be strong, but they should be fair too.
2. A blogger who is **honest** with his / her readers will probably enjoy the most respect.
3. **Clear**, **simple writing** and **short paragraphs** are easier to read.
4. **Spelling** is important online too, not just on paper.
5. Bloggers often have their own special **writing style**.
6. Readers will probably leave more **comments** if the blogger asks questions in his / her posts.
7. Headings and visuals **grab the reader's attention**.
8. People like **entertaining** posts, not boring ones.

READING

8 Comparing wiki and blog texts → WB 59/2

a) *Have a closer look at the wiki text and the blog post. Compare them in the three categories below. Then discuss them in class.*

function | language | reader interest

b) *Which of the two texts seems more reliable to you? Explain your choice. The words in the box can help you.*

Word bank

lie | fake sth | play a trick on sb / trick sb | stage a hoax | claim | be based on facts | estimate | make sth sound convincing | question somebody's motivations | think critically | informative | reliable | believable

WRITING

9 Your turn: Write your own blog response

→ △ 125/2
→ S7–9

Would you support the writer's conspiracy theory in Ex. 6 or would you argue against it? Write your own blog response.

Start like this:

- This is a comment on the … / on what you said about … | I'd like to comment on …
- I agree / disagree with you about … / with the idea that …
- In my opinion … | The way I see it, you …
- You might be right about …, but I don't think you're right about …

Tip

When you write a response, make sure you make it clear **what you're referring to**:

- the whole blog post?
- just one part of it?

Online ratings

SPEAKING

10 Reasons for rating things

Give reasons why so many people go online to rate things, e.g. films or restaurants.

READING

11 Films about space: Two film summaries

Read the two summaries below. Talk about them with a partner to make sure you both understand the plots. You need this information to deal with online ratings in Ex. 12.

Capricorn One (1978)

Imagine that the greatest moment in space exploration never happened! The NASA engineers on the Mars space program are unable to land their astronauts on the red planet. So they decide to fake the first Mars landing before the US government ends the expensive Mars program. Will NASA be able to stage the greatest hoax of all time?

The Martian (2015)

What do you do all alone on Mars, millions and millions of miles from home? After a voyage to Mars goes terribly wrong, astronaut Mark Watney (Matt Damon) is left alone to die on the red planet. Can he find a way to survive? What options are there in such a hostile environment? Will NASA even try to rescue Watney?

READING

12 Ratings on a website for film fans

a) *Read the two ratings. Describe how positive or negative each one is for its film.*

A Overall, this is a pretty good film. The plot and the acting are convincing, in my opinion. There's well-written dialogue too. But to be honest, it's a bit disappointing. I think I would have enjoyed the movie much more if I'd seen it when it was new. Back then, there weren't that many movies about space or conspiracy theories. But now there are so many great space movies.
★★★

B This is about as good as a film can get, if you ask me! As if the breathtaking visuals weren't already enough, Matt Damon has given one of his very best performances. Best of all: It's a strong, believable plot; a perfect combination of science, suspense, the power of friendship and BIG emotions. You really feel how lost and lonely a person can be. Excellent!
★★★★★

b) *Explain which rating motivates you more to watch the film. Give reasons.*

c) *Can you trust ratings? Give and explain your opinion about how reliable they are or aren't.*

READING

13 ‹ Internet research ›

→ S18

Find out as much as you can about the film above that interests you the most. Write down possible search terms before you start your search.

WRITING

14 Characteristics of ratings → WB 60/3–4

Writing skills

When you rate a film (or book), think about these points:

1. Structure your rating in **categories**. This helps you to concentrate on **what is important**, e.g. the acting | the plot | the special effects.
2. You don't need to write a summary for the film's plot; this is almost always included on the rating website already. Concentrate on **your opinion**.
3. Explain what you like or don't like, but **always be fair**. It isn't necessary to use bad language or make rude comments.
4. **Words and phrases** from other people's ratings can be very useful to help you to express your ideas. Examples from Ex. 12: *breathtaking visuals*; *well-written dialogue.*
5. Use the **simple present** to describe action and scenes (*When the story begins ...*; *The main character never knows ...* etc.).

→ △ 125/3

a) *Read the points in the skills box above. Then go back to the two ratings in Ex. 12. Find examples of points 1–4 and put them in a grid. (For point 4, you might find phrases in the box on the right to add to your grid.)*

b) *Your turn: In a group of 3–4, choose a film that three of you have recently seen. You each write a short rating (6–8 sentences) for it. Then peer-edit each other's texts. Say whose rating you like best and why!*

Useful phrases

well-developed / undeveloped / convincing characters | well-written / badly-written dialogue | a good performance / one of his / her very best performances | great / disappointing actors / acting | silly / weak / creative / believable / ... plot | In my opinion ... | If you ask me ...

WRITING

15 Options: Create wall displays

→ S7–9

Option A:
Internet research for your own wiki text

Some people believe that aliens have really landed on Earth, e.g. in Roswell, New Mexico!

a) *As a group, find one example of a UFO sighting and do research on different websites about it. Which are the most helpful and reliable?*

b) *In your group, write your own wiki text about your subject. Decide what sections your wiki text will need and divide the work up so that everyone has the same amount of work.*

c) *Arrange your wiki text as a wall display for your classroom.*

Option B:
Watch a film together and rate it

You've talked about the films on p. 104, now it's time to watch one together and then rate it.

a) *Form a group of classmates who would like to watch one of the movies you read about on p. 104.*

b) *Find the film on DVD or online.*

c) *After you've watched it, each person in your group will write a rating of the film. Don't forget to give each rating a number of stars from 1 to 5! Then peer-edit each other's texts.*

d) *When the ratings are finished, arrange them as a wall display for your classroom.*

Find more online: 9493kd

What you say and how you say it

On these pages you're going to learn about differences between American English (AE) and British English (BE). You're also going to learn how you use different words or phrases to say the same things in different situations. This is called **register**.

VOCABULARY

1 Warm-up: Which words do you use?

a) *Look at the German words below. There are different expressions for these words in different regions within Germany. Collect them.*

Brötchen | Frikadellen | Bürgersteig | Metzger

b) *Now discuss similar differences you already know about in the English language. You can look at your list from Unit 3, Ex. 18. What other differences do you know about?*

VIEWING

2 British, American and Canadian English

DVD 4/4

a) *Watch the first part of the film (00:00–02:54).*

→ S16

b) *Make a grid with the three columns below. Then watch the first part again and write down examples for each category in your grid.*

spelling | pronunciation | different words

c) *Work with a partner. Add more examples from Ex. 1b) to the grid.*

L 2/33

d) *Read the text below. The marked words are pronounced differently in AE and BE.*

Everything is so different at my new school. It starts with getting to school – my mom has to take me by car. At my old school I took the bus, but here I can't because our house is too far away! My schedule at this school is much better though – I can get up later!
So far, most of my new classes are cool; I'm just not so sure about German. But do you want to know what my biggest problem is? I'm so thirsty because I can't find the water fountain!

Tip

	BE	AE
car, other, sure, work	[-]	[r]
beautiful, little, water	[t]	[d]
new, news	[juː]	[uː]
bath, ask, can't	[ɑː]	[æː]
dog, not, lot	[ɒ]	[ɑː]
boat, know, hello	[əʊ]	[oʊ]

e) *Read the text from d) out loud with a partner. One reads it in American English, the other in British English. The tip box can help you.*

VIEWING

3 Register differences

a) *Watch the second part of the film (02:55–end). What happens in the two scenes?*

b) *Describe how register plays a role in the scenes. Explain why it is important to speak in different registers.*

c) *Your turn: In what situations do you change the way you talk? Say why and how you change it.*

VOCABULARY

4 Changing register → WB 62/1–2

a) *Match the words and phrases to the correct category:*

formal register | informal register

Hey! | How are you? | anymore | I really don't like it much. | child | Nope. | It really sucks. | Sorry, but I don't think so. | It's, like, so wild to … | I ain't … | I'm, like, … | Hello. | Totally! | Whatever! | kid | What's up? | No, I'm not. | How nice to … | no more | It's really boring. | I'm sorry. | Yes, I have. | Not in a million years! | I'm not … | It's totally not my thing.

b) *Change the register of this conversation between Brodie and his aunt June to make Brodie's words more formal and polite.*

Brodie: Whoa, sorry dude! Didn't mean to … – Oh! Hey, Auntie June! It's you! What's up?
June: Brodie! How nice to see you again. Happy Thanksgiving!
Brodie: Thanks! Same to you. It's, like, so wild to see you again.
June: How are you? You look like you've really grown in the last year.
Brodie: Totally! I'm, like, 6 feet tall now. I ain't no little kid no more!
June: How's school? Are you enjoying it?
Brodie: Nope. It's, like, so totally not my thing.
June: Well, I guess I didn't always enjoy school either.
Brodie: No. It really sucks!
June: I'm sorry you feel that way. But please mind your language!
Brodie: Whatever! The only parts I like are lunch and the final bell.
June: Maybe you can talk to one of your teachers.
Brodie: Not in a million years!

Legende

Diese Symbole und Erklärungen zeigen dir, wie du mit den Hilfen, Aufgaben und Aktivitäten auf den *Diff pool*-Seiten arbeiten kannst.

△ Hilfe zur Unit-Aufgabe | oder eine leichtere Variante der Unit-Aufgabe | oder eine zusätzliche Aufgabe

▲ eine zusätzliche Herausforderung

Unit 1

△ 1 Your turn: Your travel plans → Instead of Introduction, p. 9/4

Where would you like to spend your holiday? Choose one of these places. Find two other people who have chosen a different place. Use the phrases below to tell each other about your holiday plans.

enjoy nature | see wild animals / flowers | breathe fresh air | go for long walks / climbing | good food | …

go swimming / on a sailing trip / surfing | relax in the sun | build a sand castle | eat seafood[1] | …

go sightseeing / shopping | visit museums | travel on hop-on hop-off bus | eat international food | …

△ 2 Eating on board the ferry → After Station 1, p. 11/2

Some friends from the athletics team are talking about the different breakfasts on board the ferry. Read their conversation and answer the questions. Use ***indirect speech****.*

Fiona: I don't want to eat a French breakfast here. I've heard it's terrible.
Andrew: I tried it on my trip to France last year and it was really good.
Sally: Kevin and I are having the full English breakfast. We're really hungry because we didn't have breakfast this morning.
Andrew: Oh, I think that's too expensive. My parents only gave me €150 for the whole trip.

1. Why didn't Fiona want to have a French breakfast? 2. Why did Andrew want to eat the French breakfast? 3. Why were Kevin and Sally hungry? 4. Why couldn't Andrew afford the full Englisch breakfast?

Start like this: 1. Fiona said she … That's why she didn't want to have a French breakfast.

1 **seafood** ['si:fu:d] Meeresfrüchte

▲ 3 Trips without parents → After Station 1, p. 11/2

Most parents are very worried when their children travel alone. Would you tell your parents about everything that went wrong? Look at these problems Steve had on the trip and think of more. Then say what he told his parents and what he didn't.

1. was ten minutes late for the coach 2. paid too much for the breakfast and didn't ask for the change 3. had to borrow some money from other team members 4. had trouble with his host family because he took photos of the food 5. …

△ 4 What did she say? → Instead of Station 1, p. 12/4

Before their trip to France, Ms Woodruff told the team everything about the trip. Here's what she said – but what did the narrator tell his parents?

"I have some important information about our trip to France for you. Our coach will leave at 5 a.m., and it can't wait for people who are late – we need to catch the ferry in Dover at 8:40 a.m. We'll arrive in Calais at 9:10 a.m. There's a food court[1] on board the ferry where we can enjoy our first French breakfast. The last time I was on board a P&O ferry they also had free wifi. Some people spent most of the trip playing video games. But I hope nobody on our team wants to stare at a video screen[2] when they can enjoy the sea instead. Oh, I forgot to give you this form. All parents must sign it before we leave."

Start like this: "Ms Woodruff said she had … She told us our coach …"

△ 5 What happened? → Help with Station 1, p. 12/5a)

These words and phrases can help you to talk about the experiences of the Jones family:

Picture 1:
in Italy – go swimming – leave everything on the beach – come back – all things gone – see thief – can't catch – too far away

Picture 2:
very hot – wear shorts and tops – visit old city – go into church – want to take photos – priest[3] – tell us to leave – no shorts / tops and camera

Picture 3:
camp – long day – tired – sleep in tent[4] – suddenly hear noise – tent start to shake[5] – open – cow looking at us

△ 6 Travel situations → Help with Station 1, p. 12/5b)

These phrases can help you to talk about your travel experiences:

When I was in … last year … | During the holidays, I … | I felt very stupid / embarrassed / terrible / scared when … | Everyone / Someone was staring / looking at me / trying to explain something to me. | I was confused / upset / angry because … | I wanted to …, but I couldn't … | Next time, I'll use my mobile / ask someone about … / remember to …

1 **food court** [fu:d kɔ:t] Gastronomiebereich | 2 **screen** [skri:n] Bildschirm | 3 **priest** [pri:st] Priester | 4 **tent** [tent] Zelt | 5 **to shake** [ʃeɪk] wackeln

△ 7 A curious[1] aunt → After Station 2, p. 14/9

*At the airport, Rafiq's aunt wants to know exactly what happened. Turn her questions into **indirect speech**.*

1. "What happened at passport control?" **2.** "Why did the man become suspicious?" **3.** "Who told you to go to the side room?" **4.** "What did the security people say?" **5.** "Did they scare you?" **6.** "Have you really forgotten your birthday?" **7.** "Where's your luggage?" **8.** "Do you need help with the suitcase?" **9.** "Will you tell your parents about this?"

▲ 8 What did he ask? → After Station 2, p. 14/9

*Write down **five questions** you could ask your classmates. Then get into groups of three (Student A, B and C).*

*Student A whispers the first question on his list into the ear of Student B. Student C asks Student B: "What did he/she ask?" and Student B reports the question in **indirect speech**. Student C gives an answer, then Student B whispers a question into his ear – and Student A asks: "What did he/she say?" Take turns until you've answered all the questions on your lists.*

△ 9 I told you to call! → After Station 2, p. 14/10

When Rafiq comes back from Bangladesh, his mother is happy to see him again – but she's angry too. What did she tell him to do before he left? Complete her sentences.

Example: Did you take photos out of the plane? – I **asked you to take** photos out of the plane.

1. You didn't call when you arrived. Why not? I told you …
2. I don't think you said 'hello' to your aunt and uncle from us. But I …
3. Masud didn't take you to the old centre, did he? I know I …
4. Did you go there all alone? That's so dangerous! I …
5. I hope your aunt and uncle showed you my village. I …
6. Did Aunt Sadia cook black rice[2] for you? I …
7. I haven't got a postcard yet – did you write one? I …
8. Where is the saree[3] for me? Did you buy one? I …
9. Someone stole your money? You didn't take it to the old centre, did you? I …
10. I hope your aunt and uncle will visit us next year. Did you invite them? I …

1 curious ['kjʊəriəs] neugierig | **2 rice** [raɪs] Reis | **3 saree** ['sɑːri] Sari

▲ 10 Everyone orders me about[1] … → After Station 2, p. 14/10

*Young people hear commands from lots of different people in their lives. What commands do you get from these people? Complete the list. Then tell the class what they tell you to do. Use **indirect speech**.*

Teachers	Parents	Coach
Do your homework! …	Tidy up your room! …	Be on time for training! …

△ 11 Your turn: Travel plans → Help with Station 2, p. 15/13

You can choose from these European cities to find ideas for your plans:

	Barcelona	Dublin	Vienna
Flights from Frankfurt / Munich	1h 55 / 2h 5	2h 5 / 2h 35	1 h 20 / 1 h 5
Places of interest / Things to do	La Sagrada Familia church | Las Ramblas street | Magic Fountain[2] show | Camp Nou football stadium | beach	Ha'penny Bridge | O'Connell Street | The Book of Kells | Dublin Ghost Bus Tour | National Aquatic Centre	opera[3] house | Schönbrunn Zoo | Imperial Palace | National History Museum | Prater fun park

△ 12 Reading between the lines → After Story, p. 18/4

Read these short texts. Then decide which important information can be found between the lines.

1. It was wet outside. Very wet. Ryan looked at the kitchen clock: football training was at 4 p.m., and now it was already 3:50. He picked up his shoes and jacket, and with a sigh[4] walked out into the rain.
   a) Ryan lives close to the football stadium.
   b) Ryan hates playing football in the rain.
   c) The kitchen clock doesn't show the right time.

2. Kimberly ran all the way home, her Maths test still in her hand and a big smile on her face. "Mum!" she shouted. "You won't believe this!"
   a) Kimberly hurries home to help her mum in the kitchen.
   b) Kimberly is a very good student, especially[5] in Maths.
   c) She has a good mark in a Maths test, which is a surprise for her.

1 **to order sb about** [ˈɔːdə əˈbaʊt] jmdn. herumkommandieren | 2 **fountain** [ˈfaʊntɪn] Brunnen | 3 **opera** [ˈɒprə] Oper
4 **sigh** [saɪ] Seufzer | 5 **especially** [ɪˈspeʃli] besonders

3. Mrs Lynch looked at the students who were playing outside the school building. Laura was standing all by herself under what looked like 'her' tree now. She was staring down at her feet, as usual.
   a) Laura is unhappy because the other students don't talk to her.
   b) Mrs Lynch likes trees and students.
   c) The weather is great, so everyone can play outside.

4. Ethan checked his mobile for the tenth time – still no message. He played with the empty glass in front of him and asked himself if he should ask for another drink or give up and go home.
   a) Ethan likes drinks in restaurants and cafés.
   b) Ethan doesn't know what to do when he is alone in a restaurant.
   c) Ethan is waiting for someone, but that person doesn't come.

Text smart 1

△ 1 Theatre collocations → Instead of Introduction, p. 30/2a)

Read the following conversation between two actors and note down the theatre collocations they use.

Alex: Ian! You've forgotten your lines again! We can't give a great performance if you don't learn the lines! If you go on like that, you'll mess up the whole play.

Ian: Sorry, I just can't get into my character today. He's such a sad guy, and I'm just too happy right now.

Alex: Well, if you can't identify with your character, just try following the director's instructions, OK? They help you to understand your role. We've staged the play before – if you don't feel you can do it, Sam can play your part.

Ian: Sam? You can't be serious. He never stays in character – one moment he's a super hero, and the next a sad old man.

Alex: At least he knows how to follow the stage directions and play the scene right.

Ian: Are you sure? Remember how he forgets to use the props – he was supposed to give me the magic book in our last play but he forgot it backstage! I looked like a fool!

Alex: I don't think the audience noticed. Now just learn your role well and let's get on with our rehearsal.

△ 2 The main characters → Instead of Station 1, p. 31/5b)

Try to get into Claire's head and say what might happen.

Start like this: If I ask my parents, they'll say no. If they say no, I can't … If I can't …, Rob will …
If I tell my parents that I want to spend the night at Rob's house, …

△ 3 Telling lies → Help with Station 2, p. 33/8

*In which of the following situations are people telling a white lie? Discuss if it's OK to tell these white lies, or if it's **never** OK!*

1. Your friend has bought a new dress and looks terrible in it. She asks you if you like it and you say "It's just great!"
2. You forgot to do your homework yesterday, so you tell the teacher that you didn't understand it.
3. A friend calls, but you don't feel like talking to him and don't answer. When he asks you later why you didn't answer the phone, you say you didn't hear it.
4. You lost your mum's sunglasses, and you hadn't asked her if you could borrow them before. She asks you if you know where they are – you just tell her to take better care of her things.

△ 4 Getting into character → Help with Station 2, p. 33/9d)

Get into groups of three. One student stands in the middle. Now one of you doesn't want this student to do something, but he / she can only say "Don't!" Your partner wants the student to do it, but he / she can only say "Come on!" Keep repeating your words in as many different ways as possible to convince the student in the middle. Who is more convincing? How does the student in the middle show that?

△ 5 Acting out a scene → Help with Station 3, p. 35/12a)

Work together with another group of five. Decide who is going to play which role. Now go through the following steps together:

1. Work together with the person in the second group who has the same role as you.
2. One of you reads out the lines (reader), the other acts them (actor). If you're the reader, make sure that you read slowly and pay a lot of attention to your voice; if you're the actor, make sure that you listen carefully to the lines and pay a lot of attention to facial expressions and gestures[1].
3. Change roles and practise again.
4. Now one group acts out the scene while the other watches. Take turns. What ideas do you have to improve the scene? Try them out.

△ 6 Staying in character → Help with Station 4, p. 37/14c)

Copy these adjectives onto little pieces of paper and put them face down on the desk. Take turns to pick up a piece of paper, and use facial expressions and gestures to demonstrate[2] the feeling on your piece of paper. Don't speak! Your partner must guess which feeling you're trying to express.

angry | worried | afraid | scared | nervous | guilty | ashamed[3] | sad | shocked

disappointed | happy | confused | like an idiot | tired | fantastic

1 **gesture** [ˈdʒestʃə] Geste; Handbewegung | 2 **to demonstrate** [ˈdemənstreɪt] zeigen |
3 **ashamed** [əˈʃeɪmd] beschämt

△ 7 Bringing the story to life → Help with Options, p. 37/16

These ideas can help you with your options:

Option A:
When you act each scene, ask the students who aren't playing in that scene to watch. Pay attention to these points:

Where does each of you stand? | When do you move, and where do you go? | Who do you look at when you speak? | Make sure you don't turn your back on the audience!

Take notes for each scene and repeat the scenes with these notes in mind.

Option B:
This is what you should think about before you start:

What scenes do you want to take a photo of? | What effects can the camera angle and field size have? | What lighting do you want? | Do you need props?

When you edit the photos, these tips can be helpful:

Add the text which is necessary to understand what the scene is about (key information, dialogue, thoughts, and exclamations). | Write short texts that link the photos so that someone who doesn't know the play can understand it too.

Unit 2

△ 1 Welcome to America! → Help with Introduction, p. 43/3

*Read the questions below **before** you listen. They can help you to sum things up in Ex. 3 on p. 43.*

- Why are the European teens in America?
- Why is Josh the right person to talk to them?
- What is he going to talk about?
- Where does Josh live?
- What does he say about American apartment buildings?
- Where does he meet his friends?
- What does he say about city life?
- What is good about life in the suburbs?
- How are suburbs different from cities?
- What can you do in your free time if you live in the suburbs?
- Where will the Europeans go to school?
- What does Josh say about lockers?
- Where else do students meet?
- Do American students have to work hard?
- What does Josh say about other activities at school?
- What do Americans do in their free time?
- What else does Josh think is important?

△ 2 Different categories of gerunds → Help with Station 1, p. 45/3b)

Copy the grid into your exercise books. Complete it with the gerund phrases below.

Gerund after adjective + preposition	Gerund after verb + preposition	Gerund as sentence subject	Gerund as sentence object
I'm scared of changing		Living here isn't bad	

I miss seeing my old friends | Getting there is difficult | I like hanging out with … | We talked about organizing a party | Living here isn't bad ✔ | I miss having a garden | I'm looking forward to starting school | I enjoyed meeting you | Being in a city is cool | I love having a big bedroom | Can you imagine walking up 22 floors? | I'm scared of changing ✔ | I'm looking forward to making friends | I'm good at swimming | How about meeting up? | Stop worrying about losing your old friends | Meeting up isn't easy | I keep forgetting your dad is American | I'm getting used to living on the 22nd floor

△ 3 Do you like talking to your partner? → After Station 1, p. 46/4

Work with a partner to create little dialogues about things you like and don't like. You can use these phrases to start with. Can you think of more?

Do you like skiing? / Do you …? Are you good at playing chess? Do you feel like reading a book? Do you enjoy going for long walks? Are you crazy about texting your friends? Is dancing good for you?	✔	Yes, … is great / fantastic / fun. Yes, I love … / like … / always enjoy …
	✘	No, … takes too much time / makes me sick / is boring / isn't interesting at all. No, I hate … / don't like … at all / find … boring.

Example: Do you feel like going swimming? – No, I hate swimming.

△ 4 Gerunds to talk about likes and dislikes → Instead of Station 1, p. 46/6

*Gerunds are often helpful when you want to talk about likes and dislikes. Here, Lena is talking to her new friend, Madison. Finish the sentences below with **gerund phrases**. Each sentence with a gerund phrase should have the same meaning as the original sentence with the same number.*

Lena
1. I'm a bit shy when I meet new people, but it's OK.
2. Maybe I'll go to the mall; I'm not sure yet.
3. Mom tells me to unpack every day!
4. There's a dress code so I don't wear crazy T-shirts to school anymore.

Madison
5. My brother learned to drive when he was 16.
6. Would you like to meet some more people in the area?
7. I can't wait to plan our Thanksgiving party!
8. I listen to music all the time!

↓

Lena
1. I don't mind meeting …
2. I'm thinking of …
3. Mom keeps …
4. I've stopped …

Madison
5. My brother started …
6. Are you interested in …
7. I'm looking forward to …
8. I love …

△ 5 I like / I hate → Help with Station 1, p. 47/7

What do you like or hate? The words and phrases on the right can help you with sentences.
Write your ideas down first before you talk to your partner.

take tests | chill out with friends | travel around the world | discover new countries | go hiking | see / find dangerous animals | chill out on the sofa | text my friends | play games on my phone | watch TV | clean the kitchen | listen to music | tidy my room / the kitchen

Examples:
- I love chilling out on the sofa, but I hate washing the dishes.
- I'm really interested in …, but I'm scared of …

6 Role play: Matt, his angel and his devil → After Station 2, p. 48/9

In groups of three, write a short role play for Matt, his angel and his devil:

- Matt talks out loud about his dilemma;
- his angel and his devil try to tell him what to do from their different points of view.

The ideas below can help you to write your role play. Then act it out for the class.

hang out with geeks | (not) be an outsider | enjoy having fun | great to do sth for others | Is it really important to …? | love being part of the in-crowd | make the world a better place | What's wrong with being …?

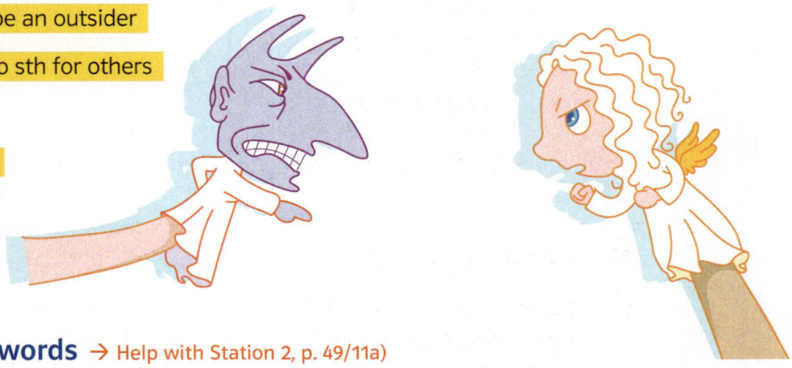

7 Infinitives with question words → Help with Station 2, p. 49/11a)

Compare A and B: Which words are left out in B? What is used instead? What else is different? This can help you to do Ex. 11a) on p. 49.

A		B
Matt asks himself a lot of questions at lunchtime:		He told his parents about it when he came home. He didn't know …
How do I pay for my lunch?	→	… how to pay for his lunch.
Where do I sit?	→	… where to sit.
What can I say to the other students?	→	… what to say to the other students.
Should I talk about the lessons?	→	… whether to talk about the lessons.

8 Do you know how to help a friend? → After Station 2, p. 49/11

*A group of kids from Matt's school is hiking in the hills of Pennsylvania. Suddenly Scott stumbles[1], falls down and doesn't get up again. Everyone is worried and asking questions. Turn their questions into **infinitive sentences**. Use words like these:*

wonder | ask themselves | not know | have no idea | not sure

Example: How can we help him? → They're wondering **how to help** him.

1. Should we feel his pulse[2]?
2. Do we have to check his breathing[3]?
3. Do we have to put up his legs?
4. Should we stay here?
5. Should we cover him with our jackets?
6. Shouldn't we try to find some adults?
7. Who can we call?
8. Where can we find some water for him?

1 **to stumble** ['stʌmbl] stolpern | 2 **pulse** [pʌls] Puls | 3 **breathing** ['bri:ðɪŋ] Atmung

▲ 9 New at our school → After Station 2, p. 49/11

a) *What kinds of things do new students want to know about their new school? Work with a partner to finish the sentences on the left with information on the right.*

1. Students who are new at our school want to know where to …
2. They wonder whether …
3. Some ask themselves how …
4. They would like to know who …
5. They don't know when …

find the cafeteria / the computer room | use the computers | borrow books | say hello to the teachers | ask for the computer passwords | bring books back to the library

b) *Work with a partner to write down questions a new student at your school might have.*

△ 10 I want you to write back! → After Station 2, p. 50/13b)

a) *Lena has told her grandma back in Germany what she is worrying about. First, read the tips and advice that her grandma wrote back.*

Liebe Lena,
ich möchte, dass du dich in Amerika zu Hause fühlst. 😀😀😀 Und ich möchte natürlich nicht, dass du traurig bist! 😢😢😢 Das tut mir so leid! Ich hätte gern, dass du Matt schreibst und ihm sagst, wie du dich fühlst. Natürlich würde ich es vorziehen, dass ER dir zuerst schreibt, aber er scheint sehr beschäftigt zu sein. Deshalb kannst du auch nicht erwarten, dass er dir sofort antwortet. Aber wenn du möchtest, dass er sich mit dir trifft, musst DU etwas tun.
Jetzt hätte ich gern, dass du mir bald antwortest! --Oma 😍😀😍

But Lena isn't so sure about her grandma's advice and wants Madison's opinion. Write what Lena could tell Madison about it.

Start like this: Grandma wants me to feel at home in America, and she doesn't …
She's really sorry for me. She'd like me to …

b) *Lots of people tell Matt what to do too. Write sentences about him:*

Eva and Scott would like Matt to …

spend the lunch break with them | go to the mall with them | not hang out with the geeks

Here's what Matt's parents expect from him:

always do his homework right after school | find new friends quickly | do what they say

And here's what Matt would prefer his friends to do:

everyone like each other | not talk bad about others | all his friends have lunch together

▲ 11 What I'd like others to do → After Station 2, p. 50/13b)

*Think of all your teachers (or classmates / parents / friends): What do they do, what don't they do? What do you like about it, what don't you like? Make a list of things you'd like them to do or not to do! Use **infinitive constructions**. Be creative!*

Examples: I'd like my English teacher to give us less homework. | I'd prefer the Math teacher to stop writing silly numbers on the board. | I expect …

△ 12 Infinitive or gerund? → Help with Station 2, p. 51/15b)

*Copy the grid into your exercise books. Then read the text below. Complete the grid with the verbs in yellow and decide: How do you write them when they're used with a **gerund**? And how do you write them with an **infinitive**? Write the German translation of the verbs into your grid.*

Verb	Gerund	Infinitive
remember	sich erinnern, etwas getan zu haben	…
…	…	…

Matt's mom remembers her last trip from England to the US: "I'll never forget losing my passport last year. I had forgotten to put it into my suitcase. I remember holding it in my hand and thinking that I shouldn't put it into my purse[1], and then I tried to open the suitcase – but the zipper[2] got stuck[3]. I tried using soap[4] on the zipper after someone had told me it helps, but it didn't. Then the doorbell rang, and I stopped to answer it. Well, once I stop doing something, I don't always remember to finish it, and that's what happened. I stopped thinking about the passport and put it into my purse. But my purse was stolen on my way to the airport! So I missed the flight *and* lost my passport!"

△ 13 Useful phrases for Lena's video chat → Help with Station 2, p. 51/16

Altkleidersammlung | keine Lust mehr haben, … zu tun | sich fragen wie … sein wird | Obdachlosenunterkunft | Kleider spenden | gut darin sein zu … / das gute Gefühl haben, … | Vorteile | von etwas profitieren | entrümpeln | etwas von jemandem erwarten

△ 14 What *really* happened at the mall → Help with Story, p. 54/4c)

These pictures and phrases can help you to write your own version of the story:

A

B

C

A	B	C
Lena sees group of young people with big signs | no Madison | the crowd pushes; Lena falls, loses her phone | sees her phone | grabs it before somebody steals it	tells officer that phone was stolen | Lena not worried; she knows she'll see the others at 5:00 | officer looks worried; tells her she might not see her phone again	Matt calls Lena's phone, Madison answers | phone was in Madison's bag the whole time | Lena waits at bench at 5:00 | Matt and Madison walk towards her

1 **purse** [pɜːs] Handtasche | 2 **zipper** [ˈzɪpə] Reißverschluss | 3 **get stuck** [stʌk] sich verhaken | 4 **soap** [səʊp] Seife

Text smart 2

△ 1 How to create an ad → Help with Station, p. 65/2b)

These words and phrases can help you to describe the ad on p. 65:

Useful phrases

- The ad for … is a typical …
- There's a large / small / funny / interesting eye-catcher on the left / right side …
- The eye-catcher shows … / is a photo of …
- It works as an eye-catcher because …
- Several photos show …
- The ad also gives / presents information on …
- The slogan is the part that says "…"
- The slogan focuses on …
- The ad copy tells the reader about …

△ 2 Talking about a target group → Help with Station, p. 66/4a)

Look at the different target groups in the first box below. Which ones would find the Fa$hion Fabulou$ ad attractive? And the Retro 4ever ad?

large families | fashion models | husbands who need a present for their wife's birthday | teachers | students | people with lots of / with little money | fashion addicts | tourists | hipsters | people who need an outfit for a wedding / for a party | skaters

These words might be able to help you to give more information about the target group:

people who want everyday / sporty[1] / cheap / nice / trendy[2] / … clothes | people who want to spend / save money | people who want …

△ 3 Improving an ad → Help with Station, p. 67/5b)

These questions might help you to find ideas for improving the ads on pages 65–66:

Visuals: Is there a link between the eye-catcher and the product? | Does the eye-catcher make the customer curious[3]? | Do the visuals cause positive / negative feelings? | Do the visuals present the product in the best possible way?

Slogan / ad copy: Does the slogan match the product? | Is the slogan catchy? | Does it tell the customer what the product is good for? | Does the ad copy tell the reader clearly where he / she can buy the product? | Does the ad copy clearly speak to a special target group?

Humor: Does the humor of the ad work for everyone? | Does it hurt anybody's feelings? | Are there ways it could be funnier?

Product: Does the ad feature enough information about the product?

Target group: Is it clear who the target group is? | Is there more than one target group? Could the target group be bigger if you changed the ad?

Effectiveness: Would you buy the product? | Do you know anybody who would buy it?

1 **sporty** ['spɔ:ti] sportlich | 2 **trendy** ['trendi] trendig | 3 **curious** ['kjʊəriəs] neugierig

Unit 3

△ 1 Big city life → Help with Introduction, p. 71/2a)

These words and phrases can help you to talk about life in a big city:

Pros: entertainment: (movie) theaters, concerts, live shows | **activities:** sports clubs, big parks | **education:** schools, museums, special offers for kids | **culture:** music, art, many nationalities[1] and cultures

Cons: people: too many people on the streets, crowded places, full buses and underground trains | **traffic:** too many cars, too much noise, pollution | **crime:** criminal gangs, violence, organized crime

△ 2 Your turn: In New York City → Help with Introduction, p. 71/3

Read the text about one of the photos from the Introduction. Which photo does it match? The text can help you to write your own text about one of the other photos.

I can hear lots of cars and voices – and so many different languages! Everyone seems to be busy. I can feel the magic of a big city with people from lots of different countries. The air smells of strange and spicy[2] food. I'm trying to catch a taxi, but that isn't so easy. Other people are waiting for a taxi too. But I'm not bored: There are so many things to discover and look at, like the colorful shop signs that I can't read and the mix of American and Chinese[3] culture.

△ 3 Tourists in New York → After Station 1, p. 73/2

*Use the phrases below to make sentences with **defining relative clauses**.*

Example: 1. Everyone **who is in New York for the first time** wants to visit the Empire State Building.

are looking for designer clothes | are interested in history | is in New York for the first time | love paintings and sculptures | want to get a great view of New York | are traveling with children | enjoy outdoor activities | don't have time

1. Everyone wants to visit the Empire State Building.
2. Most tourists spend a day in Central Park.
3. People often come to New York to visit the Museum of Modern Art.
4. Tourists love the Museum of Immigration on Ellis Island.
5. Most visitors travel by taxi.
6. Families always enjoy a visit to the Museum of Natural History.
7. Shoppers love the big department stores[4] like Bloomingdales.
8. Many tourists go up to the top of Rockefeller Center.

1 **nationality** [ˌnæʃn'æləti] Nationalität | 2 **spicy** ['spaɪsi] würzig; scharf | 3 **Chinese** [tʃaɪ'ni:z] chinesisch | 4 **department store** [dɪ'pɑ:tmənt ˌstɔ:] Kaufhaus

▲ 4 A stopover[1] in New York → After Station 1, p. 73/2

Imagine you have a two-hour stopover in Manhattan. What would you like to see and do? Write a short text. Give reasons for your choice of activities and places.

△ 5 Defining or non-defining? → After Station 1, p. 74/6

Use the phrases to make sentences about Rylee and Lea in New York City. Decide if you need ***defining*** *or* ***non-defining relative clauses****.*

Example: 1. Lea and Rylee, **who are in New York for the first time**, only have one day to spend in the city.

Diego shows the girls | Diego thinks of | is only a few blocks from Central Park | are in New York for the first time ✔ | catches Diego and the girls at the top of Rockefeller Center | calls himself 'The Naked Cowboy' | Diego and the girls visit | works in a diner

1. Lea and Rylee only have one day to spend in the city.
2. Diego takes the girls on a sightseeing tour of New York.
3. The places are for free.
4. The first place is a famous music school.
5. The man is a popular tourist attraction.
6. At the Alvin Ailey Dance Studio people take dance classes.
7. The big surprise is the view from Rockefeller Center.
8. The security man is Diego's father.

△ 6 Typical German food → Help with Station 1, p. 75/9

Match the English phrases on the left with the German expressions on the right. The English words can help you with Ex. 9 on p. 75.

black pudding | liver sausage | grow in the earth | serve with | vegetarian | point to the sky | chopped apples | the main ingredients | a popular dish

Leberwurst | die Hauptzutaten | in den Himmel ragen | ein beliebtes Gericht | Blutwurst | in der Erde wachsen | mit … servieren | vegetarisch | zerkleinerte Äpfel

△ 7 *Since* or *for*? → After Station 2, p. 77/12

Complete the sentences with ***since*** *or* ***for****.*

1. People have been calling New York 'The Big Apple' ___ a very long time.
2. A large Christmas tree has decorated Rockefeller Center every year ___ Christmas 1933.
3. Carnegie Hall has been one of the world's most famous concert halls ___ it was opened in 1891.
4. New Amsterdam has been called New York ___ Peter Stuyvesant had to give the city to the English in 1664.
5. Yellow taxis have been driving around New York ___ more than a hundred years.
6. New York has been important in foreign trade[2] ___ the opening of the Erie Canal in 1825.

1 **stopover** [ˈstɒpˌəʊvə] Zwischenstopp | 2 **foreign trade** [ˌfɒrɪn ˈtreɪd] Außenhandel

△ 8 Present perfect progressive or past perfect progressive? → After Station 2, p. 78/15

Complete the text with the right verb forms and ***since*** *or* ***for****.*

Lisa checked the time. She 1 (wait) 2 half an hour now, and still the airport bus wasn't in sight. Others were waiting with her. She noticed a woman who 3 (talk) to someone on her phone 4 20 minutes. "I 5 (live) here 6 May last year, and you haven't been here to see me once!" She'd heard her say. How could anyone not want to visit a friend in New York? Lisa 7 (dream) of coming to New York 8 she was a teenager. One day her boss had told her: "We 9 (look) for someone to take over our office in New York 10 last summer, and it seems that you're the best person for the job!" Lisa, who 11 (think of) moving to New York 12 several months, had accepted at once. "This is the chance I 13 (wait) for 14 I started working for this company," she'd told her husband. But now, after the first week in New York, she missed her husband and her kids. If only the airport bus would come …

▲ 9 Mixed bag: Different tenses → After Station 2, p. 78/15

As a taxi driver in New York, Emilio meets lots of interesting people. Here's a story he told his son Diego. Use the right tense for the verbs in brackets: ***simple past****,* ***past progressive****,* ***present perfect****,* ***past perfect*** *or* ***past perfect progressive****.*

I 1 (drive) around for a while when I 2 (pass[1]) the airport bus stop at Grand Central Station. There 3 (be) an accident on Lexington Avenue and traffic 4 (be) very slow. I 5 (notice) a family with a little boy and a teenage girl who 6 (point) at my taxi, so I 7 (stop). The man 8 (tell) me that they 9 (wait) for the airport bus for more than an hour. The family and another woman with a big suitcase 10 (get) into the taxi. They 11 (agree) to share a taxi and pay for it together. When we 12 (arrive) at the airport, the man 13 (say) he'd put it on his credit card[2]. But my credit card machine 14 (not work), so I 15 (ask) them to pay in cash[3]. Well, guess what – the family 16 (spend) all their cash and so they 17 (not be able to) pay. "Don't worry, I'll pay," the other woman 18 (say). "They can give it back to me later." She 19 (give) them her address in New York and 20 (pay): nearly $90! Isn't that cool? I 21 (never meet) such a generous person before.

△ 10 What had been happening before? → Instead of Station 2, p. 78/16

Complete the sentences with the ideas below. Use the ***past perfect progressive****.*

study hard for weeks | walk around Central Park for half an hour | look for rabbits in a muddy field for hours | chill out and talk for two hours | cry all morning | work hard all day | wait for him to call since 10 o'clock

1. I was very tired when I got home after school because I'd been …
2. Dave got the best grade on the test because he …
3. We … when there was a heavy storm and we had to go back.
4. When Kelly arrived at the café, her friends …
5. Our dog was very dirty. He …
6. Lisa thought her friend would never call. She …
7. Mary's eyes were very red. She …

1 to pass [pɑːs] vorbeikommen an | **2 credit card** [ˈkredɪt ˌkɑːd] Kreditkarte | **3 cash** [kæʃ] Bargeld

△ 11 Stylistic elements in a graphic novel → Help with Story, p. 89/3c)

Which of these stylistic elements can you find in the story? Use the prompts to talk about the effect they have in Asphalt Tribe.

set the scene | introduce the setting | create a distance / a quiet atmosphere

show action in the story | show reactions / feelings of characters

introduce fast action / speed | create suspense | make the reader live through the story

△ 12 Write the story! → Help with Story, p. 90/6

a) *Look at these beginnings of different parts of the story. What scene do they match?*

A: These streets, so busy and hectic during the day, but so dark and scary at night, were our home.

B: I ran away as fast as I could, but when I turned around, I saw that Maybe wasn't following me.

C: After a hard day in the streets we enjoyed our food – even if it was from the dumpster.

b) *Choose one of the opening sentences from a) and use the information and phrases below to continue the story.*

A: sleep under bridges | no family, only gang members | fight to survive | lonely | hard life | depressing | often hungry | invent new names

B: shout at Maybe | run at top speed | stupid rich ladies | no chance to catch us in their designer shoes | hope that handbag full of money

C: relax for a moment | glad to be with friends, not so lonely | suddenly hear police car | scared to death | drop everything and run away into the dark

Text smart 3

△ 1 Reasons → Help with Station 1, p. 102/5

There are different reasons why people would want to stage a hoax or why they believe in conspiracy theories. Maybe some of the statements below can help you with Ex. 5:

You could make a lot of money with it!

Governments or companies will do anything to look good or to cover up bad news!

When something is hard to explain, it's easy to say it was a government trick or a cover-up.

A boring person becomes interesting with a good story.

Some people will do anything for attention!

It's fun to trick people, and some will people believe anything!

△ 2 Your turn: Write your own blog response → Help with Station 1, p. 103/9

These ideas and arguments can help you to write your answer to the blog entry on the moon landing. Which ones support the blog writer? Which ones don't?

- moon landing not important → being better than the Soviet Union important
- then and now, good entertainment important → fake or real, only the show counts
- faking it → a good idea; good way to save money for a *real* trip to the moon
- flying to the moon → no benefits; too expensive
- reasons for not going anymore → other problems / challenges in world now; one successful mission enough
- clear facts → astronauts brought back stones, took photos

△ 3 A film rating gone wrong → After Station 2, p. 105/14a)

Look back at the skills box on p. 105. Then read the rating below. Talk to your partner about what's wrong here and how you could improve the text. Then write a new version.

Star Wars Episode 7: How bad can a film get?!
The film tells the story of a group of heroes who fight the dark powers and try find Luke Skywalker. On some websites people give this movie a rating of 9 or even 10 stars. Are they crazy?! Stupid?! Or both?! Were we watching the same movie?! THIS IS THE WORST STAR WARS FILM EVER! Let's start with the awful actors: Harrison Ford and Carrie Fisher are both too old and ugly to play their parts. I wish they had costumes like Chewbacca's so we wouldn't have to see their faces! Another joke: There are so many badly-done special effects! Han Solo's spaceship, the Millennium Falcon, was used in so many battles for the Rebel Alliance, especially in episodes 4 to 6, that it just looks like a silly old toy now. And can we talk about Rey, the new female[1] hero? As a girl, let me just say that it wasn't convincing for her to win a fight against Kylo Ren, Han Solo's son! Seriously! A woman who is good at mechanics[2], engineering[3] AND fighting?! Completely unbelievable!!! I wish I could give NO stars, but I have to give at least one, so here it is. ★
POSTED BY SCARY_CHICK ON DEC. 14 AT 10:08 PM

1 female [ˈfiːmeɪl] weiblich | **2 mechanics** [mɪˈkænɪks] Technik | **3 engineering** [ˌendʒɪˈnɪərɪŋ] Maschinenbau

Reading skills

S1 Schnelllesetechniken

Wenn du eine Aufgabe zu einem Text bekommst oder bestimmte Informationen suchst, liest du dir den Text ganz gezielt durch. Die folgenden Techniken können dir helfen, wenn die Zeit begrenzt ist:

Skimming („den Rahm abschöpfen“)	**Scanning („maschinell durchsuchen“)**
Wenn du danach gefragt wirst, worum es in einem Text geht, sollst du ihn nicht einfach nacherzählen, sondern nur das Wichtigste *(gist)* zusammenfassen. Dazu kannst du den ganzen Text überfliegen und darauf achten, ob bestimmte Wörter *(key words)* oder Personen häufiger vorkommen. Auch die Überschrift oder Bilder können dir helfen einzuschätzen, was wichtig ist und was nicht. Diese Art des Schnelllesens nennt man *skimming*.	Wenn du nach bestimmten Einzelheiten *(details)* in einem Text gefragt wirst, musst du ihn überfliegen und die Stellen mit den wichtigen Informationen finden. Dazu suchst du gezielt nach passenden Stichwörtern *(key words)*. Sie helfen dir dabei herauszufinden, welche Teile du genauer lesen solltest, um die gesuchten Informationen zu erhalten. Diese Art des Überfliegens nennt man auch *scanning*.

S2 Gliederung als Hilfe

Im geliehenen Buch darfst du das zwar nicht, aber auf Kopien oder in Arbeitsheften solltest du dir angewöhnen, wichtige Stellen in Texten zu markieren und Randnotizen zu machen (z. B. Fragen oder Anmerkungen). Verwende am besten verschiedene Farben:

Markiere z. B. wichtige inhaltliche Punkte grün und Informationen zu den Figuren / Charakteren blau. Diejenigen Wörter, die du nachschlagen musst, solltest du auch hervorheben. Du kannst sie unterstreichen und die richtige Übersetzung am Rand notieren. So fällt dir das erneute Lesen leichter.

Um einen Text besser zu verstehen, kann es dir auch helfen, ihn in mehrere Abschnitte zu gliedern. Orientiere dich dabei z. B. an Absätzen und inhaltlichen Punkten, die du dir markiert hast. Überlege anschließend, was in den einzelnen Teilen jeweils das Wichtigste ist und formuliere passende Überschriften. Dies erleichtert es dir, Texte zusammenzufassen oder *Mediation*-Aufgaben zu lösen.

S3 Umgang mit neuen Wörtern

Viele Wörter in einem Text kannst du verstehen, obwohl du sie noch nicht gelernt hast. Die folgenden Tipps können dir dabei helfen:

Ähnlichkeit mit Wörtern, die du schon kennst

Oft haben verwandte Wörter den gleichen Stamm, aber andere Präfixe oder Suffixe. Wenn du z. B. *usual* schon kennst, wirst du *unusual* sicher verstehen. Und wenn du das Wort *guide* als Nomen kennst, kannst du dir bestimmt denken, was das Verb *to guide* oder die Zusammensetzung *travel guide bedeutet.*

Ähnlichkeit mit Wörtern, die du aus einer anderen Sprache kennst

Viele englische Wörter gibt es genauso oder ähnlich auch im Deutschen, z. B. *computer* oder *hobby*. Manchmal hilft dir auch ein Wort, das du aus einer anderen Sprache kennst, ein englisches Wort zu verstehen, z. B. weil es ähnlich geschrieben wird oder ähnlich klingt.

Verstehen der Wörter im Zusammenhang

Manchmal kannst du dir anhand eines Bildes oder einer Überschrift denken, was ein Wort in einem Text bedeutet. Und wenn du alle Wörter in einem Satz verstehst außer einem, kann dieses oft nur eine bestimmte Bedeutung haben. Was bedeutet z. B. *ridiculous* in folgendem Satz: *That's the silliest thing I've ever heard. It's **ridiculous**!*

Auf den Zusammenhang musst du auch achten, wenn du Wörter im Wörterbuch nachschlägst, denn dort findest du meist mehrere Bedeutungen für ein Wort. Schau dir die folgenden Beispiele an:

*Take the second street on the **right**. That's the **right** way for the station.*
*I haven't got **time** to sit and chat today. We can chat when I come next **time**.*
*This is a very small **room**. There's **room** for only one bed.*

S4 Wichtige Merkmale von literarischen Texten erkennen

Story

Wenn du eine Geschichte genauer liest oder analysierst, solltest du nicht nur über die Handlung *(plot)* selbst nachdenken, sondern auch darüber, wie die Geschichte erzählt wird. Zu den wichtigsten Erzähltechniken *(narrative techniques)* gehören:

Atmosphere / Mood	Bestimmte Wörter und Beschreibungen schaffen in einer Geschichte eine gewisse Stimmung *(atmosphere* oder *mood)*. Stimmung entsteht z. B. dadurch, dass die fünf Sinne *(five senses)* angesprochen werden: Wenn man liest, was die Figuren sehen, hören, riechen, schmecken und fühlen, ist es leichter, sich in sie hineinzuversetzen.
Climax	Der Höhepunkt *(climax)* ist der Hauptwendepunkt in einer Geschichte. Die Spannung ist hier am höchsten. Die Hauptfigur befindet sich oft in einer schwierigen Situation und macht Veränderungen durch, sie wird z. B. stärker oder selbstbewusster. Siehe auch *turning point*.

Flashback	Eine Rückblende *(flashback)* erzählt Ereignisse, die vor einem bestimmten Zeitpunkt in der Geschichte stattgefunden haben. So wird z. B. die Erinnerung einer Figur an etwas Vergangenes beschrieben.
Narrative perspective	Die Wirkung, die eine Geschichte auf den Leser hat, wird stark von der Erzählperspektive *(narrative perspective)* beeinflusst. Wer ist der Erzähler und wie ist seine Einstellung zu den Figuren der Geschichte? Was erzählt er und wann? Die häufigsten Erzählperspektiven sind: **Ich-Erzähler *(first-person narrator)*** Der Ich-Erzähler erzählt aus seiner eigenen Perspektive und oft (aber nicht immer) ist er die Hauptfigur der Geschichte. Der Leser und der Ich-Erzähler erleben die Geschichte sozusagen „gemeinsam". **Er- / Sie-Erzähler *(third-person narrator)*** Dieser Erzähler erzählt die Geschichte „von außen". Die Perspektive ist nicht die der Hauptfigur.
Suspense	Spannung *(suspense)* ist eine wichtige Erzähltechnik, um den Leser in die Geschichte hineinzuziehen. Spannung kann direkt in den ersten Zeilen oder aber langsam im Verlauf der Geschichte aufgebaut werden. Sie wird z. B. durch starke, dramatische Sprache oder durch das Zurückhalten von Informationen erzeugt.
Turning point	Ein Wendepunkt *(turning point)* ist der Teil einer Geschichte, in dem eine Figur eine wichtige Entscheidung treffen muss. Diese Entscheidung beeinflusst den weiteren Verlauf der Geschichte. Sie kann für die Hauptfigur und die anderen Figuren gut oder schlecht sein. Siehe auch *climax*.

Graphic novel

In Comicromanen *(graphic novel)* wird eine Geschichte nicht nur mit Worten, sondern vor allem mit Bildern erzählt. Es ist deshalb wichtig, dass du nicht nur auf die Sprechblasen *(speech bubbles)* und die Bildtexte *(captions)* achtest, sondern auch auf die Gestaltung und Anordnung der einzelnen Bilder *(panels)*.

Poetry

Ein Gedicht ist wie eine Zeichnung oder ein Gemälde, das mit Wörtern „gemalt" wurde, daher ist bei der Interpretation jedes einzelne Wort wichtig. Denke daran: Beim Verständnis von Gedichten geht es nicht darum, die „richtige" Bedeutung zu finden – das gleiche Gedicht kann von verschiedenen Menschen ganz unterschiedlich verstanden werden. Wichtig ist aber, dass du deine Interpretation am Text belegen kannst. Dazu ist es hilfreich, auch formale Merkmale zu untersuchen und mit dem Inhalt in Verbindung zu bringen. Zu den wichtigsten Merkmalen von Gedichten gehören:

Rhyme scheme	Gedichte, die sich reimen, folgen immer einem bestimmten Reimschema *(rhyme scheme)*. Typische Reimschemata sind: **AABB** und **ABAB** sowie **ABCB**. Es gibt aber auch Gedichte, die sich nicht reimen, sogenannte *free verse poems*.
Rhythm / Stress	Ein Gedicht funktioniert nur mit dem richtigen Rhythmus *(rhythm)*. Er bestimmt, welche Stelle in jeder Zeile betont wird. Die Betonung *(stress)* liegt dann immer an der gleichen Stelle. Bei Gedichten, die sich nicht reimen, ist es wichtig, dass du selbst entscheidest, wo die Betonung liegt oder wo eine Pause gemacht werden sollte.
Symbol / Simile / Metaphor	In Gedichten spielen Symbole eine wichtige Rolle. Ein **Symbol** *(symbol)* steht stellvertretend für etwas anderes, z. B. für ein Gefühl, eine Idee oder eine Handlung. So ist das Herz ein Symbol für die Liebe. Bei einem **Vergleich** *(simile)* werden Dinge oder Personen mit etwas anderem verglichen, um auszudrücken, dass sie die gleichen Eigenschaften besitzen. Dabei wird *like* oder *as* verwendet, z. B. *Happy as a rainbow*. Eine **Metapher** *(metaphor)* ist ein verkürzter Vergleich ohne *like* oder *as*, z. B. *I'll be the light to guide you*.

Drama

Theaterstücke sind in Akte *(act)* und Szenen *(scene)* unterteilt. Sie sind dafür gedacht, von Schauspielern auf der Bühne aufgeführt zu werden. Es gibt in der Regel keinen Erzähler, der die Figuren genauer beschreibt. Stattdessen wird die Handlung direkt durch die gesprochene Sprache und durch die Darstellung der Figuren vermittelt. Deshalb ist es bei der Interpretation von Theaterstücken besonders wichtig, neben dem Text auch auf die Sprechweise, Gestik und Mimik zu achten. So kannst du Rückschlüsse auf Charaktereigenschaften, Gedanken und Gefühle der Figuren ziehen.

Characters	Die Figuren *(characters)* stellen oft klassische Typen oder Rollen dar. Auf der einen Seite gibt es einen Helden *(good guy)*, dem ein Bösewicht *(bad guy)* gegenübersteht.
Language	In Theaterstücken wird die Handlung durch gesprochene Sprache vermittelt. Die Figuren sprechen in Dialogen miteinander.
Stage directions	Alles, was nicht durch gesprochene Sprache vermittelt werden kann, wird in Regieanweisungen *(stage directions)* vorgegeben. Diese Anweisungen beschreiben, wie die Schauspieler ihre Rolle spielen und wie sie sprechen sollen. Hier werden auch Angaben zu Requisiten *(props)*, Bühnenbild und Licht gemacht. Wenn man ein Theaterstück liest, können die Regieanweisungen wichtige Hinweise z. B. auf die Stimmung der Szene und die Gefühle der Figuren geben. Sieht man das Theaterstück auf der Bühne, wird die Handlung und Stimmung des Stückes durch Körpersprache, Bewegungen, Bühnenbild, Licht, usw. getragen.

Dealing with visuals

S5 Fotos beschreiben und analysieren

Wenn du ein Foto beschreiben und analysieren sollst, kannst du in folgenden Schritten vorgehen:

1. Beschreibe, was auf dem Foto zu sehen ist. Dafür verwendest du das *simple present*. Konzentriere dich zunächst auf Personen oder Dinge, die im Vordergrund zu sehen sind, aber vergiss nicht, auch Personen oder Dinge im Hintergrund zu beschreiben. Wenn du ausdrücken willst, was auf dem Foto passiert, verwendest du das *present progressive*.
2. Nachdem du das Foto beschrieben hast, kannst du deine Meinung dazu äußern oder du kannst erklären, was es deiner Meinung nach ausdrücken möchte. Für die Analyse des Fotos verwendest du das *simple present*.

Useful phrases

Describing photos:
- At the top / bottom you can see …
- In the foreground / background / middle …
- On the left / right there is / are …
- The people in the photo are talking / having fun / celebrating / fighting / …

Analysing photos:
- I like / don't like the photo because …
- The photo is interesting / boring / exciting / … because …
- The photo shows … / represents …
- The photo tries to show … but I think a photo with … instead of … would work better because …

S6 Statistiken auswerten

Mit Diagrammen lässt sich eine Vielzahl von Informationen auf sehr kleinem Raum zusammenfassen. Häufig findest du die folgenden Diagramme, die jeweils einen anderen Schwerpunkt in der Darstellung haben:

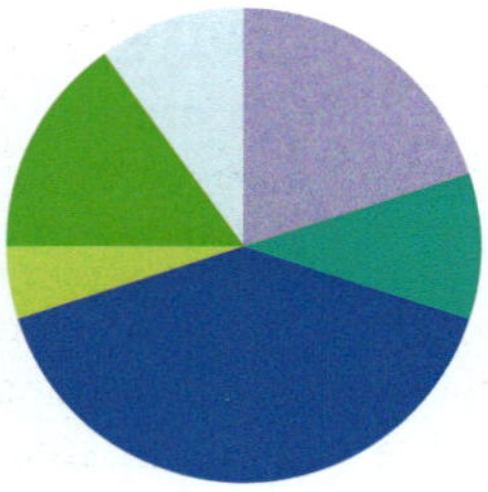

Mit einem Kuchendiagramm *(pie chart)* lassen sich Prozentzahlen darstellen, ausgehend vom gesamten Kreis (= 100 %).

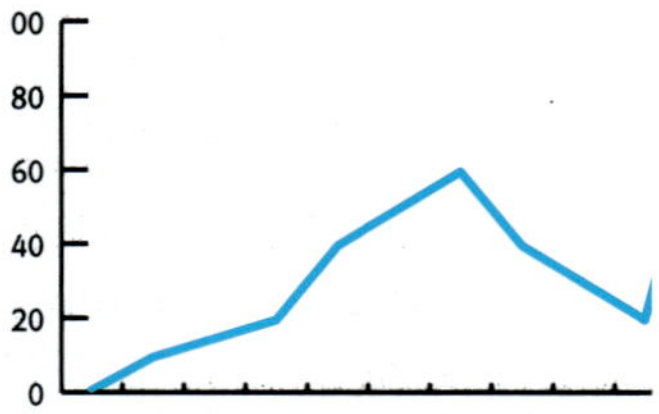

Ein Kurvendiagramm *(line graph)* verwendest du, um eine Entwicklung über einen längeren Zeitraum hinweg darzustellen.

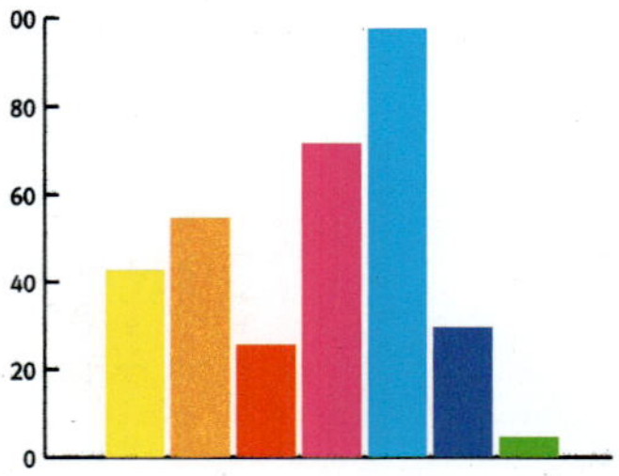

Ein Säulen- oder Balkendiagramm *(bar graph)* nutzt du, um Zahlen direkt miteinander zu vergleichen.

Wenn du deine Auswertung eines Diagramms präsentieren sollst, hilft es dir, schrittweise vorzugehen:

1. Sage zunächst, um welche Art von Diagramm es sich handelt und was es darstellt. Vergiss nicht, die Quelle und das Jahr der Veröffentlichung zu nennen.
2. Beschreibe, was du aus dem Diagramm ablesen kannst.
3. Fasse die wichtigsten Aussagen des Diagramms in 1–2 Sätzen zusammen.

Useful phrases

- The table / bar graph / line graph / pie chart / ... was published by ... in ...
- It's about ... / deals with ... / ...
- The (next) largest group of ... | The majority / minority of ... | Half of ... | Most of ... | 30 percent of the people ...
- The number of ... goes up / grows by ... / drops / goes down / doesn't change.
- The numbers / figures show / suggest that ...
- We can draw the conclusion that ...

Writing skills

S7 Textsorten und ihre Besonderheiten

Du kennst schon einige wichtige Textsorten und ihre Haupteigenschaften:

Print ads	Werbeanzeigen in Zeitungen, Zeitschriften oder auf Plakaten versuchen, den Leser davon zu überzeugen, ein bestimmtes Produkt zu kaufen. Hierzu sprechen sie den Leser direkt an und verwenden emotionale Sprache. Wichtige Elemente sind ein *eye-catcher* (ein Bild und / oder ein Text), ein ansprechender Slogan, weitere Textelemente *(ad copy)*, 1–2 Fotos des Produkts sowie Kontaktinformationen bzw. Angaben, wo das Geschäft oder die Firma zu finden ist.
Blog post	Ein Blog ist eine Art Online-Tagebuch, in dem regelmäßig Beiträge veröffentlicht werden. Es gibt unterschiedliche Arten von Blogs, z. B. Reiseblogs, Nachrichtenblogs oder Musikblogs. Meist sind Blog-Einträge aus der Ich-Perspektive geschrieben und drücken den persönlichen Standpunkt des Bloggers aus.
Dialogue / Film script	Wenn du einen Dialog schreibst, z. B. für eine Filmszene, denke daran, dass du ihn kurz hältst und echte mündliche Sprache verwendest, also z. B. *short forms*, *question tags*, verstärkende Ausdrücke, usw. Achte bei den *stage directions* für ein Film- oder Theaterskript darauf, dass du nur das angibst, was man auch sehen oder darstellen kann. Gedanken kann man nicht sehen, aber du kannst in den *stage directions* Hinweise auf die Gefühle einer Person geben, z. B. durch Anweisungen für Gesichtsausdrücke und Körpersprache.
Diary entry	Ein Tagebucheintrag erzählt und kommentiert vergangene und erwartete Ereignisse aus der ganz persönlichen Sicht einer Person und ist normalerweise nicht für andere Leser bestimmt. Verwende ausdrucksstarke Adjektive und Adverbien, um die Gedanken und Gefühle dieser Person zu beschreiben.

E-mail / Letter / Postcard / Invitation	Achte auf die richtige Anrede für den Adressaten, z. B. *Dear …*, Grußformeln am Schluss, z. B. *Yours / Love / Best wishes*, und beachte die Höflichkeitsregeln. Bei formellen E-Mails oder Briefen verwendet man eher die Langformen, z. B. *I am* statt *I'm*. Denke bei einem Brief an die Angabe der Empfänger- und Absenderadresse und an das Datum.
Flyer	Ein Flyer sollte gut lesbar sein (Schriftart- und größe) und alle wichtigen Informationen enthalten: *Who? What? When? Where? Why?* Formuliere außerdem einen ansprechenden Slogan.
Instructions	Anweisungen sind meist in mehrere, klare Schritte gegliedert. Diese Schritte können von Überschriften eingeleitet werden. Sprachlich werden vor allem Imperative und *phrases* wie *Make sure …*, *You / It must …* oder *Never …* verwendet.
News report	Konzentriere dich bei einem Tatsachenbericht auf die Fakten und spare deine persönliche Meinung aus. Achte außerdem auf eine sachliche Sprache und vermeide emotionale Ausdrücke. Die Schlagzeile *(headline)* sollte direkt auf das Thema des Artikels hinweisen und außerdem das Interesse des Lesers wecken. Beachte, dass in Zeitungsberichten häufig Passivformen verwendet werden.
Prompt cards	Wenn du dich auf eine Präsentation vorbereitest, notiere dir auf Karteikarten nur Stichwörter, die dich an die einzelnen Punkte des Vortrags erinnern. Schreibe z. B. wichtige Namen, Ereignisse, Orte und Daten auf.
Report	Bei einem Bericht ist die Vollständigkeit und Verständlichkeit der sachlichen Informationen das Wichtigste. Er wird im *simple past* geschrieben.
Review / Online rating	Eine Rezension bzw. Kritik hilft dem Leser zu entscheiden, ob es sich lohnt, einen bestimmten Film anzuschauen oder ein bestimmtes Buch zu lesen. Zuerst beschreibst du kurz die wichtigsten Details, dann folgt deine Bewertung, die du mit guten Argumenten belegen solltest.
Story	Wenn du deine eigene Geschichte schreibst, schmücke sie aus und gestalte sie sprachlich abwechslungsreich. Meistens sind Geschichten im *simple past* geschrieben. Wenn du eine Geschichte vervollständigen sollst, muss dein Teil zum vorgegebenen Text passen. Vermeide also inhaltliche Widersprüche. Außerdem sollten sich die Erzählperspektive und die Erzählzeit im Verlauf der Geschichte nicht ändern.
Wiki text	Ein Wiki-Eintrag hat zum Ziel, ähnlich wie ein Lexikonartikel Informationen zu vermitteln. Da jede beliebige Person die Texte schreiben bzw. ergänzen oder abändern kann, ist es wichtig, dass du auch nach anderen zuverlässigen Informationsquellen suchst und dich nicht nur auf die Informationen in dem Wiki verlässt.

S8 Einen eigenen Text schreiben

Es ist wichtig, dass du deine Texte gut planst und zuerst einen Entwurf schreibst, den du dann überarbeitest. So wird es für den Leser einfacher, deinen Gedanken zu folgen und deinen Text flüssig zu lesen.

1. Die Planung deines Textes

Nimm dir für diese Phase ausreichend Zeit. Lies die Aufgabenstellung genau durch und überlege, für wen dein Text bestimmt ist (Adressat) und welche Textsorte verlangt wird (Bericht, Zusammenfassung, Kommentar, usw.). Vor dem Schreiben machst du dir am besten einen Plan: Notiere in Stichwörtern, was in der Einleitung, dem Hauptteil und dem Schluss deines Textes stehen soll. So vergisst du nichts Wichtiges und findest auch leichter eine interessante Einleitung und einen passenden Schluss.

Ein guter Text besteht normalerweise aus den folgenden drei Teilen:

Einleitung *(introduction)*: Hier erfährt der Leser, worum es in deinem Text geht. Du kannst auch eine Fragestellung einführen, die in deinem Text erörtert werden soll.

Hauptteil *(main part)*: Der Hauptteil ist in mehrere Abschnitte gegliedert und beinhaltet die Details (Fakten, Argumente, Beispiele, usw.) zu deinem Thema.

Schluss *(conclusion)*: Deinen Text solltest du mit einem geeigneten Schlussteil beenden. Dies kann eine Zusammenfassung von dem sein, was du im Hauptteil geschrieben hast, oder eine persönliche Äußerung.

2. Der erste Entwurf

Auf der Grundlage deiner Planung kannst du einen ersten Entwurf schreiben. Denke daran, dass du für jede neue Idee einen eigenen Abschnitt beginnst. Tipps für einen guten Schreibstil findest du im folgenden Kapitel (→ S9).

3. Die Überarbeitung

Nachdem du den ersten Entwurf erstellt hast, ist es wichtig, dass du oder einer deiner Mitschüler den Text noch einmal kritisch durchliest. Am hilfreichsten ist es, wenn du den Text mehrmals liest, jedes Mal mit einem anderen Schwerpunkt. Dabei kann dir eine Checkliste helfen (siehe rechts).

Überarbeite anschließend die kritischen Stellen. Wenn du Feedback von einem Mitschüler bekommen hast, sieh es dir genau an und entscheide, was davon du für deinen Text übernehmen möchtest. Wenn du von einem Mitschüler gebeten wirst, seinen Text zu lesen, achte darauf, dass du bei deiner Kritik fair bleibst.

Inhalt:
- Sind alle wesentlichen Punkte enthalten?
- Gibt es keine inhaltlichen Fehler?
- Ist der Text logisch aufgebaut und hat eine klare Struktur?

Rechtschreibung:
- Sind die Wörter richtig geschrieben?
- Stimmt die Zeichensetzung?
- Ist der Text einheitlich im *British* oder *American English* geschrieben?

Grammatik:
- Stimmen die Zeitformen?
- Ist die Formenbildung richtig (z. B. Adjektive, Adverbien, usw.)?

S9 Tipps für einen guten Schreibstil

Je größer dein Wortschatz wird, desto mehr Möglichkeiten eröffnen sich dir beim Schreiben deiner eignene Texte. Lies die folgenden Tipps aufmerksam durch, bevor du mit dem Schreiben beginnst:

Adjektive und Adverbien

Du kannst deine Sätze interessanter gestalten, indem du z. B. Nomen durch Adjektive näher beschreibst. Verben kannst du durch Adverbien oder adverbiale Bestimmungen ergänzen. Vergleiche die folgenden beiden Sätze:

A *I went to the shop.*
B *I went to the big pet shop with my sister last Saturday.*

Achte darauf, dass du Adjektive wie *good*, *bad*, *nice* und *big* nicht zu häufig verwendest. In der Tabelle findest du Beispiele für Adjektive, die du stattdessen verwenden kannst:

good	*amazing, awesome, beautiful, brilliant, exciting, fantastic, fascinating, great, interesting, spectacular, wonderful*
bad	*awful, boring, terrible*
nice	*amazing, beautiful, fascinating, interesting, lovely, pretty, wonderful*
big	*gigantic, great, huge, large, wide*

Konjunktionen *(linking words)*

Ein Text liest sich leichter, wenn die Sätze darin miteinander verknüpft sind. Mit Hilfe von Konjunktionen werden logische Zusammenhänge hergestellt. Vergleiche die beiden folgenden Textausschnitte. Der erste wirkt durch die unverbundenen Hauptsätze abgehackt. Der zweite liest sich durch Satzgefüge aus Haupt- und Nebensätzen und durch Konjunktionen flüssiger. Außerdem geben die vielen Adjektive und Adverbien genauere Informationen und machen den Text interessanter.

A *I went to the shop. I wanted a guinea pig. We looked at all the guinea pigs. I didn't like them. We wanted to leave. A girl came in with a box. She brought back a guinea pig. It was cute! I bought it. I'm happy.*

B *I went to the big pet shop with my sister last Saturday because I wanted to buy a nice guinea pig. We looked at all the guinea pigs, but I didn't like them. Just when I wanted to leave, a girl came in with a box. She brought back a guinea pig which was really cute. So I bought it and I'm very happy now.*

Relativsätze *(defining and non-defining relative clauses)*

Mit Relativsätzen kannst du Sätze verbinden oder zusätzliche Informationen zu einer Person oder Sache einführen:

- *This is the food cart which sells the best hot dogs in New York. (defining relative clause)*
- *The food cart with the city's best hot dogs, which I'd never even heard about until last week, is really worth a visit. (non-defining relative clause)*

Zeitangaben *(time markers)*
Adverbiale Bestimmungen der Zeit können dem Leser helfen, sich in einem Text oder einer Geschichte zeitlich zurechtzufinden. Du kannst *time markers* auf unterschiedliche Weise einsetzen:

- um die Ereignisse zeitlich einzuordnen: *two years ago, last summer, when I came home yesterday, …*
- um zu zeigen, in welcher Reihenfolge sie passieren: *at first, next, finally, …*
- um zu verdeutlichen, wie viel Zeit zwischen den Ereignissen vergeht: *for two hours, just five minutes later, …*
- um auszudrücken, wie schnell oder langsam etwas passiert: *immediately, quickly, it took hours, …*
- um zu sagen, dass mehrere Ereignisse zeitgleich passieren: *while I was waiting, during lunch, …*

S10 Eine Zusammenfassung schreiben

Die folgenden Schritte können dir helfen, einen Text schriftlich zusammenzufassen:

1. Lies dir den Ausgangstext einmal komplett durch, damit du weißt, um was es geht. Achte dabei auch auf die Überschrift, denn sie verrät meist schon viel über den Inhalt des Textes.
2. Dann lies den Text noch einmal durch, um weitere Details zu verstehen. Erst wenn du den Text im Detail verstanden hast, kannst du entscheiden, welche Aspekte du in deiner Zusammenfassung *(summary)* erwähnen solltest und welche nicht. Du kannst dir Notizen dazu machen oder wichtige Stellen im Text markieren (wenn er nicht in deinem Englischbuch steht). Beim Verständnis des Textes können dir auch die *wh*-Fragen helfen *(Who? What? Where? When? Why?)*.
3. Entscheide, welche Informationen du in deine Zusammenfassung übernehmen möchtest. Beispiele, Zahlen, direkte Rede, Wertungen oder Interpretationen gehören nicht in eine Zusammenfassung.
4. Schreibe einen ersten Entwurf deiner Zusammenfassung. Beginne mit einer Einleitung, die wichtige Informationen wie z. B. Titel, Autor, Thema und Hauptaussage des Textes beinhaltet. Wenn du einen Zeitungsartikel zusammenfasst, solltest du hier auch die Quelle nennen. Verwende für deine Zusammenfassung das *simple present* und achte darauf, dass du nicht einfach nur den Text abschreibst, sondern deine eigenen Worte findest.

Tip

Denke daran, dass du die Personen in deiner Zusammenfassung ändern musst. Ist der Ausgangstext aus der Perspektive der 1. Person geschrieben („ich", „wir"), musst du für deine Zusammenfassung die 3. Person verwenden („er", „sie").

5. Lies deine Zusammenfassung am Ende noch einmal sorgfältig durch und vergleiche sie mit dem Ausgangstext. Hast du alle wichtigen Aspekte genannt und unwichtige Details weggelassen? Ist dein Text durchgängig im *simple present* geschrieben? Achte auch auf Rechtschreibung und grammatische Stolpersteine.

Speaking skills

S11 Gespräche führen

Es ist nicht immer leicht, sich mit Menschen zu unterhalten, die man noch nicht so lange kennt oder gerade erst kennengelernt hat. Mach dir vor dem Gespräch klar, mit wem du redest. Wenn du dich mit einem gleichaltrigen Jugendlichen unterhältst, kannst du viel informeller sprechen als wenn du mit jemand Älterem sprichst. Überlege auch, ob es kulturelle Unterschiede gibt, und passe deine Sprache entsprechend an.

Die folgenden Schritte können dir helfen, ein Gespräch zu beginnen und aufrecht zu erhalten:

1. Beginne freundlich, z. B. mit etwas, was euch beide verbindet (der Ort, die Situation, usw.).
2. Halte die Unterhaltung am Laufen. Es ist wichtig, deinem Dialogpartner immer das Gefühl zu geben, dass er einbezogen wird. Dazu dienen *feedback phrases*, Nachfragen und *question tags*, wie du anhand des folgenden Beispiels sehen kannst:

   Then we went to the new shoe shop in town, you know. And there were these amazing trainers – I showed you a photo, didn't I? Guess what Linda said when she saw them!

   Wenn du etwas nicht verstehst, frage höflich nach *(What was that you mentioned about …? Sorry, I didn't catch what you just said about …)*. Wenn du etwas nicht sagen kannst, weil dir der nötige Wortschatz fehlt, versuche es zu umschreiben oder bitte deinen Gesprächspartner um Hilfe.
3. Beende das Gespräch so freundlich, wie du es angefangen hast, und verabschiede dich. Vergiss nicht, dich zu bedanken, wenn du um Hilfe gebeten hast.

In vielen Situationen des täglichen Lebens – im Klassenzimmer, mit Freunden, in der Familie – hast du es in Diskussionen mit unterschiedlichen Meinungen zu tun. Umso wichtiger ist es, Kompromisse zu finden. Die *useful phrases* können dir helfen, typische Diskussionssituationen zu meistern.

Tip

Lass dich nicht verunsichern, wenn du beim Sprechen ins Stocken gerätst. In der gesprochenen Sprache ist es normal, dass Pausen, unvollständige Sätze, Wiederholungen oder Füllwörter vorkommen: *Well, I – I really don't know. It's – er, maybe you want to …?*

Useful phrases

Asking for an opinion: How do you feel about …? | What do you think about …?
Making a suggestion: Why don't we …? | I've got an idea. Can we …? | If we did it this way, we could …
Agreeing: Yes, we should do that. | No, I don't mind doing that.
Disagreeing: You've got a point but … | I don't think that's a good idea. It would be better to …
Finding a compromise: Can we meet halfway? | If we did it this way, we could …

S12 Eine Präsentation vorbereiten und halten

Ob in der Schule oder später im Beruf, die Fähigkeit, eine gut vorbereitete und klar strukturierte Präsentation zu halten, spielt eine wichtige Rolle. Die folgenden Schritte können dir bei der Vorbereitung und Durchführung deiner Präsentation helfen:

1. Recherchiere Informationen zu deinem Thema und strukturiere sie, indem du z. B. eine Gliederung anlegst.
2. Überlege dir, mit welchem Material du deine Präsentation unterstützen willst. Gestalte dein Poster / deine Folie / dein Handout.
3. Bereite deine Präsentation vor, indem du nummerierte Karteikarten *(prompt cards)* anlegst, auf denen du dir die wichtigsten Punkte in Stichworten notierst.
4. Übe deine Präsentation zu Hause vor dem Spiegel oder vor einem kleinen Publikum (Eltern, Großeltern, Freunde). Stoppe die Zeit, die du brauchst, damit du bei deiner Präsentation nicht in Zeitnot gerätst.
5. Wenn du deine Präsentation hältst, achte darauf, dass du die Aufmerksamkeit aller Zuhörer hast. Dann erkläre kurz, worüber du sprechen wirst und wie deine Präsentation aufgebaut ist. Sprich langsam und möglichst frei. Verwende deine *prompt cards* nur als Hilfestellung. Beende deine Präsentation mit einer kurzen Zusammenfassung der wichtigsten Punkte. Bedanke dich fürs Zuhören und frage nach, ob deine Zuhörer Fragen haben.

Useful phrases

- My presentation is about … | Today I'll talk about … | First I'd like to talk about … Then …
- Here's a new word. It's … in German.
- On my poster you can see … | The mind map shows … | I've prepared a handout for you.
- That's the end of my presentation. Do you have any questions?
- Thanks for listening.

Mediation skills

S13 Bearbeitung von *Mediation*-Aufgaben

Mediation ist die Übertragung wichtiger Informationen aus einem gesprochenen oder geschriebenen Text in eine andere Sprache, z. B. aus dem Englischen ins Deutsche oder umgekehrt. Das machst du, wenn du einen Text für jemanden zusammenfassen sollst, der die Sprache des Ausgangstextes nicht versteht. Gelegentlich kann es auch sein, dass du dolmetschen musst, also zwischen Gesprächspartnern vermittelst, die nicht dieselbe Sprache sprechen. Ganz wichtig: Es geht bei der *mediation* niemals um eine wörtliche Übersetzung *(translation)*!

Lies dir die *Mediation*-Aufgabe gut durch und beachte besonders folgende Dinge:

Adressat:
Für wen ist die Information bestimmt?
--> Je nachdem, wer die Person ist und wie viel sie schon weiß, sprichst du sie unterschiedlich an.

Zweck:
Wozu benötigt die Person die Information?
--> Du musst nur die Informationen wiedergeben, die für den Adressaten in der jeweiligen Situation wichtig sind. Alles andere kannst du weglassen. Es kann aber auch vorkommen, dass du Dinge zusätzlich erklären musst.

Beispiel: Dein Ausgangstext ist die Infobroschüre eines Museums. Wenn dein Gegenüber dich fragt, ob das Museum heute geöffnet ist, musst du nicht unbedingt alle anderen Öffnungszeiten nennen. Will die Person den Eintrittspreis wissen, kommt es auf ihr Alter an und darauf, ob sie allein oder mit einer Gruppe unterwegs ist.

Einen schriftlichen Ausgangstext kannst du in Ruhe durchlesen und die wichtigsten Informationen auswählen. Dabei helfen dir die Lesetechniken, die unter *Reading skills* beschrieben werden (→ S1). Formuliere die entsprechenden Inhalte so, dass der Adressat sie gut verstehen kann.

Tip

Achte bei einer schriftlichen *mediation* darauf, dass dein Text nicht länger als ca. 35–40 % des Ausgangstextes ist, ähnlich wie bei einer Zusammenfassung (→ **S10**).

Bei einer Dolmetschaufgabe wird eine echte mündliche Gesprächssituation simuliert. Deshalb musst du schneller reagieren, um möglichst viel von dem sinngemäß wiederzugeben, was die Gesprächspartner zueinander sagen. Nicht ganz einfach ist es, wenn du Durchsagen am Flughafen oder am Bahnhof aus dem Englischen ins Deutsche übertragen sollst, da sie oft unbekannte Wörter enthalten und durch die Hintergrundgeräusche schwer zu verstehen sind. Hier kann es dir helfen, dich auf die Namen von Personen oder Orten, Zahlen, Zeitangaben oder auf andere wichtige Schlüsselwörter *(key words)* zu konzentrieren.

S14 Paraphrasieren

Wenn du wichtige Informationen aus einer Sprache in die andere übertragen willst, kann es vorkommen, dass dir ein Wort nicht einfällt, besonders in Gesprächssituationen, wenn alles sehr schnell gehen muss. Bleibe ganz ruhig und versuche, das Wort zu umschreiben *(paraphrasing)*.

Useful phrases

- It's somebody / a person who …
- It's something that you use to …
- It's a place that / where …
- It's the same as … | It's the opposite of …

Wenn du Zeit brauchst, um das richtige Wort oder eine Umschreibung dafür zu finden, kannst du dir mit folgenden *phrases* behelfen: *Just a second …* | *Let me think …*

Listening skills

S15 Hörverstehen üben

Es ist immer sinnvoll, viele authentische englische Texte anzuhören, z. B. Nachrichten in Radio und Fernsehen oder Hörbücher. Dabei ist es nicht schlimm, wenn du nicht jedes Wort verstehst. Dir wird außerdem auffallen, wie unterschiedlich die Aussprache des Englischen je nach Herkunft des Sprechers sein kann. So gibt es neben Unterschieden zwischen britischem und amerikanischem Englisch auch innerhalb Großbritanniens verschiedene Dialekte oder regionale Akzente. Auch dann ist es nicht schlimm, wenn du nicht alles verstehst. Selbst ein Engländer aus London könnte Schwierigkeiten haben, einen Schotten aus Glasgow auf Anhieb zu verstehen.

Manchmal hilft dir beim Hörverstehen auch die Kenntnis von typischen Textsorten und Situationen. Wenn du die Textsorte des Hörtextes kennst, überlege dir, worauf es beim Telefonieren, beim Dolmetschen, bei Präsentationen, Durchsagen, Radio- oder Fernsehsendungen ankommt und welche Themen jeweils zu erwarten sind. Gelegentlich geben dir auch Bilder Hinweise zur entsprechenden Situation: Wenn z. B. bestimmte Personen oder Orte dargestellt sind, kannst du leichter einschätzen, worum es in dem Hörtext geht. Achte beim Hören auf Geräusche sowie Stimme und Tonfall des Sprechers. In echten Gesprächssituationen oder Filmen können dir Gestik und Mimik das Verständnis erleichtern.

Analog zum Lesen (→ S1) helfen dir beim Hörverstehen die folgenden Techniken:

Listening for gist	**Listening for detail**
Versuche, das Wichtigste *(gist)* in einem Hörtext zu erkennen und zusammenzufassen. Achte dabei besonders auf Wörter und Themen, die mehrmals vorkommen und vermutlich eine wichtige Rolle spielen.	Versuche gezielt, dem Text bestimmte Einzelinformationen *(details)* zu entnehmen. Achte dabei besonders auf Wörter, die du in der Antwort erwartest, und die Informationen dazu.

Viewing skills

S16 Wichtige filmische Mittel

Genre

Es gibt viele unterschiedliche Arten von Filmen, man nennt sie auch Genres. Du erkennst Filme eines Genres normalerweise daran, dass sie ähnliche Hauptmerkmale aufweisen.

Crime

Fantasy

Hier sind einige Beispiele:

Action	In Actionfilmen geht es meist um einen Helden oder eine Heldin im Kampf gegen das Böse. Dabei kommen häufig spektakuläre Stunts, Verfolgungsjagden und Gewaltszenen vor.
Crime	Im Mittelpunkt eines Kriminalfilms steht ein Verbrechen, das meist im Laufe des Films aufgeklärt wird. Dabei gibt es viele spannende Szenen und überraschende Wendungen.
Comedy	Komödien haben eine humorvolle Handlung, die zum Lachen anregt. Häufig werden die Charaktere übertrieben dargestellt und Sprachwitz spielt eine wichtige Rolle.
Fantasy	Fantasyfilme handeln von magischen oder übernatürlichen Kräften. Häufig steht ein Held oder eine Heldin im Mittelpunkt der Handlung.
Historical	Historienfilme spielen in einer bestimmten geschichtlichen Epoche. Häufig basieren sie auf wahren Begebenheiten. Die Kostüme und Requisiten sind meist aufwendig gestaltet.
Romance	In Liebesfilmen steht die Beziehung zwischen zwei Figuren im Mittelpunkt. Das Ende dieser Filme fällt meist positiv aus.
Science Fiction	Science-Fiction-Filme handeln z. B. von Erfindungen in Wissenschaft und Technik, von Zeitreisen oder Außerirdischen. Sie spielen häufig in der Zukunft und wirken unrealistisch.

Story
Wenn du einen Film anschaust, achte darauf, wo und wann der Film spielt *(setting)*, auf die Besetzung der Rollen *(cast)*, auf den Schauplatz *(location)* und die Handlung *(plot)*.

Audio-visual effects
Ein Film erzählt eine Geschichte mit Worten, aber auch mit Bildern, Geräuschen, Licht, Farben und Musik. Diese audiovisuellen Effekte *(audio-visual effects)* schaffen eine ganz bestimmte Atmosphäre *(atmosphere)* und verstärken damit die Wirkung des Gesehenen. So wird z. B. eine Actionszene meist mit schneller, lauter Musik unterlegt, eine romantische Szene eher mit ruhiger, leiser Musik.

Camera
Die Kameraeinstellung *(shot)* beeinflusst, wie wir Szenen wahrnehmen, ob z. B. Personen oder Objekte als Nahaufnahme *(close-up)*, aus der mittleren Distanz *(medium shot)* oder als Totale *(long shot)* aufgenommen sind.

Long shot

Medium shot

Close-up

Study skills

S17 Vokabeln ordnen und strukturieren

Wörter sind die Bausteine der Sprache. Du musst sie natürlich lernen und jedes für sich verstehen. Zur Beherrschung einer Sprache gehört aber auch zu wissen, welche Kombinationen dieser Bausteine möglich sind. Schreibe deshalb Wörter möglichst immer in typischen Zusammenhängen auf:

- Lerne bei Verben passende Ergänzungen mit *(collocations)*, z. B. *a dry / wet / hot / cool climate* | *to read a book / a magazine / a comic* | *to write a letter / an e-mail / a blog* | *to go swimming / shopping / home / to the cinema.*
- Schreibe dir auf, welche grammatischen Formen auf bestimmte Wörter folgen, z. B. *I would like to swim / to read / to go shopping.* | *I like swimming / reading / going shopping.*
- Notiere dir Beispiele bei Wörtern mit Präpositionen, z. B. *The party is on Friday / at seven.* | *My house is in Dover Street.* | *We're on the road to London.* | *London is on the Thames.*

Deinen Wortschatz kannst du auch erweitern, indem du die Wörter eines Wortfeldes *(word field)* lernst, da thematisch zusammenhängende Vokabeln leichter zu merken sind. Oder du kannst dir Wörter aus derselben Wortfamilie *(word family)* notieren und die Liste mit Hilfe deines Wörterbuchs ergänzen:

Wortfeld:

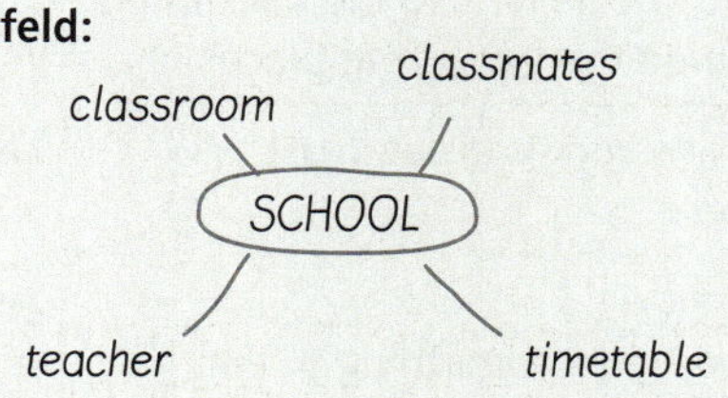

Wortfamilie:

shop – to shop – shopper – shopping
music – musician – musical
immigration – to immigrate – immigrant
colony – to colonize – colonist
information – to inform – informative

Achte beim Lesen unterschiedlicher Textsorten auf hilfreiche Formulierungen *(useful phrases)*. Diese kannst du später in eigenen Texten immer wieder verwenden.

S18 Im Internet recherchieren

Das Internet bietet eine Fülle von Informationen, die in der Regel frei zugänglich sind. Die folgenden Tipps können dir dabei helfen, genau die Informationen zu finden, die du für eine Präsentation oder für die Erstellung eines Textes brauchst:

1. Überlege dir gute Stichwörter, die du in eine Suchmaschine eingeben kannst. Wenn du z. B. eine Übersicht über das amerikanische Schulsystem suchst, kannst du als Stichwort *US school system* eingeben. Je mehr Stichwörter du eingibst, desto genauer sind deine Ergebnisse.
2. Wenn du eine Webseite mit interessanten Informationen gefunden hast, achte darauf, wer die Webseite erstellt hat. Sind die Informationen zuverlässig (Online-Lexikon, seriöse Zeitung, usw.) oder handelt es sich eher um persönliche Meinungen (Forum, Blog, usw.)?
3. Kopiere nicht einfach ganze Artikel aus dem Internet. Mache dir Notizen zu den wichtigsten Informationen und gebe sie anschließend in deinen eigenen Worten wieder.
4. Ordne dein Material und suche gezielt weiter, falls du zusätzliche Informationen brauchst.

Grammar

Liebe Schülerin, lieber Schüler,

in diesem Grammatik-Anhang findest du ausführliche Erklärungen zu allen grammatischen Themen, die in Green Line 4 behandelt werden. Die Grammatikkapitel (G) helfen dir, die Grammatik zu verstehen, einzelne Punkte nachzuholen oder bestimmte Regeln für Hausaufgaben und die Vorbereitung von Tests und Klassenarbeiten nachzuschlagen.

Regeln sind mit einem blauen Punkt (●) gekennzeichnet. Ein Ausrufezeichen (!) bedeutet, dass du hier besonders aufpassen musst. Die englische Zusammenfassung der wichtigsten Regeln findest du in der **English summary**. Mit **Test yourself** überprüfst du, ob du alles verstanden hast. Die Lösungen hierzu findest du ab Seite 259.

Grammatical terms

English term		Example	*Deutsche Bezeichnung*
defining and non-defining relative clauses	G8	Diego is the boy **who took us around New York**. Diego, who knows NY like the back of his hand, showed the girls great places.	*notwendige und nicht-notwendige Relativsätze*
gerund	G5	**Living** in New York is great. I just **love being** here.	*Gerundium*
gerund or infinitive	G7	Stop **shouting**! Let's stop **to have** something to eat.	*gerund oder Infinitiv mit* to
indirect speech	G1–G4		*Indirekte Rede*
statements	G1	They **said** (that) there **was** free wifi!	*Aussagen*
expressions of time and place	G2	He told me (that) they had been to Paris **the day before**.	*Zeit- und Ortsangaben*
questions	G3	Grandma **asked** me when my flight **was**.	*Fragen*
commands and requests	G4	She **told** him **to call** her back.	*Befehle, Aufforderungen und Bitten*
infinitive with and without *to*	G6	Would you like **to go** to the movie theater after school? – Sorry, I can't. My parents always make me come straight home.	*Infinitiv mit und ohne* to
past perfect progressive	G9	José was tired because he **had been driving** around New York all day.	*Verlaufsform des Plusquamperfekts*

Unit 1

G1 You told us there was free wifi!

→ Seiten 10–12

Aussagen in der indirekten Rede

Statements in indirect speech

Direct speech:	**Indirect speech:**
Steve's parents: We'**re** worried about Steve, Ms Woodruff. He **can't** live without **his** phone. He'**s** addicted to it.	Your parents told me (that) they **were** worried about you. They said (that) you **couldn't** live without **your** phone and they thought (that) you **were** addicted to it.

Wenn du wiedergeben möchtest, was ein anderer dir mitgeteilt hat, verwendest du gewöhnlich nicht die direkte, sondern die indirekte Rede.

- *Die indirekte Rede besteht aus einem* ***Einführungssatz*** *(Hauptsatz)* (They told me … / They said …)*, und einem* ***Nebensatz****, der mit oder ohne* that *eingeleitet werden kann* (… that they were worried about you).
- Anders *als im Deutschen steht zwischen dem Einführungssatz und dem Nebensatz* ***kein*** *Komma.*
- *Wenn du eine Aussage in der indirekten Rede wiedergibst, musst du Personalpronomen und Possessivbegleiter anpassen* (**we** → **they**; **his** → **your**).

- *Steht das Einleitungsverb im* **simple past***, ändert sich die Zeitform im Nebensatz folgendermaßen:*

Direkte Rede **Direct speech**	*Indirekte Rede* **Indirect speech**
simple present → Steve's parents: We **are** worried about Steve.	**simple past** Steve's parents told Ms Woodruff that they **were** worried about Steve.
present progressive → We think he **is spending** too much time on his phone.	**past progressive** They thought he **was spending** too much time on his phone.
present perfect → I **have tried** to take his phone away, …	**past perfect** His mum explained that she **had tried** to take his phone away, …
simple past → … but that **didn't work**.	**past perfect** … but that **hadn't worked**.
can → We **can't** help him.	**could** They said they **couldn't** help him.
will → Ms Woodruff: OK, I'**ll** talk to him.	**would** Ms Woodruff promised that she **would** talk to him.

English summary

You use indirect speech when you want to report what somebody has said.

When the reporting verb is in the simple past (He said that … / They told her that … / She thought …), the verbs used in the original speech usually move one tense further back **(present → past; past → past perfect simple; will → would; can → could)**.

Steve: *I'm on the ferry to Calais. I'll call you back later.*

Steve told Eddie that he was on the ferry to Calais and that he'd call him back later.

Test yourself **A message from Jack**

When Jack (the narrator of the story) arrived in France, he sent this message to his mother. What did she tell Jack's father when he came home?

Start like this: Jack sent me a message this afternoon. He said that …

I had a good trip and arrived safely. I haven't had time to look around yet, so I can't tell you much, but the hostel is clean and the people are very friendly. I'll call again later, but I don't know when because we're going into town for dinner and I'm not sure when we'll be back.

G2 Steve's blog

→ Seiten 10–12

Zeit- und Ortsangaben in der indirekten Rede
Expressions of time and place in indirect speech

Friday morning: Steve: We **had** horsemeat for dinner **yesterday**.	**Friday afternoon:** Steve told me that they **had had** horsemeat for dinner **yesterday**.	**A few days later:** Last Friday Steve told me that they **had had** horsemeat for dinner **the day before**.

Wenn die indirekte Rede sich auf eine Aussage aus der Vergangenheit bezieht, musst du auch die Zeit- und Ortsangaben im Satz verändern.

- *Die Zeitangaben ändern sich folgendermaßen:*

today → that day	this evening → that evening
tomorrow → the next day	three days ago → three days before
yesterday → the day before	last week / year → the week / year before
next year → the following year	now → then

- *Auch Ortsangaben ändern sich, wenn die Aussage später an einem anderen Ort wiedergegeben wird:* here → there.
- *Weitere Wörter, die meist in der indirekten Rede verändert werden, um sie dem Standpunkt des Berichtenden anzupassen, sind:* this → that; these → those; come → go *und* bring → take.

It's quite cold over **here**.
This is unusual for the time of year. So when you **come**, you shouldn't forget to **bring** some warm clothes,
Michel Lebrun

Listen boys and girls,
I've had an e-mail from Monsieur Lebrun.
He said that it was quite cold over **there**.
That was unusual for the time of year.
So when we **go**, we shouldn't forget to **take** some warm clothes.

English summary

In indirect speech, adverbs of time often change too, e.g. **today** → **that day**, **yesterday** → **the day before** etc.
But if you report something **on the same day** as it was said, the adverbs of time **don't** change.
Other words that you may need to change are:
this → that; here → there; come → go; bring → take.

Steve: *I'm going to France tomorrow.*

(the same day)
Steve said he was going to France tomorrow.

(a week later):
Steve said he was going to France the next day.

Test yourself *While Steve was in France last week, he sent this text message to his friend Eddie. A week later Eddie met Amarjit. What did he tell him?*

Start like this: Steve sent me a message from France last week. He said that …

> The athletics event started yesterday and our team is doing well. But it's very cold here. If I ever come back to this place, I'll bring warmer clothes. I wish I had listened to Ms W.

G3 He asked me what the purpose of my visit was

→ Seiten 13–15

Fragen in der indirekten Rede
Questions in indirect speech

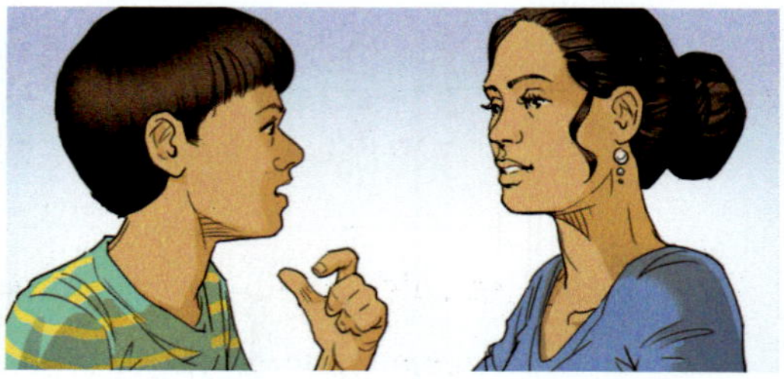

Direct question:	**Indirect speech:**
Steve's grandma: When **is** your flight, Rafiq?	Grandma **asked** me when my flight **was**.
How **are** you **getting** to the airport?	She **asked** me how I **was getting** to the airport.
Have you **weighed** your suitcase?	She **asked** me **if** I **had weighed** my suitcase.
Are you nervous about the trip?	She **asked** me **if** I **was** nervous about the trip.
Did you **find** a nice present for Aunt Sadia?	She **wanted to know if** I **had found** a nice present for Aunt Sadia.
When **will** you be back?	She **wanted to know** when I **would** be back.

Fragen werden in der indirekten Rede als Aussagesätze wiedergegeben.

- *Das Verb im **Einführungssatz** (Hauptsatz) muss deutlich machen, dass es sich um eine indirekte Frage handelt* (Grandma **asked** me … / She **wanted to know** …).
- *Das Fragewort* (what, when, where, why …) *wird in der indirekten Frage als Bindewort zwischen Haupt- und Nebensatz übernommen. Steht **kein** Fragewort, leitest du den Nebensatz mit* **if** *ein.*
- *Die Wortstellung im Nebensatz ist die gleiche wie in einem Aussagesatz: Das **Subjekt** steht immer **vor** dem **Verb**. Umschreibungen mit* do / does / did *fallen weg.*
- *Wie bei indirekten Aussagesätzen (→ G1) werden bei indirekten Fragen die Zeitformen meist um eine Zeitstufe zurückverschoben, wenn das Einleitungsverb im* simple past *steht.*

English summary

1. If you report questions that begin with a question word (what, when, how …), you use **asked / wanted to know + question word**.
2. If there is no question word, you use **if**.
3. The word order in indirect questions is the same as in statements: Subject – Verb.
4. The verb in the direct question moves one tense further back.

Steve's grandma: *How long is the flight to Dhaka?*
*Grandma **wanted to know how long** the flight to Dhaka **was**.*

Steve's grandma: *Will you be able to sleep on the plane?*
***She asked Rafiq if** he **would** be able to sleep on the plane.*

Test yourself *When Rafiq arrives at Dhaka airport, the man at passport control asks him a lot of questions. What does Rafiq tell his uncle and aunt later?*

Start like this: The man at passport control asked me …

1. Why are you travelling alone?
2. Where are you from?
3. How long do you plan to stay?
4. Do you have family in Bangladesh?
5. Can you speak Bengali?
6. Is anybody meeting you at the airport?

G4 He told me to go into a side room

→ Seiten 13–15

Befehle, Aufforderungen und Bitten in der indirekten Rede
Commands and requests in indirect speech

Direct command / request:	Indirect command / request:
Steve's grandma: Don't spend all your money in the first week. Please send me some photos from Bangladesh.	She **told** him (Rafiq) **not to spend** all his money in the first week. Grandma **asked** him (Rafiq) **to send** her some photos from Bangladesh.

Befehle, Aufforderungen und Bitten werden in der indirekten Rede als Infinitivkonstruktion mit **to** *oder* **not to** *wiedergegeben.*

- *In der indirekten Rede verwendest du meist* **tell somebody to do something** *für Befehle und Aufforderungen und* **ask somebody to do something** *für Bitten.*
- *Enthält der Befehlssatz ein Verbot (also eine Verneinung), wird* **don't** *zu* **not to** (Don't shout → … not to shout).
- *Dem Einleitungsverb* (told, asked) ***folgt*** *kein Nebensatz, sondern ein* ***Personenobjekt*** **+ to-*Infinitiv*** (She asked **Rafiq to send** …).
- *Wird* ***kein*** *Eigenname genannt, verwendest du ein* ***Pronomen*** *in der* ***Objektform*** (me, you, him, her, us, them) (She asked **him** …).

❗ *Beachte, dass es hier keine Zeitverschiebung gibt, da der Befehl selbst durch einen Infinitiv wiedergegeben wird.*
Für weitere Verben im Satz gelten jedoch die Regeln für indirekte Aussagesätze (→ G1).
Grandma: **Don't spend** all your money on things you **don't** need.
Grandma told Rafiq **not to spend** all his money on things he **didn't** need.

English summary

In indirect speech, you use **to tell somebody (not) to do something** for indirect commands and **to ask somebody (not) to do something** for indirect requests.

Flight attendant: *Fasten your seatbelt, please, and don't use your phone during take-off and landing.*
The flight attendant ***asked*** *Rafiq* ***to fasten*** *his seatbelt and* ***told*** *him* ***not to use*** *his phone during take-off and landing.*

Test yourself *What did Rafiq's mum say to him at the airport? Put her words into indirect speech.*

Start like this: Rafiq's mum asked …

1. Please say hello to everyone from us.
2. Be careful with your passport. Don't lose it.
3. Please call me as soon as you get to Dhaka.
4. Have fun while you're there and take lots of photos.

Unit 2

G5 Living here isn't bad

→ Seiten 44–46

Das Gerundium
The gerund (verb + -ing)

Living in rural Pennsylvania isn't bad. But I really **miss seeing** my friends at home and I'm **scared of changing** too much. What's Pittsburgh like? I'm **thinking of coming** to visit soon. How about **meeting up** there?

Pittsburgh is amazing. I just **love being** here. It's really cool. But I still can't **get used to living** on the 22nd floor! I'm afraid I'm very busy here, so **meeting up** isn't easy right now.

Das **gerund** (verb + -ing) *ist eine Verbform, die es im Deutschen nicht gibt.*
Im Satz kann es verschiedene Funktionen haben. Es wird folgendermaßen verwendet:
1. *als Subjekt* (**Living** here isn't …),
2. *als Objekt nach bestimmten Verben* (I miss **seeing** …),
3. *nach Präpositionen* (I'm scared of **changing** … / I'm thinking of **coming** … / How about **meeting** …).

- *Das* **gerund** *sieht aus wie das* present participle (playing, taking, running) *und wird genauso gebildet. Es gelten auch die gleichen Schreibregeln:*
  try + -ing → trying   liv**e** + -ing → liv**ing**   ge**t** + -ing → ge**tt**ing
- *Im Deutschen wird das* **gerund** *mit dem* ***Infinitiv*** *wiedergegeben:*
  I miss **seeing** my friends.   *Ich vermisse es, meine Freunde* ***zu sehen****.*
  Living here isn't bad.   *Es ist nicht schlecht hier* ***zu leben****.*

a) ***Das*** **gerund** ***als Subjekt des Satzes***

Meeting up isn't easy right now.	*Sich zu treffen ist im Moment nicht einfach.*
Finding new friends can be difficult.	*Neue Freunde zu finden kann schwierig sein.*
Living in America is awesome.	*In Amerika zu leben ist toll.*

- *Als Subjekt des Satzes steht das* **gerund** *am Satzanfang und wird wie ein Nomen gebraucht.*
- *Es kann allein stehen* (**Meeting up**), *zusammen mit einem Nomen verwendet werden* (**Finding new friends**) *und auch eine adverbiale Bestimmung bei sich haben* (**Living in America**).

b) *Das* gerund *als Objekt des Satzes nach bestimmten Verben*

Matt **enjoys**	being in Pittsburgh.	*Matt ist gerne in Pittsburgh.*
Sophie **didn't mind**	moving to America.	*Sophie hatte nichts dagegen, nach Amerika umzuziehen.*
Lena **keeps**	thinking about her friends in Germany.	*Lena denkt immer wieder an ihre Freunde in Deutschland.*
She **misses**	hanging out with them.	*Sie vermisst es, Zeit mit ihnen zu verbringen.*

- *Als Objekt des Satzes steht* ***nach bestimmten Verben*** *das* gerund *anstelle eines Infinitivs mit* to, *z.B.* Matt **enjoys** being in Pittsburgh *(nicht:* Matt enjoys to be …*).*
- *Häufig sind es Verben, die allgemeine Vorlieben oder Abneigungen ausdrücken, wie* enjoy, like, dislike, love, hate.
- *Weitere Verben, nach denen ein* ***Verb*** *als* gerund *stehen* ***muss****, sind:* keep, miss, imagine *und* suggest.

c) *Das* gerund *als Objekt nach Präpositionen*

1. ***Adjektiv + Präposition +*** gerund

Lena is **scared of**	changing too much.	*Lena hat Angst davor, sich zu sehr zu verändern.*
Sophie is **tired of**	living in the middle of nowhere.	*Sophie hat es satt, am Ende der Welt zu wohnen.*
Matt isn't **worried about**	being bored in Pittsburgh.	*Matt macht sich keine Sorgen, dass er sich in Pittsburgh langweilen könnte.*

- *Weitere Verbindungen von Adjektiv + Präposition, nach denen ein* gerund *stehen* ***muss****, sind:* good at, interested in, crazy about.

2. ***Verb + Präposition +*** gerund

Lena is **looking forward to**	seeing Matt again.	*Lena freut sich darauf, Matt wiederzusehen.*
But Matt doesn't **feel like**	meeting up with her.	*Aber Matt hat keine Lust, sich mit ihr zu treffen.*
He is **thinking of**	inviting Sophie to a baseball game.	*Er denkt darüber nach, Sophie zu einem Baseballspiel einzuladen.*

- *Weitere Verbindungen von Verb + Präposition, nach denen ein* gerund *steht, sind:* talk about, get used to, dream of, forgive somebody for, worry about.

! *Bei* look forward **to** *(sich freuen* ***auf****) und* get used **to** *(sich gewöhnen* ***an****) ist das* **to** *eine Präposition, die zum vorangestellten Verb gehört und auf die das* gerund *folgt:*
Sophie can't get used **to** sharing a room with her messy cousin.
She's looking forward **to** moving to Pittsburgh soon.

English summary

The gerund has the same form as the present participle: going, living etc. It can be used …

1. as the subject of the sentence.	**Living** in rural Pennsylvania is OK.
2. as the object of the sentence after certain verbs, e.g. *enjoy, like, hate, imagine, mind*.	Lena doesn't mind **being** there.
3. after prepositions a) adjective + preposition + gerund	She isn't worried about **having to** travel for two hours to get there.
b) verb + preposition + gerund	She's looking forward to **going** to the mall.

Test yourself *Use a gerund to rewrite the sentences.*

Example: What would you like to do today? (be interested in)
→ What would you be interested in doing today?

1. Why don't we visit a museum? (How about)
2. I don't really want to go to a museum today. (feel like)
3. OK, then, what would you like to do? (suggest)
4. Mom tells me every day about the spectacular views from Mt. Washington. (keep)
5. My mom goes there a lot too. (love)
6. She talks about the place all the time. (never stop)

G6 That's the worst thing to do!

→ Seiten 48–50

Der Infinitiv mit und ohne to
The infinitive with and without *to*

Scott and Eva don't **want me to talk** to Henry and Tyler. They say that's the **worst thing to do**. I don't **want to listen** to them. But to be honest I'm **not sure what to do**.

I'm glad I don't have your problems, Matt, but mine aren't much better, you know. I **can** never **meet** friends after school because my parents always **make me come** straight home. They won't **let me do** anything.

*Der **Infinitiv** ist die Grundform des Verbs. Im Englischen findet sich der Infinitiv in zwei Formen:* ***mit* to** *(to be, to go, to play) und* ***ohne* to** *(be, go, play).*
*Der **Infinitiv mit** **to** steht nach zahlreichen Verben, Adjektiven und Nomen.*
*Der **Infinitiv ohne** **to** wird vor allem nach Hilfsverben* (can, must, should), *aber auch nach anderen Verben wie* let *oder* make *+ Objekt gebraucht.*

a) *Der Infinitiv mit to nach bestimmten Verben*

Would you **like**	**to watch** the movie on TV this evening?
No, I'**d prefer**	**to go** to the movie theater.
OK. I'll **try**	**to get** some tickets.

- *Verben auf die der **Infinitiv mit to** folgt, können in folgende Gruppen unterteilt werden:*
  1. ***Wünsche und Absichten**, z.B.* want, would like, hope, decide, expect, offer, plan, promise
  2. ***Vorlieben**, die sich auf konkrete Situationen beziehen, z.B.* choose, prefer
  3. ***Versuche** oder **Bemühungen**, z.B.* try, learn, manage.

b) *Der Infinitiv mit to nach Verb + Fragewort oder nach* whether

Direkte Frage	*Indirekte Frage*	*mit* can, should, must, have to *mit Infinitiv* + to
Where do I have to go?	Matt doesn't **know**	where he has to go. **where to go**.
Who can I ask?	He **isn't sure**	who he can ask. **who to ask**.
Should I sit with Henry and Tyler?	He **wonders** sich fragen	**if** he should sit with Henry and Tyler. **whether to sit** with Henry and Tyler.

- *Nach* **know, be sure, decide, wonder** + ***Fragewort*** (what, when, where, which, whether) *steht der **Infinitiv mit to** oft anstelle einer indirekten Frage (mit* can, should, must, have to*).*

! *Bei Entscheidungsfragen wird bei der Infinitivkonstruktion* if *(ob) durch* **whether** *ersetzt.*

c) *Der Infinitiv mit to* nach Superlativen

Hauptsatz + Relativsatz	*Hauptsatz + Infinitiv mit* to
You are the first person who has said that.	You are **the first** (person) **to say** that.
I was the only one who ordered meat.	I was **the only one to order** meat.
That's the worst thing that you can do.	That's **the worst thing to do**.

- *Nach* **the first, the last, the only one** *und nach* ***Superlativen*** (the worst thing, the most important thing) *ersetzt der **Infinitiv mit to** einen Relativsatz.*

d) Der *Infinitiv mit to* nach Verb + Objekt

Verb	*Objekt*	*Infinitiv mit* to
Henry and Tyler **want**	**people**	**to think** about sweatshops and child labor.
They **would like**	**them**	**to join** their protest at the mall.
Scott and Eva **expect**	**Matt**	**to ignore** them.

- *Auf die folgenden Verben kann die Verbindung von **Objekt** + **Infinitiv mit to** folgen:* ask *(bitten)*, expect, prefer, tell, warn, want *und* would like.

! *Nach* want *(wollen, dass) und* would like *(möchten, dass) darfst du keinen Nebensatz mit* that *anschließen. Vergleiche:*

Matt: Scott and Eva want **me to drop** Henry and Tyler.
Scott und Eva wollen, **dass ich** Henry und Tyler fallen lasse.

e) *Der Infinitiv ohne* to *nach* let *und* make *+ Objekt*

Verb	*Objekt*	*Infinitiv ohne* to
Sophie's parents won't **let**	**her**	**meet** her friends after school.
They **make**	**her**	**come** straight home.
Do your parents **let**	**you**	**do** what you want?
Or do they **make**	**you**	**come** home early too?

- *Nach* make *+ Objekt (veranlassen, zwingen) und* let *+ Objekt (zulassen, erlauben) wird der* ***Infinitiv ohne* to** *gebraucht.* can, must, should

English summary

The infinitive with *to* is used …

1. after certain verbs, e.g. *want, expect, decide, would like / would prefer* — Sophie's parents always **want to know** where she is. They**'d like to take** control of her life.
2. after certain verbs + questions words — Sophie **isn't sure what to do**.
3. after superlatives *(the first / last / only one / the best thing)* — She's **the only one to have** parents who are so strict.
4. after *want, would like, expect, ask, tell* + object — She **would like them to relax** more.

The infinitive without *to* is used …

1. after modal verbs *(can, should, must, have to)* — They **should trust** her.
2. after *let / make* + object — They should **let her go out** with her friends.

Test yourself *Complete the second sentence so that the meaning is similar to the first. Use infinitive constructions.*

1. I'll be home before 6 p.m., I promise. — I promise …
2. I didn't know what I could say. — I didn't know what …
3. My parents say that I shouldn't watch too much TV. — My parents don't want …
4. I was surprised when he invited me to his party. — I didn't expect …
5. They always say that she can do what she wants. — They always let …
6. Our football coach says we have to train every day. — Our football coach makes …
7. The best thing that we can do is say nothing at all. — The best thing …

G7 Gerund or infinitive: It depends on the meaning

→ Seite 51

Das gerund *oder der Infinitiv mit* to: *Bedeutungsunterschiede*

*Nach einigen wenigen Verben (*forget, go on, mean, remember, stop, try*) wird je nach Bedeutung entweder ein* **gerund** *oder ein* ***Infinitiv mit* to** *verwendet.*

a) *Nach* go on, mean, stop *und* try *hängt die* **Bedeutung des Verbs** *davon ab, ob ihm ein* **gerund** *oder ein* ***Infinitiv mit* to** *folgt.*

to go on doing sth *etwas fortsetzen / weitermachen*	to go on to do sth *etwas anschließend machen*
They **went on** talking. Sie redeten weiter.	Then they **went on** to talk about child labor. Anschließend sprachen sie über Kinderarbeit.

to mean doing sth *bedeuten*	to mean to do sth *wollen, beabsichtigen*
That **means** walking. Das bedeutet, dass wir laufen müssen.	I **meant** to send you a text, but I forgot. Ich wollte dir eine SMS schicken, aber …

to stop doing sth *aufhören, etwas zu tun*	to stop to do something *anhalten, um etwas Neues zu tun*
Stop shouting! Hör auf, zu schreien!	Let's **stop** to have a drink. Lasst uns anhalten, um etwas zu trinken.

to try doing sth *eine Methode ausprobieren*	to try to do sth *eine konkrete Handlung ausprobieren*
If you can't sleep, **try** counting sheep. … probier's mal mit Schäfchen zählen.	I **tried** to sleep in the car, but it wasn't possible. Ich habe versucht, im Auto zu schlafen, aber …

b) *Nach* remember *und* forget *steht das* **gerund** *für eine Handlung, die* ***bereits stattgefunden*** *hat und an die man sich erinnert. Der* ***Infinitiv mit* to** *weist hingegen auf eine Handlung hin, die* ***beabsichtigt ist*** *und* ***noch bevorsteht****.*

to remember doing sth *sich erinnern an*	to remember to do sth *daran denken, etwas zu tun*
Sophie can't **remember visiting** London. She was too young. *Sophie kann sich nicht daran erinnern, dass sie London besucht hat. …*	Please **remember to learn** the irregular verbs for the test. *Denkt bitte daran, die unregelmäßigen Verben für den Test zu lernen.*

to forget doing sth *vergessen, wie man etwas getan hat*	to forget to do sth *vergessen, etwas zu tun*
Lena will never **forget having to say goodbye** to her friends in Hamburg. *Lena wird nie vergessen, wie sie sich von ihren Freunden … verabschieden musste.*	Please don't **forget to tidy** your room before your friends arrive. *Vergiss nicht, dein Zimmer aufzuräumen, bevor deine Freunde kommen.*

! *Nach* to begin, to start *und* to like *(im Sinne von „genießen") kann sowohl das* **gerund** *als auch der* ***Infinitiv mit* to** *stehen. Die Bedeutung ist in beiden Fällen gleich!*

It started to rain. — It started raining.
I like to go to the movie theater. — I like going to the movie theater.

English summary

Some English verbs such as *forget, go on, mean, remember, stop* and *try* can be followed by a gerund or by an infinitive with *to*, but with a change in meaning.

We **stopped to buy** some eggs from the farm.
We've **stopped buying** them from the supermarket.

Test yourself *After Lena received Matt's e-mail, this is what she wrote in her diary. Put the verb into the right form: gerund or infinitive with* to*.*

Dear Diary,
Bad news! I got a mail from Matt today and it seems he can't stop (think) about Sophie. I'm sure Matt didn't mean (hurt) me, but … When I told Madison, she said I should try (forget) him. But how? M. thinks I should try (do) yoga! She says she can remember (feel) upset about something once, and it really helped her. But I'm not sure. I'm not really sure about anything at the moment: Should I go on (write) him? Should I tell him how I feel? I don't know. The only thing I know right now is that it's really late and I mustn't forget (set) my alarm clock! Madison's mom is driving us to the mall outside Pittsburgh tomorrow. We want (get) there early and it's two hours in the car, so that means (leave) at 8 a.m.! Oh well, at least we can stop (have) breakfast somewhere on the way.

Unit 3

G8 The boy who ... / Diego, who ...

→ Seiten 72–74

Notwendige und nicht-notwendige Relativsätze
Defining and non-defining relative clauses

Diego is the boy **who took us around New York**. He showed us sights in New York **(which) you would never find in a guidebook**.	Diego, **who knows New York like the back of his hand**, showed the two girls some great places. All the sights were amazing, but Rockefeller Center, **which they visited last**, was just awesome.

Relativsätze sind Nebensätze, die ihr ***Bezugswort*** *im Hauptsatz a) näher bestimmen (***the boy*** who took us around New York) oder b) zusätzlich beschreiben (***Diego***, who knows New York like the back of his hand, ...).*
Im Englischen nennt man diese zwei Arten von Relativsätzen ***defining*** *und* ***non-defining relative clauses***.

a) Defining relative clauses

Two girls who / that are spending the day in New York visit a diner.
A boy (who / that) they meet there takes them on a tour of the city.
Some of the **sights (which / that) he shows them** are amazing.

- **Defining relative clauses** *bestimmen ihr vorangestelltes* ***Bezugswort*** *im Hauptsatz näher. Sie legen fest, wer oder was gemeint ist. Ohne den Relativsatz wäre in den obigen Beispielen nicht klar, von welchen beiden Mädchen, von welchem Jungen oder von welchen Sehenswürdigkeiten genau die Rede ist.*
- *Relativsätze, die ihr Bezugswort näher bestimmen, stehen* ***ohne Komma****. Beim Sprechen macht man keine Pause.*

- **Defining relative clauses** *werden durch Relativpronomen wie* **who** *oder* **that** *(bei Personen) und* **which** *oder* **that** *(bei Sachen) eingeleitet, wenn sie das Subjekt im Relativsatz sind. Sind die Relativpronomen* who, which, that *das Objekt im Relativsatz, können sie weggelassen werden* (a boy (**who / that**) they meet …; some of the sights (**that**) he shows …). *Diese Relativsätze nennt man* **contact clauses**.

b) Non-defining relative clauses

Rylee and Lea, **who are spending the day in New York**, visit a diner.
Diego, **who they meet there**, takes them on a tour of the city.
At **Rockefeller Center**, **which they visit last**, they have a scary experience.

- *Bei* **non-defining relative clauses** *ist das vorangestellte* ***Bezugswort bereits definiert****. Auch ohne den Relativsatz bleibt klar, wer oder was gemeint ist:* Rylee and Lea, Diego *und das* Rockefeller Center. *Die Relativsätze bestimmen daher ihr Bezugswort* ***nicht*** *näher. Sie enthalten lediglich eine zusätzliche oder ergänzende Information, die ebenso gut in Klammern stehen oder entfallen könnte, ohne dass die Aussage im Hauptsatz verändert wird.*
- *Relativsätze, die Zusatzinformationen enthalten, werden vom Hauptsatz immer* ***durch Kommas abgetrennt****. Beim Sprechen wird eine Pause gemacht.*
- *Im Gegensatz zu* defining relative clauses *beginnen* **non-defining relative clauses** ***immer mit einem Relativpronomen****: Für Personen verwendet man* **who**. *Für Dinge verwendet man* **which**. *Das Relativpronomen* **that** *ist in einem* **non-defining relative clause** ***nicht möglich***.

English summary

There are two types of relative clauses: **defining** and **non-defining**.

1.	Defining relative clauses tell you which person or thing the speaker is talking about. **No comma** is used between the noun and the relative clause.	Lea is a German girl **who / that** comes from Berlin.
2.	Non-defining relative clauses are used after nouns that are definite already. They give extra information about a person or thing. You always need a **comma** to separate the main clause from the relative clause.	Lea, **who** is German, is Rylee's cousin from Berlin.
3.	Non-defining relative clauses always begin with a relative pronoun. You use ***who*** for people and ***which*** for things. You **never** use ***that***.	They walked to the Alvin Ailey Dance Studio, **which** is close to Central Park.

Test yourself *Copy these sentences into your exercise book. Underline the noun(s) to which the relative clauses refer* (das Bezugswort) *and add commas where needed.*

1. Last year we visited New York which is the largest city in the USA.
2. We stayed with some friends who live there.
3. They showed us some amazing sights which we would never have found on our own.
4. But they also took us to famous sights like Rockefeller Center which was awesome too.
5. In Times Square we saw the Naked Cowboy who is really only *almost* naked.
6. He is a street performer who has become one of New York's biggest tourist attractions.

G9 How long had they been doing that?

→ Seiten 76–78

Die Verlaufsform des Plusquamperfekts
The past perfect progressive

When Emilio arrived home, he felt tired. He **had been working** hard all day.

Das **past perfect** *wird verwendet, um Vorzeitigkeit vor einem bestimmten Zeitpunkt in der Vergangenheit auszudrücken.*
Mit dem **past perfect simple** (I had done) *betonst du* ***das Ergebnis*** *einer abgeschlossenen Handlung, z. B.* Emilio felt tired. He **had had** a hard day.
Mit dem **past perfect progressive** (I had been doing) *betonst du den* ***Verlauf*** *oder die* ***Dauer*** *dieser Handlung, z. B.* Emilio felt tired. He **had been working** hard all day.

- *Das* past perfect progressive *bildest du aus* **had been** + **present participle** (verb + -ing)

Aussage:	He had been listening.
Verneinung:	He hadn't been listening.
Ergänzungsfrage:	How long had he been listening?
Entscheidungsfrage mit Kurzantwort:	Had he been listening? Yes, he had. / No, he hadn't.

- *Das* past perfect progressive *benutzt du für Handlungen, die vor einem Zeitpunkt in der Vergangenheit angefangen haben und bis zu diesem Zeitpunkt andauerten. Hierbei wird die Dauer der Handlung häufig durch eine Zeitangabe betont, z. B.* for ten years, since 2015, all day / week / year, all the time *usw.*

Past perfect progressive + *Zeitangabe*	*Vergangenheit*
Emilio had been waiting **for 20 minutes** *… wartete schon seit …*	before his first passenger arrived.
His second passenger hadn't been sitting in his taxi **for long** *… hatte noch nicht lange im Taxi gesessen …*	when he started to ask lots of questions.

- *Der Gebrauch des* past perfect progressive *ist mit der Verwendung des* **present perfect progressive** *vergleichbar. Die beschriebenen Handlungen dauern jedoch nicht bis in die Gegenwart an, sondern nur bis zu einem Zeitpunkt in der Vergangenheit.*

Present (now) ←←←←	Present perfect progressive
Emilio **is** tired	because he **has been driving** around New York all day.
Past (yesterday) ←←←	**Past perfect progressive**
Emilio **was** tired	because he **had been driving** around New York all day.

! *Beachte, dass du das* past perfect progressive *wie alle Verlaufsformen* ***nur bei Tätigkeitsverben*** *verwenden kannst (z. B.* wait, work, live*). Bei Verben, die keine Tätigkeit, sondern einen Zustand bezeichnen (z. B.* be, know, belong*) benutzt du das* **past perfect simple***, z. B.* Emilio had only been at the taxi stand for a few minutes when his next passenger got in.

English summary

You use the past perfect progressive to stress how long an activity continued before another event in the past happened. It is often used with an expression of time, e.g. *since, for, all day* etc.

Last week Diego found a new assistant for his diner. He **had been looking for** help since the summer.

Test yourself *Use the past perfect simple or the past perfect progressive to complete the text.*

had been walking

After Julia and Andrea from Germany (walk) around Manhattan all morning, they were very hungry. So they decided to go to Diego's Diner, which they (read) about in the guidebook they (buy) the day before. When they got there at 12:30, the diner was already very busy. Some of the people (wait) to get their lunch for quite some time. The girls (learn) English since the age of ten, so they had no language problems. But when they tried to order, nobody seemed to notice them. Finally, after they (try) to get a waiter's attention for about 15 minutes, a friendly Hispanic American came to their table and took their order.

Vocabulary

Im ***Vocabulary*** findest du alle wichtigen englischen Wörter und Redewendungen aus *Green Line* 4. Sie stehen in der Reihenfolge, in der sie im Buch vorkommen. Diese Wörter solltest du lernen und anwenden können. Andere nützliche Wörter und Begriffe (z. B. Arbeitsanweisungen), die du **nicht** auswendig lernen musst, findest du ab S. 256.
Auf das *Vocabulary* folgt das ***Dictionary (English – German, German – English)***. Falls du ein Wort vergessen hast, kannst du in diesen alphabetischen Wortlisten nachsehen.

Englische Begriffe wie *e-mail*, *cool* oder *cornflakes*, die du auch im Deutschen verwendest, stehen nicht im *Vocabulary*. Du kannst ihre Aussprache und Übersetzung aber im *Dictionary* nachschlagen. Das gleiche gilt für Wörter, die auf Englisch und Deutsch fast gleich geschrieben und ausgesprochen werden, wie z. B. *park* oder *partner*.

In den drei Teilen von ***Text smart*** musst du nicht alle neuen Vokabeln auswendig lernen. Die Wörter und Ausdrücke, die im *Vocabulary* aufgelistet sind, sind die wichtigsten und sie solltest du lernen und anwenden können. Alle anderen neuen Wörter aus *Text smart* kannst du ebenfalls hinten im *Dictionary* ab S. 191 nachschlagen.

Abkürzungen und Zeichen

pl	Mehrzahl (Plural)	↔	ist das Gegenteil von
sg	Einzahl (Singular)	→	ist verwandt mit
AE	amerikanisch-englisches Wort	=	entspricht
coll/ugs	umgangssprachlich	≠	entspricht nicht
5	In dieser Übung kommen die Wörter vor.	*Fr./Lat.*	verwandte Wörter in anderen Fremdsprachen
!	Achtung!		

Englische Laute

Konsonanten

[b]	**b**ed	[p]	**p**icture
[d]	**d**ay	[r]	**r**ed
[ð]	**th**e	[s]	**s**ix
[f]	**f**amily	[ʃ]	**sh**e
[g]	**g**o	[t]	**t**en
[ŋ]	morni**ng**	[tʃ]	**ch**air
[h]	**h**ouse	[v]	**v**ideo
[j]	**y**ou	[w]	**w**e, **o**ne
[k]	**c**an, mil**k**	[z]	eas**y**
[l]	**l**etter	[ʒ]	revi**s**ion
[m]	**m**an	[dʒ]	pa**g**e
[n]	**n**o	[θ]	**th**ank you

Vokale

[ɑː]	c**a**r	[i]	happ**y**
[æ]	**a**pple	[iː]	t**ea**cher
[e]	p**e**n	[ɒ]	d**o**g
[ə]	**a**gain	[ɔː]	b**a**ll
[ɜː]	g**ir**l	[ʊ]	b**oo**k
[ʌ]	b**u**t	[u]	Jan**u**ary
[ɪ]	**i**t	[uː]	t**oo**, tw**o**

Doppellaute

[aɪ]	**I**, m**y**
[aʊ]	n**ow**, m**ou**se
[eɪ]	n**a**me, th**ey**
[eə]	th**ere**, p**air**
[ɪə]	h**ere**, id**ea**
[əʊ]	hell**o**
[ɔɪ]	b**oy**
[ʊə]	s**ure**

[ː] der vorangehende Laut ist lang, z. B. *you* [juː]
[‿] der Bindebogen zeigt, dass zwei Wörter in der Aussprache verbunden werden
[ˈ] die folgende Silbe trägt den Hauptakzent
[ˌ] die folgende Silbe trägt den Nebenakzent

Der Aussprachestandard in *Green Line* ist *British English*. Auch Wörter, die den Zusatz *AE* haben, werden entsprechend lautschriftlich dargestellt.

Unit 1 On the move

Introduction

	on the move [ˌɒn‿ðə 'mu:v]	unterwegs	He has to travel a lot in his job. He is always *on the move*.
	travelling *(no pl)* ['trævlɪŋ]	(das) Reisen	*travelling* → to travel
1	**foreign** ['fɒrɪn]	ausländisch; fremd	A lot of British schools teach French as the first *foreign* language.
2	**seasick** ['si:sɪk]	seekrank	People sometimes feel *seasick* when they're travelling on boats or ships in bad weather.
	luggage *(no pl)* ['lʌgɪdʒ]	Gepäck	
	to **be afraid (of)** [bi‿ə'freɪd‿əv]	(sich) fürchten; Angst haben (vor)	He's *afraid of* dogs.
	plane [pleɪn]	Flugzeug	We're on our way to the airport. Our *plane* leaves in two hours.
3	**departure lounge** [dɪ'pɑ:tʃə ˌlaʊndʒ]	Abflughalle	
	passport ['pɑ:spɔ:t]	Pass; Reisepass	If you want to travel from Germany to New York, you'll need a *passport*.
	boarding card ['bɔ:dɪŋ ˌkɑ:d]	Bordkarte	A *boarding card* is the ticket you need before you get onto the plane.
	desk [desk]	Schalter	
	visa ['vi:zə], **visas** ['vi:zəz] *(pl)*	Visum, Visa *(Pl.)*; Einreisebewilligung	You can't enter the USA without a *visa*.
	passenger ['pæsndʒə]	Passagier/-in; Fahrgast	a person who is travelling by plane, train, bus, etc.
	flight attendant ['flaɪt‿əˌtendnt]	Flugbegleiter/-in	The *flight attendant* looks after the passengers on a plane.
	customs *(sg)* ['kʌstəmz]	Zoll	! *Customs* steht immer ohne Artikel und hat keine Pluralform: *Customs* **is** on your right.
	suitcase ['su:tkeɪs]	Koffer	Have you packed your *suitcase* yet? 
	ferry ['feri]	Fähre	= a boat that takes passengers and cars across a river or a narrow part of sea
	control [kən'trəʊl]	Kontrolle	If you want to travel by plane, you have to go through passport *control*.
	arrivals hall [ə'raɪvlz ˌhɔ:l]	Ankunftshalle	*arrivals hall* → arrival → to arrive
	currency ['kʌrnsi]	Währung	The *currency* in the UK is the British Pound.
	duty-free [ˌdju:ti'fri:]	zollfrei	Every airport has *duty-free* shops.

Station 1: You told us there was free wifi!

athletics *(no pl)* [æθ'letɪks]	Leichtathletik	! *Athletics* **is** an important part of PE in British schools.
vending machine ['vendɪŋ məˌʃi:n]	Automat	Let's get some drinks from the *vending machine*.
to **spill** [spɪl], **spilt** [spɪlt], **spilt** [spɪlt]	verschütten; auslaufen	Don't put too much water in the glass or you'll *spill* it.
to **hang on** [ˌhæŋ‿'ɒn]	(einen Augenblick) warten	*Hang on*. I'll ask them.
coast [kəʊst]	Küste	= where the land meets the sea *coast* → coastal path
shutter ['ʃʌtə]	Fensterladen	If it's hot outside, you should keep the *shutters* closed.
abroad [ə'brɔ:d]	im Ausland; ins Ausland	! They live *abroad*. (= im Ausland) They went *abroad*. (= ins Ausland)
groan [grəʊn]	Stöhnen	= a 'slow' sound that shows you are hurt, unhappy or disappointed
hostel ['hɒstl]	Herberge	A *hostel* is cheaper than a hotel.
addict ['ædɪkt]	Süchtige/-r; Abhängige/-r	Steve is a phone *addict*.
to **mutter** ['mʌtə]	murmeln	to speak – to talk – to shout – *to mutter*
3 **latest** ['leɪtɪst]	neueste/-r/-s	What's the *latest* news from your brother in Australia?
closed [kləʊzd]	geschlossen; zu	*closed* ↔ open *closed* → to close
big deal [bɪg 'di:l]	große Sache	That's no *big deal*. = It's not a problem.
apart from [ə'pɑ:t frəm]	abgesehen von; außer	I'm going to the supermarket later. What else do we need *apart from* bread, milk and sugar?
soup [su:p]	Suppe	A bowl of hot *soup* does you good on a cold day. 
herb [hɜ:b]	Kraut	*Herbs* are plants that people add to food to make it taste good.
garlic ['gɑ:lɪk]	Knoblauch	The soup had too much *garlic* in it.
style [staɪl]	Stil	She always wears her own *style* of clothes.
to **be called** [bi 'kɔ:ld]	heißen; genannt werden	What's your sister *called*?
sleep [sli:p]	Schlaf	*sleep* → to sleep

Station 2: Idiot nephew?

nephew ['nefju:]	Neffe	= the son of your sister or your brother
although [ɔ:l'ðəʊ]	obwohl	Jenny's father speaks very good English *although* he's German.
purpose ['pɜ:pəs]	Ziel; Absicht; Zweck	If you have a *purpose*, you have a reason to do something.
date of birth [ˌdeɪt‿əv 'bɜ:θ]	Geburtsdatum	*date of birth* → birthday

suspicious [sə'spɪʃəs]	misstrauisch; argwöhnisch	When Rafiq told the man he was only 13, he started to get *suspicious*.
side room ['saɪd ˌrʊm]	Nebenraum	We celebrated my birthday in a *side room* of the restaurant.
security [sɪ'kjʊərəti]	Sicherheit; Schutz; Wachdienst; Wach-; Sicherheits-	The *security* people at the airport are very strict.
immigration office [ˌɪmɪ'greɪʃn ˌɒfɪs]	Einwanderungsbehörde	The officials asked Rafiq's aunt to come to the *immigration office*.
immigration [ˌɪmɪ'greɪʃn]	Immigration; Einwanderung; Einreise	The USA is a popular country for *immigration*.
truth [tru:θ]	Wahrheit	*truth* ↔ lie *truth* → true
10 **quite** [kwaɪt]	ziemlich; ganz; völlig	The old centre of Dhaka is *quite* small.
traffic ['træfɪk]	Verkehr	= all the cars, buses, etc. that are moving on a road
to **search for** ['sɜ:tʃ fə]	suchen (nach)	*to search for* = to look for

Nouns and verbs with the same form

answer	to answer	hope	to hope	reply	to reply
change	to change	interest	to interest	rescue	to rescue
chat	to chat	interview	to interview	run	to run
compromise	to compromise	joke	to joke	search	to search
dance	to dance	land	to land	show	to show
design	to design	lie	to lie	smile	to smile
dream	to dream	link	to link	surprise	to surprise
drink	to drink	look	to look	talk	to talk
e-mail	to e-mail	love	to love	test	to test
end	to end	name	to name	travel	to travel
exchange	to exchange	order	to order	use	to use
film	to film	plan	to plan	visit	to visit
fight	to fight	plant	to plant	walk	to walk
guide	to guide	post	to post	work	to work
help	to help	rain	to rain		

11 **traveller** ['trævlə]	Reisende/-r	*traveller* → to travel
to **bother** ['bɒðə]	stören; belästigen	Sorry to *bother* you, but I need your help.
to **suggest** [sə'dʒest]	vorschlagen	*to suggest* → suggestion
chewing gum ['tʃu:ɪŋ ˌgʌm]	Kaugummi	*Chewing gum* isn't allowed at our school.
take-off ['teɪk‿ɒf]	Start; Abheben	
landing ['lændɪŋ]	Landung	*landing* ↔ take-off

	out of ['aʊt‿əv]	aus … heraus	Take a pencil *out of* your pencil case, please.
12	to **contain** [kən'teɪn]	enthalten	What does this box *contain*? = What's in the box?
	gate [geɪt]	Gate; Flugsteig; Ausgang	Our plane leaves from *Gate* 9.
	delay [dɪ'leɪ]	Verzögerung; Verspätung	The train will be half an hour late. We apologise for the *delay*.

At the airport

arrival(s hall)	Ankunft(shalle)
boarding (card)	Boarding/Bordkarte
customs	Zoll
delay	Verspätung
departure (lounge)	Abflug(halle)
desk	Schalter
duty free	Duty Free
flight	Flug
flight attendant	Flugbegleiter/-in
gate	Gate
immigration office	Einwanderungsbehörde
landing	Landung
passenger	Passagier/-in
passport	Pass/Ausweis
plane	Flugzeug
security control	Sicherheitskontrolle
suitcase	Koffer
take-off	Start
visa	Visum

Have you ever travelled by plane? Write 4–5 sentences.

Story: Where I belong

where I belong [ˌweər‿aɪ bɪ'lɒŋ]	wo ich hingehöre	
responsible [rɪs'pɒnsəbl]	verantwortlich; verantwortungsvoll	Who is *responsible* for the pets?
to **accept** [ək'sept]	akzeptieren; hinnehmen; annehmen	I had to *accept* my father's decision.
mask [mɑ:sk]	Maske	He showed no feelings. His face looked like a *mask*.
smuggler ['smʌglə]	Schmuggler/-in	I'm reading an exciting adventure story about *smugglers*.
overloaded [ˌəʊvə'ləʊdɪd]	überladen	The bus was completely *overloaded*.
shark [ʃɑ:k]	Hai	

crushed [krʌʃt]	eingequetscht; eingeklemmt	The girl was *crushed* between two men and couldn't move.
to **rock** [rɒk]	schaukeln	The wind was very strong and the boat *rocked* badly.
to **smash** [smæʃ]	zerschlagen; zerschmettern	The waves *smashed* against the boat.
to **be sick** [bi 'sɪk]	sich übergeben	I *was sick* in the car.
to **close oneself away from** [ˌkləʊz ə'weɪ frəm]	sich abschotten von	I *closed myself away from* what was happening around me.
to **give sb a piggyback** [gɪv‿ə 'pɪgibæk]	jmdn. Huckepack nehmen	
checkpoint ['tʃekpɔɪnt]	Kontrollpunkt	*checkpoint* → to check
seat [si:t]	Sitz; Sitzplatz	the place where you sit (in a train, plane, theatre, etc.)
except [ɪk'sept]	außer; bis auf	Everybody's here, *except* Jenny.
air-conditioning [ˌeəkən'dɪʃnɪŋ]	Klimaanlage	I'm cold. Please turn off the *air-conditioning*.
to **concentrate** ['kɒnsntreɪt]	(sich) konzentrieren	Khadija *concentrated* on what Uncle had told her.
rain [reɪn]	Regen	*rain* → to rain
steady ['stedi]	kontinuierlich; unaufhörlich	
depressing [dɪ'presɪŋ]	deprimierend; bedrückend	It rained for more than a week, which was very *depressing* for everyone.
drizzle ['drɪzl]	Nieselregen	
ground [graʊnd]	Boden; Erdboden	My phone fell onto the *ground* and broke.
to **cover** ['kʌvə]	abdecken; bedecken; zudecken	
concrete ['kɒŋkri:t]	Beton	The streets in a city are *covered* with concrete.
official [ə'fɪʃl]	Beamter/Beamtin	The *officials* just looked at her passport and then let her into the country.
to **pretend** [prɪ'tend]	vortäuschen; tun als ob	Let's *pretend* to be on holiday.
useless ['ju:sləs]	nutzlos	*useless* ↔ useful
invisible [ɪn'vɪzəbl]	unsichtbar	If something becomes *invisible*, you can't see it any more.
phone box ['fəʊn ˌbɒks]	Telefonzelle	
to **fetch** [fetʃ]	holen; abholen	Wait at the station. I'm going to *fetch* you.
button ['bʌtn]	Knopf	
Somali [sə'mɑ:li]	Somali	In Somalia people speak *Somali*.
straight [streɪt]	gerade; direkt; geradewegs	Go *straight* to school, you're late.
2 **refugee** [ˌrefjʊ'dʒi:]	Flüchtling	A lot of *refugees* have come to live in our town.
5 **climate** ['klaɪmət]	Klima	= the kind of weather that is typical of a country or area
to **be homesick** [bi 'həʊmsɪk]	Heimweh haben	*Are* you *homesick* when you're away from home?

Action UK! The guitar lesson

	guitar [gɪ'tɑ:]	Gitarre	
1	**I go wherever the wind takes me.** [aɪ ˌgəʊ weəˌrevə ðə wɪnd 'teɪks mi:]	Ich lasse mich treiben.	Let's *go wherever the wind takes us*.
2	**future** ['fju:tʃə]	zukünftig	Talk about your *future* plans.
	origin ['ɒrɪdʒɪn]	Ursprung; Herkunft; Abstammung	The girl is of African *origin*.
	destination [ˌdestɪ'neɪʃn]	Ziel; Reiseziel	Where are you travelling to? What's your *destination*?
	outgoing [aʊt'gəʊɪŋ]	kontaktfreudig	*outgoing* ↔ shy
	easy-going [ˌi:zi'gəʊɪŋ]	locker; unkompliziert	Who is more *easy-going* – your dad or your mum?
	odd [ɒd]	seltsam; komisch	*odd* = strange
3	to **be set (in)** [bi 'set ɪn]	spielen (in); seinen Schauplatz haben (in)	"Star Trek" *is set in* the future.
	unreal [ˌʌn'rɪəl]	irreal	*unreal* ↔ real
	specific [spə'sɪfɪk]	spezifisch; speziell	
	era ['ɪərə]	Ära; Zeitalter	The Industrial Revolution was an exciting *era* in British history.
	lavish ['lævɪʃ]	üppig; verschwenderisch	Only rich people can afford *lavish* lifestyles.
	magic ['mædʒɪk]	Magie; Zauberei	*magic* → magical
	supernatural ['su:pəˌnætʃrl]	übernatürlich	Fantasy stories are usually about people with magical or *supernatural* powers.
	force [fɔ:s]	Kraft; Macht	The hero couldn't defeat the supernatural *forces*.
	mythical ['mɪθɪkl]	sagenhaft; sagenumwoben	

Skills: How to tell a travel story

1	**the other day** [ði‿ʌðə 'deɪ]	neulich	! False friend: *the other day ≠ am anderen Tag*
	It turned out that ... [ɪt ˌtɜ:nd‿'aʊt ðæt]	Es stellte sich heraus, dass ...	
2	**war** [wɔ:]	Krieg	World *War* II
3	**Egyptian** [ɪ'dʒɪpʃn]	Ägypter/-in; ägyptisch	= from Egypt
	dominoes ['dɒmɪnəʊz]	Domino	
	to **order** ['ɔ:də]	bestellen	At the restaurant, I *ordered* a burger and a glass of water.
	Arab ['ærəb]	arabisch	Egypt is an *Arab* country.

Unit task: True or not true?

convincing [kən'vɪnsɪŋ]	überzeugend	The story doesn't sound *convincing*. *Lat.* convincere

Across cultures 1 Dos and don'ts

	dos and don'ts [ˌdu:z‿ənd 'dəʊnts]	Ge- und Verbote; was man tun und was man nicht tun sollte	The *dos and don'ts* are the things you should and shouldn't do.
1	**behaviour** *(no pl)* [bɪ'heɪvjə]	Verhalten; Benehmen; Betragen	*behaviour* → to behave
	to **point at sb/sth** ['pɔɪnt æt]	mit dem Finger auf jmdn./etw. zeigen	Don't *point at* people. It's rude.
	to **stand in the way of sb/sth** [ˌstænd ɪn ðə 'weɪ‿əv]	jmdm./etw. im Weg stehen	Excuse me, you*'re standing in my way*.
	to **hold open** [ˌhəʊld‿'əʊpn]	aufhalten	You should always *hold* the door *open* for others.
	to **talk with your mouth full** [ˌtɔ:k wɪð jɔ: 'maʊθ fʊl]	mit vollem Mund sprechen	Never *talk with your mouth full*.
	to **litter** ['lɪtə]	verschmutzen; verunreinigen; Müll herumliegen lassen	Don't *litter* the playground. Take your rubbish home with you.
	ear [ɪə]	Ohr	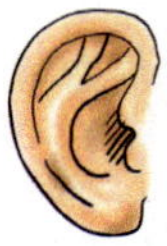
2	to **guess** [ges]	annehmen	You look tired. I *guess* you want to go home.
	custom ['kʌstəm]	Gewohnheit; Brauch; Sitte	People often wear funny costumes at Halloween. It's a *custom*.
4	**icebreaker** ['aɪsˌbreɪkə]	Eisbrecher *(Sätze, um mit jmdm. ins Gespräch zu kommen)*	*Icebreakers* are phrases which people use to start a conversation.
	glad [glæd]	froh	I'm *glad* you aren't angry with me.
	crowded ['kraʊdɪd]	überfüllt	= full of people
5	**leaflet** ['li:flət]	Broschüre; Informationsblatt; Prospekt	
	manners *(pl)* ['mænəz]	Manieren; Benehmen	It's good *manners* to say hello.

Text smart 1 Drama

Introduction

2	to **entertain** [ˌentə'teɪn]	unterhalten	Theatre plays *entertain* the audience. *to entertain* → entertainment
	to **stage** [steɪdʒ]	aufführen	This year our tutor group is going to *stage* a play by Shakespeare.
	to **mess sth up** [ˌmes‿'ʌp]	etw. durcheinanderbringen; etw. vergeigen	= to do sth badly or wrong
	performance [pə'fɔ:məns]	Aufführung; Vorstellung	All the actors gave great *performances* in the school play.

	director [dɪ'rektə]	Regisseur/-in	When a film is made, the *director* tells everyone what to do.
	lines *(pl)* [laɪnz]	Text	They've learnt their *lines* by heart.
	protagonist [prəʊ'tægnɪst]	Protagonist/-in; Hauptfigur	The *protagonist* is the main character in a play or story.

Station 1

	devil ['devl]	Teufel	
	teenage ['ti:neɪdʒ]	jugendlich; Jugend-	Your *teenage* years are the time from age 13 to age 19.
	dilemma [daɪ'lemə]	Dilemma; Zwickmühle	Claire is in a *dilemma*: should she go to the party or not?
	to **face** [feɪs]	gegenüber stehen; konfrontiert werden mit	This is a problem we have to *face*.
	angel ['eɪndʒl]	Engel	
4	to **phone** [fəʊn]	anrufen; telefonieren	*to phone* = to call *to phone* → (tele)phone
	tonight [tə'naɪt]	heute Abend; heute Nacht	*tonight* = this evening
	conscience ['kɒnʃns]	Gewissen	Does Claire have a bad *conscience* when she lies to her parents?
5	**motivation** [ˌməʊtɪ'veɪʃn]	Motivation; Beweggründe	
	unsure [ʌn'ʃʊə]	unsicher	I'm *unsure* about what to do. = I'm not sure about what I should do.
	convinced [kən'vɪnst]	überzeugt	*convinced* → to convince
	tempted ['temptɪd]	in Versuchung gebracht	She feels *tempted* to lie to her parents.
	to **tempt** [tempt]	in Versuchung führen; reizen	Rob *tempts* Claire to break the rules.

Station 2

6	**motive** ['məʊtɪv]	Motiv; Beweggrund	
	to **take a risk** [ˌteɪk‿ə 'rɪsk]	ein Risiko eingehen	If you *take a risk*, you do something that could be dangerous.
	to **exaggerate** [ɪg'zædʒreɪt]	übertreiben	If you *exaggerate* something, you make it sound better or worse than it really is. *Fr.* exagérer
	sensible ['sensɪbl]	vernünftig	! engl. *sensible* ≠ *dt. sensibel* *sensible* ↔ stupid
	Let's face it. [lets 'feɪs‿ɪt]	Machen wir uns doch nichts vor.	*Let's face it*: nobody likes this situation.

	white lie [ˌwaɪt ˈlaɪ]	Notlüge	= a small lie that you use when you don't want to hurt somebody's feelings
7	**mean** [miːn]	gemein	*mean* = nasty
	pushy [ˈpʊʃi]	aufdringlich; penetrant; aggressiv	Try to get what you want – but don't be too *pushy*!
	argument [ˈɑːgjəmənt]	Argument	You use *arguments* to explain the reasons for your opinion.
9	**tempting** [ˈtemptɪŋ]	verführerisch	*tempting* → tempted → to tempt

Station 3

10	to **warn** [wɔːn]	warnen	They *warned* me of the dangers. 
	hardly [ˈhɑːdli]	kaum	I can *hardly* believe it.
	dishonest [dɪˈsɒnɪst]	unehrlich	*dishonest* ↔ honest
	to **do well** [ˌduː ˈwel]	gute Leistungen erbringen	They would like to *do* really *well* on the project.
	schoolwork [ˈskuːlwɜːk]	Schularbeiten	
12	**bit by bit** [ˌbɪt baɪ ˈbɪt]	Stück für Stück	They've learnt their lines *bit by bit*.
	fake [feɪk]	falsch; gefälscht	A *fake* person pretends to be somebody that he or she isn't. *fake* → to fake

Station 4

13	**youth** [juːθ]	Jugend	= the period in your life before you become an adult
	to **support** [səˈpɔːt]	unterstützen	Do your parents *support* you in what you do?
	tolerant [ˈtɒlrnt]	tolerant	! Achtung Betonung.
	There's no need to ... [ˌðeəz nəʊ ˈniːd tə]	Es gibt keinen Grund zu ...	*There's no need to* shout. I'm listening to you.
	to **expect** [ɪkˈspekt]	erwarten	What you *expect* is what you think will happen.
	to **ring** [rɪŋ], **rang** [ræŋ], **rung** [rʌŋ]	anrufen	= to call sb on the phone
	out of order [ˌaʊt‿əv ˈɔːdə]	kaputt; außer Betrieb	The vending machine is *out of order*. It isn't working.
14	**shocked** [ʃɒkt]	schockiert; geschockt	
	guilty [ˈgɪlti]	schuldig	I didn't feel *guilty* because I hadn't done anything wrong.

Options

16	**casting** [ˈkɑːstɪŋ]	Casting; Rollenbesetzung	= the job of choosing actors to play particular roles

Across cultures 2 The USA: Country of contrasts

contrast ['kɒntrɑ:st]	Kontrast; Unterschied; Gegensatz	! Notice the stress on the first syllable. *Fr.* contraste *(m)*
the US (= the United States) [ðə ju:'es]	die USA (= die Vereinigten Staaten)	*The US* is a country of contrasts.
urban ['ɜ:bn]	städtisch; Stadt-	Towns and cities are *urban* areas. *Lat.* urbs *(f)*
endless ['endləs]	endlos	School lessons sometimes seem *endless*. *endless* → end
sparse [spɑ:s]	dünn; spärlich	I only have *sparse* information on this topic.
populated ['pɒpjəleɪtɪd]	bevölkert; besiedelt	
rural ['rʊərl]	ländlich	*rural* ↔ urban *Fr.* rural/-e
single ['sɪŋgl]	einzeln; einzig; alleinstehend	a *single* room = ein Einzelzimmer not a *single* person = kein einziger Mensch I'm *single*. = Ich bin alleinstehend.
tractor ['træktə]	Traktor	
desert ['dezət]	Wüste	
(the) Southwest [ˌsaʊθ'west]	(der) Südwesten; im Südwesten; südwestlich	*southwest* → northwest
temperature ['temprətʃə]	Temperatur	What's the *temperature* today? *Fr.* température *(f)*
degree Fahrenheit (°F) ['færnhaɪt]	Grad Fahrenheit	110 *°F* is about 43°C.
cactus ['kæktəs]	Kaktus	
cool [ku:l]	kühl	The weather can be cold, *cool*, warm or hot.
zone [zəʊn]	Zone	There are different climate *zones* in the US.
immigrant ['ɪmɪgrənt]	Immigrant/-in; Einwanderer/-in	! He's an *immigrant* **from** Asia. He's an *immigrant* **to** the US. *Fr.* immigrant *(m)*; *Lat.* immigrare
European [ˌjʊərə'pi:ən]	Europäer/-in; europäisch; aus Europa	*European* → Europe
cultural ['kʌltʃrl]	kulturell	There are *cultural* differences between people who come from different countries.
redwood (tree) ['redwʊd ˌtri:]	Mammutbaum	= a huge tree that grows in California
foot [fʊt], **feet** [fi:t] *(pl)*	Fuß *(Längenmaß: 30,48 cm)*	I'm 1.82 m tall, that's about 6 *feet*.

	skyscraper ['skaɪskreɪpə]	Wolkenkratzer	The Empire State Building is the most famous *skyscraper* in New York.
	state [steɪt]	Staat; Bundesstaat; Land	The US has 50 *states*.
	to **fly** [flaɪ], **flew** [flu:], **flown** [fləʊn]	hissen	Flags *are flown* on a lot of public buildings and on homes in the US.
	a (day/week/year) [ə 'deɪ/wi:k/jɪə]	pro (Tag/Woche/Jahr)	An apple *a day* keeps the doctor away. = Einen Apfel pro Tag und man bleibt gesund.
	population [ˌpɒpjə'leɪʃn]	Bevölkerung; Population	*population* → populated *Fr.* population *(f)*
	billionaire ['bɪliəneə]	Milliardär/-in	
1	**scenery** ['si:nri]	Landschaft	= what you see around you when you're somewhere with a view, e.g. out in the country
	simply ['sɪmpli]	einfach nur	Americans usually call their country *simply* 'America'.
	dense [dens]	dicht	*dense* ↔ sparse
	in the country [ˌɪn ðə 'kʌntri]	auf dem Land	
	mountainous ['maʊntɪnəs]	bergig	
	flat [flæt]	flach; platt	Countryside with no hills is *flat*.
	gigantic [dʒaɪ'gæntɪk]	gigantisch; riesig	Those mountains are *gigantic*!
	wealthy ['welθi]	wohlhabend; reich	*wealthy* ↔ poor
	wasteful ['weɪstfl]	verschwenderisch	Don't be *wasteful* with water!
	luxury ['lʌkʃri]	Luxus	Wealthy people often spend their money on all kinds of *luxury*.
	to **represent** [ˌreprɪ'zent]	repräsentieren; darstellen; stehen für	*to represent* = to stand for *Fr.* représenter
	to **symbolize** *(AE)* ['sɪmbəlaɪz]	symbolisieren	*to symbolise* → symbol *Fr.* symboliser
2	**harsh** [hɑ:ʃ]	rau; hart	Don't be so *harsh* with him. He already feels bad enough.
	extreme [ɪk'stri:m]	extrem; radikal	
	standard of living [ˌstændəd‿əv 'lɪvɪŋ]	Lebensstandard	In Germany, we enjoy a high *standard of living*.
4	to **become friends** [bɪˌkʌm‿'frendz]	sich anfreunden; Freundschaft schließen	Tristan and Callum *became friends* some years ago.
	vacation *(AE)* [və'keɪʃn]	Ferien; Urlaub	Summer *vacation* at American schools is at least two, sometimes three months.
	dude *(coll)* [du:d]	Mann; Alter *(ugs.)*	Hey, *dude*! What's up?
	awesome ['ɔ:səm]	super; spitze	*awesome* = great
	US [ˌju:'es]	US-amerikanisch	Most *US* teens don't know what it's like to have school uniforms.
	to **have no clue** [ˌhæv nəʊ 'klu:]	keine Ahnung haben	What's the time? – I *have no clue*.

route planner ['ru:t ˌplænə]	Routenplaner	
Brit [brɪt]	Brite/Britin *(ugs.)*	
colonist ['kɒlənɪst]	Siedler/-in; Kolonist/-in	*colonist* → colony *(n)*
corn [kɔ:n]	Korn; Mais; Getreide	
wheat [wi:t]	Weizen	In the Midwest you can see endless corn and *wheat* fields.
to **ride** [raɪd], **rode** [rəʊd], **ridden** ['rɪdn]	fahren; reiten	You can *ride* a bike or a horse.
epic ['epɪk]	episch; *hier:* geil	The party was *epic*!
massive ['mæsɪv]	riesig; massiv; *hier:* super	*massive* = awesome
complete [kəm'pli:t]	vollständig; komplett; völlig	Is your picture of America *complete*?

Unit 2 Kids in America

kid [kɪd]	Jugendliche/-r; Kind	Hey *kids*, let's go swimming! *kid* = child

Introduction

1	**impression** [ɪm'preʃn]	Impression; Eindruck	What is your *impression* of the US?
3	**orientation** [ˌɔ:riən'teɪʃn]	Orientierung; Orientierungs-	At the *orientation* weekend teenagers get information about teen life in the US.
	to **give a talk** [ˌgɪv‿ə 'tɔ:k]	einen Vortrag halten	I'm nervous. I have to *give a talk* at school.
	suburb ['sʌbɜ:b]	Vorort	Wimbledon is a *suburb* of London.
	suburban [sə'bɜ:bn]	Vorstadt-	*Suburban* houses often have lots of space. *suburban* → suburb
	front yard *(AE)* [ˌfrʌnt 'jɑ:d]	Vorgarten	*front yard* ↔ backyard
	shopping mall ['ʃɒpɪŋ ˌmɔ:l]	Einkaufszentrum	
	middle school *(AE)* ['mɪdl ˌsku:l]	Mittelschule *(weiterführende Schule in den USA, Mittelstufe)*	Children at *middle school* in the US are usually 13 to 14 years old.
	high school *(AE)* ['haɪ ˌsku:l]	High School *(weiterführende Schule in den USA, Oberstufe)*	= a school in the US for students between the ages of 15 and 18
	hallway ['hɔ:lweɪ]	Flur; Diele; Korridor	
	hall pass ['hɔ:l pɑ:s]	*Erlaubnis, sich während des Unterrichts auf dem Flur aufzuhalten*	During lessons students are not allowed to be in the hallway without a *hall pass*.
	dress code ['dres ˌkəʊd]	Kleiderordnung; Bekleidungsvorschriften	The school has a *dress code*, so she can't wear such a short skirt.
	restroom *(AE)* ['restrʊm]	Toilette	

Urban vs. rural

urban centers
city life
crowded, densely populated,
not enough space
short distances
skyscrapers, tall buildings, downtown
suburb, suburban

rural areas
country life, in the country
farms, corn/wheat fields, mountains
long distances, endless roads
sparsely populated,
open spaces/lots of space

Write five sentences with these words or phrases.

Station 1: Living here isn't bad

movie *(AE)* ['mu:vi]	Film	In *movies*, teen life is often shown as all fun and games.
walk-in closet [ˌwɔ:kɪn 'klɒzɪt]	begehbarer Kleiderschrank	American houses often have *walk-in closets*.
to **be around** [ˌbi: ə'raʊnd]	da sein; zusammen sein mit	There *aren't* many restaurants *around*, just a few.
not until [ˌnɒt‿ən'tɪl]	nicht vor; erst um/im	My birthday *isn't until* six weeks!
store *(AE)* [stɔ:]	Laden; Geschäft	There's a cool new *store* at the mall. Let's check it out!
drive [draɪv]	Fahrt; Anfahrt; Autofahrt	*drive* → to drive
along for the ride [əˌlɒŋ fə ðə 'raɪd]	mit dabei	My brother doesn't always want me *along for the ride*.
ride [raɪd]	Fahrt; Ritt	*ride* → to ride
curfew ['kɜ:fju:]	Sperrstunde; Ausgangssperre	In Germany, the *curfew* for teenagers between sixteen and eighteen is 10 p.m. They have to be home by 10 o'clock.
to **meet up** [ˌmi:t‿'ʌp]	sich treffen	
downtown *(AE)* [ˌdaʊn'taʊn]	im Stadtzentrum	Don't you think malls are boring? Shopping *downtown* is cooler!
to **get used to sth** [ˌget 'ju:zd tə]	sich an etw. gewöhnen	I don't like to get up early in the morning, but I *got used to* it.
floor [flɔ:]	Stockwerk	! What you call the first *floor* in Germany is the second *floor* in the US.
elevator *(AE)* ['elɪveɪtə]	Aufzug; Lift	
luckily ['lʌkɪli]	glücklicherweise	*Luckily*, he found his money and could pay for his lunch.
movie theater *(AE)* ['mu:vi ˌθɪətə]	Kino	Let's go to the movies. – OK, which *movie theater*?
soccer *(AE)* ['sɒkə]	Fußball	*Soccer* is becoming very popular in the US.
I'm afraid ... [ˌaɪm‿ə'freɪd]	Leider ...	*I'm afraid* I'm very busy right now.
to **keep in touch** [ˌki:p‿ɪn 'tʌtʃ]	in Kontakt bleiben	Let's *keep in touch*.

	to **keep** [kiːp], **kept** [kept], **kept** [kept]	*hier:* weiter tun; immer wieder tun	*Keep* smiling, and everything will be fine! = Everything feels better when you smile.
	no wonder [ˌnəʊ ˈwʌndə]	kein Wunder	Your dad is American; *no wonder* your English is so good.
2	**Pilgrim** [ˈpɪlgrɪm]	Pilger/-in	In 1620 the *Pilgrims* left England for America.
	to **practice a religion** [ˌpræktɪs‿ə rɪˈlɪdʒn]	eine Religion ausüben	
	survivor [səˈvaɪvə]	Überlebende/-r	*survivor* → to survive
	Native American [ˌneɪtɪv‿əˈmerɪkən]	Ureinwohner/-in Amerikas; Indianer/-in; indianisch	
	harvest [ˈhɑːvɪst]	Ernte	
	to **give thanks** [ˌgɪv ˈθæŋks]	danken	At Thanksgiving people *give thanks* for the good things in their lives.
	Indian [ˈɪndiən]	Indianer/-in; indianisch	! The terms ‚*Indian*' and ‚Native American' are both fine for describing the original population of what is now the US.
	menu [ˈmenjuː]	Speisekarte	
	dish [dɪʃ]	Gericht; Speise	What's your favorite *dish*?
3	**instead of** [ɪnˈsted‿əv]	statt; anstatt; an Stelle von	This year we're going to go on vacation in the winter *instead of* the summer.
4	**social media** [ˌsəʊʃl ˈmiːdiə]	soziale Netzwerke	Why aren't you on *social media* like everybody else? – Why do I have to do what everybody else does?
	to **mind** [maɪnd]	etwas dagegen haben; einem etwas ausmachen	Do you *mind* if I open the window? – No, I don't *mind*.
	in the middle of nowhere [ɪn ðə ˌmɪdl‿əv ˈnəʊweə]	mitten im Nirgendwo	
5	to **find one's way around** [ˌfaɪnd wʌnz ˌweɪ‿əˈraʊnd]	sich zurechtfinden	I know New York very well. I know how to *find my way around* in New York.
	to **be tired of** [bi ˈtaɪəd‿əv]	es müde sein (zu); es leid sein (zu); es satt haben (zu)	I'm really *tired of* cleaning up your room all the time. = I really don't want to clean up your room anymore.
6	**likes** *(pl)* [laɪks]	Vorlieben	
	dislikes *(pl)* [dɪsˈlaɪks]	Abneigungen	What are your likes and *dislikes*? = What do you like and what don't you like?
	to **unpack** [ʌnˈpæk]	auspacken	
7	to **dislike** [dɪsˈlaɪk]	nicht mögen	*to dislike* ↔ to like
	to **dream** [driːm], **dreamt** [dremt], **dreamt** [dremt]	träumen	I *dream* of having my own restaurant one day. = I really want my own restaurant one day. ! *to dream, dreamt/dreamed, dreamt/dreamed*
	to **be crazy about** [bi ˈkreɪzi‿əbaʊt]	verrückt sein nach; abfahren auf	He's *crazy about* posting new selfies. = He loves it when he can post new selfies.
	insecure [ˌɪnsɪˈkjʊə]	unsicher	Meeting new people makes me feel *insecure*.
8	**foreground** [ˈfɔːgraʊnd]	Vordergrund	*foreground* ↔ background

Likes and dislikes

There are different ways to express likes and dislikes. Sometimes you can use the same verb, sometimes there are totally different ways to express things.

I'm **interested in** meeting new friends.	I'm **interested in** new friends. / It's great to meet new friends.
Living here isn't bad / is cool.	**Life** here isn't bad/is cool.
I **like/love** having a big bedroom.	I **like/love** my big bedroom.
I **hate/dislike** sharing my room.	A bedroom on my own **would be great**.
I **miss** seeing my old friends.	I **miss** my old friends.
I'm **scared of** changing too much.	I'm **scared of** too many changes.
I **enjoyed** meeting you.	It was **great** to meet you.
How about meeting up?	**Let's** meet up.
I haven't **got used to** living on the 22nd floor.	I haven't **got used to** our apartment on the 22nd floor.
I **look forward to** starting school.	I **look forward to** my first day at school.
I'm **good at** swimming.	I'm a **good** swimmer.
Don't **worry about** losing your old friends.	Don't **worry about** your old friends; you won't lose them.
I **keep** forgetting your dad is American.	I **always forget about** the fact that your dad is American.
I **didn't mind** moving to America.	A new life in America **was no problem** for me.
I **don't feel like** going anywhere.	I don't **want to** go anywhere.
He's **tired of** answering her questions.	He **doesn't like** it when he has to answer her questions.
I **dream of** going to Australia.	I **dream of** a trip to Australia.
She's **crazy about** going shopping.	She **loves** shopping. / She **loves** it when she can go to cool stores.

Can you think of other ways to say these two sentences?

1. She talked about organizing a party.
2. Stop worrying.

Station 2: That's the worst thing to do!

committee [kəˈmɪti]	Komitee; Ausschuss	*Fr.* comité *(m)*
8th-grader *(AE)* [ˈeɪtθˌgreɪdə]	Achtklässler/-in	An *8th-grader* is a student in the 8th year of school.
period *(AE)* [ˈpɪəriəd]	Stunde; Unterrichtsstunde	At our school, first *period* starts at 8:00 a.m.
geek [giːk]	Außenseiter/-in	Just because a person isn't super popular doesn't mean he/she is a *geek*.
What a ... [ˈwɒt‿ə]	Was für ein/-e ...	*What a* dilemma!
shopper [ˈʃɒpə]	Käufer/-in	*shopper* → shopping → shop
child labor *(AE)* [ˌtʃaɪld ˈleɪbə]	Kinderarbeit	
sweatshop [ˈswetʃɒp]	Ausbeuterbetrieb	
to demonstrate [ˈdemənstreɪt]	demonstrieren	
right [raɪt]	Recht	Child labor goes against the *rights* of children.
11 **whether** [ˈweðə]	ob	*whether* = if *(in indirect speech)*

Phrases with superlatives

Why don't you come with us? You're **the only one** to stay at home.	Warum kommst du nicht mit? Du bist die Einzige, die zu Hause bleibt.
If you don't want to walk, it's **the cheapest thing** to take the bus.	Wenn du nicht zu Fuß gehen willst, ist es am günstigsten, den Bus zu nehmen.
On the weekends my dad is always **the first** to get up. My sister is **the last** to have breakfast.	Am Wochenende steht mein Vater immer als Erster auf. Meine Schwester frühstückt als Letzte.
My friends are great. They're **the funniest people** to go out with.	Meine Freunde sind toll! Mit ihnen ist es am lustigsten auszugehen.
Don't stay home alone. It's **the worst thing** to do when you're sad.	Bleib nicht allein zu Hause. Das ist das Schlimmste, was du tun kannst, wenn du traurig bist.
Should I stay or should I go? What's **the best thing** to do?	Soll ich bleiben oder gehen? Was ist am besten?

Write three more sentences with superlative phrases.

Phrases with question words

Matt didn't know **what** to think.	Er wusste nicht, **was** er davon halten sollte.
He was wondering **who** to sit with in the cafeteria.	Er fragte sich, zu **wem** er sich in der Cafeteria setzen sollte/konnte.
He wanted to know **where** to go.	Er wollte wissen, **wohin** er gehen sollte.
He wasn't sure **how much** money to bring.	Er war sich nicht sicher, **wie viel** Geld er mitbringen sollte/musste.
He didn't know **when** to use his locker.	Er wusste nicht, **wann** er seinen Spind benutzen sollte/durfte.
He didn't know **whether** to use his own laptop.	Er wusste nicht, **ob** er seinen eigenen Laptop benutzen sollte/konnte.

Write three more sentences with question words.

13	to **prefer** [prɪ'fɜː]	vorziehen	= to like more/better *Fr.* préférer
14	to **control** [kən'trəʊl]	kontrollieren; steuern	My parents *control* everything I do.
	might [maɪt]	könnte/-n (vielleicht)	Maybe he'll play well in the match. He *might* even win it!
15	to **argue** ['ɑːgjuː]	argumentieren; streiten	In a discussion, you use arguments to *argue* for or against something.
16	to **clean out** [ˌkliːn_'aʊt]	ausräumen; entrümpeln	
	clothing drive ['kləʊðɪŋ ˌdraɪv]	Kleidersammlung	Let's clean out our attic for the *clothing drive*.
	homeless shelter ['həʊmləs ˌʃeltə]	Obdachlosenunterkunft	= a place where homeless people can sleep
	homeless ['həʊmləs]	obdachlos	

to **wish** [wɪʃ]	(sich) wünschen	*to wish* → wish
to **donate** [də'neɪt]	spenden; stiften	= to give money, food, etc. to sb
benefit ['benɪfɪt]	Vorteil; Nutzen; Unterstützung	What's the *benefit* of a clothing drive?
pound [paʊnd]	Pfund *(Maßeinheit)*	In the US, people weigh things in *pounds*, not in kilos.
item ['aɪtəm]	Gegenstand; Objekt	We'll get a few cents for every *item* we donate.
drop-off ['drɒpɒf]	Abgabe	The *drop-off* point for clothes is in the cafeteria.

Story: Nightmare at the mall!

	nightmare ['naɪtmeə]	Alptraum	= a scary dream
1	**believable** [bɪ'li:vəbl]	glaubwürdig	The novel has *believable* characters. *believable* → to believe
	exaggerated [ɪg'zædʒreɪtɪd]	übertrieben	*Fr.* exagéré/-e
	unrealistic [ˌʌnrɪə'lɪstɪk]	unrealistisch	Your plan won't work because it's *unrealistic*.
	coincidence [kəʊ'ɪnsɪdns]	Zufall	There are too many unrealistic *coincidences* in this movie!
	to **open** ['əʊpn]	eröffnen	He's going to *open* a new sports store.
	to **sign** [saɪn]	unterschreiben; unterzeichnen	Please *sign* the letter. *Fr.* signer; *Lat.* signare
	amazed [ə'meɪzd]	erstaunt; verblüfft	
	scared [skeəd]	verängstigt; ängstlich	This film is scary. I feel *scared*.
	right [raɪt]	direkt	I'm looking for my pen. – It's *right* next to your exercise book.
	cheer [tʃɪə]	Jubel; Hurraruf	
	dizzy ['dɪzi]	schwindelig	Some people feel *dizzy* if they look down from a skyscraper.
	down [daʊn]	nieder	*Down* with child labor!
	to **escape (from)** [ɪ'skeɪp frəm]	fliehen; entfliehen; flüchten; entkommen	= to run away from sth or sb
	protester ['prəʊtestə]	Protestierende/-r; Demonstrant/-in	! Be careful with the pronunciaton.
	to **touch** [tʌtʃ]	berühren; antippen	Don't *touch* the dog, it bites.
	troublemaker ['trʌblmeɪkə]	Unruhestifter/-in	*troublemaker* → trouble
	to **leave sb alone** [ˌli:v‿ə'ləʊn]	jmdn. in Ruhe lassen	*Leave me alone*!
	obvious ['ɒbviəs]	offensichtlich	= easy to see or understand *obvious* = clear
	twice [twaɪs]	zweimal	= two times
2	**mess** [mes]	Unordnung; Durcheinander; Schweinerei	There's a *mess* in my room. I'll have to tidy it up.
	to **mix** [mɪks]	zusammenpassen	These colors don't *mix*.

Action USA! Go on, text her!

	Go on! [ˌgəʊ͜ˈɒn]	Los!	*Go on*, don't wait too long!
1	**attractive** [əˈtræktɪv]	attraktiv	! Be careful with the word stress.
	boyfriend [ˈbɔɪfrend]	Freund *(in einer Paarbeziehung)*	Is he just a friend, or your *boyfriend*?
	attitude [ˈætɪtjuːd]	Haltung; Einstellung	Your *attitude* to/towards life is the way you feel about it. *Fr.* attitude *(f)*
2	to **overdo** [əʊvəˈduː], **overdid** [əʊvəˈdɪd], **overdone** [əʊvəˈdʌn]	übertreiben; zu weit gehen	Don't you think that's *overdoing* it? I mean, it's a great party outfit, but for school?
3	**date** [deɪt]	Verabredung; Date	Have you got a *date* for the dance yet?

Skills: How to write in the appropriate style

1	**content** [ˈkɒntent]	Inhalt	= the information or ideas e.g. in a book, film, photo, etc.
	toothpaste [ˈtuːθpeɪst]	Zahnpasta	
3	**ironic** [ˌaɪˈrɒnɪk]	ironisch	I love writers with an *ironic* sense of humor.
	informative [ɪnˈfɔːmətɪv]	informativ	Brochures are usually *informative*.
	natural [ˈnætʃrl]	natürlich; Natur-	! Be careful with the pronunciation. *natural* → nature
	individual [ˌɪndɪˈvɪdʒuəl]	Einzelperson; Einzelne/-r; Individuum	Each person is an *individual* with his/her own personality.
	pose [pəʊz]	Pose; Haltung	
	season [ˈsiːzn]	Saison; Jahreszeit	Summer is the warmest *season*.
	championship [ˈtʃæmpiənʃɪp]	Meisterschaft	She was the youngest player ever to win the national *championship*.

Unit task: An American-style yearbook

double [ˈdʌbl]	Doppel-; zweimal	The pictures don't fit on one page, I'll need a *double* page for them.
concert [ˈkɒnsət]	Konzert	

Important differences

	AE		BE	
Different spelling	cent**er**		cent**re**	
	Dr.		Dr	
	Mr./Mrs./Ms.		Mr/Mrs/Ms	
	neighb**o**r(hood)		neighb**ou**r(hood)	
	to symboli**z**e		to symboli**s**e	
Different words	apartment	mom	flat	mum
	downtown	movie	city centre	film
	elevator	movie theater	lift	cinema
	front yard	period	garden	lesson
	high school	restroom	grammar school	bathroom, toilets
	middle school	soccer	comprehensive school	football
	8th-grader, 8th-grade student	store	Year 8 student	shop
		vacation		holiday

Text smart 2 Advertisements

ad(vertisement) [əd'vɜːtɪsmənt]	Anzeige; Werbespot	
product ['prɒdʌkt]	Produkt; Erzeugnis	! Be careful with the pronunciation. *product* → to produce
just about anywhere [ˌdʒʌst‿əˌbaʊt 'eniweə]	praktisch überall	You can see advertisements for products *just about anywhere* you look.
advertiser ['ædvətaɪzə]	Werbefachmann/-frau	
to **win** sb **over** [ˌwɪn‿'əʊvə]	jmdn. für sich gewinnen; jmdn. überzeugen	Advertisers try to *win* customers *over*.

Introduction

1 **brand** [brænd]	Marke	= a particular product or line of products made by one company and sold under a special name
immediately [ɪ'miːdiətli]	sofort; gleich	I don't want to wait any longer. Let's go *immediately*.
to **give away** [ˌɡɪv‿ə'weɪ]	verteilen; verschenken	
sample ['sɑːmpl]	Probe; Muster	My favorite chocolate company is giving away free *samples* today.
chocolate bar ['tʃɒklət ˌbɑː]	Schokoriegel	

to **fall for** ['fɔ:l fə]	hereinfallen auf	You didn't *fall for* that trick, did you?
hair [heə]	Haar; Haare	! Ihre Haare **sind** lang. = Her *hair* **is** long.
to **advertise** ['ædvətaɪz]	Werbung machen; werben; anpreisen; inserieren	Have you heard about that new phone? They *advertise* it a lot on TV.
receptive [rɪ'septɪv]	empfänglich	*receptive* → to receive
temptation [temp'teɪʃn]	Versuchung	*temptation* → to tempt
sceptical ['skeptɪkl]	skeptisch	= when you have your doubts about sth
advertising *(no pl)* ['ædvətaɪzɪŋ]	Werbung; Reklame	*advertising* → to advertise → advertisement → advertiser

You, one, they

In English there are different words for the German word 'man'. Sometimes you can also translate it with a passive sentence.

You can see advertisements for products just about anywhere **you** look.	Man sieht Werbung praktisch überall, wohin **man** schaut.
On the radio, **they** mentioned a big sale at a clothes store.	Im Radio erwähnte **man** einen großen Ausverkauf in einem Kleiderladen./Im Radio **wurde** ein großer Ausverkauf in einem Kleiderladen erwähnt.
One can never know what will happen.	**Man** kann nie wissen, was passieren wird.

'You' and 'they' are very common, but 'one' is for a more formal kind of English, e.g. for business, in formal writing and sometimes in literature too.

Station: Did you see that new ad?

	to **spice up** [ˌspaɪs_'ʌp]	aufpeppen	*Spice up* your style with some color!
	highly ['haɪli]	höchst-	*highly* = very, extremely
	brand-new [ˌbrænd'nju:]	brandneu	
	available [ə'veɪləbl]	erhältlich; verfügbar	If sth is *available*, you can get it or buy it.
	glamorous ['glæmrəs]	glamourös	She looks so *glamorous*, like a movie star!
	lovely ['lʌvli]	schön; hübsch	Thank you, that's a *lovely* present.
	nerd [nɜ:d]	Nerd *(Person, die intelligent, aber sozial unbeholfen ist)*	
2	**target** ['tɑ:gɪt]	Ziel; Ziel-	Who is the *target* group of this advertisement?
	eye-catcher ['aɪkætʃə]	Blickfang; Hingucker	Her dress is an *eye-catcher*.
	visual ['vɪʒuəl]	Bild	Ads depend a lot on *visuals*.
	ad copy ['æd ˌkɒpi]	Werbetext	We've got the visuals for the new ad, but we still need the *ad copy* for it.
	image ['ɪmɪdʒ]	Bild; Abbildung	*Fr.* image *(f)*
	billboard ['bɪlbɔ:d]	Plakatwand	= large outdoor sign for advertisements
4	**approach** [ə'prəʊtʃ]	Herangehensweise; Vorgehensweise; Ansatz; Annäherung	We get the same results but we have different *approaches*. *Fr.* approche *(f)*

	truckload ['trʌkləʊd]	Lastwagenladung	The shop gets *truckloads* of new clothes every day so the customers always find something new.
	arrival [ə'raɪvl]	Ankommende/-r; Neuzugang	*arrival* → to arrive
	to **settle for less** [ˌsetl fə 'les]	sich mit weniger zufrieden geben	I want the best, so why should I *settle for less*?
	effective [ɪ'fektɪv]	effektiv; wirkungsvoll	Featuring famous people in ads can be very *effective*.
	to **attract** [ə'trækt]	anziehen	What target group are they trying to *attract*?
	fabulous ['fæbjələs]	sagenhaft; fantastisch	*Fr.* fabuleux/fabuleuse
5	**effectiveness** [ɪ'fektɪvnəs]	Effektivität; Wirksamkeit	*effectiveness* → effective

Options

6	**trash** *(AE)* [træʃ]	Abfall; Müll	There's so much *trash* on TV!
	ugly ['ʌgli]	hässlich	*ugly* ↔ beautiful

Across cultures 3 School life – dos and don'ts

1	**corridor** ['kɒrɪdɔ:]	Gang; Flur; Korridor	
	gym(nasium) [dʒɪm; dʒɪm'neɪziəm]	Turnhalle	= the room in a school where PE lessons often take place
	lab(oratory) [læb; lə'bɒrətri]	Labor	
	cell phone *(AE)* ['selfəʊn]	Mobiltelefon; Handy	If you can't reach him at home, try him on his *cell phone*.
	to **skip** [skɪp]	auslassen; schwänzen	The girls decided to *skip* class after lunch. Bad idea! That always means trouble.
	to **cheat** [tʃi:t]	mogeln; betrügen	She *cheated* on the test, so she had to repeat it. She's *cheating* on her boyfriend. = She's going out with sb else, but her boyfriend doesn't know.
	to **get caught** [ˌget 'kɔ:t]	erwischt werden; ertappt werden	She *got caught* by the teacher while she was cheating on a test.
	principal *(AE)* ['prɪnsɪpl]	Schulleiter/-in	= the boss of a school in the US
	to **be suspended** [bi sə'spendɪd]	suspendiert werden; zeitweilig vom Unterricht ausgeschlossen werden	One of my classmates *was suspended* for two weeks for skipping class so often.
	detention [dɪ'tenʃn]	Nachsitzen; Haft; Verhaftung	The whole class got *detention* today.
2	**lunchtime** ['lʌnʃtaɪm]	Mittagszeit; Mittagspause	At *lunchtime* the students eat in the cafeteria.
	to **complete** [kəm'pli:t]	fertigstellen; vervollständigen; vollenden	After ten years the director finally *completed* his epic, 3-hour film.

	consequence ['kɒnsɪkwəns]	Konsequenz; Folge	
	otherwise ['ʌðəwaɪz]	sonst	I have to do my homework now. *Otherwise* I won't be able to go to the mall later.
3	to **stand in line** *(AE)* [ˌstænd‿ɪn 'laɪn]	anstehen; Schlange stehen; (sich) anstellen	In the US, you'll be unpopular very quicklyif you don't *stand in line*. 
	to **switch off** [ˌswɪtʃ‿'ɒf]	ausschalten	*to switch off* = to turn off
5	to **be about to do sth** [bi‿ə'baʊt tə]	im Begriff sein, etw. zu tun	Can you help me with my presentation? – I'*m about to go* shopping; I'll help you later.
	to **get into trouble** [ˌget‿ɪntə 'trʌbl]	in Schwierigkeiten geraten	
	so (that) [ˌsəʊ 'ðæt]	damit; so dass	Some students fake hall passes *so that* they can skip classes.
	cheat sheet ['tʃi:t ʃi:t]	Spickzettel	I've never used a *cheat sheet* in my life!
	You'd better ... *(= You had better)* ['ju:d ˌbetə]	Du solltest lieber ...	It's late. *I'd better* go home.
	If I were you ... [ˌɪf aɪ wɜ: 'ju:]	Wenn ich du wäre ...	*If I were you*, I wouldn't say a word to my parents.
	No risk, no fun! [nəʊ ˌrɪsk nəʊ 'fʌn]	Wer nicht wagt, der nicht gewinnt.	You never take any risks. *No risk, no fun!*
	mad [mæd]	wütend	He's *mad* at me. = He's angry with me.
	I can't see the point of ... [aɪ ˌkɑ:nt si: ðə 'pɔɪnt‿əv]	Ich sehe keinen Sinn darin ...	*I can't see the point of* talking to the teacher. He won't change his mind.
	waste [weɪst]	Verschwendung	It's a *waste* of time telling him what to do. He'll never change!

Unit 3 City of dreams: New York

Introduction

	intersection [ˌɪntə'sekʃn]	Kreuzung	= where two or more roads meet
	district ['dɪstrɪkt]	Distrikt; Bezirk	! Be careful with the word stress.
	lung [lʌŋ]	Lunge	*Lungs* need fresh air.
1	**a pocketful of** [ə 'pɒkɪtfl‿əv]	Unmengen von/an	*a pocketful of* = a lot of
	gonna (= going to) *(coll)* ['gɒnə]	wird/werden	! *Gonna* is often used in conversations and in songs.
	to **make it** ['meɪk‿ɪt]	es schaffen	If I can *make it* here, I can *make it* anywhere.
	by any means [baɪ‿enɪ 'mi:nz]	mit allen Mitteln	I'm going to make it in show business *by any means*, I don't care how!
	to **inspire** [ɪn'spaɪə]	inspirieren; anregen	= to give the idea for sth (e.g. a poem or a song)

melting pot ['meltɪŋ ˌpɒt]	Schmelztiegel	= a place where people from different origins come together to live and form a new culture
jungle ['dʒʌŋgl]	Dschungel	A lot of people call New York a 'concrete *jungle*'.

Station 1: Saving the best for last

to **save the best for last** [ˌseɪv ðə ˌbest fə 'lɑ:st]	sich das Beste bis zum Schluss aufheben	
to **take the day off** [ˌteɪk ðə ˌdeɪ‿'ɒf]	sich den Tag freinehmen	Diego isn't working. He's *taken the day off*.
diner *(AE)* ['daɪnə]	einfaches Restaurant mit Theke und Tischen	I have breakfast in the *diner* around the corner every morning before I go to work.
conference ['kɒnfrns]	Konferenz; Tagung	*Fr.* conférence *(f)*
guidebook ['gaɪdbʊk]	Reiseführer	In a *guidebook* you can find all the important sights of a city.
to **gasp** [gɑ:sp]	tief Luft holen; keuchen	"Oh no! That's terrible!" she *gasped*.
classical ['klæsɪkl]	klassisch	
bank [bæŋk]	Bank	! *bank* (Geldinstitut) ≠ *bench* (Bank zum Sitzen).
sculpture ['skʌlptʃə]	Skulptur	! Be careful with the pronunciation.
since [sɪns]	da	! '*Since*' has two meanings: – *since* I was little = seit … – *since* it's too late = da …
naked ['neɪkɪd]	nackt	! Be careful with the pronunciation: two syllables!
for free [fə 'fri:]	umsonst; kostenlos	
on a shoestring [ˌɒn‿ə 'ʃu:strɪŋ]	für/mit wenig Geld	Living *on a shoestring* isn't easy in an expensive city like New York.
to **time** [taɪm]	den richtigen Zeitpunkt wählen	If we *time* it right, we'll be at the Empire State Building before it closes.
block [blɒk]	Block; Häuserblock	= an area of land (in a town) with streets on all sides
enthusiasm [ɪn'θju:ziæzm]	Enthusiasmus; Begeisterung	He talks about his city with so much *enthusiasm*!
just in time [ˌdʒʌst‿ɪn 'taɪm]	gerade rechtzeitig	I got to the airport *just in time*. People were already getting on the plane.
sunset ['sʌnset]	Sonnenuntergang	
to **sneak** [sni:k], **snuck** [snʌk], **snuck** [snʌk]	schleichen; schmuggeln	He *snuck* into his bedroom quietly; his parents never knew he'd been gone.
service ['sɜ:vɪs]	Service; Dienstleistung; Dienst	*Fr.* service *(m)*; *Lat.* servitium *(nt)*
Leave that to me. [ˌli:v ðæt tə 'mi:]	Überlass das mir.	Oh no, what are we going to do? – *Leave that to me*. I always know what to do.
bright [braɪt]	hell; leuchtend; strahlend	In the summer, the sun is very *bright*.
2 **tour company** ['tʊə ˌkʌmpəni]	Reiseanbieter	I like *tour companies* that offer unusual tours.
3 to **be located** [bi ləʊ'keɪtɪd]	gelegen sein; liegen	Where *is* the museum *located*? = Where exactly is the museum? *to be located in* → location *(n)*

4	**subway** *(AE)* ['sʌbweɪ]	U-Bahn	
	to **groan** [grəʊn]	stöhnen	= a sound that shows you're hurt, unhappy or disappointed
6	**statue** ['stætʃu:]	Statue; Standbild	Oh look, that's not a *statue*; it's a man!
	liberty ['lɪbəti]	Freiheit	*Fr.* liberté *(f)*
	artist ['ɑ:tɪst]	Künstler/-in	*artist* → art
	tablet ['tæblət]	Tafel	The Statue of Liberty is holding a torch and a *tablet*.
	spike [spaɪk]	Spitze; Stachel	The Statue of Liberty's crown has seven *spikes*.
	to **base on** ['beɪs‿ɒn]	stützen auf	The character in the story is *based on* a real person.
	goddess ['gɒdes]	Göttin	What's the name of the Roman *goddess* of liberty?
	to **be known as** [bi 'nəʊn‿əz]	bekannt sein als	
	enlightenment [ɪn'laɪtnmənt]	Aufklärung; Erleuchtung	The Statue of Liberty's torch stands for *enlightenment*.
8	**ethnic** ['eθnɪk]	ethnisch; Volks-; *hier:* exotisch	What's your *ethnic* background? – I'm half German and half Spanish.
	from the outside [ˌfrəm ði‿aʊt'saɪd]	von außen	*From the outside*, the restaurant doesn't look very nice.
	delicious [dɪ'lɪʃəs]	köstlich	Mmm, this cake is *delicious*.
	fried [fraɪd]	gebraten *(in der Pfanne)*	*Fried* food is delicious – but you mustn't eat too much of it.
	pastry ['peɪstri]	Teig; Teigtasche	
	filling ['fɪlɪŋ]	Füllung	This pastry has a vegetarian *filling*.
	Jewish ['dʒu:ɪʃ]	jüdisch	A bagel with lox is typical *Jewish* food.
	truck *(AE)* [trʌk]	*hier:* Wagen	Are there any food *trucks* in the area?
	cart [kɑ:t]	Karrenwagen	an ice-cream *cart* 
	New Yorker [ˌnju: 'jɔ:kə]	New Yorker/-in	= a person who is from New York City
	to **combine** [kəm'baɪn]	kombinieren; verbinden	Can you *combine* red and pink?
	flavor *(AE)* ['fleɪvə]	Geschmack; Aroma	Two ice creams, please. – What *flavor*? – One chocolate and one banana.
	specialty *(AE)* ['speʃlti]	Spezialität; Besonderheit	
	combination [ˌkɒmbɪ'neɪʃn]	Kombination; Verbindung	*combination* → to combine
10	**hometown** ['həʊmtaʊn]	Heimatstadt	*hometown* → home
	spot [spɒt]	Fleck; Ort	We found a quiet *spot* in the park and sat down on the grass.

Station 2: Life is a trip

to **lift** [lɪft]	heben; hochheben; anheben	You can really hurt yourself if you try to *lift* something that's too heavy.
trunk *(AE)* [trʌŋk]	Kofferraum	

	to **be done with** [bi 'dʌn wɪð]	fertig sein mit	*I'm done with* you, I don't want to see you again!
	break [breɪk]	Durchbruch	He'd been hoping for his big *break* for five years.
	rejection [rɪ'dʒektʃn]	Ablehnung; Absage	He got one *rejection* after the other.
	to **come true** [ˌkʌm 'tru:]	wahr werden; in Erfüllung gehen	Wouldn't it be wonderful if our dreams always *came true*?
	good luck [ˌgʊd 'lʌk]	(viel) Glück	Emilio wished the man *good luck*.
	sidewalk *(AE)* ['saɪdwɔ:k]	Gehweg; Gehsteig	
	businessman ['bɪznɪsmæn]	Geschäftsmann	The passenger looked like a successful *businessman*.
	not necessarily [ˌnɒt nesə'serəli]	nicht notwendigerweise; nicht unbedingt	Seeing New York on a shoestring is impossible! – That's *not necessarily* true. Central Park, for example, is free.
	however [haʊ'evə]	jedoch	The man had lots of money. *However*, he wasn't happy with his life.
	bill *(AE)* [bɪl]	Geldschein; Rechnung	The suitcase was full of 100$ *bills*. We'd like to pay. Can you bring us the *bill*, please?
	change [tʃeɪndʒ]	Münzgeld; Wechselgeld	That'll be $8.50, please. – Here's $10.00. Keep the *change*.
	to **get in** [ˌget‿'ɪn]	einsteigen	Agree on the price before you *get in* a taxi.
	yet [jet]	doch; und trotzdem; und dennoch	*Yet* is used to add sth that seems surprising after what has been said.
	to **complain** [kəm'pleɪn]	sich beschweren; sich beklagen	My soup was cold, so I *complained*.
	to **shop** [ʃɒp]	einkaufen; shoppen	New York City is a great place to *shop*.
	needless to say [ˌni:dləs tə 'seɪ]	natürlich; selbstverständlich	When we got home, our teenage kids were having a huge, loud party. *Needless to say*, we weren't happy!
	tip [tɪp]	Trinkgeld	In the US, before you leave a café or restaurant, it's normal to leave a *tip* of at least 15%, often 20%.
16	**grade** *(AE)* [greɪd]	Note	! The best *grade* in American schools is A+; the worst is F (there's no E). Some schools use a number system: 4.00 is the best; 0.00 the worst.
18	**busker** ['bʌskə]	Straßenmusikant/-in	= sb who plays music or sings for money in city streets or stations
	to **perform** [pə'fɔ:m]	aufführen; auftreten	If you *perform* a play, you act it in front of people who come to watch it.
	freeway *(AE)* ['fri:weɪ]	Autobahn	
	to **transport** [træn'spɔ:t]	transportieren; befördern	= to take from one place to another *Fr.* transporter
	lorry ['lɒri]	Lastwagen	
19	to **fail to do sth** ['feɪl tə]	versäumen, etw. zu tun; es nicht schaffen, etw. zu tun	A lot of actors *fail to* find success.
	rags to riches [ˌrægz tə‿'rɪtʃɪz]	vom Tellerwäscher zum Millionär	There are lots of Hollywood movies with a *rags to riches* storyline.

to **make a living (from)** [ˌmeɪk‿ə 'lɪvɪŋ frəm]	seinen Lebensunterhalt bestreiten (mit)	She *makes a living* from piano lessons.
either ... or ... ['aɪðə/'i:ðə ... ɔ:]	entweder ... oder ...	You have to decide now: You can have *either* this one *or* that one, but not both.

Story: Asphalt Tribe

3	**panel** ['pænl]	Bild *(eines Comics)*	
	lead-in ['li:dɪn]	Einführung; Einleitung	
	shape [ʃeɪp]	Form	
	sequence ['si:kwəns]	Abfolge; Reihenfolge	The *sequence* of comic panels is very important.
	consecutive [kən'sekjʊtɪv]	aufeinanderfolgend; fortlaufend	The panels here are arranged *consecutively*.
	to **overlap** [ˌəʊvə'læp]	(sich) überlappen	The pictures in the book *overlap*, which I think looks cool.
	to **lay** [leɪ], **laid** [leɪd], **laid** [leɪd]	legen	
	to **make use of** [meɪk 'ju:z‿əv]	benutzen; verwenden	What tricks do they *make use of*?
	long shot ['lɒŋ ʃɒt]	Totale *(Kameraeinstellung)*	Let's use a *long shot* for this scene so we can see everything that's going on.
	medium shot ['mi:diəm ʃɒt]	Halbtotale *(Kameraeinstellung)*	
	medium ['mi:diəm]	mittel; mittelgroß	What size do you wear: small, *medium* or large?
	effect [ɪ'fekt]	Effekt; Wirkung	You should always think of the *effects* of your actions before you do something. *Fr.* effet *(m)*
	stylistic [staɪ'lɪstɪk]	Stil-; stilistisch	*stylistic* → style
	speed [spi:d]	Geschwindigkeit	This movie has a lot of *speed*.

Action USA! New Yorkers don't do things like that!

1	to **cringe** [krɪndʒ]	schaudern; sich ducken	If you *cringe* about sth, you feel very embarrassed by it. Usually, it's what sb else has done.
2	**unexpected** [ˌʌnɪk'spektɪd]	unerwartet	*unexpected* → to expect

Skills: How to conduct a podcast interview

	to **conduct** [kən'dʌkt]	durchführen; ausführen	*to conduct* an interview
1	**path** [pɑ:θ]	Pfad; Weg	Rita's *path* to success was long and hard.
2	**follow-up** ['fɒləʊʌp]	Fortsetzung; Folge-	*follow-up* → to follow → the following
	talk [tɔ:k]	Gespräch; Unterhaltung	*talk* → to talk

Important differences

	AE		BE	
Different spelling	flav**o**r, lab**o**r		flav**ou**r, lab**ou**r	
	special**t**y		special**it**y	
	to reali**z**e		to reali**s**e	
	to practi**c**e		to practi**s**e	
	trave**l**ing		trave**ll**ing	
Different words	bill	sidewalk	note	pavement
	cell phone	subway	mobile phone	underground
	freeway	trash	motorway	rubbish
	grade	truck	class	lorry
	intersection	trunk	crossroad	boot
	period	yard	lesson	garden
	principal		head teacher	

Text smart 3 Internet texts

Introduction

	reliable [rɪ'laɪəbl]	verlässlich; zuverlässig; vertrauenswürdig	He's very *reliable*. He always does what he says he'll do.
1	**inconvenient** [ˌɪnkən'viːniənt]	unbequem; lästig	Hi, can I ask you something? – Er, it's a bit *inconvenient* right now. Later?
	up-to-date [ˌʌptə'deɪt]	modern; zeitgemäß; aktuell	
	tutorial [tjuː'tɔːriəl]	Tutorium; Tutorial	I often watch *tutorials* about cooking on the Internet.
3	**moon landing** ['muːn ˌlændɪŋ]	Mondlandung	
	science [saɪəns]	Wissenschaft; Naturwissenschaft	*science* → scientist *Fr.* science *(f)*; *Lat.* scientia *(f)*
	astronaut ['æstrənɔːt]	Astronaut/-in	
	human ['hjuːmən]	Mensch	Neil Armstrong was the first *human* on the moon.
	to **be considered (to be) sth** [bi kən'sɪdəd tə]	als etw. gelten	Germany *is considered to* be one of the richest countries in the world.

Station 1: An online wiki text

	wiki (text) ['wɪkɪ ˌtekst]	Wikitext	
	mission ['mɪʃn]	Mission; Auftrag	Our *mission* as a team is to win the championship.
	to **touch down** [tʌtʃ 'daʊn]	landen	In 1969 Apollo 11 *touched down* on the moon.
	surface ['sɜːfɪs]	Oberfläche	*Fr.* surface *(f)*
	to **announce** [ə'naʊns]	ankündigen; durchsagen	*to announce* → announcement *Fr.* annoncer; *Lat.* ad + nuntiare
	to **step** [step]	treten; steigen	*to step* → step
	president ['prezɪdnt]	Präsident/-in	! Watch the word stress.
	priority [praɪ'ɒrəti]	Priorität; Vorrang	The moon landing was one of President John F. Kennedy's top *priorities*.
	to **challenge** ['tʃælɪndʒ]	herausfordern	*to challenge* → challenge
	engineer [ˌendʒɪ'nɪə]	Ingenieur/-in; Techniker/-in	
	political [pə'lɪtɪkl]	politisch	Do you like watching TV programs about *political* problems?
5	**hoax** [həʊks]	Täuschung; Trick	Some people say that the moon landing was a *hoax*.
	conspiracy [kən'spɪrəsi]	Verschwörung	Is there a *conspiracy* against the Queen? *Fr.* conspiration *(f)*; *Lat.* conspiratio *(f)*
	theory ['θɪəri]	Theorie	
	to **stage** [steɪdʒ]	inszenieren; aufführen	How difficult would it be to *stage* something like the moon landing?
	the public [ðə 'pʌblɪk]	die Öffentlichkeit	Stars sometimes want to hide from *the public*. *Fr.* public *(m)*; *Lat.* publicum *(nt)*
	to **involve** [ɪn'vɒlv]	involvieren; einbeziehen; beteiligen	If you *involve* sb in sth, you include them, e.g. in a situation or activity.
	cover-up ['kʌvərʌp]	Vertuschung	*cover-up* → to cover
	government ['gʌvnmənt]	Regierung	= a group of people whose job it is to run a country and deal with its problems
6	**complicated** ['kɒmplɪkeɪtɪd]	kompliziert	The rules of this game are too *complicated*!
	impossible [ɪm'pɒsəbl]	unmöglich	*impossible* ↔ possible *Fr.* impossible
	to **make sense** [ˌmeɪk 'sens]	Sinn ergeben; einleuchten	If sth *makes sense*, you can understand it.
	at the time [ˌət ðə 'taɪm]	damals	
	to **run** [rʌn]	betreiben; leiten; führen	My parents *run* a restaurant.
	tech [tek]	Technologie; Technik	The US is famous for its *tech* companies, e.g. in Silicon Valley or Seattle.
7	**respect** [rɪ'spekt]	Respekt	Honest bloggers will enjoy their readers' *respect*.
	entertaining [ˌentə'teɪnɪŋ]	unterhaltsam	*entertaining* ↔ boring
8	**function** ['fʌŋkʃn]	Funktion	Every text has a *function*.
	to **trick** [trɪk]	austricksen; täuschen	*to trick* → trick
	to **estimate** ['estɪmeɪt]	schätzen	I *estimate* her stay in hospital to take a week.

	to question ['kwestʃən]	fragen; hinterfragen	Our trainer always *questions* our motivation.
	critical ['krɪtɪkl]	kritisch	*critical* → self-critical

Station 2: Online ratings

10	to **rate** [reɪt]	bewerten; einstufen	*to rate* → rating
11	**space** [speɪs]	Weltraum; Weltall	There's endless space in *space*.
	space program ['speɪs ˌprəʊgræm]	Raumfahrtprogramm	There's a Mars *space program*, but will there ever really be a human on Mars?
12	**breathtaking** ['breθˌteɪkɪŋ]	atemberaubend	The visuals in the movie were *breathtaking*.
	well-written [ˌwel'rɪtn]	gut geschrieben	I think the story is *well-written*.
	disappointing [ˌdɪsə'pɔɪntɪŋ]	enttäuschend	How was the movie? – It was very *disappointing*. A waste of time!
14	**special effect** [ˌspeʃl‿ɪ'fekt]	Spezialeffekt	In action movies the *special effects* are often as important as the story.
	well-developed [ˌweldɪ'veləpt]	gut entwickelt; ausgereift	You know a character is *well-developed* when he/she seems believable, like sb you know.
	undeveloped [ˌʌndɪ'veləpt]	unentwickelt; unausgereift	*undeveloped* ↔ well-developed
	badly-written [ˌbædli'rɪtn]	schlecht geschrieben	*badly-written* ↔ well-written
	weak [wiːk]	schwach	*weak* ↔ strong

How words can start or end

You can use prefixes and suffixes to make new words from the same word family.

adjectives

in-	direct, convenient, secure	help, hope, thank, use	**-ful**
im-	possible	help, end, use	**-less**
ir-	regular	health, luck, cloud	**-y**
un-	expected, developed, realistic		
dis-	honest		

verbs

dis-	appear, agree, obey
re-	build, read, tell, write
un-	wrap, pack
mis-	behave, understand

! Be careful with the pronunciation:
In English, you don't put the stress on the prefix.
honest – dishonest

nouns

re-	action, discovery	interview, report, sing	**-er**
ex-	change	champion, friend, relation	**-ship**
in-	dependence	surf, swim(m)	**-ing**
		invent, narrat(e), surviv(e)	**-or**
		demonstrat(e), organiz(e)	**-ion/-ation**
		settle, improve	**-ment**

Write sentences with one word from each group.

Across cultures 4 What you say and how you say it

bis hier

register ['redʒɪstə]	Sprachebene; Register	It's important to change your *register* to match the situation you're in. That means you should always use the right language for the right situation.
2 **Canadian** [kə'neɪdiən]	kanadisch; Kanadier/-in	= sb or sth from Canada
to **pronounce** [prə'naʊns]	aussprechen	! Be careful with the spelling: to pron**ou**nce [aʊ] – pron**u**nciation [ʌ]
schedule *(AE)* ['ʃedju:l; 'skedʒu:l]	Stundenplan; Fahrplan; Terminkalender	
though [ðəʊ]	doch; jedoch; obwohl	I tried my best, but I just couldn't win the race. I don't mind *though*. Winning isn't everything.
water fountain ['wɔ:tə ˌfaʊntɪn]	Wasserspender	
4 **informal** [ɪn'fɔ:ml]	informell; zwanglos	*informal* ↔ formal
nope *(infml)* [nəʊp]	nee; nö	= a very informal word for 'no'
It sucks. *(slang)* [ɪt 'sʌks]	Das ist zum Kotzen.	! Only use this phrase when you talk to your friends.
ain't (= isn't/aren't) [eɪnt]	ist nicht; sind nicht	! It isn't good English to use *ain't*, but one hears it quite often. It's typical to use it in ‚double negative' sentences which are incorrect grammar: „I'm not doing anything for her!" → „I *ain't* doing nothing for her!"
totally ['təʊtli]	völlig; total	*totally* = completely
whatever [wɒt'evə]	was/wie auch immer; egal (was/welche)	
no more [ˌnəʊ 'mɔ:]	nicht mehr	*no more* = not anymore
(I) didn't mean to ... [aɪ ˌdɪdnt 'mi:n tə]	Ich wollte nicht ...	Sorry! *I didn't mean to* be rude.
auntie ['ɑ:nti]	Tantchen	
not ... either [nɒt ... 'aɪðə; nɒt ... 'i:ðə]	auch nicht	He doesn't like her. She does*n't* like him *either*.
to **mind sth** [maɪnd]	auf etw. aufpassen	*Mind* your language: Don't be rude.

Dictionary

In dieser alphabetischen Wortliste findest du das gesamte Vokabular von *Green Line* 1, 2, 3 und 4.
Namen stehen in einer extra Liste am Ende des *Dictionary*.
Einträge, die aus mehreren Wörtern bestehen, kannst du meist unter verschiedenen Stichwörtern nachschlagen. So ist z.B. *after all* unter *after* und unter *all* eingetragen.
Die Fundstellen stehen immer hinter dem jeweiligen Wort und zeigen dir an, wo es zum ersten Mal vorkommt, z. B.:
air-conditioning [ˌeəkən'dɪʃnɪŋ] Klimaanlage **IV U1,** 17 kommt zum ersten Mal vor in Band 4, Unit 1, Seite 17
advertising *(no pl)* ['ædvətaɪzɪŋ] Werbung; Reklame **IVTS2**, 64 kommt zum ersten Mal vor in Band 4, Text smart 2, Seite 64
U = Unit, AC = Across cultures, TS = Text smart
Die mit * gekennzeichneten Verben sind unregelmäßig.
Die mit ° gekennzeichneten Vokabeln sind rezeptiv.
Die mit ⟨ ⟩ gekennzeichneten Vokabeln sind fakultativ.

A

a [ə] ein/-e **I**
a bit [ə 'bɪt] ein bisschen; ein wenig **II**
a couple of [ə 'kʌpl‿əv] ein paar **I**
a few [ə 'fju:] ein paar; wenige; einige **I**
a girl from Germany [ə ˌgɜ:l frəm 'dʒɜ:məni] ein Mädchen aus Deutschland **I**
a group of three [ə ˌgru:p‿əv 'θri:] eine Dreiergruppe **I**
a little [ə 'lɪtl] ein wenig; etwas **I**
a lot [ə 'lɒt] viel **I**
a lot of [ə 'lɒt‿əv] viel/-e; eine Menge **I**
a (day/week/year) [ə 'deɪ/wi:k/jɪə] pro (Tag/Woche/Jahr) **IV AC2**, 39
a lot to learn [ə ˌlɒt tə 'lɜ:n] viel zu lernen **I**
a.m. [ˌeɪ'em] vormittags *(Uhrzeit)* **I**
*to be **able** to (do sth) [bi‿'eɪbl tə] fähig sein zu; können; dürfen **II**
aboard [ə'bɔ:d] an Bord **I**
about [ə'baʊt] ungefähr; circa; etwa **I**
out and **about** [ˌaʊt‿ən‿ə'baʊt] unterwegs **II**
about [ə'baʊt] über; von **I**
*to be **about** to do sth [bi‿ə'baʊt tə] im Begriff sein, etw. zu tun **IV AC3**, 69
What **about** …? ['wɒt‿əbaʊt] Wie wär's mit …?; Was ist mit …? **I**
What is … **about**? [ˌwɒt‿ɪz …‿ə'baʊt] Worum geht es in/im …? **I**
above [ə'bʌv] oben **II**
abroad [ə'brɔ:d] im Ausland; ins Ausland **IV U1**, 10
absolutely [ˌæbsə'lu:tli] absolut; völlig **II**
accent ['æksnt] Akzent **III**
to **accept** [ək'sept] akzeptieren; hinnehmen; annehmen **IV U1**, 16
accident ['æksɪdnt] Unfall **II**
account settings [ə'kaʊnt ˌsetɪŋz] Profileinstellungen **III**
across [ə'krɒs] auf der anderen Seite von; über; hinüber; herüber; quer durch **I**
Across cultures [əˌkrɒs 'kʌltʃəz] Interkulturelles **I**
to **act** [ækt] spielen *(Theater)* **I**; sich verhalten; handeln °**IV AC3**, 68
to **act** like ['ækt laɪk] tun als ob **II**
to **act** out [ækt 'aʊt] nachspielen **II**
acting a scene [ˌæktɪŋ‿ə 'si:n] eine Theaterszene spielen **I**
acting ['æktɪŋ] Schauspielen **III**
action ['ækʃn] Handlung; Action; Aktion **I**
active ['æktɪv] aktiv **III**
activity [æk'tɪvəti] Aktivität **I**
actor ['æktə] Schauspieler **II**
actual ['æktʃuəl] tatsächlich; wirklich; eigentlich °**IV U3**, 92
ad [əd'vɜ:tɪsmənt] Anzeige; Werbespot **IVTS2**, 64
ad copy ['æd ˌkɒpi] Werbetext **IVTS2**, 65
AD (= Anno Domini) [ˌeɪ'di:] nach Christus **III**
to **add** [æd] hinzufügen; ergänzen **I**
addict ['ædɪkt] Süchtige/-r; Abhängige/-r **IV U1**, 10
additional [ə'dɪʃnl] zusätzlich **II**
address [ə'dres] Adresse **I**
adjective ['ædʒɪktɪv] Adjektiv; Eigenschaftswort **II**
adult ['ædʌlt] Erwachsene/-r **II**
adventure [əd'ventʃə] Abenteuer **II**
adverb ['ædvɜ:b] Adverb **II**
advert ['ædvɜ:t] Anzeige; Werbespot **III**
to **advertise** ['ædvətaɪz] Werbung machen; werben; anpreisen; inserieren **IVTS2**, 64
advertisement [əd'vɜ:tɪsmənt] Anzeige; Werbespot **IVTS2**, 64
advertiser ['ædvətaɪzə] Werbefachmann/-frau **IVTS2**, 64
advertising *(no pl)* ['ædvətaɪzɪŋ] Werbung; Reklame **IVTS2**, 64
advice [əd'vaɪs] Rat; Ratschlag **II**
to **afford** [ə'fɔ:d] sich leisten **III**
*to be **afraid** (of) [bi‿ə'freɪd‿əv] (sich) fürchten; Angst haben (vor) **IV U1**, 8
I'm **afraid** … [ˌaɪm‿ə'freɪd] Leider … **IV U2**, 44
after ['ɑ:ftə] nach *(zeitlich)* **I**
after all [ˌɑ:ftər‿'ɔ:l] doch; schließlich; immerhin **I**
after that [ˌɑ:ftə 'ðæt] danach **I**
afternoon [ˌɑ:ftə'nu:n] Nachmittag **I**
this **afternoon** [ðɪs 'ɑ:ftənu:n] heute Nachmittag **II**
afterwards ['ɑ:ftəwədz] danach; hinterher °**IVTS2**, 67
again [ə'gen] wieder; noch einmal; noch mal **I**
over and over **again** [ˌəʊvər‿ən‿əʊvər‿ə'gen] immer wieder **III**
against [ə'genst] gegen **II**
against all odds [əˌgenst‿ɔ:l‿'ɒdz] entgegen allen Erwartungen **III**
age [eɪdʒ] Alter; Zeitalter **III**
Bronze **Age** ['brɒnz eɪdʒ] Bronzezeit *(ca. 2200–800 v. Chr.)* **III**
golden **age** [ˌgəʊldn 'eɪdʒ] goldenes Zeitalter **III**
travel **agency** ['trævl‿ˌeɪdʒnsi] Reisebüro **III**
travel **agent's** ['trævl‿ˌeɪdʒnts] Reisebüro **III**
aggressive [ə'gresɪv] aggressiv **II**
ago [ə'gəʊ] vor *(zeitlich)* **II**
agony aunt ['ægəni‿ˌɑ:nt] Kummerkastentante **II**
to **agree** (on) [ə'gri:] sich einigen (auf) **III**
to **agree** (with) [ə'gri:] einer Meinung sein (mit); zustimmen **II**
ain't (= isn't/aren't) [eɪnt] ist nicht; sind nicht **IV AC4**, 107
air [eə] Luft **III**
air-conditioning [ˌeəkən'dɪʃnɪŋ] Klimaanlage **IV U1**, 17
air-force base ['eəfɔ:s ˌbeɪs] Luftwaffenstützpunkt ⟨**IVTS3**, 102⟩
airport ['eəpɔ:t] Flughafen **II**
aka [ˌeɪkeɪ'eɪ] alias °**IV U3**, 79
alarm clock [ə'lɑ:m ˌklɒk] Wecker **II**
alien ['eɪliən] Außerirdische/-r; außerirdisches Wesen **I**
all [ɔ:l] alle/-s; ganz **I**
after **all** [ˌɑ:ftər‿'ɔ:l] doch; schließlich; immerhin **I**
all alone [ˌɔ:l‿ə'ləʊn] ganz allein ⟨**IVTS3**, 104⟩
all day [ˌɔ:l 'deɪ] den ganzen Tag **II**
all night [ˌɔ:l 'naɪt] die ganze Nacht **I**
all over [ˌɔ:l‿'əʊvə] überall (in) **I**

all the time [ˌɔ:l ðə 'taɪm] die ganze Zeit **II**
at **all** [ət‿'ɔ:l] überhaupt **I**
all of them ['ɔ:l‿əv ˌðem] alle **I**
all of us ['ɔ:l‿əv ˌʌs] wir alle **III**
to pledge **allegiance** [ˌpledʒ‿ə'li:dʒns] Treueschwur leisten ⟨**IV U2**, 49⟩
bowling **alley** ['bəʊlɪŋ‿æli] Bowlingbahn **I**
*to be **allowed** to (do sth) [bi‿ə'laʊd tə] dürfen **II**
almost ['ɔ:lməʊst] fast; beinahe **II**
alone [ə'ləʊn] allein; ohne fremde Hilfe **I**
all **alone** [ˌɔ:l‿ə'ləʊn] ganz allein ⟨**IV TS3**, 104⟩
*to leave sb **alone** [ˌli:v‿ə'ləʊn] jmdn. in Ruhe lassen **IV U2**, 53
along [ə'lɒŋ] entlang **I**
*to sing **along** [ˌsɪŋ‿ə'lɒŋ] mitsingen **III**
along for the ride [əˌlɒŋ fə ðə 'raɪd] mit dabei **IV U2**, 44
alphabet ['ælfəbet] Alphabet **I**
alphabetical [ˌælfə'betɪkl] alphabetisch **II**
already [ɔ:l'redi] schon; bereits **I**
also ['ɔ:lsəʊ] auch **II**
although [ɔ:l'ðəʊ] obwohl **IV U1**, 13
always ['ɔ:lweɪz] immer; ständig **I**
amazed [ə'meɪzd] erstaunt; verblüfft **IV U2**, 52
amazing [ə'meɪzɪŋ] unglaublich; toll; erstaunlich **II**
ambulance ['æmbjələns] Krankenwagen **III**
American [ə'merɪkən] Amerikanisch; amerikanisch; aus Amerika; Amerikaner/-in **II**
Native **American** [ˌneɪtɪv‿ə'merɪkən] Ureinwohner/-in Amerikas; Indianer/-in; indianisch **IV U2**, 45
among [ə'mʌŋ] unter; inmitten **III**
amount (of) [ə'maʊnt] Menge °**IV TS3**, 105
an [ən] ein/-e **I**
to **analyze** *(AE)* ['ænlaɪz] analysieren °**IV U2**, 43
ancient ['eɪnʃnt] alt; altertümlich; antik ⟨**IV TS3**, 102⟩
and [ænd; ənd] und **I**
angel ['eɪndʒl] Engel **IV TS1**, 31
anger *(no pl)* ['æŋgə] Zorn; Wut **III**
angry ['æŋgri] wütend; zornig; verärgert; böse **I**
*to make sb **angry** [meɪk 'æŋgri] jmdn. wütend machen; jmdn. verärgern **III**
animal ['ænɪməl] Tier **I**
animal shelter ['ænɪml ˌʃeltə] Tierheim **III**
ankle ['æŋkl] Fußgelenk; Fußknöchel **II**
to twist your **ankle** [ˌtwɪst jɔ:r‿'æŋkl] sich den Knöchel verrenken **II**
to **announce** [ə'naʊns] ankündigen; durchsagen **IV TS3**, 101
announcement [ə'naʊnsmənt] Ankündigung; Durchsage **III**
anonymous [ən'ɒnɪməs] anonym **II**
another [ə'nʌðə] ein/-e andere/-r/-s; noch ein/-e; ein/-e andere/-r/-s **I**
answer ['ɑ:nsə] Antwort **I**
short **answer** [ˌʃɔ:t‿'ɑ:nsə] Kurzantwort **I**
to **answer** ['ɑ:nsə] antworten; beantworten **I**
to **answer** the phone [ˌɑ:nsə ðə 'fəʊn] einen Anruf entgegennehmen **I**
answering machine ['ɑ:nsrɪŋ məˌʃi:n] Anrufbeantworter **I**
anthem ['ænθəm] Hymne **III**
any ['eni] irgendein/-e/-er; irgendwelche **I**
not **any** more [ˌnɒt‿eni 'mɔ:] nicht mehr **I**
not … **any** [nɒt … eni] kein/-e/-en **I**
not **anymore** *(AE)* [ˌnɒt‿eni'mɔ:] nicht mehr **IV AC2**, 39
anyone else [ˌeniwʌn 'els] jemand anderes **II**
Anything else? [ˌeniθɪŋ‿'els] Sonst noch etwas? **I**
not … **anything** [ˌnɒt 'eniθɪŋ] nichts **I**
anyway ['eniweɪ] trotzdem; jedenfalls; sowieso **II**
anywhere ['eniweə] irgendwo; überall (egal, wo) **II**
just about **anywhere** [ˌdʒʌst‿əˌbaʊt 'eniweə] praktisch überall **IV TS2**, 64
apart from [ə'pɑ:t frəm] abgesehen von; außer **IV U1**, 11
apartment *(AE)* [ə'pɑ:tmənt] Apartment; Wohnung **IV U2**, 43
to **apologise** [ə'pɒlədʒaɪz] sich entschuldigen **III**
app [æp] App **II**
apple ['æpl] Apfel **I**
approach [ə'prəʊtʃ] Herangehensweise; Vorgehensweise; Ansatz; Annäherung **IV TS2**, 66
appropriate [ə'prəʊpriət] angemessen **III**
April ['eɪprəl] April **I**
Arab ['ærəb] arabisch **IV U1**, 20
architect ['ɑ:kɪtekt] Architekt/-in **II**
How **are** you? [ˌhaʊ‿'ɑ: jə] Wie geht es dir?; Wie geht es euch?; Wie geht es Ihnen? **I**
area ['eəriə] Areal; Gebiet; Fläche **II**
run **area** ['rʌn ˌeəriə] Gehege; Auslauf **III**
to **argue** ['ɑ:gju:] argumentieren; streiten **IV U2**, 51
argument ['ɑ:gjəmənt] Auseinandersetzung; Streit; Argument **III**
arm [ɑ:m] Arm **II**
around [ə'raʊnd] um … herum; umher **I**
*to be **around** [ˌbi: ə'raʊnd] da sein; zusammen sein mit **IV U2**, 44
*to find one's way **around** [ˌfaɪnd wʌnz ˌweɪ‿ə'raʊnd] sich zurechtfinden **IV U2**, 46
to turn **around** [ˌtɜ:n‿(ə)'raʊnd] (sich) umdrehen; wenden **II**
to **arrange** [ə'reɪndʒ] arrangieren; anordnen **III**
to **arrest** [ə'rest] festnehmen; verhaften **II**
arrival [ə'raɪvl] Ankunft **IV U1**, 9; Ankommende/-r; Neuzugang **IV TS2**, 66
arrivals hall [ə'raɪvlz ˌhɔ:l] Ankunftshalle **IV U1**, 9
to **arrive** [ə'raɪv] ankommen **III**
arrow ['ærəʊ] Pfeil **III**
Art [ɑ:t] Kunstunterricht **I**
art [ɑ:t] Kunst **II**
article ['ɑ:tɪkl] Artikel; Bericht *(in einer Zeitschrift, Zeitung)* **II**
reference **article** ['refrns ˌɑ:tɪkl] Referenzartikel **III**
artist ['ɑ:tɪst] Künstler/-in **IV U3**, 74
as [æz; əz] als **II**
as if [əz‿'ɪf] als ob **III**
as … **as** [əz … əz] so … wie **I**
as [æz] während; indem **I**; wie **II**
as long **as** [əz 'lɒŋ‿əz] solange ⟨**IV TS1**, 34⟩
as soon **as** [əz 'su:n‿əz] sobald **II**
to **ask** [ɑ:sk] fragen; bitten **I**
Ask about … ['ɑ:sk‿əˌbaʊt] Frage/Fragt nach … **I**
to **ask** for ['ɑ:sk fə] fragen nach; bitten um **I**
*to be **asleep** [ˌbi ə'sli:p] schlafen **II**
*to fall **asleep** [ˌfɔ:l‿ə'sli:p] einschlafen **I**
aspect ['æspekt] Aspekt; Gesichtspunkt °**IV U2**, 42
asphalt ['æsfælt] Asphalt ⟨**IV U3**, 80⟩
assembly [ə'sembli] Versammlung; Morgenappell **II**
assistant [ə'sɪstnt] Assistent/-in; Verkäufer/-in **II**
astronaut ['æstrənɔ:t] Astronaut/-in **IV TS3**, 100
at [æt; ət] in; auf; bei; an; um *(bei Uhrzeitangaben)* **I**
at 7:30 [ət ˌsevn‿'θɜ:ti] um halb acht **I**
at all [ət‿'ɔ:l] überhaupt **I**
at first [ət 'fɜ:st] zuerst; zunächst **II**
at home [ət 'həʊm] zu Hause **I**
at last [ət 'lɑ:st] endlich; schließlich **I**
at least [ət 'li:st] mindestens; wenigstens **II**
at the back of [ət ðə 'bæk‿əv] hinten; am Ende; im hinteren Teil **II**
at the moment [ət ðə 'məʊmənt] im Moment; gerade **I**
at the same time [ət ðə ˌseɪm 'taɪm] zur selben Zeit; gleichzeitig **I**
at the time [ˌət ðə 'taɪm] damals **IV TS3**, 102
at the weekend [ət ðə ˌwi:k'end] am Wochenende **I**
athletics *(no pl)* [æθ'letɪks] Leichtathletik **IV U1**, 10
atlas ['ætləs] Atlas **II**
atmosphere ['ætməsfɪə] Atmosphäre; Stimmung **II**
to **attack** [ə'tæk] angreifen **III**
flight **attendant** ['flaɪt‿əˌtendnt] Flugbegleiter/-in **IV U1**, 9
attention [ə'tenʃn] Aufmerksamkeit; Beachtung **II**
*to pay **attention** to sb/sth [ˌpeɪ‿ə'tenʃn tʊ] jmdn./etw. beachten **III**
attic ['ætɪk] Dachboden **II**

attitude ['ætɪtju:d] Haltung; Einstellung **IV U2**, 55
to **attract** [ə'trækt] anziehen **IV TS2**, 66
attraction [ə'trækʃn] Attraktion; Sehenswürdigkeit **II**
attractive [ə'træktɪv] attraktiv **IV U2**, 55
audience ['ɔ:diəns] Publikum **II**
audio ['ɔ:diəʊ] Audio-; Hör- **I**
  audio tour ['ɔ:diəʊ ˌtʊə] Audioführung **II**
audio-visual effect [ˌɔ:diəʊvɪʒuəl ɪ'fekt] audiovisueller Effekt **II**
audition [ɔ:'dɪʃn] Vorsprechen; Vorsingen; Vortanzen **III**
August ['ɔ:gəst] August **I**
aunt [ɑ:nt] Tante **I**
  agony **aunt** ['ægəni‿ɑ:nt] Kummerkastentante **II**
auntie ['ɑ:nti] Tantchen **IV AC4**, 107
Australian [ɒs'treɪliən] australisch; Australier/-in **III**
author ['ɔ:θə] Autor/-in **III**
available [ə'veɪləbl] erhältlich; verfügbar **IV TS2**, 65
to **avoid** [ə'vɔɪd] vermeiden; meiden; aus dem Weg gehen **III**
to stay **awake** [ˌsteɪ‿ə'weɪk] wach bleiben ⟨**IV U3**, 90⟩
award [ə'wɔ:d] Auszeichnung; Preis **II**
to be **aware** of sth [bi‿ə'weər‿əv] sich etw. bewusst sein °**IV TS2**, 65
away [ə'weɪ] weg **I**
  *to give **away** [ˌgɪv‿ə'weɪ] verteilen; verschenken **IV TS2**, 64; verraten; preisgeben °**IV U3**, 93
  right **away** [ˌraɪt‿ə'weɪ] sofort; gleich **I**
  *to run **away** [ˌrʌn‿ə'weɪ] wegrennen **I**
  straight **away** [ˌstreɪt‿ə'weɪ] sofort; gleich **III**
  *to throw **away** [ˌθrəʊ‿ə'weɪ] wegwerfen **I**
awesome ['ɔ:səm] super; spitze **IV AC2**, 41
awful ['ɔ:fl] schrecklich; furchtbar **I**
axe [æks] Axt **III**

B

baby ['beɪbi] Baby; Säugling **I**
back [bæk] Rückseite; Rücken **III**
  at the **back** of [ət ðə 'bæk‿əv] hinten; am Ende; im hinteren Teil **II**
  back to **back** [ˌbæk tʊ 'bæk] Rücken an Rücken **I**
to **back** down [ˌbæk 'daʊn] einen Rückzieher machen ⟨**IV TS1**, 32⟩
back [bæk] zurück **I**
back then [bæk 'ðen] damals **III**
*to go right **back** to [ˌgəʊ raɪt 'bæk tə] zurückgehen auf **III**
to turn **back** [tɜ:n 'bæk] umkehren; zurückgehen **II**
backache ['bækeɪk] Rückenschmerzen; Rückenweh **II**
background ['bækgraʊnd] Hintergrund **I**
backing ['bækɪŋ] Hintergrund-; Background- **III**
  backing dancer ['bækɪŋ ˌdɑ:nsə] Backgroundtänzer/-in **III**
backpack ['bækpæk] Rucksack **III**
backyard [ˌbæk'jɑ:d] Garten; Hinterhof **III**
bacon ['beɪkn] Schinkenspeck; Speck **I**
bad [bæd] schlecht; böse; schlimm *(ugs.)* **I**
  Too **bad**! [ˌtu: 'bæd] Zu dumm!; Schade! **I**
badly-written [ˌbædli'rɪtn] schlecht geschrieben **IV TS3**, 105
badminton ['bædmɪntən] Badminton **I**
bag [bæg] Tasche; Tüte **I**
  tea **bag** ['ti: bæg] Teebeutel **III**
bagel ['beɪgl] Bagel *(weiches, ringförmiges Brötchen)* ⟨**IV U3**, 75⟩
bagpipes *(pl)* ['bægpaɪps] Dudelsack **III**
baked beans *(pl)* [ˌbeɪkt 'bi:nz] weiße Bohnen in Tomatensoße **I**
ball [bɔ:l] Ball **I**
  *to keep the **ball** bouncing [ˌki:p ðə bɔ:l 'baʊntsɪŋ] *hier:* das Gespräch am Laufen halten **III**
to **ban** [bæn] bannen; verbieten; sperren **III**
banana [bə'nɑ:nə] Banane **I**
band [bænd] Band; Musikgruppe **III**
Bang! [bæŋ] Peng! **II**
bank [bæŋk] Ufer **II**; Bank **IV U3**, 72
  word **bank** ['wɜ:d ˌbæŋk] Wortsammlung **III**
chocolate **bar** ['tʃɒklət ˌbɑ:] Schokoriegel **IV TS2**, 64
snack **bar** ['snæk ˌbɑ:] Café; Imbissstube **I**
barbed wire [ˌbɑ:bd 'waɪə] Stacheldraht ⟨**IV U3**, 90⟩
bare [beə] nackt; bloß **III**
bargain ['bɑ:gɪn] Schnäppchen **I**
to **bark** [bɑ:k] bellen **I**
air-force **base** ['eəfɔ:s ˌbeɪs] Luftwaffenstützpunkt ⟨**IV TS3**, 102⟩
to **base** on ['beɪs‿ɒn] stützen auf **IV U3**, 74
baseball ['beɪsbɔ:l] Baseball **IV U2**, 46
based on ['beɪst‿ɒn] basierend auf; beruhend auf °**IV AC2**, 40
basic ['beɪsɪk] grundlegend; Grund- **II**
basics *(pl)* ['beɪsɪks] Grundlagen **III**
basketball ['bɑ:skɪtbɔ:l] Basketball **I**
bath [bɑ:θ] Bad; Badewanne **I**
baths *(pl)* [bɑ:θs] Badehaus; Therme **III**
bathroom ['bɑ:θrʊm] Bad; Badezimmer **I**
battery ['bætri] Batterie; Akku **II**
battle ['bætl] Schlacht; Kampf **III**
BC (= before Christ) [ˌbi:'si:] vor Christus **III**
*to **be** [bi:] sein **I**
  *to **be** able to (do sth) [bi‿'eɪbl tə] fähig sein zu; können; dürfen **II**
  *to **be** about [bi:‿ə'baʊt] sich handeln um **I**
  *to **be** about to do sth [bi‿ə'baʊt tə] im Begriff sein, etw. zu tun **IV AC3**, 69
  *to **be** afraid (of) [bi‿ə'freɪd‿əv] (sich) fürchten; Angst haben (vor) **IV U1**, 8
  *to **be** allowed to (do sth) [bi‿ə'laʊd tə] dürfen **II**
  *to **be** around [ˌbi: ə'raʊnd] da sein; zusammen sein mit **IV U2**, 44
  *to **be** asleep [ˌbi ə'sli:p] schlafen **II**
  to **be** aware of sth [bi‿ə'weər‿əv] sich etw. bewusst sein °**IV TS2**, 65
  *to **be** born [bi 'bɔ:n] geboren werden **III**
  *to **be** called [bi 'kɔ:ld] heißen; genannt werden **III**
  *to **be** called to do sth [bi 'kɔ:ld tə du:] auserwählt sein, etw. zu tun **III**
  *to **be** connected [bi kə'nektɪd] zusammenhängen; in Zusammenhang stehen **II**
  *to **be** considered (to be) sth [bi kən'sɪdəd tə] als etw. gelten **IV TS3**, 100
  *to **be** crazy about [bi 'kreɪzi‿əbaʊt] verrückt sein nach; abfahren auf **IV U2**, 47
  *to **be** done with [bi 'dʌn wɪð] fertig sein mit **IV U3**, 76
  *to **be** fed up (with) [bi fed‿'ʌp wɪð] sauer sein (auf); die Nase voll haben (von) **III**
  *to **be** gone [bi: 'gɒn] verschwunden sein; weg sein **II**
  *to **be** good at [bi: 'gʊd‿ət] gut sein in **I**
  *to **be** grounded [bi 'graʊndɪd] Hausarrest haben **III**
  *to **be** hard on sb [bi 'hɑ:d‿ɒn] streng mit jmdm. sein **III**
  *to **be** homesick [bi 'həʊmsɪk] Heimweh haben **IV U1**, 18
  *to **be** in [bi‿'ɪn] dabei sein; mitmachen **II**
  *to **be** in charge (of) [bi‿ɪn 'tʃɑ:dʒ‿əv] die Verantwortung tragen (für); zuständig sein (für) **III**
  *to **be** in sb's shoes [ˌbi: ɪn sʌmbɒdɪz 'ʃu:z] an jmds. Stelle sein; in jmds. Haut stecken **III**
  *to **be** in the way [bi:‿ɪn ðə 'weɪ] im Weg sein/stehen **I**
  *to **be** interested in [bi‿'ɪntrəstɪd‿ɪn] interessiert sein an; sich interessieren für **II**
  *to **be** into [bi:‿'ɪntə] mögen; stehen auf **I**
  *to **be** jealous (of) [bi: 'dʒeləs] eifersüchtig sein (auf); neidisch sein (auf) **I**
  *to **be** known as [bi 'nəʊn‿əz] bekannt sein als **IV U3**, 74
  *to **be** late [bi: 'leɪt] zu spät dran sein; zu spät kommen **I**
  *to **be** like [bi 'laɪk] sein **III**
  *to **be** located [bi ləʊ'keɪtɪd] gelegen sein; liegen **IV U3**, 73
  *to **be** lucky [bi‿'lʌki] Glück haben **II**
  *to **be** made of [bi 'meɪd‿əv] bestehen aus **III**
  *to **be** on [bi‿'ɒn] an sein; laufen **II**
  *to **be** on fire [ˌbi:‿ɒn 'faɪə] brennen **III**
  *to **be** right [bi 'raɪt] recht haben **I**
  *to **be** scared (of) [bi: 'skeəd‿əv] Angst haben (vor) **I**
  *to **be** set (in) [bi 'set ɪn] spielen (in); seinen Schauplatz haben (in) **IV U1**, 19

*to **be** sick [bi 'sɪk] sich übergeben **IV U1**, 16
*to **be** sorry [bi: 'sɒri] leid tun **I**
*to **be** stressed out [bi ˌstrest‿'aʊt] völlig gestresst sein **III**
*to **be** surprised [bi sə'praɪzd] überrascht sein **II**
*to **be** suspended [bi sə'spendɪd] suspendiert werden; zeitweilig vom Unterricht ausgeschlossen werden **IV AC3**, 68
*to **be** tired of [bi 'taɪəd‿əv] es müde sein (zu); es leid sein (zu); es satt haben (zu) **IV U2**, 46
*to **be** trapped [bi 'træpt] eingeschlossen sein; in der Falle sitzen **III**
*to **be** unlucky [bi:‿ʌn'lʌki] Pech haben **I**
*to **be** up to [bi‿'ʌp tə] vorhaben **II**
*to **be** used to *(+ -ing)* [bi 'ju:s‿tə] gewöhnt sein an; gewohnt sein **III**
*to **be** walled in [ˌbi wɔ:ld‿'ɪn] von Wänden eingeschlossen sein ⟨**IV U3**, 90⟩
*to **be** worried [bi 'wʌrid] beunruhigt sein; besorgt sein **II**
*to **be** worth [bi: 'wɜ:θ] wert sein **I**
*to **be** wrong [bi: 'rɒŋ] unrecht haben; sich irren **I**
Be careful! [bi: 'keəfl] Vorsicht!; Pass/Passt auf! **I**
Be polite. [bi: pə'laɪt] Sei/Seid höflich. **I**
Here you **are**. [ˌhɪə ju‿'ɑ:] Bitte schön. **I**
How **are** you? [ˌhaʊ‿'ɑ: jə] Wie geht es dir?; Wie geht es euch?; Wie geht es Ihnen? **I**
How much **is/are** …? [ˌhaʊ 'mʌtʃ‿ɪz/ɑ:] Wie viel (kostet/kosten) …? **I**
I'**m** from … [ˌaɪm frɒm] Ich bin aus … **I**
Is this how you (do) …? [ɪz 'ðɪs haʊ jʊ ˌdu:] Machst du so …? **I**
beach [bi:tʃ] Strand **II**
baked **beans** *(pl)* [ˌbeɪkt 'bi:nz] weiße Bohnen in Tomatensoße **I**
bear [beə] Bär **II**
*to **beat** [bi:t] schlagen; besiegen **II**
beautiful ['bju:tɪfl] schön; hübsch; wunderbar **II**
because [bɪ'kɒz] weil; da **I**
because of [bɪ'kɒz‿əv] wegen **II**
*to **become** [bɪ'kʌm] werden **II**
*to **become** extinct [bɪˌkʌm‿ɪk'stɪŋkt] aussterben **III**
*to **become** friends [bɪˌkʌm‿'frendz] sich anfreunden; Freundschaft schließen **IV AC2**, 41
bed [bed] Bett **I**
*to go to **bed** [ˌgəʊ tə 'bed] ins Bett gehen **I**
bedroom ['bedrʊm] Schlafzimmer **I**
bee [bi:] Biene **II**
Beefeater ['bi:fˌi:tə] königlicher Leibgardist **II**
before [bɪ'fɔ:] schon einmal; vorher; zuvor **II**
before [bɪ'fɔ:] vor *(zeitlich)*; bevor **I**
*to **begin** [bɪ'gɪn] beginnen; anfangen **II**
beginning [bɪ'gɪnɪŋ] Anfang; Beginn **II**
to **behave** [bɪ'heɪv] sich benehmen; sich verhalten **III**
behavior *(no pl) (AE)* [bɪ'heɪvjə] Verhalten; Benehmen; Betragen **IV AC3**, 69
behaviour *(no pl)* [bɪ'heɪvjə] Verhalten; Benehmen; Betragen **IV AC1**, 22
behind [bɪ'haɪnd] hinter **I**
*to leave **behind** [ˌli:v‿bɪ'haɪnd] zurücklassen **III**
believable [bɪ'li:vəbl] glaubwürdig **IV U2**, 52
to **believe** [bɪ'li:v] glauben **I**
He couldn't **believe** his eyes. [hi ˌkʊdnt bɪˌli:v hɪz‿'aɪz] Er traute seinen Augen nicht. **II**
bell [bel] Glocke **II**
saved by the **bell** [ˌseɪvd baɪ ðə 'bel] noch mal Glück gehabt **III**
to **belong** (to) [bɪ'lɒŋ (tə)] gehören (zu) **II**
where I **belong** [ˌweər‿aɪ bɪ'lɒŋ] wo ich hingehöre **IV U1**, 16
below [bɪ'ləʊ] unterhalb; unten **I**
belt [belt] Gürtel **III**
bench [benʃ] Bank; Sitzbank **III**
benefit ['benɪfɪt] Vorteil; Nutzen; Unterstützung **IV U2**, 51
besides [bɪ'saɪdz] neben **III**
(the) **best** [best] (der/die/das) Beste **II**
to save the **best** for last [ˌseɪv ðə ˌbest fə 'lɑ:st] sich das Beste bis zum Schluss aufheben **IV U3**, 72
best [best] beste/-r/-s; am besten **I**
Best wishes [ˌbest 'wɪʃɪz] Viele Grüße; Herzliche Grüße **III**
the **best** … ever ['best … ˌevə] der/die/das beste … überhaupt **III**
I **bet** [aɪ 'bet] ich wette **II**
better ['betə] besser; lieber **I**
You'd **better** … *(= You had better)* ['ju:d ˌbetə] Du solltest lieber … **IV AC3**, 69
between [bɪ'twi:n] zwischen **I**
in **between** [ˌɪn bɪ'twi:n] dazwischen **III**
bicycle motocross [ˌbaɪsɪkl 'məʊtəʊkrɒs] Fahrradmotocross **II**
big [bɪg] groß **I**
big deal [bɪg 'di:l] große Sache **IV U1**, 11
bike [baɪk] Fahrrad **I**
mountain **biking** ['maʊntɪn ˌbaɪkɪŋ] Mountainbikefahren **III**
bilingual [baɪ'lɪŋgwl] zweisprachig **II**
bill *(AE)* [bɪl] Geldschein; Rechnung **IV U3**, 76
billboard ['bɪlbɔ:d] Plakatwand **IV TS2**, 65
billion ['bɪliən] Milliarde **III**
billionaire ['bɪlianeə] Milliardär/-in **IV AC2**, 39
biographical [ˌbaɪəʊ'græfɪkl] biografisch **III**
bird [bɜ:d] Vogel **II**
birdwatching ['bɜ:dˌwɒtʃɪŋ] Vogelbeobachtung **II**
date of **birth** [ˌdeɪt‿əv 'bɜ:θ] Geburtsdatum **IV U1**, 13
birthday ['bɜ:θdeɪ] Geburtstag **I**
Happy **Birthday**! [ˌhæpi 'bɜ:θdeɪ] Alles Gute zum Geburtstag!; Herzlichen Glückwunsch zum Geburtstag! **I**
biscuit ['bɪskɪt] Keks **I**
a **bit** [ə 'bɪt] ein bisschen; ein wenig **II**
bit by **bit** [ˌbɪt baɪ 'bɪt] Stück für Stück **IV TS1**, 35
to **bitch** *(coll)* [bɪtʃ] meckern; sich aufregen über ⟨**IV U3**, 87⟩
*to **bite** [baɪt] beißen **II**
black [blæk] schwarz **I**
*to go **black** [ˌgəʊ 'blæk] schwarz werden **II**
block [blɒk] Block; Häuserblock **IV U3**, 72
building **block** ['bɪldɪŋ blɒk] Baustein **II**
to **block** [blɒk] blockieren; abblocken **II**
blog [blɒg] Blog; Internettagebuch **III**
blogger ['blɒgə] Blogger/-in °**IV TS3**, 102
bloke *(fam)* [bləʊk] Typ *(ugs.)* **III**
blond [blɒnd] blond **III**
blood [blʌd] Blut **III**
*to **blow** out [ˌbləʊ‿'aʊt] ausblasen; auspusten **I**
blue [blu:] blau **I**
blurred [blɜ:d] verschwommen; verwischt **III**
BMX [ˌbi:em'eks] BMX **II**
board [bɔ:d] Brett; Tafel **III**
tourist **board** ['tʊərɪst bɔ:d] Touristeninformation **III**
boarding ['bɔ:dɪŋ] Boarding **IV U1**, 9
boarding card ['bɔ:dɪŋ ˌkɑ:d] Bordkarte **IV U1**, 9
boat [bəʊt] Boot **I**
boating lake ['bəʊtɪŋ ˌleɪk] See zum Rudern **I**
body ['bɒdi] Körper **III**
human **body** [ˌhju:mən 'bɒdi] menschlicher Körper **II**
bodyguard ['bɒdigɑ:d] Bodyguard **IV U2**, 52
bold [bəʊld] fett gedruckt **III**
bonfire ['bɒnfaɪə] Lagerfeuer; Freudenfeuer **I**
book [bʊk] Buch **I**
exercise **book** ['eksəsaɪz ˌbʊk] Übungsheft **I**
to **book** [bʊk] buchen; reservieren **III**
to **boom** [bu:m] dröhnen **III**
boot [bu:t] Stiefel; Kofferraum **III**
bored [bɔ:d] gelangweilt **I**
boring ['bɔ:rɪŋ] langweilig **I**
*to be **born** [bi 'bɔ:n] geboren werden **III**
to **borrow** ['bɒrəʊ] (sich) ausleihen **II**
boss [bɒs] Boss; Chef **III**
bossy ['bɒsi] herrisch; rechthaberisch **III**
both [bəʊθ] beide **II**
to **bother** ['bɒðə] stören; belästigen **IV U1**, 15
bottle ['bɒtl] Flasche **I**
to **bounce** [baʊnts] springen; hüpfen **III**

*to keep the ball **bouncing** [ˌki:p ðə bɔ:l ˈbaʊntsɪŋ] *hier:* das Gespräch am Laufen halten **III**
bowl [bəʊl] Schale; Schälchen; Schüssel **I**
to play **bowls** [ˌpleɪ ˈbəʊlz] Bowling spielen **III**
bowling alley [ˈbəʊlɪŋ‿æli] Bowlingbahn **I**
box [bɒks] Box; Kasten; Schachtel; Kiste **I**
phone **box** [ˈfəʊn ˌbɒks] Telefonzelle **IV U1**, 17
boxing [ˈbɒksɪŋ] Boxen **II**
round of **boxing** [ˌraʊnd‿əv ˈbɒksɪŋ] Boxrunde **II**
boy [bɔɪ] Junge **I**
cabin **boy** [ˈkæbɪn ˌbɔɪ] Schiffsjunge **I**
boyfriend [ˈbɔɪfrend] Freund *(in einer Paarbeziehung)* **IV U2**, 55
bracelet [ˈbreɪslət] Armband **I**
bracket [ˈbrækɪt] Klammer **III**
brain(s) [breɪn] Gehirn; Verstand ⟨**IV U1**, 12⟩
to **brainstorm** [ˈbreɪnstɔ:m] Ideen sammeln °**IV U2**, 57
brand [brænd] Marke **IV TS2**, 64
brand-new [ˌbrænd'nju:] brandneu **IV TS2**, 65
brave [breɪv] mutig; tapfer **I**
bread [bred] Brot **I**
bread roll [ˈbred rəʊl] Brötchen **III**
break [breɪk] Pause **II**; Durchbruch **IV U3**, 76
half-term **break** [ˌhɑ:ftɜ:m ˈbreɪk] Halbjahresferien **I**
lunch **break** [ˈlʌnʃbreɪk] Mittagspause **I**
*to **break** [breɪk] brechen; zerbrechen **I**
broken [ˈbrəʊkn] gebrochen; kaputt **I**
breakfast [ˈbrekfəst] Frühstück **I**
*to have **breakfast** [ˌhæv ˈbrekfəst] frühstücken **I**
breath [breθ] Atem; Atemzug **III**
*to take a **breath** [ˌteɪk‿ə ˈbreθ] Luft holen; Atem holen **III**
Take a deep **breath**. [ˌteɪk‿ə ˌdi:p ˈbreθ] Atme(t) tief ein. **II**
to **breathe** [bri:ð] atmen **II**
breathtaking [ˈbreθˌteɪkɪŋ] atemberaubend **IV TS3**, 104
bridge [brɪdʒ] Brücke **II**
bright [braɪt] hell; leuchtend; strahlend **IV U3**, 72
*to **bring** [brɪŋ] bringen; mitbringen **I**
*to **bring** round [ˌbrɪŋ ˈraʊnd] mitbringen ⟨**IV TS1**, 36⟩
on the **brink** of [ˌɒn ðə ˈbrɪŋk‿əv] am Rande von; kurz vor **III**
Brit [brɪt] Brite/Britin *(ugs.)* **IV AC2**, 41
British [ˈbrɪtɪʃ] britisch; Brite/Britin **I**
brochure [ˈbrəʊʃə] Broschüre; Prospekt **I**
broken [ˈbrəʊkn] gebrochen; kaputt **I**
Bronze Age [ˈbrɒnz eɪdʒ] Bronzezeit *(ca. 2200–800 v. Chr.)* **III**
brother [ˈbrʌðə] Bruder **I**
brown [braʊn] braun **I**
bucket [ˈbʌkɪt] Eimer **II**
*to **build** [bɪld] bauen **II**; aufbauen **III**
building [ˈbɪldɪŋ] Gebäude **I**
building block [ˈbɪldɪŋ blɒk] Baustein **II**
cyber **bully** [ˌsaɪbə ˈbʊli] *jemand, der andere in sozialen Netzwerken belästigt oder mobbed* **II**
*to give the **bumps** [ˌgɪv ðə ˈbʌmps] hochleben lassen **I**
a **bunch** of junk [ə‿bʌnʃ‿əv ˈdʒʌŋk] ein Haufen Müll ⟨**IV U3**, 84⟩
burger [ˈbɜ:gə] Hamburger **I**
*to **burn** [bɜ:n] brennen; verbrennen **III**
*to **burn** down [ˌbɜ:n ˈdaʊn] abbrennen; niederbrennen **III**
bus [bʌs] Bus **I**
bus station [ˈbʌs ˌsteɪʃn] Busbahnhof **I**
bush [bʊʃ] Busch *(Buschlandschaft)*; Wildnis **III**
business [ˈbɪznɪs] Geschäft; Business **III**
businessman [ˈbɪznɪsmæn] Geschäftsmann **IV U3**, 76
busker [ˈbʌskə] Straßenmusikant/-in **IV U3**, 79
busy [ˈbɪzi] belebt; beschäftigt **I**
but [bʌt] aber **I**
butter [ˈbʌtə] Butter **III**
button [ˈbʌtn] Knopf **IV U1**, 17
*to **buy** [baɪ] kaufen **I**
buyer [ˈbaɪə] Käufer/-in **I**
by [baɪ] bei; neben; an; von **III**
by *(bike)* [baɪ] mit *(dem Fahrrad)* **I**
by the river [baɪ ðə ˈrɪvə] am Fluss **II**
by any means [baɪ‿eni ˈmi:nz] mit allen Mitteln **IV U3**, 70
Bye! [baɪ] Tschüss! **II**

C

cabin boy [ˈkæbɪn ˌbɔɪ] Schiffsjunge **I**
cache [kæʃ] Cache **III**
cactus [ˈkæktəs] Kaktus **IV AC2**, 38
café [ˈkæfeɪ] Café **I**
cafeteria [ˌkæfəˈtɪəriə] Cafeteria **I**
cake [keɪk] Kuchen; Torte **I**
calendar [ˈkæləndə] Kalender **III**
(phone) **call** [ˈfəʊn ˌkɔ:l] Anruf; Telefonanruf **I**
to **call** [kɔ:l] nennen; anrufen; rufen **I**
*to be **called** [bi ˈkɔ:ld] heißen; genannt werden **III**
*to be **called** to do sth [bi ˈkɔ:ld tə du:] auserwählt sein, etw. zu tun **III**
caller [ˈkɔ:lə] Anrufer/-in **I**
call-in [ˈkɔ:lɪn] *Sendung, bei der sich das Publikum telefonisch beteiligen kann* **III**
to **calm** down [ˌkɑ:m ˈdaʊn] sich beruhigen **II**
camel racing [ˈkæml ˌreɪsɪŋ] Kamelrennen **II**
camera [ˈkæmrə] Fotoapparat; Kamera **II**
caught on **camera** [ˌkɔ:t‿ɒn ˈkæmrə] ertappt; mit der Kamera festgehalten **II**
summer **camp** [ˈsʌmə kæmp] Sommerferienlager **II**
to **camp** [kæmp] campen; zelten **III**
to **campaign** (for) [kæmˈpeɪn fɔ:] demonstrieren (für); aufmerksam machen (auf); sich engagieren (für) **III**
camping [ˈkæmpɪŋ] Camping; Zelten **II**
can [kæn] Dose; Büchse **I**
tin **can** [ˈtɪn kæn] Blechdose **III**
can [kæn; kən] können; dürfen **I**
can't [kɑ:nt] kann nicht; können nicht **I**
Can you name …? [ˈkæn jʊ ˌneɪm] Kannst du … nennen? **I**
Canadian [kəˈneɪdiən] kanadisch; Kanadier/-in **IV AC4**, 106
candle [ˈkændl] Kerze **I**
candlelight *(no pl)* [ˈkændlaɪt] Kerzenlicht **II**
cannot [ˈkænɒt] kann nicht; können nicht **II**
capital [ˈkæpɪtl] Hauptstadt **II**
capital letter [ˌkæpɪtl ˈletə] Großbuchstabe **I**
capitalistic [ˌkæpɪtlˈɪstɪk] kapitalistisch ⟨**IV U3**, 87⟩
captain [ˈkæptɪn] Kapitän/-in; Mannschaftsführer/-in **I**
caption [ˈkæpʃn] Bildunterschrift; Untertitel **III**
to **capture** [ˈkæptʃə] ergreifen; einfangen **III**
car [kɑ:] Auto **I**
card [kɑ:d] Karte; Spielkarte **I**
boarding **card** [ˈbɔ:dɪŋ ˌkɑ:d] Bordkarte **IV U1**, 9
prompt **card** [ˈprɒmpt kɑ:d] Stichwortkarte; Rollenkarte **II**
*to take **care** of sb [ˌteɪk ˈkeər‿əv] sich um jmdn. kümmern; für jmdn. sorgen **III**
to **care** (about) [ˈkeər‿əˌbaʊt] wichtig nehmen; sich kümmern (um); sich interessieren (für) **II**
career [kəˈrɪə] Beruf; Laufbahn; Karriere **III**
careful [ˈkeəfl] vorsichtig; sorgfältig **II**
Be **careful**! [bi: ˈkeəfl] Vorsicht!; Pass/Passt auf! **I**
carnival [ˈkɑ:nɪvl] Karneval **II**
carpet [ˈkɑ:pɪt] Teppich **II**
carrot [ˈkærət] Karotte; Möhre **I**
to **carry** [ˈkæri] tragen **III**
cart [kɑ:t] Karren **IV U3**, 75
cartoon [kɑ:ˈtu:n] Cartoon; Zeichentrickfilm **III**
cash *(no pl)* [kæʃ] Bargeld ⟨**IV U3**, 84⟩
plaster **cast** [ˈplɑ:stə kɑ:st] Gipsverband **III**
casting [ˈkɑ:stɪŋ] Casting; Rollenbesetzung **IV TS1**, 37
castle [ˈkɑ:sl] Schloss; Burg **II**
cat [kæt] Katze **I**
*to **catch** [kætʃ] fangen **II**; mitbekommen *(ugs.)*; mitkriegen *(ugs.)* **III**; erwischen ⟨**IV U3**, 83⟩
catchy [ˈkætʃi] eingängig; einprägsam **III**
category [ˈkætəgri] Kategorie; Klasse **II**
caught on camera [ˌkɔ:t‿ɒn ˈkæmrə] ertappt; mit der Kamera festgehalten **II**
*to get **caught** [ˌget ˈkɔ:t] erwischt werden; ertappt werden **IV AC3**, 68

to **cause** [kɔ:z] verursachen **II**
cave [keɪv] Höhle **III**
to **celebrate** ['seləbreɪt] feiern **I**
celebration [ˌselə'breɪʃn] Feier ⟨**IV U3**, 90⟩
celebrity [sə'lebrəti] Prominente/-r; berühmte Person **III**
cell [sel] Zelle ⟨**IV U3**, 90⟩
cell phone *(AE)* ['selfəʊn] Mobiltelefon; Handy **IV AC3**, 68
Celt [kelt] Kelte/Keltin **III**
Celtic ['keltɪk; 'seltɪk] keltisch **II**
cent [sent] Cent *(Währung)* **I**
center *(AE)* ['sentə] Zentrum; Center **IV AC2**, 38
central ['sentrl] zentral; Zentral- **II**
centre ['sentə] Zentrum; Center **I**
community **centre** [kə'mju:nəti ˌsentə] Gemeindezentrum **I**
leisure **centre** ['leʒə ˌsentə] Freizeitzentrum **I**
tourist information **centre** [ˌtʊərɪst ɪnfə'meɪʃn ˌsentə] Touristeninformation **I**
century ['senʃri] Jahrhundert **II**
cereal *(no pl)* ['sɪəriəl] Frühstückszerealie; Getreideprodukt *(z. B. Cornflakes oder Müsli)* **I**
chair [tʃeə] Stuhl; Sessel **I**
challenge ['tʃælɪndʒ] Herausforderung **II**
to **challenge** ['tʃælɪndʒ] herausfordern **IV TS3**, 101
champion ['tʃæmpiən] Gewinner/-in; Sieger/-in; Champion **III**
championship ['tʃæmpiənʃɪp] Meisterschaft **IV U2**, 56
chance [tʃɑ:ns] Chance; Gelegenheit; Möglichkeit **II**
change [tʃeɪndʒ] Änderung; Veränderung; Wechsel **III**; Münzgeld; Wechselgeld **IV U3**, 76
to **change** [tʃeɪndʒ] wechseln; (sich) ändern **II**
to **change** one's mind [ˌtʃeɪndʒ wʌnz 'maɪnd] seine Meinung ändern **III**
to **change** (onto) [tʃeɪndʒ ('ɒntʊ)] umsteigen (in) **II**
chant [tʃɑ:nt] Sprechgesang **II**
chaos ['keɪɒs] Chaos; Durcheinander **III**
chapter ['tʃæptə] Kapitel **III**
character ['kærəktə] Charakter; Figur **I**
characteristic [ˌkærəktə'rɪstɪk] typisches Merkmal °**IV TS3**, 103
*to be in **charge** (of) [bi ɪn 'tʃɑ:dʒ əv] die Verantwortung tragen (für); zuständig sein (für) **III**
charity ['tʃærɪti] Wohltätigkeitsverein; wohltätige Zwecke; Wohlfahrt **I**
charity shop ['tʃærɪti ʃɒp] Second-Hand-Laden **I**
lucky **charm** [ˌlʌki 'tʃɑ:m] Glücksbringer; Talisman **I**
to **chase** [tʃeɪs] jagen; nachjagen **I**
chat [tʃæt] Chat **III**
chat room ['tʃæt rʊm] Chatroom **II**
video **chat** ['vɪdiəʊ ˌtʃæt] Videochat **II**
to **chat** [tʃæt] plaudern; chatten *(sich online unterhalten)* **I**
cheap [tʃi:p] billig; preiswert **I**
to **cheat** [tʃi:t] mogeln; betrügen **IV AC3**, 68
cheat sheet ['tʃi:t ʃi:t] Spickzettel **IV AC3**, 69
to **check** [tʃek] überprüfen; prüfen; kontrollieren **I**
to **check** out *(coll)* [ˌtʃek 'aʊt] prüfen; abchecken; auschecken **III**
to **check** with ['tʃek wɪð] nachfragen bei ⟨**IV TS1**, 34⟩
Check-in ['tʃekɪn] Einchecken **I**
checklist ['tʃeklɪst] Checkliste **II**
Check-out ['tʃekaʊt] Auschecken **I**
checkpoint ['tʃekpɔɪnt] Kontrollpunkt **IV U1**, 16
cheer [tʃɪə] Jubel; Hurraruf **IV U2**, 52
to **cheer** [tʃɪə] anfeuern; jubeln; zujubeln **II**
to **cheer** sb up [ˌtʃɪər 'ʌp] jmdn. aufheitern **III**
Cheers! [tʃɪəz] Danke! **III**
cheese [tʃi:z] Käse **I**
chess [tʃes] Schach **II**
chewing gum ['tʃu:ɪŋ ˌgʌm] Kaugummi **IV U1**, 15
chick *(slang)* [tʃɪk] Puppe *(Jargon)*; Mieze *(Jargon)* ⟨**IV U3**, 84⟩
chicken ['tʃɪkɪn] Huhn; Hähnchen **I**
chicken tikka masala [ˌtʃɪkɪn ˌtɪkə mə'sɑ:lə] *indisches Hühnchengericht* **I**
child, **children** *(pl)* ['tʃaɪld; 'tʃɪldrən] Kind **I**
child labor *(AE)* [ˌtʃaɪld 'leɪbə] Kinderarbeit **IV U2**, 48
only **child** ['əʊnli ˌtʃaɪld] Einzelkind **I**
to **chill** out [tʃɪl 'aʊt] chillen **III**
chimney ['tʃɪmni] Kamin; Schornstein **III**
chips *(pl)* *(BE)* [tʃɪps] Pommes frites **I**
chocolate ['tʃɒklət] Schokolade **I**
chocolate bar ['tʃɒklət ˌbɑ:] Schokoriegel **IV TS2**, 64
choice [tʃɔɪs] Wahl; Auswahl **II**
*to **choose** [tʃu:z] auswählen; wählen **II**
chorus ['kɔ:rəs] Refrain **III**
in **chorus** [ɪn 'kɔ:rəs] im Chor **IV TS1**, 33
Christmas ['krɪsməs] Weihnachten **I**
church [tʃɜ:tʃ] Kirche **I**
cinema ['sɪnəmə] Kino **I**
circle ['sɜ:kl] Kreis; Ring **I**
*to go round in **circles** [gəʊ ˌraʊnd ɪn 'sɜ:klz] sich im Kreis drehen **III**
city ['sɪti] Stadt; Großstadt **I**
to **claim** [kleɪm] behaupten °**IV TS3**, 102
to **clap** [klæp] klatschen **I**
Clap your hands. [ˌklæp jɔ: 'hændz] Klatsch/Klatscht in die Hände. **I**
clarification [ˌklærɪfɪ'keɪʃn] Klärung; Klarstellung **IV U1**, 15
class [klɑ:s] Klasse; Schulklasse **I**; *hier:* Unterricht **II**
class display ['klɑ:s dɪˌspleɪ] Ausstellung in der Klasse **I**
class poster ['klɑ:s ˌpəʊstə] Klassenposter **I**
classical ['klæsɪkl] klassisch **IV U3**, 72
classmate ['klɑ:smeɪt] Klassenkamerad/-in; Mitschüler/-in **I**
classroom ['klɑ:srʊm] Klassenzimmer **I**
contact **clause** ['kɒntækt ˌklɔ:z] *Relativsatz ohne Relativpronomen* **II**
defining relative **clause** [dɪˌfaɪnɪŋ 'relətɪv ˌklɔ:z] notwendiger Relativsatz **II**
if-**clause** ['ɪfˌklɔ:z] if-Satz **III**
main **clause** ['meɪn ˌklɔ:z] Hauptsatz **III**
non-defining relative **clause** [ˌnɒndɪfaɪnɪŋ 'relətɪv ˌklɔ:z] nicht notwendiger Relativsatz °**IV U3**, 73
clay pipe ['kleɪ paɪp] Tonpfeife **II**
to **clean** [kli:n] säubern; reinigen **I**
to **clean** out [ˌkli:n 'aʊt] ausräumen; entrümpeln **IV U2**, 51
clean [kli:n] sauber **III**
to **clear** out [ˌklɪər 'aʊt] ausräumen; entrümpeln **I**
clear [klɪə] klar; deutlich **I**
clever ['klevə] schlau; klug **II**
click [klɪk] Klicken; Klick **II**
to **click** on ['klɪk ˌɒn] anklicken **III**
cliff [klɪf] Klippe; Kliff **III**
climate ['klaɪmət] Klima **IV U1**, 18
climax ['klaɪmæks] Höhepunkt **III**
to **climb** [klaɪm] klettern; besteigen; steigen **I**
climbing ['klaɪmɪŋ] Klettern **II**
clique [kli:k] Clique **IV U2**, 48
clock [klɒk] Uhr **I**
alarm **clock** [ə'lɑ:m ˌklɒk] Wecker **II**
o'**clock** [ə'klɒk] Uhr *(Zeitangabe bei vollen Stunden)* **I**
to **clone** [kləʊn] klonen **III**
close [kləʊs] schmaler Durchgang **III**
to **close** [kləʊz] schließen; zumachen **I**
to **close** oneself away from [ˌkləʊz ə'weɪ frəm] sich abschotten von **IV U1**, 16
close [kləʊs] eng; knapp **I**; nahe **II**
Look **closely** … [ˌlʊk 'kləʊsli] Schau(t) genau … **II**
That was **close**! [ˌðæt wəz 'kləʊs] Das war knapp! **I**
closed [kləʊzd] geschlossen; zu **IV U1**, 11
closet ['klɒzɪt] Schrank; Wandschrank **IV U2**, 44
walk-in **closet** [ˌwɔ:kɪn 'klɒzɪt] begehbarer Kleiderschrank **IV U2**, 44
close-up ['kləʊsʌp] Nahaufnahme **II**
clothes *(pl)* [kləʊðz] Kleider; Kleidung **I**
clothing ['kləʊðɪŋ] Kleidung **IV U2**, 51
clothing drive ['kləʊðɪŋ ˌdraɪv] Kleidersammlung **IV U2**, 51
cloud [klaʊd] Wolke **III**
word **cloud** ['wɜ:d ˌklaʊd] Wörterwolke **II**
cloudy ['klaʊdi] bedeckt; bewölkt **II**

clown [klaʊn] Clown **II**
club [klʌb] Klub; Verein; AG **I**
Cooking **Club** ['kʊkɪŋ ˌklʌb] Koch-AG **I**
clue [klu:] Hinweis; Spur **II**
*to have no **clue** [ˌhæv nəʊ 'klu:] keine Ahnung haben **IV AC2**, 41
coach [kəʊtʃ] Trainer/-in **I**; Reisebus **II**
coast [kəʊst] Küste **IV U1**, 10
coastal path [ˌkəʊstl 'pɑ:θ] Küstenweg **III**
coastline ['kəʊstlaɪn] Küste; Küstenverlauf **III**
coconut ['kəʊkənʌt] Kokosnuss **II**
dress **code** ['dres ˌkəʊd] Kleiderordnung; Bekleidungsvorschriften **IV U2**, 43
coffee ['kɒfi] Kaffee **I**
coin [kɔɪn] Münze **I**
coincidence [kəʊ'ɪnsɪdns] Zufall **IV U2**, 52
coke ['kəʊk] Cola **I**
cold [kəʊld] Erkältung **II**; Kälte ⟨**IV U3**, 90⟩
cold [kəʊld] kalt **II**
to **collect** [kə'lekt] sammeln **I**
collection [kə'lekʃn] Kollektion; Sammlung **II**
collocation [ˌkɒlə'keɪʃn] Wortverbindung **II**
colonist ['kɒlənɪst] Siedler/-in; Kolonist/-in **IV AC2**, 41
colony ['kɒləni] Kolonie **II**
colour ['kʌlə] Farbe **I**
What **colour** is …? [ˌwɒt 'kʌlər‿ɪz] Welche Farbe hat …? **I**
colourful ['kʌləfl] farbenfroh; bunt **I**
column ['kɒləm] Spalte **III**
combination [ˌkɒmbɪ'neɪʃn] Kombination; Verbindung **IV U3**, 75
to **combine** [kəm'baɪn] kombinieren; verbinden **IV U3**, 75
*to **come** [kʌm] kommen **I**
*to **come** down [ˌkʌm 'daʊn] herunterkommen **I**
*to **come** in [ˌkʌm‿'ɪn] hereinkommen **III**
*to **come** true [ˌkʌm 'tru:] wahr werden; in Erfüllung gehen **IV U3**, 76
*to **come** up [ˌkʌm‿'ʌp] vorkommen **III**
Come off it! [ˌkʌm‿'ɒf‿ɪt] Komm wieder runter! ⟨**IV U3**, 86⟩
Come on! [ˌkʌm‿'ɒn] Komm schon!; Komm jetzt! **I**
comedian [kə'mi:diən] Komiker/-in; Comedian **II**
comedy ['kɒmədi] Komödie **III**
comedy show ['kɒmədi ˌʃəʊ] Comedy Show **II**
comfortable ['kʌmftəbl] komfortabel; bequem **II**
comic ['kɒmɪk] Comicheft **II**
comma ['kɒmə] Komma °**IV U3**, 73
command [kə'mɑ:nd] Befehl **IV U1**, 9
command module [kə'mɑ:nd ˌmɒdju:l] Kommandokapsel ⟨**IV TS3**, 101⟩
commander [kə'mɑ:ndə] Kommandant/-in ⟨**IV TS3**, 101⟩
comment ['kɒment] Kommentar **II**
to **comment** (on) ['kɒment‿(ɒn)] kommentieren **II**
committee [kə'mɪti] Komitee; Ausschuss **IV U2**, 48
*to have in **common** [ˌhæv‿ɪn 'kɒmən] gemeinsam haben **III**
to **communicate** [kə'mju:nɪkeɪt] kommunizieren; sich verständigen **II**
communication [kəˌmju:nɪ'keɪʃn] Kommunikation **II**
community centre [kə'mju:nəti ˌsentə] Gemeindezentrum **I**
company ['kʌmpəni] Gesellschaft; Firma; Unternehmen **III**
tour **company** ['tʊə ˌkʌmpəni] Reiseanbieter **IV U3**, 73
comparative [kəm'pærətɪv] Komparativ **II**
to **compare** (with/to) [kəm'peə] vergleichen (mit) **I**
comparison [kəm'pærɪsn] Vergleich **II**
to **compete** (with) [kəm'pi:t] konkurrieren (mit); sich messen (mit); in Wettbewerb treten (mit) **III**
competition [ˌkɒmpə'tɪʃn] Wettbewerb; Turnier **II**
competitive [kəm'petɪtɪv] leistungsorientiert; konkurrierend **III**
to **complain** [kəm'pleɪn] sich beschweren; sich beklagen **IV U3**, 76
to **complete** [kəm'pli:t] fertigstellen; vervollständigen; vollenden **IV AC3**, 68
complete [kəm'pli:t] vollständig; komplett; völlig **IV AC2**, 41
completely [kəm'pli:tli] völlig **III**
complicated ['kɒmplɪkeɪtɪd] kompliziert **IV TS3**, 102
compound word ['kɒmpaʊnd wɜ:d] Kompositum *(zusammengesetztes Wort)* **II**
compromise ['kɒmprəmaɪz] Kompromiss **II**
to **compromise** ['kɒmprəmaɪz] Kompromisse eingehen **III**
computer [ˌkəm'pju:tə] Computer **I**
computing power [ˌkəm'pju:tɪŋ ˌpaʊə] Rechenleistung ⟨**IV TS3**, 102⟩
con [kɒn] Argument dagegen **II**
to **concentrate** ['kɒnsntreɪt] (sich) konzentrieren **IV U1**, 17
concert ['kɒnsət] Konzert **IV U2**, 57
concrete ['kɒŋkri:t] Beton **IV U1**, 17
conditional sentence [kənˌdɪʃnl 'sentəns] Bedingungssatz **III**
to **conduct** [kən'dʌkt] durchführen; ausführen **IV U3**, 92
conference ['kɒnfrns] Konferenz; Tagung **IV U3**, 72
confident ['kɒnfɪdnt] selbstsicher; selbstbewusst **II**
confused [kən'fju:zd] verwirrt; wirr; konfus **III**
*to be **connected** [bi kə'nektɪd] zusammenhängen; in Zusammenhang stehen **II**
connection [kə'nekʃn] Verbindung **III**
conscience ['kɒnʃns] Gewissen **IV TS1**, 31
consecutive [kən'sekjʊtɪv] aufeinanderfolgend; fortlaufend **IV U3**, 89
consequence ['kɒnsɪkwəns] Konsequenz; Folge **IV AC3**, 68
*to be **considered** (to be) sth [bi kən'sɪdəd tə] als etw. gelten **IV TS3**, 100
conspiracy [kən'spɪrəsi] Verschwörung **IV TS3**, 102
construction [kən'strʌkʃn] Konstruktion °**IV U2**, 43
contact ['kɒntækt] Kontakt **II**
contact clause ['kɒntækt ˌklɔ:z] *Relativsatz ohne Relativpronomen* **II**
to **contain** [kən'teɪn] enthalten **IV U1**, 15
content ['kɒntent] Inhalt **IV U2**, 56
contest ['kɒntest] Wettkampf; Wettbewerb **I**
continent ['kɒntɪnənt] Kontinent; Erdteil **IV U3**, 74
to **continue** [kən'tɪnju:] fortfahren; andauern; weitermachen **III**; weitergehen **IV U1**, 18
contrast ['kɒntrɑ:st] Kontrast; Unterschied; Gegensatz **IV AC2**, 38
control [kən'trəʊl] Kontrolle **IV U1**, 9
mission **control** [ˌmɪʃn kən'trəʊl] Bodenkontrollzentrum ⟨**IV TS3**, 101⟩
to **control** [kən'trəʊl] kontrollieren; beherrschen ⟨**IV U1**, 12⟩; steuern **IV U2**, 50
conversation [ˌkɒnvə'seɪʃn] Konversation; Gespräch; Unterhaltung **I**
to hog a **conversation** [ˌhɒg‿ə kənvə'seɪʃn] ein Gespräch für sich in Beschlag nehmen; ein Gespräch dominieren **III**
to **convert** [kən'vɜ:t] umwandeln; verwandeln; umsetzen in ⟨**IV U3**, 90⟩
to **convince** [kən'vɪns] überzeugen **II**
convinced [kən'vɪnst] überzeugt **IV TS1**, 31
convincing [kən'vɪnsɪŋ] überzeugend **IV U1**, 21
to **cook** [kʊk] kochen **II**
cooker ['kʊkə] Herd **I**
cooking ['kʊkɪŋ] Kochen **I**
Cooking Club ['kʊkɪŋ ˌklʌb] Koch-AG **I**
*to leave it to **cool** [li:v‿ɪt tə 'ku:l] kalt stellen **I**
cool [ku:l] cool; super **I**; kühl **IV AC2**, 38
cop *(coll)* [kɒp] Polizist/-in *(ugs.)* ⟨**IV U3**, 88⟩
ad **copy** ['æd ˌkɒpi] Werbetext **IV TS2**, 65
to **copy** ['kɒpi] abschreiben; kopieren **I**
corn [kɔ:n] Korn; Mais; Getreide **IV AC2**, 41
corner ['kɔ:nə] Ecke **II**
Cornish ['kɔ:nɪʃ] in Cornwall **III**
Correct … [kə'rekt] Korrigiere/Korrigiert … **I**
correct [kə'rekt] richtig; korrekt **I**
corridor ['kɒrɪdɔ:] Gang; Flur; Korridor **IV AC3**, 68
*to **cost** [kɒst] kosten **I**
costume ['kɒstju:m] Kostüm **I**
cough [kɒf] Husten **II**
could [kʊd] könnte/-n **II**; konnte/-n **III**
to **count** (on) ['kaʊnt‿ɒn] zählen (auf) **I**

country, **countries** *(pl)* ['kʌntri; 'kʌntriz] Land **I**
in the **country** [ˌɪn ðə 'kʌntri] auf dem Land **IV AC2**, 40
countryside ['kʌntrisaɪd] Land **III**
couple ['kʌpl] Paar **III**
a **couple** of [ə 'kʌpl‿əv] ein paar **I**
course [kɔːs] Kurs **II**
of **course** [əv 'kɔːs] natürlich; selbstverständlich **I**
court [kɔːt] Spielfeld **II**
cousin ['kʌzn] Cousin/Cousine **I**
cover ['kʌvə] Cover; Titelblatt **III**
cover version ['kʌvə ˌvɜːʃn] Coverversion **III**
to **cover** ['kʌvə] abdecken; bedecken; zudecken **III**
to **cover** up for sb [ˌkʌvər‿'ʌp fə] jmdn. decken ⟨**IV TS1**, 31⟩
cover-up ['kʌvərʌp] Vertuschung **IV TS3**, 102
cow [kaʊ] Kuh **III**
cowboy ['kaʊbɔɪ] Cowboy; Rinderhirte **IV U3**, 72
crack [kræk] Knacken; Krachen **III**
cracking ['krækɪŋ] knackend; brechend **III**
cramp [kræmp] Krampf **II**
cranberry ['krænbri] Cranberry ⟨**IV U2**, 45⟩
crane [kreɪn] Kran **III**
to **crash** [kræʃ] abstürzen **II**; zusammenstoßen **III**
crazy ['kreɪzi] verrückt **I**
*to be **crazy** about [bi 'kreɪzi‿əbaʊt] verrückt sein nach; abfahren auf **IV U2**, 47
*to go **crazy** [ˌgəʊ 'kreɪzi] ausflippen; durchdrehen; verrückt werden **II**
cream [kriːm] Creme; Sahne **I**
ice **cream** [ˌaɪs 'kriːm] Eis; Eiscreme **I**
to **create** [kri'eɪt] schaffen; erschaffen; erfinden **I**
creative [kri'eɪtɪv] kreativ **I**
credit ['kredɪt] Guthaben **II**
cricket ['krɪkɪt] Cricket **II**
crime [kraɪm] Verbrechen; Kriminalität **III**
criminal ['krɪmɪnəl] Kriminelle/-r; Verbrecher/-in **III**
to **cringe** [krɪndʒ] schaudern; sich ducken **IV U3**, 91
crisp *(BE)* [krɪsp] Kartoffelchip **I**
criterion [kraɪ'tɪəriən], **criteria** [kraɪ'tɪəriə] *(pl)* Kriterium; Argument **III**
critical ['krɪtɪkl] kritisch **IV TS3**, 103
croissant ['krwæsɑ̃ŋ] Croissant ⟨**IV U3**, 75⟩
cronut ['krəʊnʌt] Cronut ⟨**IV U3**, 75⟩
to **crop** (a photo) [krɒp] (ein Foto) zurechtschneiden **III**
cross [krɒs] Kreuz **III**
to **cross** [krɒs] überqueren; kreuzen **II**
*to keep your fingers **crossed** [ˌkiːp jɔː ˌfɪŋgəz 'krɒst] die Daumen drücken **I**
crowd [kraʊd] Menschenmenge **II**
crowded ['kraʊdɪd] überfüllt **IV AC1**, 23
crown [kraʊn] Krone **III**
crown jewels [ˌkraʊn 'dʒuːəlz] Kronjuwelen **II**
cruel ['kruːəl] grausam **III**
crushed [krʌʃt] eingequetscht; eingeklemmt **IV U1**, 16
to **cry** [kraɪ] schreien; rufen **II**; weinen **III**
CU *(= See you)* ['siː ju] Bis dann!; Bis … **I**
cultural ['kʌltʃrl] kulturell **IV AC2**, 38
culture ['kʌltʃə] Kultur **I**
Across **cultures** [əˌkrɒs 'kʌltʃəz] Interkulturelles **I**
cup [kʌp] Tasse **III**
cupboard ['kʌbəd] Küchenschrank; Schrank **I**
curfew ['kɜːfjuː] Sperrstunde; Ausgangssperre **IV U2**, 44
currency ['kʌrnsi] Währung **IV U1**, 9
curry ['kʌri] Curry *(Gewürz oder Gericht)* **I**
custard ['kʌstəd] Vanillesoße; Vanillepudding **I**
custom ['kʌstəm] Gewohnheit; Brauch; Sitte **IV AC1**, 22
customer ['kʌstəmə] Kunde/Kundin **III**
customs *(sg)* ['kʌstəmz] Zoll **IV U1**, 9
*to **cut** (off) [kʌt (ɒf)] schneiden; abschneiden **II**
*to **cut** up [kʌt‿'ʌp] zerschneiden °**IV U3**, 91
cute [kjuːt] niedlich; süß **I**
cyber **bully** [ˌsaɪbə 'bʊli] *jemand, der andere in sozialen Netzwerken belästigt oder mobbed* **II**
to **cycle** ['saɪkl] Fahrrad fahren **IV U2**, 46
cycling ['saɪklɪŋ] Radfahren **I**

D

dad [dæd] Papa **I**
dance [dɑːns] Tanz; Tanzveranstaltung **III**
to **dance** [dɑːns] tanzen **I**
to **dance** to ['dɑːns tə] tanzen zu **III**
I like singing and **dancing**. [ˌaɪ laɪk ˌsɪŋɪŋ‿ənd 'dɑːnsɪŋ] Ich singe und tanze gern. **I**
dancer ['dɑːnsə] Tänzer/-in **II**
backing **dancer** ['bækɪŋ ˌdɑːnsə] Backgroundtänzer/-in **III**
danger ['deɪndʒə] Gefahr **III**
dangerous ['deɪndʒrəs] gefährlich **I**
the **dark** [ðə 'dɑːk] Dunkelheit **II**
dark [dɑːk] dunkel **II**
darkness ['dɑːknəs] Dunkelheit **III**
date [deɪt] Datum **I**; Verabredung; Date **IV U2**, 55
date of birth [ˌdeɪt‿əv 'bɜːθ] Geburtsdatum **IV U1**, 13
daughter ['dɔːtə] Tochter **III**
day [deɪ] Tag **I**
all **day** [ˌɔːl 'deɪ] den ganzen Tag **II**
one **day** [wʌn 'deɪ] eines Tages **II**
*to take the **day** off [ˌteɪk ðə ˌdeɪ‿'ɒf] sich den Tag freinehmen **IV U3**, 72
the other **day** [ði‿ˌʌðə 'deɪ] neulich **IV U1**, 20
these **days** [ˌðiːz 'deɪz] zurzeit **III**
a (**day**/week/year) [ə 'deɪ/wiːk/jɪə] pro (Tag/Woche/Jahr) **IV AC2**, 39
a **day** out in … [ə ˌdeɪ‿'aʊt ɪn] ein Tag in … **II**
the next **day** [ðə ˌnekst 'deɪ] am nächsten Tag **II**
dead [ded] tot **II**
big **deal** [bɪg 'diːl] große Sache **IV U1**, 11
*to **deal** (with) [diːl] sich befassen mit; umgehen mit **II**
Oh **dear**! [ˌəʊ 'dɪə] Oje! **III**
Dear … [dɪə] Lieber …; Liebe … *(Anrede in Briefen)* **I**
Dear Sir or Madam [dɪə ˌsɜːr‿ɔː 'mædəm] Sehr geehrte Dame, sehr geehrter Herr **III**
death [deθ] Tod **III**
December [dɪ'sembə] Dezember **I**
to **decide** [dɪ'saɪd] (sich) entscheiden **I**
decision [dɪ'sɪʒn] Entscheidung **III**
*to make a **decision** [ˌmeɪk‿ə dɪ'sɪʒn] eine Entscheidung treffen **II**
deck [dek] Deck **I**
to **decorate** ['dekəreɪt] dekorieren; verzieren; schmücken **I**
decorations *(pl)* [ˌdekə'reɪʃnz] Dekoration; Schmuck **I**
deep [diːp] tief **III**
to **defeat** [dɪ'fiːt] besiegen **III**
defining relative clause [dɪˌfaɪnɪŋ 'relətɪv ˌklɔːz] notwendiger Relativsatz **II**
definitely ['defɪnətli] bestimmt; definitiv; eindeutig **III**
definition [ˌdefɪ'nɪʃn] Definition **III**
degree Fahrenheit (°F) ['færnhaɪt] Grad Fahrenheit **IV AC2**, 38
delay [dɪ'leɪ] Verzögerung; Verspätung **IV U1**, 15
to **delete** [dɪ'liːt] löschen **III**
deli ['deli] Feinkostgeschäft ⟨**IV U3**, 85⟩
delicate ['delɪkət] empfindlich ⟨**IV U3**, 86⟩
delicious [dɪ'lɪʃəs] köstlich **IV U3**, 75
to **demonstrate** ['demənstreɪt] demonstrieren **IV U2**, 48
dense [dens] dicht **IV AC2**, 40
to **depart** [dɪ'pɑːt] abfahren **III**
departure [dɪ'pɑːtʃə] Abflug; Abreise **IV U1**, 9
departure lounge [dɪ'pɑːtʃə ˌlaʊndʒ] Abflughalle **IV U1**, 9
to **depend** (on) [dɪ'pend‿(ɒn)] abhängen von **III**
depressing [dɪ'presɪŋ] deprimierend; bedrückend **IV U1**, 17
to **describe** [dɪ'skraɪb] beschreiben **I**
description [dɪ'skrɪpʃn] Beschreibung **II**
desert ['dezət] Wüste **IV AC2**, 38
to **deserve** [dɪ'zɜːv] verdienen **II**
design [dɪ'zaɪn] Design; Gestaltung; Entwurf **II**
to **design** [dɪ'zaɪn] entwerfen; gestalten **II**
designer [dɪ'zaɪnə] Designer/-in **III**
web **designer** ['web dɪˌzaɪnə] Webdesigner **III**

desk [desk] Schalter **IV U1**, 9
destination [ˌdestɪ'neɪʃn] Ziel; Reiseziel **IV U1**, 19
detail ['di:teɪl] Detail; Einzelheit **II**
detective [dɪ'tektɪv] Detektiv/-in; Detektivgeschichte; Kriminalroman; Kriminalfilm; Krimi **III**
private **detective** [ˌpraɪvət dɪ'tektɪv] Privatdetektiv/-in **III**
detention [dɪ'tenʃn] Nachsitzen; Haft; Verhaftung **IV AC3**, 68
devil ['devl] Teufel **IV TS1**, 31
diagram ['daɪəgræm] Diagramm **I**
dialect ['daɪəlekt] Dialekt **III**
dialogue ['daɪəlɒg] Dialog; Gespräch **I**
diary ['daɪəri] Tagebuch **III**
diary entry ['daɪəri entri] Tagebucheintrag **III**
dice [daɪs] Würfel **II**
Roll two **dice**. [ˌrəʊl ˌtu: 'daɪs] Würfle/Würfelt mit zwei Würfeln. **I**
throw the **dice** twice [ˌθrəʊ ðə daɪs 'twaɪs] würfle zweimal **II**
dictionary ['dɪkʃnri] Wörterbuch **I**
to **die** [daɪ] sterben **III**
difference ['dɪfrəns] Unterschied **I**
different ['dɪfrnt] anders; unterschiedlich; verschieden **I**
difficult ['dɪfɪklt] schwierig **II**
*to **dig** [dɪg] graben **II**
dilemma [daɪ'lemə] Dilemma; Zwickmühle **IV TS1**, 31
diner *(AE)* ['daɪnə] einfaches Restaurant mit Theke und Tischen **IV U3**, 72
dinner ['dɪnə] Abendessen **I**
dinosaur ['daɪnəsɔ:] Dinosaurier **II**
direct [dɪ'rekt] direkt **III**
direct speech [dɪˌrekt 'spi:tʃ] direkte Rede **IV U1**, 11
direction [dɪ'rekʃn] Richtung **I**
stage **direction** ['steɪdʒ dɪˌrekʃn] Regieanweisung **III**
director [dɪ'rektə] Regisseur/-in **IV TS1**, 30
dirt [dɜ:t] Schmutz; Dreck **III**
dirty ['dɜ:ti] dreckig; schmutzig **II**
to **disagree** [ˌdɪsə'gri:] anderer Meinung sein; nicht einverstanden sein **III**
disappointed [ˌdɪsə'pɔɪntɪd] enttäuscht **I**
disappointing [ˌdɪsə'pɔɪntɪŋ] enttäuschend **IV TS3**, 104
disaster [dɪ'zɑ:stə] Desaster; Katastrophe; Unglück **II**
to **discover** [dɪ'skʌvə] entdecken **II**
discovery [dɪ'skʌvri] Entdeckung **III**
to **discuss** [dɪ'skʌs] diskutieren **I**
discussion [dɪ'skʌʃn] Diskussion **II**
dish [dɪʃ] Gericht; Speise **IV U2**, 45
dishonest [dɪ'sɒnɪst] unehrlich **IV TS1**, 34
to **dislike** [dɪs'laɪk] nicht mögen **IV U2**, 47
dislikes *(pl)* [dɪs'laɪks] Abneigungen **IV U2**, 46

to **disobey** [ˌdɪsə'beɪ] nicht gehorchen; ungehorsam sein **III**
display [dɪ'spleɪ] Ausstellung **II**
class **display** ['klɑ:s dɪˌspleɪ] Ausstellung in der Klasse **I**
distance ['dɪstns] Distanz; Entfernung **II**
district ['dɪstrɪkt] Distrikt; Bezirk **IV U3**, 70
to **divide** (up) [dɪ'vaɪd] aufteilen **III**
dizzy ['dɪzi] schwindelig **IV U2**, 52
DJ [ˌdi:'dʒeɪ] DJ; Discjockey **III**
*to **do** [du:] machen; tun **I**
*to be **done** with [bi 'dʌn wɪð] fertig sein mit **IV U3**, 76
*to **do** about ['du:‿əˌbaʊt] unternehmen wegen **II**
*to **do** our hair [ˌdu:‿aʊə 'heə] uns frisieren; unsere Haare machen **I**
*to **do** the shopping [ˌdu: ðə 'ʃɒpɪŋ] Einkäufe machen; Besorgungen machen **III**
*to **do** well [ˌdu: 'wel] gute Leistungen erbringen **IV TS1**, 34
Don't worry! [ˌdəʊnt 'wʌri] Keine Sorge! **I**
dos and **don'ts** [ˌdu:z‿ənd 'dəʊnts] Ge- und Verbote; was man tun und was man nicht tun sollte **IV AC1**, 22
We **did** it! [ˌwi: 'dɪd‿ɪt] Wir haben es geschafft! **II**
You can **do** it! [ju: kən 'du: ɪt] Du schaffst es! **III**
doctor ['dɒktə] Arzt/Ärztin **II**
to **document** ['dɒkjəment] dokumentieren; festhalten ⟨**IV TS3**, 101⟩
dog [dɒg] Hund **I**
hot **dog** ['hɒt ˌdɒg] Hot Dog *(Würstchen im Brötchen)* ⟨**IV U3**, 75⟩
to walk the **dog** [ˌwɔ:k ðə 'dɒg] den Hund ausführen; mit dem Hund spazieren gehen **I**
I'm **dog-tired**. [ˌaɪm ˌdɒg'taɪəd] Ich bin hundemüde. **I**
dollar ['dɒlə] Dollar *(Währung)* **III**
dolphin ['dɒlfɪn] Delfin **III**
dominoes ['dɒmɪnəʊz] Domino **IV U1**, 20
to **donate** [də'neɪt] spenden; stiften **IV U2**, 51
door [dɔ:] Tür **I**
front **door** [ˌfrʌnt 'dɔ:] Haustür **II**
next **door** [ˌnekst 'dɔ:] (von) nebenan **III**
doorbell ['dɔ:bel] Türklingel **III**
double ['dʌbl] Doppel-; zweimal **IV U2**, 57
doubt [daʊt] Zweifel **III**
doughnut ['dəʊnʌt] Donut *(frittierter Teigkringel)* ⟨**IV U3**, 75⟩
down [daʊn] nach unten; herunter; hinunter **II**; nieder **IV U2**, 52
*to come **down** [ˌkʌm 'daʊn] herunterkommen **I**
*to go **down** [ˌgəʊ 'daʊn] hinuntergehen; nach unten gehen; entlanggehen **I**
to note **down** [ˌnəʊt 'daʊn] notieren; aufschreiben **II**

to pull **down** [ˌpʊl‿'daʊn] abreißen **III**
*to sit **down** [ˌsɪt 'daʊn] sich hinsetzen; sich setzen **I**
to slow **down** [ˌsləʊ 'daʊn] langsamer werden; bremsen ⟨**IV U3**, 90⟩
to touch **down** [tʌtʃ 'daʊn] landen **IV TS3**, 101
*to write **down** [ˌraɪt 'daʊn] aufschreiben **I**
to **download** [ˌdaʊn'ləʊd] herunterladen *(aus dem Internet)* **II**
downstairs [ˌdaʊn'steəz] nach unten; im Untergeschoss; unten **II**
downtown *(AE)* [ˌdaʊn'taʊn] im Stadtzentrum **IV U2**, 44
draft [drɑ:ft] Entwurf; Konzept **I**
drama ['drɑ:mə] Theater; Drama **II**
dramatic [drə'mætɪk] dramatisch **II**
*to **draw** [drɔ:] zeichnen **I**; ziehen **III**
*to **draw** the reader into the story/action [ˌdrɔ: ðə ˌri:də ɪntə ðə 'stɔ:ri/'ækʃn] den Leser/die Leserin in die Geschichte/Handlung hineinziehen **III**
drawing ['drɔ:ɪŋ] Zeichnung **I**
dreadlocks *(pl)* ['dredlɒks] Rastalocken ⟨**IV U3**, 90⟩
dream [dri:m] Traum **II**
*to **dream** [dri:m] träumen **IV U2**, 47
dress [dres] Kleid **III**
dress code ['dres ˌkəʊd] Kleiderordnung; Bekleidungsvorschriften **IV U2**, 43
fancy **dress** ['fænsi dres] Verkleidung; Kostüm **II**
to **drift** [drɪft] schweben; treiben ⟨**IV U1**, 12⟩
drink [drɪŋk] Getränk **I**
*to **drink** [drɪŋk] trinken **I**
drive [draɪv] Fahrt; Anfahrt; Autofahrt **IV U2**, 44
clothing **drive** ['kləʊðɪŋ ˌdraɪv] Kleidersammlung **IV U2**, 51
*to **drive** [draɪv] fahren **III**
*to **drive** off [draɪv‿'ɒf] wegfahren **III**
driver ['draɪvə] Fahrer/-in **II**
drizzle ['drɪzl] Nieselregen **IV U1**, 17
to **drop** [drɒp] fallen (lassen) **II**
to **drop** out (of) [ˌdrɒp 'aʊt‿əv] abbrechen **III**
drop-off ['drɒpɒf] Abgabe **IV U2**, 51
to **drown** [draʊn] ertrinken; ertränken **III**
drums *(pl)* [drʌmz] Schlagzeug **III**
dry [draɪ] trocken **III**
dude *(coll)* [du:d] Mann; Alter *(ugs.)* **IV AC2**, 41
dumpster ['dʌmpstə] Müllcontainer ⟨**IV U3**, 85⟩
during *(+ noun)* ['djʊərɪŋ] während *(+ Nomen)* **II**
duty-free [ˌdju:ti'fri:] zollfrei **IV U1**, 9
DVD [ˌdi:vi:'di:] DVD **I**

E

e.g. *(= for example)* [ˌiːˈdʒiː] z.B. *(= zum Beispiel)* **I**
each [iːtʃ] jede/-r/-s **I**
each other [iːtʃ‿ˈʌðə] einander; sich; sich gegenseitig **I**
each [iːtʃ] pro Person; pro Stück **I**
ear [ɪə] Ohr **IV AC1**, 22
early [ˈɜːli] früh **I**
this **early** [ˈðɪs ˌɜːli] so früh **III**
to **earn** [ɜːn] verdienen **I**
earth [ɜːθ] Erdboden; Erde; die Erde **II**
What on **earth** …? [ˌwɒtː‿ɒn‿ˈɜːθ] Was um alles in der Welt …? **II**
east [iːst] Osten; Ost- **I**
Easter [ˈiːstə] Ostern **I**
easy [ˈiːzi] einfach; leicht **I**
easy-going [ˌiːziˈgəʊɪŋ] locker; unkompliziert **IV U1**, 19
*to **eat** [iːt] essen; fressen **I**
Eco [ˈiːkəʊ] Öko- **II**
to **edit** out [ˌedɪt‿ˈaʊt] herausschneiden **III**
education *(no pl)* [ˌedʒʊˈkeɪʃn] Erziehung; Bildung **III**
effect [ɪˈfekt] Effekt; Wirkung **IV U3**, 89
audio-visual **effect** [ˌɔːdiəʊvɪʒuəl ɪˈfekt] audiovisueller Effekt **II**
special **effect** [ˌspeʃl‿ɪˈfekt] Spezialeffekt **IV TS3**, 105
effective [ɪˈfektɪv] effektiv; wirkungsvoll **IV TS2**, 66
effectiveness [ɪˈfektɪvnəs] Effektivität; Wirksamkeit **IV TS2**, 67
egg [eg] Ei **I**
Egyptian [ɪˈdʒɪpʃn] Ägypter/-in; ägyptisch **IV U1**, 20
eight [eɪt] acht **I**
not … **either** [nɒt … ˈaɪðə; nɒt … ˈiːðə] auch nicht **IV AC4**, 107
either … or … [ˈaɪðə/ˈiːðə … ɔː] entweder … oder … **IV U3**, 79
elderly [ˈeldəli] älter **III**
electric [ɪˈlektrɪk] elektrisch **III**
electrician [ˌelɪkˈtrɪʃn] Elektriker/-in **III**
electricity [ˌelɪkˈtrɪsəti] Elektrizität; Strom **III**
electrics [ɪˈlektrɪks] Elektrik **III**
electronic [ˌelekˈtrɒnɪk] elektronisch **II**
element [ˈelɪmənt] Element **III**
elephant [ˈelɪfənt] Elefant **III**
elevator *(AE)* [ˈelɪveɪtə] Aufzug; Lift **IV U2**, 44
eleven [ɪˈlevn] elf **I**
else [els] andere/-r/-s; sonst noch **III**
nobody **else** [ˈnəʊbədi els] niemand anderes **III**
what **else** [ˌwɒt‿ˈels] was sonst; was noch **I**
e-mail [ˈiːmeɪl] E-Mail **I**
to **e-mail** [ˈiːmeɪl] mailen; per E-Mail schicken **II**
embarrassed [ɪmˈbærəst] verlegen **II**
embarrassing [ɪmˈbærəsɪŋ] peinlich **II**
emotion [ɪˈməʊʃn] Gefühl; Emotion ⟨**IV TS3**, 104⟩
emotional [ɪˈməʊʃnl] emotional; Gefühls- **III**
emperor [ˈemprə] Kaiser **III**
empire [ˈempaɪə] Reich; Kaiserreich **III**
empty [ˈemti] leer **III**
encyclopaedia [ɪnˌsaɪkləˈpiːdiə] Enzyklopädie; Lexikon °**IV TS3**, 101
end [end] Ende; Schluss **I**
in the **end** [ˌɪn ði‿ˈend] schließlich; zum Schluss **II**
to **end** [end] enden; beenden **II**
to **end** up [ˌend‿ˈʌp] enden; landen **II**
ending [ˈendɪŋ] Ende; Schluss *(einer Geschichte)* **I**
happy **ending** [ˌhæpi ˈendɪŋ] Happy End **III**
endless [ˈendləs] endlos **IV AC2**, 38
enemy [ˈenəmi] Feind/-in **III**
energy [ˈenədʒi] Energie; Kraft **III**
search **engine** [ˈsɜːtʃ‿endʒɪn] Suchmaschine °**IV U2**, 42
steam **engine** [ˈstiːm‿endʒɪn] Dampfmaschine **III**
engineer [ˌendʒɪˈnɪə] Ingenieur/-in; Techniker/-in **IV TS3**, 101
engineering [ˌendʒɪˈnɪərɪŋ] Technik; Maschinenbau ⟨**IV TS3**, 102⟩
English [ˈɪŋglɪʃ] englisch; Englisch; aus England; Engländer/-in **I**
English-speaking [ˈɪŋglɪʃˌspiːkɪŋ] englischsprachig **I**
I'm **English**. [aɪm‿ˈɪŋglɪʃ] Ich bin Engländer/-in. **I**
to **enjoy** [ɪnˈdʒɔɪ] genießen; sich freuen an **II**
to **enjoy** oneself [ɪnˈdʒɔɪ] Spaß haben; sich amüsieren **III**
enlightenment [ɪnˈlaɪtnmənt] Aufklärung; Erleuchtung **IV U3**, 74
enough [ɪˈnʌf] genug; genügend **I**
to **enter** [ˈentə] hineingehen; betreten; eintreten; *hier:* mitmachen **II**
to **entertain** [ˌentəˈteɪn] unterhalten **IV TS1**, 30
entertainer [ˌentəˈteɪnə] Entertainer/-in; Unterhaltungskünstler/-in **IV U3**, 72
entertaining [ˌentəˈteɪnɪŋ] unterhaltsam **IV TS3**, 103
entertainment *(no pl)* [ˌentəˈteɪnmənt] Unterhaltung **III**
enthusiasm [ɪnˈθjuːziæzm] Enthusiasmus; Begeisterung **IV U3**, 72
entrance [ˈentrəns] Eingang; Eintritt **III**
entry [ˈentri] Eintrag **III**
diary **entry** [ˈdaɪəri entri] Tagebucheintrag **III**
environment [ɪnˈvaɪrnmənt] Umwelt; Umgebung **III**
epic [ˈepɪk] episch; *hier:* geil **IV AC2**, 41
equipment [ɪˈkwɪpmənt] Ausstattung; Ausrüstung **II**
er [ɜː] äh **I**
era [ˈɪərə] Ära; Zeitalter **IV U1**, 19
escalator [ˈeskəleɪtə] Rolltreppe **I**
escape [ɪˈskeɪp] Flucht **III**
to **escape** (from) [ɪˈskeɪp frəm] fliehen; entfliehen; flüchten; entkommen **IV U2**, 52
to **estimate** [ˈestɪmeɪt] schätzen **IV TS3**, 103
etc. *(= et cetera)* [ɪtˈsetrə] usw. *(= und so weiter)* **II**
ethnic [ˈeθnɪk] ethnisch; Volks-; *hier:* exotisch **IV U3**, 75
euro [ˈjʊərəʊ] Euro *(Währung)* **I**
European [ˌjʊərəˈpiːən] Europäer/-in; europäisch; aus Europa **IV AC2**, 38
even [ˈiːvn] sogar; selbst **I**
evening [ˈiːvnɪŋ] Abend **I**
in the **evenings** [ɪn ði‿ˈiːvnɪŋz] abends **I**
event [ɪˈvent] Ereignis; Veranstaltung **I**
ever [ˈevə] jemals **II**
the best … **ever** [ˈbest … ˌevə] der/die/das beste … überhaupt **III**
every [ˈevri] jede/-r/-s **I**
everybody [ˈevribɒdi] jeder; alle **II**
everyday [ˈevrideɪ] alltäglich **III**
everyone [ˈevriwʌn] jeder; alle **I**
everything [ˈevriθɪŋ] alles **I**
everywhere [ˈevriweə] überall **I**
exactly [ɪgˈzæktli] genau **II**
to **exaggerate** [ɪgˈzædʒreɪt] übertreiben **IV TS1**, 32
exaggerated [ɪgˈzædʒreɪtɪd] übertrieben **IV U2**, 52
exam [ɪgˈzæm] Examen; Prüfung **II**
example [ɪgˈzɑːmpl] Beispiel **I**
for **example** [fər‿ɪgˈzɑːmpl] zum Beispiel **II**
excellent [ˈekslnt] exzellent; hervorragend ⟨**IV TS3**, 104⟩
excellent piece of quick thinking [ˌekslnt piːs‿əv kwɪk ˈθɪŋkɪŋ] ausgezeichnete Reaktionsschnelligkeit ⟨**IV TS1**, 36⟩
except [ɪkˈsept] außer; bis auf **IV U1**, 17
excerpt [ˈeksɜːpt] Auszug °**IV U3**, 89
exchange [ɪksˈtʃeɪndʒ] Austausch; Austausch- **III**
exchange student [ɪksˈtʃeɪndʒ ˌstjuːdnt] Austauschschüler/-in **III**
student **exchange** [ˈstjuːdnt ɪksˌtʃeɪndʒ] Schüleraustausch **III**
to **exchange** [ɪksˈtʃeɪndʒ] austauschen **II**
excited [ɪkˈsaɪtɪd] aufgeregt; begeistert **I**
excitement *(no pl)* [ɪkˈsaɪtmənt] Aufregung **III**
exciting [ɪkˈsaɪtɪŋ] spannend; aufregend **I**
Excuse me … [ɪkˈskjuːz mi] Entschuldigung!; Entschuldigen Sie! **I**
exercise [ˈeksəsaɪz] Übung; Aufgabe **I**
exercise book [ˈeksəsaɪz ˌbʊk] Übungsheft **I**
to **expect** [ɪkˈspekt] erwarten **III**
expectation [ˌekspekˈteɪʃn] Erwartung °**IV U2**, 50
expensive [ɪkˈspensɪv] teuer **I**

experience [ɪk'spɪəriəns] Erfahrung **II**
to **experience** [ɪk'spɪəriəns] erfahren; erleben **III**
expert ['ekspɜ:t] Experte/Expertin **II**
to **explain** [ɪk'spleɪn] erklären **I**
exploration [ˌeksplə'reɪʃn] Erforschung; Erkundung ⟨**IVTS3**, 104⟩
to **explore** [ɪk'splɔ:] auf Entdeckungsreise gehen; sich umschauen; erkunden; erforschen **I**
to **express** [ɪk'spres] ausdrücken **II**
expression [ɪk'spreʃn] Ausdruck; Wendung; Äußerung **II**
facial **expression** [ˌfeɪʃl ɪk'spreʃn] Gesichtsausdruck **III**
*to become **extinct** [bɪˌkʌm‿ɪk'stɪŋkt] aussterben **III**
extinction *(no pl)* [ɪks'tɪŋkʃn] Aussterben **III**
extra ['ekstrə] extra; zusätzlich **I**
extreme [ɪk'stri:m] extrem; radikal **IV AC2**, 40
eye [aɪ] Auge **II**
to roll one's **eyes** [ˌrəʊl wʌnz‿'aɪz] die Augen verdrehen **III**
He couldn't believe his **eyes**. [hi ˌkʊdnt bɪˌli:v hɪz‿'aɪz] Er traute seinen Augen nicht. **II**
eyebrow ['aɪbraʊ] Augenbraue ⟨**IV U3**, 90⟩
eye-catcher ['aɪkætʃə] Blickfang; Hingucker **IVTS2**, 65
eyewitness ['aɪwɪtnəs] Augenzeuge/Augenzeugin **II**

F

fabulous ['fæbjələs] sagenhaft; fantastisch **IVTS2**, 66
face [feɪs] Gesicht **I**
Put ... **face** down. [pʊt ˌfeɪs 'daʊn] Lege/Legt ... umgedreht hin. **I**
to **face** [feɪs] gegenüber stehen; konfrontiert werden mit **IVTS1**, 31
Let's **face** it. [lets 'feɪs‿ɪt] Machen wir uns doch nichts vor. **IVTS1**, 32
face-to-face [ˌfeɪstə'feɪs] *hier:* persönlich; von Angesicht zu Angesicht **II**
facial expression [ˌfeɪʃl ɪk'spreʃn] Gesichtsausdruck **III**
fact [fækt] Fakt; Tatsache **II**
factory ['fæktri] Fabrik; Werk **III**
factual ['fæktʃʊəl] sachlich **III**
factual text [ˌfæktʃʊəl 'tekst] Sachtext **III**
degree **Fahrenheit** (°F) ['færnhaɪt] Grad Fahrenheit **IV AC2**, 38
to **fail** to do sth ['feɪl tə] versäumen, etw. zu tun; es nicht schaffen, etw. zu tun **IV U3**, 79
fair [feə] gerecht; fair **I**
fair play [feə 'pleɪ] Fairplay **III**
to **fake** [feɪk] vortäuschen; fälschen **II**
fake [feɪk] falsch; gefälscht **IVTS1**, 35
*to **fall** [fɔ:l] fallen; hinfallen **I**
*to **fall** asleep [ˌfɔ:l‿ə'sli:p] einschlafen **I**
*to **fall** down [ˌfɔ:l‿'daʊn] stürzen; hinunterfallen **III**
*to **fall** for ['fɔ:l fə] hereinfallen auf **IVTS2**, 64
*to **fall** off [ˌfɔ:l‿'ɒf] herunterfallen; hinunterfallen **II**
*to **fall** over [ˌfɔ:l‿'əʊvə] hinfallen; umkippen **I**
family ['fæmli] Familie **I**
family tree ['fæmli ˌtri:] Stammbaum **I**
host **family** ['həʊst ˌfæmli] Gastfamilie **III**
famous ['feɪməs] berühmt **I**
fan [fæn] Fan; Anhänger/-in **II**
to **fancy** *(+ ing) (infml) (BE)* ['fænsi] Lust haben zu ⟨**IVTS1**, 31⟩
fancy dress ['fænsi dres] Verkleidung; Kostüm **II**
fantastic [fæn'tæstɪk] fantastisch; großartig **II**
fantasy ['fæntəsi] Fantasie; Traum- **I**; Fantasy **III**
fanzine [fæn'zi:n] Fanzeitschrift **II**
FAQ [ˌefeɪ'kju:] Liste mit häufig gestellten Fragen **III**
in the **far** west [ɪn ðə fɑ: 'west] im äußersten Westen **III**
far [fɑ:] weit **II**
so **far** [ˌsəʊ 'fɑ:] bis jetzt **II**
fare [feə] Fahrpreis **III**
farewell [ˌfeə'wel] Lebewohl; Abschied ⟨**IVTS1**, 36⟩
farm [fɑ:m] Farm; Bauernhof **I**
farmer ['fɑ:mə] Farmer/-in; Landwirt/-in **II**
fascinating ['fæsɪneɪtɪŋ] faszinierend **III**
fashion ['fæʃn] Mode **II**
fast [fɑ:st] schnell **I**
father ['fɑ:ðə] Vater **I**
their **fault** [ˌdeə 'fɔ:lt] ihre Schuld ⟨**IVTS1**, 36⟩
favourite ['feɪvrɪt] Favorit/-in; Günstling **III**
favourite ['feɪvrɪt] Lieblings- **I**
My **favourite** ... [maɪ 'feɪvrɪt] Mein/e Lieblings ... **I**
What's your **favourite** ...? ['wɒts jə ˌfeɪvrɪt] Was ist dein/-e Lieblings...? **I**
fear [fɪə] Angst; Furcht; Befürchtung **II**
fearful ['fɪəfl] ängstlich **III**
feast [fi:st] Festmahl ⟨**IV U3**, 85⟩
feather ['feðə] Feder **III**
feature ['fi:tʃə] Eigenschaft; Merkmal **III**
to **feature** ['fi:tʃə] zeigen; aufweisen **III**
February ['februri] Februar **I**
*to be **fed** up (with) [bi fed‿'ʌp wɪð] sauer sein (auf); die Nase voll haben (von) **III**
fee [fi:] Gebühr **III**
school **fees** *(pl)* ['sku:l fi:z] Schulgeld; Schulgebühren **III**
*to **feed** [fi:d] füttern; ernähren **III**
feedback ['fi:dbæk] Feedback; Rückmeldung **II**
*to **feel** [fi:l] fühlen; sich fühlen **I**
*to **feel** left out [ˌfi:l left‿'aʊt] sich ausgeschlossen fühlen **II**
*to **feel** sick [ˌfi:l 'sɪk] Übelkeit verspüren; sich schlecht fühlen **II**
*to **feel** sorry for [ˌfi:l 'sɒri fɔ:] Mitleid haben mit; bedauern **III**
feeling ['fi:lɪŋ] Gefühl **II**
ferry ['feri] Fähre **IV U1**, 9
festival ['festɪvl] Festival; Fest **I**
to **fetch** [fetʃ] holen; abholen **IV U1**, 17
fever ['fi:və] Fieber **II**
few [fju:] wenige **II**
a **few** [ə 'fju:] ein paar; wenige; einige **I**
fiction *(no pl)* ['fɪkʃn] Erzählliteratur; Erfindung; Prosa; Fiktion **III**
science **fiction** [ˌsaɪəns 'fɪkʃn] Science-Fiction *(Zukunftsdichtung)* **II**
fictional ['fɪkʃnl] fiktional; fiktiv; erdichtet **III**
field [fi:ld] Feld; Spielfeld; Wiese; Weide; Acker **II**
fifteen [ˌfɪf'ti:n] fünfzehn **I**
fight [faɪt] Kampf; Streit **II**
*to **fight** [faɪt] kämpfen; (sich) streiten **II**
figure ['fɪgə] Figur; Gestalt **II**; Ziffer; Zahl **III**
wax **figure** ['wæks ˌfɪgə] Wachsfigur **II**
to **fill** [fɪl] (sich) füllen **III**
to **fill** in [ˌfɪl‿'ɪn] ausfüllen **II**
filling ['fɪlɪŋ] Füllung **IV U3**, 75
film [fɪlm] Film **I**
to **film** [fɪlm] filmen; drehen **III**
filmmaker ['fɪlmˌmeɪkə] Filmemacher/-in **II**
final ['faɪnl] endgültig **II**; letzte/-r/-s **III**
finally ['faɪnli] schließlich; endlich; zum Schluss; letztlich **II**
*to **find** [faɪnd] finden; herausfinden **I**
*to **find** one's way around [ˌfaɪnd wʌnz ˌweɪ‿ə'raʊnd] sich zurechtfinden **IV U2**, 46
*to **find** out [ˌfaɪnd‿'aʊt] herausfinden **I**
fine [faɪn] gut; in Ordnung; schön **I**
I'm **fine**. [ˌaɪm 'faɪn] Mir geht's gut. **I**
finger ['fɪŋgə] Finger **I**
*to keep your **fingers** crossed [ˌki:p jɔ: ˌfɪŋgəz 'krɒst] die Daumen drücken **I**
finish line ['fɪnɪʃ ˌlaɪn] Ziellinie **II**
to **finish** ['fɪnɪʃ] beenden; enden; fertigstellen; aufhören **I**
finished ['fɪnɪʃt] fertig **II**
fire [faɪə] Feuer **III**
*to be on **fire** [ˌbi:‿ɒn 'faɪə] brennen **III**
fireworks *(pl)* ['faɪəwɜ:ks] Feuerwerk **I**
first [fɜ:st] zuerst; als Erstes; erste/-r/-s **I**
at **first** [ət 'fɜ:st] zuerst; zunächst **II**
first language [ˌfɜ:st 'læŋgwɪdʒ] Muttersprache **II**
first person narrator [ˌfɜ:st ˌpɜ:sn nə'reɪtə] Ich-Erzähler/-in **III**
fish, fish *(pl)* [fɪʃ] Fisch **I**
fishing ['fɪʃɪŋ] Angeln; Fischen; Fischerei **III**
to **fit** [fɪt] passen **II**
*to get **fit** [ˌget 'fɪt] in Form kommen; fit werden **I**
five [faɪv] fünf **I**

to **fix** [fɪks] reparieren; befestigen **II**
flag [flæg] Flagge; Fahne **III**
flair [fleə] Flair; Atmosphäre **II**
flame [fleɪm] Flamme **III**
flash [flæʃ] Blitz; Lichtblitz **III**
flashback ['flæʃbæk] Rückblende; Flashback **III**
flat [flæt] Wohnung **I**
flat [flæt] flach; platt **IV AC2**, 40
flavor *(AE)* ['fleɪvə] Geschmack; Aroma **IV U3**, 75
flea market ['fli: ˌmɑ:kɪt] Flohmarkt **I**
flight [flaɪt] Flug **III**
flight attendant ['flaɪt‿əˌtendnt] Flugbegleiter/-in **IV U1**, 9
floor [flɔ:] Fußboden **I**; Stockwerk **IV U2**, 44
to **flow** out [fləʊ‿'aʊt] hinausfließen **II**
flower ['flaʊə] Blume **II**
*to **fly** [flaɪ] fliegen **III**
*to **fly** [flaɪ] hissen **IV AC2**, 39
flyer ['flaɪə] Flyer **I**
focus ['fəʊkəs] Blickpunkt; Schwerpunkt; Fokus **III**
out of **focus** [ˌaʊt‿əv 'fəʊkəs] unscharf **III**
to **focus** (on) ['fəʊkəs‿ɒn] sich konzentrieren (auf) **II**
folder ['fəʊldə] Ordner; Mappe **I**
to **follow** ['fɒləʊ] folgen; hinterhergehen; befolgen **II**
the **following** [ðə 'fɒləʊɪŋ] folgende/-r/-s **III**
follow-up ['fɒləʊʌp] Fortsetzung; Folge- **IV U3**, 92
food [fu:d] Essen; Lebensmittel **I**; Futter **III**
foot [fʊt], **feet** [fi:t] *(pl)* Fuß *(Längenmaß: 30,48 cm)* **IV AC2**, 39
*to keep one's **feet** or hands still [ˌki:p wʌnz: 'fi:t‿ɔ: 'hændz stɪl] die Beine und Hände ruhig halten **III**
on **foot** [ɒn 'fʊt] zu Fuß **II**
foot, feet *(pl)* [fʊt; fi:t] Fuß **I**
football ['fʊtbɔ:l] Fußball **I**
for [fɔ:; fə] für **I**; wegen **II**
for *(+ Zeitraum)* [fɔ:; fə] seit **III**
for example [fər‿ɪg'zɑ:mpl] zum Beispiel **II**
for free [fə 'fri:] umsonst; kostenlos **IV U3**, 72
for ... [fɔ:; fə] ... lang **II**
force [fɔ:s] Kraft; Macht **IV U1**, 19
weather **forecast** ['weðə ˌfɔ:kɑ:st] Wettervorhersage **III**
foreground ['fɔ:graʊnd] Vordergrund **IV U2**, 47
foreign ['fɒrɪn] ausländisch; fremd **IV U1**, 8
foreign language [ˌfɒrɪn 'læŋgwɪdʒ] Fremdsprache **II**
forest ['fɒrɪst] Wald **II**
forever [fə'revə] für immer; ewig **II**
*to **forget** [fə'get] vergessen **I**
*to **forgive** [fə'gɪv] vergeben; verzeihen **II**
fork [fɔ:k] Gabel **III**
form [fɔ:m] Form **I**; Formular **III**
negative **form** ['negətɪv ˌfɔ:m] verneinte Form **I**
past **form** ['pɑ:st fɔ:m] Vergangenheitsform **II**
possessive **form** [pəˌsesɪv 'fɔ:m] Possessivform **I**
short **form** ['ʃɔ:t fɔ:m] Kurzform **I**
to **form** [fɔ:m] formen; bilden **II**
formal ['fɔ:ml] formal; formell; förmlich **II**
forum ['fɔ:rəm] Forum **II**
forward ['fɔ:wəd] vorwärts **III**
to look **forward** to [ˌlʊk 'fɔ:wəd tə] sich freuen auf **II**
to **found** [faʊnd] gründen **III**
water **fountain** ['wɔ:tə ˌfaʊntɪn] Wasserspender **IV AC4**, 106
four [fɔ:] vier **I**
Four and six is ten. [ˌfɔ:r‿ənd ˌsɪks‿ɪz 'ten] Vier plus sechs ist zehn. **I**
four-walled ['fɔ:wɔ:ld] mit vier Wänden ⟨**IV U3**, 90⟩
fox [fɒks] Fuchs **II**
freeze frame ['fri:z ˌfreɪm] Standbild **III**
free [fri:] frei; kostenlos **I**
free time [ˌfri: 'taɪm] Freizeit **I**
for **free** [fə 'fri:] umsonst; kostenlos **IV U3**, 72
freedom *(no pl)* ['fri:dəm] Freiheit; Unabhängigkeit **III**
freeway *(AE)* ['fri:weɪ] Autobahn **IV U3**, 79
freeze frame ['fri:z ˌfreɪm] Standbild **III**
French [frenʃ] französisch; Französisch **II**
frequently asked [ˌfri:kwəntli‿'ɑ:skt] häufig gefragt **I**
fresh [freʃ] frisch **I**
Friday ['fraɪdeɪ] Freitag **I**
fridge [frɪdʒ] Kühlschrank **I**
fried [fraɪd] gebraten *(in der Pfanne)* **IV U3**, 75
friend [frend] Freund/-in **I**
*to become **friends** [bɪˌkʌm‿'frendz] sich anfreunden; Freundschaft schließen **IV AC2**, 41
*to make **friends** [ˌmeɪk 'frendz] Freundschaft schließen **II**
That's what **friends** are for. [ˌðæts wɒt 'frendz‿ɑ: ˌfɔ:] Dafür sind Freunde da. **I**
friendly ['frendli] freundlich; nett **II**
friendship ['frendʃɪp] Freundschaft **II**
fringe [frɪndʒ] Rand-; Alternativ- **III**
from [frɒm; frəm] aus; von **I**
from the outside [ˌfrəm ði‿aʊt'saɪd] von außen **IV U3**, 75
from ... to [frəm ... tə] von ... bis **I**
Where ... **from**? [ˌweə ... 'frɒm] Woher ...? **I**
from around the world [frɒm əˌraʊnd ðə 'wɜ:ld] aus aller Welt **III**
front [frʌnt] Vorderseite; Front-; Vorder- **III**
front door [ˌfrʌnt 'dɔ:] Haustür **II**
front yard *(AE)* [ˌfrʌnt 'jɑ:d] Vorgarten **IV U2**, 43
in **front** of [ɪn 'frʌnt‿əv] vor **I**
fruit [fru:t] Frucht; Obst **I**
full (of) [fʊl‿əv] voll (von) **I**
to talk with your mouth **full** [ˌtɔ:k wɪð jɔ: 'maʊθ fʊl] mit vollem Mund sprechen **IV AC1**, 22
fun [fʌn] Freude; Spaß **I**
*to have **fun** [ˌhæv 'fʌn] Spaß haben; sich amüsieren **I**
It's **fun**. [ɪts 'fʌn] Es macht Spaß. **I**
No risk, no **fun**! [nəʊ ˌrɪsk nəʊ 'fʌn] Wer nicht wagt, der nicht gewinnt. **IV AC3**, 69
fun [fʌn] lustig; witzig; fröhlich **I**
function ['fʌŋkʃn] Funktion **IV TS3**, 103
funny ['fʌni] lustig; witzig **I**; merkwürdig; komisch **III**
further ['fɜ:ðə] weiter (weg) **III**
future ['fju:tʃə] Zukunft **III**
future ['fju:tʃə] zukünftig **IV U1**, 19

G

gadget ['gædʒɪt] Gerät; technische Spielerei **III**
Gaelic ['geɪlɪk] gälisch; Gälisch **III**
gallery walk ['gælri ˌwɔ:k] Museumsrundgang; Vernissage **I**
game [geɪm] Spiel **I**
guessing **game** ['gesɪŋ ˌgeɪm] Ratespiel **II**
gap [gæp] Lücke; Spalt; Abstand **I**
garage ['gærɑ:ʒ] Garage **I**
garden ['gɑ:dn] Garten **I**
garlic ['gɑ:lɪk] Knoblauch **IV U1**, 11
to **gasp** [gɑ:sp] tief Luft holen; keuchen **IV U3**, 72
gate [geɪt] Gate; Flugsteig; Ausgang **IV U1**, 15
geek [gi:k] Außenseiter/-in **IV U2**, 48
general ['dʒenrl] allgemein °**IV U3**, 92
generation [ˌdʒenə'reɪʃn] Generation **III**
generous ['dʒenrəs] großzügig **III**
genius ['dʒi:niəs] Genie **II**
genre ['ʒɑ̃:nrə] Gattung **III**
gentleman ['dʒentlmən], **gentlemen** ['dʒentlmen] *(pl)* Gentleman; feiner Herr **III**
geocaching ['dʒi:əʊkæʃɪŋ] Geocaching **III**
geography [dʒi'ɒgrəfi] Geografie; Erdkunde **III**
German ['dʒɜ:mən] deutsch; Deutsch; aus Deutschland; Deutsche/-r **I**
gerund ['dʒernd] Gerundium °**IV U2**, 43
gesture ['dʒestʃə] Geste; Gebärde **IV TS1**, 33
*to **get** [get] holen; bringen; bekommen; besorgen; kaufen **I**; werden **III**
*to **get** around [ˌget‿ə'raʊnd] *hier:* sich fortbewegen **II**
*to **get** away with [ˌget‿ə'weɪ wɪð] davonkommen mit **II**
*to **get** caught [ˌget 'kɔ:t] erwischt werden; ertappt werden **IV AC3**, 68

*to **get** fit [ˌget ˈfɪt] in Form kommen; fit werden **I**
*to **get** in [ˌget‿ˈɪn] einsteigen **IV U3**, 76
*to **get** in the way [ˌget‿ɪn ðə ˈweɪ] stören; im Weg stehen **II**
*to **get** into [ˌget‿ˈɪntə] einsteigen; hineingelangen **I**
*to **get** into trouble [ˌget‿ɪntə ˈtrʌbl] in Schwierigkeiten geraten **IV AC3**, 69
*to **get** involved with sb [ˌget‿ɪnˈvɒlvd wɪð] sich einlassen mit jmdm. ⟨**IV TS1**, 34⟩
*to **get** lost [ˌget ˈlɒst] verloren gehen; sich verirren **III**
*to **get** off (a bus/train) [ˌget‿ˈɒf] aussteigen (aus einem Bus/Zug) **II**
*to **get** on (the bus) [ˌget‿ˈɒn] einsteigen (in den Bus) **III**
*to **get** on people's nerves [ˌget‿ɒn sʌmbɒdiz ˈnɜːvz] jemandem auf die Nerven gehen **I**
*to **get** organised [get ˈɔːgənaɪzd] sich organisieren **III**
*to **get** out of [get ˌaʊt‿əv] aussteigen **II**
*to **get** right [get ˈraɪt] richtig beantworten **III**
*to **get** started [ˌget ˈstɑːtɪd] anfangen **II**
*to **get** sth out of one's head [get ˌaʊt‿əv wʌnz ˈhed] etw. aus dem Kopf bekommen **III**
*to **get** there [ˈget ðeə] hinkommen **I**
*to **get** to [ˈget tə] kommen zu; kommen nach; erreichen **I**
*to **get** to know [ˌget tə ˈnəʊ] kennenlernen **III**
*to **get** up [ˌget‿ˈʌp] aufstehen *(aus dem Bett)* **I**
*to **get** used to sth [ˌget ˈjuːzd tə] sich an etw. gewöhnen **IV U2**, 44
Time to **get** up! [ˌtaɪm tə ˌget‿ˈʌp] Es ist Zeit aufzustehen! **I**

ghost [gəʊst] Geist **II**
giant [dʒaɪənt] Riesen-; riesig ⟨**IV TS3**, 101⟩
gig [gɪg] Auftritt; Gig **III**
gigantic [dʒaɪˈgæntɪk] gigantisch; riesig **IV AC2**, 40
girl [gɜːl] Mädchen **I**
a **girl** from Germany [ə ˌgɜːl frəm ˈdʒɜːməni] ein Mädchen aus Deutschland **I**
girlfriend [ˈgɜːlfrend] Freundin *(in einer Paarbeziehung)* **II**
gist [dʒɪst] das Wesentliche **II**
*to **give** [gɪv] geben; schenken **I**
*to **give** a talk [ˌgɪv‿ə ˈtɔːk] einen Vortrag halten **IV U2**, 43
*to **give** away [ˌgɪv‿əˈweɪ] verteilen; verschenken **IV TS2**, 64; verraten; preisgeben °**IV U3**, 93
*to **give** reasons [ˌgɪv ˈriːznz] Gründe nennen/angeben ⟨**IV U3**, 90⟩
*to **give** sb a piggyback [gɪv‿ə ˈpɪgibæk] jmdn. Huckepack nehmen **IV U1**, 16
*to **give** sb funny looks [ˌgɪv fʌni ˈlʊks] jmdn. schief anschauen **III**
*to **give** thanks [ˌgɪv ˈθæŋks] danken **IV U2**, 45
*to **give** the bumps [ˌgɪv ðə ˈbʌmps] hochleben lassen **I**
*to **give** up [ˌgɪv‿ˈʌp] aufgeben **III**

glad [glæd] froh **IV AC1**, 23
glamorous [ˈglæmrəs] glamourös **IV TS2**, 65
to **glance** at [ˈglɑːns‿ət] einen Blick werfen auf; blicken auf ⟨**IV U3**, 90⟩
glass [glɑːs] Glas **I**
glasses *(pl)* [ˈglɑːsɪz] Brille **II**
to **glint** [glɪnt] glitzern ⟨**IV U3**, 90⟩
glossary [ˈglɒsri] Glossar; Stichwortverzeichnis **IV TS1**, 30
glove [glʌv] Handschuh **I**
*to **go** [gəʊ] gehen; fahren **I**
*to **go** black [ˌgəʊ ˈblæk] schwarz werden **II**
*to **go** crazy [ˌgəʊ ˈkreɪzi] ausflippen; durchdrehen; verrückt werden **II**
*to **go** down [ˌgəʊ ˈdaʊn] hinuntergehen; nach unten gehen; entlanggehen **I**
*to **go** for a walk [ˌgəʊ fər‿ə ˈwɔːk] spazieren gehen **II**
*to **go** on [ˌgəʊ‿ˈɒn] weitergehen; weitermachen; weiterführen; fortfahren **I**
*to **go** out [ˌgəʊ‿ˈaʊt] ausgehen; hinausgehen **III**
*to **go** over to [ˌgəʊ ˈəʊvə tə] hinübergehen zu; zu jmdm. nach Hause gehen **II**
*to **go** right back to [ˌgəʊ raɪt ˈbæk tə] zurückgehen auf **III**
*to **go** round in circles [gəʊ ˌraʊnd ɪn ˈsɜːklz] sich im Kreis drehen **III**
*to **go** shopping [ˌgəʊ ˈʃɒpɪŋ] einkaufen gehen **I**
*to **go** swimming [ˌgəʊ ˈswɪmɪŋ] Schwimmen gehen **I**
*to **go** to bed [ˌgəʊ tə ˈbed] ins Bett gehen **I**
*to **go** together [ˌgəʊ təˈgeðə] zueinander passen; zueinander gehören **I**
*to **go** with [ˈgəʊ wɪð] passen zu; gehören zu **I**
*to **go** wrong [ˌgəʊ ˈrɒŋ] schiefgehen **I**
*to let **go** (of) [ˌlet ˈgəʊ (əv)] loslassen **II**
Go on! [ˌgəʊ‿ˈɒn] Los! **IV U2**, 55
It's **gone**. [ɪts ˈgɒn] Es ist weg. **II**
What's **going** on? [wɒts ˌgəʊɪŋ‿ˈɒn] Was ist los?; Was geht ab? **III**

goal [gəʊl] Tor; Ziel **I**
God [gɒd] Gott ⟨**IV U2**, 49⟩
goddess [ˈgɒdes] Göttin **IV U3**, 74
gold [gəʊld] Gold **III**
golden [ˈgəʊldn] golden; Gold- ⟨**IV U1**, 12⟩
golden age [ˌgəʊldn ˈeɪdʒ] goldenes Zeitalter **III**
golf [gɒlf] Golf **III**
*to be **gone** [biː ˈgɒn] verschwunden sein; weg sein **II**
gonna (= going to) *(coll)* [ˈgɒnə] wird/werden **IV U3**, 70
good [gʊd] gut **I**
*to be **good** at [biː ˈgʊd‿ət] gut sein in **I**
good luck [ˌgʊd ˈlʌk] viel Glück **IV U3**, 76
Good morning. [ˌgʊd ˈmɔːnɪŋ] Guten Morgen. **I**

goodbye [gʊdˈbaɪ] auf Wiedersehen **I**
gorge scrambling [ˈgɔːdʒ ˌskræmblɪŋ] Schluchtenklettern **II**
government [ˈgʌvnmənt] Regierung **IV TS3**, 102
to **grab** [græb] greifen; ergreifen; schnappen **II**
grade *(AE)* [greɪd] Note **IV U3**, 78
8th-grader *(AE)* [ˈeɪtθˌgreɪdə] Achtklässler/-in **IV U2**, 48
grammar [ˈgræmə] Grammatik **II**
grammar school [ˈgræmə ˌskuːl] Gymnasium **III**
grandad [ˈgrændæd] Opa **I**
grandma [ˈgrænmɑː] Oma **I**
grandparents *(pl)* [ˈgrænˌpeərənts] Großeltern **I**
granny [ˈgræni] Oma **I**
graphic novel [ˌgræfɪk ˈnɒvl] Bildergeschichte; Comic **III**
gratitude [ˈgrætɪtjuːd] Dankbarkeit **III**
great [greɪt] großartig; toll; super **I**
It's **great** for ... [ɪts ˈgreɪt fə] Es ist super zum/für ... **I**

green [griːn] grün **I**
Greenwich Mean Time *(= GMT)* [ˌgrenɪdʒ ˈmiːn ˌtaɪm] westeuropäische Zeit **I**
greeting [ˈgriːtɪŋ] Gruß **I**
grey [greɪ] grau **I**
grid [grɪd] Gitter; Tabelle; Raster **I**
groan [grəʊn] Stöhnen **IV U1**, 10
to **groan** [grəʊn] stöhnen **IV U3**, 74
ground [graʊnd] Boden; Erdboden **IV U1**, 17
*to be **grounded** [bi ˈgraʊndɪd] Hausarrest haben **III**
group [gruːp] Gruppe; Klasse **I**
a **group** of three [ə ˌgruːp‿əv ˈθriː] eine Dreiergruppe **I**
tutor **group** [ˈtjuːtə ˌgruːp] Klasse *(in einer englischen Schule)* **I**

to **group** (around) [gruːp (əˈraʊnd)] gruppieren (um) **III**
*to **grow** [grəʊ] wachsen; anbauen; züchten **III**
*to **grow** up [ˌgrəʊ‿ˈʌp] aufwachsen; erwachsen werden **III**

guard [gɑːd] Wache; Wächter/-in **II**
to **guess** [ges] raten; erraten; vermuten **I**; annehmen **IV AC1**, 22
guessing game [ˈgesɪŋ ˌgeɪm] Ratespiel **II**
guest [gest] Gast **III**
guide [gaɪd] Führer/-in; Reiseführer **II**
to **guide** [gaɪd] führen; leiten **III**
guidebook [ˈgaɪdbʊk] Reiseführer **IV U3**, 72
guilty [ˈgɪlti] schuldig **IV TS1**, 37

guinea pig ['gɪni: ˌpɪg] Meerschweinchen **I**
guitar [gɪ'tɑ:] Gitarre **IV U1**, 19
chewing **gum** ['tʃu:ɪŋ ˌgʌm] Kaugummi **IV U1**, 15
guy [gaɪ] Typ; Kerl; *(Pl.)* Leute **II**
gym(nasium) [dʒɪm; dʒɪm'neɪziəm] Turnhalle **IV AC3**, 68

H

haggis ['hægɪs] Haggis *(schottisches Gericht aus in einem Schafsmagen gekochten Schafsinnereien und Haferschrot)* **III**
hair [ˌdu:ˌaʊə 'heə] Haar(e) **I**
*to do our **hair** [ˌdu:ˌaʊə 'heə] uns frisieren; unsere Haare machen **I**
hair [heə] Haar; Haare **IV TS2**, 64
hairbrush ['heəbrʌʃ] Haarbürste **III**
half, **halves** *(pl)* (of) [hɑ:f; hɑ:vz] die Hälfte **I**
half an hour [ˌhɑ:fˌənˌ'aʊər] eine halbe Stunde **III**
half [hɑ:f] halb **I**
half past [ˌhɑ:f 'pɑ:st] halb *(bei Uhrzeitangaben)* **I**
half-sister ['hɑ:fˌsɪstə] Halbschwester **I**
half-term break [ˌhɑ:ftɜ:m 'breɪk] Halbjahresferien **I**
*to meet **halfway** [ˌmi:t hɑ:f'weɪ] sich auf halbem Weg treffen **III**
hall [hɔ:l] Halle; Saal **II**; Flur; Diele; Korridor **III**
arrivals **hall** [ə'raɪvlz ˌhɔ:l] Ankunftshalle **IV U1**, 9
hall pass ['hɔ:l pɑ:s] *Erlaubnis, sich während des Unterrichts auf dem Flur aufzuhalten* **IV U2**, 43
hallway ['hɔ:lweɪ] Flur; Diele; Korridor **IV U2**, 43
ham [hæm] Schinken **III**
hammer ['hæmə] Hammer **II**
hand [hænd] Hand **I**
Clap your **hands**. [ˌklæp jɔ: 'hændz] Klatsch/Klatscht in die Hände. **I**
On the one **hand** …, (but) on the other **hand** … [ɒn ðəˌ'wʌn ˌhænd … (bʌt) ɒn ðiˌ'ʌðə ˌhænd …] Einerseits …, (aber) andererseits … **II**
*to **hang** on [ˌhæŋˌ'ɒn] (einen Augenblick) warten **IV U1**, 10
*to **hang** out (with) *(infml)* [ˌhæŋˌ'aʊt wɪð] sich herumtreiben (mit); rumhängen (mit); sich treffen (mit) **III**
*to **hang** up [ˌhæŋˌ'ʌp] aufhängen **II**
to **happen** ['hæpn] geschehen; passieren **I**
happy ['hæpi] glücklich; froh; fröhlich **I**
happy ending [ˌhæpi 'endɪŋ] Happy End **III**
Happy Birthday! [ˌhæpi 'bɜ:θdeɪ] Alles Gute zum Geburtstag!; Herzlichen Glückwunsch zum Geburtstag! **I**
harbour ['hɑ:bə] Hafen **III**
hard [hɑ:d] hart; schwer; schwierig; *hier:* stark **II**
*to be **hard** on sb [bi 'hɑ:dˌɒn] streng mit jmdm. sein **III**
hardly ['hɑ:dli] kaum **IV TS1**, 34
harsh [hɑ:ʃ] rau; hart **IV AC2**, 40
harvest ['hɑ:vɪst] Ernte **IV U2**, 45
hat [hæt] Hut **I**
to **hate** [heɪt] hassen; nicht mögen **II**
*to **have** [hæv] haben **I**
*to **have** a look (at) [ˌhævˌə 'lʊk] anschauen **II**
*to **have** a point [ˌhævˌə 'pɔɪnt] nicht ganz unrecht haben **III**
*to **have** breakfast [ˌhæv 'brekfəst] frühstücken **I**
*to **have** fun [ˌhæv 'fʌn] Spaß haben; sich amüsieren **I**
*to **have** got [hæv 'gɒt] besitzen; haben **I**
*to **have** in common [ˌhævˌɪn 'kɒmən] gemeinsam haben **III**
*to **have** no clue [ˌhæv nəʊ 'klu:] keine Ahnung haben **IV AC2**, 41
*to **have** to ['hæv tə] müssen **II**
Have a good time. [ˌhævˌə gʊd 'taɪm] Viel Spaß. ⟨**IV TS1**, 36⟩
*to **have** *(a sweet)* [hæv] *(ein Bonbon)* nehmen; *(ein Bonbon)* essen **I**
he [hi:] er **I**
head [hed] Kopf **I**
*to get sth out of one's **head** [get ˌaʊtˌəv wʌnz 'hed] etw. aus dem Kopf bekommen **III**
head of state [ˌhedˌəv 'steɪt] Staatsoberhaupt **II**
With a very big **head**! [ˌwɪð ə ˌveri bɪg 'hed] Und ein Angeber! **II**
to **head** for ['hed fə] zusteuern auf ⟨**IV TS1**, 34⟩
headache *(no pl)* ['hedeɪk] Kopfschmerzen; Kopfweh **II**
heading ['hedɪŋ] Überschrift; Titel **I**
headline ['hedlaɪn] Schlagzeile **III**
headphones *(pl)* ['hedfəʊnz] Kopfhörer **II**
health [helθ] Gesundheit **II**
healthy ['helθi] gesund **I**
*to **hear** [hɪə] hören **I**
I **hear** … [aɪ 'hɪə] Ich habe gehört, dass … **I**
heart [hɑ:t] Herz; *hier:* Zentrum **II**
*to learn … by **heart** [ˌlɜ:n baɪ 'hɑ:t] auswendig lernen **I**
heating ['hi:tɪŋ] Heizung **III**
underfloor **heating** *(no pl)* [ˌʌndəflɔ: 'hi:tɪŋ] Fußbodenheizung **III**
heavy ['hevi] schwer; stark **III**
hectic ['hektɪk] hektisch ⟨**IV U3**, 81⟩
hedgehog ['hedʒhɒg] Igel **III**
height [haɪt] Höhe ⟨**IV TS3**, 102⟩
Hello. [hel'əʊ] Hallo. **I**
*to say **hello** (to) [ˌseɪ hel'əʊ tə] grüßen; Grüße ausrichten (an) **I**
help [help] Hilfe **I**
to **help** [help] helfen **I**
to **help** out [ˌhelpˌ'aʊt] aushelfen **III**
helpful ['helpfl] hilfsbereit; hilfreich **I**
helpless ['helpləs] hilflos **I**
her [hɜ:] ihr/-e; sie **I**
herb [hɜ:b] Kraut **IV U1**, 11
here [hɪə] hier **I**
right **here** [ˌraɪt 'hɪə] genau hier **II**
Here you are. [ˌhɪə juˌ'ɑ:] Bitte schön. **I**
Here's … [hɪəz] Hier ist … **I**
hero, **heroes** *(pl)* ['hɪərəʊ, 'hɪərəʊz] Held **III**
heroine ['herəʊɪn] Heldin **III**
to **hesitate** ['hezɪteɪt] zögern **III**
Hey! [heɪ] Hi.; He!; Hallo. **I**
Hi. [haɪ] Hi.; Hallo. **I**
hibernation [ˌhaɪbə'neɪʃn] Winterschlaf **III**
*to **hide** [haɪd] (sich) verstecken **III**
high [haɪ] hoch; groß **II**
high school *(AE)* ['haɪ ˌsku:l] High School *(weiterführende Schule in den USA, Oberstufe)* **IV U2**, 43
high tide ['haɪ ˌtaɪd] Flut **II**
the **high** street [ðə 'haɪ ˌstri:t] die Haupteinkaufsstraße **III**
highlight ['haɪlaɪt] Highlight; Höhepunkt **II**
highly ['haɪli] höchst- **IV TS2**, 65
hiking ['haɪkɪŋ] Wandern **III**
hill [hɪl] Berg; Hügel **III**
him [hɪm] ihn; ihm **I**
himself [hɪm'self] er/sich (selbst); selber **II**
hint [hɪnt] Hinweis; Andeutung; Tipp **III**
his [hɪz] sein/-e **I**
historic [hɪ'stɒrɪk] historisch **III**
historical [hɪ'stɒrɪkl] historisch; geschichtlich **I**
history ['hɪstri] Geschichte **II**
living **history** show [ˌlɪvɪŋ 'hɪstəri ˌʃəʊ] *Show, in der historischer Alltag nachgespielt wird* **III**
*to **hit** [hɪt] schlagen; treffen **I**
hoax [həʊks] Täuschung; Trick **IV TS3**, 102
hobby, **hobbies** *(pl)* ['hɒbi; 'hɒbiz] Hobby **I**
hockey [hɒki] Hockey **II**
to **hog** a conversation [ˌhɒgˌə kɒnvə'seɪʃn] ein Gespräch für sich in Beschlag nehmen; ein Gespräch dominieren **III**
*to **hold** [həʊld] halten; festhalten **I**
*to **hold** onto [ˌhəʊldˌ'ɒntə] (sich) festhalten an **III**
*to **hold** open [ˌhəʊldˌ'əʊpn] aufhalten **IV AC1**, 22
hole [həʊl] Loch **II**
holiday ['hɒlədeɪ] Urlaub; Feiertag **I**
holidays *(pl)* ['hɒlədeɪz] Ferien **I**
home [həʊm] Zuhause; Heim **I**
at **home** [ət 'həʊm] zu Hause **I**
home [həʊm] nach Hause **I**
homeless ['həʊmləs] obdachlos **IV U2**, 51
homeless shelter ['həʊmləs ˌʃeltə] Obdachlosenunterkunft **IV U2**, 51
homepage ['həʊmpeɪdʒ] Homepage **I**

*to be **homesick** [bi 'həʊmsɪk] Heimweh haben **IV U1**, 18
hometown ['həʊmtaʊn] Heimatstadt **IV U3**, 75
homework ['həʊmwɜ:k] Hausaufgabe(n) **I**
honest ['ɒnɪst] ehrlich **III**
honey ['hʌni] Honig **III**
to **hook** [hʊk] *hier:* fesseln **III**
hope [həʊp] Hoffnung **II**
to **hope** [həʊp] hoffen **I**
hopeful ['həʊpfl] hoffnungsvoll **I**
horn [hɔ:n] Horn **III**
horrified ['hɒrɪfaɪd] entsetzt **I**
horror ['hɒrə] Horrorgeschichte; Horrorfilm; Horror **III**
horse [hɔ:s] Pferd **I**
hospital ['hɒspɪtl] Hospital; Krankenhaus **II**
host family ['həʊst ˌfæmli] Gastfamilie **III**
hostel ['hɒstl] Herberge **IV U1**, 10
hostile ['hɒstaɪl] feindlich; ablehnend ⟨**IV TS3**, 104⟩
hot [hɒt] heiß **III**
hot dog ['hɒt ˌdɒg] Hot Dog *(Würstchen im Brötchen)* ⟨**IV U3**, 75⟩
hotel [həʊ'tel] Hotel **II**
hour [aʊə] Stunde **II**
half an **hour** [ˌhɑ:f‿ən‿'aʊər] eine halbe Stunde **III**
house [haʊs] Haus **I**
to move (**house**) [mu:v (haʊs)] umziehen **III**
how [haʊ] wie **I**
How many …? [ˌhaʊ 'meni] Wie viele …? **I**
How are you? [ˌhaʊ‿'ɑ: jə] Wie geht es dir?; Wie geht es euch?; Wie geht es Ihnen? **I**
How much (is/are) …? [ˌhaʊ 'mʌtʃ‿ɪz/ɑ:] Wie viel (kostet/kosten) …? **I**
How old are you? [haʊ‿'əʊld‿ə ˌju:] Wie alt bist du?; Wie alt sind Sie? **I**
How to … ['haʊ tə] Wie man … **I**
Is this **how** you (do) …? [ɪz 'ðɪs haʊ jʊ ˌdu:] Machst du so …? **I**
that's **how** [ðæts 'haʊ] so **II**
however [haʊ'evə] jedoch **IV U3**, 76
to **hug** [hʌg] umarmen **I**
huge [hju:dʒ] riesig; riesengroß; gewaltig **II**
to **hum** [hʌm] summen **II**
human ['hju:mən] Mensch **IV TS3**, 100
human body [ˌhju:mən 'bɒdi] menschlicher Körper **II**
Humanities *(pl)* [hju:'mænətiz] Sozialwissenschaften **II**
humour *(no pl)* ['hju:mə] Humor; Stimmung **III**
sense of **humour** *(no pl)* [ˌsens‿əv 'hju:mə] Sinn für Humor **III**
hundreds of ['hʌndrədz‿əv] Hunderte (von) **III**
hungry ['hʌŋgri] hungrig **I**
to **hurry** ['hʌri] eilen; sich beeilen **I**
*to **hurt** [hɜ:t] verletzen; weh tun **II**
hurt [hɜ:t] verletzt **II**
husband ['hʌzbənd] Ehemann **II**

I

I [aɪ] ich **I**
I don't know! [ˌaɪ ˌdəʊnt 'nəʊ] Ich weiß (es) nicht! **I**
I don't like … [aɪ 'dəʊnt laɪk] Ich mag … nicht.; Ich mache … nicht gern. **I**
I hear … [aɪ 'hɪə] Ich habe gehört, dass … **I**
I like … [aɪ 'laɪk] Mir gefällt …; Ich mag … **I**
I love you. [aɪ 'lʌv ju] Ich liebe dich.; Ich mag dich. **I**
I love … [aɪ 'lʌv] Ich liebe …; Ich mag … total gern. **I**
I'd like to … *(= I would like to)* [aɪd 'laɪk tə] Ich möchte …; Ich würde gern … **I**
I'd rather [aɪd 'rɑ:ðə] ich würde lieber **III**
I'm (not) scared of … [ˌaɪm (nɒt) 'skeəd‿əv] Ich habe (keine) Angst vor … **I**
I'm afraid … [ˌaɪm‿ə'freɪd] Leider … **IV U2**, 44
I'm dog-tired. [ˌaɪm ˌdɒg'taɪəd] Ich bin hundemüde. **I**
I'm English. [aɪm‿'ɪŋglɪʃ] Ich bin Engländer/-in. **I**
I'm fine. [ˌaɪm 'faɪn] Mir geht's gut. **I**
I'm from … [ˌaɪm frɒm] Ich bin aus … **I**
I'm sorry! [ˌaɪm 'sɒri] Tut mir leid! **I**
I'm … [aɪm] Ich bin … **I**
ice [aɪs] Eis **I**
ice cream [ˌaɪs 'kri:m] Eis; Eiscreme **I**
ice rink ['aɪs ˌrɪŋk] Eisbahn; Schlittschuhbahn **I**
icebreaker ['aɪsˌbreɪkə] Eisbrecher *(Sätze, um mit jmdm. ins Gespräch zu kommen)* **IV AC1**, 23
idea [aɪ'dɪə] Idee; Einfall **I**
no **idea** [ˌnəʊ‿aɪ'dɪə] keine Ahnung **II**
to **identify** with [aɪ'dentɪfaɪ wɪð] sich identifizieren mit **III**
identity [aɪ'dentəti] Identität **II**
idiot ['ɪdiət] Idiot/-in **II**
if [ɪf] wenn; falls; ob **I**
as **if** [əz‿'ɪf] als ob **III**
if-clause ['ɪfˌklɔ:z] if-Satz **III**
If I were you … [ˌɪf aɪ wɜ: 'ju:] Wenn ich du wäre … **IV AC3**, 69
to **ignore** [ɪg'nɔ:] ignorieren; außer Acht lassen **III**
ill [ɪl] krank **III**
illegal [ɪ'li:gl] illegal; unrechtmäßig; rechtswidrig **III**
image ['ɪmɪdʒ] Bild; Abbildung **IV TS2**, 65
imagination [ɪˌmædʒɪ'neɪʃn] Fantasie; Vorstellungskraft **III**
imaginative [ɪ'mædʒɪnətɪv] einfallsreich; fantasievoll **III**
to **imagine** [ɪ'mædʒɪn] sich (etwas) vorstellen **I**
immediately [ɪ'mi:diətli] sofort; gleich **IV TS2**, 64
immigrant ['ɪmɪgrənt] Immigrant/-in; Einwanderer/-in **IV AC2**, 38
immigration [ˌɪmɪ'greɪʃn] Immigration; Einwanderung; Einreise **IV U1**, 13
immigration office [ˌɪmɪ'greɪʃn ˌɒfɪs] Einwanderungsbehörde **IV U1**, 13
imperative [ɪm'perətɪv] Imperativ; Befehlsform **III**
impolite [ˌɪmp'laɪt] unhöflich **III**
important [ɪm'pɔ:tnt] wichtig **I**
impossible [ɪm'pɒsəbl] unmöglich **IV TS3**, 102
impressed [ɪm'prest] beeindruckt **II**
impression [ɪm'preʃn] Impression; Eindruck **IV U2**, 42
to **improve** [ɪm'pru:v] sich verbessern; verbessern **I**
improvement [ɪm'pru:vmənt] Verbesserung °**IV TS2**, 67
in [ɪn] in; im; rein; herein **I**
in between [ˌɪn bɪ'twi:n] dazwischen **III**
in chorus [ɪn 'kɔ:rəs] im Chor **IV TS1**, 33
in front of [ɪn 'frʌnt‿əv] vor **I**
in need [ɪn 'ni:d] bedürftig; in Not **II**
in secret [ɪn 'si:krət] heimlich **II**
in the country [ˌɪn ðə 'kʌntri] auf dem Land **IV AC2**, 40
in the end [ˌɪn ði‿'end] schließlich; zum Schluss **II**
in the evenings [ɪn ði‿'i:vnɪŋz] abends **I**
in the mornings [ˌɪn ðə 'mɔ:nɪŋz] morgens; vormittags **I**
in the photo(s) [ˌɪn ðə 'fəʊtəʊ(z)] auf dem Foto/den Fotos **I**
in the street [ˌɪn ðə 'stri:t] in der Straße; auf der Straße **I**
to **include** [ɪn'klu:d] einschließen; beinhalten; aufnehmen; einbeziehen **III**
inconvenient [ˌɪnkən'vi:niənt] unbequem; lästig **IV TS3**, 100
in-crowd ['ɪnkraʊd] Szene; die Angesagten; die Beliebten **III**
independence *(no pl)* [ˌɪndɪ'pendəns] Unabhängigkeit **III**
independent [ˌɪndɪ'pendənt] unabhängig **III**
Indian ['ɪndiən] Inder/-in; indisch **I**; Indianer/-in; indianisch **IV U2**, 45
indirect ['ɪndɪrekt] indirekt **IV U1**, 11
indirect speech [ˌɪndɪrekt 'spi:tʃ] indirekte Rede **IV U1**, 11
individual [ˌɪndɪ'vɪdʒuəl] Einzelperson; Einzelne/-r; Individuum **IV U2**, 56
individual [ˌɪndɪ'vɪdʒuəl] individuell; einzeln **II**
indivisible [ˌɪndɪ'vɪzəbl] unteilbar ⟨**IV U2**, 49⟩
industry ['ɪndəstri] Industrie; Branche; Gewerbe **III**
infinitive [ɪn'fɪnətɪv] Infinitiv **I**

to **influence** ['ɪnfluəns] beeinflussen **II**
informal [ɪn'fɔ:ml] informell; zwanglos **IV AC4**, 107
information *(no pl)* [ˌɪnfə'meɪʃn] Information; Informationen **I**
informative [ɪn'fɔ:mətɪv] informativ **IV U2**, 56
ingredient [ɪn'gri:diənt] Zutat **III**
injury ['ɪndʒəri] Verletzung **II**
inline skating ['ɪnlaɪn ˌskeɪtɪŋ] Inlineskatefahren **I**
insecure [ˌɪnsɪ'kjʊə] unsicher **IV U2**, 47
inside [ˌɪn'saɪd] innen; im Innern; hinein; nach drinnen; in; drin **I**
to **inspire** [ɪn'spaɪə] inspirieren; anregen **IV U3**, 70
instead [ɪn'sted] stattdessen **III**
instead of [ɪn'sted‿əv] statt; anstatt; an Stelle von **IV U2**, 45
instruction [ɪn'strʌkʃn] Instruktion; Anweisung **I**
instructor [ɪn'strʌktə] Lehrer/-in; Betreuer/-in **II**
interest ['ɪntrəst] Interesse **II**
to **interest** ['ɪntrəst] (sich) interessieren **II**
*to be **interested** in [bi‿'ɪntrəstɪd‿ɪn] interessiert sein an; sich interessieren für **II**
interesting ['ɪntrəstɪŋ] interessant **I**
international [ˌɪntə'næʃnl] international **I**
internet ['ɪntənet] Internet **I**
intersection [ˌɪntə'sekʃn] Kreuzung **IV U3**, 70
interview ['ɪntəvju:] Interview; Befragung **I**
to **interview** ['ɪntəvju:] interviewen; befragen **I**
interviewee [ˌɪntəvju'i:] Befragte/-r; Interviewte/-r °**IV U3**, 93
interviewer ['ɪntəvju:ə] Interviewer/-in; Befrager/-in °**IV U3**, 92
into ['ɪntə] in; in … hinein **I**
*to be **into** [bi:‿'ɪntə] mögen; stehen auf **I**
You're **into** … ['jɔ:r‿ˌɪntə] Du magst …; Du stehst auf … **I**
to **introduce** [ˌɪntrə'dju:s] einführen; einleiten **IV U1**, 11
Introduce … [ˌɪntrə'dju:s] Stelle/Stellt … vor. **I**
introduction [ˌɪntrə'dʌkʃn] Einführung; Einleitung; Vorstellung **II**
to **invade** [ɪn'veɪd] einmarschieren (in); eindringen (in); überfallen **III**
to **invent** [ɪn'vent] erfinden **III**
invention [ɪn'venʃn] Erfindung **III**
inventor [ɪn'ventə] Erfinder/-in **III**
invisible [ɪn'vɪzəbl] unsichtbar **IV U1**, 17
invitation [ˌɪnvɪ'teɪʃn] Einladung **I**
to **invite** [ɪn'vaɪt] einladen **I**
to **involve** [ɪn'vɒlv] involvieren; einbeziehen; beteiligen **IV TS3**, 102
*to get **involved** with sb [ˌget‿ɪn'vɒlvd wɪð] sich einlassen mit jmdm. ⟨**IV TS1**, 34⟩
inward ['ɪnwəd] ankommend **III**
Irish ['aɪrɪʃ] irisch; Irisch **III**
ironic [ˌaɪ'rɒnɪk] ironisch **IV U2**, 56
irregular [ɪ'regjələ] unregelmäßig **I**
Is this how you (do) …? [ɪz 'ðɪs haʊ jʊ ˌdu:] Machst du so …? **I**
island ['aɪlənd] Insel **III**
it [ɪt] es **I**
*to make **it** ['meɪk‿ɪt] es schaffen **IV U3**, 70
It's fun. [ɪts 'fʌn] Es macht Spaß. **I**
It's great for … [ɪts 'greɪt fə] Es ist super zum/für … **I**
It's your turn. [ˌɪts 'jɔ: tɜ:n] Du bist dran. **I**
It's, like, so wild to … [ˌɪts laɪk səʊ 'waɪld tə] Es ist echt klasse … ⟨**IV AC4**, 107⟩
It's …/They're … [ɪts/ðeə] Es kostet …/Sie kosten … **I**
IT *(= Information Technology)* [ˌaɪ'ti:] Informatik; Informationstechnik **III**
item ['aɪtəm] Gegenstand; Objekt **IV U2**, 51
its [ɪts] sein/-e; ihr/-e **I**
ivory *(no pl)* ['aɪvri] Elfenbein **III**

J

jacket ['dʒækɪt] Jacke **III**
jam [dʒæm] Marmelade; Konfitüre **III**
January ['dʒænjuri] Januar **I**
*to be **jealous** (of) [bi: 'dʒeləs] eifersüchtig sein (auf); neidisch sein (auf) **I**
jelly ['dʒeli] Tortenguss; Götterspeise; Wackelpudding; Gelee **I**
jewel ['dʒu:əl] Juwel; Edelstein **III**
crown **jewels** [ˌkraʊn 'dʒu:əlz] Kronjuwelen **II**
jewellery ['dʒu:əlri] Schmuck **I**
Jewish ['dʒu:ɪʃ] jüdisch **IV U3**, 75
job [dʒɒb] Arbeit; Aufgabe; Job **I**
mouth **jogging** ['maʊθ ˌdʒɒgɪŋ] Training für den Mund **I**
to **join** [dʒɔɪn] beitreten; sich anschließen; verbinden **II**
joke [dʒəʊk] Witz **I**
to **joke** [dʒəʊk] scherzen **II**
journey ['dʒɜ:ni] Reise; Fahrt **III**
to **judge** [dʒʌdʒ] beurteilen; bewerten **III**
juggling ['dʒʌglɪŋ] Jonglieren **II**
juice [dʒu:s] Saft **I**
July [dʒʊ'laɪ] Juli **I**
to **jump** [dʒʌmp] springen **I**
to **jump** back [ˌdʒʌmp‿'bæk] zurückspringen; *hier:* zurückschrecken **II**
to **jump** the queue [ˌdʒʌmp ðə 'kju:] sich vordrängeln **I**
June [dʒu:n] Juni **I**
jungle ['dʒʌŋgl] Dschungel **IV U3**, 70
a bunch of **junk** [əˌbʌnʃ‿əv 'dʒʌŋk] ein Haufen Müll ⟨**IV U3**, 84⟩
piece of **junk** [ˌpi:s‿əv 'dʒʌŋk] Stück Schrott **III**
just [dʒʌst] gerade; nur; einfach **I**
just about anywhere [ˌdʒʌst‿əˌbaʊt 'eniweə] praktisch überall **IV TS2**, 64
just in time [ˌdʒʌst‿ɪn 'taɪm] gerade rechtzeitig **IV U3**, 72
justice ['dʒʌstɪs] Gerechtigkeit ⟨**IV U2**, 49⟩
juvenile ['dʒu:vnaɪl] Jugend- ⟨**IV U3**, 88⟩

K

keen [ki:n] begeistert; leidenschaftlich ⟨**IV TS1**, 36⟩
*to **keep** [ki:p] behalten; aufbewahren; halten **I**
*to **keep** away from [ˌki:p‿ə'weɪ frəm] (sich) fernhalten von **III**
*to **keep** going [ˌki:p 'gəʊɪŋ] aufrechterhalten **II**
*to **keep** in mind [ˌki:p‿ɪn 'maɪnd] beachten; im Gedächtnis behalten °**IV U3**, 79
*to **keep** in touch [ˌki:p‿ɪn 'tʌtʃ] in Kontakt bleiben **IV U2**, 44
*to **keep** one's feet or hands still [ˌki:p wʌnz: 'fi:t‿ɔ: 'hændz stɪl] die Beine und Hände ruhig halten **III**
*to **keep** out (of) [ˌki:p‿'aʊt əv] draußen bleiben; draußen halten **III**
*to **keep** the ball bouncing [ˌki:p ðə bɔ:l 'baʊntsɪŋ] *hier:* das Gespräch am Laufen halten **III**
*to **keep** up (with) [ˌki:p‿'ʌp (wɪð)] mithalten (mit); Schritt halten (mit) **II**
*to **keep** your fingers crossed [ˌki:p jɔ: ˌfɪŋgəz 'krɒst] die Daumen drücken **I**
*to **keep** [ki:p] *hier:* weiter tun; immer wieder tun **IV U2**, 44
key [ki:] Schlüssel **II**
key ring ['ki: ˌrɪŋ] Schlüsselbund; Schlüsselanhänger **III**
key word ['ki: wɜ:d] Stichwort; Schlüsselbegriff **I**
to **kick** [kɪk] schießen; treten **II**
kid [kɪd] Jugendliche/-r; Kind **IV U2**, 42
to **kill** [kɪl] töten; umbringen **III**
kilometre (km) ['kɪləˌmi:tə; kɪ'lɒmɪtə] Kilometer **III**
kilt [kɪlt] Kilt; Schottenrock **III**
kind [kaɪnd] Art; Sorte **I**
kind of ['kaɪnd‿əv] ziemlich ⟨**IV U3**, 90⟩
king [kɪŋ] König **I**
kitchen ['kɪtʃɪn] Küche **I**
knife [naɪf], **knives** [naɪvz] *(pl)* Messer **III**
knight [naɪt] Ritter **III**
knob [nɒb] Griff **II**
*to **know** [nəʊ] kennen; wissen **I**
*to be **known** as [bi 'nəʊn‿əz] bekannt sein als **IV U3**, 74
*to get to **know** [ˌget tə 'nəʊ] kennenlernen **III**
I don't **know**! [ˌaɪ ˌdəʊnt 'nəʊ] Ich weiß (es) nicht! **I**
You **know** how to … [ju: 'nəʊ ˌhaʊ tə] Du weißt, wie man …; Ihr wisst, wie man … **I**
koala [kəʊ'ɑ:lə] Koala **III**

Korean [kəˈriːən] koreanisch; Koreanisch; Koreaner/-in **II**
South **Korean** [ˌsaʊθ kəˈriːən] Südkoreaner/-in; südkoreanisch; Südkoreanisch **II**

L

lab(oratory) [læb; ləˈbɒrətri] Labor **IV AC3**, 68
child **labor** *(AE)* [ˌtʃaɪld ˈleɪbə] Kinderarbeit **IV U2**, 48
laboratory [læb; ləˈbɒrətri] Labor **IV AC3**, 68
ladder [ˈlædə] Leiter **II**
lady [ˈleɪdi] Lady; Dame **III**
lady-in-waiting [ˌleɪdiɪnˈweɪtɪŋ] Hofdame **III**
laid-back [ˌleɪdˈbæk] entspannt; locker **III**
lake [leɪk] See **I**
boating **lake** [ˈbəʊtɪŋ ˌleɪk] See zum Rudern **I**
lamb [læm] Lamm; Lämmchen **I**
land [lænd] Land **I**
to **land** [lænd] landen **II**
landing [ˈlændɪŋ] Landung **IV U1**, 15
moon **landing** [ˈmuːn ˌlændɪŋ] Mondlandung **IV TS3**, 100
landscape [ˈlændskeɪp] Landschaft **III**
language [ˈlæŋgwɪdʒ] Sprache **I**
first **language** [ˌfɜːst ˈlæŋgwɪdʒ] Muttersprache **II**
foreign **language** [ˌfɒrɪn ˈlæŋgwɪdʒ] Fremdsprache **II**
official **language** [əˌfɪʃl ˈlæŋgwɪdʒ] Amtssprache **II**
laptop [ˈlæptɒp] Laptop **II**
large [lɑːdʒ] groß; riesig **II**
lassi [ˈlʌsi] Lassi **I**
last [lɑːst] letzte/-r/-s **I**
at **last** [ət ˈlɑːst] endlich; schließlich **I**
to save the best for **last** [ˌseɪv ðə ˌbest fə ˈlɑːst] sich das Beste bis zum Schluss aufheben **IV U3**, 72
late [leɪt] spät; zu spät **I**
*to be **late** [biː ˈleɪt] zu spät dran sein; zu spät kommen **I**
later [ˈleɪtə] später **I**
latest [ˈleɪtɪst] neueste/-r/-s **IV U1**, 11
to **laugh** [lɑːf] lachen **I**
lavish [ˈlævɪʃ] üppig; verschwenderisch **IV U1**, 19
*to **lay** [leɪ] legen **IV U3**, 89
layer (of) [ˈleɪər‿əv] Schicht (aus); Lage (aus) **III**
layout [ˈleɪaʊt] Layout; Anordnung **III**
lazy [ˈleɪzi] faul **III**
lead part [ˌliːd ˈpɑːt] Hauptrolle **III**
*to **lead** [liːd] führen; anführen **III**
*to **lead** off [liːd‿ˈɒf] wegführen **III**
lead [liːd] Haupt- **III**
lead-in [ˈliːdɪn] Einführung; Einleitung **IV U3**, 89
leaflet [ˈliːflət] Broschüre; Informationsblatt; Prospekt **IV AC1**, 23

leap [liːp] Sprung; Satz ⟨**IV TS3**, 101⟩
*to **learn** [lɜːn] lernen **I**
*to **learn** a lesson from [ˌlɜːn‿ə ˈlesn frəm] lernen aus ⟨**IV U3**, 86⟩
*to **learn** about [ˈlɜːn‿əˌbaʊt] erfahren über **III**
*to **learn** … by heart [ˌlɜːn baɪ ˈhɑːt] auswendig lernen **I**
a lot to **learn** [əˌlɒt tə ˈlɜːn] viel zu lernen **I**
at **least** [ət ˈliːst] mindestens; wenigstens **II**
*to **leave** [liːv] verlassen; lassen; abfahren; losgehen **II**
*to **leave** a message [ˌliːv‿ə ˈmesɪdʒ] eine Nachricht hinterlassen **I**
*to **leave** behind [ˌliːv‿bɪˈhaɪnd] zurücklassen **III**
*to **leave** it to cool [ˌliːv‿ɪt tə ˈkuːl] kalt stellen **I**
*to **leave** out [ˌliːv‿ˈaʊt] auslassen; weglassen °**IV U2**, 54
*to **leave** sb alone [ˌliːv‿əˈləʊn] jmdn. in Ruhe lassen **IV U2**, 53
*to **leave** space [liːv ˈspeɪs] Platz lassen **I**
Leave that to me. [ˌliːv ðæt tə ˈmiː] Überlass das mir. **IV U3**, 72
left [left] linke/-r/-s; links **I**
on the **left** [ɒn ðə ˈleft] auf der linken Seite; links **I**
left [left] übrig **I**
left-hand [ˈlefthænd] linke/-r/-s °**IV U2**, 45
leg [leg] Bein **II**
legend [ˈledʒənd] Legende; Sage **III**
leisure [ˈleʒə] Freizeit; Freizeit- **I**
leisure centre [ˈleʒə ˌsentə] Freizeitzentrum **I**
lemon [ˈlemən] Zitrone **II**
lemonade [ˌleməˈneɪd] Limonade **I**
*to **lend** [ˈlend tə] leihen; verleihen **III**
less [les] weniger **III**
to settle for **less** [ˌsetl fə ˈles] sich mit weniger zufrieden geben **IV TS2**, 66
lesson [ˈlesn] Unterrichtsstunde; Schulstunde; Unterricht **I**
*to learn a **lesson** from [ˌlɜːn‿ə ˈlesn frəm] lernen aus ⟨**IV U3**, 86⟩
*to **let** [let] lassen **I**
*to **let** go (of) [ˌlet ˈgəʊ (əv)] loslassen **II**
Let's face it. [lets ˈfeɪs‿ɪt] Machen wir uns doch nichts vor. **IV TS1**, 32
Let's … [lets] Lass/Lasst uns … **I**
letter [ˈletə] Buchstabe **I**; Brief **II**
capital **letter** [ˌkæpɪtl ˈletə] Großbuchstabe **I**
liberty [ˈlɪbəti] Freiheit **IV U3**, 74
library [ˈlaɪbri] Bibliothek; Bücherei **III**
lie [laɪ] Lüge **III**
white **lie** [ˌwaɪt ˈlaɪ] Notlüge **IV TS1**, 32
to **lie** [laɪ] lügen **II**
*to **lie** [laɪ] liegen **II**
life, **lives** *(pl)* [laɪf, laɪvz] Leben **II**
lifeboat [ˈlaɪfbəʊt] Rettungsboot **I**

lifebuoy [ˈlaɪfbɔɪ] Rettungsring **I**
lifestyle [ˈlaɪfstaɪl] Lebensstil; Lifestyle **III**
to **lift** [lɪft] heben; hochheben; anheben **IV U3**, 76
light [laɪt] Licht; Lampe **II**
light [laɪt] leicht **III**
to **lighten** [ˈlaɪtn] aufhellen **III**
lightning *(no pl)* [ˈlaɪtnɪŋ] Blitz **II**
to **like** [laɪk] mögen; gern haben **I**
would **like** [wʊd ˈlaɪk] würde/-st/-n/-t gern; hätte/-st/-n/-t gern **I**
I don't **like** … [aɪ ˈdəʊnt laɪk] Ich mag … nicht.; Ich mache … nicht gern. **I**
I **like** singing and dancing. [ˌaɪ laɪk ˌsɪŋɪŋ‿ənd ˈdɑːnsɪŋ] Ich singe und tanze gern. **I**
I **like** … [aɪ ˈlaɪk] Mir gefällt …; Ich mag … **I**
I'd **like** to … *(= I would like to)* [aɪd ˈlaɪk tə] Ich möchte …; Ich würde gern … **I**
Would you **like** …? [ˌwʊd jʊ ˈlaɪk] Möchtest du …?; Möchten Sie …?; Möchtet ihr …? **II**
like [laɪk] wie **I**
*to be **like** [bi ˈlaɪk] sein **III**
like that [laɪk ˈðæt] so **I**
like this [laɪk ˈðɪs] so **I**
What was it **like**? [ˌwɒt wɒz‿ɪt ˈlaɪk] Wie war es? **III**
likes *(pl)* [laɪks] Vorlieben **IV U2**, 46
limit [ˈlɪmɪt] Limit; Grenze **III**
line [laɪn] Zeile; Linie **I**
finish **line** [ˈfɪnɪʃ ˌlaɪn] Ziellinie **II**
opening **line** [ˈəʊpnɪŋ‿laɪn] der erste Satz **III**
*to stand in **line** *(AE)* [ˌstænd‿ɪn ˈlaɪn] anstehen; Schlange stehen; (sich) anstellen **IV AC3**, 69
time **line** [ˈtaɪm ˌlaɪn] Zeitstrahl **I**
lines *(pl)* [laɪnz] Text **IV TS1**, 30
to **line** up [laɪn‿ˈʌp] (sich) aufstellen **III**
link [lɪŋk] Link; Verbindung **II**
to **link** [lɪŋk] verbinden **II**
linking word [ˈlɪŋkɪŋ ˌwɜːd] Bindewort **I**
lion [ˈlaɪən] Löwe **II**
list [lɪst] Liste **I**
to **listen** (to) [ˈlɪsn] zuhören; anhören **I**
Listen again. [ˌlɪsn‿əˈgen] Hör/Hört noch einmal zu. **I**
to **listen** for [ˈlɪsn fə] horchen auf **I**
listener [ˈlɪsənə] Zuhörer/-in **II**
listening [ˈlɪsnɪŋ] Hören **I**
litre (l) [ˈliːtə] Liter **III**
to **litter** [ˈlɪtə] verschmutzen; verunreinigen; Müll herumliegen lassen **IV AC1**, 22
little [ˈlɪtl] klein **I**
a **little** [ə ˈlɪtl] ein wenig; etwas **I**
little [ˈlɪtl] wenig °**IV U3**, 91
to **live** [lɪv] wohnen; leben **I**
standard of **living** [ˌstændəd‿əv ˈlɪvɪŋ] Lebensstandard **IV AC2**, 40
live [laɪv] live **III**
lively [ˈlaɪvli] lebendig **II**

living room ['lɪvɪŋ rʊm] Wohnzimmer **I**
*to make a living (from) [ˌmeɪk‿ə 'lɪvɪŋ frəm] seinen Lebensunterhalt bestreiten (mit) **IV U3**, 79
living history show [ˌlɪvɪŋ 'hɪstəri ˌʃəʊ] *Show, in der historischer Alltag nachgespielt wird* **III**
local ['ləʊkl] örtlich; lokal **III**
*to be located [bi ləʊ'keɪtɪd] gelegen sein; liegen **IV U3**, 73
location [ləʊ'keɪʃn] Handlungsort; Lage; Standort **II**
loch [lɒx; lɒk] See *(in Schottland)* **III**
locked [lɒkt] abgeschlossen **II**
locker ['lɒkə] Schließfach; Spind **I**
loft [lɒft] Dachboden **I**
logbook ['lɒgbʊk] Logbuch °**IV TS3**, 102
logic ['lɒdʒɪk] Logik **III**
LOL (= laughing out loud) [lɒl] LOL **II**
Londoner ['lʌndənə] Londoner/-in **I**
lonely ['ləʊnli] einsam **I**
long [lɒŋ] lang **I**
as **long** as [əz 'lɒŋ‿əz] solange ⟨**IV TS1**, 34⟩
long shot ['lɒŋ ˌʃɒt] Totale *(Kameraeinstellung)* **IV U3**, 89
(not) any **longer** [nɒt‿eni 'lɒŋgə] (nicht) mehr; (nicht) länger **III**
look [lʊk] Blick **I**
*to give sb funny **looks** [ˌgɪv fʌni 'lʊks] jmdn. schief anschauen **III**
*to have a **look** (at) [ˌhæv‿ə 'lʊk] anschauen **II**
*to take a **look** at [ˌteɪk‿ə 'lʊk‿æt] einen Blick werfen auf **II**
to look [lʊk] schauen; sehen; aussehen **I**
Look! [lʊk] Schau/Schaut mal! **I**
to **look** after [ˌlʊk‿'ɑːftə] aufpassen auf; hüten; sich kümmern um **I**
to **look** at ['lʊk‿ət] anschauen; ansehen **I**
to **look** for ['lʊk fɔː] suchen nach **I**
to **look** forward to [ˌlʊk 'fɔːwəd tə] sich freuen auf **II**
to **look** out [ˌlʊk‿'aʊt] aufpassen **II**
to **look** up [ˌlʊk‿'ʌp] nachschlagen; nachschauen **I**
Look closely … [ˌlʊk 'kləʊsli] Schau(t) genau … **II**
what the man **looked** like [ˌwɒt ðə mæn 'lʊkt laɪk] wie der Mann aussah **II**
looks *(pl)* [lʊks] Aussehen **III**
lord [lɔːd] Lord; Herr **III**
lorry ['lɒri] Lastwagen **IV U3**, 79
*to lose [luːz] verlieren **II**
lost [lɒst] verloren ⟨**IV TS3**, 104⟩
*to get **lost** [ˌget 'lɒst] verloren gehen; sich verirren **III**
a lot [ə 'lɒt] viel **I**
a lot of [ə 'lɒt‿əv] viel/-e; eine Menge **I**
lots (of) ['lɒts‿əv] viel/-e; jede Menge **I**
loud [laʊd] laut **I**
*to read/sing out **loud** [ˌriːd/sɪŋ‿aʊt 'laʊd] laut vorsingen **III**

departure lounge [dɪ'pɑːtʃə ˌlaʊndʒ] Abflughalle **IV U1**, 9
love [lʌv] Liebe **III**
Love … [lʌv] Liebe Grüße *(am Briefende)*; Herzliche Grüße *(am Briefende)* **I**
to love [lʌv] lieben; gern mögen **I**
would **love** [wʊd 'lʌv] würde/-st/-n/-t sehr gern; hätte/-st-/-n/-t sehr gern **I**
I **love** you. [aɪ 'lʌv ju] Ich liebe dich.; Ich mag dich. **I**
I **love** … [aɪ 'lʌv] Ich liebe …; Ich mag … total gern. **I**
lovebirds *(pl)* ['lʌvˌbɜːdz] Turteltauben **II**
lovely ['lʌvli] schön; hübsch **IV TS2**, 65
low [ləʊ] niedrig **II**
low tide ['ləʊ ˌtaɪd] Ebbe **II**
lox [lɑːks] Räucherlachs ⟨**IV U3**, 75⟩
good luck [ˌgʊd 'lʌk] viel Glück **IV U3**, 76
What luck! [wɒt 'lʌk] Was für ein Glück! **III**
luckily ['lʌkɪli] glücklicherweise **IV U2**, 44
lucky … ['lʌki] … der/die Glückliche **I**
*to be **lucky** [bi‿'lʌki] Glück haben **II**
lucky charm [ˌlʌki 'tʃɑːm] Glücksbringer; Talisman **I**
… is/are **lucky**. [ɪz/ɑː 'lʌki] … hat/haben Glück. **I**
luggage *(no pl)* ['lʌgɪdʒ] Gepäck **IV U1**, 8
lunch [lʌnʃ] Mittagessen **I**
lunch break ['lʌnʃbreɪk] Mittagspause **I**
lunchtime ['lʌnʃtaɪm] Mittagszeit; Mittagspause **IV AC3**, 68
lung [lʌŋ] Lunge **IV U3**, 71
the lungs *(pl)* [ðə 'lʌŋz] die Lunge **III**
luxury ['lʌkʃri] Luxus **IV AC2**, 40
(song) lyrics *(pl)* [sɒŋ 'lɪrɪks] Liedtext **III**

M

machine [mə'ʃiːn] Automat; Maschine; Apparat; Gerät **I**
answering **machine** ['ɑːnsrɪŋ məˌʃiːn] Anrufbeantworter **I**
vending **machine** ['vendɪŋ məˌʃiːn] Automat **IV U1**, 10
washing **machine** ['wɒʃɪŋ məˌʃiːn] Waschmaschine **II**
mad [mæd] verrückt **II**; wütend **IV AC3**, 69
Dear Sir or Madam [dɪə ˌsɜːr‿ɔː 'mædəm] Sehr geehrte Dame, sehr geehrter Herr **III**
made up from [ˌmeɪd‿'ʌp frəm] zusammengesetzt aus °**IV TS3**, 102
magazine [ˌmægə'ziːn] Zeitschrift **I**
maggot ['mægət] Made ⟨**IV U3**, 86⟩
magic ['mædʒɪk] Magie; Zauberei **IV U1**, 19
magical ['mædʒɪkəl] magisch; Zauber- **III**
to mail ['iːmeɪl] mailen; per E-Mail schicken **II**
main [meɪn] Haupt- **I**
main clause ['meɪn ˌklɔːz] Hauptsatz **III**
*to make [meɪk] machen; tun; bilden; *hier:* ergeben **I**

*to be **made** of [bi 'meɪd‿əv] bestehen aus **III**
*to **make** a decision [ˌmeɪk‿ə dɪ'sɪʒn] eine Entscheidung treffen **II**
*to **make** a living (from) [ˌmeɪk‿ə 'lɪvɪŋ frəm] seinen Lebensunterhalt bestreiten (mit) **IV U3**, 79
*to **make** a wish [ˌmeɪk‿ə 'wɪʃ] sich etwas wünschen **I**
*to **make** friends [ˌmeɪk 'frendz] Freundschaft schließen **II**
*to **make** it ['meɪk‿ɪt] es schaffen **IV U3**, 70
*to **make** money [ˌmeɪk 'mʌni] Geld verdienen **I**
*to **make** notes [ˌmeɪk 'nəʊts] Notizen machen **I**
*to **make** sb angry [meɪk 'æŋgri] jmdn. wütend machen; jmdn. verärgern **III**
*to **make** sense [ˌmeɪk 'sens] Sinn ergeben; einleuchten **IV TS3**, 102
*to **make** somebody do something [meɪk] jmdn. dazu bringen, etw. zu tun **II**
*to **make** sure [ˌmeɪk 'ʃɔː] sich versichern **I**
*to **make** trouble [ˌmeɪk 'trʌbl] Ärger machen; in Schwierigkeiten bringen **I**
*to **make** use of [meɪk 'juːz‿əv] benutzen; verwenden **IV U3**, 89
shopping mall ['ʃɒpɪŋ ˌmɔːl] Einkaufszentrum **IV U2**, 43
man, men *(pl)* [mæn; men] Mann **I**
what the **man** looked like [ˌwɒt ðə mæn 'lʊkt laɪk] wie der Mann aussah **II**
manga ['mæŋgə] Manga *(japanischer Comic)* **II**
mango ['mæŋgəʊ] Mango **I**
manicure ['mænɪkjʊə] Maniküre ⟨**IV U3**, 86⟩
mankind [mæn'kaɪnd] Menschheit ⟨**IV TS3**, 101⟩
manners *(pl)* ['mænəz] Manieren; Benehmen **IV AC1**, 23
software manual ['sɒftweə ˌmænjuəl] Softwarehandbuch **III**
many ['meni] viele **I**
How **many** …? [ˌhaʊ 'meni] Wie viele …? **I**
map [mæp] Stadtplan; Landkarte **I**
mind **map** ['maɪnd mæp] Wörternetz *(eine Art Schaubild)* **I**
marathon ['mærəθn] Marathon **II**
March [mɑːtʃ] März **I**
to march [mɑːtʃ] marschieren **III**
mark [mɑːk] Note **III**
marked [mɑːkt] markiert °**IV AC4**, 106
market ['mɑːkɪt] Markt **I**
flea **market** ['fliː ˌmɑːkɪt] Flohmarkt **I**
marmalade ['mɑːməleɪd] Marmelade aus Zitrusfrüchten **III**
to marry ['mæri] heiraten **III**
mashed potatoes *(pl)* [ˌmæʃt pə'teɪtəʊz] Kartoffelpüree **III**
mask [mɑːsk] Maske **IV U1**, 16
massive ['mæsɪv] riesig; massiv; *hier:* super **IV AC2**, 41

raven **master** ['reɪvn ˌmɑːstə] Herr der Raben **II**
match [mætʃ] Spiel; Match **II**
to **match** [mætʃ] zuordnen; passen zu; entsprechen **I**
mate [meɪt] Schiffsoffizier; Maat **I**
material [mə'tɪəriəl] Material **II**
Maths [mæθs] Mathematik; Mathe **II**
What's the **matter?** [ˌwɒts ðə 'mætə] Was ist los?; Was hast du? **III**
It doesn't **matter.** [ɪt ˌdʌznt 'mætə] Es ist egal. **III**
May [meɪ] Mai **I**
may [meɪ] (vielleicht) können; dürfen **II**
maybe ['meɪbi] vielleicht **I**
mayo ['meɪəʊ] Mayonnaise ⟨**IV U3**, 87⟩
me [miː] ich; mich; mir **I**
meal [miːl] Mahlzeit; Essen **II**
ready **meal** [ˌredi 'miːl] Fertiggericht **I**
*to **mean** [miːn] bedeuten; meinen **II**
(I) didn't **mean** to … [aɪ ˌdɪdnt 'miːn tə] Ich wollte nicht … **IV AC4**, 107
mean [miːn] gemein **IV TS1**, 33
meaning ['miːnɪŋ] Bedeutung; Sinn **II**
by any **means** [baɪ ˌeni 'miːnz] mit allen Mitteln **IV U3**, 70
meat *(no pl)* [miːt] Fleisch **III**
mechanic [mə'kænɪk] Mechaniker/-in; Kfz-Mechaniker/-in **II**
media ['miːdiə] Medien **II**
social **media** [ˌsəʊʃl 'miːdiə] soziale Netzwerke **IV U2**, 46
mediation [ˌmiːdi'eɪʃn] Sprachmittlung **I**
medicine *(no pl)* ['medsn] Medizin; Medikamente **III**
medieval [ˌmedi'iːvl] mittelalterlich **III**
medium ['miːdiəm] mittel; mittelgroß **IV U3**, 89
medium shot ['miːdiəm ʃɒt] Halbtotale *(Kameraeinstellung)* **IV U3**, 89
*to **meet** [miːt] treffen; sich treffen **I**
*to **meet** halfway [ˌmiːt hɑːf'weɪ] sich auf halbem Weg treffen **III**
*to **meet** up [ˌmiːt‿'ʌp] sich treffen **IV U2**, 44
melody ['melədi] Melodie **III**
melting pot ['meltɪŋ ˌpɒt] Schmelztiegel **IV U3**, 70
member ['membə] Mitglied **II**
memory ['memri] Erinnerung; Gedächtnis **II**
menacing ['menɪsɪŋ] drohend ⟨**IV U3**, 90⟩
to **mention** ['menʃn] erwähnen **II**
menu ['menjuː] Speisekarte **IV U2**, 45
merchant ['mɜːtʃənt] Kaufmann; Händler **II**
mess [mes] Unordnung; Durcheinander; Schweinerei **IV U2**, 54
to **mess** sth up [ˌmes‿'ʌp] etw. durcheinanderbringen; etw. vergeigen **IV TS1**, 30
message ['mesɪdʒ] Botschaft; Nachricht **I**
*to leave a **message** [ˌliːv‿ə 'mesɪdʒ] eine Nachricht hinterlassen **I**
*to take a **message** [ˌteɪk‿ə 'mesɪdʒ] eine Nachricht entgegennehmen; jmdm. etw. ausrichten **I**
text (**message**) ['tekst ˌmesɪdʒ] SMS; Kurznachricht **I**
messy ['mesi] unordentlich **III**
metre ['miːtə] Meter **II**
middle ['mɪdl] Mitte **I**
middle school *(AE)* ['mɪdl ˌskuːl] Mittelschule *(weiterführende Schule in den USA, Mittelstufe)* **IV U2**, 43
in the **middle** of nowhere [ɪn ðə ˌmɪdl‿əv 'nəʊweə] mitten im Nirgendwo **IV U2**, 46
midnight ['mɪdnaɪt] Mitternacht **III**
might [maɪt] könnte/-n (vielleicht) **IV U2**, 50
It **might** as well be … [ˌɪt maɪt əs 'wel biː …] Es könnte/-n auch … sein. **III**
mile [maɪl] Meile *(brit. Längenmaß)* **II**
milk [mɪlk] Milch **I**
to **milk** [mɪlk] melken **III**
million ['mɪljən] Million **II**
I've done this a **million** times before. [ˌaɪv dʌn ðɪs ə ˌmɪljən taɪmz bɪ'fɔː] Ich habe das schon eine Million Mal gemacht. **II**
millionaire [ˌmɪljə'neə] Millionär/-in **III**
mind [maɪnd] Geist; Verstand **III**
to change one's **mind** [ˌtʃeɪndʒ wʌnz 'maɪnd] seine Meinung ändern **III**
*to keep in **mind** [ˌkiːp‿ɪn 'maɪnd] beachten; im Gedächtnis behalten °**IV U3**, 79
mind map ['maɪnd mæp] Wörternetz *(eine Art Schaubild)* **I**
*to rise up in one's **mind** [raɪz‿ʌp ɪn wʌnz 'maɪnd] jmdm. in den Sinn kommen **III**
to **mind** [maɪnd] etwas dagegen haben; einem etwas ausmachen **IV U2**, 46
to **mind** sth [maɪnd] auf etw. aufpassen **IV AC4**, 107
I don't **mind** … *(+ -ing)* [ˌaɪ dəʊnt 'maɪnd] Ich habe nichts dagegen (zu) …; Mir macht es nichts aus (zu) … **III**
mine [maɪn] Mine **III**
mine [maɪn] mein/-er/-e/-es **II**
mini [mɪni] Mini- **II**
mining ['maɪnɪŋ] Bergbau **III**
minute ['mɪnɪt] Minute **I**
mirror ['mɪrə] Spiegel **III**
miserable ['mɪzrəbl] elend; armselig; jämmerlich ⟨**IV TS1**, 32⟩
Miss [mɪs] Fräulein *(Anrede)* **III**
to **miss** [mɪs] verpassen; versäumen **II**; vermissen **III**
missing ['mɪsɪŋ] fehlend; verschwunden **II**
What is **missing**? [ˌwɒt‿ɪz 'mɪsɪŋ] Was fehlt? **I**
mission ['mɪʃn] Mission; Auftrag **IV TS3**, 101
mission control [ˌmɪʃn kən'trəʊl] Bodenkontrollzentrum ⟨**IV TS3**, 101⟩
mist [mɪst] Nebel; Dunst ⟨**IV U3**, 90⟩
mistake [mɪ'steɪk] Fehler **I**
misunderstood [ˌmɪsʌndə'stʊd] missverstanden **III**
mix [mɪks] Mix **III**
to **mix** [mɪks] Umgang haben ⟨**IV TS1**, 34⟩; zusammenpassen **IV U2**, 54
to **mix** (up) [mɪks‿'ʌp] mischen; vermischen **III**
mobile ['məʊbaɪl] Handy; Mobiltelefon **II**
modal ['məʊdl] Modalverb **II**
model ['mɒdl] Modell; Tonmodell; Model **I**
modelling ['mɒdəlɪŋ] Modeln **III**
modern ['mɒdn] modern **II**
module ['mɒdjuːl] Modul; Element ⟨**IV TS3**, 101⟩
command **module** [kə'mɑːnd ˌmɒdjuːl] Kommandokapsel ⟨**IV TS3**, 101⟩
mom *(AE)* [mɒm] Mama **IV AC2**, 41
moment ['məʊmənt] Moment; Augenblick **II**
at the **moment** [ət ðə 'məʊmənt] im Moment; gerade **I**
monarch ['mɒnək] Monarch/-in **III**
Monday ['mʌndeɪ] Montag **I**
on **Mondays** [ɒn 'mʌndeɪz] montags **I**
money ['mʌni] Geld **I**
*to make **money** [ˌmeɪk 'mʌni] Geld verdienen **I**
pocket **money** ['pɒkɪt ˌmʌni] Taschengeld **I**
to raise **money** [ˌreɪz 'mʌni] Geld sammeln **II**
monster ['mɒnstə] Monster; Ungeheuer **I**
montage [mɒn'tɑːʒ] Montage °**IV U3**, 91
month [mʌnθ] Monat **II**
monument ['mɒnjəmənt] Monument; Denkmal **III**
mood [muːd] Stimmung; Laune **II**
moon [muːn] Mond **IV TS3**, 100
moon landing ['muːn ˌlændɪŋ] Mondlandung **IV TS3**, 100
moonlight ['muːnlaɪt] Mondlicht **III**
more [mɔː] mehr; weitere **I**
no **more** [ˌnəʊ 'mɔː] nicht mehr **IV AC4**, 107
not any **more** [ˌnɒt‿eni 'mɔː] nicht mehr **I**
more … than ['mɔː ðən] mehr … als **I**
morning ['mɔːnɪŋ] Morgen; Vormittag **I**
in the **mornings** [ˌɪn ðə 'mɔːnɪŋz] morgens; vormittags **I**
Good **morning**. [ˌgʊd 'mɔːnɪŋ] Guten Morgen. **I**
(the) **most** [ðə 'məʊst] der/die/das meiste; die meisten **I**
mother ['mʌðə] Mutter **I**
to **motivate** ['məʊtɪveɪt] motivieren **I**
motivation [ˌməʊtɪ'veɪʃn] Motivation; Beweggründe **IV TS1**, 31
motive ['məʊtɪv] Motiv; Beweggrund **IV TS1**, 32
bicycle **motocross** [ˌbaɪsɪkl 'məʊtəʊkrɒs] Fahrradmotocross **II**
mountain ['maʊntɪn] Berg **II**
mountain biking ['maʊntɪn ˌbaɪkɪŋ] Mountainbikefahren **III**
mountainous ['maʊntɪnəs] bergig **IV AC2**, 40

mouse *(sg)*, **mice** *(pl)* [maʊs; maɪs] Maus/Mäuse **I**
mouth [maʊθ] Mund **I**
mouth jogging ['maʊθ ˌdʒɒgɪŋ] Training für den Mund **I**
to talk with your **mouth** full [ˌtɔːk wɪð jɔː 'maʊθ fʊl] mit vollem Mund sprechen **IV AC1**, 22
move [muːv] Bewegung **I**
on the **move** [ˌɒn‿ðə 'muːv] unterwegs **IV U1**, 8
to **move** [muːv] (sich) bewegen **I**
to **move** in/into [ˌmuːv‿'ɪn/'ɪntə] einziehen in **III**
to **move** (house) [muːv (haʊs)] umziehen **III**
movie *(AE)* ['muːvi] Film **IV U2**, 44
movie theater *(AE)* ['muːvi ˌθɪətə] Kino **IV U2**, 44
Mr ['mɪstə] Herr *(Anrede)* **I**
Mrs ['mɪsɪz] Frau *(Anrede)* **I**
much [mʌtʃ] viel **I**
that **much** [ðæt 'mʌtʃ] so viel **III**
mud [mʌd] Schlamm **II**
muddy ['mʌdi] schlammig **II**
mudlark ['mʌdlɑːk] *jemand, der im Schlamm nach Sachen sucht, die er dann verkaufen kann* **II**
muesli ['mjuːzli] Müsli **III**
mug [mʌg] Becher **III**
multi-ethnic [ˌmʌlti'eθnɪk] Vielvölker-; international **II**
mum [mʌm] Mama **I**
mummy ['mʌmi] Mama; Mami; Mutti **III**
murder ['mɜːdə] Mord **III**
museum [mjuː'ziːəm] Museum **I**
music ['mjuːzɪk] Musik **I**
musical ['mjuːzɪkl] musikalisch; Musik- **III**
musician [mjuː'zɪʃn] Musiker/-in **II**
must [mʌst] müssen **I**
mustn't ['mʌsnt] nicht dürfen **I**
to **mutter** ['mʌtə] murmeln **IV U1**, 10
my [maɪ] mein/-e **I**
My favourite … [maɪ 'feɪvrɪt] Mein/e Lieblings … **I**
My name is … [maɪ 'neɪm‿ɪz] Ich heiße … **I**
myself [maɪ'self] ich/mir/mich (selbst); selber **II**
mysterious [mɪ'stɪəriəs] mysteriös; geheimnisvoll **III**
mystery ['mɪstri] Mysterium; Rätsel; Geheimnis **III**
mythical ['mɪθɪkl] sagenhaft; sagenumwoben **IV U1**, 19

N

naked ['neɪkɪd] nackt **IV U3**, 72
name [neɪm] Name **I**
name day ['neɪm ˌdeɪ] Namenstag **I**
My **name** is … [maɪ 'neɪm‿ɪz] Ich heiße … **I**
What's your **name**? [ˌwɒts jə 'neɪm] Wie heißt du?; Wie heißen Sie? **I**
to **name** [neɪm] nennen; benennen **I**
narrative perspective [ˌnærətɪv pə'spektɪv] Erzählperspektive **III**
narrator [nə'reɪtə] Erzähler/-in **III**
first person **narrator** [ˌfɜːst ˌpɜːsn nə'reɪtə] Ich-Erzähler/-in **III**
third person **narrator** [ˌθɜːd ˌpɜːsn nə'reɪtə] Er/Sie-Erzähler/-in **III**
narrow ['nærəʊ] eng; schmal **III**
NASA *(= National Aeronautics and Space Administration)* ['næsə] NASA **IV TS3**, 100
nasty ['nɑːsti] garstig; gemein **II**
nation ['neɪʃn] Nation ⟨**IV U2**, 49⟩
national ['næʃnl] national; landesweit **I**
Native American [ˌneɪtɪv‿ə'merɪkən] Ureinwohner/-in Amerikas; Indianer/-in; indianisch **IV U2**, 45
natural ['nætʃrl] natürlich; Natur- **IV U2**, 56
nature ['neɪtʃə] Natur **II**
near [nɪə] nahe; in der Nähe von **I**
nearly ['nɪəli] fast; annähernd **II**
not **necessarily** [ˌnɒt nesə'serəli] nicht notwendigerweise; nicht unbedingt **IV U3**, 76
necessary ['nesəsri] nötig; notwendig; erforderlich °**IV TS3**, 105
neck [nek] Hals; Nacken; Genick ⟨**IV U3**, 90⟩
necklace ['nekləs] Halskette **III**
in **need** [ɪn 'niːd] bedürftig; in Not **II**
There's no **need** to … [ˌðeəz nəʊ 'niːd tə] Es gibt keinen Grund zu … **IV TS1**, 36
with special **needs** [wɪð ˌspeʃl 'niːdz] behindert **II**
to **need** (to do) [niːd] (tun) müssen **I**
needn't ['niːdnt] nicht brauchen; nicht müssen **I**
to **need** (to) [niːd] brauchen; benötigen **I**
needless to say [ˌniːdləs tə 'seɪ] natürlich; selbstverständlich **IV U3**, 76
negative ['negətɪv] negativ; verneint **III**
negative form ['negətɪv ˌfɔːm] verneinte Form **I**
neighborhood *(AE)* ['neɪbəhʊd] Nachbarschaft **IV U2**, 43
neighbour *(BE)* ['neɪbə] Nachbar/-in **I**
neighbourhood ['neɪbəhʊd] Nachbarschaft **III**
nephew ['nefjuː] Neffe **IV U1**, 13
nerd [nɜːd] Nerd *(Person, die intelligent, aber sozial unbeholfen ist)* **IV TS2**, 65
*to get on people's **nerves** [ˌget‿ɒn sʌmbɒdiz 'nɜːvz] jemandem auf die Nerven gehen **I**
nervous ['nɜːvəs] nervös; aufgeregt **II**
net [net] Netz **II**
netball ['netbɔːl] Korbball **I**
social **network** [ˌsəʊʃl 'netwɜːk] soziales Netzwerk **II**
never ['nevə] nie; niemals **I**
new [njuː] neu **I**
New Year's Eve [ˌnjuː‿jɪəz‿'iːv] Silvester ⟨**IV U3**, 90⟩
New Yorker [ˌnjuː 'jɔːkə] New Yorker/-in **IV U3**, 75
news *(sg)* [njuːz] Nachrichten; Neuigkeiten **II**
news report ['njuːz rɪˌpɔːt] Tatsachenbericht; Nachrichtenbeitrag; Meldung **III**
newspaper ['njuːsˌpeɪpə] Zeitung **III**
next [nekst] nächste/-r/-s; der/die Nächste(n) **I**
next door [ˌnekst 'dɔː] (von) nebenan **III**
next to ['nekst tə] neben **I**
the **next** day [ðə ˌnekst 'deɪ] am nächsten Tag **II**
next [nekst] als Nächstes **I**
nice [naɪs] nett; schön; lieb **I**
night [naɪt] Nacht **I**
all **night** [ˌɔːl 'naɪt] die ganze Nacht **I**
night walk ['naɪt wɔːk] Nachtwanderung **II**
nightmare ['naɪtmeə] Alptraum **IV U2**, 52
nine [naɪn] neun **I**
2nite *(= tonight)* [tə'naɪt] heute Abend **I**
no [nəʊ] kein/-e **I**
no more [ˌnəʊ 'mɔː] nicht mehr **IV AC4**, 107
no way [ˌnəʊ 'weɪ] auf keinen Fall; keineswegs ⟨**IV U2**, 54⟩; keine Möglichkeit; kein Weg ⟨**IV TS3**, 102⟩
no idea [ˌnəʊ‿aɪ'dɪə] keine Ahnung **II**
no wonder [ˌnəʊ 'wʌndə] kein Wunder **IV U2**, 44
no [nəʊ] nein **I**
nobody ['nəʊbədi] niemand **II**
nobody else ['nəʊbədi els] niemand anderes **III**
noise [nɔɪz] Lärm; Geräusch **II**
noisy ['nɔɪzi] laut **III**
non- [nɒn] nicht- **II**
non-defining relative clause [ˌnɒndɪfaɪnɪŋ 'relətɪv ˌklɔːz] nicht notwendiger Relativsatz °**IV U3**, 73
nope *(infml)* [nəʊp] nee; nö **IV AC4**, 107
normal ['nɔːml] normal **II**
normally ['nɔːmli] normalerweise **IV AC1**, 22
Norman ['nɔːmən] Normanne/Normannin; normannisch **III**
north [nɔːθ] Norden; Nord- **II**
north [nɔːθ] nördlich; im Norden **III**
nose [nəʊz] Nase **II**
to wrinkle one's **nose** [ˌrɪŋkl wʌnz 'nəʊz] die Nase rümpfen ⟨**IV U3**, 90⟩
not [nɒt] nicht **I**
not any more [ˌnɒt‿eni 'mɔː] nicht mehr **I**
not anymore *(AE)* [ˌnɒt‿eni'mɔː] nicht mehr **IV AC2**, 39
not necessarily [ˌnɒt nesə'serəli] nicht notwendigerweise; nicht unbedingt **IV U3**, 76
not until [ˌnɒt‿ən'tɪl] nicht vor; erst um/im **IV U2**, 44
not … any [nɒt … eni] kein/-e/-en **I**

not … anything [ˌnɒt ˈeniθɪŋ] nichts **I**
not … either [nɒt … ˈaɪðə; nɒt … ˈiːðə] auch nicht **IV AC4**, 107
not … yet [nɒt ˈjet] noch nicht **II**
note [nəʊt] Notiz; Anmerkung **I**
*to make **notes** [ˌmeɪk ˈnəʊts] Notizen machen **I**
*to take **notes** [ˌteɪk ˈnəʊts] sich Notizen machen **I**
to **note** down [ˌnəʊt ˈdaʊn] notieren; aufschreiben **II**
nothing [ˈnʌθɪŋ] nichts **I**
to **notice** [ˈnəʊtɪs] bemerken; wahrnehmen **II**
noticeboard [ˈnəʊtɪsbɔːd] schwarzes Brett **II**
noun [naʊn] Nomen; Hauptwort **I**
novel [ˈnɒvl] Roman **III**
graphic **novel** [ˌɡræfɪk ˈnɒvl] Bildergeschichte; Comic **III**
November [nəˈvembə] November **I**
now [naʊ] jetzt; nun **I**
right **now** [ˌraɪt ˈnaʊ] jetzt gleich; sofort; gerade **II**
nowhere [ˈnəʊweə] nirgendwo; nirgendwohin **III**
in the middle of **nowhere** [ɪn ðə ˌmɪdl‿əv ˈnəʊweə] mitten im Nirgendwo **IV U2**, 46
number [ˈnʌmbə] Zahl; Nummer **I**
nurse [nɜːs] Krankenschwester; Krankenpfleger **III**
nut [nʌt] Nuss **I**

O

o'clock [əˈklɒk] Uhr *(Zeitangabe bei vollen Stunden)* **I**
oak [əʊk] Eiche **III**
object [ˈɒbdʒɪkt] Objekt **II**; Gegenstand **III**
object pronoun [ˌɒbdʒɪkt ˈprəʊnaʊn] Objektpronomen **III**
obvious [ˈɒbviəs] offensichtlich **IV U2**, 53
October [ɒkˈtəʊbə] Oktober **I**
against all **odds** [əˌɡenst‿ɔːl ˈɒdz] entgegen allen Erwartungen **III**
odd [ɒd] seltsam; komisch **IV U1**, 19
of [ɒv; əv] von **I**
of course [əv ˈkɔːs] natürlich; selbstverständlich **I**
of one's own [əv wʌnz‿ˈəʊn] eigen **III**
*to take **off** [ˌteɪk‿ˈɒf] abnehmen; herunternehmen; ausziehen **I**
*to take the day **off** [ˌteɪk ðə ˌdeɪ‿ˈɒf] sich den Tag freinehmen **IV U3**, 72
to turn **off** [ˌtɜːn‿ˈɒf] abschalten; ausschalten **II**
special **offer** [ˌspeʃl‿ˈɒfə] Sonderangebot **I**
to **offer** [ˈɒfə] anbieten **II**
office [ˈɒfɪs] Büro **I**
immigration **office** [ˌɪmɪˈɡreɪʃn ˌɒfɪs] Einwanderungsbehörde **IV U1**, 13
ticket **office** [ˈtɪkɪt ˌɒfɪs] Kartenschalter **III**

police **officer** [pəˈliːs‿ˌɒfɪsə] Polizeibeamter; Polizist/-in **II**
official [əˈfɪʃl] Schiedsrichter/-in **II**; Beamter/Beamtin **IV U1**, 17
official [əˈfɪʃl] offiziell **III**
official language [əˌfɪʃl ˈlæŋɡwɪdʒ] Amtssprache **II**
offline [ˈɒflaɪn] offline **II**
often [ˈɒfn] oft; häufig **I**
oh [əʊ] null *(bei Telefonnummern und Uhrzeitangaben)* **I**
Oh! [əʊ] O! **I**
Oh dear! [əʊ ˈdɪə] Oje! **III**
ointment [ˈɔɪntmənt] Salbe **II**
OK [əʊˈkeɪ] o.k.; in Ordnung **I**
okay [əˈkeɪ] okay **IV TS1**, 31
old [əʊld] alt **I**
How **old** are you? [haʊ‿ˈəʊld‿ə ˌjuː] Wie alt bist du?; Wie alt sind Sie? **I**
11-year-**old** [ɪˌlevnˈjɪərəʊld] 11-Jährige/-r **II**
OMG! (Oh my god!) [ˌəʊ maɪ ˈɡɒd] OMG! (Oh mein Gott!) **IV U2**, 56
*to put **on** [ˌpʊt‿ˈɒn] anziehen **III**
on [ɒn] auf; an; am; in; im **I**
*to be **on** [bi‿ˈɒn] an sein; laufen **II**
on Mondays [ɒn ˈmʌndeɪz] montags **I**
on my own [ˌɒn maɪ‿ˈəʊn] allein; für mich **II**
on the brink of [ˌɒn ðə ˈbrɪŋk‿əv] am Rande von; kurz vor **III**
on the left [ɒn ðə ˈleft] auf der linken Seite; links **I**
on the right [ɒn ðə ˈraɪt] auf der rechten Seite; rechts **I**
on time [ɒn ˈtaɪm] pünktlich **II**
on top [ɒn ˈtɒp] oben; obendrauf **I**
Come **on!** [ˌkʌm‿ˈɒn] Komm schon!; Komm jetzt! **I**
on a shoestring [ˌɒn‿ə ˈʃuːstrɪŋ] für/mit wenig Geld **IV U3**, 72
on the move [ˌɒn‿ðə ˈmuːv] unterwegs **IV U1**, 8
once [wʌns] einmal; einst **I**
one [wʌn] eins **I**
one *(sg)*/**ones** *(pl)* [wʌn/wʌnz] eine/-r/-s **II**
one-way ticket [ˈwʌnweɪ ˌtɪkɪt] einfache Fahrkarte **III**
online [ˌɒnˈlaɪn] online **II**
only [ˈəʊnli] einzige/-r/-s **II**
only [ˈəʊnli] erst; bloß; nur **I**
only child [ˈəʊnli ˌtʃaɪld] Einzelkind **I**
onto [ˈɒntə] auf … hinauf ⟨**IV TS3**, 101⟩
Oops! [uːps] Hoppla!; Huch! **I**
to **open** [ˈəʊpn] öffnen; aufmachen **I**; *hier:* beginnen **III**; eröffnen **IV U2**, 52
open [ˈəʊpn] offen; geöffnet; aufgeschlagen **I**
*to hold **open** [ˌhəʊld‿ˈəʊpn] aufhalten **IV AC1**, 22
opening [ˈəʊpnɪŋ] Öffnung; Beginn **III**
opening line [ˈəʊpnɪŋ‿ˌlaɪn] der erste Satz **III**

opinion [əˈpɪnjən] Meinung **II**
opposite [ˈɒpəzɪt] gegenüber; auf der anderen Seite von **I**
optimistic [ˌɒptɪˈmɪstɪk] optimistisch **III**
option [ˈɒpʃn] Möglichkeit; Wahl; Option **III**
or [ɔː] oder **I**
either … **or** … [ˈaɪðə/ˈiːðə … ɔː] entweder … oder … **IV U3**, 79
orange [ˈɒrɪndʒ] Orange **I**
orange [ˈɒrɪndʒ] orange **I**
orbit [ˈɔːbɪt] Umlaufbahn; Orbit ⟨**IV TS3**, 101⟩
order [ˈɔːdə] Reihenfolge; Ordnung **I**; Befehl **III**
out of **order** [ˌaʊt‿əv ˈɔːdə] kaputt; außer Betrieb **IV TS1**, 36
word **order** [ˈwɜːd‿ˌɔːdə] Wortstellung; Satzstellung **I**
to **order** [ˈɔːdə] bestellen **IV U1**, 20
organisation [ˌɔːɡnaɪˈzeɪʃn] Organisation **III**
to **organise** [ˈɔːɡənaɪz] organisieren **I**
*to get **organised** [get ˈɔːɡənaɪzd] sich organisieren **III**
orientation [ˌɔːriənˈteɪʃn] Orientierung; Orientierungs- **IV U2**, 43
origin [ˈɒrɪdʒɪn] Ursprung; Herkunft; Abstammung **IV U1**, 19
original [əˈrɪdʒnl] Original **III**
original [əˈrɪdʒnl] original; ursprünglich **III**
originally [əˈrɪdʒnli] ursprünglich **II**
other [ˈʌðə] anders; andere/-r/-s; weitere **I**
each **other** [ˌiːtʃ‿ˈʌðə] einander; sich; sich gegenseitig **I**
the **others** [ði‿ˈʌðəz] die anderen **I**
otherwise [ˈʌðəwaɪz] sonst **IV AC3**, 68
Ouch! [aʊtʃ] Aua! **II**
our [aʊə; ɑː] unser/-e **I**
out [aʊt] außerhalb; heraus; hinaus; nach draußen **I**
to clean **out** [ˌkliːn‿ˈaʊt] ausräumen; entrümpeln **IV U2**, 51
to clear **out** [ˌklɪər‿ˈaʊt] ausräumen; entrümpeln **I**
to drop **out** (of) [ˌdrɒp ˈaʊt‿əv] abbrechen **III**
*to hang **out** (with) *(infml)* [ˌhæŋ‿ˈaʊt wɪð] sich herumtreiben (mit); rumhängen (mit); sich treffen (mit) **III**
*to leave **out** [ˌliːv‿ˈaʊt] auslassen; weglassen °**IV U2**, 54
out and about [ˌaʊt‿ən‿əˈbaʊt] unterwegs **II**
out of [ˈaʊt‿əv] aus … heraus **IV U1**, 15
out of focus [ˌaʊt‿əv ˈfəʊkəs] unscharf **III**
out of order [ˌaʊt‿əv ˈɔːdə] kaputt; außer Betrieb **IV TS1**, 36
a day **out** in … [ə ˌdeɪ‿ˈaʊt ɪn] ein Tag in … **II**
outdoor [ˌaʊtˈdɔː] Freiluft-; Outdoor- **II**
outfit [ˈaʊtfɪt] Outfit; Kleidung **II**
outgoing [aʊtˈɡəʊɪŋ] kontaktfreudig **IV U1**, 19

outlaw ['aʊtlɔ:] Geächtete/-r; Gesetzlose/-r **III**
out-of-character [ˌaʊtəv'kærəktə] ungewöhnlich °**IV U2**, 54
from the **outside** [ˌfrəm ðiˌaʊt'saɪd] von außen **IV U3**, 75
outside [aʊt'saɪd] nach draußen; draußen; außerhalb **I**
outward ['aʊtwəd] abfahrend **III**
over ['əʊvə] hinüber; über **I**; vorüber; vorbei **II**
*to go **over** to [ˌgəʊ 'əʊvə tə] hinübergehen zu; zu jmdm. nach Hause gehen **II**
over and **over** again [ˌəʊvər‿ən‿ˌəʊvər‿ə'gen] immer wieder **III**
*to win sb **over** [ˌwɪn‿'əʊvə] jmdn. für sich gewinnen; jmdn. überzeugen **IV TS2**, 64
overall [ˌəʊvr'ɔ:l] insgesamt ⟨**IV TS3**, 104⟩
*to **overdo** [əʊvə'du:] übertreiben; zu weit gehen **IV U2**, 55
to **overlap** [ˌəʊvə'læp] (sich) überlappen **IV U3**, 89
overloaded [ˌəʊvə'ləʊdɪd] überladen **IV U1**, 16
overnight [ˌəʊvə'naɪt] über Nacht **III**
to **overreact** [ˌəʊvəri'ækt] überreagieren **II**
own [əʊn] eigene/-r/-s **I**
of one's **own** [ˌəv wʌnz‿'əʊn] eigen **III**
on my **own** [ˌɒn maɪ‿'əʊn] allein; für mich **II**

P

p.m. [ˌpi:'em] nachmittags *(Uhrzeit)*; abends *(Uhrzeit)* **I**
packet ['pækɪt] Päckchen; Paket; Packung **I**
page [peɪdʒ] Seite **I**
pain [peɪn] Schmerz **II**
to **paint** [peɪnt] anmalen; malen **I**
painting ['peɪntɪŋ] Malerei; Gemälde **II**
pair [peə] Paar **I**
pair work ['peə wɜ:k] Partnerarbeit **II**
to **pair** [peə] Paare bilden **III**
palm tree ['pɑ:m ˌtri:] Palme **III**
panel ['pænl] Bild *(eines Comics)* **IV U3**, 89
to **panic** ['pænɪk] panisch werden **II**
piece of **paper** [ˌpi:s‿əv 'peɪpə] Stück Papier **I**
paper ['peɪpə] Papier **I**
paradise ['pærədaɪs] Paradies **II**
paragraph ['pærəgrɑ:f] Paragraf; Absatz °**IV TS3**, 103
parcel ['pɑ:sl] Paket; Päckchen **I**
parents *(pl)* ['peərənts] Eltern **I**
park [pɑ:k] Park **I**
part [pɑ:t] Teil; Stadtteil **I**; Rolle **III**
lead **part** [ˌli:d 'pɑ:t] Hauptrolle **III**
*to take **part** (in) [ˌteɪk 'pɑ:t (ɪn)] teilnehmen (an) **II**
partially sighted [ˌpɑ:ʃəli 'saɪtɪd] sehbehindert **II**
to **participate** [pɑ:'tɪsɪpeɪt] teilnehmen **II**
past **participle** [ˌpɑ:st pɑ:'tɪsɪpl] Partizip **II**
particular [pə'tɪkjələ] bestimmte/-r/-s **III**
partly ['pɑ:tli] teilweise ⟨**IV TS1**, 32⟩
partner ['pɑ:tnə] Partner/-in **I**
party ['pɑ:ti] Party; Feier **I**; Partei **III**
hall **pass** ['hɔ:l pɑ:s] *Erlaubnis, sich während des Unterrichts auf dem Flur aufzuhalten* **IV U2**, 43
to **pass** [pɑ:s] zupassen; zuspielen **II**
to **pass** (on) [ˌpɑ:s‿'ɒn] weitergeben **I**
passenger ['pæsndʒə] Passagier/-in; Fahrgast **IV U1**, 9
passive ['pæsɪv] Passiv **III**
passive ['pæsɪv] passiv **III**
passport ['pɑ:spɔ:t] Pass; Reisepass **IV U1**, 9
past [pɑ:st] Vergangenheit **II**
past form ['pɑ:st fɔ:m] Vergangenheitsform **II**
past participle [ˌpɑ:st pɑ:'tɪsɪpl] Partizip **II**
past perfect [ˌpɑ:st 'pɜ:fɪkt] Plusquamperfekt **III**
past perfect progressive [ˌpɑ:st ˌpɜ:fɪkt prə'gresɪv] Verlaufsform des Plusquamperfekts °**IV U3**, 77
past progressive [ˌpɑ:st prə'gresɪv] Verlaufsform der Vergangenheit **II**
simple **past** [ˌsɪmpl 'pɑ:st] Vergangenheitsform **II**
past [pɑ:st] nach *(bei Uhrzeitangaben)*; vorbei (an); vorüber (an) **I**
half **past** [ˌhɑ:f 'pɑ:st] halb *(bei Uhrzeitangaben)* **I**
quarter **past**/to ['kwɔ:tə pɑ:st/tə] Viertel nach/vor **I**
pasta ['pæstə] Pasta; Nudeln **I**
pastry ['peɪstri] Teig; Teigtasche **IV U3**, 75
patchwork ['pætʃwɜ:k] Flicken-; Patchwork- ⟨**IV U3**, 90⟩
path [pɑ:θ] Pfad; Weg **IV U3**, 92
coastal **path** [ˌkəʊstl 'pɑ:θ] Küstenweg **III**
pattern ['pætn] Muster **III**
pause [pɔ:z] Pause **III**
pawn shop ['pɔ:n ʃɒp] Pfandhaus; Pfandleihe **III**
*to **pay (for)** [peɪ] bezahlen **I**
*to **pay** attention to sb/sth [ˌpeɪ‿ə'tenʃn tʊ] jmdn./etw. beachten **III**
*to **pay** out [peɪ‿'aʊt] ausgeben ⟨**IV TS1**, 34⟩
PC *(= Personal Computer)* [pi:'si:] PC **II**
PE *(= Physical Education)* [ˌpi:'i:; ˌfɪzɪkl‿edʒʊ'keɪʃn] Sportunterricht **II**
peach [pi:tʃ] Pfirsich **III**
peer pressure ['pɪə ˌpreʃe] Gruppenzwang **III**
to **peer-edit** ['pɪər‿edɪt] gegenseitig kontrollieren **II**
pen [pen] Füller **I**
penny, **pence** *(pl)* ['peni; pens] Penny *(brit. Währungseinheit)*; Pence *(brit. Währungseinheit)* **I**
pencil ['pensl] Bleistift; Buntstift **I**
pencil-case ['pensl ˌkeɪs] Federmäppchen; Mäppchen **I**
penicillin [ˌpenɪ'sɪlɪn] Penicillin **III**
penny, **pence** *(pl)* ['peni; pens] Penny *(brit. Währungseinheit)*; Pence *(brit. Währungseinheit)* **I**
penthouse ['penthaʊs] Penthouse; Wohnung mit Dachterrasse **IV U3**, 79
people *(pl)* ['pi:pl] Leute; Menschen **I**
per [pɜ:; pə] pro **III**
past **perfect** [ˌpɑ:st 'pɜ:fɪkt] Plusquamperfekt **III**
past **perfect** progressive [ˌpɑ:st ˌpɜ:fɪkt prə'gresɪv] Verlaufsform des Plusquamperfekts °**IV U3**, 77
present **perfect** [ˌpreznt 'pɜ:fɪkt] das Perfekt **II**
present **perfect** progressive [ˌpreznt ˌpɜ:fɪkt prə'gresɪv] Verlaufsform des Perfekts **III**
perfect ['pɜ:fɪkt] perfekt; vollkommen **I**
to **perform** [pə'fɔ:m] aufführen; auftreten **IV U3**, 79
performance [pə'fɔ:məns] Aufführung; Vorstellung **IV TS1**, 30
perhaps [pə'hæps] vielleicht **III**
period ['pɪəriəd] Periode; Zeitspanne **III**
period *(AE)* ['pɪəriəd] Stunde; Unterrichtsstunde **IV U2**, 48
person, **people** *(pl)* ['pɜ:sn; 'pi:pl] Person; Mensch **I**
first **person** narrator [ˌfɜ:st ˌpɜ:sn nə'reɪtə] Ich-Erzähler/-in **III**
third **person** narrator [ˌθɜ:d ˌpɜ:sn nə'reɪtə] Er/Sie-Erzähler/-in **III**
personal ['pɜ:snl] persönlich **I**
personality [ˌpɜ:sn'æləti] Persönlichkeit **III**
perspective [pə'spektɪv] Perspektive; Blickwinkel **II**
narrative **perspective** [ˌnærətɪv pə'spektɪv] Erzählperspektive **III**
to **persuade** [pə'sweɪd] überreden **II**
persuasive [pə'sweɪsɪv] überzeugend **III**
pet [pet] Haustier **I**
phone [fəʊn] Telefon; Handy **I**
to answer the **phone** [ˌɑ:nsə ðə 'fəʊn] einen Anruf entgegennehmen **I**
cell **phone** *(AE)* ['selfəʊn] Mobiltelefon; Handy **IV AC3**, 68
phone box ['fəʊn ˌbɒks] Telefonzelle **IV U1**, 17
phone call ['fəʊn ˌkɔ:l] Anruf; Telefonanruf **I**
rotary **phone** ['rəʊtri fəʊn] Telefon mit Wählscheibe **III**
to **phone** [fəʊn] anrufen; telefonieren **IV TS1**, 31
photo ['fəʊtəʊ] Foto; Fotografie **I**
in the **photo**(s) [ˌɪn ðə 'fəʊtəʊ(z)] auf dem Foto/den Fotos **I**
photo shoot ['fəʊtəʊ ˌʃu:t] Fotoshooting; Fotoaufnahmen **III**
photo story ['fəʊtəʊ ˌstɔ:ri] Fotostory; Bildgeschichte **I**

*to take **photos** [ˌteɪk ˈfəʊtəʊz] fotografieren; Fotos machen **I**
to **photobomb** [ˈfəʊtəʊbɒm] ins Foto laufen **III**
photographer [fəˈtɒgrəfə] Fotograf/-in **III**
phrase [freɪz] Redewendung; Ausdruck; Satz **I**
Useful **phrases** [ˌju:sfl ˈfreɪsɪz] nützliche Ausdrücke **I**
piano [piˈænəʊ] Klavier; Piano **IV U3**, 77
to **pick** [pɪk] auswählen; aussuchen **II**
to **pick** up [ˌpɪk ˈʌp] aufheben; mitnehmen; abholen **III**
pick-up [ˈpɪkʌp] Pick-up; Wiederaufnehmen **I**
picnic [ˈpɪknɪk] Picknick **I**
picture [ˈpɪktʃə] Bild; Foto **I**
pie [paɪ] Kuchen; Pastete **I**
pumpkin **pie** [ˌpʌmpkɪn ˈpaɪ] Kürbiskuchen ⟨**IV U2**, 45⟩
piece [pi:s] Stück **I**
excellent **piece** of quick thinking [ˌekslnt pi:s əv kwɪk ˈθɪŋkɪŋ] ausgezeichnete Reaktionsschnelligkeit ⟨**IV TS1**, 36⟩
piece of junk [ˌpi:s əv ˈdʒʌŋk] Stück Schrott **III**
piece of paper [ˌpi:s əv ˈpeɪpə] Stück Papier **I**
pier [pɪə] Pier; Hafendamm **I**
piercing [ˈpɪəsɪŋ] Piercing ⟨**IV U3**, 90⟩
pig [pɪg] Schwein **I**
guinea **pig** [ˈgɪni: ˌpɪg] Meerschweinchen **I**
*to give sb a **piggyback** [gɪv ə ˈpɪgibæk] jmdn. Huckepack nehmen **IV U1**, 16
Pilgrim [ˈpɪlgrɪm] Pilger/-in **IV U2**, 45
pill [pɪl] Pille; Tablette **II**
pilot [ˈpaɪlət] Pilot/-in **II**
pineapple [ˈpaɪnæpl] Ananas **III**
pink [pɪŋk] pink; rosa **I**
pipe [paɪp] Rohr; Rohrleitung; Pfeife **II**
clay **pipe** [ˈkleɪ paɪp] Tonpfeife **II**
pitch [pɪtʃ] Spielfeld; Platz **II**
pizza [ˈpi:tsə] Pizza **I**
place [pleɪs] Ort; Stelle; Platz **I**
starting **place** [ˈstɑ:tɪŋ pleɪs] Startpunkt **III**
*to take **place** [ˌteɪk ˈpleɪs] stattfinden **I**
to **place** [pleɪs] legen **III**
placemat [ˈpleɪsmæt] Placemat; Platzdeckchen **I**
plan [plæn] Plan; Entwurf **I**
to **plan** [plæn] planen **I**
plane [pleɪn] Flugzeug **IV U1**, 8
planet [ˈplænɪt] Planet **II**
planner [ˈplænə] Handbuch; Kalender **I**
route **planner** [ˈru:t ˌplænə] Routenplaner **IV AC2**, 41
plant [plɑ:nt] Pflanze **III**
to **plant** [plɑ:nt] pflanzen; anpflanzen **II**
plaster cast [ˈplɑ:stə kɑ:st] Gipsverband **III**
plate [pleɪt] Teller **III**
platform [ˈplætfɔ:m] Plattform; Bahnsteig **III**
play [pleɪ] Theaterstück **III**
fair **play** [feə ˈpleɪ] Fairplay **III**
play on words [ˌpleɪ ɒn ˈwɜ:dz] Wortspiel **III**
role **play** [ˈrəʊl ˌpleɪ] Rollenspiel **I**
to **play** [pleɪ] spielen **I**
to **play** a trick (on) [ˌpleɪ ə ˈtrɪk ɒn] einen Streich spielen **I**
to **play** bowls [ˌpleɪ ˈbəʊlz] Bowling spielen **III**
player [ˈpleɪə] Spieler/-in; Mitspieler/-in **II**
Please. [pli:z] Bitte. **I**
to **pledge** allegiance [ˌpledʒ əˈli:dʒns] Treueschwur leisten ⟨**IV U2**, 49⟩
plot [plɒt] Handlung **III**
plumber [ˈplʌmə] Installateur/-in; Klempner/-in **III**
plumbing [ˈplʌmɪŋ] Sanitärarbeit **III**
plural [ˈplʊərəl] Plural; Mehrzahl **I**
poaching *(no pl)* [ˈpəʊtʃɪŋ] Wilderei **III**
pocket [ˈpɒkɪt] Tasche; Hosentasche **III**
pocket money [ˈpɒkɪt ˌmʌni] Taschengeld **I**
a **pocketful** of [ə ˈpɒkɪtfl əv] Unmengen von/an **IV U3**, 70
podcast [ˈpɒdkɑ:st] Podcast **IV U3**, 92
poem [ˈpəʊɪm] Gedicht **I**
point [pɔɪnt] Punkt; Zeitpunkt **II**
*to have a **point** [ˌhæv ə ˈpɔɪnt] nicht ganz unrecht haben **III**
point of view [ˌpɔɪnt əv ˈvju:] Standpunkt; Ansicht; Perspektive **II**
to the **point** [tə ðə ˈpɔɪnt] prägnant; treffend **III**
turning **point** [ˈtɜ:nɪŋ ˌpɔɪnt] Wendepunkt **III**
I can't see the **point** of … [aɪ ˌkɑ:nt si: ðə ˈpɔɪnt əv] Ich sehe keinen Sinn darin … **IV AC3**, 69
to **point** at sb/sth [ˈpɔɪnt æt] mit dem Finger auf jmdn./etw. zeigen **IV AC1**, 22
to **point** out sth [ˌpɔɪnt ˈaʊt] hinweisen auf etw. °**IV AC2**, 41
Point to … [ˈpɔɪnt tə] Zeige/Zeigt auf … **I**
Point. [pɔɪnt] Zeige/Zeigt darauf. **I**
police [pəˈli:s] Polizei **II**
police officer [pəˈli:s ɒfɪsə] Polizeibeamter; Polizist/-in **II**
polite [pəˈlaɪt] höflich **I**
Be **polite**. [bi: pəˈlaɪt] Sei/Seid höflich. **I**
political [pəˈlɪtɪkl] politisch **IV TS3**, 101
pollution [pəˈlu:ʃn] Verschmutzung **II**
pond [pɒnd] Teich **II**
pony [ˈpəʊni] Pony **I**
pony trekking [ˈpəʊni ˌtrekɪŋ] Ponyreiten im Gelände **III**
swimming **pool** [ˈswɪmɪŋ ˌpu:l] Swimmingpool; Schwimmbecken **III**
the **poor** [ðə pʊə] die Armen **III**
poor [pɔ:; pʊə] arm **III**
popular [ˈpɒpjələ] beliebt; populär **I**
populated [ˈpɒpjəleɪtɪd] bevölkert; besiedelt **IV AC2**, 38
population [ˌpɒpjəˈleɪʃn] Bevölkerung; Population **IV AC2**, 39
pose [pəʊz] Pose; Haltung **IV U2**, 56
positive [ˈpɒzətɪv] positiv **II**
possessive form [pəˌsesɪv ˈfɔ:m] Possessivform **I**
possibility [ˌpɒsəˈbɪləti] Möglichkeit **III**
possible [ˈpɒsəbl] möglich **I**
post [pəʊst] Post *(Eintrag im Internet)* **I**
to **post** [pəʊst] online stellen; posten **II**
postcard [ˈpəʊstkɑ:d] Postkarte **III**
poster [ˈpəʊstə] Poster **I**
class **poster** [ˈklɑ:s ˌpəʊstə] Klassenposter **I**
postman [ˈpəʊstmən] Briefträger **II**
melting **pot** [ˈmeltɪŋ ˌpɒt] Schmelztiegel **IV U3**, 70
potato [pəˈteɪtəʊ], **potatoes** [pəˈteɪtəʊz] *(pl)* Kartoffel **III**
mashed **potatoes** *(pl)* [ˌmæʃt pəˈteɪtəʊz] Kartoffelpüree **III**
sweet **potatoes** *(pl)* [ˈswi:t pəˌteɪtəʊz] Süßkartoffeln ⟨**IV U2**, 45⟩
pound [paʊnd] Pfund *(Maßeinheit)* **IV U2**, 51
pound (£) [paʊnd] Pfund *(brit. Währungseinheit)* **I**
to **pour** [pɔ:] einschenken; eingießen; schütten **I**
power [paʊə] Kraft; Macht; Stärke **III**
computing **power** [ˌkəmˈpju:tɪŋ ˌpaʊə] Rechenleistung ⟨**IV TS3**, 102⟩
power cut [ˈpaʊə ˌkʌt] Stromausfall **II**
Word **power** [ˈwɜ:d ˌpaʊə] die Kraft der Wörter *(Wortschatzübung)* **I**
those in **power** [ˌðəʊz ɪn ˈpaʊə] die Regierenden; die Herrschenden **III**
powerful [ˈpaʊəfl] stark; mächtig **III**
practical [ˈpræktɪkl] praktisch **II**
practice [ˈpræktɪs] Training; Übung **III**
to **practice** *(AE)* [ˈpræktɪs] üben; ausüben; praktizieren; trainieren **IV U2**, 45
to **practice** a religion [ˌpræktɪs ə rɪˈlɪdʒn] eine Religion ausüben **IV U2**, 45
to **practise** [ˈpræktɪs] üben; trainieren **I**
practising [ˈpræktɪsɪŋ] Üben **I**
to **pray** [preɪ] beten **III**
to **preach** [pri:tʃ] predigen ⟨**IV TS1**, 36⟩
prediction [prɪˈdɪkʃn] Vorhersage; Voraussage **III**
to **prefer** [prɪˈfɜ:] vorziehen **IV U2**, 50
prehistoric [ˌpri:hɪˈstɒrɪk] vorgeschichtlich **III**
to **prepare** [prɪˈpeə] vorbereiten; zubereiten **I**
preposition [ˌprepəˈzɪʃn] Präposition **I**
pre-reading [ˌpri:ˈri:dɪŋ] vor dem Lesen **I**
prescription [prɪˈskrɪpʃn] Rezept *(für Arzneimittel)* **II**

present ['preznt] Geschenk **I**; Gegenwart; Präsens **II**
present perfect [ˌpreznt 'pɜ:fɪkt] das Perfekt **II**
present progressive [ˌpreznt prə'gresɪv] Verlaufsform des Präsens/der Gegenwart **I**
present perfect progressive [ˌpreznt ˌpɜ:fɪkt prə'gresɪv] Verlaufsform des Perfekts **III**
simple **present** [ˌsɪmpl 'preznt] Gegenwart; Präsens **I**
to **present** [prɪ'zent] präsentieren; vorstellen **I**
present ['preznt] heutig; Gegenwarts- **III**
presentation [ˌprezn'teɪʃn] Präsentation; Vortrag **I**
presenter [prɪ'zentə] Moderator/-in **I**
president ['prezɪdnt] Präsident/-in **IV TS3**, 101
to **press** [pres] drücken; pressen **II**
peer **pressure** ['pɪə ˌpreʃə] Gruppenzwang **III**
to **pretend** [prɪ'tend] vortäuschen; tun als ob **IV U1**, 17
pretty ['prɪti] hübsch **III**
pretty ['prɪti] ziemlich; ganz schön ⟨**IV TS3**, 104⟩
price [praɪs] Preis **I**
primary school ['praɪmri ˌsku:l] Grundschule **I**
principal *(AE)* ['prɪnsɪpl] Schulleiter/-in **IV AC3**, 68
print [prɪnt] gedruckt; Druck- **II**
priority [praɪ'ɒrəti] Priorität; Vorrang **IV TS3**, 101
prison ['prɪzn] Gefängnis **II**
prisoner ['prɪznə] Gefangene/-r ⟨**IV U3**, 90⟩
private detective [ˌpraɪvət dɪ'tektɪv] Privatdetektiv/-in **III**
prize [praɪz] Preis; Gewinn **I**
pro [prəʊ] Argument dafür **II**
probably ['prɒbəbli] möglicherweise; wahrscheinlich **II**
problem ['prɒbləm] Problem; Schwierigkeit **I**
to **produce** [prə'dju:s] herstellen; produzieren **III**
product ['prɒdʌkt] Produkt; Erzeugnis **IV TS2**, 64
production [prə'dʌkʃn] Produktion; Inszenierung **IV TS1**, 30
profile ['prəʊfaɪl] Profil; Porträt **I**
program *(AE)* ['prəʊgræm] Programm; Sendung **IV TS3**, 104
space **program** ['speɪs ˌprəʊgræm] Raumfahrtprogramm **IV TS3**, 104
programme ['prəʊgræm] Programm; Sendung **II**
progress ['prəʊgres] Fortschritt **II**
past perfect **progressive** [ˌpɑ:st ˌpɜ:fɪkt prə'gresɪv] Verlaufsform des Plusquamperfekts °**IV U3**, 77
past **progressive** [ˌpɑ:st prə'gresɪv] Verlaufsform der Vergangenheit **II**
present perfect **progressive** [ˌpreznt ˌpɜ:fɪkt prə'gresɪv] Verlaufsform des Perfekts **III**
present **progressive** [ˌpreznt prə'gresɪv] Verlaufsform des Präsens/der Gegenwart **I**
project ['prɒdʒekt] Projekt **I**
to **promise** ['prɒmɪs] versprechen **III**
prompt [prɒmpt] Stichwort **III**
prompt card ['prɒmpt kɑ:d] Stichwortkarte; Rollenkarte **II**
pronoun ['prəʊnaʊn] Pronomen; Fürwort °**IV U2**, 50
object **pronoun** [ˌɒbdʒɪkt 'prəʊnaʊn] Objektpronomen **III**
reflexive **pronoun** [rɪˌfleksɪv 'prəʊnaʊn] Reflexivpronomen **III**
relative **pronoun** [ˌrelətɪv 'prəʊnaʊn] Relativpronomen **II**
to **pronounce** [prə'naʊns] aussprechen **IV AC4**, 106
pronunciation [prəˌnʌnsi'eɪʃn] Aussprache **I**
prop [prɒp] Requisite **III**
protagonist [prəʊ'tægnɪst] Protagonist/-in; Hauptfigur **IV TS1**, 30
protest ['prəʊtest] Protest **III**
protester ['prəʊtestə] Protestierende/-r; Demonstrant/-in **IV U2**, 52
proud (of) ['praʊd‿əv] stolz (auf) **II**
the **public** [ðə 'pʌblɪk] die Öffentlichkeit **IV TS3**, 102
public ['pʌblɪk] öffentlich **II**
public transport *(no pl)* [ˌpʌblɪk 'trænspɔ:t] öffentliche Verkehrsmittel **II**
pudding ['pʊdɪŋ] Pudding; Nachtisch **I**
to **pull** [pʊl] ziehen **I**
to **pull** down [ˌpʊl‿'daʊn] abreißen **III**
pumpkin pie [ˌpʌmpkɪn 'paɪ] Kürbiskuchen ⟨**IV U2**, 45⟩
purple ['pɜ:pl] violett; lila **I**
purpose ['pɜ:pəs] Ziel; Absicht; Zweck **IV U1**, 13
to **push** [pʊʃ] stoßen; schieben; schubsen **II**
to **push** oneself ['pʊʃ wʌnˌself] sich alles abverlangen; sich Mühe geben **III**
pushy ['pʊʃi] aufdringlich; penetrant; aggressiv **IV TS1**, 33
*to **put** [pʊt] setzen; stellen; legen **I**
Put in … [pʊt‿'ɪn] Setze/Setzt ein … **I**
Put it in … [ˌpʊt‿ɪt‿'ɪn] Lege/Legt es in …; Stelle/Stellt es in … **I**
*to **put** on [pʊt‿'ɒn] anziehen **III**
*to **put** through [pʊt‿'θru:] verbinden **I**
*to **put** up [pʊt‿'ʌp] aufstellen; errichten; aufhängen **II**
Put … face down. [pʊt ˌfeɪs 'daʊn] Lege/Legt … umgedreht hin. **I**
puzzle ['pʌzl] Rätsel; Puzzle **I**
pyjamas *(pl)* [pɪ'dʒɑ:məz] Schlafanzug; Pyjama **II**

Q

quality ['kwɒləti] Qualität **I**
quarter past/to ['kwɔ:tə pɑ:st/tə] Viertel nach/vor **I**
queen [kwi:n] Königin **II**
question ['kwestʃən] Frage **I**
question tag ['kwestʃən ˌtæg] Frageanhängsel; Bestätigungsfrage **II**
to **question** ['kwestʃən] fragen; hinterfragen **IV TS3**, 103
questionnaire [ˌkwestʃə'neə] Fragebogen **III**
queue [kju:] Schlange; Warteschlange **I**
to jump the **queue** [ˌdʒʌmp ðə 'kju:] sich vordrängeln **I**
quick [kwɪk] schnell **I**
quickly ['kwɪkli] schnell **II**
quiet [kwaɪət] still; ruhig; leise **I**
quill [kwɪl] Federkiel **III**
quite [kwaɪt] ziemlich; ganz; völlig **IV U1**, 14
quiz [kwɪz] Quiz; Rätsel **I**
quotation [kwə'teɪʃn] Zitat; Belegstelle °**IV U3**, 79
quote [kwəʊt] Zitat **II**

R

rabbit ['ræbɪt] Kaninchen **I**
race [reɪs] Wettlauf; Rennen **II**
camel **racing** ['kæml ˌreɪsɪŋ] Kamelrennen **II**
racquet ['rækɪt] Schläger **II**
radio ['reɪdiəʊ] Radio **II**
raffle ['ræfl] Tombola **I**
rags to riches [ˌrægz tə‿'rɪtʃɪz] vom Tellerwäscher zum Millionär **IV U3**, 79
rain [reɪn] Regen **IV U1**, 17
to **rain** [reɪn] regnen **II**
rainbow ['reɪnbəʊ] Regenbogen **III**
raincoat ['reɪnkəʊt] Regenmantel **III**
to **raise** money [ˌreɪz 'mʌni] Geld sammeln **II**
rap [ræp] Rap **I**
to **rap** [ræp] rappen **I**
rat [ræt] Ratte **I**
to **rate** [reɪt] bewerten; einstufen **IV TS3**, 104
I'd **rather** [aɪd 'rɑ:ðə] ich würde lieber **III**
rating ['reɪtɪŋ] Kritik **III**
raven ['reɪvn] Rabe **II**
raven master ['reɪvn ˌmɑ:stə] Herr der Raben **II**
RE *(= Religious Education)* [ˌɑ:r'i:; rɪˌlɪdʒəs‿edʒʊ'keɪʃn] Religion *(Schulfach)* **II**
to **reach** [ri:tʃ] erreichen; dran kommen **II**
to **react** [ri'ækt] reagieren **III**
reaction [ri'ækʃn] Reaktion **II**
*to **read** [ri:d] lesen **I**
*to **read** out loud [ˌri:d/sɪŋ‿aʊt 'laʊd] laut vorsingen **III**
reader ['ri:də] Leser/-in **I**
*to draw the **reader** into the story/action [ˌdrɔ: ðə ˌri:də ɪntə ðə 'stɔ:ri/'ækʃn] den

Leser/die Leserin in die Geschichte/ Handlung hineinziehen **III**
reading ['ri:dɪŋ] Lesen **I**
ready ['redi] fertig; bereit **II**
ready meal [ˌredi 'mi:l] Fertiggericht **I**
real [rɪəl] echt; richtig; wirklich **II**
to **realise** ['rɪəlaɪz] erkennen; realisieren **III**
realistic [ˌrɪə'lɪstɪk] realistisch **II**
to **realize** *(AE)* ['rɪəlaɪz] erkennen; realisieren **IV U2**, 52
really ['rɪəli] wirklich **I**
reason ['ri:zn] Grund **II**
*to give **reasons** [ˌgɪv 'ri:znz] Gründe nennen/angeben ⟨**IV U3**, 90⟩
*to **rebuild** [ˌri:'bɪld] wieder aufbauen **III**
to **receive** [rɪ'si:v] empfangen; erhalten; bekommen **II**
recently ['ri:sntli] kürzlich; neulich °**IV TS3**, 105
receptive [rɪ'septɪv] empfänglich **IV TS2**, 64
recipe ['resɪpi] Rezept **III**
to **recite** [rɪ'saɪt] vortragen; rezitieren **III**
to **record** [rɪ'kɔ:d] aufnehmen; aufzeichnen **II**
recorder [rɪ'kɔ:də] Flöte **III**
recording [rɪ'kɔ:dɪŋ] Aufnahme; Aufzeichnung **I**
recording studio [rɪ'kɔ:dɪŋ ˌstju:diəʊ] Aufnahmestudio; Tonstudio **I**
recycling [ˌri:'saɪklɪŋ] Recycling; Wiederaufbereitung **II**
red [red] rot **I**
redwood (tree) ['redwʊd ˌtri:] Mammutbaum **IV AC2**, 39
to **reef** the sails [ˌri:f ðə 'seɪlz] die Segel einholen **I**
to **refer** to [rɪ'fɜ: tə] sich beziehen auf °**IV TS3**, 103
reference article ['refrns ˌɑ:tɪkl] Referenzartikel **III**
referendum [ˌrefr'endəm] Referendum; Volksentscheid **III**
reflexive [rɪ'fleksɪv] reflexiv; Reflexiv- **III**
reflexive pronoun [rɪˌfleksɪv 'prəʊnaʊn] Reflexivpronomen **III**
refugee [ˌrefjʊ'dʒi:] Flüchtling **IV U1**, 18
region ['ri:dʒn] Region; Gegend **II**
register ['redʒɪstə] Sprachebene; Register **IV AC4**, 106
registration [ˌredʒɪs'treɪʃn] Anwesenheitskontrolle **II**
regular ['regjələ] regelmäßig; gleichmäßig **I**
regulator ['regjəleɪtə] Regulator/-in; Aufsicht führende Person °**IV TS3**, 101
to **rehearse** [rɪ'hɜ:s] proben **III**
reign [reɪn] Herrschaft; Regierungszeit **III**
to **reign** [reɪn] herrschen; regieren **III**
rejection [rɪ'dʒektʃn] Ablehnung; Absage **IV U3**, 76
to **relate** to [rɪ'leɪt tə] Zugang finden zu **III**
relationship [rɪ'leɪʃnʃɪp] Beziehung **II**
defining **relative** clause [dɪˌfaɪnɪŋ 'relətɪv ˌklɔ:z] notwendiger Relativsatz **II**
non-defining **relative** clause [ˌnɒndɪfaɪnɪŋ 'relətɪv ˌklɔ:z] nicht notwendiger Relativsatz °**IV U3**, 73
relative pronoun [ˌrelətɪv 'prəʊnaʊn] Relativpronomen **II**
to **relax** [rɪ'læks] sich entspannen; sich ausruhen; sich beruhigen **II**
reliable [rɪ'laɪəbl] verlässlich; zuverlässig; vertrauenswürdig **IV TS3**, 100
religion [rɪ'lɪdʒn] Religion **IV U2**, 45
to practice a **religion** [ˌpræktɪs ə rɪ'lɪdʒn] eine Religion ausüben **IV U2**, 45
religious [rɪ'lɪdʒəs] religiös; gläubig **I**
to **rely** (on) [rɪ'laɪ ɒn] sich verlassen (auf); vertrauen (auf) **III**
to **remember** [rɪ'membə] sich erinnern (an); sich merken; denken an **I**
Remember? [rɪ'membə] Erinnerst du dich?; Erinnert ihr euch? **I**
to **remind** (sb of sth/sb) [rɪ'maɪnd əv] (jmdn. an etw./jmdn.) erinnern **III**
to **rent** (out) [ˌrent 'aʊt] mieten **III**
to **repeat** [rɪ'pi:t] wiederholen **II**
repetition [ˌrepɪ'tɪʃn] Wiederholung **IV U1**, 15
to **replace** (by/with) [rɪ'pleɪs] ersetzen (durch) ⟨**IV U3**, 90⟩
reply [rɪ'plaɪ] Antwort; Erwiderung; Entgegnung **I**
to **reply** [rɪ'plaɪ] antworten; erwidern; entgegnen **I**
report [rɪ'pɔ:t] Bericht; Meldung **II**
news **report** ['nju:z rɪˌpɔ:t] Tatsachenbericht; Nachrichtenbeitrag; Meldung **III**
travel **report** [ˌtrævl rɪ'pɔ:t] Reisebericht **II**
to **report** [rɪ'pɔ:t] berichten; wiedergeben **IV U1**, 9
reporter [rɪ'pɔ:tə] Reporter/-in **II**
to **represent** [ˌreprɪ'zent] repräsentieren; darstellen; stehen für **IV AC2**, 40
republic [rɪ'pʌblɪk] Republik ⟨**IV U2**, 49⟩
request [rɪ'kwest] Bitte **IV U1**, 9
*to **reread** ['ri:ri:d] noch einmal lesen **III**
rescue ['reskju:] Rettung **II**
to **rescue** ['reskju:] retten **III**
research *(no pl)* [rɪ'sɜ:tʃ] Recherche; Forschung; Untersuchung **III**
respect [rɪ'spekt] Respekt **IV TS3**, 103
response [rɪ'spɒns] Antwort; Erwiderung; Rückmeldung °**IV TS3**, 103
responsible [rɪs'pɒnsəbl] verantwortlich; verantwortungsvoll **IV U1**, 16
the **rest** [rest] der Rest **I**
restaurant ['restrɒnt] Restaurant; Gaststätte **I**
restroom *(AE)* ['restrʊm] Toilette **IV U2**, 43
result [rɪ'zʌlt] Ergebnis; Resultat **II**
*to **retell** [ˌri:'tel] nacherzählen; nochmals erzählen **I**
return ticket [rɪ'tɜ:n ˌtɪkɪt] Hin- und Rückfahrkarte **III**
to **return** [rɪ'tɜ:n] zurückkehren; zurückfahren **III**
revision [rɪ'vɪʒn] Wiederholung **II**
*to **rewrite** [ˌri:'raɪt] umschreiben; neu schreiben **III**
rhino ['raɪnəʊ] Rhinozeros; Nashorn **III**
rhyme [raɪm] Reim **I**
rhyme scheme ['raɪm ski:m] Reimschema **III**
to **rhyme** [raɪm] (sich) reimen **III**
rhyming ['raɪmɪŋ] sich reimend **III**
rhythm ['rɪðm] Rhythmus **I**
the **rich** [ðə rɪtʃ] die Reichen **III**
rich [rɪtʃ] reich **III**
rags to **riches** [ˌrægz tə ˈrɪtʃɪz] vom Tellerwäscher zum Millionär **IV U3**, 79
ride [raɪd] Fahrt; Ritt **IV U2**, 44
along for the **ride** [əˌlɒŋ fə ðə 'raɪd] mit dabei **IV U2**, 44
*to **ride** [raɪd] fahren; reiten **IV AC2**, 41
rigging ['rɪgɪŋ] Takelage **I**
right [raɪt] Recht **IV U2**, 48
right [raɪt] richtig; korrekt; rechts; rechte/-r/-s **I**
*to be **right** [bi 'raɪt] recht haben **I**
*to get **right** [get 'raɪt] richtig beantworten **III**
on the **right** [ɒn ðə 'raɪt] auf der rechten Seite; rechts **I**
right away [ˌraɪt ə'weɪ] sofort; gleich **I**
right here [ˌraɪt 'hɪə] genau hier **II**
right now [ˌraɪt 'naʊ] jetzt gleich; sofort; gerade **II**
right [raɪt] direkt **IV U2**, 52
ring [rɪŋ] Ring **III**
key **ring** ['ki: ˌrɪŋ] Schlüsselbund; Schlüsselanhänger **III**
*to **ring** [rɪŋ] klingeln; läuten **I**; anrufen **IV TS1**, 36
ice **rink** ['aɪs ˌrɪŋk] Eisbahn; Schlittschuhbahn **I**
*to **rise** [raɪz] steigen; sich erheben **III**
*to **rise** up in one's mind [raɪz ʌp ɪn wʌnz 'maɪnd] jmdm. in den Sinn kommen **III**
No **risk**, no fun! [nəʊ ˌrɪsk nəʊ 'fʌn] Wer nicht wagt, der nicht gewinnt. **IV AC3**, 69
*to take a **risk** [ˌteɪk ə 'rɪsk] ein Risiko eingehen **IV TS1**, 32
river ['rɪvə] Fluss **I**
by the **river** [baɪ ðə 'rɪvə] am Fluss **II**
road [rəʊd] Straße **II**
to **roar** [rɔ:] dröhnen; brüllen; rauschen **III**
roaring ['rɔ:rɪŋ] dröhnend; tosend; donnernd **III**
roast turkey [rəʊst 'tɜ:ki] Putenbraten ⟨**IV U2**, 45⟩
robber ['rɒbə] Räuber/-in **III**
robot ['rəʊbɒt] Roboter; Automat ⟨**IV U3**, 90⟩
rock [rɒk] Fels; Stein ⟨**IV TS3**, 101⟩
rock [rɒk] Rock *(Musik)* **III**
rock 'n' roll [ˌrɒk ən 'rəʊl] Rock 'n' Roll **II**
to **rock** [rɒk] schaukeln **IV U1**, 16

rocky ['rɒki] felsig; steinig **III**
role [rəʊl] Rolle **I**
role play ['rəʊl ˌpleɪ] Rollenspiel **I**
to swap **roles** [ˌswɒp 'rəʊlz] Rollen tauschen **I**
bread **roll** ['bred rəʊl] Brötchen **III**
rock 'n' **roll** [ˌrɒk‿ən 'rəʊl] Rock 'n' Roll **II**
to **roll** off [rəʊl] hinunterrollen; herunterrollen **II**
to **roll** one's eyes [ˌrəʊl wʌnz‿'aɪz] die Augen verdrehen **III**
Roll two dice. [ˌrəʊl ˌtu: 'daɪs] Würfle/Würfelt mit zwei Würfeln. **I**
Roman ['rəʊmən] Römer/-in; römisch **II**
romance [rə'mæns] Liebesgeschichte; Liebesfilm **III**
Romanian [rʊ'meɪniən] Rumäne/Rumänin; rumänisch; Rumänisch **II**
roof [ru:f] Dach **III**
room [ru:m; rʊm] Zimmer; Raum **I**
chat **room** ['tʃæt rʊm] Chatroom **II**
living **room** ['lɪvɪŋ rʊm] Wohnzimmer **I**
side **room** ['saɪd ˌrʊm] Nebenraum **IV U1**, 13
roommate ['ru:mmeɪt] Zimmergenosse/Zimmergenossin **I**
rope [rəʊp] Seil **III**
rotary phone ['rəʊtri fəʊn] Telefon mit Wählscheibe **III**
rough [rʌf] rau; derb; grob ⟨**IV TS1**, 31⟩
round [raʊnd] Runde **II**
round of boxing [ˌraʊnd‿əv 'bɒksɪŋ] Boxrunde **II**
the **Round** Table [ðə ˌraʊnd 'teɪbl] die Tafelrunde **III**
*to bring **round** [ˌbrɪŋ‿'raʊnd] mitbringen ⟨**IV TS1**, 36⟩
*to go **round** in circles [gəʊ ˌraʊnd ɪn 'sɜ:klz] sich im Kreis drehen **III**
to turn **round** [ˌtɜ:n‿(ə)'raʊnd] (sich) umdrehen; wenden **II**
round [raʊnd] um … herum **II**
route [ru:t] Strecke; Route **II**
route planner ['ru:t ˌplænə] Routenplaner **IV AC2**, 41
routine [ru:'ti:n] Routine **IV U1**, 16
royal ['rɔɪəl] königlich **I**
rubber ['rʌbə] Radiergummi **I**
rubbish ['rʌbɪʃ] Müll; Gerümpel **I**
rude [ru:d] unhöflich; unverschämt **I**
rugby ['rʌgbi] Rugby **II**
to ruin ['ru:ɪn] ruinieren; zerstören **II**
rule [ru:l] Regel **I**
What's the **rule** for …? [ˌwɒts ðə 'ru:l fə] Was ist die Regel für …? **I**
to **rule** [ru:l] herrschen; regieren **III**
ruler ['ru:lə] Lineal **I**
run [rʌn] Rennen; Lauf **II**
run area ['rʌn ˌeəriə] Gehege; Auslauf **III**
*to **run** [rʌn] rennen; laufen **I**; betreiben; leiten; führen **IV TS3**, 102
*to **run** away [ˌrʌn‿ə'weɪ] wegrennen **I**
runner ['rʌnə] Läufer/-in **II**
running ['rʌnɪŋ] Laufen; Rennen **II**
rural ['rʊərl] ländlich **IV AC2**, 38

S

sad [sæd] traurig **I**
safe [seɪf] sicher; ungefährlich **II**
to reef the **sails** [ˌri:f ðə 'seɪlz] die Segel einholen **I**
to **sail** [seɪl] segeln; umsegeln **III**
sailboat ['seɪlbəʊt] Segelboot **III**
sailor ['seɪlə] Seemann; Matrose **I**
salad ['sæləd] Salat **I**
sale [seɪl] Verkauf **II**
the **same** [ðə 'seɪm] der-/die-/dasselbe; der/die/das gleiche **I**
the **same** way as [ˌðə seɪm 'weɪ æz] genauso wie **II**
samosa [sə'məʊsə] *mit Kartoffeln oder Hackfleisch gefüllte indische Teigtasche* ⟨**IV U3**, 75⟩
sample ['sɑ:mpl] Probe; Muster **IV TS2**, 64
sandal ['sændl] Sandale **III**
sandwich ['sænwɪdʒ] Sandwich; belegtes Brot **I**
sandy ['sændi] sandig; Sand- **III**
Saturday ['sætədeɪ] Samstag **I**
sauce [sɔ:s] Soße **III**
sausage ['sɒsɪdʒ] Wurst; Bratwurst **III**
to **save** [seɪv] retten; bergen **I**; sparen **III**
to **save** the best for last [ˌseɪv ðə ˌbest fə 'lɑ:st] sich das Beste bis zum Schluss aufheben **IV U3**, 72
saved by the bell [ˌseɪvd baɪ ðə 'bel] noch mal Glück gehabt **III**
sax ['sæks] Saxofon **I**
saxophone ['sæksəfəʊn] Saxofon **I**
*to **say** [seɪ] sagen; aufsagen; sprechen **I**
needless to **say** [ˌni:dləs tə 'seɪ] natürlich; selbstverständlich **IV U3**, 76
*to **say** hello (to) [ˌseɪ hel'əʊ tə] grüßen; Grüße ausrichten (an) **I**
saying ['seɪɪŋ] Redensart; Sprichwort **III**
to **scan** [skæn] scannen; nach Details durchsuchen **II**
scared [skeəd] verängstigt; ängstlich **IV U2**, 52
*to be **scared** (of) [bi: 'skeəd‿əv] Angst haben (vor) **I**
I'm (not) **scared** of … [ˌaɪm (nɒt) 'skeəd‿əv] Ich habe (keine) Angst vor … **I**
scary ['skeəri] unheimlich; gruselig; beängstigend **II**
scene [si:n] Szene **I**; Schauplatz **II**
acting a **scene** [ˌæktɪŋ‿ə 'si:n] eine Theaterszene spielen **I**
scenery ['si:nri] Landschaft **IV AC2**, 40
sceptical ['skeptɪkl] skeptisch **IV TS2**, 64
schedule *(AE)* ['ʃedju:l; 'skedʒu:l] Stundenplan; Fahrplan; Terminkalender **IV AC4**, 106
rhyme **scheme** ['raɪm ski:m] Reimschema **III**
schnitzel ['ʃnɪtsl] Schnitzel ⟨**IV U3**, 75⟩
school [sku:l] Schule **I**
grammar **school** ['græmə ˌsku:l] Gymnasium **III**
high **school** *(AE)* ['haɪ ˌsku:l] High School *(weiterführende Schule in den USA, Oberstufe)* **IV U2**, 43
middle **school** *(AE)* ['mɪdl ˌsku:l] Mittelschule *(weiterführende Schule in den USA, Mittelstufe)* **IV U2**, 43
primary **school** ['praɪmri ˌsku:l] Grundschule **I**
school fees *(pl)* ['sku:l fi:z] Schulgeld; Schulgebühren **III**
schoolbag ['sku:lbæg] Schultasche **I**
schoolwork ['sku:lwɜ:k] Schularbeiten **IV TS1**, 34
Science [saɪəns] Naturwissenschaften **II**
science [saɪəns] Wissenschaft; Naturwissenschaft **IV TS3**, 100
science fiction [ˌsaɪəns 'fɪkʃn] Science-Fiction *(Zukunftsdichtung)* **II**
scientist ['saɪəntɪst] Wissenschaftler/-in **III**
score [skɔ:] Punktestand; Spielstand **II**
Scot [skɒt] Schotte/Schottin **III**
Scottish ['skɒtɪʃ] schottisch **III**
gorge **scrambling** ['gɔ:dʒ ˌskræmblɪŋ] Schluchtenklettern **II**
to **scream** [skri:m] schreien; kreischen **II**
script [skrɪpt] Drehbuch; Skript **III**
sculpture ['skʌlptʃə] Skulptur **IV U3**, 72
sea [si:] Meer **I**
search [sɜ:tʃ] Suche; Such- **II**
search engine ['sɜ:tʃ‿endʒɪn] Suchmaschine °**IV U2**, 42
to **search** for ['sɜ:tʃ fə] suchen (nach) **IV U1**, 14
seasick ['si:sɪk] seekrank **IV U1**, 8
season ['si:zn] Saison; Jahreszeit **IV U2**, 56
seat [si:t] Sitz; Sitzplatz **IV U1**, 16
second ['seknd] zweite/-r/-s **I**
secret ['si:krət] Geheimnis **II**
in **secret** [ɪn 'si:krət] heimlich **II**
secret ['si:krət] geheim **III**
section ['sekʃn] Abschnitt; Paragraf **II**
security [sɪ'kjʊərəti] Sicherheit; Schutz; Wachdienst; Wach-; Sicherheits- **IV U1**, 13
*to **see** [si:] sehen **I**
See you! ['si: jə] Bis dann!; Bis … **I**
I can't **see** the point of … [aɪ ˌkɑ:nt si: ðə 'pɔɪnt‿əv] Ich sehe keinen Sinn darin … **IV AC3**, 69
Wait and **see**! [ˌweɪt‿ənd 'si:] Warte ab! **I**
to **seem** [si:m] scheinen **III**
self [self], **selves** [selvz] *(pl)* das Selbst **III**
self-critical [ˌselfˈkrɪtɪkl] selbstkritisch **II**
self-evaluation [ˌselfɪˌvælju'eɪʃn] Selbsteinschätzung **I**
selfie ['selfi] Selfie **II**
*to **sell** [sel] verkaufen **I**

seller ['selə] Verkäufer/-in *(auf einem Flohmarkt)* **I**
*to **send** [send] schicken; senden **I**
*to **send** off [send ̮'ɒf] abschicken **III**
sense [sens] Sinn **III**
*to make **sense** [ˌmeɪk 'sens] Sinn ergeben; einleuchten **IV TS3**, 102
sense of humour *(no pl)* [ˌsens ̮əv 'hju:mə] Sinn für Humor **III**
sensible ['sensɪbl] vernünftig **IV TS1**, 32
sentence ['sentəns] Satz **I**
conditional **sentence** [kənˌdɪʃnl 'sentəns] Bedingungssatz **III**
to **separate** ['sepreɪt] (sich) trennen °**IV U3**, 73
separate ['seprət] separat; getrennt; verschieden **II**
September [sep'tembə] September **I**
sequence ['si:kwəns] Sequenz; Szene **III**; Abfolge; Reihenfolge **IV U3**, 89
series ['sɪəri:z], **series** ['sɪəri:z] *(pl)* Serie **III**
serious ['sɪəriəs] ernsthaft; ernst **I**
service ['sɜ:vɪs] Service; Dienstleistung; Dienst **IV U3**, 72
set [set] Umgebung; Rahmen; Aufnahmeort; Drehort **III**
a **set** of [ə 'set ̮əv] eine Liste von **III**
*to be **set** (in) [bi 'set ɪn] spielen (in); seinen Schauplatz haben (in) **IV U1**, 19
*to **set** off [ˌset ̮'ɒf] *hier:* ein Feuerwerk zünden **III**
*to **set** up [ˌset ̮'ʌp] einrichten; aufbauen **I**
setting ['setɪŋ] Schauplatz; Rahmen **II**
account **settings** [ə'kaʊnt ˌsetɪŋz] Profileinstellungen **III**
to **settle** for less [ˌsetl fə 'les] sich mit weniger zufrieden geben **IV TS2**, 66
seven ['sevn] sieben **I**
several ['sevrl] einige; mehrere; verschiedene **II**
shadow ['ʃædəʊ] Schatten **III**
*to **shake** [ʃeɪk] schütteln ⟨**IV U3**, 90⟩
shampoo [ʃæm'pu:] Shampoo **IV TS2**, 64
shape [ʃeɪp] Form **IV U3**, 89
to **share** [ʃeə] teilen **II**
shark [ʃɑ:k] Hai **IV U1**, 16
sharp [ʃɑ:p] scharf; schneidend **III**
she [ʃi:] sie **I**
sheep, **sheep** *(pl)* [ʃi:p] Schaf **II**
cheat **sheet** ['tʃi:t ʃi:t] Spickzettel **IV AC3**, 69
animal **shelter** ['ænɪml ˌʃeltə] Tierheim **III**
homeless **shelter** ['həʊmləs ˌʃeltə] Obdachlosenunterkunft **IV U2**, 51
*to **shine** [ʃaɪn] scheinen; glänzen **II**
shinty ['ʃɪnti] Shinty *(eine Art Hockey)* **III**
ship [ʃɪp] Schiff **I**
shipbuilding ['ʃɪpbɪldɪŋ] Schiffsbau **III**
shit *(vulg)* [ʃɪt] Scheiße; Scheißdreck ⟨**IV U3**, 84⟩
shock [ʃɒk] Schock **II**
shocked [ʃɒkt] schockiert; geschockt **IV TS1**, 37

shoe [ʃu:] Schuh **I**
*to be in sb's **shoes** [ˌbi: ɪn sʌmbɒdɪz 'ʃu:z] an jmds. Stelle sein; in jmds. Haut stecken **III**
in Jay's **shoes** [ɪn dʒeɪz 'ʃu:z] an Jays Stelle **III**
on a **shoestring** [ˌɒn ̮ə 'ʃu:strɪŋ] für/mit wenig Geld **IV U3**, 72
photo **shoot** ['fəʊtəʊ ˌʃu:t] Fotoshooting; Fotoaufnahmen **III**
*to **shoot** [ʃu:t ̮(ət)] schießen (auf) **III**
shop [ʃɒp] Geschäft; Laden **I**
charity **shop** ['tʃærɪti ʃɒp] Second-Hand-Laden **I**
pawn **shop** ['pɔ:n ʃɒp] Pfandhaus; Pfandleihe **III**
to **shop** [ʃɒp] einkaufen; shoppen **IV U3**, 76
shopper ['ʃɒpə] Käufer/-in **IV U2**, 48
shopping ['ʃɒpɪŋ] Einkaufen; Einkäufe **I**
*to do the **shopping** [ˌdu: ðə 'ʃɒpɪŋ] Einkäufe machen; Besorgungen machen **III**
*to go **shopping** [ˌgəʊ 'ʃɒpɪŋ] einkaufen gehen **I**
shopping mall ['ʃɒpɪŋ ˌmɔ:l] Einkaufszentrum **IV U2**, 43
shore [ʃɔ:] Ufer; Küste **II**
short [ʃɔ:t] kurz **I**
short answer [ˌʃɔ:t ̮'ɑ:nsə] Kurzantwort **I**
short form ['ʃɔ:t fɔ:m] Kurzform **I**
shorts *(pl)* [ʃɔ:ts] Shorts; kurze Hose **II**
shot [ʃɒt] Einstellung; Kameraeinstellung **II**; Aufnahme **III**
long **shot** ['lɒŋ ʃɒt] Totale *(Kameraeinstellung)* **IV U3**, 89
medium **shot** ['mi:diəm ʃɒt] Halbtotale *(Kameraeinstellung)* **IV U3**, 89
should [ʃʊd] sollte; solltest; sollten; solltet **II**
shouldn't ['ʃʊdnt] sollte(n) nicht **II**
shoulder ['ʃəʊldə] Schulter **II**
to **shout** [ʃaʊt] schreien; rufen **I**
show [ʃəʊ] Show; Schau; Aufführung **II**
comedy **show** ['kɒmədi ˌʃəʊ] Comedy Show **II**
living history **show** [ˌlɪvɪŋ 'hɪstəri ˌʃəʊ] *Show, in der historischer Alltag nachgespielt wird* **III**
talent **show** ['tælənt ˌʃəʊ] Talentwettbewerb **I**
to **show** [ʃəʊ] zeigen **I**
to **show** off [ʃəʊ ̮'ɒf] angeben **II**
shower ['ʃaʊə] Dusche **I**
show-off ['ʃəʊ ̮ɒf] Angeber/-in **III**
to **shuffle** ['ʃʌfl] mischen **III**
shutter ['ʃʌtə] Fensterladen **IV U1**, 10
shy [ʃaɪ] schüchtern **II**
sick [sɪk] krank; unwohl **II**
*to be **sick** [bi 'sɪk] sich übergeben **IV U1**, 16
*to feel **sick** [ˌfi:l 'sɪk] Übelkeit verspüren; sich schlecht fühlen **II**
side [saɪd] Seite **II**

side room ['saɪd ˌrʊm] Nebenraum **IV U1**, 13
sidewalk *(AE)* ['saɪdwɔ:k] Gehweg; Gehsteig **IV U3**, 76
sight [saɪt] Sehenswürdigkeit; Anblick **II**; *hier:* Blick **III**
sighting ['saɪtɪŋ] Sichten °**IV TS3**, 105
sightseeing ['saɪtsi:ɪŋ] Sightseeing-; Besichtigungs- **II**
sign [saɪn] Zeichen; Schild **II**
to **sign** [saɪn] unterschreiben; unterzeichnen **IV U2**, 52
signal ['sɪgnl] Signal; Empfang **III**
signal word ['sɪgnəl ˌwɜ:d] Signalwort **I**
silence *(no pl)* ['saɪləns] Stille; Schweigen; Ruhe **III**
silent ['saɪlənt] still; ruhig; schweigsam; stumm **III**
silk [sɪlk] Seide ⟨**IV TS1**, 34⟩
silly ['sɪli] Dummkopf **II**
silly ['sɪli] dumm; doof; albern **I**
silver ['sɪlvə] Silber **II**
similar ['sɪmɪlə] ähnlich **II**
similarity [ˌsɪmɪ'lærəti] Ähnlichkeit; Gemeinsamkeit °**IV TS2**, 67
simple ['sɪmpl] einfach; simpel **III**
simple past [ˌsɪmpl 'pɑ:st] Vergangenheitsform **II**
simple present [ˌsɪmpl 'preznt] Gegenwart; Präsens **I**
simply ['sɪmpli] einfach nur **IV AC2**, 40
since [sɪns] da **IV U3**, 72
since *(+ Zeitpunkt)* [sɪns] seit; seitdem **III**
*to **sing** [sɪŋ] singen **I**
*to **sing** along [ˌsɪŋ ̮ə'lɒŋ] mitsingen **III**
*to **sing** out loud [ˌri:d/sɪŋ ̮aʊt 'laʊd] laut vorsingen **III**
I like **singing** and dancing. [ˌaɪ laɪk ˌsɪŋɪŋ ̮ənd 'dɑ:nsɪŋ] Ich singe und tanze gern. **I**
singer ['sɪŋə] Sänger/-in **II**
single ['sɪŋgl] einzeln; einzig; alleinstehend **IV AC2**, 38
single ticket ['sɪŋgl ˌtɪkɪt] einfache Fahrkarte **III**
*to **sink** [sɪŋk] untergehen; sinken **III**
Dear **Sir** or Madam [dɪə ˌsɜ:r ̮ɔ: 'mædəm] Sehr geehrte Dame, sehr geehrter Herr **III**
sister ['sɪstə] Schwester **I**
half-**sister** ['hɑ:fˌsɪstə] Halbschwester **I**
*to **sit** [sɪt] sitzen **I**
Sit! [sɪt] Sitz! *(Befehl für Hunde)*; Platz! *(Befehl für Hunde)* **I**
*to **sit** down [ˌsɪt 'daʊn] sich hinsetzen; sich setzen **I**
*to **sit** face to face [ˌsɪt feɪs tə ˌfeɪs] sich gegenüber sitzen **I**
site [saɪt] Webseite **II**
situation [ˌsɪtju'eɪʃn] Situation **I**
six [sɪks] sechs **I**
Four and **six** is ten. [ˌfɔ:r ̮ənd ˌsɪks ̮ɪz 'ten] Vier plus sechs ist zehn. **I**
size [saɪz] Größe; Kleidergröße **I**

to **skate** [skeɪt] Inlineskates fahren; Schlittschuh laufen **I**
skateboard ['skeɪtbɔ:d] Skateboard **II**
skateboarding ['skeɪtbɔ:dɪŋ] Skateboardfahren **I**
skates *(pl)* [skeɪts] Inlineskates; Rollschuhe; Schlittschuhe **I**
(inline) **skating** ['ɪnlaɪn ˌskeɪtɪŋ] Inlineskatefahren **I**
skill [skɪl] Fertigkeit; Geschick **I**
to **skim** [skɪm] überfliegen **II**
to **skip** [skɪp] auslassen; schwänzen **IV AC3**, 68
skirt [skɜ:t] Rock **III**
sky [skaɪ] Himmel **III**
skyscraper ['skaɪskreɪpə] Wolkenkratzer **IV AC2**, 39
slave [sleɪv] Sklave/Sklavin **III**
sleep [sli:p] Schlaf **IV U1**, 11
*to **sleep** [sli:p] schlafen **I**
sleepover ['sli:pˌəʊvə] Übernachtung **I**
to **slice** [slaɪs] in Scheiben schneiden **I**
slide [slaɪd] Rutschbahn **I**
water **slide** ['wɔ:tə ˌslaɪd] Wasserrutsche **I**
*to **slide** [slaɪd] gleiten lassen ⟨**IV U3**, 90⟩
to **slip** into [slɪp‿'ɪntə] schlüpfen in °**IV TS2**, 67
slogan ['sləʊgən] Slogan; Werbespruch **II**
time **slot** ['taɪm slɒt] Zeitfenster **II**
to **slow** down [ˌsləʊ 'daʊn] langsamer werden; bremsen ⟨**IV U3**, 90⟩
slow [sləʊ] langsam **I**
to step into a story **slowly** [step‿ˌɪntʊ ə ˌstɔ:ri 'sləʊli] eine Geschichte langsam entwickeln **III**
small [smɔ:l] klein **I**
small talk ['smɔ:l ˌtɔ:k] Smalltalk **III**
smart [smɑ:t] schlau; klug; intelligent **III**
smartcard ['smɑ:tkɑ:d] Chipkarte **II**
smartphone ['smɑ:tfəʊn] Smartphone **II**
to **smash** [smæʃ] zerschlagen; zerschmettern **IV U1**, 16
*to **smell** [smel] riechen; duften **III**
smile [smaɪl] Lächeln **I**
to **smile** [smaɪl] lächeln **I**
smoke [sməʊk] Rauch **III**
smoky ['sməʊki] verraucht **III**
smuggler ['smʌglə] Schmuggler/-in **IV U1**, 16
snack [snæk] Snack; Imbiss **I**
snack bar ['snæk ˌbɑ:] Café; Imbissstube **I**
word **snake** ['wɜ:d ˌsneɪk] Wortschlange **I**
to **sneak** around [ˌsni:k‿ə'raʊnd] herumschleichen **II**
*to **sneak** [sni:k] schleichen; schmuggeln **IV U3**, 72
to **snore** [snɔ:] schnarchen **I**
snow [snəʊ] Schnee **III**
so [səʊ] so; also **I**
so far [ˌsəʊ 'fɑ:] bis jetzt **II**
so is ['səʊ ɪz] ebenso wie **III**
so (that) [ˌsəʊ 'ðæt] damit; so dass **IV AC3**, 69
to **soak** up [səʊk‿'ʌp] aufsaugen **III**
soccer *(AE)* ['sɒkə] Fußball **IV U2**, 44
social ['səʊʃl] sozial; gesellschaftlich **IV U2**, 46
social media [ˌsəʊʃl 'mi:diə] soziale Netzwerke **IV U2**, 46
social network [ˌsəʊʃl 'netwɜ:k] soziales Netzwerk **II**
society [sə'saɪəti] Verein; Gesellschaft **III**
sofa ['səʊfə] Sofa; Couch **I**
software ['sɒftweə] Software *(Computerprogramme)* ⟨**IV TS3**, 102⟩
software manual ['sɒftweə ˌmænjuəl] Softwarehandbuch **III**
soldier ['səʊldʒə] Soldat/-in **III**
solution [sə'lu:ʃn] Lösung **II**
to **solve** [sɒlv] lösen **III**
Somali [sə'mɑ:li] Somali **IV U1**, 17
some [sʌm; səm] einige; ein paar; etwas **I**
somebody ['sʌmbədi] jemand **I**
someone ['sʌmwʌn] jemand **II**
something ['sʌmθɪŋ] etwas **I**
sometimes ['sʌmtaɪmz] manchmal **I**
somewhere ['sʌmweə] irgendwo **II**
son [sʌn] Sohn **III**
song [sɒŋ] Song; Lied **I**
theme **song** ['θi:m sɒŋ] Titelmelodie °**IV U3**, 91
soon [su:n] bald **II**
as **soon** as [əz 'su:n‿əz] sobald **II**
Sorry! ['sɒri] Entschuldigung!; Tut mir leid! **I**
*to be **sorry** [bi: 'sɒri] leid tun **I**
*to feel **sorry** for [ˌfi:l 'sɒri fɔ:] Mitleid haben mit; bedauern **III**
I'm **sorry**! [ˌaɪm 'sɒri] Tut mir leid! **I**
sort [sɔ:t] Sorte; Art ⟨**IV TS1**, 34⟩
to **sort** into [sɔ:t 'ɪntʊ] einsortieren; sortieren nach **III**
sound [saʊnd] Ton; Geräusch; Klang **I**
to **sound** [saʊnd] klingen **I**
soup [su:p] Suppe **IV U1**, 11
source [sɔ:s] Quelle **III**
south [saʊθ] Süden; Süd- **II**
South Korean [ˌsaʊθ kə'ri:ən] Südkoreaner/-in; südkoreanisch; Südkoreanisch **II**
(the) **Southwest** [ˌsaʊθ'west] (der) Südwesten; im Südwesten; südwestlich **IV AC2**, 38
souvenir [ˌsu:vn'ɪə] Souvenir; Andenken **II**
space [speɪs] Raum; Fläche; Platz; Ort **II**
*to leave **space** [li:v 'speɪs] Platz lassen **I**
space [speɪs] Weltraum; Weltall **IV TS3**, 104
space program ['speɪs ˌprəʊgræm] Raumfahrtprogramm **IV TS3**, 104
spaceship ['speɪsʃɪp] Raumschiff **II**
Spanish ['spænɪʃ] spanisch; Spanisch; die Spanier **III**
sparse [spɑ:s] dünn; spärlich **IV AC2**, 38
*to **speak** [spi:k] sprechen **I**
speaker ['spi:kə] Redner/-in; Sprecher/-in **I**
speaking ['spi:kɪŋ] Sprechen **I**
spear [spɪə] Speer **III**
special ['speʃl] besonders; speziell **I**
special effect [ˌspeʃl‿ɪ'fekt] Spezialeffekt **IV TS3**, 105
special offer [ˌspeʃl‿'ɒfə] Sonderangebot **I**
with **special** needs [wɪð ˌspeʃl 'ni:dz] behindert **II**
specialty *(AE)* ['speʃlti] Spezialität; Besonderheit **IV U3**, 75
specific [spə'sɪfɪk] spezifisch; speziell **IV U1**, 19
spectacular [spek'tækjələ] spektakulär **III**
speech [spi:tʃ] Rede **III**
direct **speech** [dɪˌrekt 'spi:tʃ] direkte Rede **IV U1**, 11
indirect **speech** [ˌɪndɪrekt 'spi:tʃ] indirekte Rede **IV U1**, 11
speech bubble ['spi:tʃ ˌbʌbl] Sprechblase **I**
speed [spi:d] Geschwindigkeit **IV U3**, 89
*to **spell** [spel] buchstabieren **I**
spelling ['spelɪŋ] Rechtschreibung **I**
*to **spend** [spend] ausgeben *(Geld)* **I**; verbringen *(Zeit)* **II**
to **spice** up [ˌspaɪs‿'ʌp] aufpeppen **IV TS2**, 65
spider ['spaɪdə] Spinne **III**
spike [spaɪk] Spitze; Stachel **IV U3**, 74
*to **spill** [spɪl] verschütten; auslaufen **IV U1**, 10
spoken ['spəʊkn] gesprochen **II**
sponge [spʌndʒ] Rühr-; Biskuit- **I**
spontaneous [spɒn'teɪniəs] spontan **III**
spoon [spu:n] Löffel **III**
sport [spɔ:t] Sport; Sportart **I**
spot [spɒt] Fleck; Ort **IV U3**, 75
spray [spreɪ] Spray ⟨**IV U3**, 86⟩
spring [sprɪŋ] Frühling **III**
squirrel ['skwɪrəl] Eichhörnchen **I**
stadium ['steɪdiəm] Stadion **II**
stage [steɪdʒ] Bühne **III**
stage direction ['steɪdʒ dɪˌrekʃn] Regieanweisung **III**
to **stage** [steɪdʒ] aufführen **IV TS1**, 30; inszenieren **IV TS3**, 102
stairs *(pl)* [steəz] Treppe **III**
*to **stand** [stænd] stehen **I**
*to **stand** in line *(AE)* [ˌstænd‿ɪn 'laɪn] anstehen; Schlange stehen; (sich) anstellen **IV AC3**, 69
*to **stand** in the way of sb/sth [ˌstænd ɪn ðə 'weɪ‿əv] jmdm./etw. im Weg stehen **IV AC1**, 22
*to **stand** up [ˌstænd‿'ʌp] aufstehen *(von einer Sitzgelegenheit)* **I**
standard of living [ˌstændəd‿əv 'lɪvɪŋ] Lebensstandard **IV AC2**, 40
star [stɑ:] Star; Stern **I**
to **stare** [steə] starren; anstarren **I**
start [stɑ:t] Anfang; Start **III**
to **start** [stɑ:t] anfangen; beginnen; starten **I**; *hier:* gründen **III**
*to get **started** [ˌget 'stɑ:tɪd] anfangen **II**
starting place ['stɑ:tɪŋ pleɪs] Startpunkt **III**

state [steɪt] Staat; Bundesstaat; Land **IV AC2**, 39
head of **state** [ˌhed_əv 'steɪt] Staatsoberhaupt **II**
statement ['steɪtmənt] Aussage; Behauptung; Erklärung **II**
station ['steɪʃn] Haltestelle; Bahnhof; Station **I**; Sender **II**
bus **station** ['bʌs ˌsteɪʃn] Busbahnhof **I**
statue ['stætʃu:] Statue; Standbild **IV U3**, 74
to **stay** [steɪ] bleiben **I**; übernachten **III**
to **stay** awake [ˌsteɪ_ə'weɪk] wach bleiben ⟨**IV U3**, 90⟩
to **stay** away from [ˌsteɪ_ə'weɪ frəm] fernbleiben von; meiden **II**
to **stay** in touch (with) [ˌsteɪ ɪn 'tʌtʃ (wɪð)] in Kontakt bleiben (mit) **II**
to **stay** with ['steɪ wɪð] wohnen bei **II**
Stay the way you are. [ˌsteɪ ðə weɪ ju 'ɑ:] Bleib wie du bist. **III**
steady ['stedi] kontinuierlich; unaufhörlich **IV U1**, 17
steak [steɪk] Steak **I**
*to **steal** [sti:l] stehlen **II**
steam [sti:m] Dampf **III**
steam engine ['sti:m_endʒɪn] Dampfmaschine **III**
step [step] Stufe; Schritt **I**
step-by-**step** [ˌstepbaɪ'step] Schritt-für-Schritt- **II**
to **step** [step] treten; steigen **IV TS3**, 101
to **step** into a story slowly [step_ɪntʊ ə ˌstɔ:ri 'sləʊli] eine Geschichte langsam entwickeln **III**
stepmum ['stepmʌm] Stiefmutter **I**
*to **stick** [stɪk] stecken ⟨**IV U3**, 88⟩
still [stɪl] Standbild **II**
still [stɪl] still **I**
still [stɪl] noch; immer noch **I**; dennoch **II**
*to keep one's feet or hands **still** [ˌki:p wʌnz: 'fi:t_ɔ: 'hændz stɪl] die Beine und Hände ruhig halten **III**
*to **sting** [stɪŋ] stechen **III**
stomach ['stʌmək] Magen; Bauch **II**
stomachache ['stʌməkeɪk] Bauchschmerzen; Bauchweh **II**
stone [stəʊn] Stein; Stein- **III**
stop [stɒp] Haltestelle; Halt **II**
to **stop** [stɒp] aufhören (mit); anhalten; stoppen **I**
Stop and think [ˌstɒp_ənd 'θɪŋk] Warte/Wartet und denk/denkt nach. **I**
Stop it! ['stɒp_ɪt] Mach/Macht das aus!; Hör/Hört auf! **I**
store *(AE)* [stɔ:] Laden; Geschäft **IV U2**, 44
storm [stɔ:m] Sturm **I**
story, **stories** *(pl)* ['stɔ:ri; 'stɔ:riz] Story; Geschichte; Erzählung **I**
photo **story** ['fəʊtəʊ ˌstɔ:ri] Fotostory; Bildgeschichte **I**

to step into a **story** slowly [step_ɪntʊ ə ˌstɔ:ri 'sləʊli] eine Geschichte langsam entwickeln **III**
storyline ['stɔ:rilaɪn] Handlung °**IV U2**, 54
straight [streɪt] gerade; direkt; geradewegs **IV U1**, 17
straight away [ˌstreɪt_ə'weɪ] sofort; gleich **III**
straight on [streɪt_'ɒn] geradeaus **I**
strange [streɪndʒ] fremd; seltsam; merkwürdig **I**
street [stri:t] Straße *(in der Stadt)* **I**
in the **street** [ˌɪn ðə 'stri:t] in der Straße; auf der Straße **I**
the high **street** [ðə 'haɪ ˌstri:t] die Haupteinkaufsstraße **III**
streetlight ['stri:tlaɪt] Straßenlampe ⟨**IV U3**, 90⟩
stress [stres] Betonung **III**
to **stress** [stres] betonen; hervorheben **III**
*to be **stressed** out [bi ˌstrest_'aʊt] völlig gestresst sein **III**
strict [strɪkt] streng; strikt **III**
stringy ['strɪŋi] strähnig ⟨**IV U3**, 90⟩
strong [strɒŋ] stark **II**
structure ['strʌktʃə] Struktur; Aufbau; Gliederung **III**
to **structure** ['strʌktʃə] strukturieren; gliedern °**IV TS3**, 105
stuck in the middle of … [ˌstʌk ɪn ðə 'mɪdl_əv] mitten in … stecken; feststecken in … **III**
student ['stju:dnt] Schüler/-in; Student/-in **I**
exchange **student** [ɪks'tʃeɪndʒ ˌstju:dnt] Austauschschüler/-in **III**
student exchange ['stju:dnt ɪksˌtʃeɪndʒ] Schüleraustausch **III**
studies *(pl)* ['stʌdiz] Studium; Lernen; Arbeit für die Schule **II**
studio ['stju:diəʊ] Studio; Atelier **IV U3**, 72
recording **studio** [rɪ'kɔ:dɪŋ ˌstju:diəʊ] Aufnahmestudio; Tonstudio **I**
to **study** ['stʌdi] studieren; lernen **III**
stuff [stʌf] Zeug **I**
stupid ['stju:pɪd] dumm; blöd **II**
style [staɪl] Stil **IV U1**, 11
stylistic [staɪ'lɪstɪk] Stil-; stilistisch **IV U3**, 89
subject ['sʌbdʒɪkt] Schulfach; Subjekt; Satzgegenstand **II**; Thema **III**
substitute ['sʌbstɪtju:t] Ersatz; Ersatz- **II**
suburb ['sʌbɜ:b] Vorort **IV U2**, 43
suburban [sə'bɜ:bn] Vorstadt- **IV U2**, 43
subway *(AE)* ['sʌbweɪ] U-Bahn **IV U3**, 74
to **succeed** (in) [sək'si:d_ɪn] Erfolg haben (in/bei/mit) **III**
success [sək'ses] Erfolg **III**
successful [sək'sesfl] erfolgreich **III**
such [sʌtʃ] solch; solche/-r/-s **II**
It **sucks**. *(slang)* [ɪt 'sʌks] Das ist zum Kotzen. **IV AC4**, 107
suddenly ['sʌdnli] plötzlich; auf einmal **I**
sugar ['ʃʊgə] Zucker **III**

to **suggest** [sə'dʒest] vorschlagen **IV U1**, 15
suggestion [sə'dʒestʃn] Vorschlag; Anregung **I**
suitcase ['su:tkeɪs] Koffer **IV U1**, 9
to **sum** up [ˌsʌm_'ʌp] zusammenfassen **II**
summary ['sʌmri] Zusammenfassung **IV TS1**, 37
summer ['sʌmə] Sommer **II**
summer camp ['sʌmə kæmp] Sommerferienlager **II**
sun [sʌn] Sonne **II**
Sunday ['sʌndeɪ] Sonntag **I**
sunflower ['sʌnflaʊə] Sonnenblume **III**
sunset ['sʌnset] Sonnenuntergang **IV U3**, 72
super ['su:pə] super **IV U2**, 44
superlative [su:'pɜ:lətɪv] Superlativ **II**
supermarket ['su:pəˌmɑ:kɪt] Supermarkt **I**
supernatural ['su:pəˌnætʃrl] übernatürlich **IV U1**, 19
superpower ['su:pəˌpaʊə] Supermacht **II**
supper ['sʌpə] spätes Abendessen ⟨**IV U3**, 86⟩
to **supply** [sə'plaɪ] versorgen **III**
to **support** [sə'pɔ:t] unterstützen **IV TS1**, 36
sure [ʃʊə; ʃɔ:] sicher **I**
*to make **sure** [ˌmeɪk 'ʃɔ:] sich versichern **I**
I'm (not) **sure** … [ˌaɪm nɒt 'ʃʊə] Ich bin mir (nicht) sicher … **III**
surface ['sɜ:fɪs] Oberfläche **IV TS3**, 101
surfing ['sɜ:fɪŋ] Surfen **III**
surgery ['sɜ:dʒəri] Arztpraxis; Praxis; Praxisräume **I**
surprise [sə'praɪz] Überraschung **I**
to **surprise** [sə'praɪz] überraschen **II**
*to be **surprised** [bi sə'praɪzd] überrascht sein **II**
surprising [sə'praɪzɪŋ] überraschend **II**
survey ['sɜ:veɪ] Umfrage; Studie **I**
to **survive** [sə'vaɪv] überleben **III**
survivor [sə'vaɪvə] Überlebende/-r **IV U2**, 45
*to be **suspended** [bi sə'spendɪd] suspendiert werden; zeitweilig vom Unterricht ausgeschlossen werden **IV AC3**, 68
suspense [sə'spens] Spannung **III**
suspicious [sə'spɪʃəs] misstrauisch; argwöhnisch **IV U1**, 13
to **swap** [swɒp] tauschen °**IV TS2**, 67
to **swap** roles [ˌswɒp 'rəʊlz] Rollen tauschen **I**
sweatshop ['swetʃɒp] Ausbeuterbetrieb **IV U2**, 48
sweet [swi:t] süß **I**
sweet potatoes *(pl)* ['swi:t pəˌteɪtəʊz] Süßkartoffeln ⟨**IV U2**, 45⟩
sweets *(pl)* [swi:ts] Süßigkeiten; Bonbons **I**
*to **swim** [swɪm] schwimmen **I**
swimming ['swɪmɪŋ] Schwimmen **I**
*to go **swimming** [ˌgəʊ 'swɪmɪŋ] Schwimmen gehen **I**
swimming pool ['swɪmɪŋ ˌpu:l] Swimmingpool; Schwimmbecken **III**
switch [swɪtʃ] Schalter **III**

to switch off [ˌswɪtʃ‿ˈɒf] ausschalten IV AC3, 69
syllable [ˈsɪləbl] Silbe **III**
symbol [ˈsɪmbl] Symbol **II**
to symbolize *(AE)* [ˈsɪmbəlaɪz] symbolisieren IV AC2, 40
system [ˈsɪstəm] System ⟨IV U3, 90⟩

T

table [ˈteɪbl] Tisch **I**
the Round **Table** [ðə ˌraʊnd ˈteɪbl] die Tafelrunde **III**
tablet [ˈtæblət] Tablet **II**; Tafel **IV U3**, 74
taco [ˈtækəʊ] Taco *(mexikanische gefüllte Teigtasche)* ⟨IV U3, 75⟩
taekwondo [ˌtækwʌnˈduː] Taekwondo **II**
question **tag** [ˈkwestʃən ˌtæg] Frageanhängsel; Bestätigungsfrage **II**
tail [teɪl] Schwanz; Schweif **I**
*to **take** [teɪk] nehmen; mitnehmen; wegnehmen; bringen; mitbringen **I**; dauern; (Zeit) brauchen **II**
*to **take** a breath [ˌteɪk‿ə ˈbreθ] Luft holen; Atem holen **III**
*to **take** a look at [ˌteɪk‿ə ˈlʊk‿æt] einen Blick werfen auf **II**
*to **take** a message [ˌteɪk‿ə ˈmesɪdʒ] eine Nachricht entgegennehmen; jmdm. etw. ausrichten **I**
*to **take** a risk [ˌteɪk‿ə ˈrɪsk] ein Risiko eingehen **IV TS1**, 32
*to **take** a test [ˌteɪk‿ə ˈtest] einen Test machen **II**
*to **take** a vote [ˌteɪk‿ə ˈvəʊt] abstimmen **I**
*to **take** care of sb [ˌteɪk‿ˈkeər‿əv] sich um jmdn. kümmern; für jmdn. sorgen **III**
*to **take** notes [teɪk ˈnəʊts] sich Notizen machen **I**
*to **take** off [ˌteɪk‿ˈɒf] abnehmen; herunternehmen; ausziehen **I**
*to **take** part (in) [ˌteɪk ˈpɑːt (ɪn)] teilnehmen (an) **II**
*to **take** photos [ˌteɪk ˈfəʊtəʊz] fotografieren; Fotos machen **I**
*to **take** place [ˌteɪk ˈpleɪs] stattfinden **I**
*to **take** the day off [ˌteɪk ðə ˌdeɪ‿ˈɒf] sich den Tag freinehmen **IV U3**, 72
Take turns. [ˌteɪk ˈtɜːnz] Wechselt euch ab. **I**
Take a deep breath. [ˌteɪk‿ə ˌdiːp ˈbreθ] Atme(t) tief ein. **II**
take-off [ˈteɪk‿ɒf] Start; Abheben **IV U1**, 15
talent [ˈtælənt] Talent **I**
talent show [ˈtælənt ˌʃəʊ] Talentwettbewerb **I**
talk [tɔːk] Vortrag; Rede **IV U2**, 43; Gespräch; Unterhaltung **IV U3**, 92
*to give a **talk** [ˌgɪv‿ə ˈtɔːk] einen Vortrag halten **IV U2**, 43
small **talk** [ˈsmɔːl ˌtɔːk] Smalltalk **III**
to talk [tɔːk] sprechen; reden **I**
to **talk** about … [ˈtɔːk‿əbaʊt] sprechen über; erzählen von **I**
to **talk** to [ˈtɔːk tə] reden mit **I**
to **talk** with your mouth full [ˌtɔːk wɪð jɔː ˈmaʊθ fʊl] mit vollem Mund sprechen **IV AC1**, 22
talker [ˈtɔːkə] Sprecher/-in **III**
talking [ˈtɔːkɪŋ] Sprechen **I**
tall [tɔːl] groß; hoch **II**
to tap [tæp] antippen **II**
target [ˈtɑːgɪt] Ziel; Ziel- **IV TS2**, 65
tartan [ˈtɑːtn] Schottenkaro *(bestimmtes Muster eines Clans)*; karierter Schottenstoff **III**
task [tɑːsk] Aufgabe; Auftrag **I**
to taste [teɪst] schmecken; probieren **III**
tattoo [tætˈuː] Tattoe; Tätowierung **III**
to tattoo [tætˈuː] tätowieren ⟨IV U3, 90⟩
taxi [ˈtæksi] Taxi **II**
tea [tiː] Tee **I**
tea bag [ˈtiː bæg] Teebeutel **III**
***to teach** [tiːtʃ] unterrichten; lehren; beibringen **II**
*to **teach** somebody a lesson [ˌtiːtʃ‿ə ˈlesn] jmdm. eine Lehre/Lektion erteilen **II**
teacher [ˈtiːtʃə] Lehrer/-in **I**
team [tiːm] Team; Gruppe **II**
tear [tɪə] Träne ⟨IV U3, 84⟩
to tease sb [tiːz] jmdn. aufziehen; jmdn. hänseln; jmdn. ärgern **III**
tech [tek] Technologie; Technik **IV TS3**, 102
technique [tekˈniːk] Methode; Technik °**IV U3**, 91
Technology [tekˈnɒlədʒi] Technik; Computerunterricht **II**
technology [tekˈnɒlədʒi] Technologie **II**
teen [tiːn] Jugend- **II**; Teenager; Jugendliche/-r **III**
teenage [ˈtiːneɪdʒ] jugendlich; Jugend- **IV TS1**, 31
teenager [ˈtiːnˌeɪdʒə] Teenager; Jugendliche/-r **I**
telephone [ˈtelɪfəʊn] Telefon **I**
***to tell** [tel] erzählen; sagen; mitteilen **I**
Tell me about … [ˈtel miː‿əˌbaʊt] Erzähle mir von … **I**
temperature [ˈtemprətʃə] Temperatur **IV AC2**, 38
to tempt [tempt] in Versuchung führen; reizen **IV TS1**, 31
temptation [tempˈteɪʃn] Versuchung **IV TS2**, 64
tempted [ˈtemptɪd] in Versuchung gebracht **IV TS1**, 31
tempting [ˈtemptɪŋ] verführerisch **IV TS1**, 33
ten [ten] zehn **I**
ten times [ten ˈtaɪmz] zehnmal **I**
Four and six is **ten.** [ˌfɔːr‿ənd ˌsɪks‿ɪz ˈten] Vier plus sechs ist zehn. **I**
tennis [ˈtenɪs] Tennis **I**
tense [tens] Zeit; Zeitform *(grammatisch)* **II**
term [tɜːm] Begriff **IV TS1**, 30
terrible [ˈterəbl] schrecklich; schlimm; furchtbar ⟨IV TS1, 34⟩; ⟨IV TS3, 104⟩
test [test] Test; Klassenarbeit; Prüfung **I**
*to take a **test** [ˌteɪk‿ə ˈtest] einen Test machen **II**
to test [test] testen; prüfen **III**
text [tekst] Text **I**
factual **text** [ˌfæktʃʊəl ˈtekst] Sachtext **III**
text (message) [ˈtekst ˌmesɪdʒ] SMS; Kurznachricht **I**
wiki **(text)** [ˈwɪkɪ ˌtekst] Wikitext **IV TS3**, 101
to text [tekst] eine SMS schicken **II**
than [ðæn] als *(bei Vergleichen)* **II**
more … **than** [ˈmɔː ðən] mehr … als **I**
***to give thanks** [ˌgɪv ˈθæŋks] danken **IV U2**, 45
to thank [θæŋk] danken **II**
Thank you. [ˈθæŋk ju] Danke. **I**
thankful [ˈθæŋkfl] dankbar **I**
Thanks. [θæŋks] Danke. **I**
that [ðæt] so *(Betonung)* **III**
that much [ðæt ˈmʌtʃ] so viel **III**
that [ðæt; ðət] dass **I**
so **(that)** [ˌsəʊ ˈðæt] damit; so dass **IV AC3**, 69
that [ðæt] das; jenes **I**
after **that** [ˌɑːftə ˈðæt] danach **I**
like **that** [laɪk ˈðæt] so **I**
That was close! [ˌðæt wəz ˈkləʊs] Das war knapp! **I**
that's how [ðæts ˈhaʊ] so **II**
That's what friends are for. [ˌðæts wɒt ˈfrendz‿ɑː ˌfɔː] Dafür sind Freunde da. **I**
that's why [ðæts ˈwaɪ] deshalb **II**
That's … [ðæts] Das macht … **I**
that [ðæt] der; dem; den; die; das *(Relativpronomen)* **II**
the [ðə; ði] der; die *(auch Pl.)*; das **I**
the others [ði‿ˈʌðəz] die anderen **I**
the same [ðə ˈseɪm] der-/die-/dasselbe; der/die/das gleiche **I**
the … **the** [ðə … ðə] je … desto **II**
theater *(AE)* [ˈθɪətə] Theater **IV U3**, 70
movie **theater** *(AE)* [ˈmuːvi ˌθɪətə] Kino **IV U2**, 44
theatre [ˈθɪətə] Theater **I**
their [ðeə] ihr/-e *(Pl.)* **I**
their fault [ˌdeə ˈfɔːlt] ihre Schuld ⟨IV TS1, 36⟩
them [ðem] sie *(Pl.)*; ihnen **I**
theme [θiːm] Thema; Motto **I**
theme song [ˈθiːm sɒŋ] Titelmelodie °**IV U3**, 91
then [ðen] dann; danach **I**
back **then** [bæk ˈðen] damals **III**
theorist [ˈθɪərist] Theoretiker/-in ⟨IV TS3, 102⟩
theory [ˈθɪəri] Theorie **IV TS3**, 102
there [ðeə] da; dort; dahin; dorthin **I**
there is/are [ðər‿ˈɪz/ˈɑː] da ist/sind; es gibt **I**
There's no need to … [ˌðeəz nəʊ ˈniːd tə] Es gibt keinen Grund zu … **IV TS1**, 36

these [ði:z] diese (hier) **I**
these days [ˌði:z 'deɪz] zurzeit **III**
they [ðeɪ] sie *(Pl.)* **I**
It's .../**They**'re ... [ɪts/ðeə] Es kostet .../ Sie kosten ... **I**
thick [θɪk] dick *(nicht für Personen)* **III**
thief [θi:f], **thieves** [θi:vz] *(pl)* Dieb/-in ⟨**IV U3**, 82⟩
thing [θɪŋ] Ding; Sache **I**
*to **think** [θɪŋk] denken; nachdenken; glauben **I**
Stop and **think** [ˌstɒp‿ənd 'θɪŋk] Warte/ Wartet und denk/denkt nach. **I**
*to **think** of ['θɪŋk‿əv] halten von; denken über **I**
*to **think** of ['θɪŋk‿əv] (sich) ausdenken; sich etwas einfallen lassen **II**
Think of ... ['θɪŋk‿əv] Denke/Denkt an ... **I**
*to **think** up [θɪŋk‿'ʌp] (sich) ausdenken; sich einfallen lassen °**IVTS2**, 66
excellent piece of quick **thinking** [ˌekslnt pi:s‿əv kwɪk 'θɪŋkɪŋ] ausgezeichnete Reaktionsschnelligkeit ⟨**IVTS1**, 36⟩
third [θɜ:d] dritte/-r/-s **I**
third person narrator [ˌθɜ:d ˌpɜ:sn nə'reɪtə] Er/Sie-Erzähler/-in **III**
thirsty ['θɜ:sti] durstig **III**
thirteen [ˌθɜ:'ti:n] dreizehn **I**
this [ðɪs] dies; diese/-r/-s **I**
this afternoon [ðɪs 'ɑ:ftənu:n] heute Nachmittag **II**
this early ['ðɪs ˌɜ:li] so früh **III**
This is ... ['ðɪs‿ɪz] Das (hier) ist ... **I**
thistle ['θɪsl] Distel **III**
those [ðəʊz] diese dort; jene **I**
those in power [ˌðəʊz ɪn 'paʊə] die Regierenden; die Herrschenden **III**
though [ðəʊ] doch; jedoch; obwohl **IV AC4**, 106
thought [θɔ:t] Gedanke **II**
thousands of ['θaʊzndz‿əv] tausende (von) **I**
three [θri:] drei **I**
through [θru:] durch **I**
*to **throw** (at) [θrəʊ] werfen (nach) **I**
*to **throw** away [ˌθrəʊ‿ə'weɪ] wegwerfen **I**
throw the dice twice [ˌθrəʊ ðə daɪs 'twaɪs] würfle zweimal **II**
thumb [θʌm] Daumen **II**
thunder *(no pl)* ['θʌndə] Donner **II**
Thursday ['θɜ:zdeɪ] Donnerstag **I**
to **tick** [tɪk] abhaken **II**
ticket ['tɪkɪt] Los; Ticket; Eintrittskarte **I**; Fahrschein **III**
one-way **ticket** ['wʌnweɪ ˌtɪkɪt] einfache Fahrkarte **III**
return **ticket** [rɪ'tɜ:n ˌtɪkɪt] Hin- und Rückfahrkarte **III**
single **ticket** ['sɪŋgl ˌtɪkɪt] einfache Fahrkarte **III**
ticket office ['tɪkɪt ˌɒfɪs] Kartenschalter **III**

high **tide** ['haɪ ˌtaɪd] Flut **II**
low **tide** ['ləʊ ˌtaɪd] Ebbe **II**
to **tidy** *(a room)* ['taɪdi] aufräumen; in Ordnung bringen **I**
to **tie** (to) ['taɪ tə] binden (an); fesseln (an) **III**
tight [taɪt] eng ⟨**IV U3**, 90⟩
till [tɪl] bis **I**
time [taɪm] Zeit **I**; Mal **II**
all the **time** [ˌɔ:l ðə 'taɪm] die ganze Zeit **II**
at the same **time** [ət ðə ˌseɪm 'taɪm] zur selben Zeit; gleichzeitig **I**
at the **time** [ˌət ðə 'taɪm] damals **IVTS3**, 102
free **time** [ˌfri: 'taɪm] Freizeit **I**
on **time** [ɒn 'taɪm] pünktlich **II**
ten **times** [ten 'taɪmz] zehnmal **I**
time line ['taɪm ˌlaɪn] Zeitstrahl **I**
time slot ['taɪm slɒt] Zeitfenster **II**
Have a good **time**. [ˌhæv‿ə gʊd 'taɪm] Viel Spaß. ⟨**IVTS1**, 36⟩
I can't wait till next **time**. [aɪ kɑ:nt ˌweɪt tɪl nekst 'taɪm] Ich kann es bis zum nächsten Mal kaum erwarten. **II**
just in **time** [ˌdʒʌst‿ɪn 'taɪm] gerade rechtzeitig **IV U3**, 72
Time to get up! [ˌtaɪm tə ˌget‿'ʌp] Es ist Zeit aufzustehen! **I**
What **time**? [ˌwɒt 'taɪm] Um wie viel Uhr? **I**
What's the **time**? [ˌwɒts ðə 'taɪm] Wie spät ist es?; Wie viel Uhr ist es? **I**
to **time** [taɪm] den richtigen Zeitpunkt wählen **IV U3**, 72
timetable ['taɪmˌteɪbl] Stundenplan; Fahrplan **I**
tin [tɪn] Zinn **III**
tin can ['tɪn kæn] Blechdose **III**
tinned [tɪnd] Dosen-; aus der Dose **I**
tiny ['taɪni] klein; winzig **III**
tip [tɪp] Tipp; Ratschlag **I**; Trinkgeld **IV U3**, 76
to **tiptoe** ['tɪptəʊ] auf Zehenspitzen gehen **II**
tired [taɪəd] müde **I**
*to be **tired** of [bi 'taɪəd‿əv] es müde sein (zu); es leid sein (zu); es satt haben (zu) **IV U2**, 46
title ['taɪtl] Titel; Überschrift **II**
to [tʊ; tə] zu; nach; auf; in; vor *(bei Uhrzeitangaben)* **I**
from ... **to** [frəm ... tə] von ... bis **I**
quarter past/**to** ['kwɔ:tə pɑ:st/tə] Viertel nach/vor **I**
to the point [tə ðə 'pɔɪnt] prägnant; treffend **III**
toast [təʊst] Toast **I**
tobacco *(no pl)* [tə'bækəʊ] Tabak **III**
today [tə'deɪ] heute **I**
together [tə'geðə] zusammen; miteinander; gemeinsam **I**
toilet ['tɔɪlət] Toilette **I**
tolerant ['tɒlrnt] tolerant **IVTS1**, 36
tomato, **tomatoes** *(pl)* [tə'mɑ:təʊ; tə'mɑ:təʊz] Tomate **I**

tomorrow [tə'mɒrəʊ] morgen **I**
tone [təʊn] Ton; Signalton °**IV U2**, 56
tonight [tə'naɪt] heute Abend; heute Nacht **IVTS1**, 31
too [tu:] auch; zu **I**
Too bad! [ˌtu: 'bæd] Zu dumm!; Schade! **I**
You **too**? [ju: 'tu:] Du auch? **I**
tool [tu:l] Werkzeug; Gerät **III**
toothpaste ['tu:θpeɪst] Zahnpasta **IV U2**, 56
top [tɒp] Spitze; oberer Teil; oberes Ende **I**
on **top** [ɒn 'tɒp] oben; obendrauf **I**
to **top** up [tɒp‿'ʌp] aufladen **II**
topic ['tɒpɪk] Thema **II**
torch [tɔ:tʃ] Fackel; Taschenlampe **II**
totally ['təʊtli] völlig; total **IV AC4**, 107
*to keep in **touch** [ˌki:p‿ɪn 'tʌtʃ] in Kontakt bleiben **IV U2**, 44
to stay in **touch** (with) [ˌsteɪ ɪn 'tʌtʃ (wɪð)] in Kontakt bleiben (mit) **II**
to **touch** [tʌtʃ] berühren; antippen **IV U2**, 52
to **touch** down [tʌtʃ 'daʊn] landen **IVTS3**, 101
tour [tʊə] Tour; Fahrt; Rundgang **II**
audio **tour** ['ɔ:diəʊ ˌtʊə] Audioführung **II**
tour company ['tʊə ˌkʌmpəni] Reiseanbieter **IV U3**, 73
tourism ['tʊərɪzm] Tourismus **III**
tourist ['tʊərɪst] Tourist/-in **I**
tourist board ['tʊərɪst bɔ:d] Touristeninformation **III**
tourist information centre [ˌtʊərɪst ɪnfə'meɪʃn ˌsentə] Touristeninformation **I**
towards [tə'wɔ:dz] in Richtung; auf ... zu; darauf zu **II**
tower [taʊə] Turm **III**
town [taʊn] Stadt **I**
toy [tɔɪ] Spielzeug **I**
to **trace** [treɪs] verfolgen; nachspüren **I**
tractor ['træktə] Traktor **IV AC2**, 38
to **trade** [treɪd] austauschen **II**
tradition [trə'dɪʃn] Tradition **I**
traditional [trə'dɪʃnl] traditionell **III**
traffic ['træfɪk] Verkehr **IV U1**, 14
walking **trail** ['wɔ:kɪŋ treɪl] Wanderweg **III**
train [treɪn] Zug **I**
to **train** [treɪn] trainieren **II**
trainer ['treɪnə] Turnschuh **III**
training ['treɪnɪŋ] Training **II**
to **translate** [trænz'leɪt] übersetzen **I**
translation [trænz'leɪʃn] Übersetzung **I**
transport ['trænspɔ:t] Verkehrsmittel; Transport **III**
public **transport** *(no pl)* [ˌpʌblɪk 'trænspɔ:t] öffentliche Verkehrsmittel **II**
to **transport** [træn'spɔ:t] transportieren; befördern **IV U3**, 79
*to be **trapped** [bi 'træpt] eingeschlossen sein; in der Falle sitzen **III**
trash *(AE)* [træʃ] Abfall; Müll **IVTS2**, 67
travel ['trævl] (das) Reisen; Reise **II**
travel agency ['trævl‿eɪdʒnsi] Reisebüro **III**

travel agent's [ˈtrævl͜ˌeɪdʒnts] Reisebüro **III**
travel report [ˌtrævl rɪˈpɔ:t] Reisebericht **II**
to **travel** [ˈtrævl] fahren; reisen **II**
traveller [ˈtrævlə] Reisende/-r **IV U1**, 15
travelling *(no pl)* [ˈtrævlɪŋ] (das) Reisen **IV U1**, 9
treasure [ˈtreʒə] Schatz **II**
treat [tri:t] *hier:* Leckerli; Belohnung **III**
tree [tri:] Baum **I**
family **tree** [ˈfæmli ˌtri:] Stammbaum **I**
palm **tree** [ˈpɑ:m ˌtri:] Palme **III**
redwood **tree** [ˈredwʊd ˌtri:] Mammutbaum **IV AC2**, 39
pony **trekking** [ˈpəʊni ˌtrekɪŋ] Ponyreiten im Gelände **III**
trial [traɪəl] Qualifikation **II**
tribe [traɪb] Stamm; Volksstamm **III**
trick [trɪk] Trick; Streich **I**
to play a **trick** (on) [ˌpleɪ͜ə ˈtrɪk͜ɒn] einen Streich spielen **I**
to **trick** [trɪk] austricksen; täuschen **IV TS3**, 103
trifle [ˈtraɪfl] Trifle *(englischer Nachtisch)* **I**
trip [trɪp] Trip; Reise; Ausflug; Fahrt **II**
triumph [ˈtraɪəmf] Triumph ⟨**IV TS3**, 101⟩
trouble [ˈtrʌbl] Ärger; Probleme; Schwierigkeiten **II**
*to get into **trouble** [ˌget͜ɪntə ˈtrʌbl] in Schwierigkeiten geraten **IV AC3**, 69
*to make **trouble** [ˌmeɪk ˈtrʌbl] Ärger machen; in Schwierigkeiten bringen **I**
troublemaker [ˈtrʌblmeɪkə] Unruhestifter/-in **IV U2**, 53
trousers *(pl)* [ˈtraʊzəz] Hose **III**
trowel [ˈtraʊəl] kleiner Spaten **II**
truck *(AE)* [trʌk] *hier:* Wagen **IV U3**, 75
truckload [ˈtrʌkləʊd] Lastwagenladung **IV TS2**, 66
true [tru:] wahr **II**
*to come **true** [ˌkʌm ˈtru:] wahr werden; in Erfüllung gehen **IV U3**, 76
trunk *(AE)* [trʌŋk] Kofferraum **IV U3**, 76
to **trust** [trʌst] vertrauen **III**
truth [tru:θ] Wahrheit **IV U1**, 13
to **try** [traɪ] versuchen; probieren **I**
to **try** on [ˌtraɪ͜ˈɒn] anprobieren **II**
to **try** out [ˌtraɪ͜ˈaʊt] ausprobieren **III**
Try … [traɪ] Versuch es mal mit …; Probier mal … **I**
T-shirt [ˈti:ʃɜ:t] T-Shirt **I**
the **Tube** [ðə ˈtju:b] die Londoner U-Bahn **II**
Tudor [ˈtju:də] Tudor- **III**
Tuesday [ˈtju:zdeɪ] Dienstag **I**
tune [tju:n] Melodie **III**
tunnel [ˈtʌnl] Tunnel **I**
roast **turkey** [rəʊst ˈtɜ:ki] Putenbraten ⟨**IV U2**, 45⟩
It's your **turn**. [ˌɪts ˈjɔ: tɜ:n] Du bist dran. **I**
Take **turns**. [ˌteɪk ˈtɜ:nz] Wechselt euch ab. **I**
Your **turn**. [ˈjɔ: tɜ:n] Du bist dran. **I**
to **turn** [tɜ:n] einbiegen; abbiegen **I**
to **turn** (a)round [ˌtɜ:n͜(ə)ˈraʊnd] (sich) umdrehen; wenden **II**
to **turn** back [tɜ:n ˈbæk] umkehren; zurückgehen **II**
to **turn** into [ˌtɜ:n͜ˈɪntə] ändern in; umwandeln in **IV U1**, 14
to **turn** off [ˌtɜ:n͜ˈɒf] abschalten; ausschalten **II**
to **turn** to [ˈtɜ:n tə] sich wenden an; sich zuwenden **III**
turning point [ˈtɜ:nɪŋ ˌpɔɪnt] Wendepunkt **III**
It **turned** out that … [ɪt ˌtɜ:nd͜ˈaʊt ðæt] Es stellte sich heraus, dass … **IV U1**, 20
to **turn** [tɜ:n] drehen; (sich) umdrehen **III**
tusk [tʌsk] Stoßzahn **III**
tutor [ˈtju:tə] Klassenlehrer/-in **I**
tutor group [ˈtju:tə ˌgru:p] Klasse *(in einer englischen Schule)* **I**
tutorial [tju:ˈtɔ:riəl] Tutorium; Tutorial **IV TS3**, 100
TV [ˌti:ˈvi:] Fernsehen; Fernseher **I**
to watch **TV** [ˌwɒtʃ ti:ˈvi:] fernsehen **I**
twelve [twelv] zwölf **I**
twice [twaɪs] zweimal **IV U2**, 53
twin [twɪn] Zwilling; Zwillings- **III**
to **twist** your ankle [ˌtwɪst jɔ:r͜ˈæŋkl] sich den Knöchel verrenken **II**
two [tu:] zwei **I**
the **two** of them [ðə ˈtu:͜əv ðəm] beide **II**
two of which [ˈtu:͜əv wɪtʃ] zwei von ihnen **III**
type [taɪp] Typ; Art; Sorte **III**
typical [ˈtɪpɪkl] typisch **I**
typically [ˈtɪpɪkli] typisch **III**

U

u *(= you)* [ju:; jə] du; Sie; ihr **I**
UFO [ˌju:efˈəʊ] UFO **II**
ugly [ˈʌgli] hässlich **IV TS2**, 67
umbrella [ʌmˈbrelə] Regenschirm ⟨**IV U3**, 90⟩
unable [ʌnˈeɪbl] unfähig; nicht in der Lage ⟨**IV TS3**, 104⟩
unbelievable [ˌʌnbɪˈli:vəbl] unglaublich; unglaubwürdig ⟨**IV TS3**, 102⟩
uncle [ˈʌŋkl] Onkel **I**
under [ˈʌndə] unter **I**
underfloor heating *(no pl)* [ˌʌndəflɔ: ˈhi:tɪŋ] Fußbodenheizung **III**
underground [ˈʌndəgraʊnd] U-Bahn **II**
to **underline** [ˌʌndəˈlaɪn] unterstreichen **III**
*to **understand** [ˌʌndəˈstænd] verstehen **I**
understanding [ˌʌndəˈstændɪŋ] Verständnis **II**
undeveloped [ˌʌndɪˈveləpt] unentwickelt; unausgereift **IV TS3**, 105
unexpected [ˌʌnɪkˈspektɪd] unerwartet **IV U3**, 91
unfair [ʌnˈfeə] unfair **II**
unfamiliar [ˌʌnfəˈmɪliə] nicht vertraut; unbekannt **III**
unfriendly [ʌnˈfrendli] unfreundlich **II**
uniform [ˈju:nɪfɔ:m] Uniform **I**
unit [ˈju:nɪt] Lektion; Kapitel; Einheit **I**
*to be **unlucky** [bi:͜ʌnˈlʌki] Pech haben **I**
unofficial [ˌʌnəˈfɪʃl] inoffiziell **III**
to **unpack** [ʌnˈpæk] auspacken **IV U2**, 46
unreal [ˌʌnˈrɪəl] irreal **IV U1**, 19
unrealistic [ˌʌnrɪəˈlɪstɪk] unrealistisch **IV U2**, 52
unsure [ʌnˈʃʊə] unsicher **IV TS1**, 31
until [ʌnˈtɪl] bis; erst wenn **II**
not **until** [ˌnɒt͜ənˈtɪl] nicht vor; erst um/im **IV U2**, 44
to **unwrap** [ʌnˈræp] auswickeln; auspacken **I**
up [ʌp] hinauf; nach oben **II**
*to cut **up** [kʌt͜ˈʌp] zerschneiden °**IV U3**, 91
to end **up** [ˌend͜ˈʌp] enden; landen **II**
*to get **up** [ˌget͜ˈʌp] aufstehen *(aus dem Bett)* **I**
*to give **up** [ˌgɪv͜ˈʌp] aufgeben **III**
to look **up** [ˌlʊk͜ˈʌp] nachschlagen; nachschauen **I**
What's **up**? [ˌwɒts͜ˈʌp] Was ist los? **III**
*to **upset** [ʌpˈset] aus der Fassung bringen **III**
upset [ʌpˈset] aufgebracht; bestürzt **II**
upstairs [ʌpˈsteəz] nach oben; im Obergeschoss; oben **II**
up-to-date [ˌʌptəˈdeɪt] modern; zeitgemäß; aktuell **IV TS3**, 100
urban [ˈɜ:bn] städtisch; Stadt- **IV AC2**, 38
us [ʌs] uns **I**
US [ˌju:ˈes] US-amerikanisch **IV AC2**, 41
use [ju:s] Verwendung; Gebrauch; Nutzen °**IV U3**, 77
*to make **use** of [meɪk ˈju:z͜əv] benutzen; verwenden **IV U3**, 89
to **use** [ju:z] benutzen; verwenden; gebrauchen **I**
*to be **used** to *(+ -ing)* [bi ˈju:s͜tə] gewöhnt sein an; gewohnt sein **III**
*to get **used** to sth [ˌget ˈju:zd tə] sich an etw. gewöhnen **IV U2**, 44
useful [ˈju:sfl] nützlich; hilfreich **I**
Useful phrases [ˌju:sfl ˈfreɪsɪz] nützliche Ausdrücke **I**
useless [ˈju:sləs] nutzlos **IV U1**, 17
usual [ˈju:ʒl] üblich **III**
usually [ˈju:ʒli] normalerweise; gewöhnlich; meistens **I**

V

vacation *(AE)* [vəˈkeɪʃn] Ferien; Urlaub **IV AC2**, 41
van [væn] Lieferwagen; Transporter; Kleinbus ⟨**IV U3**, 88⟩
vegetable [ˈvedʒtəbl] Gemüse **III**
vegetarian [ˌvedʒɪˈteəriən] Vegetarier/-in **III**
vegetarian [ˌvedʒɪˈteəriən] vegetarisch **III**
vending machine [ˈvendɪŋ məˌʃi:n] Automat **IV U1**, 10

verb [vɜ:b] Verb **I**
verse [vɜ:s] Vers; Strophe **III**
version ['vɜ:ʃn] Version **III**
cover **version** ['kʌvə ˌvɜ:ʃn] Coverversion **III**
versus (vs.) ['vɜ:səs] gegen **III**
very ['veri] sehr **I**
very much [ˌveri 'mʌtʃ] sehr **I**
vet [vet] Tierarzt/Tierärztin **I**
Victorian [vɪk'tɔ:riən] viktorianisch; Viktorianer/-in **III**
video ['vɪdiəʊ] Video **II**
video chat ['vɪdiəʊ ˌtʃæt] Videochat **II**
view [vju:] Aussicht; Sicht; Ausblick; Blick **II**
point of **view** [ˌpɔɪnt‿əv 'vju:] Standpunkt; Ansicht; Perspektive **II**
viewer ['vju:ə] Zuschauer/-in **II**
viewing ['vju:ɪŋ] Hör-/Sehverstehen **I**
village ['vɪlɪdʒ] Dorf **I**
villain ['vɪlən] Bösewicht **III**
violence *(no pl)* ['vaɪəlns] Gewalt **III**
violent ['vaɪəlnt] gewaltsam; gewalttätig; brutal **III**
visa ['vi:zə], **visas** ['vi:zəz] *(pl)* Visum, Visa *(Pl.)*; Einreisebewilligung **IV U1**, 9
visit ['vɪzɪt] Besuch **I**
to **visit** ['vɪzɪt] besichtigen; besuchen **I**
visitor ['vɪzɪtə] Besucher/-in **I**
visual ['vɪʒuəl] Bild **IV TS2**, 65
vitamin ['vɪtəmɪn] Vitamin **III**
vocabulary [və'kæbjəlri] Vokabular; Wortschatz **I**
voice [vɔɪs] Stimme **I**
volleyball ['vɒlibɔ:l] Volleyball **I**
*to take a **vote** [ˌteɪk‿ə 'vəʊt] abstimmen **I**
to **vote** [vəʊt] abstimmen; wählen **I**
voyage ['vɔɪɪdʒ] Reise; Fahrt ⟨**IV TS3**, 104⟩

W

to **wait** (for) [weɪt] warten (auf) **I**
I can't **wait** till next time. [aɪ kɑ:nt ˌweɪt tɪl nekst 'taɪm] Ich kann es bis zum nächsten Mal kaum erwarten. **II**
Wait and see! [ˌweɪt‿ənd 'si:] Warte ab! **I**
*to **wake** up [weɪk‿'ʌp] aufwachen; aufwecken **III**
gallery **walk** ['gæləri ˌwɔ:k] Museumsrundgang; Vernissage **I**
*to go for a **walk** [ˌgəʊ fər‿ə 'wɔ:k] spazieren gehen **II**
night **walk** ['naɪt wɔ:k] Nachtwanderung **II**
to **walk** [wɔ:k] gehen; laufen **I**
to **walk** the dog [ˌwɔ:k ðə 'dɒg] den Hund ausführen; mit dem Hund spazieren gehen **I**
walk-in closet [ˌwɔ:kɪn 'klɒzɪt] begehbarer Kleiderschrank **IV U2**, 44
walking ['wɔ:kɪŋ] Wandern **II**
walking trail ['wɔ:kɪŋ treɪl] Wanderweg **III**
wall [wɔ:l] Wand; Mauer **I**; Online-Pinnwand **III**

*to be **walled** in [ˌbi wɔ:ld‿'ɪn] von Wänden eingeschlossen sein ⟨**IV U3**, 90⟩
wanna *(= want to) (infml)* ['wɒnə] will/wollen ⟨**IV U1**, 12⟩
to **want** (to) ['wɒnt tə] wollen; mögen **I**
war [wɔ:] Krieg **IV U1**, 20
wardrobe ['wɔ:drəʊb] Kleiderschrank **I**
to **warm** up [ˌwɔ:m‿'ʌp] aufwärmen; sich aufwärmen **I**
warm [wɔ:m] warm **III**
warm-up ['wɔ:m‿ˌʌp] Aufwärmübung **I**
to **warn** [wɔ:n] warnen **IV TS1**, 34
warrior ['wɒriə] Krieger **III**
to **wash** [wɒʃ] waschen; sich waschen **I**
to **wash** up [ˌwɒʃ‿'ʌp] angespült werden **II**
washing machine ['wɒʃɪŋ məˌʃi:n] Waschmaschine **II**
waste [weɪst] Verschwendung **IV AC3**, 69
to **waste** [weɪst] verschwenden **II**
wasteful ['weɪstfl] verschwenderisch **IV AC2**, 40
to **watch** [wɒtʃ] beobachten; (sich) ansehen; zuschauen **I**
to **watch** TV [ˌwɒtʃ ti:'vi:] fernsehen **I**
water ['wɔ:tə] Wasser **I**
water fountain ['wɔ:tə ˌfaʊntɪn] Wasserspender **IV AC4**, 106
water slide ['wɔ:tə ˌslaɪd] Wasserrutsche **I**
wave [weɪv] Welle **I**
wax [wæks] Wachs **II**
wax figure ['wæks ˌfɪgə] Wachsfigur **II**
way [weɪ] Weg; Art und Weise **I**
*to be in the **way** [bi:‿ɪn ðə 'weɪ] im Weg sein/stehen **I**
*to find one's **way** around [ˌfaɪnd wʌnz ˌweɪ‿ə'raʊnd] sich zurechtfinden **IV U2**, 46
*to get in the **way** [ˌget‿ɪn ðə 'weɪ] stören; im Weg stehen **II**
no **way** [ˌnəʊ 'weɪ] auf keinen Fall; keineswegs ⟨**IV U2**, 54⟩; keine Möglichkeit; kein Weg ⟨**IV TS3**, 102⟩
in other **ways** [ɪn‿'ʌðə weɪz] auf andere Weise **II**
the same **way** as [ˌðə seɪm 'weɪ æz] genauso wie **II**
we [wi:; wi] wir **I**
We're from … ['wɪə frəm] Wir sind aus … **I**
weak [wi:k] schwach **IV TS3**, 105
wealthy ['welθi] wohlhabend; reich **IV AC2**, 40
weapon ['wepən] Waffe **III**
*to **wear** [weə] anhaben; tragen *(Kleidung)* **I**
weather ['weðə] Wetter **I**
weather forecast ['weðə ˌfɔ:kɑ:st] Wettervorhersage **III**
web [web] Netz; Spinnennetz **III**
web designer ['web dɪˌzaɪnə] Webdesigner **III**
website ['websaɪt] Website; Internetauftritt **I**
wedding ['wedɪŋ] Hochzeit **I**

Wednesday ['wenzdeɪ] Mittwoch **I**
week [wi:k] Woche **I**
weekday ['wi:kdeɪ] Wochentag **II**
weekend [ˌwi:k'end] Wochenende **I**
at the **weekend** [ət ðə ˌwi:k'end] am Wochenende **I**
to **weigh** [weɪ] wiegen **III**
weight [weɪt] Gewicht **III**
weird [wɪəd] merkwürdig; seltsam; sonderbar **II**
Welcome! ['welkəm] Willkommen! **II**
to **welcome** ['welkəm] willkommen heißen **II**
You're **welcome**. [ˌjɔ: 'welkəm] Bitte schön.; Nichts zu danken.; Gern geschehen. **I**
*to do **well** [ˌdu: 'wel] gute Leistungen erbringen **IV TS1**, 34
well-developed [ˌweldɪ'veləpt] gut entwickelt; ausgereift **IV TS3**, 105
well-written [ˌwel'rɪtn] gut geschrieben **IV TS3**, 104
well [wel] tja; nun **I**
Welsh [welʃ] walisisch; Walisisch; Waliser/-in **II**
west [west] Westen; West- **I**
in the far **west** [ɪn ðə fɑ: 'west] im äußersten Westen **III**
wet [wet] nass **II**
what [wɒt] was; welche/-r/-s; was für ein **I**
What a … ['wɒt‿ə] Was für ein/-e … **IV U2**, 48
What about … ? ['wɒt‿əbaʊt] Wie wär's mit …?; Was ist mit …? **I**
What are …? ['wɒt‿ɑ:] Welche … sind es? **I**
What colour is …? [ˌwɒt 'kʌlər‿ɪz] Welche Farbe hat …? **I**
what else [ˌwɒt‿'els] was sonst; was noch **I**
What is missing? [ˌwɒt‿ɪz 'mɪsɪŋ] Was fehlt? **I**
What is … about? [ˌwɒt‿ɪz …‿ə'baʊt] Worum geht es in/im …? **I**
what it's like [ˌwɒt‿ɪts 'laɪk] wie das ist **II**
What luck! [wɒt 'lʌk] Was für ein Glück! **III**
What on earth …? [ˌwɒt:‿ɒn‿'ɜ:θ] Was um alles in der Welt …? **II**
What time? [ˌwɒt 'taɪm] Um wie viel Uhr? **I**
what to … ['wɒt tə] was man … **I**
What was it like? [ˌwɒt wɒz‿ɪt 'laɪk] Wie war es? **III**
What's that? [wɒts 'ðæt] Was ist das? **I**
What's the rule for …? [ˌwɒts ðə 'ru:l fə] Was ist die Regel für …? **I**
What's up? [ˌwɒts‿'ʌp] Was ist los? **III**
What's your favourite …? ['wɒts jə ˌfeɪvrɪt] Was ist dein/-e Lieblings…? **I**
What's your name? [ˌwɒts jə 'neɪm] Wie heißt du?; Wie heißen Sie? **I**
What's going on? [wɒts ˌgəʊɪŋ‿'ɒn] Was ist los?; Was geht ab? **III**
What's the matter? [ˌwɒts ðə 'mætə] Was ist los?; Was hast du? **III**

What's the time? [ˌwɒts ðə 'taɪm] Wie spät ist es?; Wie viel Uhr ist es? **I**
… **what** to do. ['wɒt tə du:] … was ich tun soll. **II**
what the man looked like [ˌwɒt ðə mæn 'lʊkt laɪk] wie der Mann aussah **II**
whatever [wɒt'evə] wie auch immer; egal (was/welche) **IV AC4**, 107
wheat [wi:t] Weizen **IV AC2**, 41
wheel [wi:l] Rad; Steuerrad; Steuer **I**
wheelchair ['wi:ltʃeə] Rollstuhl **II**
when [wen] wenn; wann; als **I**
whenever [wen'evə] wann immer; jedes Mal, wenn; so oft **II**
where [weə] wo; wohin **I**
Where … from? [ˌweə … 'frɒm] Woher …? **I**
where I belong [ˌweər‿aɪ bɪ'lɒŋ] wo ich hingehöre **IV U1**, 16
… **where** to go. [ˌweə tə 'gəʊ] … wohin ich gehen kann. **II**
I go **wherever** the wind takes me. [aɪ ˌgəʊ weəˌrevə ðə wɪnd 'teɪks mi:] Ich lasse mich treiben. **IV U1**, 19
whether ['weðə] ob **IV U2**, 49
which [wɪtʃ] welche/-r/-s **I**
which [wɪtʃ] der; die; das; dem; den *(Relativpronomen)* **II**
a **while** [ə 'waɪl] eine Weile **II**
while [waɪl] während **I**
to **whip** [wɪp] schlagen **I**
whisky ['wɪski] Whisky **III**
to **whisper** ['wɪspə] flüstern **I**
white [waɪt] weiß **I**
white lie [ˌwaɪt 'laɪ] Notlüge **IV TS1**, 32
who [hu:] wer; wem; wen **I**
Who … for? [ˌhu: 'fɔ:] Für wen …? **I**
Who is it? [ˌhu:‿'ɪz‿ɪt] Wer ist es? **I**
Who's in? [hu:z‿'ɪn] Wer macht mit?; Wer ist dabei? **II**
who [hu:] der; dem; den; die *(Relativpronomen)* **II**
whole [həʊl] ganz **I**
whom [hu:m] wem; wen **IV TS1**, 37
whoosh [wʊʃ] wusch **I**
whose [hu:z] wessen °**IV U2**, 44
whose [hu:z] dessen; deren *(Relativpronomen)* **II**
why [waɪ] warum **I**
that's **why** [ðæts 'waɪ] deshalb **II**
wide [waɪd] breit; weit; ausgedehnt **III**
wife, **wives** *(pl)* [waɪf, waɪvz] Ehefrau **II**
wifi ['waɪfaɪ] WLAN **IV U1**, 10
wiki (text) ['wɪkɪ ˌtekst] Wikitext **IV TS3**, 101
wild [waɪld] wild **III**
It's, like, so **wild** to … [ˌɪts laɪk səʊ 'waɪld tə] Es ist echt klasse … ⟨**IV AC4**, 107⟩
wildlife ['waɪldlaɪf] Tierwelt *(in freier Wildbahn)* **II**
will [wɪl] werden *(futurisch)* **III**
*to **win** [wɪn] gewinnen; siegen **I**
*to **win** sb over [wɪn‿'əʊvə] jmdn. für sich gewinnen; jmdn. überzeugen **IV TS2**, 64
wind [wɪnd] Wind **III**
I go wherever the **wind** takes me. [aɪ ˌgəʊ weəˌrevə ðə wɪnd 'teɪks mi:] Ich lasse mich treiben. **IV U1**, 19
window ['wɪndəʊ] Fenster **I**
windsurfing ['wɪndsɜ:fɪŋ] Windsurfen **III**
wine [waɪn] Wein **I**
winner ['wɪnə] Gewinner/-in; Sieger/-in **I**
winter ['wɪntə] Winter **III**
barbed **wire** [ˌbɑ:bd 'waɪə] Stacheldraht ⟨**IV U3**, 90⟩
wish [wɪʃ] Wunsch **I**
*to make a **wish** [ˌmeɪk‿ə 'wɪʃ] sich etwas wünschen **I**
Best **wishes** [ˌbest 'wɪʃɪz] Viele Grüße; Herzliche Grüße **III**
to **wish** [wɪʃ] (sich) wünschen **IV U2**, 51
with [wɪð] mit; bei **I**
within [wɪ'ðɪn] innerhalb °**IV AC4**, 106
without [wɪ'ðaʊt] ohne **I**
witness ['wɪtnəs] Zeuge/Zeugin **II**
wizard ['wɪzəd] Zauberer **III**
wobbly ['wɒbli] wackelig **II**
woman, **women** *(pl)* ['wʊmən; 'wɪmɪn] Frau **I**
no **wonder** [ˌnəʊ 'wʌndə] kein Wunder **IV U2**, 44
wonderful ['wʌndəfl] wunderbar **II**
wood [wʊd] Wald; Wäldchen **III**
wood [wʊd] Holz **III**
wooden ['wʊdn] hölzern; aus Holz **III**
Woof! [wʊf] Wau! **I**
word [wɜ:d] Wort **I**
compound **word** ['kɒmpaʊnd wɜ:d] Kompositum *(zusammengesetztes Wort)* **II**
key **word** ['ki: wɜ:d] Stichwort; Schlüsselbegriff **I**
linking **word** ['lɪŋkɪŋ ˌwɜ:d] Bindewort **I**
play on **words** [ˌpleɪ‿ɒn 'wɜ:dz] Wortspiel **III**
signal **word** ['sɪgnəl ˌwɜ:d] Signalwort **I**
word bank ['wɜ:d ˌbæŋk] Wortsammlung **III**
word cloud ['wɜ:d ˌklaʊd] Wörterwolke **II**
word order ['wɜ:d‿ˌɔ:də] Wortstellung; Satzstellung **I**
Word power ['wɜ:d ˌpaʊə] die Kraft der Wörter *(Wortschatzübung)* **I**
word snake ['wɜ:d ˌsneɪk] Wortschlange **I**
word-building ['wɜ:dˌbɪldɪŋ] Wortbildung **II**
work [wɜ:k] Arbeit **I**
pair **work** ['peə wɜ:k] Partnerarbeit **II**
to **work** [wɜ:k] arbeiten **I**; funktionieren **II**
to **work** out [ˌwɜ:k‿'aʊt] herausfinden; ausarbeiten **II**; funktionieren; klappen **III**
workbook ['wɜ:kbʊk] Arbeitsheft; Übungsheft **IV TS1**, 37
workshop ['wɜ:kʃɒp] Workshop **I**
world [wɜ:ld] Erde; Welt **I**
from around the **world** [frɒm əˌraʊnd ðə 'wɜ:ld] aus aller Welt **III**
worm [wɜ:m] Wurm **I**
worried ['wʌrid] beunruhigt; besorgt **III**
*to be **worried** [bi 'wʌrid] beunruhigt sein; besorgt sein **II**
to **worry** ['wʌri] sich Sorgen machen **II**
Don't **worry**! [ˌdəʊnt 'wʌri] Keine Sorge! **I**
the **worst** [ðə 'wɜ:st] der/die/das schlimmste; der/die/das schlechteste **II**
*to be **worth** [bi: 'wɜ:θ] wert sein **I**
would [wʊd] würde/-st/-n/-t **III**
would like [wʊd 'laɪk] würde/-st/-n/-t gern; hätte/-st/-n/-t gern **I**
would love [wʊd 'lʌv] würde/-st/-n/-t sehr gern; hätte/-st-/-n/-t sehr gern **I**
Would you like …? [ˌwʊd jʊ 'laɪk] Möchtest du …?; Möchten Sie …?; Möchtet ihr …? **II**
wounded ['wu:ndɪd] verwundet; verletzt **III**
Wow! [waʊ] Wow! **I**
to **wrap** [ræp] einwickeln; einpacken **I**
wrapping ['ræpɪŋ] Verpackung; Hülle **I**
to **wrinkle** one's nose [ˌrɪŋkl wʌnz 'nəʊz] die Nase rümpfen ⟨**IV U3**, 90⟩
wrist [rɪst] Handgelenk **II**
*to **write** [raɪt] schreiben **I**
*to **write** down [ˌraɪt 'daʊn] aufschreiben **I**
writer ['raɪtə] Autor/-in; Verfasser/-in **III**
writing ['raɪtɪŋ] Schreiben **I**
wrong [rɒŋ] falsch **I**
*to be **wrong** [bi: 'rɒŋ] unrecht haben; sich irren **I**
*to go **wrong** [ˌgəʊ 'rɒŋ] schiefgehen **I**

X

XOXO [ˌhʌgz‿ən 'kɪsɪz] Umarmungen und Küsse *(am Ende von E-Mails und SMS)* **I**

Y

yard [jɑ:d] Garten; Hof **IV U2**, 43
front **yard** *(AE)* [ˌfrʌnt 'jɑ:d] Vorgarten **IV U2**, 43
yeah *(infml)* [jeə] ja **I**
year [jɪə] Jahr; Schuljahr **I**
New **Year's** Eve [ˌnju:‿jɪəz‿'i:v] Silvester ⟨**IV U3**, 90⟩
11-**year-old** [ɪˌlevn'jɪərəʊld] 11-Jährige/-r **II**
18-**year-old** [ˌeɪti:n 'jɪər‿əʊld] 18-jährig **II**
yearbook ['jɪəbʊk] Jahrbuch **II**
yellow ['jeləʊ] gelb **I**
yes [jes] ja **I**
yesterday ['jestədeɪ] gestern **II**
yet [jet] schon; noch **II**
not … **yet** [nɒt 'jet] noch nicht **II**
yet [jet] doch; und trotzdem; und dennoch **IV U3**, 76
yoghurt ['jɒgət] Joghurt **I**
you [ju:; jə] du; ihr; Sie **I**

You know how to … [ju: 'nəʊ ˌhaʊ tə] Du weißt, wie man …; Ihr wisst, wie man … **I**
You too? [ju: 'tu:] Du auch? **I**
You'd better … *(= You had better)* ['ju:d ˌbetə] Du solltest lieber … **IV AC3**, 69
You're into … ['jɔ:r‿ˌɪntə] Du magst …; Du stehst auf … **I**
You're welcome. [ˌjɔ: 'welkəm] Bitte schön.; Nichts zu danken.; Gern geschehen. **I**
You're … [jɔ:r] Sie sind …; Du bist … **I**
young [jʌŋ] jung **I**
your [jɔ:; jə] dein/-e; euer/eure; Ihr/-e **I**
What's **your** name? [ˌwɒts jə 'neɪm] Wie heißt du?; Wie heißen Sie? **I**
Your turn. ['jɔ: tɜ:n] Du bist dran. **I**
yours [jɔ:z] dein/-er/-e/-es; eure/-r/-s; Ihr/-e **II**
Yours … [jɔ:z] Viele Grüße … *(am Ende von Briefen und Mails)* **II**
yourself [jɔ:'self] du/dir/dich/Sie/sich (selbst); selber **I**
yourselves [jɔ:'selvz] ihr/euch/Sie/sich (selbst); selber **III**
youth [ju:θ] Jugend **IV TS1**, 36

Z

zero ['zɪərəʊ] null **I**
zone [zəʊn] Zone **IV AC2**, 38
zoo [zu:] Zoo; Tierpark **II**
to zoom in (on) [ˌzu:m‿'ɪn ɒn] heranzoomen (auf) **III**

Boys' names

Abdi ['æbdi] **IV U1**, 16
Abdirahman [ˌæbdirə'mɑ:n] **IV U1**, 17
Ahmed ['æmed] **IV U1**, 16
Amarjit [ə'mɑ:dʒɪt] **IV U1**, 10
Amir [ˌɑ:'mi:r] **II**
Austin ['ɒstɪn] **IV U2**, 56
Ben [ben] **I**
Bob [bɒb] **I**
Brad [bræd] **III**
Brodie ['brəʊdi] **IV AC4**, 107
Callum ['kæləm] **IV AC2**, 41
Damian ['deɪmiən] **I**
Daniel ['dænjəl] **IV U3**, 92
Dave [deɪv] **I**
David ['deɪvɪd] **I**
Desmond ['dezmənd] **I**
Diego [di'eɪgəʊ] **IV U3**, 72
Ed [ed] **II**
Eddie ['edi] **IV U1**, 10
Emilio [ɪ'mɪliəʊ] **IV U3**, 76
Ethan ['i:θn] **III**
Finn [fɪn] **III**
Frank [fræŋk] **II**
Harrison ['hærɪsn] **IV U3**, 79
Henry ['henri] **I**
Jack [dʒæk] **I**
Jago ['dʒeɪgəʊ] **III**
James [dʒeɪmz] **II**
Jamie ['dʒeɪmi] **I**
Jay [dʒeɪ] **I**
Jim [dʒɪm] **III**
John [dʒɒn] **II**
Josh [dʒɒʃ] **IV U2**, 43
Lawrence ['lɔ:rəns] **IV U3**, 91
Luke [lu:k] **I**
Mario ['mæriəʊ] **III**
Mark [mɑ:k] **IV TS3**, 104
Marley ['mɑ:li] **II**
Marlon ['mɑ:lən] **IV TS3**, 100
Masud [mə'su:d] **IV U1**, 14
Matt [mæt] **III**
Max [mæks] **III**
Mick [mɪk] **II**
Mike [maɪk] **II**
Nathan ['neɪθn] **II**
Nick [nɪk] **II**
Peter ['pi:tə] **II**
Rick [rɪk] **III**
Rob [rɒb] **IV TS1**, 31
Scott [skɒt] **IV U2**, 48
Sean [ʃɔ:n] **III**
Shahid [ʃɑ:'hi:d] **I**
Simon ['saɪmən] **IV TS1**, 30
Steve [sti:v] **I**
Stuart ['stu:ət] **III**
Thomas ['tɒməs] **III**
Tim [tɪm] **IV TS3**, 100
Todd [tɒd] ⟨**IV U3**, 90⟩
Tony ['təʊni] **I**
Tristan ['trɪstən] **IV AC2**, 41
Tyler ['taɪlə] **I**
Wesley ['wezli] **IV U2**, 55
Will [wɪl] **II**

Girls' names

Alice ['ælɪs] **II**
Alicia [ə'lɪsiə; ə'lɪʃə] **I**
Alva ['ælvə] **III**
Amber ['æmbə] **I**
Anna ['ænə] **I**
Anne [æn] **I**
Annie ['æni] **III**
Anya ['ænjə] **IV U1**, 13
Ashley ['æʃli] **IV U3**, 73
Carol ['kærəl] **I**
Ceri ['keri] **II**
Christine [krɪ'sti:n] **IV U3**, 91
Ciara [s'jærə] **IV U1**, 19
Claire ['kleə] **I**
Emily ['emɪli] **I**
Eva ['i:və] **IV U2**, 48
Fowsia [faʊ'ziɑ] **IV U1**, 16
Frances ['frɑ:nsɪs] **I**
Gwen [gwen] **II**
Hayley ['heɪli] **IV U1**, 19
Helen ['helɪn] **III**
Holly ['hɒli] **I**
Irina [ɪ'ri:nə] **I**
Ivy ['aɪvi] **III**
Janie ['dʒeɪni] **IV U2**, 56
Jean [dʒi:n] **III**
Jenny ['dʒeni] **IV U1**, 15
Jessica ['dʒesɪkə] **IV U2**, 55
Judith ['dʒu:dɪθ] **III**
Julie ['dʒu:li] **I**
June [dʒu:n] **IV AC4**, 107
Kate [keɪt] **II**
Kelly ['keli] **IV U3**, 78
Khadija [kə'di:dʒə] **IV U1**, 16
Kirsty ['kɜ:sti] **III**
Laura ['lɔ:rə] **I**
Lauren ['lɔ:rən] **II**
Leanne [li'æn] **IV U2**, 55
Lou [lu:] **I**
Lucy ['lu:si] **I**
Madison ['mædɪsn] **IV U2**, 44
Maisie ['meɪzi] **II**
Margaret ['mɑ:grət] **III**
Mary ['meəri] **II**
Maryan ['mærjən] **IV U1**, 16
Megan ['megən] **III**
Meredith ['merədɪθ] **IV U3**, 77
Mila ['mi:lə] **I**
Mina ['mi:nə] **II**
Nancy ['nænsi] **IV U3**, 74
Olivia [ɒl'ɪviə] **I**
Pia ['pi:ə] **I**
Polly ['pɒli] **II**
Rita ['ri:tə] **IV U3**, 92
Rose [rəʊz] **I**
Ruby ['ru:bi] **II**
Rylee ['raɪli] **IV U3**, 72
Sabra ['sæbrə] **IV U1**, 16
Sadia ['seɪdjə] **IV U1**, 14
Sally ['sæli] **I**
Sarah ['seərə] **IV U3**, 91
Sophie ['səʊfi] **IV U2**, 44
Tamara [tə'mɑ:rə] **III**
Tina ['ti:nə] **III**
Violet ['vaɪələt] **III**
Vivien ['vɪvjən] **III**

Surnames

Ashton ['æʃtən] **II**
Azad [ə'zɑ:d] **I**
Blanchard ['blænʃəd] **IV U3**, 79
Elliot ['eliət] **I**
Ford [fɔ:d] **IV U2**, 56
Francis ['frɑ:nsɪs] **III**
Fraser ['freɪzə] **I**
Green [gri:n] **I**
Jones [dʒəʊnz] **IV U1**, 12
Karp [kɑ:p] **III**
King [kɪŋ] **III**
Mahmoud [mæ'mu:d] **IV U1**, 17
Miller ['mɪlə] **III**
Moreno [mə'ri:nəʊ] **IV U3**, 92

Mussa ['mu:sə] **IV U1**, 16
Nicholls ['nɪkəlz] **III**
Parker ['pɑ:kə] **II**
Preston ['prestən] **I**
Pulsford ['pʌlsfɔ:d] **III**
Richardson ['rɪtʃədsn] **I**
Strasser ['stræsə] ⟨**IV U3**, 90⟩
Swindon ['swɪndən] **I**
Thompson ['tɒmsən] **II**
Walker ['wɔ:kə] **I**
Watney ['wɒtni] **IV TS3**, 104
Woodruff ['wʊdrʌf] **IV U1**, 10
Wright [raɪt] **II**

Place names

Aberdeen [ˌæbə'di:n] *Stadt in Schottland* **III**
Bedloe Island [ˌbedləʊ‿'aɪlənd] **IV U3**, 74
Birchview ['bɜ:tʃvju:] *Stadt in den USA* **IV U2**, 44
Birmingham ['bɜ:mɪŋəm] **III**
Boston ['bɒstn] *Stadt in den USA* **IV AC2**, 41
Bradford ['brædfəd] **II**
Bristol ['brɪstl] **III**
Broadway ['brɔ:dweɪ] *Straße in NYC* **IV AC2**, 41
Brooklyn ['brʊklɪn] *Stadtteil von New York* **IV TS2**, 65
Calais ['kæleɪ] *frz. Küstenstadt am Ärmelkanal* **IV U1**, 10
Cambridge ['keɪmbrɪdʒ] *Stadt in den USA* **IV U2**, 44
Camden Market ['kæmdən ˌmɑ:kɪt] **II**
Chicago [ʃɪ'kɑ:gəʊ] *Stadt in den USA* **IV AC2**, 39
Cologne [kə'ləʊn] Köln **I**
Covent Garden [ˌkɒvnt 'gɑ:dn] **II**
Cracow ['krækɒv; 'krɑ:kaʊ] Krakau **I**
Dhaka ['dɑ:kə] **IV U1**, 14
Dover ['dəʊvə] *englische Küstenstadt am Ärmelkanal* **IV U1**, 10
Dubai [du:'baɪ] **IV U1**, 16
Edinburgh ['edɪnbrə] **III**
Ellis Island [ˌelɪs‿'aɪlənd] *Insel vor New York City* **IV AC2**, 38
Glasgow ['glɑ:zgəʊ] *Stadt in Schottland* **III**
Heathrow [ˌhi:θ'rəʊ] *Flughafen in London* **IV U1**, 15
Hollywood ['hɒliwʊd] **II**
Houston ['hju:stn] *Stadt in den USA* **IV TS3**, 101
Hyde Park [ˌhaɪd 'pɑ:k] **II**
Isle of Man [ˌaɪl‿əv 'mæn] **III**
Lakeview ['leɪkvju:] *Stadt in den USA* **IV U2**, 51
Liberty Island [ˌlɪbəti‿'aɪlənd] **IV U3**, 74
Liverpool ['lɪvəpu:l] **III**
London ['lʌndən] **I**
Lower Manhattan [ˌləʊə mæn'hætn] **IV U3**, 74
Manhattan [mæn'hætn] *Stadtteil von New York* **IV TS2**, 65
Midtown Manhattan [ˌmɪdtaʊn mæn'hætn] **IV U3**, 71
New York [ˌnju: 'jɔ:k] **III**
Nottingham ['nɒtɪŋəm] **III**
Philadelphia [ˌfɪlə'delfiə] *Stadt in den USA* **IV TS2**, 65
Pittsburgh ['pɪtsbɜ:g] *Stadt in den USA* **IV U2**, 44
Roswell ['rɒzwel] *Stadt in den USA* **IV TS3**, 105
San Diego [ˌsæn di'eɪgəʊ] *Stadt in den USA* **IV AC2**, 41
Seattle [si'ætl] **IV U1**, 15
Stratford-upon-Avon [ˌstrætfədəpɒn'eɪvn] *Geburtsort Shakespeares* **III**
Washington, D.C. [ˌwɒʃɪŋtən ˌdi:'si:] *Hauptstadt der USA* **IV TS2**, 65
Wimbledon ['wɪmbldən] **I**

Geographical names

Africa ['æfrɪkə] Afrika **III**
Alabama [ˌælə'bæmə] *US-amerik. Bundesstaat* **IV U3**, 72
America [ə'merɪkə] **II**
Arizona [ˌærɪ'zəʊnə] *US-Bundesstaat* **IV AC2**, 38
Asia ['eɪʒə] Asien **IV AC2**, 38
Atlantic Ocean [ətˌlæntɪk 'əʊʃn] Atlantischer Ozean **III**
Australia [ɒs'treɪliə] Australien **II**
Austria ['ɔ:strɪə] Österreich **II**
Bangladesh [ˌbæŋglə'deʃ] Bangladesch **IV U1**, 13
Britain ['brɪtn] Großbritannien **I**
British Empire [ˌbrɪtɪʃ‿'empaɪə] britisches Königreich **II**
British Isles [ˌbrɪtɪʃ‿'aɪlz] Britische Inseln **III**
California [ˌkælɪ'fɔ:niə] Kalifornien *(US-amerik. Bundesstaat)* **IV AC2**, 39
Canada ['kænədə] Kanada **I**
China ['tʃaɪnə] China **I**
Cornwall ['kɔ:nwɔ:l] **III**
Cuba ['kju:bə] Kuba **IV U3**, 92
Egypt ['i:dʒɪpt] Ägypten **IV U1**, 20
England ['ɪŋglənd] England **I**
European Union (EU) [ˌjʊərəpiən 'ju:njən (i:ju:)] Europäische Union **II**
France [frɑ:ns] Frankreich **II**
Germany ['dʒɜ:məni] Deutschland **I**
Great Britain (GB) [ˌgreɪt 'brɪtn] Großbritannien **III**
India ['ɪndiə] Indien **II**
Italy ['ɪtəli] Italien **II**
Kenya ['kenjə] Kenia **IV U1**, 16
Latin America [ˌlætɪn ə'merɪkə] Lateinamerika **IV AC2**, 38
Loch Ness [ˌlɒx 'nes; ˌlɒk 'nes] *See in Schottland* **III**
(the) **Midwest** [ˌmɪd'west] (der) Mittlere Westen **IV AC2**, 41
Mount Rainier [ˌmaʊnt reɪ'niə] *Berg in den USA* **IV AC2**, 38
New Mexico [ˌnju: 'meksɪkəʊ] *US-amerik. Bundesstaat* **IV TS3**, 105
North Sea [ˌnɔ:θ 'si:] Nordsee **III**
Northern Ireland [ˌnɔ:ðn‿'aɪələnd] Nordirland **III**
the **Pacific Northwest** [ðə pəˌsɪfɪk nɔ:θ'west] Pazifischer Nordwesten **IV AC2**, 38
Pennsylvania [ˌpensɪl'veɪniə] *US-amerik. Bundesstaat* **IV U2**, 44
Poland ['pəʊlənd] Polen **I**
Republic of Ireland [rɪˌpʌblɪk‿əv‿'aɪələnd] Republik Irland **III**
the **Rockies** (= the Rocky Mountains) [ðə 'rɒkiz] *Gebirge in the USA* **IV AC2**, 41
Russia ['rʌʃə] Russland **IV AC2**, 39
Scandinavia [ˌskændɪ'neɪviə] Skandinavien **III**
Scotland ['skɒtlənd] Schottland **III**
Somalia [sə'mɑ:liə] Somalia **IV U1**, 16
South Africa [ˌsaʊθ‿'æfrɪkə] Südafrika **II**
Soviet Union [ˌsəʊviət 'ju:njən] Sowjetunion **IV TS3**, 101
Spain [speɪn] Spanien **II**
Sweden ['swi:dn] Schweden **IV AC2**, 39
Thames [temz] **I**
United Kingdom (UK) [ju:'keɪ] Vereinigtes Königreich von Großbritannien und Nordirland **I**
the **US** (= the United States) [ðə ˌju:'es] die USA (= die Vereinigten Staaten) **IV AC2**, 38
USA (United States of America) [ˌju:es'eɪ (ju:ˌnaɪtɪd ˌsteɪts‿əv‿ə'merɪkə)] USA (Vereinigte Staaten von Amerika) **II**
Wales [weɪlz] **II**
Washington State [ˌwɒʃɪŋtən 'steɪt] *US-Bundesstaat* **IV AC2**, 38
Wisconsin [wɪ'skɒnsɪn] *US-amerik. Bundesstaat* **IV U3**, 76

Other names

Apollo 11 [əˌpɒləʊ ɪ'levn] *Raumfähre* **IV TS3**, 101
Area 51 [ˌeəriə ˌfɪfti'wʌn] **IV TS3**, 102
Astor Place Cube [ˌæstə pleɪs 'kju:b] *Kunstwerk* **IV U3**, 72
Auguste Bartholdi [ɔ:ˌgʊst bɑ:'təʊldi] *frz. Bildhauer* **IV U3**, 74
Big Ben [ˌbɪg 'ben] **II**
British Airways [ˌbrɪtɪʃ‿'eəweɪz] *Fluggesellschaft* **IV U1**, 15
Buckingham Palace [ˌbʌkɪŋəm 'pælɪs] **II**
Capricorn One [ˌkæprɪkɔ:n 'wʌn] *Filmtitel* **IV TS3**, 104
Central Park [ˌsentrl 'pɑ:k] *Park in New York* **IV U3**, 71
Chinatown ['tʃaɪnətaʊn] **IV U3**, 71
Chrysler Building ['kraɪslə ˌbɪldɪŋ] *Wolkenkratzer in New York* **IV U3**, 71

Cold War [ˌkəʊld 'wɔ:] Kalter Krieg **IV TS3**, 101
Columbia [kə'lʌmbiə] *Raumkapsel* **IV TS3**, 101
Docklands Light Railway *(DLR)* [ˌdɒklændz ˌlaɪt 'reɪlweɪ] *Regionalbahn im Osten Londons* **I**
Eagle ['i:gl] *Raumkapsel* **IV TS3**, 101
Empire State Building [ˌempaɪə 'steɪt ˌbɪldɪŋ] *Wolkenkratzer in NYC* **IV AC2**, 39
Empire State of Mind [ˌempaɪə ˌsteɪt‿əv 'maɪnd] *Liedtitel* **IV U3**, 70
Fashion Fabulous [ˌfæʃn 'fæbjələs] **IV TS2**, 66
the **Globe Theatre** [ðə ˌgləʊb 'θɪətə] **III**
God Save the Queen ['gɒd seɪv ðə ˌkwi:n] Gott schütze die Königin *(britische Nationalhymne)* **III**
the **Houses of Parliament** [ðə ˌhaʊzɪz‿əv 'pɑ:ləmənt] *britisches Parlamentsgebäude* **II**
Independence Day [ˌɪndɪ'pendəns ˌdeɪ] amerikanischer Unabhängigkeitstag **IV AC2**, 41
Industrial Revolution [ɪnˌdʌstriəl revl'u:ʃn] die industrielle Revolution **III**
Juillard School ['dʒu:ljəd ˌsku:l] *Hochschule für Tanz* **IV U3**, 72
London Eye [ˌlʌndən‿'aɪ] **II**
Mars [mɑ:z] **IV TS3**, 104
Meridian Line [məˌrɪdiən 'laɪn] Nullmeridian **I**
Metropolitan Museum of Art [metrəˌpɒlɪtn mju:ˌzi:əm‿əv‿'ɑ:t] *Museum in New York* **IV U3**, 72
OG [əʊ'dʒi:] **IV U3**, 79
Park Avenue [ˌpɑ:k‿'ævənju:] *Straße in New York* **IV U3**, 76
Pledge of Allegiance [ˌpledʒ‿əv‿ə'li:dʒns] *Treueeid auf die amerikanische Flagge* **IV U2**, 48
Retro 4ever [ˌretrəʊ fə'revə] **IV TS2**, 65
Rockefeller Center [ˌrɒkəfelə 'sentə] *Gebäude in New York* **IV U3**, 72
Statue of Liberty [ˌstætʃu:‿əv 'lɪbəti] Freiheitsstatue **IV U3**, 74
Thanksgiving [ˌθæŋks'gɪvɪŋ] *amerik. Erntedankfest* **IV U2**, 44
The Martian [ðə 'mɑ:ʃn] *Filmtitel* **IV TS3**, 104
The Naked Cowboy [ðə ˌneɪkɪd 'kaʊbɔɪ] **IV U3**, 72
The Wind in the Willows [ðə ˌwɪnd ɪn ðə 'wɪləʊz] *engl. Kinderbuchklassiker* **IV TS1**, 30
Times Square [ˌtaɪmz 'skweə] *Platz in New York* **IV U3**, 70
the **Tower of London** [ðə ˌtaʊər‿əv 'lʌndən] **II**
Wall Street ['wɔ:l ˌstri:t] *Straße in New York* **IV U3**, 74
Wayne Larson [ˌweɪn 'lɑ:sn] **IV U2**, 52
Weezer ['wi:zə] **IV U1**, 12
World War II [ˌwɜ:ld ˌwɔ: 'tu:] Zweiter Weltkrieg **II**

Famous names

Alicia Keys [əˌlɪʃə 'ki:z] *US-amerik. Sängerin* **IV U3**, 70
Alvin Ailey [ˌælvɪn 'eɪli] *Tänzer* **IV U3**, 72
Anne Boleyn [ˌæn 'bɒlɪn] *Mutter von Elizabeth I.* **III**
Anne Hathaway [ˌæn 'hæðəweɪ] *Shakespeares Frau* **III**
Buzz Aldrin [ˌbʌz 'ɔ:ldrɪn] *amerik. Astronaut* **IV TS3**, 101
Dave Draper [ˌdeɪv 'dreɪpə] **IV TS1**, 31
Elizabeth I [ɪˌlɪzəbəθ ðə 'fɜ:st] **II**
Francis Drake [ˌfrɑ:nsɪs 'dreɪk] **III**
Henry VIII [ˌhenri ði 'eɪtθ] Heinrich VIII. **III**
John F. Kennedy (JFK) [ˌdʒɒn‿ef 'kenədi; dʒeɪ‿ef keɪ] **IV U3**, 74
King Arthur [ˌkɪŋ‿'ɑ:θə] König Artus **III**
King Edward [kɪŋ 'edwəd] **III**
Matt Damon [ˌmæt 'deɪmən] *US-amerik. Schauspieler* **IV TS3**, 104
Michael Collins [ˌmaɪkl 'kɒlɪnz] *amerik. Astronaut* **IV TS3**, 101
Neil Armstrong [ˌni:l‿'ɑ:mstrɒŋ] *amerik. Astronaut* **IV TS3**, 100
Prince Albert [ˌprɪns 'ælbət] **II**
Queen Victoria [ˌkwi:n vɪk'tɔ:riə] **II**
Sherlock Holmes [ˌʃɜ:lɒk 'həʊmz] **III**
William Shakespeare [ˌwɪljəm 'ʃeɪkspɪə] *englischer Dramatiker (1564–1616)* **III**
William the Conqueror [ˌwɪljəm ðə 'kɒŋkrə] **II**

A

abbiegen to turn **I**
Abbildung image **IV TS2**, 65
abblocken to block **II**
abbrechen to drop out (of) **III**
abbrennen *to burn down **III**
abchecken to check out *(coll)* **III**
abdecken to cover **III**
Abend evening **I**
heute **Abend** 2nite *(= tonight)* **I**; tonight **IV TS1**, 31
Abendessen dinner **I**
abends in the evenings **I**
abends *(Uhrzeit)* p.m. **I**
Abenteuer adventure **II**
aber but **I**
abfahren *to leave **II**; to depart **III**
abfahren auf *to be crazy about **IV U2**, 47
abfahrend outward **III**
Abfall trash *(AE)* **IV TS2**, 67
Abflug departure **IV U1**, 9
Abflughalle departure lounge **IV U1**, 9
Abfolge sequence **IV U3**, 89
Abgabe drop-off **IV U2**, 51
abgeschlossen locked **II**
abgesehen von apart from **IV U1**, 11
abhaken to tick **II**
abhängen von to depend (on) **III**
Abhängige/-r addict **IV U1**, 10
Abheben take-off **IV U1**, 15
abholen to pick up **III**; to fetch **IV U1**, 17
Ablehnung rejection **IV U3**, 76
abnehmen *to take off **I**
Abneigungen dislikes *(pl)* **IV U2**, 46
Abreise departure **IV U1**, 9
abreißen to pull down **III**
Absage rejection **IV U3**, 76
abschalten to turn off **II**
abschicken *to send off **III**
abschneiden *to cut (off) **II**
Abschnitt section **II**
sich abschotten von to close oneself away from **IV U1**, 16
abschreiben to copy **I**
Absicht purpose **IV U1**, 13
absolut absolutely **II**
Abstammung origin **IV U1**, 19
Abstand gap **I**
abstimmen *to take a vote; to vote **I**
abstürzen to crash **II**
sich alles abverlangen to push oneself **III**
außer Acht lassen to ignore **III**
acht eight **I**
Achtklässler/-in 8th-grader *(AE)* **IV U2**, 48
Acker field **II**
Action action **I**
Adjektiv adjective **II**
Adresse address **I**
Adverb adverb **II**
AG club **I**
aggressiv aggressive **II**; pushy **IV TS1**, 33
Ägypter/-in Egyptian **IV U1**, 20
ägyptisch Egyptian **IV U1**, 20
äh er **I**
ähnlich similar **II**
keine Ahnung no idea **II**
keine Ahnung haben *to have no clue **IV AC2**, 41
Akku battery **II**
Aktion action **I**
aktiv active **III**
Aktivität activity **I**
aktuell up-to-date **IV TS3**, 100
Akzent accent **III**
akzeptieren to accept **IV U1**, 16
albern silly **I**
alle all of them; everyone **I**; everybody **II**
alle/-s all **I**
wir **alle** all of us **III**
allein alone **I**; on my own **II**
alleinstehend single **IV AC2**, 38
alles everything **I**
alltäglich everyday **III**
Alphabet alphabet **I**
alphabetisch alphabetical **II**
Alptraum nightmare **IV U2**, 52
als as **II**
als *(bei Vergleichen)* than **II**
als when **I**
als ob as if **III**
also so **I**
alt old **I**
Wie **alt** bist du? How old are you? **I**
Wie **alt** sind Sie? How old are you? **I**
Alter age **III**
Alter *(ugs.)* dude *(coll)* **IV AC2**, 41
älter elderly **III**
Alternativ- fringe **III**
am on **I**
am besten best **I**
am Fluss by the river **II**
am Wochenende at the weekend **I**
aus Amerika American **II**
Ureinwohner/-in **Amerikas** Native American **IV U2**, 45
Amerikaner/-in American **II**
amerikanisch American **II**
Amtssprache official language **II**
sich amüsieren *to have fun **I**; to enjoy oneself **III**
an on; at **I**; by **III**
an Bord aboard **I**
an Stelle von instead of **IV U2**, 45
an sein *to be on **II**
Ananas pineapple **III**
anbauen *to grow **III**
anbieten to offer **II**
Anblick sight **II**
andauern to continue **III**
Andenken souvenir **II**
die anderen the others **I**
andere/-r/-s other **I**; else **III**
ein/-e **andere**/-r/-s another **I**
Einerseits ..., (aber) andererseits ... On the one hand ..., (but) on the other hand ... **II**
ändern in to turn into **IV U1**, 14
seine Meinung **ändern** to change one's mind **III**
(sich) **ändern** to change **II**
anders different; other **I**
Änderung change **III**
Andeutung hint **III**
Anfahrt drive **IV U2**, 44
Anfang beginning **II**; start **III**
anfangen to start **I**; *to get started; *to begin **II**
anfeuern to cheer **II**
sich anfreunden *to become friends **IV AC2**, 41
anführen *to lead **III**
angeben to show off **II**
Angeber/-in show-off **III**
Und ein **Angeber**! With a very big head! **II**
Angeln fishing **III**
angemessen appropriate **III**
die Angesagten in-crowd **III**
von Angesicht zu Angesicht face-to-face **II**
angespült werden to wash up **II**
angreifen to attack **III**
Angst fear **II**
Angst haben (vor) *to be scared (of) **I**; *to be afraid (of) **IV U1**, 8
Ich habe (keine) **Angst** vor ... I'm (not) scared of ... **I**
ängstlich fearful **III**; scared **IV U2**, 52
anhaben *to wear **I**
anhalten to stop **I**
Anhänger/-in fan **II**
anheben to lift **IV U3**, 76
anhören to listen (to) **I**
anklicken to click on **III**
ankommen to arrive **III**
ankommend inward **III**
Ankommende/-r arrival **IV TS2**, 66
ankündigen to announce **IV TS3**, 101
Ankündigung announcement **III**
Ankunft arrival **IV U1**, 9
Ankunftshalle arrivals hall **IV U1**, 9
anmalen to paint **I**
Anmerkung note **I**
annähernd nearly **II**
Annäherung approach **IV TS2**, 66
annehmen to accept **IV U1**, 16; to guess **IV AC1**, 22
anonym anonymous **II**
anordnen to arrange **III**
Anordnung layout **III**
anpflanzen to plant **II**
anpreisen to advertise **IV TS2**, 64
anprobieren to try on **II**
anregen to inspire **IV U3**, 70
Anregung suggestion **I**
Anruf phone call **I**

einen **Anruf** entgegennehmen to answer the phone **I**
Anrufbeantworter answering machine **I**
anrufen to call **I**; to phone **IV TS1**, 31; *to ring **IV TS1**, 36
Anrufer/-in caller **I**
Ansatz approach **IV TS2**, 66
anschauen to look at **I**; *to have a look (at) **II**
jmdn. schief/komisch **anschauen** *to give sb funny looks **III**
sich **anschließen** to join **II**
ansehen to look at **I**
(sich) **ansehen** to watch **I**
Ansicht point of view **II**
anstarren to stare **I**
anstatt instead of **IV U2**, 45
anstehen *to stand in line *(AE)* **IV AC3**, 69
(sich) **anstellen** *to stand in line *(AE)* **IV AC3**, 69
antippen to tap **II**; to touch **IV U2**, 52
Antwort answer; reply **I**
antworten to answer; to reply **I**
Anweisung instruction **I**
Anwesenheitskontrolle registration **II**
Anzeige advert **III**; ad **IV TS2**, 64
anziehen *to put on **III**; to attract **IV TS2**, 66
Apartment apartment *(AE)* **IV U2**, 43
Apfel apple **I**
App app **II**
Apparat machine **I**
April April **I**
Ära era **IV U1**, 19
arabisch Arab **IV U1**, 20
Arbeit job; work **I**
Arbeit für die Schule studies *(pl)* **II**
arbeiten to work **I**
Arbeitsheft workbook **IV TS1**, 37
Architekt/-in architect **II**
Areal area **II**
Ärger trouble **II**
Ärger machen *to make trouble **I**
jmdn. **ärgern** to tease sb **III**
Argument criterion, criteria *(pl)*; argument **III**
Argument dafür pro **II**
Argument dagegen con **II**
argumentieren to argue **IV U2**, 51
argwöhnisch suspicious **IV U1**, 13
Arm arm **II**
arm poor **III**
die **Armen** the poor **III**
armselig miserable ⟨**IV TS1**, 32⟩
Aroma flavor *(AE)* **IV U3**, 75
arrangieren to arrange **III**
Art kind **I**; type **III**
Art und Weise way **I**
Artikel article **II**
Arzt/**Ärztin** doctor **II**
Arztpraxis surgery **I**
Assistent/-in assistant **II**
Astronaut/-in astronaut **IV TS3**, 100
Atelier studio **IV U3**, 72
Atem breath **III**
Atem holen *to take a breath **III**
atemberaubend breathtaking **IV TS3**, 104
Atemzug breath **III**
Atlantischer Ozean Atlantic Ocean **III**
Atlas atlas **II**
atmen to breathe **II**
Atmosphäre flair; atmosphere **II**
Attraktion attraction **II**
attraktiv attractive **IV U2**, 55
Aua! Ouch! **II**
auch too **I**; also **II**
auch nicht not … either **IV AC4**, 107
Du **auch**? You too? **I**
Audio- audio **I**
Audioführung audio tour **II**
audiovisueller Effekt audio-visual effect **II**
auf on; at; to **I**
auf dem Foto/den Fotos in the photo(s) **I**
auf der anderen Seite von across; opposite **I**
auf der Straße in the street **I**
auf einmal suddenly **I**
auf Wiedersehen goodbye **I**
auf … zu towards **II**
Aufbau structure **III**
aufbauen *to set up **I**; *to build **III**
wieder **aufbauen** *to rebuild **III**
aufbewahren *to keep **I**
aufdringlich pushy **IV TS1**, 33
aufeinanderfolgend consecutive **IV U3**, 89
aufführen to stage **IV TS1**, 30; **IV TS3**, 102; to perform **IV U3**, 79
Aufführung show **II**; performance **IV TS1**, 30
Aufgabe task; exercise; job **I**
aufgeben *to give up **III**
aufgebracht upset **II**
aufgeregt excited **I**; nervous **II**
aufgeschlagen open **I**
aufhalten *to hold open **IV AC1**, 22
aufhängen *to put up; *to hang up **II**
aufheben to pick up **III**
jmdn. **aufheitern** to cheer sb up **III**
aufhellen to lighten **III**
aufhören to finish **I**
Hör/**Hört** auf! Stop it! **I**
aufhören (mit) to stop **I**
Aufklärung enlightenment **IV U3**, 74
aufladen to top up **II**
aufmachen to open **I**
aufmerksam machen (auf) to campaign (for) **III**
Aufmerksamkeit attention **II**
Aufnahme recording **I**; shot **III**
Aufnahmeort set **III**
Aufnahmestudio recording studio **I**
aufnehmen to record **II**; to include **III**
auf etw. **aufpassen** to mind sth **IV AC4**, 107
aufpassen auf to look after **I**
Pass/**Passt auf**! Be careful! **I**
aufpassen to look out **II**
aufpeppen to spice up **IV TS2**, 65
aufräumen to tidy *(a room)* **I**
aufrechterhalten *to keep going **II**
aufregend exciting **I**
Aufregung excitement *(no pl)* **III**
aufsagen *to say **I**
aufsaugen to soak up **III**
aufschreiben *to write down **I**; to note down **II**
aufstehen *(aus dem Bett)* *to get up **I**
Es ist Zeit **aufzustehen**! Time to get up! **I**
aufstehen *(von einer Sitzgelegenheit)* *to stand up **I**
aufstellen *to put up **II**
(sich) **aufstellen** to line up **III**
aufteilen to divide (up) **III**
Auftrag task **I**; mission **IV TS3**, 101
auftreten to perform **IV U3**, 79
Auftritt gig **III**
aufwachen *to wake up **III**
aufwachsen *to grow up **III**
aufwärmen to warm up **I**
sich **aufwärmen** to warm up **I**
Aufwärmübung warm-up **I**
aufwecken *to wake up **III**
aufweisen to feature **III**
aufzeichnen to record **II**
Aufzeichnung recording **I**
jmdn. **aufziehen** to tease sb **III**
Aufzug elevator *(AE)* **IV U2**, 44
Auge eye **II**
die **Augen** verdrehen to roll one's eyes **III**
Er traute seinen **Augen** nicht. He couldn't believe his eyes. **II**
Augenblick moment **II**
Augenzeuge/**Augenzeugin** eyewitness **II**
August August **I**
aus from **I**
aus Cornwall Cornish **III**
aus … heraus out of **IV U1**, 15
aus aller Welt from around the world **III**
ausarbeiten to work out **II**
Ausbeuterbetrieb sweatshop **IV U2**, 48
ausblasen *to blow out **I**
Ausblick view **II**
Auschecken Check-out **I**
auschecken to check out *(coll)* **III**
(sich) **ausdenken** *to think of **II**
Ausdruck phrase **I**; expression **II**
nützliche **Ausdrücke** Useful phrases **I**
ausdrücken to express **II**
Auseinandersetzung argument **III**
auserwählt sein, etw. zu tun *to be called to do sth **III**
ausflippen *to go crazy **II**
Ausflug trip **II**
ausführen to conduct **IV U3**, 92
den Hund **ausführen** to walk the dog **I**
ausfüllen to fill in **II**
Ausgang gate **IV U1**, 15
Ausgangssperre curfew **IV U2**, 44
ausgeben *(Geld)* *to spend **I**
ausgedehnt wide **III**

ausgehen *to go out III
ausgereift well-developed IV TS3, 105
sich ausgeschlossen fühlen *to feel left out II
zeitweilig vom Unterricht ausgeschlossen werden *to be suspended IV AC3, 68
aushelfen to help out III
im Ausland abroad IV U1, 10
ins Ausland abroad IV U1, 10
ausländisch foreign IV U1, 8
auslassen to skip IV AC3, 68
Auslauf run area III
auslaufen *to spill IV U1, 10
(sich) ausleihen to borrow II
einem etwas ausmachen to mind IV U2, 46
Mach/Macht das aus! Stop it! I
auspacken to unwrap I; to unpack IV U2, 46
ausprobieren to try out III
auspusten *to blow out I
ausräumen to clear out I; to clean out IV U2, 51
jmdm. etw. ausrichten *to take a message I
sich ausruhen to relax II
Ausrüstung equipment II
Aussage statement II
ausschalten to turn off II; to switch off IV AC3, 69
Ausschuss committee IV U2, 48
aussehen to look I
Aussehen looks *(pl)* III
von außen from the outside IV U3, 75
Außenseiter/-in geek IV U2, 48
außer Acht lassen to ignore III
außer apart from IV U1, 11; except IV U1, 17
außer Betrieb out of order IV TS1, 36
im äußersten Westen in the far west III
außerhalb outside; out I
Außerirdische/-r alien I
Äußerung expression II
Aussicht view II
Aussprache pronunciation I
aussprechen to pronounce IV AC4, 106
Ausstattung equipment II
aussteigen *to get out of II
aussteigen (aus einem Bus/Zug) *to get off (a bus/train) II
Ausstellung display II
Ausstellung in der Klasse class display I
Aussterben extinction *(no pl)* III
aussterben *to become extinct III
aussuchen to pick II
Austausch exchange III
Austausch- exchange III
austauschen to exchange; to trade II
Austauschschüler/-in exchange student III
Australier/-in Australian III
australisch Australian III
austricksen to trick IV TS3, 103
ausüben to practice *(AE)* IV U2, 45
eine Religion ausüben to practice a religion IV U2, 45
Auswahl choice II
auswählen *to choose; to pick II
auswendig lernen *to learn … by heart I
auswickeln to unwrap I
Auszeichnung award II
ausziehen *to take off I
Auto car I
Autobahn freeway *(AE)* IV U3, 79
Autofahrt drive IV U2, 44
Automat machine I; vending machine IV U1, 10
Autor/-in author; writer III
Axt axe III

B

Baby baby I
Background- backing III
Backgroundtänzer/-in backing dancer III
Bad bath I
Badehaus baths *(pl)* III
Badewanne bath I
Badezimmer bathroom I
Badminton badminton I
Bahnhof station I
Bahnsteig platform III
bald soon II
Ball ball I
Banane banana I
Band band III
Bank bench III; bank IV U3, 72
bannen to ban III
Bär bear II
Baseball baseball IV U2, 46
Basketball basketball I
Batterie battery II
Bauch stomach II
Bauchschmerzen stomachache II
Bauchweh stomachache II
bauen *to build II
Bauernhof farm I
Baum tree I
Baustein building block II
jmdn./etw. beachten *to pay attention to sb/sth III
Beachtung attention II
Beamter/Beamtin official IV U1, 17
beängstigend scary II
beantworten to answer I
richtig beantworten *to get right III
Becher mug III
bedauern *to feel sorry for III
bedecken to cover III
bedeckt cloudy II
bedeuten *to mean II
Bedeutung meaning II
Bedingungssatz conditional sentence III
bedrückend depressing IV U1, 17
bedürftig in need II
sich beeilen to hurry I
beeindruckt impressed II
beeinflussen to influence II
beenden to finish I; to end II
sich befassen mit *to deal (with) II
Befehl order III; command IV U1, 9
Befehlsform imperative III
befestigen to fix II
befolgen to follow II
befördern to transport IV U3, 79
befragen to interview I
Befragung interview I
Befürchtung fear II
begehbarer Kleiderschrank walk-in closet IV U2, 44
begeistert excited I
Begeisterung enthusiasm IV U3, 72
Beginn beginning II; opening III
beginnen to start I; *to begin II
Begriff term IV TS1, 30
im Begriff sein, etw. zu tun *to be about to do sth IV AC3, 69
behalten *to keep I
Behauptung statement II
behindert with special needs II
bei with; at I; by III
beibringen *to teach II
beide both II
beide the two of them II
Bein leg II
die Beine und Hände ruhig halten *to keep one's feet or hands still III
beinahe almost II
beinhalten to include III
Beispiel example I
zum Beispiel for example II
beißen *to bite II
beitreten to join II
bekannt sein als *to be known as IV U3, 74
sich beklagen to complain IV U3, 76
Bekleidungsvorschriften dress code IV U2, 43
bekommen *to get I; to receive II
etw. aus dem Kopf bekommen *to get sth out of one's head III
belästigen to bother IV U1, 15
belebt busy I
beliebt popular I
die Beliebten in-crowd III
bellen to bark I
Belohnung treat III
bemerken to notice II
Benehmen behaviour *(no pl)* IV AC1, 22; manners *(pl)* IV AC1, 23; behavior *(no pl) (AE)* IV AC3, 69
sich benehmen to behave III
benötigen to need (to) I
benutzen to use I; *to make use of IV U3, 89
beobachten to watch I
bequem comfortable II
bereit ready II
bereits already I
Berg mountain II; hill III
Bergbau mining III
bergen to save I
bergig mountainous IV AC2, 40

Bericht report **II**
Bericht *(in einer Zeitschrift, Zeitung)* article **II**
berichten to report **IV U1**, 9
Beruf career **III**
sich beruhigen to relax; to calm down **II**
berühmt famous **I**
 berühmte Person celebrity **III**
berühren to touch **IV U2**, 52
beschäftigt busy **I**
beschreiben to describe **I**
Beschreibung description **II**
sich beschweren to complain **IV U3**, 76
besichtigen to visit **I**
Besichtigungs- sightseeing **II**
besiedelt populated **IV AC2**, 38
besiegen *to beat **II**; to defeat **III**
besitzen *to have got **I**
Besonderheit specialty *(AE)* **IV U3**, 75
besonders special **I**
besorgen *to get **I**
besorgt worried **III**
 besorgt sein *to be worried **II**
Besorgungen machen *to do the shopping **III**
besser better **I**
Bestätigungsfrage question tag **II**
(der/die/das) Beste (the) best **II**
 sich das **Beste** bis zum Schluss aufheben to save the best for last **IV U3**, 72
bestehen aus *to be made of **III**
besteigen to climb **I**
bestellen to order **IV U1**, 20
beste/-r/-s best **I**
 am **besten** best **I**
 der/die/das **beste** … überhaupt the best … ever **III**
bestimmt definitely **III**
bestimmte/-r/-s particular **III**
bestürzt upset **II**
Besuch visit **I**
besuchen to visit **I**
Besucher/-in visitor **I**
beteiligen to involve **IV TS3**, 102
beten to pray **III**
Beton concrete **IV U1**, 17
betonen to stress **III**
Betonung stress **III**
Betragen behaviour *(no pl)* **IV AC1**, 22; behavior *(no pl) (AE)* **IV AC3**, 69
betreiben *to run **IV TS3**, 102
betreten to enter **II**
Betreuer/-in instructor **II**
außer Betrieb out of order **IV TS1**, 36
betrügen to cheat **IV AC3**, 68
Bett bed **I**
 ins **Bett** gehen *to go to bed **I**
beunruhigt worried **III**
 beunruhigt sein *to be worried **II**
beurteilen to judge **III**
bevölkert populated **IV AC2**, 38
Bevölkerung population **IV AC2**, 39
bevor before **I**
(sich) bewegen to move **I**
Beweggrund motive **IV TS1**, 32
Beweggründe motivation **IV TS1**, 31
Bewegung move **I**
bewerten to judge **III**; to rate **IV TS3**, 104
bewölkt cloudy **II**
bezahlen *to pay (for) **I**
Beziehung relationship **II**
 eine **Beziehung** finden zu to relate to **III**
Bezirk district **IV U3**, 70
Bibliothek library **III**
Biene bee **II**
Bild picture **I**; visual; image **IV TS2**, 65
Bild *(eines Comics)* panel **IV U3**, 89
bilden *to make **I**; to form **II**
Bildergeschichte graphic novel **III**
Bildgeschichte photo story **I**
Bildung education *(no pl)* **III**
Bildunterschrift caption **III**
billig cheap **I**
binden (an) to tie (to) **III**
Bindewort linking word **I**
biografisch biographical **III**
Bis … CU *(= See you)*; See you! **I**
 Bis dann! CU *(= See you)*; See you! **I**
bis till **I**; until **II**
 bis jetzt so far **II**
 von … **bis** from … to **I**
 bis auf except **IV U1**, 17
Biskuit- sponge **I**
ein bisschen a bit **II**
Bitte request **IV U1**, 9
Bitte. Please. **I**
 Bitte schön. Here you are.; You're welcome. **I**
bitten to ask **I**
 bitten um to ask for **I**
blau blue **I**
Blechdose tin can **III**
bleiben to stay **I**
 draußen **bleiben** *to keep out (of) **III**
 Bleib wie du bist. Stay the way you are. **III**
Bleistift pencil **I**
Blick look **I**; view **II**
 einen **Blick** werfen auf *to take a look at **II**
hier: Blick sight **III**
Blickfang eye-catcher **IV TS2**, 65
Blickpunkt focus **III**
Blickwinkel perspective **II**
Blitz lightning *(no pl)* **II**; flash **III**
Block block **IV U3**, 72
blockieren to block **II**
blöd stupid **II**
Blog blog **III**
blond blond **III**
bloß bare **III**
bloß only **I**
Blume flower **II**
Blut blood **III**
BMX BMX **II**
Boarding boarding **IV U1**, 9
Boden ground **IV U1**, 17
Bodyguard bodyguard **IV U2**, 52
weiße Bohnen in Tomatensoße baked beans *(pl)* **I**
Bonbons sweets *(pl)* **I**
Boot boat **I**
an Bord aboard **I**
Bordkarte boarding card **IV U1**, 9
böse angry; bad **I**
Bösewicht villain **III**
Boss boss **III**
Botschaft message **I**
Bowling spielen to play bowls **III**
Bowlingbahn bowling alley **I**
Box box **I**
Boxen boxing **II**
Boxrunde round of boxing **II**
Branche industry **III**
brandneu brand-new **IV TS2**, 65
Bratwurst sausage **III**
Brauch custom **IV AC1**, 22
brauchen to need (to) **I**
 nicht **brauchen** needn't **I**
 (Zeit) **brauchen** *to take **II**
braun brown **I**
brechen *to break **I**
brechend cracking **III**
breit wide **III**
brennen *to burn; *to be on fire **III**
Brett board **III**
 schwarzes **Brett** noticeboard **II**
Brief letter **II**
Briefträger postman **II**
Brille glasses *(pl)* **II**
bringen *to bring; *to get; *to take **I**
 in Schwierigkeiten **bringen** *to make trouble **I**
 jmdn. dazu **bringen**, etw. zu tun *to make somebody do something **II**
Brite/Britin British **I**
britisch British **I**
Bronzezeit *(ca. 2200–800 v. Chr.)* Bronze Age **III**
Broschüre brochure **I**; leaflet **IV AC1**, 23
Brot bread **I**
 belegtes **Brot** sandwich **I**
Brötchen bread roll **III**
Brücke bridge **II**
Bruder brother **I**
brüllen to roar **III**
brutal violent **III**
Buch book **I**
buchen to book **III**
Bücherei library **III**
Büchse can **I**
Buchstabe letter **I**
buchstabieren *to spell **I**
Bühne stage **III**
Bundesstaat state **IV AC2**, 39
bunt colourful **I**
Buntstift pencil **I**
Burg castle **II**

Büro office I
Bus bus I
Busbahnhof bus station I
Busch *(Buschlandschaft)* bush III
Business business III
Butter butter III

C

Cache cache III
Café café; snack bar I
Cafeteria cafeteria I
campen to camp III
Camping camping II
Cartoon cartoon III
Casting casting **IV TS1**, 37
Cent *(Währung)* cent I
Center centre I; center *(AE)* **IV AC2**, 38
Champion champion III
Chance chance II
Chaos chaos III
Charakter character I
Chat chat III
Chatroom chat room II
chatten *(sich online unterhalten)* to chat I
Checkliste checklist II
Chef boss III
chillen to chill out III
Chipkarte smartcard II
im Chor in chorus **IV TS1**, 33
nach Christus AD (= Anno Domini) III
vor Christus BC (= before Christ) III
circa about I
Clique clique **IV U2**, 48
Clown clown II
Cola coke I
Comedian comedian II
Comedy Show comedy show II
Comic comic II; graphic novel III
Comicheft comic II
Computer computer I
Computerunterricht Technology II
cool cool I
aus Cornwall Cornish III
Couch sofa I
Cousin/Cousine cousin I
Cover cover III
Coverversion cover version III
Cowboy cowboy **IV U3**, 72
Creme cream I
Cricket cricket II
Curry *(Gewürz oder Gericht)* curry I

D

da sein *to be around **IV U2**, 44
da because I; since **IV U3**, 72
da there I
  da ist/sind there is/are I
dabei sein *to be in II
  mit **dabei** along for the ride **IV U2**, 44
Dach roof III
Dachboden loft I; attic II
Wohnung mit Dachterrasse penthouse **IV U3**, 79
etwas dagegen haben to mind **IV U2**, 46
  Ich habe nichts **dagegen** (zu) … I don't mind … *(+ -ing)* III
dahin there I
damals back then III; at the time **IV TS3**, 102
Dame lady III
  Sehr geehrte **Dame**, sehr geehrter Herr Dear Sir or Madam III
damit so (that) **IV AC3**, 69
Dampf steam III
Dampfmaschine steam engine III
danach then; after that I
dankbar thankful I
Dankbarkeit gratitude III
Danke! Cheers! III
Danke. Thank you.; Thanks. I
danken to thank II; *to give thanks **IV U2**, 45
  Nichts zu **danken**. You're welcome. I
dann then I
darauf zu towards II
darstellen to represent **IV AC2**, 40
das the I
das that I
  Das (hier) ist … This is … I
  Das macht … That's … I
  Das war knapp! That was close! I
das *(Relativpronomen)* which II
dass that I
Date date **IV U2**, 55
Datum date I
dauern *to take II
Daumen thumb II
  die **Daumen** drücken *to keep your fingers crossed I
davonkommen mit *to get away with II
dazwischen in between III
Deck deck I
Definition definition III
definitiv definitely III
dein/-e your I
dein/-er/-e/-es yours II
Dekoration decorations *(pl)* I
dekorieren to decorate I
Delfin dolphin III
dem *(Relativpronomen)* who; which II
Demonstrant/-in protester **IV U2**, 52
demonstrieren to demonstrate **IV U2**, 48
  demonstrieren (für) to campaign (for) III
den *(Relativpronomen)* who; which II
denken *to think I
  Denke/Denkt an … Think of … I
  denken an to remember I
  denken über *to think of I
Denkmal monument III
dennoch still II
  und **dennoch** yet **IV U3**, 76
deprimierend depressing **IV U1**, 17
der the I
der; dem; den; die; das *(Relativpronomen)* that II
der *(Relativpronomen)* who; which II
deren *(Relativpronomen)* whose II
der-/die-/dasselbe the same I
Desaster disaster II
deshalb that's why II
Design design II
Designer/-in designer III
dessen *(Relativpronomen)* whose II
Detail detail II
  nach **Details** durchsuchen to scan II
Detektiv/-in detective III
Detektivgeschichte detective III
deutlich clear I
Deutsch German I
deutsch German I
Deutsche/-r German I
aus Deutschland German I
Dezember December I
Diagramm diagram I
Dialekt dialect III
Dialog dialogue I
dicht dense **IV AC2**, 40
dick *(nicht für Personen)* thick III
die *(auch Pl.)* the I
die *(Relativpronomen)* who; which II
Diele hall III; hallway **IV U2**, 43
Dienst service **IV U3**, 72
Dienstag Tuesday I
Dienstleistung service **IV U3**, 72
dies this I
diese (hier) these I
  diese dort those I
diese/-r/-s this I
Dilemma dilemma **IV TS1**, 31
Ding thing I
Dinosaurier dinosaur II
direkt direct III
direkte Rede direct speech **IV U1**, 11
direkt straight **IV U1**, 17; right **IV U2**, 52
Discjockey DJ III
Diskussion discussion II
diskutieren to discuss I
Distanz distance II
Distel thistle III
Distrikt district **IV U3**, 70
DJ DJ III
doch after all I
doch yet **IV U3**, 76; though **IV AC4**, 106
dokumentieren to document ⟨**IV TS3**, 101⟩
Dollar *(Währung)* dollar III
ein Gespräch dominieren to hog a conversation III
Domino dominoes **IV U1**, 20
Donner thunder *(no pl)* II
donnernd roaring III
Donnerstag Thursday I
doof silly I
Doppel- double **IV U2**, 57
Dorf village I
dort there I

dorthin there I
Dose can I
aus der Dose tinned I
Dosen- tinned I
Drama drama II
dramatisch dramatic II
dran kommen to reach II
Du bist dran. Your turn.; It's your turn. I
draußen outside I
draußen bleiben *to keep out (of) III
draußen halten *to keep out (of) III
nach draußen out I
Dreck dirt III
dreckig dirty II
Drehbuch script III
drehen to film; to turn III
sich im Kreis drehen *to go round in circles III
Drehort set III
drei three I
eine Dreiergruppe a group of three I
dreizehn thirteen I
drin inside I
dritte/-r/-s third I
dröhnen to boom; to roar III
dröhnend roaring III
Druck- print II
drücken to press II
die Daumen drücken *to keep your fingers crossed I
Dschungel jungle IV U3, 70
du you; u *(= you)* I
Du auch? You too? I
Du bist dran. Your turn.; It's your turn. I
Du bist … You're … I
Du solltest lieber … You'd better … *(= You had better)* IV AC3, 69
Du weißt, wie man … You know how to … I
du/dir/dich/Sie/sich (selbst) yourself I
sich ducken to cringe IV U3, 91
Dudelsack bagpipes *(pl)* III
duften *to smell III
dumm silly I; stupid II
Zu dumm! Too bad! I
Dummkopf silly II
dunkel dark II
Dunkelheit the dark II; darkness III
dünn sparse IV AC2, 38
Dunst mist ⟨IV U3, 90⟩
durch through I
Durchbruch break IV U3, 76
durchdrehen *to go crazy II
Durcheinander chaos III; mess IV U2, 54
etw. durcheinanderbringen to mess sth up IV TS1, 30
durchführen to conduct IV U3, 92
schmaler Durchgang close III
Durchsage announcement III
durchsagen to announce IV TS3, 101
nach Details durchsuchen to scan II

dürfen can I; *to be allowed to (do sth); *to be able to (do sth); may II
nicht dürfen mustn't I
durstig thirsty III
Dusche shower I
DVD DVD I

E

Ebbe low tide II
ebenso wie so is III
echt real II
Ecke corner II
Edelstein jewel III
(der Garten) Eden Eden III
Effekt effect IV U3, 89
audiovisueller Effekt audio-visual effect II
effektiv effective IV TS2, 66
Effektivität effectiveness IV TS2, 67
egal (was/welche) whatever IV AC4, 107
Es ist egal. It doesn't matter. III
Ehefrau wife, wives *(pl)* II
Ehemann husband II
ehrlich honest III
Ei egg I
Eiche oak III
Eichhörnchen squirrel I
eifersüchtig sein (auf) *to be jealous (of) I
eigen of one's own III
eigene/-r/-s own I
Eigenschaft feature III
Eigenschaftswort adjective II
eilen to hurry I
Eimer bucket II
ein/-e a; an I
ein paar a couple of I
ein wenig a little I
ein/-e andere/-r/-s another I
noch ein/-e another I
einander each other I
einbeziehen to include III; to involve IV TS3, 102
einbiegen to turn I
Einchecken Check-in I
eindeutig definitely III
eindringen (in) to invade III
Eindruck impression IV U2, 42
eine/-r/-s one *(sg)*/ones *(pl)* II
Einerseits …, (aber) andererseits … On the one hand …, (but) on the other hand … II
einfach easy I; simple III
einfache Fahrkarte one-way ticket; single ticket III
einfach nur simply IV AC2, 40
einfach just I
Einfall idea I
sich etwas einfallen lassen *to think of II
einfallsreich imaginative III
einfangen to capture III
einführen to introduce IV U1, 11

Einführung introduction II; lead-in IV U3, 89
Eingang entrance III
eingängig catchy III
eingeklemmt crushed IV U1, 16
eingequetscht crushed IV U1, 16
eingeschlossen sein *to be trapped III
eingießen to pour I
Einheit unit I
die Segel einholen to reef the sails I
einige some; a few I; several II
sich einigen (auf) to agree (on) III
Einkäufe machen *to do the shopping III
Einkäufe shopping I
Einkaufen shopping I
einkaufen to shop IV U3, 76
einkaufen gehen *to go shopping I
Einkaufszentrum shopping mall IV U2, 43
einladen to invite I
Einladung invitation I
einleiten to introduce IV U1, 11
Einleitung introduction II; lead-in IV U3, 89
einleuchten *to make sense IV TS3, 102
einmal once I
einmarschieren (in) to invade III
einpacken to wrap I
einprägsam catchy III
Einreise immigration IV U1, 13
Einreisebewilligung visa, visas *(pl)* IV U1, 9
einrichten *to set up I
eins one I
einsam lonely I
einschenken to pour I
einschlafen *to fall asleep I
einschließen to include III
einsortieren to sort into III
einst once I
einsteigen *to get into I; *to get in IV U3, 76
einsteigen (in den Bus) *to get on (the bus) III
Einstellung shot II; attitude IV U2, 55
einstufen to rate IV TS3, 104
Eintrag entry III
eintreten to enter II
Eintritt entrance III
Eintrittskarte ticket I
nicht einverstanden sein to disagree III
Einwanderer/-in immigrant IV AC2, 38
Einwanderung immigration IV U1, 13
Einwanderungsbehörde immigration office IV U1, 13
einwickeln to wrap I
Einzelheit detail II
Einzelkind only child I
einzeln individual II; single IV AC2, 38
Einzelne/-r individual IV U2, 56
Einzelperson individual IV U2, 56
einziehen in to move in/into III
einzig single IV AC2, 38
einzige/-r/-s only II
Eis ice; ice cream I
Eisbahn ice rink I

Eisbrecher *(Sätze, um mit jmdm. ins Gespräch zu kommen)* icebreaker **IV AC1**, 23
Eiscreme ice cream **I**
Elefant elephant **III**
Elektrik electrics **III**
Elektriker/-in electrician **III**
elektrisch electric **III**
Elektrizität electricity **III**
elektronisch electronic **II**
Element element **III**
elf eleven **I**
Elfenbein ivory *(no pl)* **III**
Eltern parents *(pl)* **I**
E-Mail e-mail **I**
per **E-Mail** schicken to mail **II**
emotional emotional **III**
Empfang signal **III**
empfangen to receive **II**
empfänglich receptive **IV TS2**, 64
Ende ending; end **I**
am **Ende** at the back of **II**
enden to finish **I**; to end up; to end **II**
endgültig final **II**
endlich at last **I**; finally **II**
endlos endless **IV AC2**, 38
Energie energy **III**
eng close **I**; narrow **III**
sich **engagieren** (für) to campaign (for) **III**
Engel angel **IV TS1**, 31
aus **England** English **I**
Brite/**Britin** *(ugs.)* Brit **IV AC2**, 41
Engländer/-in English **I**
Ich bin **Engländer**/-in. I'm English. **I**
Englisch English **I**
englisch English **I**
englischsprachig English-speaking **I**
entdecken to discover **II**
Entdeckung discovery **III**
auf **Entdeckungsreise** gehen to explore **I**
Entertainer/-in entertainer **IV U3**, 72
Entfernung distance **II**
entfliehen to escape (from) **IV U2**, 52
entgegen allen Erwartungen against all odds **III**
eine Nachricht **entgegennehmen** *to take a message **I**
einen Anruf **entgegennehmen** to answer the phone **I**
entgegnen to reply **I**
Entgegnung reply **I**
enthalten to contain **IV U1**, 15
Enthusiasmus enthusiasm **IV U3**, 72
entkommen to escape (from) **IV U2**, 52
entlang along **I**
entlanggehen *to go down **I**
entrümpeln to clear out **I**; to clean out **IV U2**, 51
(sich) **entscheiden** to decide **I**
Entscheidung decision **III**
eine **Entscheidung** treffen *to make a decision **II**

Entschuldigen Sie! Excuse me ... **I**
sich **entschuldigen** to apologise **III**
Entschuldigung! Sorry!; Excuse me ... **I**
entsetzt horrified **I**
sich **entspannen** to relax **II**
entspannt laid-back **III**
entsprechen to match **I**
enttäuschend disappointing **IV TS3**, 104
enttäuscht disappointed **I**
entweder ... oder ... either ... or ... **IV U3**, 79
entwerfen to design **II**
eine Geschichte langsam **entwickeln** to step into a story slowly **III**
gut **entwickelt** well-developed **IV TS3**, 105
Entwurf plan; draft **I**; design **II**
episch epic **IV AC2**, 41
er he **I**
Erdboden earth **II**; ground **IV U1**, 17
Erde world **I**; earth **II**
die **Erde** earth **II**
erdichtet fictional **III**
Erdkunde geography **III**
Erdteil continent **IV U3**, 74
Ereignis event **I**
erfahren to experience **III**
erfahren über *to learn about **III**
Erfahrung experience **II**
erfinden to create **I**; to invent **III**
Erfinder/-in inventor **III**
Erfindung invention; fiction *(no pl)* **III**
Erfolg success **III**
Erfolg haben (in/bei/mit) to succeed (in) **III**
erfolgreich successful **III**
erforschen to explore **I**
in **Erfüllung** gehen *to come true **IV U3**, 76
ergänzen to add **I**
Ergebnis result **II**
ergreifen to grab **II**; to capture **III**
erhalten to receive **II**
erhältlich available **IV TS2**, 65
sich **erheben** *to rise **III**
(jmdn. an etw./jmdn.) **erinnern** to remind (sb of sth/sb) **III**
sich **erinnern** (an) to remember **I**
Erinnerst du dich? Remember? **I**
Erinnert ihr euch? Remember? **I**
Erinnerung memory **II**
Erkältung cold **II**
erkennen to realise **III**; to realize *(AE)* **IV U2**, 52
erklären to explain **I**
Erklärung statement **II**
erkunden to explore **I**
Erlaubnis, *sich während des Unterrichts auf dem Flur aufzuhalten* hall pass **IV U2**, 43
erleben to experience **III**
Erleuchtung enlightenment **IV U3**, 74
ernähren *to feed **III**
ernst serious **I**
ernsthaft serious **I**

Ernte harvest **IV U2**, 45
eröffnen to open **IV U2**, 52
erraten to guess **I**
erreichen *to get to **I**; to reach **II**
errichten *to put up **II**
Ersatz substitute **II**
Ersatz- substitute **II**
erschaffen to create **I**
erst only **I**
erst um/im not until **IV U2**, 44
erst wenn until **II**
erstaunlich amazing **II**
erstaunt amazed **IV U2**, 52
erste/-r/-s first **I**
als **Erstes** first **I**
ertappt caught on camera **II**
ertappt werden *to get caught **IV AC3**, 68
ertränken to drown **III**
ertrinken to drown **III**
erwachsen werden *to grow up **III**
Erwachsene/-r adult **II**
erwähnen to mention **II**
erwarten to expect **III**
entgegen allen **Erwartungen** against all odds **III**
erwidern to reply **I**
Erwiderung reply **I**
erwischt werden *to get caught **IV AC3**, 68
erzählen *to tell **I**
erzählen von to talk about ... **I**
nochmals **erzählen** *to retell **I**
Erzähle mir von ... Tell me about ... **I**
Erzähler/-in narrator **III**
Er/Sie-**Erzähler**/-in third person narrator **III**
Erzählliteratur fiction *(no pl)* **III**
Erzählperspektive narrative perspective **III**
Erzählung story, stories *(pl)* **I**
Erzeugnis product **IV TS2**, 64
Erziehung education *(no pl)* **III**
es it **I**
Essen food **I**; meal **II**
(ein Bonbon) **essen** *to have *(a sweet)* **I**
essen *to eat **I**
ethnisch ethnic **IV U3**, 75
etwa about **I**
etwas some; something; a little **I**
euer/**eure** your **I**
eure/-r/-s yours **II**
Euro *(Währung)* euro **I**
aus **Europa** European **IV AC2**, 38
Europäer/-in European **IV AC2**, 38
europäisch European **IV AC2**, 38
ewig forever **II**
Examen exam **II**
hier: **exotisch** ethnic **IV U3**, 75
Experte/**Expertin** expert **II**
extra extra **I**
extrem extreme **IV AC2**, 40

F

Fabrik factory **III**
Fackel torch **II**
fähig sein zu *to be able to (do sth) **II**
Fahne flag **III**
Fähre ferry **IV U1**, 9
fahren *to go **I**; to travel **II**; *to drive **III**; *to ride raid **IV AC2**, 41
  Fahrrad **fahren** to cycle **IV U2**, 46
Grad **Fahrenheit** degree Fahrenheit (°F) **IV AC2**, 38
Fahrer/-in driver **II**
Fahrgast passenger **IV U1**, 9
einfache **Fahrkarte** one-way ticket; single ticket **III**
Fahrplan timetable **I**; schedule *(AE)* **IV AC4**, 106
Fahrpreis fare **III**
Fahrrad bike **I**
  Fahrrad fahren to cycle **IV U2**, 46
Fahrradmotocross bicycle motocross **II**
Fahrschein ticket **III**
Fahrt trip; tour **II**; journey **III**; drive; ride **IV U2**, 44
fair fair **I**
Fairplay fair play **III**
Fakt fact **II**
in der **Falle** sitzen *to be trapped **III**
fallen *to fall **I**
  fallen (lassen) to drop **II**
falls if **I**
falsch wrong **I**; fake **IV TS1**, 35
fälschen to fake **II**
Familie family **I**
Fan fan **II**
fangen *to catch **II**
Fantasie fantasy **I**; imagination **III**
fantasievoll imaginative **III**
fantastisch fantastic **II**; fabulous **IV TS2**, 66
Fantasy fantasy **III**
Fanzeitschrift fanzine **II**
Farbe colour **I**
  Welche **Farbe** hat …? What colour is …? **I**
farbenfroh colourful **I**
Farm farm **I**
Farmer/-in farmer **II**
aus der **Fassung** bringen *to upset **III**
fast nearly; almost **II**
Fastnachtsdienstag Shrove Tuesday **I**
faszinierend fascinating **III**
faul lazy **III**
Favorit/-in favourite **III**
Februar February **I**
Feder feather **III**
Federkiel quill **III**
Federmäppchen pencil-case **I**
Feedback feedback **II**
Was **fehlt**? What is missing? **I**
fehlend missing **II**
Fehler mistake **I**
Feier party **I**
feiern to celebrate **I**
Feiertag holiday **I**
Feind/-in enemy **III**
Feld field **II**
felsig rocky **III**
Fenster window **I**
Fensterladen shutter **IV U1**, 10
Ferien holidays *(pl)* **I**; vacation *(AE)* **IV AC2**, 41
fernbleiben von to stay away from **II**
(sich) **fernhalten** von *to keep away from **III**
Fernsehen TV **I**
fernsehen to watch TV **I**
Fernseher TV **I**
fertig ready; finished **II**
  fertig sein mit *to be done with **IV U3**, 76
Fertiggericht ready meal **I**
Fertigkeit skill **I**
fertigstellen to finish **I**; to complete **IV AC3**, 68
fesseln (an) to tie (to) **III**
Fest festival **I**
festhalten *to hold **I**
  (sich) **festhalten** an *to hold onto **III**
Festival festival **I**
festnehmen to arrest **II**
feststecken in … stuck in the middle of … **III**
fett gedruckt bold **III**
Feuer fire **III**
Feuerwerk fireworks *(pl)* **I**
  hier: ein **Feuerwerk** zünden *to set off **III**
Fieber fever **II**
Figur character **I**; figure **II**
Fiktion fiction *(no pl)* **III**
fiktional fictional **III**
fiktiv fictional **III**
Film film **I**; movie *(AE)* **IV U2**, 44
Filmemacher/-in filmmaker **II**
filmen to film **III**
finden *to find **I**
Finger finger **I**
Firma company **III**
Fisch fish, fish *(pl)* **I**
Fischen fishing **III**
Fischerei fishing **III**
fit werden *to get fit **I**
flach flat **IV AC2**, 40
Fläche space; area **II**
Flagge flag **III**
Flair flair **II**
Flamme flame **III**
Flasche bottle **I**
Flashback flashback **III**
Fleck spot **IV U3**, 75
Fleisch meat *(no pl)* **III**
fliegen *to fly **III**
fliehen to escape (from) **IV U2**, 52
Flohmarkt flea market **I**
Flöte recorder **III**
Flucht escape **III**
flüchten to escape (from) **IV U2**, 52
Flüchtling refugee **IV U1**, 18
Flug flight **III**
Flugbegleiter/-in flight attendant **IV U1**, 9
Flughafen airport **II**
Flugsteig gate **IV U1**, 15
Flugzeug plane **IV U1**, 8
Flur hall **III**; hallway **IV U2**, 43; corridor **IV AC3**, 68
Fluss river **I**
  am **Fluss** by the river **II**
flüstern to whisper **I**
Flut high tide **II**
Flyer flyer **I**
Fokus focus **III**
Folge consequence **IV AC3**, 68
Folge- follow-up **IV U3**, 92
folgen to follow **II**
folgende/-r/-s the following **III**
Form form **I**; shape **IV U3**, 89
  in **Form** kommen *to get fit **I**
  verneinte **Form** negative form **I**
formal formal **II**
formell formal **II**
formen to form **II**
förmlich formal **II**
Formular form **III**
Forschung research *(no pl)* **III**
hier: sich **fortbewegen** *to get around **II**
fortfahren *to go on **I**; to continue **III**
fortlaufend consecutive **IV U3**, 89
Fortschritt progress **II**
Fortsetzung follow-up **IV U3**, 92
Forum forum **II**
Foto photo; picture **I**
  auf dem **Foto**/den **Fotos** in the photo(s) **I**
  Fotos machen *to take photos **I**
  ins **Foto** laufen to photobomb **III**
Fotoapparat camera **II**
Fotoaufnahmen photo shoot **III**
Fotograf/-in photographer **III**
Fotografie photo **I**
fotografieren *to take photos **I**
Fotoshooting photo shoot **III**
Fotostory photo story **I**
Frage question **I**
Frageanhängsel question tag **II**
Fragebogen questionnaire **III**
fragen to ask **I**; to question **IV TS3**, 103
  Frage/Fragt nach … Ask about … **I**
  fragen nach to ask for **I**
Französisch French **II**
französisch French **II**
Frau woman, women *(pl)* **I**
Frau *(Anrede)* Mrs **I**
Fräulein *(Anrede)* Miss **III**
frei free **I**
Freiheit freedom *(no pl)* **III**; liberty **IV U3**, 74
Freiluft- outdoor **II**
sich den Tag **freinehmen** *to take the day off **IV U3**, 72
Freitag Friday **I**
Freizeit free time; leisure **I**

Freizeitzentrum leisure centre **I**
fremd strange **I**; foreign **IV U1**, 8
Fremdsprache foreign language **II**
fressen *to eat **I**
Freude fun **I**
Freudenfeuer bonfire **I**
sich **freuen** auf to look forward to **II**
sich **freuen** an to enjoy **II**
Freund *(in einer Paarbeziehung)* boyfriend **IV U2**, 55
Freund/-in friend **I**
Dafür sind **Freunde** da. That's what friends are for. **I**
Freundin *(in einer Paarbeziehung)* girlfriend **II**
freundlich friendly **II**
Freundschaft friendship **II**
Freundschaft schließen *to make friends **II**; *to become friends **IV AC2**, 41
frisch fresh **I**
uns **frisieren** *to do our hair **I**
froh happy **I**; glad **IV AC1**, 23
fröhlich happy; fun **I**
Front- front **III**
Frucht fruit **I**
früh early **I**
so **früh** this early **III**
Frühling spring **III**
Frühstück breakfast **I**
frühstücken *to have breakfast **I**
Frühstückszerealie cereal *(no pl)* **I**
Fuchs fox **II**
fühlen *to feel **I**
sich **fühlen** *to feel **I**
sich ausgeschlossen **fühlen** *to feel left out **II**
sich schlecht **fühlen** *to feel sick **II**
führen to guide; *to lead **III**; *to run **IV TS3**, 102
Führer/-in guide **II**
(sich) **füllen** to fill **III**
Füller pen **I**
Füllung filling **IV U3**, 75
fünf five **I**
fünfzehn fifteen **I**
Funktion function **IV TS3**, 103
funktionieren to work **II**; to work out **III**
für for **I**
für mich on my own **II**
Für wen …? Who … for? **I**
Furcht fear **II**
furchtbar awful **I**
(sich) **fürchten** *to be afraid (of) **IV U1**, 8
Fuß foot, feet *(pl)* **I**
zu **Fuß** on foot **II**
Fuß *(Längenmaß: 30,48 cm)* foot, feet *(pl)* **IV AC2**, 39
Fußball football **I**; soccer *(AE)* **IV U2**, 44
Fußboden floor **I**
Fußbodenheizung underfloor heating *(no pl)* **III**
Fußgelenk ankle **II**
Fußknöchel ankle **II**
Futter food **III**
füttern *to feed **III**

G

Gabel fork **III**
Gälisch Gaelic **III**
gälisch Gaelic **III**
Gang corridor **IV AC3**, 68
ganz all **I**
den **ganzen** Tag all day **II**
ganz quite **IV U1**, 14
ganz whole **I**
Garage garage **I**
garstig nasty **II**
Garten garden **I**; backyard **III**; yard **IV U2**, 43
Gast guest **III**
Gastfamilie host family **III**
Gaststätte restaurant **I**
Gate gate **IV U1**, 15
Gattung genre **III**
Geächtete/-r outlaw **III**
Gebärde gesture **IV TS1**, 33
Gebäude building **I**
geben *to give **I**
es **gibt** there is/are **I**
Gebiet area **II**
geboren werden *to be born **III**
Ge- und Verbote dos and don'ts **IV AC1**, 22
gebraten *(in der Pfanne)* fried **IV U3**, 75
gebrauchen to use **I**
gebrochen broken **I**
Gebühr fee **III**
Geburtsdatum date of birth **IV U1**, 13
Geburtstag birthday **I**
Alles Gute zum **Geburtstag**! Happy Birthday! **I**
Herzlichen Glückwunsch zum **Geburtstag**! Happy Birthday! **I**
Gedächtnis memory **II**
Gedanke thought **II**
Gedicht poem **I**
gedruckt print **II**
Sehr **geehrte** Dame, sehr **geehrter** Herr Dear Sir or Madam **III**
Gefahr danger **III**
gefährlich dangerous **I**
Mir **gefällt** … I like … **I**
gefälscht fake **IV TS1**, 35
Gefängnis prison **II**
Gefühl feeling **II**
Gefühls- emotional **III**
gegen against **II**; versus (vs.) **III**
Gegend region **II**
Gegensatz contrast **IV AC2**, 38
sich **gegenseitig** each other **I**
Gegenstand object **III**; item **IV U2**, 51
gegenüber stehen to face **IV TS1**, 31
gegenüber opposite **I**
Gegenwart present **II**
Gegenwarts- present **III**
Gehege run area **III**
geheim secret **III**
Geheimnis secret **II**; mystery **III**
geheimnisvoll mysterious **III**
gehen *to go; to walk **I**
aus dem Weg **gehen** to avoid **III**
ins Bett **gehen** *to go to bed **I**
nach unten **gehen** *to go down **I**
zu jmdm. nach Hause **gehen** *to go over to **II**
Wie **geht** es dir? How are you? **I**
Wie **geht** es euch? How are you? **I**
Wie **geht** es Ihnen? How are you? **I**
nicht **gehorchen** to disobey **III**
gehören (zu) to belong (to) **II**
gehören zu *to go with **I**
zueinander **gehören** *to go together **I**
Gehsteig sidewalk *(AE)* **IV U3**, 76
Gehweg sidewalk *(AE)* **IV U3**, 76
hier: **geil** epic **IV AC2**, 41
Geist ghost **II**; mind **III**
gelangweilt bored **I**
gelb yellow **I**
Geld money **I**
Geld sammeln to raise money **II**
Geld verdienen *to make money **I**
für/mit wenig **Geld** on a shoestring **IV U3**, 72
Geldschein bill *(AE)* **IV U3**, 76
Gelee jelly **I**
Gelegenheit chance **II**
als etw. **gelten** *to be considered (to be) sth **IV TS3**, 100
Gemälde painting **II**
gemein nasty **II**; mean **IV TS1**, 33
Gemeindezentrum community centre **I**
gemeinsam together **I**
gemeinsam haben *to have in common **III**
Gemüse vegetable **III**
genannt werden *to be called **III**
genau exactly **II**
genau hier right here **II**
genauso wie the same way as **II**
Generation generation **III**
Genie genius **II**
genießen to enjoy **II**
Gentleman gentleman, gentlemen *(pl)* **III**
genug enough **I**
genügend enough **I**
Geocaching geocaching **III**
geöffnet open **I**
Geografie geography **III**
Gepäck luggage *(no pl)* **IV U1**, 8
gerade straight **IV U1**, 17
gerade just; at the moment **I**; right now **II**
gerade rechtzeitig just in time **IV U3**, 72
geradeaus straight on **I**
geradewegs straight **IV U1**, 17
Gerät machine **I**; tool; gadget **III**
Geräusch sound **I**; noise **II**
gerecht fair **I**

Gericht dish **IV U2**, 45
Gern geschehen. You're welcome. **I**
gern haben to like **I**
 gern mögen to love **I**
 hätte/-st/-n/-t **gern** would like **I**
 hätte/-st-/-n/-t sehr **gern** would love **I**
 würde/-st/-n/-t **gern** would like **I**
 würde/-st/-n/-t sehr **gern** would love **I**
Gerümpel rubbish **I**
Geschäft shop **I**; business **III**; store *(AE)* **IV U2**, 44
Geschäftsmann businessman **IV U3**, 76
geschehen to happen **I**
Geschenk present **I**
Geschichte story, stories *(pl)* **I**; history **II**
 eine **Geschichte** langsam entwickeln to step into a story slowly **III**
geschichtlich historical **I**
Geschick skill **I**
geschlossen closed **IV U1**, 11
Geschmack flavor *(AE)* **IV U3**, 75
geschockt shocked **IV TS1**, 37
gut **geschrieben** well-written **IV TS3**, 104
 schlecht **geschrieben** badly-written **IV TS3**, 105
Geschwindigkeit speed **IV U3**, 89
Gesellschaft society; company **III**
gesellschaftlich social **IV U2**, 46
Gesetzlose/-r outlaw **III**
Gesicht face **I**
Gesichtsausdruck facial expression **III**
Gespräch dialogue; conversation **I**; talk **IV U3**, 92
 ein **Gespräch** dominieren to hog a conversation **III**
 ein **Gespräch** für sich in Beschlag nehmen to hog a conversation **III**
 hier: das **Gespräch** am Laufen halten *to keep the ball bouncing **III**
gesprochen spoken **II**
Gestalt figure **II**
gestalten to design **II**
Gestaltung design **II**
Geste gesture **IV TS1**, 33
gestern yesterday **II**
völlig **gestresst** sein *to be stressed out **III**
gesund healthy **I**
Gesundheit health **II**
Getränk drink **I**
Getreide corn **IV AC2**, 41
getrennt separate **II**
Gewalt violence *(no pl)* **III**
gewaltig huge **II**
gewaltsam violent **III**
gewalttätig violent **III**
Gewerbe industry **III**
Gewicht weight **III**
Gewinn prize **I**
gewinnen *to win **I**
 jmdn. für sich **gewinnen** *to win sb over **IV TS2**, 64
Gewinner/-in winner **I**; champion **III**
Gewissen conscience **IV TS1**, 31
sich an etw. **gewöhnen** *to get used to sth **IV U2**, 44
Gewohnheit custom **IV AC1**, 22
gewöhnlich usually **I**
gewohnt sein *to be used to *(+ -ing)* **III**
gewöhnt sein an *to be used to *(+ -ing)* **III**
Gig gig **III**
gigantisch gigantic **IV AC2**, 40
Gipsverband plaster cast **III**
Gitarre guitar **IV U1**, 19
Gitter grid **I**
glamourös glamorous **IV TS2**, 65
glänzen *to shine **II**
Glas glass **I**
glauben *to think; to believe **I**
gläubig religious **I**
glaubwürdig believable **IV U2**, 52
der/die/das **gleiche** the same **I**
gleich right away **I**; straight away **III**; immediately **IV TS2**, 64
 jetzt **gleich** right now **II**
gleichmäßig regular **I**
gleichzeitig at the same time **I**
Gliederung structure **III**
Glocke bell **II**
Glossar glossary **IV TS1**, 30
Glück haben *to be lucky **II**
 noch mal **Glück** gehabt saved by the bell **III**
 (viel) **Glück** good luck **IV U3**, 76
 Was für ein **Glück**! What luck! **III**
 … hat/haben **Glück**. … is/are lucky. **I**
glücklich happy **I**
glücklicherweise luckily **IV U2**, 44
Glücksbringer lucky charm **I**
Gold gold **III**
goldenes Zeitalter golden age **III**
Golf golf **III**
Götterspeise jelly **I**
Göttin goddess **IV U3**, 74
graben *to dig **II**
Grad Fahrenheit degree Fahrenheit (°F) **IV AC2**, 38
Grammatik grammar **II**
grau grey **I**
grausam cruel **III**
greifen to grab **II**
Grenze limit **III**
Griff knob **II**
groß big **I**; tall; high; large **II**
 große Sache big deal **IV U1**, 11
großartig great **I**; fantastic **II**
Großbuchstabe capital letter **I**
Größe size **I**
Großeltern grandparents *(pl)* **I**
Großstadt city **I**
großzügig generous **III**
grün green **I**
Grund reason **II**
 Es gibt keinen **Grund** zu … There's no need to … **IV TS1**, 36
Grund- basic **II**
gründen to found **III**; to start **III**
Grundlagen basics *(pl)* **III**
grundlegend basic **II**
Grundschule primary school **I**
Gruppe group **I**; team **II**
Gruppenzwang peer pressure **III**
gruppieren (um) to group (around) **III**
gruselig scary **II**
Gruß greeting **I**
 Grüße ausrichten (an) *to say hello (to) **I**
 Herzliche **Grüße** Best wishes **III**
 Herzliche **Grüße** *(am Briefende)* Love … **I**
 Liebe **Grüße** *(am Briefende)* Love … **I**
 Viele **Grüße** Best wishes **III**
 Viele **Grüße** … *(am Ende von Briefen und Mails)* Yours … **II**
grüßen *to say hello (to) **I**
Günstling favourite **III**
Gürtel belt **III**
gut good; fine **I**
 gut entwickelt well-developed **IV TS3**, 105
 gut geschrieben well-written **IV TS3**, 104
 gut sein in *to be good at **I**
 gute Leistungen erbringen *to do well **IV TS1**, 34
 Guten Morgen. Good morning. **I**
 Mir geht's **gut**. I'm fine. **I**
Guthaben credit **II**
Gymnasium grammar school **III**

H

Haar hair **IV TS2**, 64
Haar(e) hair **I**
Haarbürste hairbrush **III**
Haare hair **IV TS2**, 64
 unsere **Haare** machen *to do our hair **I**
haben *to have got; *to have **I**
 hätte/-st/-n/-t gern would like **I**
 hätte/-st-/-n/-t sehr gern would love **I**
 nicht ganz Unrecht **haben** *to have a point **III**
Hafen harbour **III**
Hafendamm pier **I**
Haft detention **IV AC3**, 68
Haggis *(schottisches Gericht aus in einem Schafsmagen gekochten Schafsinnereien und Haferschrot)* haggis **III**
Hähnchen chicken **I**
Hai shark **IV U1**, 16
halb half **I**
 halb *(bei Uhrzeitangaben)* half past **I**
 eine **halbe** Stunde half an hour **III**
Halbjahresferien half-term break **I**
Halbschwester half-sister **I**
Halbtotale *(Kameraeinstellung)* medium shot **IV U3**, 89
die **Hälfte** half, halves *(pl)* (of) **I**
Halle hall **II**
Hallo. Hello.; Hi.; Hey! **I**
Halskette necklace **III**

Halt stop **II**
halten *to hold; *to keep **I**
  halten von *to think of **I**
Haltestelle station **I**; stop **II**
Haltung attitude **IV U2**, 55; pose **IV U2**, 56
Hamburger burger **I**
Hammer hammer **II**
Hand hand **I**
  Klatsch/Klatscht in die **Hände**. Clap your hands. **I**
Handbuch planner **I**
sich **handeln** um *to be about **I**
Handgelenk wrist **II**
Händler merchant **II**
Handlung action **I**; plot **III**
Handlungsort location **II**
Handschuh glove **I**
Handy phone **I**; mobile **II**; cell phone *(AE)* **IV AC3**, 68
jmdn. **hänseln** to tease sb **III**
Happy End happy ending **III**
hart hard **II**; harsh **IV AC2**, 40
hassen to hate **II**
hässlich ugly **IV TS2**, 67
häufig often **I**
  häufig gefragt frequently asked **I**
Haupt- main **I**; lead **III**
die **Haupteinkaufsstraße** the high street **III**
Hauptfigur protagonist **IV TS1**, 30
Hauptrolle lead part **III**
Hauptsatz main clause **III**
Hauptstadt capital **II**
Hauptwort noun **I**
Haus house **I**
  nach **Hause** home **I**
  zu **Hause** at home **I**
  zu jmdm. nach **Hause** gehen *to go over to **II**
Hausarrest haben *to be grounded **III**
Hausaufgabe(n) homework **I**
Häuserblock block **IV U3**, 72
Haustier pet **I**
Haustür front door **II**
in jmds. **Haut** stecken *to be in sb's shoes **III**
He! Hey! **I**
heben to lift **IV U3**, 76
Heim home **I**
Heimatstadt hometown **IV U3**, 75
heimlich in secret **II**
Heimweh haben *to be homesick **IV U1**, 18
heiraten to marry **III**
heiß hot **III**
heißen *to be called **III**
  Ich **heiße** … My name is … **I**
  Wie **heißen** Sie? What's your name? **I**
  Wie **heißt** du? What's your name? **I**
Heizung heating **III**
Held hero, heroes *(pl)* **III**
Heldin heroine **III**
helfen to help **I**
hell bright **IV U3**, 72
Herangehensweise approach **IV TS2**, 66
heranzoomen (auf) to zoom in (on) **III**
heraus out **I**
herausfinden *to find; *to find out **I**; to work out **II**
herausfordern to challenge **IV TS3**, 101
Herausforderung challenge **II**
herausschneiden to edit out **III**
Es **stellte** sich **heraus**, dass … It turned out that … **IV U1**, 20
Herberge hostel **IV U1**, 10
Herd cooker **I**
herein in **I**
hereinfallen auf *to fall for **IV TS2**, 64
hereinkommen *to come in **III**
Herkunft origin **IV U1**, 19
Herr lord **III**
  feiner **Herr** gentleman, gentlemen *(pl)* **III**
  Herr der Raben raven master **II**
  Sehr geehrte Dame, sehr geehrter **Herr** Dear Sir or Madam **III**
Herr *(Anrede)* Mr **I**
herrisch bossy **III**
Herrschaft reign **III**
herrschen to rule; to reign **III**
die **Herrschenden** those in power **III**
herstellen to produce **III**
um … **herum** around **I**
herumschleichen to sneak around **II**
sich **herumtreiben** (mit) *to hang out (with) *(infml)* **III**
herunter down **II**
herunterfallen *to fall off **II**
herunterkommen *to come down **I**
herunterladen *(aus dem Internet)* to download **II**
herunternehmen *to take off **I**
herunterrollen to roll off **II**
hervorheben to stress **III**
Herz heart **II**
Herzliche Grüße Best wishes **III**
  Herzliche Grüße *(am Briefende)* Love … **I**
heute today **I**
  heute Abend 2nite *(= tonight)* **I**; tonight **IV TS1**, 31
  heute Nachmittag this afternoon **II**
  heute Nacht tonight **IV TS1**, 31
heutig present **III**
Hi. Hi.; Hey! **I**
hier here **I**
  genau **hier** right here **II**
  Hier ist … Here's … **I**
High School *(weiterführende Schule in den USA, Oberstufe)* high school *(AE)* **IV U2**, 43
Highlight highlight **II**
Hilfe help **I**
  ohne fremde **Hilfe** alone **I**
hilflos helpless **I**
hilfreich useful; helpful **I**
hilfsbereit helpful **I**
Himmel sky **III**
hinauf up **II**
hinaus out **I**
hinausfließen to flow out **II**
hinausgehen *to go out **III**
hinein inside **I**
hineingehen to enter **II**
hineingelangen *to get into **I**
den Leser/die Leserin in die Geschichte/Handlung **hineinziehen** *to draw the reader into the story/action **III**
Hin- und Rückfahrkarte return ticket **III**
hinfallen *to fall over; *to fall **I**
wo ich **hingehöre** where I belong **IV U1**, 16
Hingucker eye-catcher **IV TS2**, 65
hinkommen *to get there **I**
hinnehmen to accept **IV U1**, 16
sich **hinsetzen** *to sit down **I**
hinten at the back of **II**
hinter behind **I**
hinterfragen to question **IV TS3**, 103
Hintergrund background **I**
Hintergrund- backing **III**
hinterhergehen to follow **II**
Hinterhof backyard **III**
hinüber over; across **I**
hinübergehen zu *to go over to **II**
hinunter down **II**
hinunterfallen *to fall off **II**; *to fall down **III**
hinuntergehen *to go down **I**
hinunterrollen to roll off **II**
Hinweis clue **II**; hint **III**
hinzufügen to add **I**
hissen *to fly flaɪ **IV AC2**, 39
historisch historical **I**; historic **III**
Hobby hobby, hobbies *(pl)* **I**
hoch tall; high **II**
hochheben to lift **IV U3**, 76
hochleben lassen *to give the bumps **I**
höchst- highly **IV TS2**, 65
Hochzeit wedding **I**
Hockey hockey **II**
Hof yard **IV U2**, 43
Hofdame lady-in-waiting **III**
hoffen to hope **I**
Hoffnung hope **II**
hoffnungsvoll hopeful **I**
höflich polite **I**
  Sei/Seid **höflich**. Be polite. **I**
Höhepunkt highlight **II**; climax **III**
Höhle cave **III**
holen *to get **I**; to fetch **IV U1**, 17
Holz wood **III**
  aus **Holz** wooden **III**
hölzern wooden **III**
Homepage homepage **I**
Honig honey **III**
Hoppla! Oops! **I**
Hör- audio **I**
horchen auf to listen for **I**
Hören listening **I**
hören *to hear **I**
  Ich habe **gehört**, dass … I hear … **I**
Horn horn **III**
Horror horror **III**

Horrorfilm horror III
Horrorgeschichte horror III
Hör-/Sehverstehen viewing I
Hose trousers *(pl)* III
kurze **Hose** shorts *(pl)* II
Hosentasche pocket III
Hospital hospital II
Hotel hotel II
hübsch beautiful II; pretty III; lovely IVTS2, 65
Huch! Oops! I
jmdn. **Huckepack** nehmen *to give sb a piggyback IV U1, 16
Hügel hill III
Huhn chicken I
Hülle wrapping I
Humor humour *(no pl)* III
Sinn für **Humor** sense of humour *(no pl)* III
Hund dog I
den **Hund** ausführen to walk the dog I
mit dem **Hund** spazieren gehen to walk the dog I
Ich bin **hundemüde**. I'm dog-tired. I
Hunderte (von) hundreds of III
hungrig hungry I
hüpfen to bounce III
Hurraruf cheer IV U2, 52
Husten cough II
Hut hat I
hüten to look after I
Hymne anthem III

I

ich I; me I
Ich bin aus … I'm from … I
Ich bin Engländer/-in. I'm English. I
Ich heiße … My name is … I
Ich mache … nicht gern. I don't like … I
Ich mag … nicht. I don't like … I
Ich möchte … I'd like to … *(= I would like to)* I
Ich weiß (es) nicht! I don't know! I
Ich würde gern … I'd like to … *(= I would like to)* I
ich würde lieber I'd rather III
Ich-Erzähler/-in first person narrator III
Idee idea I
sich **identifizieren** mit to identify with III
Identität identity II
Idiot/-in idiot II
if-Satz if-clause III
Igel hedgehog III
ignorieren to ignore III
ihm him I
ihn him I
ihnen them I
ihr you; u *(= you)* I
Ihr/-e your I; yours II
ihr/-e her; its I
ihr/-e *(Pl.)* their I
illegal illegal III
im in; on I
im Begriff sein, etw. zu tun *to be about to do sth IV AC3, 69
im Chor in chorus IVTS1, 33
im Innern inside I
im Moment at the moment I
im Weg sein/stehen *to be in the way I
Imbiss snack I
Imbissstube snack bar I
immer always I
für **immer** forever II
immer noch still I
immer wieder over and over again III
immer wieder tun *to keep ki:p IV U2, 44
immerhin after all I
Immigrant/-in immigrant IV AC2, 38
Immigration immigration IV U1, 13
Imperativ imperative III
Impression impression IV U2, 42
in in; on; at; to; into; inside I
in Cornwall Cornish III
in der Nähe von near I
in der Straße in the street I
in Kontakt bleiben *to keep in touch IV U2, 44
in Not in need II
in … hinein into I
in Ordnung OK; fine I
indem as I
Inder/-in Indian I
Indianer/-in Native American; Indian IV U2, 45
indianisch Native American; Indian IV U2, 45
indirekt indirect IV U1, 11
indirekte Rede indirect speech IV U1, 11
indisch Indian I
individuell individual II
Individuum individual IV U2, 56
Industrie industry III
Infinitiv infinitive I
Informatik IT *(= Information Technology)* III
Information information *(no pl)* I
Informationen information *(no pl)* I
Informationsblatt leaflet IV AC1, 23
Informationstechnik IT *(= Information Technology)* III
informativ informative IV U2, 56
informell informal IV AC4, 107
Ingenieur/-in engineer IVTS3, 101
Inhalt content IV U2, 56
Inlineskates fahren to skate I
Inlineskatefahren inline skating I
Inlineskates skates *(pl)* I
inmitten among III
innen inside I
inoffiziell unofficial III
Insel island III
inserieren to advertise IVTS2, 64
inspirieren to inspire IV U3, 70
Installateur/-in plumber III
Instruktion instruction I
inszenieren to stage IVTS3, 102
Inszenierung production IVTS1, 30
intelligent smart III
interessant interesting I
Interesse interest II
(sich) **interessieren** to interest II
sich **interessieren** (für) to care (about) II
sich **interessieren** für *to be interested in II
interessiert sein an *to be interested in II
Interkulturelles Across cultures I
international international I; multi-ethnic II
Internet internet I
Internetauftritt website I
Internettagebuch blog III
Interview interview I
interviewen to interview I
involvieren to involve IVTS3, 102
irgendein/-e/-er any I
irgendwelche any I
irgendwo anywhere; somewhere II
Irisch Irish III
irisch Irish III
ironisch ironic IV U2, 56
irreal unreal IV U1, 19
sich **irren** *to be wrong I

J

ja yes; yeah *(infml)* I
Jacke jacket III
jagen to chase I
Jahr year I
Jahrbuch yearbook II
Jahreszeit season IV U2, 56
Jahrhundert century II
18-jährig 18-year-old II
11-Jährige/-r 11-year-old II
Januar January I
je … desto the … the II
jedenfalls anyway II
jede/-r/-s every; each I
jeder everyone I; everybody II
jede Menge lots (of) I
jedes Mal, wenn whenever II
jedoch however IV U3, 76; though IV AC4, 106
jemals ever II
jemand somebody I; someone II
jemand anderes anyone else II
jene those I
jenes that I
jetzt now I
jetzt gleich right now II
Job job I
Joghurt yoghurt I
Jonglieren juggling II
Jubel cheer IV U2, 52
jubeln to cheer II
jüdisch Jewish IV U3, 75
Jugend youth IVTS1, 36
Jugend- teen II; teenage IVTS1, 31
jugendlich teenage IVTS1, 31

Jugendliche/-r teenager **I**; teen **III**; kid **IV U2**, 42
Juli July **I**
jung young **I**
Junge boy **I**
Juni June **I**
Juwel jewel **III**

K

Kaffee coffee **I**
Kaiser emperor **III**
Kaiserreich empire **III**
Kaktus cactus **IV AC2**, 38
Kalender planner **I**; calendar **III**
kalt cold **II**
kalt stellen *to leave it to cool **I**
Kamelrennen camel racing **II**
Kamera camera **II**
mit der **Kamera** festgehalten caught on camera **II**
Kameraeinstellung shot **II**
Kamin chimney **III**
Kampf fight **II**; battle **III**
kämpfen *to fight **II**
Kanadier/-in Canadian **IV AC4**, 106
kanadisch Canadian **IV AC4**, 106
Kaninchen rabbit **I**
Kapitän/-in captain **I**
Kapitel unit **I**; chapter **III**
kaputt broken **I**; out of order **IV TS1**, 36
Karneval carnival **II**
Karotte carrot **I**
Karren cart **IV U3**, 75
Karriere career **III**
Karte card **I**
Kartenschalter ticket office **III**
Kartoffel potato, potatoes *(pl)* **III**
Kartoffelchip crisp *(BE)* **I**
Kartoffelpüree mashed potatoes *(pl)* **III**
Käse cheese **I**
Kasten box **I**
Katastrophe disaster **II**
Kategorie category **II**
Katze cat **I**
kaufen *to buy; *to get **I**
Käufer/-in buyer **I**; shopper **IV U2**, 48
Kaufmann merchant **II**
Kaugummi chewing gum **IV U1**, 15
kaum hardly **IV TS1**, 34
kein/-e no **I**
kein Wunder no wonder **IV U2**, 44
keine Ahnung no idea **II**
keine Ahnung haben *to have no clue **IV AC2**, 41
Keine Sorge! Don't worry! **I**
kein/-e/-en not … any **I**
Keks biscuit **I**
Kelte/Keltin Celt **III**
keltisch Celtic **II**
kennen *to know **I**
kennenlernen *to get to know **III**
Kerl guy **II**
Kerze candle **I**
Kerzenlicht candlelight *(no pl)* **II**
keuchen to gasp **IV U3**, 72
Kfz-Mechaniker/-in mechanic **II**
Kilometer kilometre (km) **III**
Kilt kilt **III**
Kind child, children *(pl)* **I**; kid **IV U2**, 42
Kinderarbeit child labor *(AE)* **IV U2**, 48
Kino cinema **I**; movie theater *(AE)* **IV U2**, 44
Kirche church **I**
Kiste box **I**
Klammer bracket **III**
Klang sound **I**
klappen to work out **III**
klar clear **I**
Klarstellung clarification **IV U1**, 15
Klärung clarification **IV U1**, 15
Klasse group; class **I**
Klasse *(in einer englischen Schule)* tutor group **I**
Ausstellung in der **Klasse** class display **I**
Klassenarbeit test **I**
Klassenkamerad/-in classmate **I**
Klassenlehrer/-in tutor **I**
Klassenposter class poster **I**
Klassenzimmer classroom **I**
klassisch classical **IV U3**, 72
klatschen to clap **I**
Klatsch/Klatscht in die Hände. Clap your hands. **I**
Klavier piano **IV U3**, 77
Kleid dress **III**
Kleider clothes *(pl)* **I**
Kleidergröße size **I**
Kleiderordnung dress code **IV U2**, 43
Kleidersammlung clothing drive **IV U2**, 51
Kleiderschrank wardrobe **I**
begehbarer **Kleiderschrank** walk-in closet **IV U2**, 44
Kleidung clothes *(pl)* **I**; outfit **II**; clothing **IV U2**, 51
klein small; little **I**; tiny **III**
Klempner/-in plumber **III**
Klettern climbing **II**
klettern to climb **I**
Klick click **II**
Klicken click **II**
Kliff cliff **III**
Klima climate **IV U1**, 18
Klimaanlage air-conditioning **IV U1**, 17
klingeln *to ring **I**
klingen to sound **I**
Klippe cliff **III**
klonen to clone **III**
Klub club **I**
klug clever **II**; smart **III**
Knacken crack **III**
knackend cracking **III**
knapp close **I**
Das war **knapp**! That was close! **I**
Knoblauch garlic **IV U1**, 11
sich den Knöchel verrenken to twist your ankle **II**
Knopf button **IV U1**, 17
Koala koala **III**
Koch-AG Cooking Club **I**
Kochen cooking **I**
kochen to cook **II**
Koffer suitcase **IV U1**, 9
Kofferraum boot **III**; trunk *(AE)* **IV U3**, 76
Kokosnuss coconut **II**
Kollektion collection **II**
Kolonie colony **II**
Kolonist/-in colonist **IV AC2**, 41
Kombination combination **IV U3**, 75
kombinieren to combine **IV U3**, 75
komfortabel comfortable **II**
Komiker/-in comedian **II**
komisch funny **III**; odd **IV U1**, 19
jmdn. **komisch** anschauen *to give sb funny looks **III**
Komitee committee **IV U2**, 48
kommen *to come **I**
kommen nach *to get to **I**
kommen zu *to get to **I**
Komm jetzt! Come on! **I**
Komm schon! Come on! **I**
Kommentar comment **II**
kommentieren to comment (on) **II**
Kommunikation communication **II**
kommunizieren to communicate **II**
Komödie comedy **III**
Komparativ comparative **II**
komplett complete **IV AC2**, 41
kompliziert complicated **IV TS3**, 102
Kompositum *(zusammengesetztes Wort)* compound word **II**
Kompromiss compromise **II**
Kompromisse eingehen to compromise **III**
Konferenz conference **IV U3**, 72
Konfitüre jam **III**
konfrontiert werden mit to face **IV TS1**, 31
konfus confused **III**
König king **I**
Königin queen **II**
königlich royal **I**
königlicher Leibgardist Beefeater **II**
konkurrieren (mit) to compete (with) **III**
konkurrierend competitive **III**
können can **I**; *to be able to (do sth) **II**
kann nicht can't **I**; cannot **II**
können nicht can't **I**; cannot **II**
könnte/-n could **II**
könnte/-n (vielleicht) might **IV U2**, 50
(vielleicht) **können** may **II**
Es **könnte/-n** auch … sein. It might as well be … **III**
konnte/-n could **III**
Konsequenz consequence **IV AC3**, 68
Kontakt contact **II**
in **Kontakt** bleiben *to keep in touch **IV U2**, 44

in **Kontakt** bleiben (mit) to stay in touch (with) II
kontaktfreudig outgoing IV U1, 19
Kontinent continent IV U3, 74
kontinuierlich steady IV U1, 17
Kontrast contrast IV AC2, 38
Kontrolle control IV U1, 9
kontrollieren to check I; to control IV U2, 50
gegenseitig **kontrollieren** to peer-edit II
Kontrollpunkt checkpoint IV U1, 16
Konversation conversation I
(sich) **konzentrieren** to concentrate IV U1, 17
sich **konzentrieren** (auf) to focus (on) II
Konzept draft I
Konzert concert IV U2, 57
Kopf head I
etw. aus dem **Kopf** bekommen *to get sth out of one's head III
Kopfhörer headphones *(pl)* II
Kopfschmerzen headache *(no pl)* II
Kopfweh headache *(no pl)* II
kopieren to copy I
Korbball netball I
Koreaner/-in Korean II
Koreanisch Korean II
koreanisch Korean II
Korn corn IV AC2, 41
Körper body III
menschlicher **Körper** human body II
korrekt correct; right I
Korridor hall III; hallway IV U2, 43; corridor IV AC3, 68
Korrigiere/**Korrigiert** … Correct … I
kosten *to cost I
Es **kostet** …/Sie **kosten** … It's …/They're … I
Wie viel **kostet**/**kosten** …? How much is/are …? I
kostenlos free I; for free IV U3, 72
köstlich delicious IV U3, 75
Kostüm costume I; fancy dress II
Das ist zum **Kotzen**. It sucks. *(slang)* IV AC4, 107
Krachen crack III
Kraft power; energy III; force IV U1, 19
Krampf cramp II
Kran crane III
krank sick II; ill III
Krankenhaus hospital II
Krankenpfleger nurse III
Krankenschwester nurse III
Krankenwagen ambulance III
Kraut herb IV U1, 11
kreativ creative I
Kreis circle I
sich im **Kreis** drehen *to go round in circles III
kreischen to scream II
Kreuz cross III
kreuzen to cross II
Kreuzung intersection IV U3, 70
Krieg war IV U1, 20
Krieger warrior III
Krimi detective III
Kriminalfilm detective III
Kriminalität crime III
Kriminalroman detective III
Kriminelle/-r criminal III
Kriterium criterion, criteria *(pl)* III
Kritik rating III
kritisch critical IV TS3, 103
Krone crown III
Kronjuwelen crown jewels II
Küche kitchen I
Kuchen cake; pie I
Küchenschrank cupboard I
Kuh cow III
kühl cool IV AC2, 38
Kühlschrank fridge I
Kultur culture I
kulturell cultural IV AC2, 38
Kummerkastentante agony aunt II
sich **kümmern** (um) to care (about) II
sich **kümmern** um to look after I
sich um jmdn. **kümmern** *to take care of sb III
Kunde/**Kundin** customer III
Kunst art II
Künstler/-in artist IV U3, 74
Kunstunterricht Art I
Kurs course II
kurz short I
kurz vor on the brink of III
Kurzantwort short answer I
Kurzform short form I
Kurznachricht text (message) I
Küste shore II; coastline III; coast IV U1, 10
Küstenverlauf coastline III
Küstenweg coastal path III

L

Labor laboratory IV AC3, 68
Lächeln smile I
lächeln to smile I
lachen to laugh I
Laden shop I; store *(AE)* IV U2, 44
Lady lady III
Lage location II
Lage (aus) layer (of) III
Lagerfeuer bonfire I
Lamm lamb I
Lämmchen lamb I
Lampe light II
Land country, countries *(pl)*; land I; countryside III; state IV AC2, 39
auf dem **Land** in the country IV AC2, 40
landen to end up; to land II; to touch down IV TS3, 101
landesweit national I
Landkarte map I
ländlich rural IV AC2, 38
Landschaft landscape III; scenery IV AC2, 40
Landung landing IV U1, 15
Landwirt/-in farmer II
lang long I
(nicht) **länger** (not) any longer III
… **lang** for … II
langsam slow I
eine Geschichte **langsam** entwickeln to step into a story slowly III
langweilig boring I
Laptop laptop II
Lärm noise II
lassen *to let I; *to leave II
Lass/**Lasst** uns … Let's … I
Lassi lassi I
lästig inconvenient IV TS3, 100
Lastwagen lorry IV U3, 79
Lastwagenladung truckload IV TS2, 66
Lauf run II
Laufbahn career III
Laufen running II
laufen *to run; to walk I; *to be on II
ins Foto **laufen** to photobomb III
Läufer/-in runner II
Laune mood II
laut loud I; noisy III
laut vorsingen *to sing out loud III
läuten *to ring I
Layout layout III
Leben life, lives *(pl)* II
leben to live I
lebendig lively II
Lebensmittel food I
Lebensstandard standard of living IV AC2, 40
seinen **Lebensunterhalt** bestreiten (mit) *to make a living (from) IV U3, 79
hier: **Leckerli** treat III
leer empty III
legen *to put I; to place III; *to lay lei IV U3, 89
Lege/**Legt** es in … Put it in … I
Legende legend III
jmdm. eine **Lehre**/**Lektion** erteilen *to teach somebody a lesson II
lehren *to teach II
Lehrer/-in teacher I; instructor II
königlicher **Leibgardist** Beefeater II
leicht easy I; light III
Leichtathletik athletics *(no pl)* IV U1, 10
es **leid** sein (zu) *to be tired of IV U2, 46
leid tun *to be sorry I
Tut mir **leid**! Sorry!; I'm sorry! I
Leider … I'm afraid … IV U2, 44
leihen *to lend III
leise quiet I
sich **leisten** to afford III
gute **Leistungen** erbringen *to do well IV TS1, 34
leistungsorientiert competitive III
leiten to guide III; *to run IV TS3, 102
Leiter ladder II
Lektion unit I

jmdm. eine Lehre/**Lektion** erteilen *to teach somebody a lesson **II**
Lernen studies *(pl)* **II**
lernen *to learn **I**; to study **III**
viel zu **lernen** a lot to learn **I**
auswendig **lernen** *to learn … by heart **I**
Lesen reading **I**
vor dem **Lesen** pre-reading **I**
lesen *to read **I**
noch einmal **lesen** *to reread **III**
Leser/-in reader **I**
den **Leser**/die **Leserin** in die Geschichte/Handlung hineinziehen *to draw the reader into the story/action **III**
letzte/-r/-s last **I**; final **III**
letztlich finally **II**
leuchtend bright **IV U3**, 72
Leute people *(pl)* **I**
Licht light **II**
Lichtblitz flash **III**
lieb nice **I**
Lieber … Dear … **I**
Liebe … *(Anrede in Briefen)* Dear … **I**
Liebe Grüße *(am Briefende)* Love … **I**
Liebe love **III**
lieben to love **I**
Ich **liebe** dich. I love you. **I**
Ich **liebe** … I love … **I**
lieber better **I**
ich würde **lieber** I'd rather **III**
Liebesfilm romance **III**
Liebesgeschichte romance **III**
Lieblings- favourite **I**
Mein/e **Lieblings …** My favourite … **I**
Was ist dein/-e **Lieblings**…? What's your favourite …? **I**
Lied song **I**
Liedtext (song) lyrics *(pl)* **III**
liegen *to lie **II**; *to be located **IV U3**, 73
gelegen sein *to be located **IV U3**, 73
Lifestyle lifestyle **III**
Lift elevator *(AE)* **IV U2**, 44
lila purple **I**
Limit limit **III**
Limonade lemonade **I**
Lineal ruler **I**
Linie line **I**
Link link **II**
linke/-r/-s left **I**
auf der **linken** Seite on the left **I**
links on the left; left **I**
Liste list **I**
eine **Liste** von a set of **III**
Liste mit häufig gestellten Fragen FAQ **III**
Liter litre (l) **III**
live live **III**
Loch hole **II**
locker laid-back **III**; easy-going **IV U1**, 19
Löffel spoon **III**
Logik logic **III**
lokal local **III**
LOL LOL (= laughing out loud) **II**
Londoner/-in Londoner **I**
Lord lord **III**
Los ticket **I**
Los! Go on! **IV U2**, 55
löschen to delete **III**
lösen to solve **III**
losgehen *to leave **II**
loslassen *to let go (of) **II**
Lösung solution **II**
Löwe lion **II**
Lücke gap **I**
Luft air **III**
Luft holen *to take a breath **III**
tief **Luft** holen to gasp **IV U3**, 72
Lüge lie **III**
lügen to lie **II**
die Lunge the lungs *(pl)* **III**; lung **IV U3**, 71
lustig funny; fun **I**
Luxus luxury **IV AC2**, 40

M

Maat mate **I**
machen *to do; *to make **I**
Fotos **machen** *to take photos **I**
sich Notizen **machen** *to take notes **I**
Machen wir uns doch nichts vor. Let's face it. **IV TS1**, 32
Machst du so …? Is this how you (do) …? **I**
Mir **macht** es nichts aus (zu) … I don't mind … *(+ -ing)* **III**
Macht power **III**; force **IV U1**, 19
mächtig powerful **III**
Mädchen girl **I**
Magen stomach **II**
Magie magic **IV U1**, 19
magisch magical **III**
Mahlzeit meal **II**
Mai May **I**
mailen to mail **II**
Mais corn **IV AC2**, 41
Mal time **II**
malen to paint **I**
Malerei painting **II**
Mama mum **I**; mummy **III**; mom *(AE)* **IV AC2**, 41
Mami mummy **III**
Mammutbaum redwood tree **IV AC2**, 39
manchmal sometimes **I**
Manga *(japanischer Comic)* manga **II**
Mango mango **I**
Manieren manners *(pl)* **IV AC1**, 23
Mann man, men *(pl)* **I**; dude *(coll)* **IV AC2**, 41
Mannschaftsführer/-in captain **I**
Mäppchen pencil-case **I**
Mappe folder **I**
Marathon marathon **II**
Marke brand **IV TS2**, 64
Markt market **I**
Marmelade jam **III**
Marmelade aus Zitrusfrüchten marmalade **III**
marschieren to march **III**
März March **I**
Maschine machine **I**
Maske mask **IV U1**, 16
massiv massive **IV AC2**, 41
Match match **II**
Material material **II**
Mathe Maths **II**
Mathematik Maths **II**
Matrose sailor **I**
Mauer wall **I**
Maus/Mäuse mouse *(sg)*, mice *(pl)* **I**
Mechaniker/-in mechanic **II**
Medien media **II**
Medikamente medicine *(no pl)* **III**
Medizin medicine *(no pl)* **III**
Meer sea **I**
Meerschweinchen guinea pig **I**
mehr more **I**
nicht **mehr** no more **IV AC4**, 107
(nicht) **mehr** (not) any longer **III**
mehr … als more … than **I**
mehrere several **II**
Mehrzahl plural **I**
meiden to stay away from **II**; to avoid **III**
Meile *(brit. Längenmaß)* mile **II**
mein/-e my **I**
Mein/e Lieblings… My favourite … **I**
mein/-er/-e/-es mine **II**
meinen *to mean **II**
Meinung opinion **II**
anderer **Meinung** sein to disagree **III**
einer **Meinung** sein (mit) to agree (with) **II**
seine **Meinung** ändern to change one's mind **III**
die meisten (the) most **I**
der/die/das meiste (the) most **I**
meistens usually **I**
Meisterschaft championship **IV U2**, 56
Meldung report **II**; news report **III**
melken to milk **III**
Melodie tune; melody **III**
eine Menge a lot of **I**
jede **Menge** lots (of) **I**
Mensch person, people *(pl)* **I**; human **IV TS3**, 100
Menschen people *(pl)* **I**
Menschenmenge crowd **II**
menschlicher Körper human body **II**
sich merken to remember **I**
Merkmal feature **III**
merkwürdig strange **I**; weird **II**; funny **III**
sich messen (mit) to compete (with) **III**
Messer knife, knives *(pl)* **III**
Meter metre **II**
mich me **I**
mieten to rent (out) **III**
Milch milk **I**
Milliardär/-in billionaire **IV AC2**, 39

Milliarde billion **III**
Million million **II**
Ich habe das schon eine **Million** Mal gemacht. I've done this a million times before. **II**
Millionär/-in millionaire **III**
vom Tellerwäscher zum **Millionär** rags to riches **IV U3**, 79
mindestens at least **II**
Mine mine **III**
Mini- mini **II**
Minute minute **I**
mir me **I**
Mir geht's gut. I'm fine. **I**
mischen to shuffle; to mix (up) **III**
Mission mission **IV TS3**, 101
misstrauisch suspicious **IV U1**, 13
missverstanden misunderstood **III**
mit with **I**
mit allen Mitteln by any means **IV U3**, 70
mit dabei along for the ride **IV U2**, 44
mit *(dem Fahrrad)* by *(bike)* **I**
mitbekommen *(ugs.)* *to catch **III**
mitbringen *to bring; *to take **I**
miteinander together **I**
Mitglied member **II**
mithalten (mit) *to keep up (with) **II**
mitkriegen *(ugs.)* *to catch **III**
Mitleid haben mit *to feel sorry for **III**
mitmachen *to be in **II**; to enter **II**
mitnehmen *to take **I**; to pick up **III**
Mitschüler/-in classmate **I**
mitsingen *to sing along **III**
Mitspieler/-in player **II**
Mittagessen lunch **I**
Mittagspause lunch break **I**; lunchtime **IV AC3**, 68
Mittagszeit lunchtime **IV AC3**, 68
Mitte middle **I**
mitteilen *to tell **I**
mit allen **Mitteln** by any means **IV U3**, 70
mittel medium **IV U3**, 89
mittelalterlich medieval **III**
mittelgroß medium **IV U3**, 89
Mittelschule *(weiterführende Schule in den USA, Mittelstufe)* middle school *(AE)* **IV U2**, 43
mitten im Nirgendwo in the middle of nowhere **IV U2**, 46
mitten in … stecken stuck in the middle of … **III**
Mitternacht midnight **III**
Mittwoch Wednesday **I**
Mix mix **III**
Mobiltelefon mobile **II**; cell phone *(AE)* **IV AC3**, 68
Modalverb modal **II**
Mode fashion **II**
Model model **I**
Modell model **I**
Modeln modelling **III**
Moderator/-in presenter **I**
modern modern **II**; up-to-date **IV TS3**, 100
mogeln to cheat **IV AC3**, 68
mögen to like; *to be into; to want (to) **I**
gern **mögen** to love **I**
nicht **mögen** to hate **II**; to dislike **IV U2**, 47
Du **magst** … You're into … **I**
Ich **mag** dich. I love you. **I**
Ich **mag** … I like … **I**
Ich **mag** … nicht. I don't like … **I**
Ich **mag** … total gern. I love … **I**
Ich **möchte** … I'd like to … *(= I would like to)* **I**
Möchten Sie …? Would you like …? **II**
Möchtest du …? Would you like …? **II**
Möchtet ihr …? Would you like …? **II**
möglich possible **I**
möglicherweise probably **II**
Möglichkeit chance **II**; possibility; option **III**
Möhre carrot **I**
Moment moment **II**
im **Moment** at the moment **I**
Monarch/-in monarch **III**
Monat month **II**
Mond moon **IV TS3**, 100
Mondlandung moon landing **IV TS3**, 100
Mondlicht moonlight **III**
Monster monster **I**
Montag Monday **I**
montags on Mondays **I**
Monument monument **III**
Mord murder **III**
Morgen morning **I**
Guten **Morgen**. Good morning. **I**
morgen tomorrow **I**
morgens in the mornings **I**
Motiv motive **IV TS1**, 32
Motivation motivation **IV TS1**, 31
motivieren to motivate **I**
Motto theme **I**
Mountainbikefahren mountain biking **III**
müde tired **I**
es **müde** sein (zu) *to be tired of **IV U2**, 46
sich **Mühe** geben to push oneself **III**
Müll rubbish **I**; trash *(AE)* **IV TS2**, 67
Müll herumliegen lassen to litter **IV AC1**, 22
Mund mouth **I**
mit vollem **Mund** sprechen to talk with your mouth full **IV AC1**, 22
Münze coin **I**
Münzgeld change **IV U3**, 76
murmeln to mutter **IV U1**, 10
Museum museum **I**
Museumsrundgang gallery walk **I**
Musik music **I**
Musik- musical **III**
musikalisch musical **III**
Musiker/-in musician **II**
Musikgruppe band **III**
Müsli muesli **III**
müssen must **I**; *to have to **II**
(tun) **müssen** to need (to do) **I**
nicht **müssen** needn't **I**
Muster pattern **III**; sample **IV TS2**, 64
mutig brave **I**
Mutter mother **I**
Muttersprache first language **II**
Mutti mummy **III**
mysteriös mysterious **III**
Mysterium mystery **III**

N

nach to **I**
nach draußen outside; out **I**
nach drinnen inside **I**
nach Hause home **I**
nach oben up; upstairs **II**
nach unten down **II**; downstairs **II**
nach *(bei Uhrzeitangaben)* past **I**
nach *(zeitlich)* after **I**
Nachbar/-in neighbour *(BE)* **I**
Nachbarschaft neighbourhood **III**; neighborhood *(AE)* **IV U2**, 43
nachdenken *to think **I**
Warte/Wartet und **denk/denkt nach**. Stop and think **I**
nacherzählen *to retell **I**
nachjagen to chase **I**
Nachmittag afternoon **I**
heute **Nachmittag** this afternoon **II**
nachmittags *(Uhrzeit)* p.m. **I**
Nachricht message **I**
eine **Nachricht** entgegennehmen *to take a message **I**
eine **Nachricht** hinterlassen *to leave a message **I**
Nachrichten news *(sg)* **II**
Nachrichtenbeitrag news report **III**
nachschauen to look up **I**
nachschlagen to look up **I**
Nachsitzen detention **IV AC3**, 68
nachspielen to act out **II**
nachspüren to trace **I**
nächste/-r/-s next **I**
der/die **Nächste(n)** next **I**
als **Nächstes** next **I**
am **nächsten** Tag the next day **II**
Nacht night **I**
die ganze **Nacht** all night **I**
heute **Nacht** tonight **IV TS1**, 31
über **Nacht** overnight **III**
Nachtisch pudding **I**
Nachtwanderung night walk **II**
nackt bare **III**; naked **IV U3**, 72
Nahaufnahme close-up **II**
in der **Nähe** von near **I**
nahe near **I**; close **II**
Name name **I**
Namenstag name day **I**
Nase nose **II**
die **Nase** voll haben (von) *to be fed up (with) **III**

Nashorn rhino **III**
nass wet **II**
national national **I**
Natur nature **II**
Natur- natural **IV U2**, 56
natürlich natural **IV U2**, 56
natürlich of course **I**; needless to say **IV U3**, 76
Naturwissenschaft science **IV TS3**, 100
Naturwissenschaften Science **II**
neben next to **I**; besides; by **III**
(von) nebenan next door **III**
Nebenraum side room **IV U1**, 13
nee nope *(infml)* **IV AC4**, 107
Neffe nephew **IV U1**, 13
negativ negative **III**
nehmen *to take **I**
(ein Bonbon) **nehmen** *to have *(a sweet)* **I**
neidisch sein (auf) *to be jealous (of) **I**
nein no **I**
benennen to name **I**
nennen to name; to call **I**
Nerd *(Person, die intelligent, aber sozial unbeholfen ist)* nerd **IV TS2**, 65
jemandem auf die Nerven gehen *to get on people's nerves **I**
nervös nervous **II**
nett nice **I**; friendly **II**
Netz net **II**; web **III**
soziale Netzwerke social media **IV U2**, 46
soziales Netzwerk social network **II**
neu new **I**
neu schreiben *to rewrite **III**
neueste/-r/-s latest **IV U1**, 11
Neuigkeiten news *(sg)* **II**
neulich the other day **IV U1**, 20
neun nine **I**
Neuzugang arrival **IV TS2**, 66
New Yorker/-in New Yorker **IV U3**, 75
nicht not **I**
auch **nicht** not … either **IV AC4**, 107
nicht gehorchen to disobey **III**
nicht mehr not any more **I**; not anymore *(AE)* **IV AC2**, 39; no more **IV AC4**, 107
nicht mögen to hate **II**; to dislike **IV U2**, 47
nicht notwendigerweise not necessarily **IV U3**, 76
nicht unbedingt not necessarily **IV U3**, 76
nicht vor not until **IV U2**, 44
noch **nicht** not … yet **II**
nicht- non- **II**
nichts nothing; not … anything **I**
Nichts zu danken. You're welcome. **I**
nie never **I**
nieder down **IV U2**, 52
niederbrennen *to burn down **III**
niedlich cute **I**
niedrig low **II**
niemals never **I**
niemand nobody **II**
niemand anderes nobody else **III**
Nieselregen drizzle **IV U1**, 17
mitten im Nirgendwo in the middle of nowhere **IV U2**, 46
nirgendwo nowhere **III**
nirgendwohin nowhere **III**
nö nope *(infml)* **IV AC4**, 107
noch still **I**; yet **II**
noch ein/-e another **I**
noch einmal again **I**
noch mal again **I**
noch nicht not … yet **II**
noch mal Glück gehabt saved by the bell **III**
Nomen noun **I**
Nord- north **II**
Norden north **II**
im **Norden** north **III**
nördlich north **III**
Nordsee North Sea **III**
normal normal **II**
normalerweise usually **I**; normally **IV AC1**, 22
Normanne/Normannin Norman **III**
normannisch Norman **III**
in Not in need **II**
Note mark **III**; grade *(AE)* **IV U3**, 78
notieren to note down **II**
Notiz note **I**
Notizen machen *to make notes **I**
sich **Notizen** machen *to take notes **I**
Notlüge white lie **IV TS1**, 32
notwendiger Relativsatz defining relative clause **II**
nicht notwendigerweise not necessarily **IV U3**, 76
November November **I**
Nudeln pasta **I**
null zero **I**
null *(bei Telefonnummern und Uhrzeitangaben)* oh **I**
Nullmeridian Meridian Line **I**
Nummer number **I**
nun now **I**
nun well **I**
nur only; just **I**
Nuss nut **I**
Nutzen benefit **IV U2**, 51
nützlich useful **I**
nützliche Ausdrücke Useful phrases **I**
nutzlos useless **IV U1**, 17

O

O! Oh! **I**
o.k. OK **I**
ob if **I**; whether **IV U2**, 49
obdachlos homeless **IV U2**, 51
Obdachlosenunterkunft homeless shelter **IV U2**, 51
oben on top **I**; above; upstairs **II**
nach **oben** up **II**
obendrauf on top **I**
oberer Teil top **I**
oberes Ende top **I**
Oberfläche surface **IV TS3**, 101
im Obergeschoss upstairs **II**
Objekt object **II**; item **IV U2**, 51
Objektpronomen object pronoun **III**
Obst fruit **I**
obwohl although **IV U1**, 13; though **IV AC4**, 106
oder or **I**
entweder … **oder** … either … or … **IV U3**, 79
offen open **I**
offensichtlich obvious **IV U2**, 53
öffentlich public **II**
die Öffentlichkeit the public **IV TS3**, 102
offiziell official **III**
offline offline **II**
öffnen to open **I**
Öffnung opening **III**
oft often **I**
so **oft** whenever **II**
ohne without **I**
ohne fremde Hilfe alone **I**
Ohr ear **IV AC1**, 22
Oje! Oh dear! **III**
okay okay **IV TS1**, 31
Öko- Eco **II**
Oktober October **I**
Oma grandma; granny **I**
OMG! (Oh mein Gott!) OMG! (Oh my god!) **IV U2**, 56
Onkel uncle **I**
Online-Pinnwand wall **III**
online stellen to post **II**
online online **II**
Opa grandad **I**
optimistisch optimistic **III**
Option option **III**
Orange orange **I**
orange orange **I**
Ordner folder **I**
Ordnung order **I**
in **Ordnung** fine **I**
in **Ordnung** bringen to tidy *(a room)* **I**
Organisation organisation **III**
organisieren to organise **I**
sich **organisieren** *to get organised **III**
Orientierung orientation **IV U2**, 43
Orientierungs- orientation **IV U2**, 43
Original original **III**
original original **III**
Ort place **I**; space **II**; spot **IV U3**, 75
örtlich local **III**
Ost- east **I**
Osten east **I**
Ostern Easter **I**
Outdoor- outdoor **II**
Outfit outfit **II**

P

Paar pair **I**; couple **III**
Paare bilden to pair **III**

ein **paar** some; a few; a couple of **I**
Päckchen packet; parcel **I**
Packung packet **I**
Paket packet; parcel **I**
Palme palm tree **III**
panisch werden to panic **II**
Papa dad **I**
Papier paper **I**
Stück **Papier** piece of paper **I**
Paradies paradise **II**
Paragraf section **II**
Park park **I**
Partei party **III**
Partizip past participle **II**
Partner/-in partner **I**
Partnerarbeit pair work **II**
Party party **I**
Pass passport **IV U1**, 9
Passagier/-in passenger **IV U1**, 9
passen to fit **II**
passen zu *to go with; to match **I**
zueinander **passen** *to go together **I**
passieren to happen **I**
Passiv passive **III**
Pasta pasta **I**
Pastete pie **I**
Pause break **II**; pause **III**
PC PC *(= Personal Computer)* **II**
Pech haben *to be unlucky **I**
peinlich embarrassing **II**
Pence *(brit. Währungseinheit)* penny, pence *(pl)* **I**
penetrant pushy **IV TS1**, 33
Penicillin penicillin **III**
Penny *(brit. Währungseinheit)* penny, pence *(pl)* **I**
Penthouse penthouse **IV U3**, 79
perfekt perfect **I**
Periode period **III**
Person person, people *(pl)* **I**
berühmte **Person** celebrity **III**
pro **Person** each **I**
persönlich personal **I**; face-to-face **II**
Persönlichkeit personality **III**
Perspektive perspective; point of view **II**
Pfad path **IV U3**, 92
Pfandhaus pawn shop **III**
Pfandleihe pawn shop **III**
Pfeife pipe **II**
Pfeil arrow **III**
Pferd horse **I**
Pfirsich peach **III**
Pflanze plant **III**
pflanzen to plant **II**
Pfund *(brit. Währungseinheit)* pound (£) **I**
Pfund *(Maßeinheit)* pound **IV U2**, 51
Piano piano **IV U3**, 77
Picknick picnic **I**
Pick-up pick-up **I**
Pier pier **I**
Pilger/-in Pilgrim **IV U2**, 45
Pille pill **II**
Pilot/-in pilot **II**
pink pink **I**
Online-**Pinnwand** wall **III**
Pizza pizza **I**
Placemat placemat **I**
Platzdeckchen placemat **I**
Plakatwand billboard **IV TS2**, 65
Plan plan **I**
planen to plan **I**
Planet planet **II**
platt flat **IV AC2**, 40
Plattform platform **III**
Platz place **I**; space; pitch **II**
Platz! *(Befehl für Hunde)* Sit! **I**
plaudern to chat **I**
plötzlich suddenly **I**
Plural plural **I**
Plusquamperfekt past perfect **III**
Podcast podcast **IV U3**, 92
Polen Poland **I**
politisch political **IV TS3**, 101
Polizei police **II**
Polizeibeamter police officer **II**
Polizist/-in police officer **II**
Pommes frites chips *(pl) (BE)* **I**
Pony pony **I**
Ponyreiten im Gelände pony trekking **III**
populär popular **I**
Population population **IV AC2**, 39
Porträt profile **I**
Pose pose **IV U2**, 56
positiv positive **II**
Possessivform possessive form **I**
Post *(Eintrag im Internet)* post **I**
Poster poster **I**
Postkarte postcard **III**
prägnant to the point **III**
praktisch practical **II**
praktisch überall just about anywhere **IV TS2**, 64
praktizieren to practice *(AE)* **IV U2**, 45
Präposition preposition **I**
Präsens present **II**
Präsentation presentation **I**
präsentieren to present **I**
Präsident/-in president **IV TS3**, 101
Praxis surgery **I**
Praxisräume surgery **I**
Preis price; prize **I**; award **II**
preiswert cheap **I**
pressen to press **II**
Priorität priority **IV TS3**, 101
Privatdetektiv/-in private detective **III**
pro per **III**
pro Person each **I**
pro Stück each **I**
pro (Tag/Woche/Jahr) a (day/week/year) **IV AC2**, 39
Probe sample **IV TS2**, 64
proben to rehearse **III**
probieren to try **I**; to taste **III**
Problem problem **I**
Probleme trouble **II**
Produkt product **IV TS2**, 64
Produktion production **IV TS1**, 30
produzieren to produce **III**
Profil profile **I**
Profileinstellungen account settings **III**
Programm programme **II**; program *(AE)* **IV TS3**, 104
Projekt project **I**
Prominente/-r celebrity **III**
Prosa fiction *(no pl)* **III**
Prospekt brochure **I**; leaflet **IV AC1**, 23
Protagonist/-in protagonist **IV TS1**, 30
Protest protest **III**
Protestierende/-r protester **IV U2**, 52
prüfen to check **I**; to test; to check out *(coll)* **III**
Prüfung test **I**; exam **II**
Publikum audience **II**
Pudding pudding **I**
Punkt point **II**
Punktestand score **II**
pünktlich on time **II**
Puzzle puzzle **I**
Pyjama pyjamas *(pl)* **II**

Q

Qualifikation trial **II**
Qualität quality **I**
Quelle source **III**
quer durch across **I**
Quiz quiz **I**

R

Rabe raven **II**
Herr der **Raben** raven master **II**
Rad wheel **I**
Radfahren cycling **I**
Radiergummi rubber **I**
radikal extreme **IV AC2**, 40
Radio radio **II**
Rahmen setting **II**; set **III**
am **Rande** von on the brink of **III**
Rand- fringe **III**
Rap rap **I**
rappen to rap **I**
Raster grid **I**
Rat advice **II**
raten to guess **I**
Ratespiel guessing game **II**
Ratschlag tip **I**; advice **II**
Rätsel puzzle; quiz **I**; mystery **III**
Ratte rat **I**
rau harsh **IV AC2**, 40
Räuber/-in robber **III**
Rauch smoke **III**
Raum room **I**; space **II**
Raumfahrtprogramm space program **IV TS3**, 104
Raumschiff spaceship **II**

rauschen to roar **III**
reagieren to react **III**
Reaktion reaction **II**
realisieren to realise **III**; to realize *(AE)* **IV U2**, 52
realistisch realistic **II**
Recherche research *(no pl)* **III**
Rechnung bill *(AE)* **IV U3**, 76
Recht right **IV U2**, 48
recht haben *to be right **I**
rechte/-r/-s right **I**
rechthaberisch bossy **III**
rechts on the right; right **I**
auf der **rechten** Seite on the right **I**
Rechtschreibung spelling **I**
rechtswidrig illegal **III**
gerade rechtzeitig just in time **IV U3**, 72
Recycling recycling **II**
Rede speech **III**; talk **IV U2**, 43
direkte **Rede** direct speech **IV U1**, 11
indirekte **Rede** indirect speech **IV U1**, 11
reden to talk **I**
reden mit to talk to **I**
Redensart saying **III**
Redewendung phrase **I**
Redner/-in speaker **I**
Referendum referendum **III**
Referenzartikel reference article **III**
reflexiv reflexive **III**
Reflexiv- reflexive **III**
Reflexivpronomen reflexive pronoun **III**
Refrain chorus **III**
Regel rule **I**
regelmäßig regular **I**
Regen rain **IV U1**, 17
Regenbogen rainbow **III**
Regenmantel raincoat **III**
Regieanweisung stage direction **III**
regieren to rule; to reign **III**
die Regierenden those in power **III**
Regierung government **IV TS3**, 102
Regierungszeit reign **III**
Region region **II**
Regisseur/-in director **IV TS1**, 30
Register register **IV AC4**, 106
regnen to rain **II**
Reich empire **III**
reich rich **III**; wealthy **IV AC2**, 40
die Reichen the rich **III**
Reihenfolge order **I**; sequence **IV U3**, 89
Reim rhyme **I**
(sich) reimen to rhyme **III**
sich reimend rhyming **III**
Reimschema rhyme scheme **III**
rein in **I**
reinigen to clean **I**
Reise trip; travel **II**; journey **III**
Reiseanbieter tour company **IV U3**, 73
Reisebericht travel report **II**
Reisebüro travel agent's; travel agency **III**
Reisebus coach **II**
Reiseführer guide **II**; guidebook **IV U3**, 72
(das) Reisen travel **II**; travelling *(no pl)* **IV U1**, 9
reisen to travel **II**
Reisende/-r traveller **IV U1**, 15
Reisepass passport **IV U1**, 9
Reiseziel destination **IV U1**, 19
reiten *to ride raɪd **IV AC2**, 41
reizen to tempt **IV TS1**, 31
Reklame advertising *(no pl)* **IV TS2**, 64
Relativpronomen relative pronoun **II**
notwendiger Relativsatz defining relative clause **II**
Religion religion **IV U2**, 45
eine **Religion** ausüben to practice a religion **IV U2**, 45
Religion *(Schulfach)* RE *(= Religious Education)* **II**
religiös religious **I**
Rennen race; running; run **II**
rennen *to run **I**
reparieren to fix **II**
Reporter/-in reporter **II**
repräsentieren to represent **IV AC2**, 40
Requisite prop **III**
reservieren to book **III**
Respekt respect **IV TS3**, 103
der Rest the rest **I**
Restaurant restaurant **I**
einfaches **Restaurant** mit Theke und Tischen diner *(AE)* **IV U3**, 72
Resultat result **II**
retten to save **I**; to rescue **III**
Rettung rescue **II**
Rettungsboot lifeboat **I**
Rettungsring lifebuoy **I**
Rezept recipe **III**
Rezept *(für Arzneimittel)* prescription **II**
rezitieren to recite **III**
Rhinozeros rhino **III**
Rhythmus rhythm **I**
richtig correct; right **I**; real **II**
richtig beantworten *to get right **III**
Richtung direction **I**
in **Richtung** towards **II**
riechen *to smell **III**
riesengroß huge **II**
riesig huge; large **II**; gigantic **IV AC2**, 40; massive **IV AC2**, 41
Rinderhirte cowboy **IV U3**, 72
Ring circle **I**; ring **III**
ein Risiko eingehen *to take a risk **IV TS1**, 32
Ritt ride **IV U2**, 44
Ritter knight **III**
Rock skirt **III**
Rock *(Musik)* rock **III**
Rock 'n' Roll rock 'n' roll **II**
Rohr pipe **II**
Rohrleitung pipe **II**
Rolle role **I**; part **III**
Rollen tauschen to swap roles **I**
Rollenbesetzung casting **IV TS1**, 37
Rollenkarte prompt card **II**
Rollenspiel role play **I**
Rollschuhe skates *(pl)* **I**
Rollstuhl wheelchair **II**
Rolltreppe escalator **I**
Roman novel **III**
Römer/-in Roman **II**
römisch Roman **II**
rosa pink **I**
rot red **I**
Route route **II**
Routenplaner route planner **IV AC2**, 41
Routine routine **IV U1**, 16
Rückblende flashback **III**
Rücken back **III**
Rücken an **Rücken** back to back **I**
Rückenschmerzen backache **II**
Rückenweh backache **II**
Hin- und Rückfahrkarte return ticket **III**
Rückmeldung feedback **II**
Rucksack backpack **III**
Rückseite back **III**
rufen to shout; to call **I**; to cry **II**
Rugby rugby **II**
Ruhe silence *(no pl)* **III**
jmdn. in **Ruhe** lassen *to leave sb alone **IV U2**, 53
ruhig quiet **I**; silent **III**
die Beine und Hände **ruhig** halten *to keep one's feet or hands still **III**
Rühr- sponge **I**
ruinieren to ruin **II**
Rumäne/Rumänin Romanian **II**
Rumänisch Romanian **II**
rumänisch Romanian **II**
rumhängen (mit) *to hang out (with) *(infml)* **III**
Runde round **II**
Rundgang tour **II**
Rutschbahn slide **I**

S

Saal hall **II**
Sache thing **I**
große **Sache** big deal **IV U1**, 11
sachlich factual **III**
Sachtext factual text **III**
Saft juice **I**
Sage legend **III**
sagen *to say; *to tell **I**
sagenhaft mythical **IV U1**, 19; fabulous **IV TS2**, 66
sagenumwoben mythical **IV U1**, 19
Sahne cream **I**
Saison season **IV U2**, 56
Salat salad **I**
Salbe ointment **II**
sammeln to collect **I**
Geld **sammeln** to raise money **II**
Sammlung collection **II**
Samstag Saturday **I**
Sand- sandy **III**

Sandale sandal **III**
sandig sandy **III**
Sandwich sandwich **I**
Sänger/-in singer **II**
Sanitärarbeit plumbing **III**
es **satt** haben (zu) *to be tired of **IV U2**, 46
Satz phrase; sentence **I**
if-**Satz** if-clause **III**
der erste **Satz** opening line **III**
Satzgegenstand subject **II**
Satzstellung word order **I**
sauber clean **III**
säubern to clean **I**
sauer sein (auf) *to be fed up (with) **III**
Säugling baby **I**
Saxofon saxophone; sax **I**
scannen to scan **II**
Schach chess **II**
Schachtel box **I**
Schade! Too bad! **I**
Schaf sheep, sheep *(pl)* **II**
schaffen to create **I**
es nicht **schaffen**, etw. zu tun to fail to do sth **IV U3**, 79
es **schaffen** *to make it **IV U3**, 70
Du **schaffst** es! You can do it! **III**
Wir haben es **geschafft**! We did it! **II**
Schälchen bowl **I**
Schale bowl **I**
Schalter switch **III**; desk **IV U1**, 9
scharf sharp **III**
Schatten shadow **III**
Schatz treasure **II**
schätzen to estimate **IV TS3**, 103
Schau show **II**
schaudern to cringe **IV U3**, 91
schauen to look **I**
Schau/Schaut mal! Look! **I**
Schau(t) genau ... Look closely ... **II**
schaukeln to rock **IV U1**, 16
Schauplatz setting; scene **II**
seinen **Schauplatz** haben (in) *to be set (in) **IV U1**, 19
Schauspielen acting **III**
Schauspieler actor **II**
in **Scheiben** schneiden to slice **I**
scheinen *to shine **II**; to seem **III**
schenken *to give **I**
scherzen to joke **II**
Schicht (aus) layer (of) **III**
schicken *to send **I**
schieben to push **II**
Schiedsrichter/-in official **II**
jmdn. **schief** anschauen *to give sb funny looks **III**
schiefgehen *to go wrong **I**
schießen to kick **II**
schießen (auf) *to shoot **III**
Schiff ship **I**
Schiffsbau shipbuilding **III**
Schiffsjunge cabin boy **I**
Schiffsoffizier mate **I**
Schild sign **II**
Schinken ham **III**
Schinkenspeck bacon **I**
Schlacht battle **III**
Schlaf sleep **IV U1**, 11
Schlafanzug pyjamas *(pl)* **II**
schlafen *to sleep **I**; *to be asleep **II**
Schlafzimmer bedroom **I**
schlagen *to hit; to whip **I**; *to beat **II**
Schläger racquet **II**
Schlagzeile headline **III**
Schlagzeug drums *(pl)* **III**
Schlamm mud **II**
schlammig muddy **II**
Schlange queue **I**
Schlange stehen *to stand in line *(AE)* **IV AC3**, 69
schlau clever **II**; smart **III**
schlecht bad **I**
der/die/das **schlechteste** the worst **II**
schlecht geschrieben badly-written **IV TS3**, 105
sich **schlecht** fühlen *to feel sick **II**
schleichen *to sneak **IV U3**, 72
schließen to close **I**
Schließfach locker **I**
schließlich at last; after all **I**; in the end; finally **II**
schlimm *(ugs.)* bad **I**
der/die/das **schlimmste** the worst **II**
Schlittschuh laufen to skate **I**
Schlittschuhbahn ice rink **I**
Schlittschuhe skates *(pl)* **I**
Schloss castle **II**
Schluchtenklettern gorge scrambling **II**
Schluss end **I**
zum **Schluss** in the end; finally **II**
sich das Beste bis zum **Schluss** aufheben to save the best for last **IV U3**, 72
Schluss *(einer Geschichte)* ending **I**
Schlüssel key **II**
Schlüsselanhänger key ring **III**
Schlüsselbegriff key word **I**
Schlüsselbund key ring **III**
schmal narrow **III**
schmaler Durchgang close **III**
schmecken to taste **III**
Schmelztiegel melting pot **IV U3**, 70
Schmerz pain **II**
Schmuck jewellery; decorations *(pl)* **I**
schmücken to decorate **I**
schmuggeln *to sneak **IV U3**, 72
Schmuggler/-in smuggler **IV U1**, 16
Schmutz dirt **III**
schmutzig dirty **II**
Schnäppchen bargain **I**
schnappen to grab **II**
schnarchen to snore **I**
Schnee snow **III**
schneiden *to cut (off) **II**
in Scheiben **schneiden** to slice **I**
schneidend sharp **III**
schnell fast; quick **I**
schnell quickly **II**
Schock shock **II**
schockiert shocked **IV TS1**, 37
Schokolade chocolate **I**
Schokoriegel chocolate bar **IV TS2**, 64
schön nice; fine **I**; beautiful **II**; lovely **IV TS2**, 65
schon already **I**; yet **II**
schon einmal before **II**
High **School** *(weiterführende Schule in den USA, Oberstufe)* high school *(AE)* **IV U2**, 43
Schornstein chimney **III**
Schotte/Schottin Scot **III**
Schottenkaro *(bestimmtes Muster eines Clans)* tartan **III**
Schottenrock kilt **III**
karierter **Schottenstoff** tartan **III**
schottisch Scottish **III**
Schrank cupboard **I**; closet **IV U2**, 44
schrecklich awful **I**
Schreiben writing **I**
schreiben *to write **I**
schreien to shout **I**; to scream; to cry **II**
Schritt step **I**
Schritt halten (mit) *to keep up (with) **II**
Schritt-für-**Schritt**- step-by-step **II**
Stück **Schrott** piece of junk **III**
schubsen to push **II**
schüchtern shy **II**
Schuh shoe **I**
Schularbeiten schoolwork **IV TS1**, 34
schuldig guilty **IV TS1**, 37
Schule school **I**
Schüler/-in student **I**
Schüleraustausch student exchange **III**
Schulfach subject **II**
Schulgebühren school fees *(pl)* **III**
Schulgeld school fees *(pl)* **III**
Schuljahr year **I**
Schulklasse class **I**
Schulleiter/-in principal *(AE)* **IV AC3**, 68
Schulstunde lesson **I**
Schultasche schoolbag **I**
Schulter shoulder **II**
Schüssel bowl **I**
schütten to pour **I**
Schutz security **IV U1**, 13
schwach weak **IV TS3**, 105
Schwanz tail **I**
schwänzen to skip **IV AC3**, 68
schwarz black **I**
schwarz werden *to go black **II**
schwarzes Brett noticeboard **II**
Schweif tail **I**
Schweigen silence *(no pl)* **III**
schweigsam silent **III**
Schwein pig **I**
Schweinerei mess **IV U2**, 54
schwer hard **II**; heavy **III**
Schwerpunkt focus **III**
Schwester sister **I**

schwierig hard; difficult **II**
Schwierigkeit problem **I**
Schwierigkeiten trouble **II**
in **Schwierigkeiten** bringen *to make trouble **I**
in **Schwierigkeiten** geraten *to get into trouble **IV AC3**, 69
Schwimmbecken swimming pool **III**
Schwimmen swimming **I**
Schwimmen gehen *to go swimming **I**
schwimmen *to swim **I**
schwindelig dizzy **IV U2**, 52
Science-Fiction *(Zukunftsdichtung)* science fiction **II**
sechs six **I**
Second-Hand-Laden charity shop **I**
See lake **I**
See zum Rudern boating lake **I**
seekrank seasick **IV U1**, 8
Seemann sailor **I**
die Segel einholen to reef the sails **I**
Segelboot sailboat **III**
segeln to sail **III**
sehbehindert partially sighted **II**
sehen *to see; to look **I**
Ich **sehe** keinen Sinn darin … I can't see the point of … **IV AC3**, 69
Sehenswürdigkeit sight; attraction **II**
sehr very; very much **I**
Sehr geehrte Dame, **sehr** geehrter Herr Dear Sir or Madam **III**
Hör-/Sehverstehen viewing **I**
Seil rope **III**
sein *to be **I**; *to be like **III**
ist nicht ain't (= isn't/aren't) **IV AC4**, 107
Sei/Seid höflich. Be polite. **I**
sind nicht ain't (= isn't/aren't) **IV AC4**, 107
sein/-e his; its **I**
seit for *(+ Zeitraum)* **III**; since *(+ Zeitpunkt)* **III**
seitdem since *(+ Zeitpunkt)* **III**
Seite page **I**; side **II**
auf der anderen **Seite** von across; opposite **I**
selber yourself **I**; himself; myself **II**; yourselves **III**
das Selbst self self, selves selvz *(pl)* **III**
selbst even **I**
du/dir/dich/Sie/sich (**selbst**) yourself **I**
ihr/euch/Sie/sich (**selbst**) yourselves **III**
er/sich (**selbst**) himself **II**
ich/mir/mich (**selbst**) myself **II**
selbstbewusst confident **II**
Selbsteinschätzung self-evaluation **I**
selbstkritisch self-critical **II**
selbstsicher confident **II**
selbstverständlich of course **I**; needless to say **IV U3**, 76
Selfie selfie **II**
seltsam strange **I**; weird **II**; odd **IV U1**, 19
senden *to send **I**
Sender station **II**
Sendung programme **II**; program *(AE)* **IV TS3**, 104
separat separate **II**
September September **I**
Sequenz sequence **III**
Serie series, series *(pl)* **III**
Service service **IV U3**, 72
Sessel chair **I**
setzen *to put **I**
sich **setzen** *to sit down **I**
Shampoo shampoo **IV TS2**, 64
Shinty *(eine Art Hockey)* shinty **III**
shoppen to shop **IV U3**, 76
Shorts shorts *(pl)* **II**
Show show **II**
Comedy **Show** comedy show **II**
sich each other **I**
sicher sure **I**; safe **II**
Ich bin mir (nicht) **sicher** … I'm (not) sure … **III**
Sicherheit security **IV U1**, 13
Sicherheits- security **IV U1**, 13
Sicht view **II**
Sie you; u *(= you)* **I**
sie her; she **I**
sie *(Pl.)* they **I**; them **I**
sieben seven **I**
Siedler/-in colonist **IV AC2**, 41
siegen *to win **I**
Sieger/-in winner **I**; champion **III**
Sightseeing- sightseeing **II**
Signal signal **III**
Signalwort signal word **I**
Silbe syllable **III**
Silber silver **II**
simpel simple **III**
singen *to sing **I**
sinken *to sink **III**
Sinn meaning **II**; sense **III**
jmdm. in den **Sinn** kommen *to rise up in one's mind **III**
Sinn ergeben *to make sense **IV TS3**, 102
Sinn für Humor sense of humour *(no pl)* **III**
Ich sehe keinen **Sinn** darin … I can't see the point of … **IV AC3**, 69
Sitte custom **IV AC1**, 22
Situation situation **I**
Sitz seat **IV U1**, 16
Sitzbank bench **III**
Sitz! *(Befehl für Hunde)* Sit! **I**
sitzen *to sit **I**
sich gegenüber **sitzen** *to sit face to face **I**
Sitzplatz seat **IV U1**, 16
Skateboard skateboard **II**
Skateboardfahren skateboarding **I**
skeptisch sceptical **IV TS2**, 64
Sklave/Sklavin slave **III**
Skript script **III**
Skulptur sculpture **IV U3**, 72
Slogan slogan **II**
Smalltalk small talk **III**
Smartphone smartphone **II**
SMS text (message) **I**
eine **SMS** schicken to text **II**
Snack snack **I**
so like this; so; like that **I**; that's how **II**
so dass so (that) **IV AC3**, 69
so früh this early **III**
so oft whenever **II**
so … wie as … as **I**
so viel that much **III**
sobald as soon as **II**
Sofa sofa **I**
sofort right away **I**; right now **II**; straight away **III**; immediately **IV TS2**, 64
Softwarehandbuch software manual **III**
sogar even **I**
Sohn son **III**
solch such **II**
solche/-r/-s such **II**
Soldat/-in soldier **III**
sollte/sollten/solltest/solltet should **II**
Du **solltest** lieber … You'd better … *(= You had better)* **IV AC3**, 69
sollte(n) nicht shouldn't **II**
Somali Somali **IV U1**, 17
Sommer summer **II**
Sommerferienlager summer camp **II**
Sonderangebot special offer **I**
sonderbar weird **II**
Song song **I**
Sonne sun **II**
Sonnenblume sunflower **III**
Sonnenuntergang sunset **IV U3**, 72
Sonntag Sunday **I**
sonst otherwise **IV AC3**, 68
sonst noch else **III**
Sonst noch etwas? Anything else? **I**
Keine Sorge! Don't worry! **I**
sich Sorgen machen to worry **II**
für jmdn. sorgen *to take care of sb **III**
sorgfältig careful **II**
Sorte kind **I**; type **III**
sortieren nach to sort into **III**
Soße sauce **III**
Souvenir souvenir **II**
sowieso anyway **II**
sozial social **IV U2**, 46
soziale Netzwerke social media **IV U2**, 46
soziales Netzwerk social network **II**
Sozialwissenschaften Humanities *(pl)* **II**
Spalt gap **I**
Spalte column **III**
die Spanier Spanish **III**
Spanisch Spanish **III**
spanisch Spanish **III**
spannend exciting **I**
Spannung suspense **III**
sparen to save **III**
spärlich sparse **IV AC2**, 38
Spaß fun **I**
Spaß haben *to have fun **I**; to enjoy oneself **III**

Es macht **Spaß**. It's fun. **I**
spät late **I**
zu **spät** late **I**
zu **spät** kommen *to be late **I**
Wie **spät** ist es? What's the time? **I**
zu **spät** dran sein *to be late **I**
kleiner **Spaten** trowel **II**
später later **I**
spazieren gehen *to go for a walk **II**
mit dem Hund **spazieren** gehen to walk the dog **I**
Speck bacon **I**
Speer spear **III**
Speise dish **IV U2**, 45
Speisekarte menu **IV U2**, 45
spektakulär spectacular **III**
spenden to donate **IV U2**, 51
sperren to ban **III**
Sperrstunde curfew **IV U2**, 44
Spezialeffekt special effect **IV TS3**, 105
Spezialität specialty *(AE)* **IV U3**, 75
speziell special **I**; specific **IV U1**, 19
spezifisch specific **IV U1**, 19
Spickzettel cheat sheet **IV AC3**, 69
Spiegel mirror **III**
Spiel game **I**; match **II**
spielen to play **I**
einen Streich **spielen** to play a trick (on) **I**
spielen (in) *to be set (in) **IV U1**, 19
spielen *(Theater)* to act **I**
eine Theaterszene **spielen** acting a scene **I**
Spieler/-in player **II**
technische **Spielerei** gadget **III**
Spielfeld field; court; pitch **II**
Spielkarte card **I**
Spielstand score **II**
Spielzeug toy **I**
Spind locker **I**
Spinne spider **III**
Spinnennetz web **III**
Spitze top **I**; spike **IV U3**, 74
spitze awesome **IV AC2**, 41
spontan spontaneous **III**
Sport sport **I**
Sportart sport **I**
Sportunterricht PE *(= Physical Education)* **II**
Sprache language **I**
Sprachebene register **IV AC4**, 106
Sprachmittlung mediation **I**
Sprechblase speech bubble **I**
Sprechen speaking; talking **I**
sprechen *to say; to talk; *to speak **I**
mit vollem Mund **sprechen** to talk with your mouth full **IV AC1**, 22
sprechen über to talk about … **I**
Sprecher/-in speaker **I**; talker **III**
Sprechgesang chant **II**
Sprichwort saying **III**
springen to jump **I**; to bounce **III**
Spur clue **II**
Staat state **IV AC2**, 39
Staatsoberhaupt head of state **II**
Stachel spike **IV U3**, 74
Stadion stadium **II**
Stadt city; town **I**
Stadt- urban **IV AC2**, 38
städtisch urban **IV AC2**, 38
Stadtplan map **I**
Stadtteil part **I**
im **Stadtzentrum** downtown *(AE)* **IV U2**, 44
Stamm tribe **III**
Stammbaum family tree **I**
Standbild still **II**; freeze frame **III**; statue **IV U3**, 74
ständig always **I**
Standort location **II**
Standpunkt point of view **II**
Star star **I**
stark strong **II**; powerful; heavy **III**
Stärke power **III**
starren to stare **I**
Start start **III**; take-off **IV U1**, 15
starten to start **I**
Startpunkt starting place **III**
Station station **I**
statt instead of **IV U2**, 45
stattdessen instead **III**
stattfinden *to take place **I**
Statue statue **IV U3**, 74
Steak steak **I**
stechen *to sting **III**
mitten in **stecken** stuck in the middle of … **III**
stehen *to stand **I**
gegenüber **stehen** to face **IV TS1**, 31
jmdm./etw. im Weg **stehen** *to stand in the way of sb/sth **IV AC1**, 22
stehen auf *to be into **I**
stehen für to represent **IV AC2**, 40
Du **stehst** auf … You're into … **I**
stehlen *to steal **II**
steigen to climb **I**; *to rise **III**; to step **IV TS3**, 101
Stein stone **III**
Stein- stone **III**
steinig rocky **III**
Stelle place **I**
an **Stelle** von instead of **IV U2**, 45
an Jays **Stelle** in Jay's shoes **III**
an jmds. **Stelle** sein *to be in sb's shoes **III**
stellen *to put **I**
online **stellen** to post **II**
Stelle/Stellt es in … Put it in … **I**
sterben to die **III**
Stern star **I**
Steuer wheel **I**
steuern to control **IV U2**, 50
Steuerrad wheel **I**
Stichwort key word **I**; prompt **III**
Stichwortkarte prompt card **II**
Stichwortverzeichnis glossary **IV TS1**, 30
Stiefel boot **III**
Stiefmutter stepmum **I**
stiften to donate **IV U2**, 51
Stil style **IV U1**, 11
Stil- stylistic **IV U3**, 89
stilistisch stylistic **IV U3**, 89
still quiet; still **I**; silent **III**
Stille silence *(no pl)* **III**
Stimme voice **I**
Stimmung mood; atmosphere **II**; humour *(no pl)* **III**
Stockwerk floor **IV U2**, 44
Stöhnen groan **IV U1**, 10
stöhnen to groan **IV U3**, 74
stolz (auf) proud (of) **II**
stoppen to stop **I**
stören *to get in the way **II**; to bother **IV U1**, 15
Story story, stories *(pl)* **I**
stoßen to push **II**
Stoßzahn tusk **III**
strahlend bright **IV U3**, 72
Strand beach **II**
Straße road **II**
Straße *(in der Stadt)* street **I**
auf der **Straße** in the street **I**
in der **Straße** in the street **I**
Straßenmusikant/-in busker **IV U3**, 79
Strecke route **II**
Streich trick **I**
einen **Streich** spielen to play a trick (on) **I**
Streit fight **II**; argument **III**
streiten to argue **IV U2**, 51
(sich) **streiten** *to fight **II**
streng strict **III**
streng mit jmdm. sein *to be hard on sb **III**
strikt strict **III**
Strom electricity **III**
Stromausfall power cut **II**
Strophe verse **III**
Struktur structure **III**
Stück piece **I**
pro **Stück** each **I**
Stück für **Stück** bit by bit **IV TS1**, 35
Stück Papier piece of paper **I**
Stück Schrott piece of junk **III**
Student/-in student **I**
Studie survey **I**
studieren to study **III**
Studio studio **IV U3**, 72
Studium studies *(pl)* **II**
Stufe step **I**
Stuhl chair **I**
stumm silent **III**
Stunde hour **II**; period *(AE)* **IV U2**, 48
eine halbe **Stunde** half an hour **III**
Stundenplan timetable **I**; schedule *(AE)* **IV AC4**, 106
Sturm storm **I**
stürzen *to fall down **III**
stützen auf to base on **IV U3**, 74
Such- search **II**
Suche search **II**

suchen (nach) to search for **IV U1**, 14
  suchen nach to look for **I**
Süchtige/-r addict **IV U1**, 10
Süd- south **II**
Süden south **II**
Südkoreaner/-in South Korean **II**
Südkoreanisch South Korean **II**
südkoreanisch South Korean **II**
(der) **Südwesten** (the) Southwest **IV AC2**, 38
im **Südwesten** (the) Southwest **IV AC2**, 38
südwestlich (the) Southwest **IV AC2**, 38
summen to hum **II**
super great; cool **I**; awesome **IV AC2**, 41; massive **IV AC2**, 41; super **IV U2**, 44
Superlativ superlative **II**
Supermacht superpower **II**
Supermarkt supermarket **I**
Suppe soup **IV U1**, 11
Surfen surfing **III**
suspendiert werden *to be suspended **IV AC3**, 68
süß cute; sweet **I**
Süßigkeiten sweets *(pl)* **I**
Swimmingpool swimming pool **III**
Symbol symbol **II**
symbolisieren to symbolize *(AE)* **IV AC2**, 40
Szene scene **I**; in-crowd; sequence **III**

T

Tabak tobacco *(no pl)* **III**
Tabelle grid **I**
Tablet tablet **II**
Tablette pill **II**
Taekwondo taekwondo **II**
Tafel board **III**; tablet **IV U3**, 74
die **Tafelrunde** the Round Table **III**
Tag day **I**
  sich den **Tag** freinehmen *to take the day off **IV U3**, 72
  am nächsten **Tag** the next day **II**
  den ganzen **Tag** all day **II**
  ein **Tag** in … a day out in … **II**
  eines **Tages** one day **II**
  pro (**Tag**/Woche/Jahr) a (day/week/year) **IV AC2**, 39
Tagebuch diary **III**
Tagebucheintrag diary entry **III**
Tagung conference **IV U3**, 72
Takelage rigging **I**
Talent talent **I**
Talentwettbewerb talent show **I**
Talisman lucky charm **I**
Tantchen auntie **IV AC4**, 107
Tante aunt **I**
Tanz dance **III**
tanzen to dance **I**
  tanzen zu to dance to **III**
Tänzer/-in dancer **II**
Tanzveranstaltung dance **III**
tapfer brave **I**
Tasche bag **I**; pocket **III**
Taschengeld pocket money **I**
Taschenlampe torch **II**
Tasse cup **III**
Tätowierung tattoo **III**
Tatsache fact **II**
Tatsachenbericht news report **III**
Tattoe tattoo **III**
Rollen **tauschen** to swap roles **I**
täuschen to trick **IV TS3**, 103
Täuschung hoax **IV TS3**, 102
tausende (von) thousands of **I**
Taxi taxi **II**
Team team **II**
Technik Technology **II**; engineering; tech **IV TS3**, 102
Techniker/-in engineer **IV TS3**, 101
technische Spielerei gadget **III**
Technologie technology **II**; tech **IV TS3**, 102
Tee tea **I**
Teebeutel tea bag **III**
Teenager teenager **I**; teen **III**
Teich pond **II**
Teig pastry **IV U3**, 75
Teigtasche pastry **IV U3**, 75
Teil part **I**
  im hinteren **Teil** at the back of **II**
teilen to share **II**
teilnehmen to participate **II**
teilnehmen (an) *to take part (in) **II**
Telefon phone; telephone **I**
  Telefon mit Wählscheibe rotary phone **III**
Telefonanruf phone call **I**
telefonieren to phone **IV TS1**, 31
Telefonzelle phone box **IV U1**, 17
Teller plate **III**
vom **Tellerwäscher** zum Millionär rags to riches **IV U3**, 79
Temperatur temperature **IV AC2**, 38
Tennis tennis **I**
Teppich carpet **II**
Terminkalender schedule *(AE)* **IV AC4**, 106
Test test **I**
  einen **Test** machen *to take a test **II**
testen to test **III**
teuer expensive **I**
Teufel devil **IV TS1**, 31
Text text **I**; lines *(pl)* **IV TS1**, 30
Theater theatre **I**; drama **II**; theater *(AE)* **IV U3**, 70
Theaterstück play **III**
eine **Theaterszene** spielen acting a scene **I**
Thema theme **I**; topic **II**; subject **III**
Theorie theory **IV TS3**, 102
Therme baths *(pl)* **III**
Ticket ticket **I**
tief deep **III**
  tief Luft holen to gasp **IV U3**, 72
Tier animal **I**
Tierarzt/Tierärztin vet **I**
Tierheim animal shelter **III**
Tierpark zoo **II**
Tierwelt *(in freier Wildbahn)* wildlife **II**
Tipp tip **I**; hint **III**
Tisch table **I**
Titel heading **I**; title **II**
Titelblatt cover **III**
tja well **I**
Toast toast **I**
Tochter daughter **III**
Tod death **III**
Toilette toilet **I**; restroom *(AE)* **IV U2**, 43
tolerant tolerant **IV TS1**, 36
toll great **I**; amazing **II**
Tomate tomato, tomatoes *(pl)* **I**
Tombola raffle **I**
Ton sound **I**
Tonmodell model **I**
Tonpfeife clay pipe **II**
Tonstudio recording studio **I**
Tor goal **I**
Torte cake **I**
Tortenguss jelly **I**
tosend roaring **III**
tot dead **II**
total totally **IV AC4**, 107
Totale *(Kameraeinstellung)* long shot **IV U3**, 89
töten to kill **III**
Tour tour **II**
Tourismus tourism **III**
Tourist/-in tourist **I**
Touristeninformation tourist information centre **I**; tourist board **III**
Tradition tradition **I**
traditionell traditional **III**
tragen to carry **III**
tragen *(Kleidung)* *to wear **I**
Trainer/-in coach **I**
trainieren to practise **I**; to train **II**; to practice *(AE)* **IV U2**, 45
Training training **II**; practice **III**
Traktor tractor **IV AC2**, 38
Transport transport **III**
transportieren to transport **IV U3**, 79
Er **traute** seinen Augen nicht. He couldn't believe his eyes. **II**
Traum dream **II**
Traum- fantasy **I**
träumen *to dream dri:m **IV U2**, 47
traurig sad **I**
treffen *to meet; *to hit **I**
  sich auf halbem Weg **treffen** *to meet halfway **III**
  sich **treffen** *to meet **I**; *to meet up **IV U2**, 44
  sich **treffen** (mit) *to hang out (with) *(infml)* **III**
treffend to the point **III**
Ich lasse mich **treiben**. I go wherever the wind takes me. **IV U1**, 19
Treppe stairs *(pl)* **III**
treten to kick **II**; to step **IV TS3**, 101
Trick trick **I**; hoax **IV TS3**, 102
Trifle *(englischer Nachtisch)* trifle **I**

trinken *to drink **I**
Trinkgeld tip **IV U3**, 76
Trip trip **II**
trocken dry **III**
trotzdem anyway **II**
und **trotzdem** yet **IV U3**, 76
Tschüss! Bye! **II**
T-Shirt T-shirt **I**
Tudor- Tudor **III**
tun *to do; *to make **I**
tun als ob to act like **II**; to pretend **IV U1**, 17
was man **tun** und was man nicht **tun** sollte dos and don'ts **IV AC1**, 22
Tunnel tunnel **I**
Tür door **I**
Türklingel doorbell **III**
Turm tower **III**
Turnhalle gym(nasium) **IV AC3**, 68
Turnier competition **II**
Turnschuh trainer **III**
Turteltauben lovebirds *(pl)* **II**
Tüte bag **I**
Tutorial tutorial **IV TS3**, 100
Tutorium tutorial **IV TS3**, 100
Typ guy **II**; type **III**
Typ *(ugs.)* bloke *(fam)* **III**
typisch typical **I**
typisch typically **III**

U

U-Bahn underground **II**; subway *(AE)* **IV U3**, 74
die Londoner **U-Bahn** the Tube **II**
Übelkeit verspüren *to feel sick **II**
Üben practising **I**
üben to practise **I**; to practice *(AE)* **IV U2**, 45
über about; over; across **I**
über Nacht overnight **III**
überall everywhere **I**
überall (in) all over **I**
überall (egal, wo) anywhere **II**
praktisch **überall** just about anywhere **IV TS2**, 64
überfallen to invade **III**
überfliegen to skim **II**
überfüllt crowded **IV AC1**, 23
sich übergeben *to be sick **IV U1**, 16
überhaupt at all **I**
überladen overloaded **IV U1**, 16
(sich) überlappen to overlap **IV U3**, 89
Überlass das mir. Leave that to me. **IV U3**, 72
überleben to survive **III**
Überlebende/-r survivor **IV U2**, 45
übernachten to stay **III**
Übernachtung sleepover **I**
übernatürlich supernatural **IV U1**, 19
überprüfen to check **I**
überqueren to cross **II**
überraschen to surprise **II**
überraschend surprising **II**
überrascht sein *to be surprised **II**
Überraschung surprise **I**
überreagieren to overreact **II**
überreden to persuade **II**
Überschrift heading **I**; title **II**
übersetzen to translate **I**
Übersetzung translation **I**
übertreiben to exaggerate **IV TS1**, 32; *to overdo **IV U2**, 55
übertrieben exaggerated **IV U2**, 52
jmdn. **überzeugen** *to win sb over **IV TS2**, 64
überzeugen to convince **II**
überzeugend persuasive **III**; convincing **IV U1**, 21
überzeugt convinced **IV TS1**, 31
üblich usual **III**
übrig left **I**
Übung exercise **I**; practice **III**
Übungsheft exercise book **I**; workbook **IV TS1**, 37
Ufer bank; shore **II**
UFO UFO **II**
Uhr clock **I**
Um wie viel **Uhr**? What time? **I**
Wie viel **Uhr** ist es? What's the time? **I**
Uhr *(Zeitangabe bei vollen Stunden)* o'clock **I**
um *(bei Uhrzeitangaben)* at **I**
um halb acht at 7:30 **I**
um … herum around **I**; round **II**
Um wie viel Uhr? What time? **I**
umarmen to hug **I**
umbringen to kill **III**
(sich) umdrehen to turn round **II**; to turn **III**
Umfrage survey **I**
Umgebung environment; set **III**
umgehen mit *to deal (with) **II**
umher around **I**
umkehren to turn back **II**
umkippen *to fall over **I**
sich umschauen to explore **I**
umschreiben *to rewrite **III**
umsegeln to sail **III**
umsonst for free **IV U3**, 72
umsteigen (in) to change (onto) **II**
umwandeln in to turn into **IV U1**, 14
Umwelt environment **III**
umziehen to move (house) **III**
unabhängig independent **III**
Unabhängigkeit freedom *(no pl)*; independence *(no pl)* **III**
unaufhörlich steady **IV U1**, 17
unausgereift undeveloped **IV TS3**, 105
nicht **unbedingt** not necessarily **IV U3**, 76
unbekannt unfamiliar **III**
unbequem inconvenient **IV TS3**, 100
und and **I**
unehrlich dishonest **IV TS1**, 34
unentwickelt undeveloped **IV TS3**, 105
unerwartet unexpected **IV U3**, 91
unfair unfair **II**
Unfall accident **II**
unfreundlich unfriendly **II**
ungefähr about **I**
ungefährlich safe **II**
Ungeheuer monster **I**
ungehorsam sein to disobey **III**
unglaublich amazing **II**
Unglück disaster **II**
unheimlich scary **II**
unhöflich rude **I**; impolite **III**
Uniform uniform **I**
unkompliziert easy-going **IV U1**, 19
Unmengen von/an a pocketful of **IV U3**, 70
unmöglich impossible **IV TS3**, 102
unordentlich messy **III**
Unordnung mess **IV U2**, 54
unrealistisch unrealistic **IV U2**, 52
nicht ganz **unrecht** haben *to have a point **III**
unrecht haben *to be wrong **I**
unrechtmäßig illegal **III**
unregelmäßig irregular **I**
Unruhestifter/-in troublemaker **IV U2**, 53
uns us **I**
unscharf out of focus **III**
unser/-e our **I**
unsicher unsure **IV TS1**, 31; insecure **IV U2**, 47
unsichtbar invisible **IV U1**, 17
unten downstairs **II**
nach **unten** down **II**
nach **unten** gehen *to go down **I**
unten below **I**
unter under **I**; among **III**
untergehen *to sink **III**
im **Untergeschoss** downstairs **II**
unterhalb below **I**
unterhalten to entertain **IV TS1**, 30
unterhaltsam entertaining **IV TS3**, 103
Unterhaltung conversation **I**; entertainment *(no pl)* **III**; talk **IV U3**, 92
Unterhaltungskünstler/-in entertainer **IV U3**, 72
Unternehmen company **III**
unternehmen wegen *to do about **II**
Unterricht lesson **I**; class **II**
zeitweilig vom **Unterricht** ausgeschlossen werden *to be suspended **IV AC3**, 68
unterrichten *to teach **II**
Unterrichtsstunde lesson **I**; period *(AE)* **IV U2**, 48
Unterschied difference **I**; contrast **IV AC2**, 38
unterschiedlich different **I**
unterschreiben to sign **IV U2**, 52
unterstreichen to underline **III**
unterstützen to support **IV TS1**, 36
Unterstützung benefit **IV U2**, 51
Untersuchung research *(no pl)* **III**
Untertitel caption **III**
unterwegs out and about **II**; on the move **IV U1**, 8
unterzeichnen to sign **IV U2**, 52
unverschämt rude **I**
unwohl sick **II**

üppig lavish **IV U1**, 19
Ureinwohner/-in Amerikas Native American **IV U2**, 45
Urlaub holiday **I**; vacation *(AE)* **IV AC2**, 41
Seid ihr im **Urlaub**? Are you on holiday? **I**
Sind Sie im **Urlaub**? Are you on holiday? **I**
Ursprung origin **IV U1**, 19
ursprünglich original **III**
ursprünglich originally **II**
US-amerikanisch US **IV AC2**, 41
usw. *(= und so weiter)* etc. *(= et cetera)* **II**

V

Vanillepudding custard **I**
Vanillesoße custard **I**
Vater father **I**
Vegetarier/-in vegetarian **III**
vegetarisch vegetarian **III**
Verabredung date **IV U2**, 55
Veränderung change **III**
verängstigt scared **IV U2**, 52
Veranstaltung event **I**
verantwortlich responsible **IV U1**, 16
die **Verantwortung** tragen (für) *to be in charge (of) **III**
verantwortungsvoll responsible **IV U1**, 16
jmdn. **verärgern** *to make sb angry **III**
verärgert angry **I**
Verb verb **I**
verbessern to improve **I**
sich **verbessern** to improve **I**
verbieten to ban **III**
verbinden *to put through **I**; to join; to link **II**; to combine **IV U3**, 75
Verbindung link **II**; connection **III**; combination **IV U3**, 75
verblüfft amazed **IV U2**, 52
Ge- und **Verbote** dos and don'ts **IV AC1**, 22
Verbrechen crime **III**
Verbrecher/-in criminal **III**
verbrennen *to burn **III**
verbringen *(Zeit)* *to spend **II**
verdienen to earn **I**; to deserve **II**
Geld **verdienen** *to make money **I**
die Augen **verdrehen** to roll one's eyes **III**
Verein club **I**; society **III**
Verfasser/-in writer **III**
verfolgen to trace **I**
verfügbar available **IV TS2**, 65
verführerisch tempting **IV TS1**, 33
Vergangenheit past **II**
Vergangenheitsform simple past; past form **II**
vergeben *to forgive **II**
etw. **vergeigen** to mess sth up **IV TS1**, 30
vergessen *to forget **I**
Vergleich comparison **II**
vergleichen (mit) to compare (with/to) **I**
verhaften to arrest **II**
Verhaftung detention **IV AC3**, 68
Verhalten behaviour *(no pl)* **IV AC1**, 22; behavior *(no pl) (AE)* **IV AC3**, 69
sich **verhalten** to behave **III**
sich **verirren** *to get lost **III**
Verkauf sale **II**
verkaufen *to sell **I**
Verkäufer/-in assistant **II**
Verkäufer/-in *(auf einem Flohmarkt)* seller **I**
Verkehr traffic **IV U1**, 14
Verkehrsmittel transport **III**
öffentliche **Verkehrsmittel** public transport *(no pl)* **II**
Verkleidung fancy dress **II**
verlassen *to leave **II**
sich **verlassen** (auf) to rely (on) **III**
verlässlich reliable **IV TS3**, 100
verlegen embarrassed **II**
verleihen *to lend **III**
verletzen *to hurt **II**
verletzt hurt **II**; wounded **III**
Verletzung injury **II**
verlieren *to lose **II**
verloren gehen *to get lost **III**
vermeiden to avoid **III**
vermieten to rent (out) **III**
vermischen to mix (up) **III**
vermissen to miss **III**
vermuten to guess **I**
verneint negative **III**
verneinte Form negative form **I**
Vernissage gallery walk **I**
vernünftig sensible **IV TS1**, 32
Verpackung wrapping **I**
verpassen to miss **II**
verraucht smoky **III**
sich den Knöchel **verrenken** to twist your ankle **II**
verrückt crazy **I**; mad **II**
verrückt sein nach *to be crazy about **IV U2**, 47
verrückt werden *to go crazy **II**
Vers verse **III**
Versammlung assembly **II**
versäumen to miss **II**
versäumen, etw. zu tun to fail to do sth **IV U3**, 79
verschenken *to give away **IV TS2**, 64
verschieden different **I**; separate **II**
verschiedene several **II**
verschmutzen to litter **IV AC1**, 22
Verschmutzung pollution **II**
verschütten *to spill **IV U1**, 10
verschwenden to waste **II**
verschwenderisch lavish **IV U1**, 19; wasteful **IV AC2**, 40
Verschwendung waste **IV AC3**, 69
verschwommen blurred **III**
Verschwörung conspiracy **IV TS3**, 102
verschwunden missing **II**
verschwunden sein *to be gone **II**
sich **versichern** *to make sure **I**
Version version **III**
versorgen to supply **III**
Verspätung delay **IV U1**, 15
versprechen to promise **III**
Verstand mind **III**
sich **verständigen** to communicate **II**
Verständnis understanding **II**
(sich) **verstecken** *to hide **III**
verstehen *to understand **I**
versuchen to try **I**
Versuchung temptation **IV TS2**, 64
in **Versuchung** führen to tempt **IV TS1**, 31
in **Versuchung** gebracht tempted **IV TS1**, 31
verteilen *to give away **IV TS2**, 64
vertrauen to trust **III**
vertrauen (auf) to rely (on) **III**
vertrauenswürdig reliable **IV TS3**, 100
nicht **vertraut** unfamiliar **III**
Vertuschung cover-up **IV TS3**, 102
verunreinigen to litter **IV AC1**, 22
verursachen to cause **II**
vervollständigen to complete **IV AC3**, 68
verwenden to use **I**; *to make use of **IV U3**, 89
verwirrt confused **III**
verwischt blurred **III**
verwundet wounded **III**
verzeihen *to forgive **II**
verzieren to decorate **I**
Verzögerung delay **IV U1**, 15
Video video **II**
Videochat video chat **II**
viel/-e lots (of); a lot of **I**
viel a lot **I**; much **I**
so **viel** that much **III**
viel zu lernen a lot to learn **I**
viel Glück good luck **IV U3**, 76
viele many **I**
Viele Grüße Best wishes **III**
vielleicht maybe **I**; perhaps **III**
Vielvölker- multi-ethnic **II**
vier four **I**
Viertel nach/vor quarter past/to **I**
Viktorianer/-in Victorian **III**
viktorianisch Victorian **III**
violett purple **I**
Visum, **Visa** *(Pl.)* visa, visas *(pl)* **IV U1**, 9
Vitamin vitamin **III**
Vogel bird **II**
Vogelbeobachtung birdwatching **II**
Vokabular vocabulary **I**
Volks- ethnic **IV U3**, 75
Volksentscheid referendum **III**
Volksstamm tribe **III**
voll (von) full (of) **I**
vollenden to complete **IV AC3**, 68
Volleyball volleyball **I**
völlig complete **IV AC2**, 41
völlig absolutely **II**; completely **III**; quite **IV U1**, 14; totally **IV AC4**, 107
vollkommen perfect **I**
vollständig complete **IV AC2**, 41

von from; about; of **I**; by **III**
von … bis from … to **I**
vor in front of **I**
vor *(bei Uhrzeitangaben)* to **I**
vor *(zeitlich)* before **I**; ago **II**
nicht **vor** not until **IV U2**, 44
vor dem Lesen pre-reading **I**
Voraussage prediction **III**
vorbei over **II**
vorbei (an) past **I**
vorbereiten to prepare **I**
Vorder- front **III**
Vordergrund foreground **IV U2**, 47
Vorderseite front **III**
sich **vordrängeln** to jump the queue **I**
Vorgarten front yard *(AE)* **IV U2**, 43
Vorgehensweise approach **IV TS2**, 66
vorgeschichtlich prehistoric **III**
vorhaben *to be up to **II**
vorher before **II**
Vorhersage prediction **III**
vorkommen *to come up **III**
laut **vorlesen** *to read out loud **III**
Vorlieben likes *(pl)* **IV U2**, 46
Vormittag morning **I**
vormittags in the mornings **I**
vormittags *(Uhrzeit)* a.m. **I**
Vorort suburb **IV U2**, 43
Vorrang priority **IV TS3**, 101
Vorschlag suggestion **I**
vorschlagen to suggest **IV U1**, 15
Vorsicht! Be careful! **I**
vorsichtig careful **II**
Vorsingen audition **III**
laut **vorsingen** *to sing out loud **III**
Vorsprechen audition **III**
Vorstadt- suburban **IV U2**, 43
vorstellen to present **I**
sich (etwas) **vorstellen** to imagine **I**
Stelle/Stellt … **vor**. Introduce … **I**
Vorstellung introduction **II**; performance **IV TS1**, 30
Vorstellungskraft imagination **III**
Vortanzen audition **III**
vortäuschen to fake **II**; to pretend **IV U1**, 17
Vorteil benefit **IV U2**, 51
Vortrag presentation **I**; talk **IV U2**, 43
einen **Vortrag** halten *to give a talk **IV U2**, 43
vortragen to recite **III**
vorüber over **II**
vorüber (an) past **I**
vorwärts forward **III**
vorziehen to prefer **IV U2**, 50

W

Wach- security **IV U1**, 13
Wachdienst security **IV U1**, 13
Wache guard **II**
Wachs wax **II**
wachsen *to grow **III**
Wachsfigur wax figure **II**
Wächter/-in guard **II**
wackelig wobbly **II**
Wackelpudding jelly **I**
Waffe weapon **III**
hier: **Wagen** truck *(AE)* **IV U3**, 75
Wer nicht **wagt**, der nicht gewinnt. No risk, no fun! **IV AC3**, 69
Wahl choice **II**; option **III**
wählen to vote **I**; *to choose **II**
den richtigen Zeitpunkt **wählen** to time **IV U3**, 72
Telefon mit **Wählscheibe** rotary phone **III**
wahr true **II**
wahr werden *to come true **IV U3**, 76
während *(+ Nomen)* during *(+ noun)* **II**
während while; as **I**
Wahrheit truth **IV U1**, 13
wahrnehmen to notice **II**
wahrscheinlich probably **II**
Währung currency **IV U1**, 9
Wald forest **II**; wood **III**
Wäldchen wood **III**
Waliser/-in Welsh **II**
Walisisch Welsh **II**
walisisch Welsh **II**
Wand wall **I**
Wandern walking **II**; hiking **III**
Wanderweg walking trail **III**
Wandschrank closet **IV U2**, 44
wann when **I**
wann immer whenever **II**
warm warm **III**
warnen to warn **IV TS1**, 34
warten (auf) to wait (for) **I**
(einen Augenblick) **warten** *to hang on **IV U1**, 10
Warte/Wartet und denk/denkt nach. Stop and think **I**
Warte ab! Wait and see! **I**
Warteschlange queue **I**
warum why **I**
was what **I**
was auch immer whatever **IV AC4**, 107
was für ein what **I**
Was fehlt? What is missing? **I**
Was für ein Glück! What luck! **III**
Was für ein/-e … What a … **IV U2**, 48
Was geht ab? What's going on? **III**
Was hast du? What's the matter? **III**
Was ist das? What's that? **I**
Was ist dein/-e Lieblings…? What's your favourite …? **I**
Was ist die Regel für …? What's the rule for …? **I**
Was ist los? What's the matter?; What's up?; What's going on? **III**
Was ist mit …? What about …? **I**
was noch what else **I**
was sonst what else **I**
Was um alles in der Welt …? What on earth …? **II**
waschen to wash **I**
sich **waschen** to wash **I**
Waschmaschine washing machine **II**
Wasser water **I**
Wasserrutsche water slide **I**
Wasserspender water fountain **IV AC4**, 106
Wau! Woof! **I**
Webdesigner web designer **III**
Webseite site **II**
Website website **I**
Wechsel change **III**
Wechselgeld change **IV U3**, 76
wechseln to change **II**
Wechselt euch ab. Take turns. **I**
Wecker alarm clock **II**
Weg way **I**; path **IV U3**, 92
im **Weg** sein/stehen *to be in the way **I**
im **Weg** stehen *to get in the way **II**
weg away **I**
weg sein *to be gone **II**
Es ist **weg**. It's gone. **II**
wegen because of; for **II**
wegfahren *to drive off **III**
wegführen *to lead off **III**
wegnehmen *to take **I**
wegrennen *to run away **I**
wegwerfen *to throw away **I**
weh tun *to hurt **II**
Weide field **II**
Weihnachten Christmas **I**
weil because **I**
eine **Weile** a while **II**
Wein wine **I**
weinen to cry **III**
auf andere **Weise** in other ways **II**
weiß white **I**
weit far **II**; wide **III**
weiter (weg) further **III**
zu **weit** gehen *to overdo **IV U2**, 55
hier: **weiter** tun *to keep **IV U2**, 44
weitere more; other **I**
weiterführen *to go on **I**
weitergeben to pass (on) **I**
weitergehen *to go on **I**; to continue **IV U1**, 18
weitermachen *to go on **I**; to continue **III**
Weizen wheat **IV AC2**, 41
welche/-r/-s what; which **I**
Welche Farbe hat …? What colour is …? **I**
Welche … sind es? What are …? **I**
Welle wave **I**
Welt world **I**
aus aller **Welt** from around the world **III**
Was um alles in der **Welt** …? What on earth …? **II**
Weltall space **IV TS3**, 104
Weltraum space **IV TS3**, 104
wem who **I**; whom **IV TS1**, 37
wen who **I**; whom **IV TS1**, 37
Für **wen** …? Who … for? **I**
wenden to turn round **II**
sich **wenden** an to turn to **III**

Wendepunkt turning point **III**
Wendung expression **II**
ein **wenig** a little **I**; a bit **II**
für/mit **wenig** Geld on a shoestring **IV U3**, 72
wenige a few **I**; few **II**
weniger less **III**
wenigstens at least **II**
wenn when; if **I**
Wenn ich du wäre … If I were you … **IV AC3**, 69
wer who **I**
Wer ist dabei? Who's in? **II**
Wer ist es? Who is it? **I**
Wer macht mit? Who's in? **II**
Werbefachmann/-frau advertiser **IV TS2**, 64
werben to advertise **IV TS2**, 64
Werbespot advert **III**; ad **IV TS2**, 64
Werbespruch slogan **II**
Werbetext ad copy **IV TS2**, 65
Werbung advertising *(no pl)* **IV TS2**, 64
Werbung machen to advertise **IV TS2**, 64
werden *to become **II**; *to get **III**
werden *(futurisch)* will **III**
wird/**werden** gonna (= going to) *(coll)* **IV U3**, 70
würde/-st/-n/-t would **III**
werfen (nach) *to throw (at) **I**
Werk factory **III**
Werkzeug tool **III**
wert sein *to be worth **I**
das **Wesentliche** gist **II**
West- west **I**
Westen west **I**
im äußersten **Westen** in the far west **III**
westeuropäische Zeit Greenwich Mean Time *(= GMT)* **I**
Wettbewerb contest **I**; competition **II**
in **Wettbewerb** treten (mit) to compete (with) **III**
ich **wette** I bet **II**
Wetter weather **I**
Wettervorhersage weather forecast **III**
Wettkampf contest **I**
Wettlauf race **II**
Whisky whisky **III**
wichtig important **I**
wichtig nehmen to care (about) **II**
wie like **I**; as **II**
wie how **I**
wie auch immer whatever **IV AC4**, 107
Wie viele …? How many …? **I**
Wie alt bist du? How old are you? **I**
Wie alt sind Sie? How old are you? **I**
wie das ist what it's like **II**
Wie geht es dir? How are you? **I**
Wie geht es euch? How are you? **I**
Wie geht es Ihnen? How are you? **I**
Wie heißen Sie? What's your name? **I**
Wie heißt du? What's your name? **I**
Wie man … How to … **I**
Wie spät ist es? What's the time? **I**
Wie viel (kostet/kosten) …? How much is/are …? **I**
Wie viel Uhr ist es? What's the time? **I**
Wie war es? What was it like? **III**
Wie wär's mit …? What about …? **I**
wieder again **I**
Wiederaufbereitung recycling **II**
Wiederaufnehmen pick-up **I**
wiedergeben to report **IV U1**, 9
wiederholen to repeat **II**
Wiederholung revision **II**; repetition **IV U1**, 15
auf **Wiedersehen** goodbye **I**
wiegen to weigh **III**
Wiese field **II**
Wikitext wiki (text) **IV TS3**, 101
wild wild **III**
Wilderei poaching *(no pl)* **III**
Wildnis bush **III**
Willkommen! Welcome! **II**
willkommen heißen to welcome **II**
Wind wind **III**
Windsurfen windsurfing **III**
Winter winter **III**
Winterschlaf hibernation **III**
winzig tiny **III**
wir we **I**
Wir sind aus … We're from … **I**
wirklich real **II**
wirklich really **I**
Wirksamkeit effectiveness **IV TS2**, 67
Wirkung effect **IV U3**, 89
wirkungsvoll effective **IV TS2**, 66
wirr confused **III**
wissen *to know **I**
Du **weißt**, wie man … You know how to … **I**
Ich **weiß** (es) nicht! I don't know! **I**
Ihr **wisst**, wie man … You know how to … **I**
Wissenschaft science **IV TS3**, 100
Wissenschaftler/-in scientist **III**
Witz joke **I**
witzig funny; fun **I**
WLAN wifi **IV U1**, 10
wo where **I**
wo ich hingehöre where I belong **IV U1**, 16
Woche week **I**
Wochenende weekend **I**
am **Wochenende** at the weekend **I**
Wochentag weekday **II**
Woher …? Where … from? **I**
wohin where **I**
Wohlfahrt charity **I**
wohlhabend wealthy **IV AC2**, 40
wohltätige Zwecke charity **I**
Wohltätigkeitsverein charity **I**
wohnen to live **I**
wohnen bei to stay with **II**
Wohnung flat **I**; apartment *(AE)* **IV U2**, 43
Wohnung mit Dachterrasse penthouse **IV U3**, 79
Wohnzimmer living room **I**
Wolke cloud **III**
Wolkenkratzer skyscraper **IV AC2**, 39
wollen to want (to) **I**
Ich **wollte** nicht … (I) didn't mean to … **IV AC4**, 107
Workshop workshop **I**
Wort word **I**
Wortbildung word-building **II**
Wörterbuch dictionary **I**
Wörternetz *(eine Art Schaubild)* mind map **I**
Wörterwolke word cloud **II**
Wortsammlung word bank **III**
Wortschatz vocabulary **I**
Wortschlange word snake **I**
Wortspiel play on words **III**
Wortstellung word order **I**
Wortverbindung collocation **II**
Worum geht es in/im …? What is … about? **I**
Wow! Wow! **I**
kein **Wunder** no wonder **IV U2**, 44
wunderbar beautiful; wonderful **II**
Wunsch wish **I**
(sich) **wünschen** to wish **IV U2**, 51
sich etwas **wünschen** *to make a wish **I**
würde/-st/-n/-t gern would like **I**
Ich **würde** gern … I'd like to … *(= I would like to)* **I**
würde/-st/-n/-t sehr gern would love **I**
Würfel dice **II**
würfle zweimal throw the dice twice **II**
Würfle/Würfelt mit zwei Würfeln. Roll two dice. **I**
Wurm worm **I**
Wurst sausage **III**
wusch whoosh **I**
Wüste desert **IV AC2**, 38
Wut anger *(no pl)* **III**
wütend angry **I**; mad **IV AC3**, 69
jmdn. **wütend** machen *to make sb angry **III**

Z

z.B. *(= zum Beispiel)* e.g. *(= for example)* **I**
Zahl number **I**; figure **III**
zählen (auf) to count (on) **I**
Zahnpasta toothpaste **IV U2**, 56
Zauber- magical **III**
Zauberei magic **IV U1**, 19
Zauberer wizard **III**
auf **Zehenspitzen** gehen to tiptoe **II**
zehn ten **I**
zehnmal ten times **I**
Zeichen sign **II**
Zeichentrickfilm cartoon **III**
zeichnen *to draw **I**
Zeichnung drawing **I**
zeigen to show **I**; to feature **III**
mit dem Finger auf jmdn./etw. **zeigen** to point at sb/sth **IV AC1**, 22

Zeige/Zeigt auf ... Point to ... **I**
Zeige/Zeigt darauf. Point. **I**
Zeile line **I**
Zeit time **I**; tense **II**
(**Zeit**) brauchen *to take **II**
zur selben **Zeit** at the same time **I**
die ganze **Zeit** all the time **II**
Es ist **Zeit** aufzustehen! Time to get up! **I**
Zeitalter age **III**; era **IV U1**, 19
goldenes **Zeitalter** golden age **III**
Zeitfenster time slot **II**
Zeitform *(grammatisch)* tense **II**
zeitgemäß up-to-date **IV TS3**, 100
Zeitpunkt point **II**
den richtigen **Zeitpunkt** wählen to time **IV U3**, 72
Zeitschrift magazine **I**
Zeitspanne period **III**
Zeitstrahl time line **I**
Zeitung newspaper **III**
zeitweilig vom Unterricht ausgeschlossen werden *to be suspended **IV AC3**, 68
Zelten camping **II**
zelten to camp **III**
zentral central **II**
Zentral- central **II**
Zentrum centre **I**; center *(AE)* **IV AC2**, 38
zerbrechen *to break **I**
zerschlagen to smash **IV U1**, 16
zerschmettern to smash **IV U1**, 16
zerstören to ruin **II**
Zeug stuff **I**
Zeuge/Zeugin witness **II**
ziehen to pull **I**; *to draw **III**
Ziel goal **I**; purpose **IV U1**, 13; destination **IV U1**, 19; target **IV TS2**, 65
Ziel- target **IV TS2**, 65
Ziellinie finish line **II**
ziemlich quite **IV U1**, 14
Ziffer figure **III**
Zimmer room **I**
Zimmergenosse/Zimmergenossin roommate **I**
Zinn tin **III**
Zitrone lemon **II**
zögern to hesitate **III**
Zoll customs *(sg)* **IV U1**, 9
zollfrei duty-free **IV U1**, 9
Zone zone **IV AC2**, 38
Zoo zoo **II**
Zorn anger *(no pl)* **III**
zornig angry **I**
zu closed **IV U1**, 11
zu too **I**
Zu dumm! Too bad! **I**
zu to **I**
zu Hause at home **I**
zubereiten to prepare **I**
züchten *to grow **III**
Zucker sugar **III**
zudecken to cover **III**
zuerst first **I**; at first **II**
Zufall coincidence **IV U2**, 52
sich mit weniger **zufrieden** geben to settle for less **IV TS2**, 66
Zug train **I**
Zugang finden zu to relate to **III**
Zuhause home **I**
zuhören to listen (to) **I**
Zuhörer/-in listener **II**
zujubeln to cheer **II**
Zukunft future **III**
zukünftig future **IV U1**, 19
zum Beispiel for example **II**
zumachen to close **I**
zunächst at first **II**
hier: ein Feuerwerk **zünden** *to set off **III**
zuordnen to match **I**
zupassen to pass **II**
sich **zurechtfinden** *to find one's way around **IV U2**, 46
(ein Foto) **zurechtschneiden** to crop (a photo) **III**
zurück back **I**
zurückfahren to return **III**
zurückgehen to turn back **II**
zurückgehen auf *to go right back to **III**
zurückkehren to return **III**
zurücklassen *to leave behind **III**
hier: **zurückschrecken** to jump back **II**
zurückspringen to jump back **II**
zurzeit these days **III**
zusammen sein mit *to be around **IV U2**, 44
zusammen together **I**
zusammenfassen to sum up **II**
Zusammenfassung summary **IV TS1**, 37
in **Zusammenhang** stehen *to be connected **II**
zusammenhängen *to be connected **II**
zusammenpassen to mix **IV U2**, 54
zusammenstoßen to crash **III**
zusätzlich extra **I**; additional **II**
zuschauen to watch **I**
Zuschauer/-in viewer **II**
zuspielen to pass **II**
zuständig sein (für) *to be in charge (of) **III**
zustimmen to agree (with) **II**
Zutat ingredient **III**
zuverlässig reliable **IV TS3**, 100
zuvor before **II**
sich **zuwenden** to turn to **III**
zwanglos informal **IV AC4**, 107
Zweck purpose **IV U1**, 13
zwei two **I**
zwei von ihnen two of which **III**
Zweifel doubt **III**
zweimal twice **IV U2**, 53; double **IV U2**, 57
zweisprachig bilingual **II**
zweite/-r/-s second **I**
Zwickmühle dilemma **IV TS1**, 31
Zwilling twin **III**
Zwillings- twin **III**
zwischen between **I**
zwölf twelve **I**

In the classroom

Tip

Die Wörter und Ausdrücke auf diesen Seiten musst du nicht auswendig lernen. Aber in vielen Situationen im Klassenzimmer wirst du sie nützlich finden!

Asking for help and information

Can you help me, please?	Kannst du / Können Sie mir bitte helfen?
How do you do this exercise?	Wie macht man diese Übung?
How do you spell …, please?	Wie schreibt man …, bitte?
Is this right? I'm not sure.	Ist das richtig? Ich bin mir nicht sicher.
Is it OK to …?	Ist es in Ordnung, wenn ich / wir …?
Is it true or false?	Ist das richtig oder falsch?
Sorry, I don't know. Ask …	Tut mir leid, das weiß ich nicht. Frag …
Sorry. Can you say that again, please?	Wie bitte? Können Sie das bitte wiederholen?
What does that mean?	Was bedeutet das?
What's for homework?	Was haben wir als Hausaufgabe auf?
What's that in English / German?	Was heißt das auf Englisch / Deutsch?

Vocabulary for instructions and activities

(Die mit * gekennzeichneten Begriffe werden im Fachlehrplan von mindestens einem Bundesland als Operatoren definiert. Die Verwendung der geforderten Operatoren in Green Line beginnt in Band 1 und wird Band für Band ausgebaut.)

Act (out) one of the scenes. / Act (out) the dialogues.	Spiele eine der Szenen. / Spiele die Dialoge.
Add more words / ideas.	Füge weitere Wörter / Ideen hinzu.
Ask your partner questions.	Stelle deinem Partner / deiner Partnerin Fragen.
Answer your partner's questions.	Beantworte die Fragen deines Partners / deiner Partnerin.
Check your partner's text.	Überprüfe den Text deines Partners / deiner Partnerin.
Choose a character / one of the situations / options.	Wähle eine Figur / eine der Situationen / Optionen.
Collect ideas.	Sammle Ideen.
***Compare** English and German.	Vergleiche das Englische und Deutsche.
Complete the answers.	Vervollständige die Antworten.
Copy the grid / the mind map.	Schreibe die Tabelle / das Wörternetz ab.
Correct the wrong sentences.	Korrigiere die falschen Sätze.
***Describe** what you see / how it makes you feel.	Beschreibe, was du siehst / wie du dich dabei fühlst.
Decide who writes which part.	Entscheidet, wer welchen Teil schreibt.

*__Discuss__ different ideas.	Diskutiert verschiedene Ideen.
Divide your class up into two groups.	Teilt eure Klasse in zwei Gruppen auf.
Draw a picture.	Zeichne ein Bild.
Exchange your flyers / questions.	Tauscht eure Flyer / Fragen untereinander aus.
*__Explain__ your answer. / Explain why.	Erkläre deine Antwort. / Erkläre warum.
Fill in your grid / the form.	Fülle deine Tabelle / das Formular aus.
Find the rule / the right word order.	Finde die Regel / die richtige Wortstellung.
Finish your brochure.	Stelle deine Broschüre fertig.
Form expert groups.	Bildet Expertengruppen.
Get organised.	Organisiert euch.
Give reasons. / Give examples / feedback.	Nenne Gründe. / Gib Beispiele / ein Feedback.
Go back to your home group.	Gehe zurück zu deiner ersten Gruppe.
Guess the new words.	Errate die neuen Wörter.
Imagine you're one of the people in the story.	Stelle dir vor, du bist eine der Personen in der Geschichte.
Improve your text / part of the report.	Verbessere deinen Text / Teil des Berichts.
Learn your text by heart.	Lerne deinen Text auswendig.
Listen to the sentences / the dialogue.	Höre dir die Sätze / den Dialog an.
Look at the picture / the examples.	Schau dir das Bild / die Beispiele an.
*__Look up__ the words.	Schlage die Wörter nach.
Make a poster / a grid / a mind map / notes.	Fertige ein Poster / eine Tabelle / ein Wörternetz / Notizen an.
*__Match__ the sentence parts.	Ordne die Satzteile einander zu.
Note down what is missing.	Notiere, was fehlt.
Plan the scenes.	Plane die Szenen.
Practise your scenes / the dialogues.	Übe deine Szenen / die Dialoge.
*__Present__ the information from your text.	Präsentiere die Informationen aus deinem Text.
Put in the correct forms.	Setze die richtigen Formen ein.
Put the verbs in the right / correct form.	Bringe die Verben in die richtige Form.
Read your text aloud. / Read your text out loud.	Lies deinen Text laut vor.
Record your final report / dialogue.	Nehmt euren fertigen Bericht / Dialog auf.
Repeat the sentences / the dialogues.	Wiederhole die Sätze / die Dialoge.
*__Report__ what the people say.	Berichte, was die Leute sagen.
Say the words / the sounds.	Sage die Wörter / die Laute.
Scan the text for details.	Suche den Text nach Details ab.
Share the information with your partner.	Teile die Informationen mit deinem Partner / deiner Partnerin.
Skim the text for the gist.	Überfliege den Text und finde die wichtigsten Aussagen.
*__Sum up / Summarise__ what happens in the story.	Fasse zusammen, was in der Geschichte passiert.
Swap roles.	Tauscht die Rollen.
Take notes.	Mache dir Notizen.
Take turns.	Wechselt euch ab.
*__Talk__ with / to your partner (about …).	Sprich mit deinem Partner / deiner Partnerin (über …).

Tell your partner about your experiences.	Erzähle deinem Partner / deiner Partnerin von deinen Erfahrungen.
Think - pair - share.	Nachdenken - Paare bilden - teilen / austauschen.
Think about different problems.	Denke über die verschiedenen Probleme nach.
Think of ideas for …	Überlege dir Ideen für …
Translate the words / sentences.	Übersetze die Wörter / Sätze.
Underline the words that change.	Unterstreiche die Wörter, die sich ändern.
Use the ideas / the vocabulary.	Verwende die Ideen / die Vokabeln.
Watch the film.	Sieh dir den Film an.
Work with a partner or in a group.	Arbeite mit einem Partner / einer Partnerin oder in einer Gruppe.
Write dialogues / a short text / a reply / a summary.	Schreibe Dialoge / einen kurzen Text / eine Antwort / eine Zusammenfassung.
Write about your friends.	Schreibe über deine Freunde.
Write down your ideas / key words.	Schreibe deine Ideen / Schlüsselwörter auf.

Useful words

activity - Aktivität	presentation - Präsentation; Vortrag
answer - Antwort	prompt card - Rollenkarte
class display - Ausstellung in der Klasse	puzzle - Rätsel; Puzzle
collocation - Wortverbindung	pros and cons - Vor- und Nachteile
description - Beschreibung	question - Frage
dialogue - Dialog	quiz - Quiz; Rätsel
dice - Würfel	quote - Zitat
draft - Entwurf; Konzept	report - Bericht
drawing - Zeichnung	revision - Wiederholung
example - Beispiel	rhyme - Reim
fact - Tatsache; Fakt	role play - Rollenspiel
folder - Ordner; Mappe	rule - Regel
game - Spiel	scene - Szene
grid - Gitter; Tabelle; Raster	signal word - Signalwort
heading - Überschrift	slogan - Slogan; Werbespruch
information - Information(en)	speech bubble - Sprechblase
key word - Schlüsselwort	story - Geschichte; Erzählung
list - Liste	task - Aufgabe
mind map - Wörternetz	theme - Thema
order - Reihenfolge	title - Titel; Überschrift
perspective - Perspektive	unit - Lektion; Kapitel
phrase - Redewendung; Ausdruck	useful phrases - nützliche Ausdrücke
picture story - Bildergeschichte	vocabulary - Vokabular; Wortschatz
point of view - Standpunkt; Ansicht	word bank - Wortsammlung

Grammar solutions

Unit 1

G1 You told us there was free wifi!

A message from Jack

Jack's mother: Jack sent me a message this afternoon. He said that **he'd had** a good trip and that **he'd arrived** safely. **He hadn't had** time to look around yet, so **he couldn't tell me** much, but he said that the hostel **was** clean and the people **were** very friendly. He said **he'd call** again later, but **he didn't know** when because **they were going** into town for dinner and **he wasn't sure** when **they'd be back**.

G2 Steve's blog

Eddie: Steve sent me a message from France last week. He said that the athletics event **had started the day before** and that **their** team **was** doing well. But it **was** very cold **there**. He said that if **he** ever **came back** to **that** place, **he'd bring** warmer clothes. **He wished he'd listened** to Ms W.

G3 He asked me what the purpose of my visit was

1. The man at passport control asked me **why I was** travelling alone.
2. He wanted to know **where I was from**.
3. He asked me **how long I planned** to stay.
4. He wanted to know **if I had** family in Bangladesh.
5. He asked **if I could speak** Bengali.
6. He wanted to know **if anybody was meeting me** at the airport.

G4 He told me to go into a side room

1. Rafiq's mum **asked him to say hello** to everyone from **them**.
2. She **told him to be careful** with his passport and **not to lose it**.
3. She **asked him to call her** as soon as **he got to** Dhaka.
4. She **told him to have fun** while **he was** there and **to take** lots of photos.

Unit 2

G5 Living here isn't bad

1. How about visiting a museum?
2. I don't really feel like going to a museum today.
3. OK, then, what would you suggest doing?
4. Mom keeps telling me about the spectacular views from Mt. Washington.
5. My mom loves going there too.
6. She never stops talking about the place.

G6 That's the worst thing to do!

1. I promise to be home before 6 p.m.
2. I didn't know what to say.
3. My parents don't want me to watch too much TV.
4. I didn't expect him to invite me to his party.
5. They always let her do what she wants.
6. Our football coach makes us train every day.
7. The best thing to do is say nothing at all.

G7 Gerund or infinitive: It depends on the meaning

Dear Diary,
Bad news! I got a mail from Matt today and it seems he can't stop **thinking** about Sophie. I'm sure Matt didn't mean **to hurt** me, but … When I told Madison, she said I should try **to forget** him. But how? M. thinks I should try **doing** yoga! She says she can remember **feeling** upset about something once, and it really helped her. But I'm not sure. I'm not really sure about anything at the moment: Should I go on **writing** to him? Should I tell him how I feel? I don't know. The only thing I know right now is that it's really late and I mustn't forget **to set** my alarm clock! Madison's mom is driving us to the mall outside Pittsburgh tomorrow. We want **to get** there early and it's two hours in the car, so that means **leaving** at 8 a.m.! Oh well, at least we can stop **to have** breakfast somewhere on the way.

Unit 3

G8 The boy who … / Diego, who …

1. Last year we visited **New York**, which is the largest city in the USA.
2. We stayed with **some friends** who live there.
3. They showed us **some amazing sights** which we would never have found on our own.
4. But they also took us to famous sights like **Rockefeller Center**, which was awesome too.
5. In Times Square we saw **the Naked Cowboy**, who is really only almost naked.
6. He is a **street performer** who has become one of New York's biggest tourist attractions.

G9 How long had they been doing that?

After Julia and Andrea from Germany **had been walking** around Manhattan all morning, they were very hungry. So they decided to go to Diego's Diner, which they **had read** about in the guidebook they **had bought** the day before. When they got there at 12:30, the diner was already very busy. Some of the people **had been waiting** to get their lunch for quite some time. The girls **had been learning** English since the age of ten, so they had no language problems. But when they tried to order, nobody seemed to notice them. Finally, after they **had been trying** to get a waiter's attention for about 15 minutes, a friendly Hispanic American came to their table and took their order.

Find more online: 8x6wn6

Irregular verbs

■ ■ ■ Grundform, *simple past* und *past participle* sind identisch
■ ● ● Grundform unterscheidet sich vom *simple past* und *past participle*
■ ● ■ Grundform und *past participle* sind identisch, nur das *simple past* hat eine andere Form
■ ● ▲ Grundform, *simple past* und *past participle* haben alle eine andere Form

■ Grundform	■ simple past	■ past participle	Deutsch
cost [kɒst]	cost [kɒst]	cost [kɒst]	kosten
cut [kʌt]	cut [kʌt]	cut [kʌt]	schneiden
hit [hɪt]	hit [hɪt]	hit [hɪt]	schlagen, treffen
hurt [hɜ:t]	hurt [hɜ:t]	hurt [hɜ:t]	verletzen, sich weh tun
let [let]	let [let]	let [let]	lassen
put [pʊt]	put [pʊt]	put [pʊt]	legen, setzen, stellen
set up ['set ˌʌp]	set up ['set ˌʌp]	set up ['set ˌʌp]	erbauen, errichten
upset [ʌp'set]	upset [ʌp'set]	upset [ʌp'set]	aus der Fassung bringen

■ Grundform	● simple past	● past participle	Deutsch
bring [brɪŋ]	brought [brɔ:t]	brought [brɔ:t]	(mit)bringen
build [bɪld]	built [bɪlt]	built [bɪlt]	bauen
burn [bɜ:n]	burnt [bɜ:nt]	burnt [bɜ:nt]	(ver)brennen
buy [baɪ]	bought [bɔ:t]	bought [bɔ:t]	kaufen
catch [kætʃ]	caught [kɔ:t]	caught [kɔ:t]	fangen; mitbekommen
dream [dri:m]	dreamed [dri:md] / dreamt [dremt]	dreamed [dri:md] / dreamt [dremt]	träumen
feel [fi:l]	felt [felt]	felt [felt]	fühlen
find [faɪnd]	found [faʊnd]	found [faʊnd]	finden
get [get]	got [gɒt]	got [gɒt]	holen, bringen, bekommen; werden
hang [hæŋ]	hung [hʌŋ]	hung [hʌŋ]	hängen
have [hæv]	had [hæd]	had [hæd]	haben
hear [hɪə]	heard [hɜ:d]	heard [hɜ:d]	hören
hold [həʊld]	held [held]	held [held]	halten
keep [ki:p]	kept [kept]	kept [kept]	(auf)bewahren, behalten
lead [li:d]	led [led]	led [led]	(an)führen
learn [lɜ:n]	learned [lɜ:nd] / learnt [lɜ:nt]	learned [lɜ:nd] / learnt [lɜ:nt]	lernen
leave [li:v]	left [left]	left [left]	(ver)lassen
lend [lend]	lent [lent]	lent [lent]	(ver)leihen
make [meɪk]	made [meɪd]	made [meɪd]	machen, tun
meet [mi:t]	met [met]	met [met]	treffen
pay [peɪ]	paid [peɪd]	paid [peɪd]	(be)zahlen
read [ri:d]	read [red]	read [red]	lesen
say [seɪ]	said [sed]	said [sed]	sagen
sell [sel]	sold [səʊld]	sold [səʊld]	verkaufen
send [send]	sent [sent]	sent [sent]	senden, verschicken
shoot [ʃu:t]	shot [ʃɒt]	shot [ʃɒt]	schießen (auf)
sit [sɪt]	sat [sæt]	sat [sæt]	sitzen

sleep [sli:p]	slept [slept]	slept [slept]	schlafen
smell [smel]	smelt [smelt]	smelt [smelt]	riechen, duften
spell [spel]	spelt [spelt]	spelt [spelt]	buchstabieren
spend [spend]	spent [spent]	spent [spent]	ausgeben, verbringen
spill [spɪl]	spilt [spɪlt]	spilt [spɪlt]	verschütten, auslaufen
stand (up) [stænd]	stood (up) [stʊd]	stood (up) [stʊd]	(auf)stehen
sting [stɪŋ]	stung [stʌŋ]	stung [stʌŋ]	stechen
tell [tel]	told [təʊld]	told [təʊld]	erzählen
think [θɪŋk]	thought [θɔ:t]	thought [θɔ:t]	(nach)denken, glauben
understand [ˌʌndəˈstænd]	understood [ˌʌndəˈstʊd]	understood [ˌʌndəˈstʊd]	verstehen
win [wɪn]	won [wʌn]	won [wʌn]	gewinnen, siegen

■ Grundform	● simple past	■ past participle	Deutsch
become [bɪˈkʌm]	became [bɪˈkeɪm]	become [bɪˈkʌm]	werden
come [kʌm]	came [keɪm]	come [kʌm]	kommen
run [rʌn]	ran [ræn]	run [rʌn]	laufen, rennen

■ Grundform	● simple past	▲ past participle	Deutsch
be [bi:]	was / were [wɒz / wɜ:]	been [bi:n]	sein
blow (out) [bləʊ]	blew [blu:]	blown [bləʊn]	(aus)blasen, (aus)pusten
break [breɪk]	broke [brəʊk]	broken [ˈbrəʊkn]	(zer)brechen, kaputt machen
choose [tʃu:z]	chose [tʃəʊz]	chosen [tʃəʊzn]	(aus)wählen
do [du:]	did [dɪd]	done [dʌn]	machen, tun
draw [drɔ:]	drew [dru:]	drawn [drɔ:n]	zeichnen
drink [drɪŋk]	drank [dræŋk]	drunk [drʌŋk]	trinken
drive [draɪv]	drove [drəʊv]	driven [ˈdrɪvn]	fahren
eat [i:t]	ate [et]	eaten [i:tn]	essen
fall [fɔ:l]	fell [fel]	fallen [ˈfɔ:lən]	fallen
fly [flaɪ]	flew [flu:]	flown [fləʊn]	fliegen
forget [fəˈget]	forgot [fəˈgɒt]	forgotten [fəˈgɒtn]	vergessen
give [gɪv]	gave [geɪv]	given[ˈgɪvn]	geben
go [gəʊ]	went [went]	gone [gɒn]	gehen, fahren
grow [grəʊ]	grew [gru:]	grown [grəʊn]	wachsen; anbauen
know [nəʊ]	knew [nju:]	known [nəʊn]	kennen, wissen
ring [rɪŋ]	rang [ræŋ]	rung [rʌŋ]	klingeln; anrufen
rise [raɪz]	rose [rəʊz]	risen [ˈrɪzn]	steigen, sich erheben
see [si:]	saw [sɔ:]	seen [si:n]	sehen
show [ʃəʊ]	showed [ʃəʊd]	shown [ʃəʊn]	zeigen
sing [sɪŋ]	sang [sæŋ]	sung [sʌŋ]	singen
sink [sɪŋk]	sank [sæŋk]	sunk [sʌŋk]	sinken, untergehen
speak [spi:k]	spoke [spəʊk]	spoken [ˈspəʊkn]	sprechen
swim [swɪm]	swam [swæm]	swum [swʌm]	schwimmen
take [teɪk]	took [tʊk]	taken [ˈteɪkn]	nehmen
throw [θrəʊ]	threw [θru:]	thrown [θrəʊn]	werfen
wake up [ˌweɪk‿ˈʌp]	woke up [ˌwəʊk‿ˈʌp]	woken up [ˌwəʊkn‿ˈʌp]	aufwachen; aufwecken
wear [weə]	wore [wɔ:]	worn [wɔ:n]	anhaben, tragen
write [raɪt]	wrote [rəʊt]	written [ˈrɪtn]	schreiben

The US school system

For most kids in the US, school starts at the age of 3–4 with pre-school (or nursery school), which can be compared to German *Kindergarten*. Different to Germany, kindergarten in the US comes after pre-school.

School systems differ around the US, but everywhere high school ends with the **high school diploma** after 12th grade. Then students can decide if they want to find a job or continue their education at college or university. A dual vocational training[1] like in Germany doesn't exist in the US.

State-run schools in the US are called **public schools**. The others are **private schools** mostly operated by religious institutions and organizations.

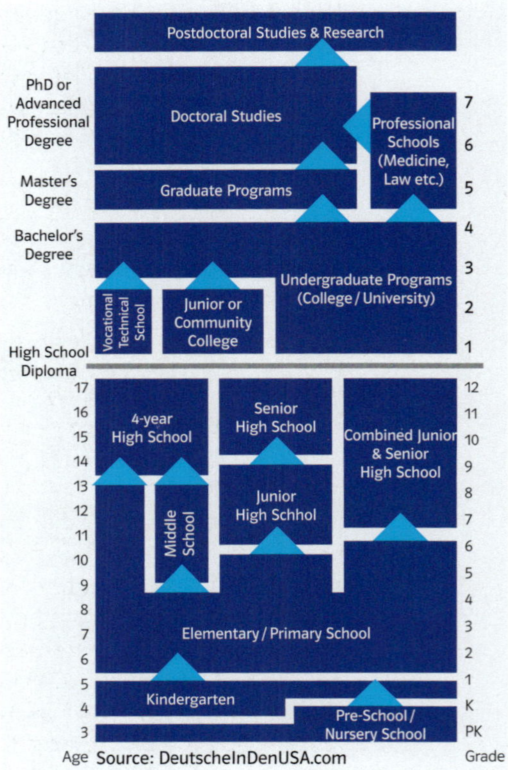

Source: DeutscheInDenUSA.com

School takes up a lot of time

In America kids are at school all day. How early the day starts depends on how they get to school – with a school bus, by public or private transportation. Either the kids bring a bag lunch from home or eat a hot lunch in the school cafeteria. But even when classes are over in the afternoon, a lot of kids still don't go home because there are all kinds of activities going on. If you don't have sports practice for a school team, you might have a drama or chess club meeting. That means that many students don't get home until the evening.

Even on the weekend students spend a lot of time at school. Going to school sports events is a big social activity that involves a lot of different students, especially at the high school level. The school band plays at the game, the cheerleaders cheer, the dance team performs at half-time and the school newspaper photographer takes pictures.

High schools typically have formal dances several times a year. The most popular are the homecoming[2] dance after a football game and the prom[3] at the end of the school year.

Other school activities have more to do with the community. The students might organize a food or clothing drive to help poor families. Or they spend their weekend helping to build a playground in the neighborhood. Most of the students really do want to help, but they also know that participating in these activities will look good on their college applications[4]. Getting into a good college or university can be very competitive and kids start thinking about it at the beginning of high school already!

Surprising facts

- About 2 million students are home-schooled in America.
- Going to a private school can cost $50,000 a year.
- The largest high school in America has over 8,000 students.

1 dual vocational training [du'a:l voʊ'keɪʃnl 'treɪnɪŋ] duale Berufsausbildung | **2 homecoming** ['həʊmˌkʌmɪŋ] Ehemaligentreffen | **3 prom** [prɒm] *Ball am Ende des Schuljahres* | **4 application** [ˌæplɪ'keɪʃn] Bewerbung

New York, New York

New York City, which was originally founded as a trading post in 1624, is the largest city in America with an estimated population of 8.6 million people (Berlin has about 3.5 million). In area, New York City is about half the size of Saarland.

The city is divided into five sections called **boroughs**[1]. The borough with the third-largest population is the smallest – **Manhattan**. This is home to the city's famous skyscrapers and three of the world's ten most-visited tourist attractions (Times Square, Central Park and the Grand Central Terminal). About 60 million tourists visit the city each year.

The least-populated borough and probably the most different compared to Manhattan is **Staten Island**. Most of the island is a residential[2] area. It is connected to Brooklyn by a bridge and the free Staten Island Ferry.

The **Bronx** is home to the world's largest metro zoo and the New York Yankees professional baseball team. However, it's probably most well-known as the birthplace of rap and hip-hop culture. More than half of the population is Hispanic.

Queens is the largest borough in area and is considered the most ethnically diverse[3] urban area in the world. Almost 50 % of the residents are foreign-born and 50 % of New York City's Asian population lives here. Queens annually hosts the US Open tennis tournament at Flushing Meadows. Two of the world's busiest airports, John F. Kennedy and LaGuardia, are also located here.

The most populous borough is **Brooklyn**. There is wide cultural, social and ethnic diversity. The rapidly growing Chinese-American population has established[4] several Chinatowns. Brooklyn is also home to a strong independent art scene but also to many high-tech start-ups.

Surprising facts

- New York was originally called New Amsterdam.
- The name 'Manhattan' goes back to the Native American tribe that lived in the area, called the Mannahatta.
- Almost half of the city's residents over the age of five speak a language other than English.

New York's importance in the world

New York City is often called the cultural and financial center of the world. The city is home to the world's two largest stock exchanges[5], where global trading goes on continuously. The United Nations has been located in New York since soon after its creation in 1945. The world's perhaps most famous theater district is simply known by the street that hosts it – Broadway. This is the place to go for plays and musicals. Besides performing arts like the symphony and ballet, there are also important art museums in NY, like the Museum of Modern Art, or MoMA for short. New York City has a huge advertising industry too. It used to be concentrated on Madison Avenue, but has now spread out across the city.

1 **borough** ['bʌrə] Stadtteil | 2 **residential** [ˌrezɪ'denʃl] Wohn- | 3 **diverse** [daɪ'vɜːs] vielfältig | 4 **to establish** [ɪ'stæblɪʃ] gründen | 5 **stock exchange** ['stɑk ɪksˌtʃeɪndʒ] Börse

Bildquellennachweis:

U1.1 plainpicture GmbH & Co. KG (Kniel Synnatzschke), Hamburg; **U1.2** shutterstock (Sean Pavone), New York, NY; **2.1**; **30.2** Ullstein Bild GmbH (ArenaPAL), Berlin; **4.1** Corbis, Berlin; **8.1** Thinkstock (brians**101**), München; **9.1** Getty Images (Marco Di Lauro), München; **9.2** Thinkstock (Creatas), München; **9.3** Getty Images (E+), München; **14.1** iStockphoto (Tarzan**9280**), Calgary, Alberta; **19.1**; **23.1**; **23.2**; **23.3**; February Films, London; **20.1** shutterstock (Dave Allen Photography), New York, NY; **21.1** Klett-Archiv (Peter Niehoff), Stuttgart; **26.1** shutterstock (Art Konovalov), New York, NY; **26.2** Fotolia.com (Ekaterina Pokrovsky), New York; **28.1** shutterstock (saiko3p), New York, NY; **29.1** shutterstock (Syda Productions), New York, NY; **29.2** shutterstock (Cesar Augusto), New York, NY; **29.3** shutterstock (Jack Frog), New York, NY; **30.1** Fotolia.com (Katrina Brown), New York; **31.1**; **32.1**; **34.1**; **34.2**; **36.1** Clemens Weisshaar, Bisingen-Zimmern; **38.1** shutterstock (granata1111), New York, NY; **38.2** Corbis (Matt Mawson), Berlin; **38.3** Corbis (Bill Stormont), Berlin; **38.4** shutterstock (Pi-Lens), New York, NY; **38.5** Corbis (Nick Roush), Berlin; **38.6** shutterstock (Everett Historical), New York, NY; **39.1** Corbis (Louie Psihoyos), Berlin; **39.2** Corbis (Gavin Hellier/JAI), Berlin; **39.3** Corbis (Hill Street Studios/Blend Images), Berlin; **39.4** Corbis (Lynn Christiansen), Berlin; **39.5** Corbis (David Butow), Berlin; **41.1** Corbis (Robert Niedring), Berlin; **42.1** Corbis (Kevin Dodge/Masterfile), Berlin; **41.2**; **47.2** Corbis (Hero Images), Berlin; **42.2** shutterstock (LizCoughlan), New York, NY; **43.1** shutterstock (Monkey Business Images), New York, NY; **149.1**; **151.2**; **154.1**; **44.1** Fotolia.com (jackfrog), New York; **44.2**; **149.2** Corbis (**237**/Paul Bradbury/Ocean), Berlin; **45.1** Corbis (GraphicaArtis), Berlin; **45.2** shutterstock (Karen Grigoryan), New York, NY; **46.1** shutterstock (Lucky Business), New York, NY; **47.1** Thinkstock (ikick), München; **49.1** Corbis (Tetra Images), Berlin; **51.1** Corbis (KidStock/Blend Images), Berlin; **55.1**; **55.2**; **68.1**; **106**; **107.1**; **107.2**; JDM Productions Inc, New York; **56.1**; **56.3** shutterstock (Veronica Louro), New York, NY; **56.2** Corbis (DreamPictures/VStock/Blend Images/), Berlin; **57.1** Getty Images (Vivien Killilea), München; **58.1** iStockphoto (wickedberlin), Calgary, Alberta; **58.2** Alamy Stock Photo (Vespasian), Abingdon, Oxon; **60.1** Fotolia.com (Monkey Business), New York; **60.2** shutterstock (JuliusKielaitis), New York, NY; **60.3** shutterstock (Palenque), New York, NY; **61.1** www.CartoonStock.com (Schwadron, Harley), Bath; **62.1** shutterstock (Gary Whitton), New York, NY; **62.2** shutterstock (Gimas), New York, NY; **62.3** iStockphoto (Pgiam), Calgary, Alberta; **63.1** Thinkstock (lisafx), München; **63.2** Picture-Alliance (Maja Hitij), Frankfurt; **63.3** Alamy Stock Photo (Jim West), Abingdon, Oxon; **63.4** shutterstock (ducu59us), New York, NY; **65.1** Thinkstock (darak77), München; **65.2** shutterstock (yurok), New York, NY; **65.3** Getty Images (fStop), München; **65.4** shutterstock (InesBazdar), New York, NY; **65.5** shutterstock (Fotoatelie), New York, NY; **65.6**; **66.1** Thinkstock (shironosov), München; **67.1** Getty Images (DEA / A. DAGLI ORTI/De Agostini), München; **67.2**; **67.3** shutterstock (Maridav), New York, NY; **69.1** shutterstock (HBRH), New York, NY; **70.1** shutterstock (Luciano Mortula), New York, NY; **71.1** Getty Images (Visions of America/UIG), München; **71.2** shutterstock (digishoots), New York, NY; **71.3** Thinkstock (stu99), München; **71.4** iStockphoto (carterdayne), Calgary, Alberta; **73.1** shutterstock (DrimaFilm), New York, NY; **75.1** shutterstock (martiapunts), New York, NY; **75.2** shutterstock (Erika Cross), New York, NY; **79.1** shutterstock (oneinchpunch), New York, NY; **79.2** shutterstock (FashionStock.com), New York, NY; **80.1**; **81.1**; **82.1**; **83.1**; **84.1**; **85.1**; **86.1**; **87.1**; **88.1**; **124.2**; **124.3**; **124.1** Stefani Kampmann / Morton Rhue: Asphalt Tribe ¿ Eine Graphic Novel © **2011** by Ravensburger Buchverlag Otto Maier GmbH, Ravensburg; **90.1** Alamy Stock Photo (Sean Pavone), Abingdon, Oxon; **91.1**; **91.2** shutterstock (Antonio Guillem), New York, NY; **92.1** shutterstock (Kamira), New York, NY; **94.1** iStockphoto (Jitalia17), Calgary, Alberta; **95.1** shutterstock (Vacclav), New York, NY; **95.2** shutterstock (Christopher Penler), New York, NY; **97.1** shutterstock (View Apart), New York, NY; **98.1** shutterstock (Kaesler Media), New York, NY; **99.1** akg-images (Jason Hook), Berlin; **99.2** Corbis (Matt Moyer), Berlin; **99.3** shutterstock (pisaphotography), New York, NY; **100.1** Getty Images (Hero Images), München; **101.1** NASA (PD), Washington , D.C.; **101.2** Getty Images (CBS Photo Archive), München; **102.1** Getty Images (Barry King/WireImage), München; **104.1** Getty Images (Moviepix), München; **104.2** ddp images GmbH (Capital Pictures), Hamburg; **108.1** shutterstock (In Tune), New York, NY; **108.2** iStockphoto (RF/Ischa Gast), Calgary, Alberta; **108.3** shutterstock (Bikeworldtravel), New York, NY; **121.1** shutterstock (Northfoto), New York, NY; **135.1** Thinkstock (Comstock), München; **136.1** Thinkstock (Tom Ackerman), München; **137.1** iStockphoto (clu), Calgary, Alberta; **139.1** dreamstime.com (Edward Bartel), Brentwood, TN; **139.2** akg-images (Album), Berlin; **151.1** Getty Images (Corbis), München; **154.2** Thinkstock (Wavebreakmedia Ltd), München; **156.1** Fotolia.com (Pierre brillot), New York; **173.1** Thinkstock (LUNAMARINA), München; **173.2** Fotolia.com (spiritofamerica), New York; **256.1** Thinkstock (Creatas Images), München; **262.1** Klett-Archiv (DeutscheInDenUSA.com), Stuttgart; **263.1** shutterstock (Rainer Lesniewski), New York, NY;

Sollte es in einem Einzelfall nicht gelungen sein, den korrekten Rechteinhaber ausfindig zu machen, so werden berechtigte Ansprüche selbstverständlich im Rahmen der üblichen Regelungen abgegolten.

Textquellen:

12 "Island in the sun" Text: CUOMO, RIVERS Copyright E O Smith Music, Melodie der Welt J. Michel GmbH & Co. KG Musikverlag, Frankfurt; **16–17** From *Where I belong* by Gillian Cross, Oxford University Press, April 2010; **31–36** "Claire's Devil": First published by Utbildningsstaden AB, Sweden, 1995 © Dave Draper 1995; **70** Song: "Empire State of Mind" Text: Carter, Shawn/Hunte, Angela/Keyes, Bert/Keys, Alicia/Robinson, Sylvia/Sewell, Janet Andrea/Shuckburgh, Alexander William, © Carter Boys Music/EMI April Music/Foray Music/Gambi Music Inc/Global Talent Publishing/J Sewell Publishing/Lellow Productions Inc/Masani El Shabazz, EMI Music Publishing Germany GmbH, Berlin/Rolf Budde Musikverlag GmbH, Berlin/Neue Welt Musikverlag GmbH, Hamburg; **90** Reprinted with the permission of Simon & Schuster Books for Young Readers, an imprint of Simon & Schuster Children's Publishing Division, from CAN'T GET THERE FROM HERE by Todd Strasser. Copyright © 2004 by Todd Strasser. All rights reserved.; **96** http://www.twc.org/about-us/a-poem-as-big-as-nyc/a-poem-as-big-as-nyc-poems/

NEW YORK
THE BRONX
W 155th St.
Harlem River Dr.
W 145th St.
HARLEM
W 125th St.
Henry Hudson Pkwy.
Broadway
7th Avenue
Lenox Avenue
MANHATTAN
Park Avenue
2nd Avenue
1st Avenue
Amsterdam Ave.
Central Park
E 106th St.
Hudson River
UPPER
WEST
SIDE
W 81st St.
5th Avenue
E 96th St.
The Metropolitan Museum of Art
E 84th St.
UPPER
EAST
SIDE
The Juilliard School
Lincoln Center
Broadway
E 79th St.
10th Avenue
Park Avenue
3rd Avenue
2nd Avenue
1st Avenue
E 66th St.
Central Park S.
Lincoln Tunnel
Alvin Ailey American Dance Theater
9th Avenue
QUEENS
12th Avenue
W 42nd St.
Avenue of the Americas
Museum of Modern Art
Rockefeller Center
Queensboro Bridge
Times Square
W 34th St.
5th Avenue
Chrysler Building
The High Line
E 42nd St.
MIDTOWN
United Nations
Empire State Building
Queens Midtown Tunnel
NEW JERSEY
9th Avenue
8th Avenue
7th Avenue
Broadway
W 14th St.
E 23rd St.
West Side Highway
Bleecker St.
Greenwich Village
E 14th St.
Hudson St.
Holland Tunnel
Soho
Broadway
Astor Place
Avenue D
LOWER
WEST
SIDE
Broome St.
Little Italy
E Houston St.
East River
Canal St.
LOWER
EAST
SIDE
Chinatown
Bowery
Williamsburg Bridge
One World Trade Center
9/11 Memorial
FDR Drive
Brooklyn Bridge
Manhattan Bridge
Ellis Island
Brooklyn Battery Tunnel
Liberty Island
Statue of Liberty
BROOKLYN
MANHATTAN
THE BRONX
NEW JERSEY
QUEENS
STATEN ISLAND
BROOKLYN

ALASKA
Denali
CANADA
CANADA
Seattle
Portland
WASHINGTON
Rocky Mountains
MONTANA
NORTH DAKOTA
OREGON
IDAHO
WYOMING
SOUTH DAKOTA
NEBRASKA
NEVADA
UTAH
San Francisco
Denver
CALIFORNIA
COLORADO
Las Vegas
HOLLYWOOD
ARIZONA
Los Angeles
Pacific Ocean
San Diego
Phoenix
NEW MEXICO
TEXAS
HAWAII
MEXICO

THE UNITED STATES OF AMERICA